MERCADOS

MERCA

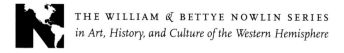

THE WILLIAM & BETTYE NOWLIN SERIES
in Art, History, and Culture of the Western Hemisphere

DOS

RECIPES FROM THE MARKETS OF MEXICO

—

DAVID STERLING

with Mario Canul

UNIVERSITY OF TEXAS PRESS ❖ AUSTIN

A few recipes in this book include information describing varying levels of toxicity in the suggested ingredients, and care should be taken when using them. Interested readers should consult other sources of information before eating any of these ingredients. Neither the author nor the publisher claims responsibility for adverse effects resulting from the use of these recipes and/or information found within this book.

Requests for permission to reproduce material
from this work should be sent to:
    Permissions
    University of Texas Press
    P.O. Box 7819
    Austin, TX 78713-7819
    utpress.utexas.edu/rp-form

♾ The paper used in this book meets the minimum
requirements of ANSI/NISO Z39.48-1992 (R1997)
(Permanence of Paper).

LIBRARY OF CONGRESS
CATALOGING-IN-PUBLICATION DATA

Names: Sterling, David, 1951–2016, author.
Title: Mercados : recipes from the markets of Mexico
    / David Sterling.
Description: First edition. | Austin : University
    of Texas Press, 2019. | Includes bibliographical
    references and index.
Identifiers: LCCN 2018013078
ISBN 978-1-4773-1040-3 (cloth : alk. paper)
ISBN 978-1-4773-1808-9 (library e-book)
ISBN 978-1-4773-1809-6 (nonlibrary e-book)
Subjects: LCSH: Cooking, Mexican. | Cooking—
    Mexico. | Markets—Mexico. | Mexico—
    Description and travel. | Mexico—Social life
    and customs.
Classification: LCC TX716.M4 S689 2019 |
    DDC 641.5972—dc23
LC record available at https://lccn.loc.gov/2018013078

doi:10.7560/310403

PHOTO CREDITS

The initials next to photos represent the following individuals:

DCC = Daniel Caballero Cerón
DS = David Sterling
EC = Eduardo Cervantes
KH = Keith Heitke
LP = Leonardo Palafox
MC = Mario Canul
MR = Mark Randall
TA = Thomas F. Aleto

Photos by Ricardo Espinosa-reo are credited as follows: CPTM/Foto: Ricardo Espinosa-reo.

For other photo sources, see Photo Credits (page 560).

CONTENTS

3

THE GULF COAST
209

4

CENTRAL HIGHLANDS
289

5

PACIFIC REGION
431

MARKET FUNDAMENTALS
524

GLOSSARY
534

BIBLIOGRAPHY
540

INDEX TO RECIPES BY CATEGORY
547

GENERAL INDEX
552

PHOTO CREDITS
560

PUBLISHER'S NOTE

D AVID STERLING'S *Yucatán: Recipes from a Culinary Expedition* received some of the culinary world's highest honors: the James Beard Foundation's Cookbook of the Year award and the inaugural Art of Eating Prize. When David died in November 2016, *Yucatán* was rightly recognized as "a wonderful legacy" by Rick Bayless and other luminaries. Fortunately, David's legacy now includes another book.

Mercados, this exploration of some of the regional markets of Mexico, was in the latter stages of being drafted when David passed. The photography was complete, the recipes had been written, and the manuscript was glowing with David's passion and spirit. His collaborators—Keith Heitke, his partner; Mark Randall, his longtime friend and photographer; and Mario Canul, his sous chef—confirmed it was David's wish to see the book in print, and the University of Texas Press committed to bringing *Mercados* to publication.

This book would still be languishing in David's computer, however, if not for Mario Canul, who excavated every file in the months after David's passing. But Mario's influence began years earlier. He accompanied David on research trips across Mexico, and took many of the photos gathered here. As we edited the book, we relied on Mario to clarify recipe instructions, and to retest dishes so that, as he wrote, "they had the flavor I remember from those trips." No recipes have been added or substantively changed, but there were missing quantities for some ingredients and it was Mario who ensured that those recipes now taste true to their sources and inspirations. The book you have in your hands is very much as David envisioned it—thanks to Mario.

While we hope to honor David by bringing this book into the world, we know David, rightly, would remind us that *Mercados* is meant to honor the fascinating, diverse, and gifted cooks in the Mexican markets that he loved. We have attributed the recipes to their creators wherever possible.

INTRODUCTION

I traveled Mexico for years on end, from market to market. Because Mexico is in its markets . . .

PABLO NERUDA

THIS BOOK BEGINS with a simple premise, as lyrically described by the Chilean poet Pablo Neruda: that Mexico—or perhaps any country—can best be known by exploring its markets. And so, following in Neruda's footsteps, I set out traveling through magical Mexico "for years on end, from market to market"—a colossal shopping spree—savoring foods and collecting recipes along the way.

Markets are boundless repositories—not just of goods for sale, but also of cultural proclivities, tolerances, and biases; of human relationships, interactions, and conflicts; of the histories of human societies and their physical, spiritual, and emotional needs and desires.

Mexican markets are particularly interesting because they represent a continuous cultural/gastronomic/economic tradition that is hundreds if not thousands of years old. Frederick A. Peterson of the New World Archaeological Foundation highlighted this fact during his visits to Mexican markets in the mid-twentieth century:

I have surveyed several of the Indian markets of Mexico and found that about four-fifths of the goods sold are the same as those used in pre-Hispanic times, or are close equivalents. Manufactured goods of metal are the main items of non-Indian manufacture, with printed cloth running a close second. Some substitutes for pre-Hispanic goods are modern mirrors, cheap jewellery [sic], knives, shoes, and clothing. Otherwise the market is as Bernal Díaz and Cortés described it in the early 1500s. . . . One of the delights of a modern tourist is to wander around the markets of Mexico, where the eye, ear, and nose thrill to pre-Hispanic vibrations. The market is one of the most impressive survivals of ancient Mexico. (Peterson, Ancient Mexico: An Introduction to the Pre-Hispanic Cultures, 180)

Even though Peterson published this statement in 1959, more recent scholarship has corroborated his observations. As far as food plants are concerned, contemporary scholars have found examples in today's markets that trace their genetics to some of Mesoamerica's most ancient crops and were described by colonial chroniclers in the sixteenth century, thereby stretching a continuous gastronomic thread from ancient times to the present.

Market days were and still are times when all strata of society come together to share not just the essentials for survival but also cultural values—and even gossip. These kinds of exchanges are enriching to all participants, and it is this richness that one senses when one enters the Mexican market. Perhaps most important, though, going to market is simply fun! Regional market days in Mexico are in fact regular major social events—the primary opportunity for campesino and urbanite alike to socialize, joke, scout for potential spouses—all against a backdrop of food and eating. Perhaps the sixteenth-century Dominican clergyman Fray Diego Durán expressed it best when he wrote about the great Aztec markets:

The markets were so inviting, pleasurable, appealing, and gratifying to these people that great crowds attended, and still attend, them, especially during the big feasts, as is well known to all. I suspect that if I said to a market woman accustomed to going from market to market: "Look, today is market day in such and such a town. What would you rather do, go from here right to Heaven or to that market?" I believe this would be her answer: "Allow me to go to that market first, and then I will go to Heaven." (Durán, Book of the Gods and Rites and the Ancient Calendar)

ABOUT THE MARKETS IN THIS BOOK

So, how does one go on a shopping spree through an entire country? And not just any country, but one of the most culturally rich and ecologically diverse countries in the world? Where to start?

The great urban hubs of Mexico always feature grand market complexes—all sprawling and labyrinthine, colorful and wonderfully funky. Yet even the smallest town will also usually have some kind of market, even if it is simply a crate set up on a front stoop with a few wilted vegetables spread humbly atop yesterday's newspaper, or shanks of pork from a freshly slaughtered pig dangling from the eaves.

My "Goldilocks Zone" for exploring the country's markets turned out to be towns with a population of around 30,000 or less—not too big, not too small, but just right. Among those, I sought towns that are known throughout the country for encapsulating a beauty, culture, and history unique to the town and that collectively contribute to the legendary magic of Mexico. I also included in my criteria towns that exhibit a continuous commitment to preserving tangible and intangible local folkways such as crafts, dance, music, and gastronomy. Several of these towns are known as Pueblos Mágicos (Magical Towns)—a designation given by the national secretary of tourism to towns that meet those criteria. In the end, I couldn't resist visiting the markets in some of Mexico's dynamic cities, too: we based our travels in several of the country's great state capitals before venturing farther afield to visit the smaller villages, and we took advantage of our time in these urban hubs to eat and shop voraciously. Natural limits of time and resources imposed on a project of this scale restricted our investigation. The Northern Highlands, for example, which is a vast region, has a history and gastronomy so rich and varied, fused as it is with influences from north of the border, that it should warrant its own volume one day.

So, what constitutes a market? In Mexico, it is often but not always a brick-and-mortar building; it may be a cluster of portable stalls with canvas awning covers—known as a *tianguis*—and in that case the markets may simply spread from spot to spot and spill out onto the sidewalks and into surrounding squares. In some places, such as Huasca de Ocampo, Hidalgo (p. 356), the whole tiny town is a market!

In most markets, big or small, there are at least a few permanent food stalls, known as *comedores*, that serve dishes made from the wonderfully fresh produce sold elsewhere in the market. Many of these *comedores* are multigenerational family businesses, and their gifted cooks shared recipes and knowledge as well as delicious food with us. We'll also meet *ambulantes*, the roving vendors that move through the aisles with their wares in their arms, adding to the ordered chaos that makes markets so compelling. Finally, from time to time we'll venture beyond the pueblo or urban setting into the countryside to visit local producers: not only is it enlightening to see how and where foods found in the markets are produced, but also many market vendors are what are known as *propios*—those who produce or harvest their own goods elsewhere and then sell them in the market, an enduring tradition in Mexico, predating the "farm-to-table" trend by millennia.

Scattered as they are across Mexico's richly varied terrain—each with its own terroir and each with an agenda of culinary preservation—the pueblos we will visit are natural strongholds of regional and local Mexican cuisines. And in turn, it is in the markets of these pueblos where perhaps the most unique and representative foods can be found—both raw ingredients and prepared dishes, linked synergistically. Of course, all the regions of Mexico are united by the many species they share—maize, beans, squash, chiles, and so on—but each region and locale also features its own unique ingredients—and therefore dishes and flavors—that cannot readily be found elsewhere. For the purposes of the recipes in this book, I present the reader with many of these unique ingredients for educational value, and, of course, when they are called for in a recipe, I suggest excellent substitutions.

As we tour this great country together, you will become acquainted with each region through its food and come to understand how regional foods contribute to regional cultural differences and, on the flip side, how unique cultures and histories inform regional gastronomies. The indigenous peoples that we will meet in the markets—those who developed and maintain these gastronomic traditions—will therefore be of vital interest and importance. In the Southern Highlands and the Yucatán Peninsula, we will see how many interpretations there can be for the "holy trinity" of maize, beans, and squash, one of the oldest traditions in the country and still the basis of the diet of the indigenous Mayas; in the Central Highlands, cactus fruits, flowers,

and plants have created what we might call a "desert cuisine," which has sustained nomadic tribes since prehistory and still contributes to the diet and the economy of the Otomí-Chichimeca groups; in the Pacific Region, we'll find mountain lakes full of fish and bouquets blooming with wild herbs, mushrooms, and *huitlacoche*—corn fungus—signatures of the cuisine of the Mazahua and P'urhépecha peoples; and in the Gulf Coast region, the scent of vanilla produced by the Totonacs will become the mnemonic that transports us to the beginning of time in Mexico.

THE MARKETS OF PRE-COLUMBIAN MEXICO

In April 1519, thirty-four-year-old Hernán Cortés and some six hundred warriors landed on the Mexican mainland at a natural harbor he christened La Villa Rica de la Vera Cruz; within days, his army began the overland march into the Central Highlands toward the Valley of Mexico and its crown jewel, the great Aztec capital of Tenochtitlán, today Mexico City. By the end of that year, with the empire's ruler Moctezuma safely under house arrest, Cortés took a break to go shopping.

The legendary market of Tlatelolco was situated on an island it shared with the regal city of Tenochtitlán, connected by canals and a grand causeway that plied through Lake Texcoco. What Cortés and his retinue saw at the teeming market astounded them, and reports to Spain were breathless and full of wonder. In 1520, in his Second Letter to Charles V, Cortés wrote, "Every kind of merchandise such as may be met with in every land is for sale." He went on to describe in vivid detail a bounty of fruits, vegetables, animals, cloth, even gold and silver, and his further elaboration is impressive indeed:

> This city has many public squares, in which are situated the markets and other places for buying and selling. There is one square twice as large as that of the city of Salamanca, surrounded by porticoes, where are daily assembled more than sixty thousand souls, engaged in buying and selling; and where are found all kinds of merchandise that the world affords, embracing the necessaries of life, as for instance articles of food, as well as jewels of gold and silver, lead, brass, copper, tin, precious stones, bones, shells, snails, and feathers. . . . There is a street for game, where every variety of birds in the country are sold, as fowls, partridges, quails, wild ducks, fly-catchers, widgeons, turtledoves,

The great market of Tlatelolco, with the causeway leading to Tenochtitlán in the background. Mural by Diego Rivera located in the Palacio Nacional, Mexico City.

pigeons, reed-birds, parrots, sparrows, eagles, hawks, owls, and kestrels; they sell likewise the skins of some birds of prey, with their feathers, head, beak, and claws. There are also sold rabbits, hares, deer, and little dogs, which are raised for eating. There is also an herb street, where may be obtained all sorts of roots and medicinal herbs that the country affords. There are apothecaries' shops, where prepared medicines, liquids, ointments, and plasters are sold; barbers' shops, where they wash and shave the head; and restaurateurs that furnish food and drink at a certain price. There is also a class of men like those called in Castile porters, for carrying burdens . . .

There are all kinds of green vegetables, especially onions, leeks, garlic, watercresses, nasturtium, borage, sorrel, artichokes, and golden thistle; fruits also of numerous descriptions, amongst which are cherries and plums, similar to those in Spain; honey and wax from bees, and from the stalks of maize, which are as sweet as the sugar-cane; honey is also extracted from the plant called maguey, which is superior to sweet or new wine; from the same plant they extract sugar and wine, which they also sell. . . . Painters' colors, as numerous as can be found in Spain, and as fine shades; deerskins dressed and undressed, dyed different colors; earthen-ware of a large size and excellent quality; large and small jars, jugs, pots, bricks, and endless variety of vessels, all made of fine clay, and all or most of them glazed and painted; maize or Indian corn, in the grain and in the form of bread . . . ; pâtés of birds and fish . . . ; the eggs of hens, geese, and of all the other birds I have mentioned, in great abundance, and cakes made of eggs; finally, everything that can be found throughout the whole country is sold in the markets . . . (Cortés, Letters from Mexico)

Several of the foods noted—for example, onions, leeks, and garlic—were introduced to the New World by the Spanish in the mid-sixteenth century, so we should perhaps not assume that, by 1520, these had assimilated themselves into the market; rather, it is more likely that the author (as did so many of the time) simply attributed familiar names to unfamiliar things—and there were unquestionably a myriad of unfamiliar things for the Spanish to note and taste.

The great Aztec market offered raw ingredients from throughout the region, as well as prepared food and drink. Another important Spanish chronicler of the time, the Franciscan friar Bernardino de Sahagún, wrote a paean to Mexican food in stream-of-consciousness style. It almost seems as though he narrated his account to a scribe, since the language is casual, unpolished, and repetitive. Still, he expresses in his repetitiveness what must have seemed to the average Spaniard of the time an overwhelming choice of prepared foods for sale in the market, particularly the variety of maize offerings. Many foods on his list can still be recognized in today's Mexican markets.

Variety of fruits and other foodstuffs in a colonial market.

> *He sells meat tamales . . . plain tamales; tamales cooked in an earth oven; those cooked in an olla . . . frog tamales . . . axolotl (a kind of larval salamander) tamales, tadpoles with grains of maize, mushrooms with grains of maize, tuna cactus with grains of maize, rabbit tamales . . . pocket gopher tamales: tasty—tasty, very tasty, very well made, always tasty, savory, of pleasing odor; made with a very pleasing odor, very savory.*
>
> *He sells tamales of maize softened in wood ashes . . . tamales of maize softened in lime—narrow tamales, fruit tamales, cooked bean tamales . . . [tamales of] broken, cracked grains of maize . . . pointed tamales . . . turkey egg tamales . . . tamales of tender maize, tamales of green maize, brick-shaped tamales, braised ones; plain tamales, honey tamales, bee tamales . . . squash tamales . . . maize flower tamales . . .*
>
> *The food seller sells tortillas which [are] thick, thickish, thick overall, extremely thick; he sells thin [ones]—thin tortillas, stretched-out tortillas; disklike, straight . . . with shelled beans . . . with shelled beans mashed; chile with maize, tortillas with meat and grains of maize, folded . . . with chile—chile wrapped, gathered in the hand . . .*
>
> *He sells foods, sauces, hot sauces; fried [food], olla-cooked [food], juices . . . shredded [food] with chile, with squash seeds, with tomatoes, with smoked chile . . . with hot chile sauce, with "bird excrement" sauce, sauce of smoked chile, heated [sauces], bean sauce; [he sells] toasted beans, cooked beans, mushroom sauce, sauce of small squash, sauce of large tomatoes, sauce of ordinary tomatoes, sauce of various kinds of sour herbs, avocado sauce. (Sahagún, The Florentine Codex)*

The great Aztec market of Tlatelolco—while by all accounts grand—was in truth simply the hub of a highly elaborated network of markets that operated throughout Mesoamerica. In the Yucatán Peninsula, the Mayas operated markets, too, established not only for local and regional trade but also for trade with the great highland centers of Guatemala and the Valley of Mexico, where the Mayas enjoyed what was a virtual monopoly on several coveted goods—salt and cacao, among others—that were much in demand. Although less was written about them by the colonial chroniclers, we do get glimpses of the presence of Maya markets from the Franciscan friar Diego de Landa, who arrived in Yucatán in 1549:

Their favorite occupation was trading, whereby they brought in salt; also cloths and slaves from Tabasco and Ulúa. In their bartering they used cacao and stone counters which they had for money, and with which they bought slaves and other fine and beautiful stones, such as the chiefs wore as jewels on festal occasions. They had also certain red shells for use as money and jewels for wearing; these they carried in network purses. In their markets they dealt in all the products of the country; they gave credit, borrowed and paid promptly and without usury. (Landa, An Account of the Things of Yucatán)

Considering the fact that marketplaces are difficult to find in the archaeological record due to the organic nature of most of the products sold, it is interesting to note that in contrast to the Aztec marketplace, we know more about the Maya markets from archaeological studies than we do from the written reports of colonial chroniclers.

Perhaps the most compelling physical evidence that reveals to us the ancient Maya market is a dramatic painted mural dating to 700–620 BCE that had been perfectly preserved inside a structure at Calakmul in the modern state of Campeche on the Yucatán Peninsula. The mural is unusual in that—unlike most representations of Maya society—it portrays the "lower echelons" rather than the elites, folks obviously going about the daily business of passing, receiving, and consuming diverse foods.

THE MARKET AS SPECTACLE

The extrapolations we are able to make about the pre-Columbian Aztec and Maya markets from both colonial sources and the archaeological record leave us with an image of a vibrant commercial and social landscape that had evolved over thousands of years to take its place among the crowning achievements of these great civilizations.

As noted earlier, attendance at the market fulfilled needs beyond the gustatory. The marketplace was a stage upon which all the dramas and farces of the human condition were enacted. People came to see what was for sale, perhaps to buy something, but as much as anything, just to watch the passing spectacle.

In his fascinating summary of colonial reports, Scott R. Hutson of the University of Kentucky paints a vivid portrait of the color and chaos of the markets. For example, he explains that public executions were morbid

This detail of a mural in Structure 1, Calakmul, Campeche, illustrates a thriving Maya market with vendors and buyers exchanging everything from maize and salt to tamales and tobacco. The hieroglyph at left signifies "maize gruel person" and depicts an atole vendor with a large pot, a dish, and a spoon.

Tianguis in Mexico City, 1885. The word in Nahuatl (language of the peoples known as Aztecs) for "marketplace" is tiankistli *(or tianquistli). Nowadays, throughout Mexico the term* tianguis *is used to refer to open-air or periodic markets. Roving vendors known as* ambulantes *move from locale to locale, extending the shopping experience beyond the setting of the market or tianguis.*

forms of entertainment, and market goers seemed to eagerly await the bad behaviors of their neighbors. Thieves, market cheats, adulterers, and anyone found drinking pulque (p. 365) were just a few to feel the executioner's sting. Stoning, bludgeoning, strangulation, or burning were typical punishments, and traitors were hacked to bits, their pieces laughingly tossed about the market and played with by children like toys.

Market cheats provided ample fuel for the bloodlust of the populace. The tricks they resorted to were clever and plentiful. Cacao merchants smeared bad beans in ashes to lend them a more natural color; those who sold amaranth seeds were reported to mix rancid seeds with the good ones; and sellers of syrups frequently diluted them. Sahagún let spew his righteous venom regarding these "bad merchants":

[They are] stingy, avaricious, greedy, thrifty, grasping, deceiving; a misrepresenter of things to others; evil tongued, one who becomes insistent, who over-praises things, who exaggerates things; a usurer, a profiteer, a thief, a misrepresenter, a liar— dog-like, deceitful, profiting excessively. (Sahagún, vol. 10 of The Florentine Codex, *43, 65, 67, 74)*

The excitement to be found in the market wasn't restricted to criminal activity and mob bloodthirstiness. Sex was another major attraction. Young people went in search of partners; marriages were often contracted in the marketplace; prostitution was present. The sexual tension of the marketplace was evidenced in a report by Durán, in which sons of Tenochtitlán lords (whom he refers to as "bachelor menaces") chanced upon some daughters of Tlatelolco royalty and began to playfully tease and mock them. The young women responded in kind, and as they left the market, they were pursued by the overheated males, who treated them dishonorably and violated their innocence.

According to Hutson, special market days with their concomitant festivals held particular attraction. Fray Juan de Torquemada tells of one such festival in which the merchants danced and then performed farcical skits for the audience. In one skit, the merchant pretended to be a mosquito, making buzzing sounds and even playing at biting the flesh of shoppers, all the while quipping with the audience. Another merchant, acting as a dung beetle, smeared himself in excrement. Durán, too, reported on the immense popularity of these entertainments.

While public drunkenness was often punished, it was just as frequently tolerated, and drinking during the special festivals offered another raucous diversion. In fact, the Aztec market was associated at least in name with the "400 Rabbits," described in the *Florentine Codex* as the "gods of wine and feasting, patrons of drunkards and the masters of drunkenness." Interestingly, "400 Rabbits" was the colloquial term for the constellation of the Pleiades, the formal name of which in Nahuatl was *tianquiztli*, or "marketplace."

Perhaps the ribaldry and spectacle of the marketplace served as a relief valve for Aztec society, which was rigidly structured and defined by rank. All levels of society were divided into strict classes. No wonder, then, that the average Aztec citizen may have sought an escape in the rowdier aspects of the market, where the revelry, the vulgarity, and the inversion of the normal order of things at least momentarily suspended these social hierarchies—an aspect not lost in today's markets.

THE MEXICAN MARKET: TODAY AND TOMORROW

The changes that have impacted the Mexican market are inevitable, if at times unfortunate. The proliferation of new products creates new desires and demand: cheap plastic toys and blinking tree lights from China flood the markets every year at Christmastime, screaming for attention, and knockoff "designer" items elbow out locally made goods. Biodegradation, deforestation, and other environmental challenges threaten to disrupt traditional farming methods and, in turn, the markets. More important, shifting politics between Mexico and its looming neighbor to the north shape new destinies for agriculture, as the life of the average Mexican rides in the balance.

One change in the Mexican market simply has to do with scale: increased population as well as the proliferation of novel goods has resulted in the expansion of markets not only into larger physical complexes but also outward into neighboring areas or even adjacent towns. For example, shoppers can rely on collecting the basic daily necessities at their neighborhood market—generally local produce or a few artisanally crafted products—but for imported or manufactured goods, such as hardware, clothing, or electronics, they must travel to other parts of town or sometimes to distant, often larger, market centers.

Similarly, the giant self-service supermarkets that surged in popularity in the middle of the twentieth century continue to extend their enterprise throughout the country, providing consumers with a broad range of comestibles and durable goods—often in a convenient "one-stop-shopping" context. Furthermore, the demands of growing populations, increases in industrialized farming, and expanding transportation networks have all contributed to changes in Mexico's markets. The implementation of the North American Free Trade Agreement (NAFTA) on January 1, 1994, catapulted Mexico from being a relatively small player in exports to the United States to being its second-largest source of imports of agricultural goods. Among those goods exported from Mexico to the United States are beef, tropical fruits, avocados, and tomatoes. The increased US demand has resulted in the abandonment of smaller terrains and traditional farming methods in favor of more lucrative large-scale industrial agriculture and its concomitant environmental and economical hazards.

Clearly, not all of these changes are welcome, and Mexico's farmers are fighting for their right to have a voice in the decisions that affect them. In October 2013, just two days after thousands in Mexico took to the streets to protest genetically modified maize, a federal judge ruled that Monsanto, DuPont, and other companies will no longer be allowed to plant or sell their products in Mexico. Shortly thereafter, on March 11, 2014, a federal judge in the state of Campeche in the Yucatán Peninsula settled a two-year battle of indigenous farmers against Monsanto's aggressive overtures to introduce transgenic soybeans to the state.

The richness and variety of Mexico's regional cuisines result directly from a unique confluence of geology and terroir, culture and history. The geological composition of the country is complex, creating one of the world's most diverse biotas: Mexico is one of twelve countries in the world that collectively contain between 60 and 70 percent of the total diversity of the planet—a phenomenon described as "megadiverse." It is one of the eight global centers of the domestication of edible plants, including maize, beans, vanilla, cacao, avocado, tomato, and many others. Apart from geographical and ecological diversity, Mexico is also home to some 25.7 million indigenous people who speak many different languages that shape discrete ethnic groups and form distinct cultural areas. Ecological and cultural diversity merged to make Mexico a laboratory for the interaction of human cultures and plants for millennia, in turn shaping unique regional gastronomies, dating to the earliest appearance of Mesoamerican civilizations.

Both rulings have hopefully established a legal precedent that will now be followed nationwide in similar cases and ensure that the foods we find in markets in the future will carry forward age-old genes and traditions.

In spite of these dramatic and sometimes horrific sea changes, I remain optimistic about the future of the Mexican market. One thing that gives me hope is the knowledge, as detailed above, that these markets have survived conquest and exploitation—as well as great environmental shifts—through many hundreds of years, often thriving in the same place and form since precontact times. And if ever I doubt the outcome of the Mexican market, all I have to do is look at the foods I see there. The markets we will visit in this book are full of local products, a not insignificant percentage of which are produced within a 50-mile (80 km) radius of where they are sold; still others may have been harvested in family compounds on the outskirts of town. The Mexican people are tenacious, yes, but even more so they are steeped in traditions that are not so easily conquered.

The geographical characteristics of Mexico may be divided into two broad categories: highlands and lowlands. Both the highlands and the lowlands of Mexico are defined by great mountain ranges that create a shape rather like an enormous horseshoe: the highlands fill the interior of the horseshoe, and the lowlands outline its exterior.

THE HIGHLANDS

This region is composed of three sections: the Northern Highlands, the Central Highlands, and the Southern Highlands.

The Central Mexican Plateau—also known as the Altiplano—averages between 3,280 and 9,005 feet (1,000–2,745 m) above sea level. It fills the interior of the horseshoe, almost literally squeezed between the two great mountain ranges that formed it through volcanism and tectonics some 65 million years ago: the Sierra Madre Occidental and the Sierra Madre Oriental. The Altiplano is further subdivided into two primary sections, separated by a low mountain range that crosses the state of Zacatecas: the Mesa del Norte (which I will call the Northern Highlands) and the Mesa Central (Central Highlands). The Eje Volcánico Transversal (Trans-Mexican Volcanic Belt) and the Sierra Madre del Sur in the south bring an abrupt halt to the Altiplano and

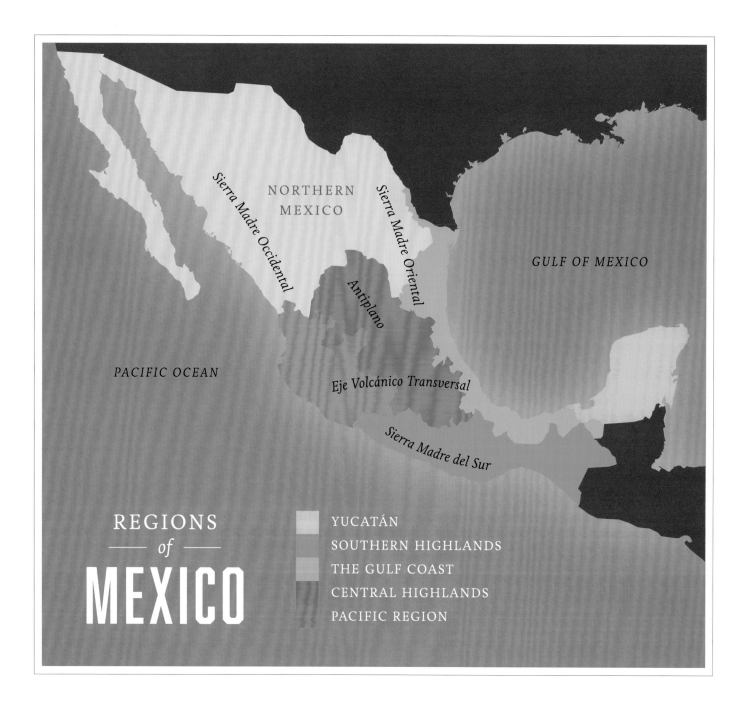

REGIONS
— of —
MEXICO

Sierra Madre Occidental

NORTHERN
MEXICO

Sierra Madre Oriental

GULF OF MEXICO

Antiplano

PACIFIC OCEAN

Eje Volcánico Transversal

Sierra Madre del Sur

YUCATÁN
SOUTHERN HIGHLANDS
THE GULF COAST
CENTRAL HIGHLANDS
PACIFIC REGION

together form the northernmost edge of the third section of the highland region: the Southern Highlands.

THE LOWLANDS

This region pertains almost exclusively to the coastal areas, those that outline the exterior of the horseshoe: the Pacific Region and the Gulf Coast Lowlands. The Yucatán Peninsula is also part of the lowland region, outlined by the Gulf of Mexico and the Caribbean Sea. The lowlands range in altitude between sea level and 3,280 feet (1,000 m).

Because of the proximity of the western ranges of the Sierra Madre to the Pacific Ocean and the abruptness of their descent into the sea, several states in the west straddle the line between highlands and lowlands, further complexifying their diversity.

CULTURAL GROUPS OF MEXICO

According to *Ethnologue: Languages of the World*, there are at present 289 individual languages in Mexico, of which 285 are living and 4 extinct; most of these are grouped into twenty larger language families, and all are further grouped into 62 categories unified by environment and cultural similarities—"ethnolinguistic groups," or "cultural groups."

It is essential to consider these cultural groups if one hopes to achieve an understanding of regional Mexican cuisine. The distinct regions of Mexico are defined as much by the people who live in them as they are by topography and climate. The resources of each region inform how people live within them; in turn, people interact with and impact the region. They fashion foods that are determined by regional resources and select for cultivation those resources that function best as food. And, importantly, the foods they fashion are frequently manifestations of their cosmologies and may play important roles in rituals and celebrations. It is this symbiosis of land and belief-driven human beings that is the germplasm for what we know as the most elemental basis of "regional cuisine."

For example, dishes incorporating *chaya* (*Cnidoscolus aconitifolius*), or tree spinach, may typically be associated with the Yukatek or Southern Highlands Mayas, who have traditionally used the plant medicinally and in rituals as well as consumed it as food; similarly, the Yukatek Mayas still consider maize to be lifeblood, and initiation rituals for weaned infants involve foods of maize and *chaya*. The *pejelagarto* (*Atractosteus tropicus*), a freshwater garfish, was highly symbolic to the Olmecs, who used its sharp teeth for bloodletting rituals that opened the door to the underworld; for their heirs, the Chontales of Tabasco, the *pejelagarto* is still tightly interwoven with their culture and gastronomy. And the mammoth tamale known as *zacahuil*—often measuring 6 and a half feet (2 m) in length—is identified with the peoples of the region known as La Huasteca and has traditionally been consumed during rituals blessing the earth.

You will be introduced to many of Mexico's indigenous cultural groups as we travel from one region to the next throughout this book.

ABOUT THE RECIPES AND HOW TO USE THIS BOOK

I've organized this book by state, beginning with my home state of Yucatán and moving westward across Mexico. We enjoyed many, many unique dishes that never appear outside the market where we encountered them. However, some of the foods herein can be found, in identical or easily recognizable form, in more than one state. *Carnitas*, for instance, are enjoyed throughout Mexico. Nonetheless, *carnitas* are so strongly associated with the state of Michoacán that it would be inappropriate to include them anywhere but the chapter on Michoacán. In cases where a dish is not so clearly cultural property—*ensalada de nopales*, for instance—I've placed it where we found a particularly compelling example (in this case, Querétaro). But the basic recipes for both *carnitas* and *ensalada de nopales*, among others, are cross-referenced as part of dishes in other states where needed. Finally, a handful of basic salsas and foundational recipes—Masa para tamales, Enriched Pot Beans—appear so frequently that I've collected them into their own chapter for easy reference, along with some common techniques that you will use throughout the book.

1

YUCATÁN

Valladolid. [CPTM/FOTO: RICARDO ESPINOSA-REO]

INTRODUCTION

FOR MANY CENTURIES, the Mayas of the Yucatán Peninsula enjoyed a monopoly on the profitable trade in salt and cacao in precontact Mesoamerica. Their control of these coveted goods was a happy accident resulting from the geography of their homeland: a vast peninsula whose shores were encrusted with the salt deposits left by evaporating seawater, and whose ocean waterways served as natural routes for Maya merchants to travel by canoe to distant trade nodes, especially to the cacao-producing region of Chontalpa on the Gulf Coast. During its five-hundred-year ascendancy, the powerful city of Chichén Itzá—anchored imposingly in the center of the peninsula— likely controlled this trade. Its expansion was further underwritten by the Mayas' mastery of agriculture in what would appear to be a thoroughly inhospitable environment.

Hundreds of years later, terrain and topography would combine once more to generate wealth for the region's inhabitants, leading to some surprising culinary repercussions. On the eve of the twentieth century, boundless plantations of the native henequen—*Agave fourcroydes*, the plant that yields the lucrative fiber sisal, known locally as *oro verde* (green gold)—stretched endlessly toward the horizon from every direction outward from Mérida, making Yucatán the wealthiest and most modernized state in Mexico. During the Gilded Age, Yucatán's wealth, coupled with its peninsular location, offered the opportunity for much global exchange: due to the nexus of port/railway links, it was far easier for a Yucatecan to travel to Europe than it was for someone from central Mexico. Freighters and passenger ships arriving at Gulf Coast ports brought new cultures, new influences. In fact, in at least two notable instances, whole mansions were fabricated in France and imported—down to the nails—on ships that sailed from Marseilles; French maids, cooks, and housekeepers were "imported," too, to staff these grand homes. Cookbooks and recipes came with them.

Not only French but also a wide array of global culinary influences had easy access to the shores of the Yucatán Peninsula, impacting its culture and cuisine: from Africa came the cowpea (black-eyed pea), known as *x'pelón*; from the Antilles, the famously fiery *chile habanero*; from Portugal, the dried sausage linguiça, here brick red and smoky and called *longaniza*; from Holland came the bright red ball cheese, Edam, the most frequently used cheese in Yucatán; and, perhaps surprisingly, the classic Moorish/Andalusian staples of garbanzo beans, capers, raisins, olives, almonds, and Asian spices stocked the holds of the first ships from Spain. Native maize, beans, squash, and squash seeds, as well as tomatoes and chiles still form the basis of the indigenous Maya diet and coexist peaceably side by side with the introduced European fare.

PHYSICAL ENVIRONMENT AND AGRICULTURE

Most of the vast limestone slab of the Yucatán Peninsula lies at sea level or just slightly above; due to its mammoth size—some 76,300 square miles (197,600 sq. km)—it is like a solid ocean that stretches across the horizon seemingly endlessly, into the Gulf of Mexico on the north and west and the Caribbean on the east.

Weaknesses in the limestone caused by a cataclysmic meteorite impact some 65 million years ago have resulted in sinkholes (cenotes) filled with freshwater; many of these form the junctions of an extensive network of underground rivers, providing the main water source for the Mayas. The peninsula is covered by subtropical dry broadleaf forest—the largest in Mexico—and is traced by 1,100 miles (1,700 km) of coastline rich in marine life. Both forest and ocean environments provided peninsular peoples with abundant resources, which—coupled with an advanced agricultural system—allowed the native Mayas to build one of the greatest civilizations in Mesoamerica.

A visit to any market in the peninsula will illustrate the impressive agricultural and gastronomical richness of Yucatán. Piles of spiny, fluorescent-colored *pitahaya* or sandy brown jicama; tubs brimming with guava and papaya and lima beans; burlap bags heaving with allspice and cacao beans—these and many of Mexico's other most prized fruits, vegetables, and flavorings are indigenous to the peninsula or have been cultivated here since at least 3400 BCE. Today, among the top agricultural products are pork, poultry, maize, honey, papaya, citrus, *chile habanero*, coconut, and avocado. Agricultural production by small-scale family farmers using simple tools is by far the primary economic activity of the region. When we find native fruits in the markets, we know that local campesino families grew them, since most native fruit tree species are seasonally harvested primarily for auto-consumption and to a lesser extent for subsistence trading.

ETHNOLINGUISTIC GROUP

Unlike any other region in Mexico, the Yucatán Peninsula has traditionally been dominated by one single cultural group—the Mayas. The Mayas are one of the oldest extant cultural groups in Mesoamerica, and they remain the second-largest ethnolinguistic group in Mexico, after the Nahuas. More than 1.5 million people in Mexico speak some form of the Mayan language (there are 28 distinct strands of Mayan; the Yucatán Peninsula is dominated by Yukatek Mayan speakers). Because the Maya Empire encompassed such a large swath of territory, extending into Chiapas and other parts of Mexico as well as neighboring countries, it's important to remember that the Peninsula includes only a portion of the diverse Maya world. Within Yucatán, however, evidence of its Maya heritage is everywhere, from the breathtaking archaeological sites to the foods, like *sikil p'aak* (a paste made from tomatoes and squash seeds), that retain their Mayan names.

IZAMAL

As WE HEAD EAST out of Mérida toward Izamal, the faint gray-green of the hene-quen fields—the source of great wealth during Yucatán's gilded age—gradually fades behind us. Entering Izamal, the color scheme brightens to a warm and welcoming gold. Every building in the town—from schools and restaurants to banks and churches—is equalized behind a coat of sunny ocher, outlined in pert white trim. Izamal acquired its notable palette—color coordinated to that of the Vatican, by the way—in 1993, as residents prepared for the visit of Pope John Paul II, who came to bestow his blessings on the festivities surrounding the International Year of the World's Indigenous People. A small museum still displays the tiny silver crown that the Pope gave to honor the Virgin of the Immaculate Conception—or Nuestra Señora de Izamal—the town's patron saint. It would seem that what was good for the Pope is good for tourism, since town authorities have maintained the gilded color scheme, and travel guidebooks now promote "The Yellow City."

The centerpiece of town, its principal milestone and main tourist attraction is the impressive Franciscan convent of San Antonio de Padua, founded in 1553 by Fray Diego de Landa. It is distinctive for several reasons, not least of which is that it perches atop the base of an ancient Maya pyramid known as Pop Hol Chak. The platform was too mighty a mass for the Spaniards to level, as they did so many others, so instead they decided simply to build the church on the summit, quarrying whatever stone they might need from the existing structure. Strolling through the hushed cloisters, visitors pass evidence of the pilferage, as carved hieroglyphic stones peek out here and there, whispering ancient Mayan messages at every turn.

[EC]

MERCADO MUNICIPAL

The tidy municipal market (center background)—yellow inside and out—seems to bow reverentially at the hem of the looming stone platform of Pop Hol Chak, while the convent above righteously radiates the same auriferous tone as the more secular buildings below. A statue of Fray Diego de Landa—the bishop of Yucatán contradictorily reviled for having burned the Maya codices in 1562, and honored for having repented and written a history of the Mayas in a compensatory act—stands staunchly in the center of a traffic circle, daring any traveler to circumvent his supercilious gaze.

(above) The colonnade of the market mirrors that of the looming convent behind. Terraces that rim the market are filled with ambulantes—*roving vendors—who sell everything from fruits and vegetables to plants and seeds. These are people of Yukatek Maya descent, and the goods they offer are typically from their own gardens.* [EC] *(below) Inside the market, rhythmical colonnades of golden arches neatly define individual vendors' stalls, some stacked high with impeccably displayed produce, others more modestly dressed with a few simple vegetables from the family garden.* [EC]

CHILE DE MILPA/CHILE VERDE

BOTANICAL: *Capsicum annuum*/Family Solanaceae
ENGLISH: none | **MAYAN:** *ya'ax iik*

A Maya vendor on the market terrace was selling these green chiles, freshly plucked from his milpa; he aptly called them *chiles de milpa*. The Mayan name means simply "green chile." Next to the habanero (p. 29), this is the most popular chile in Yucatán, and it is frequently planted to one side of the maize, beans, and squash. The finger-shaped chile measures about 1½ inches (4 cm) in length and ½ inch (1.5 cm) in width; it is moderately hot, ranging from 5,000 to 15,000 Scoville Heat Units. When dried, it is known as *chile seco* or *chile país*. It is the dried chile that is burned to ash, then ground with a few other herbs and spices to make Yucatán's signature seasoning blend, *recado negro*.

[PHOTOS BY MC]

The line forms early at Lonchería "San José" for the cheapest food in the market. [EC]

"EMPANADITAS" DE SAN JOSÉ

CRISPY "EMPANADAS" WITH VEGETARIAN TOPPINGS

At a tiny stall in the humble Izamal market, ample platters were filled with what appeared to be two kinds of picadillo, or chopped meat: one a meaty-looking brown color (beef?), the other an appetizing reddish color (pork?). And to one side were Yucatán's requisite and ubiquitous purple pickled onions—or so I thought. A casual chat with the stall's friendly owner, José Camaal Sosa, revealed the magician's secret: one of the imposter "meats" was actually made from tofu; the other, eggs scrambled with achiote then finely chopped. And the onions? Not onions at all, but rather finely chopped cabbage stained fluorescent fuchsia with thick slices of beet. I was astonished that in this land of die-hard carnivores, a vegetarian *puesto* (stall) would be so popular, as this one obviously was. However, the clever vendor readily confided that his creations had nothing to do with appealing to herbivores, but instead was a way to carve out a competitive niche in a market visited by folk of humble means. His famous "Empanaditas" de San José are cheap—just 2 pesos each (about 15 cents).

Prepare-ahead note: The tofu needs to be frozen at least 24 hours to reduce water content. You should prepare the fillings and keep them warm while you form and fry the empanadas.

YIELD: 8 SERVINGS/2 DOZEN EMPANADAS

FOR THE GARNISH

¼ small cabbage (9 oz./260 g), finely chopped

1 small beet (4½ oz./125 g), peeled and thickly sliced

½ cup (125 mL) white vinegar

½ teaspoon (3 g) sea salt

FOR THE FILLINGS

"Picadillo" de tofu

14 ounces (400 g) tofu

2 tablespoons (30 mL) vegetable oil

1 tablespoon (2 g) dried whole Mexican oregano *plus* ¼ teaspoon (0.75 g) cumin seed, lightly toasted and ground together

¼ teaspoon (1.25 g) freshly ground black pepper

½ teaspoon (3 g) sea salt

"Picadillo" de huevo

6 eggs

2 tablespoons (30 g) recado rojo ("de achiote")

1 tablespoon (15 mL) water

1 tablespoon (15 mL) vegetable oil

PREPARE THE GARNISH

Combine the ingredients in a nonreactive mixing bowl; allow to macerate for at least 30 minutes, tossing occasionally to distribute the color from the beets.

PREPARE THE FILLINGS

"Picadillo" de tofu

With the tofu in its original wrapping, freeze it for at least 24 hours. On the day you will be preparing the filling, bring the tofu to room temperature until completely soft. Remove the tofu from the package and pour off the water. Line a fine-mesh sieve with a piece of cheesecloth; place the tofu in the cheesecloth and use your fingers to squeeze out as much liquid as possible. Rinse the tofu, use your fingers to squeeze out the liquid again, and repeat this process until the liquid runs clear. When the liquid is clear, gather the ends of the cheesecloth, twist, and squeeze until virtually no liquid passes through.

Heat the vegetable oil in a large nonstick skillet until shimmering; transfer the tofu from the cheesecloth to the skillet and immediately begin to break it apart and crumble it with a wooden spoon or spatula; the texture should resemble ground pork or beef. Add the spices, stir to incorporate, and continue cooking another 2–3 minutes or until dry. Check seasonings and add salt if needed. Keep warm until ready to serve.

"Picadillo" de huevo

In a small mixing bowl, thoroughly beat the eggs and set aside; mix the *recado* with the water until completely dissolved. Beat the *recado* mixture into the eggs until thoroughly incorporated.

Heat the vegetable oil in a medium nonstick skillet until shimmering. Pour in the beaten egg mixture and immediately begin to stir it with a wooden spoon to scramble the eggs. Continue stirring until completely cooked. (*Note*: Commercial *recado* already contains salt, but you will want to check the seasonings anyway and add salt if necessary.)

An employee finely chops cabbage for the faux pickled onions. [MC]

FOR THE "EMPANADITAS"
2 cups (500 g) masa harina
½ teaspoon (3 g) sea salt
2 cups (500 mL) water
Vegetable oil for frying

FOR SERVING
Chile sauce of your choice

Transfer the scrambled eggs to a cutting board; chop the eggs finely, then return them to the skillet to keep warm until time to serve.

PREPARE AND FRY THE "EMPANADITAS"
Combine the masa harina, salt, and water thoroughly and let the dough rest for 15 minutes before proceeding. Form the dough into 24 balls weighing 0.7 oz. (20 g) each; keep them covered loosely with a towel as you work. Meanwhile, prepare a tortilla press: slit open a small plastic sandwich bag along the two sides; open it and place it onto the bottom round of the opened press: half of the plastic should rest on the bottom of the press, the other flap should extend toward the handle.

Pour 2 inches (5 cm) of vegetable oil into a large skillet; heat to a temperature of 375°F (190°C). Place one ball of dough in the center of the plastic, and fold the other half of the plastic to cover the ball. Lower the lever of the tortilla press, and gently press to form a tortilla about 4 inches (10 cm) in diameter. Use the plastic to lift the tortilla; place the tortilla on the palm of one hand while you peel away the plastic with the other. Add about 2 tablespoons of the tofu or egg mixture, fold the tortilla in half to resemble an empanada ("half-moon" shape), seal the edge of the empanada with your hands, then immediately plunge it into the hot oil. Fry only 3 or 4 *empanaditas* at a time, basting them with hot oil and turning once until golden brown, about 2–3 minutes. Remove to paper towels to drain.

TO SERVE
Plate 3 *empanaditas* per person, overlapping the corners slightly. Top with 2 tablespoons (12 g) of the cabbage garnish. Diners add chile sauce to taste if desired.

Venison is extremely rare—almost never seen—in Yucatán's markets in spite of its traditional popularity in the diet. So, the bright yellow signs hawking *venado de cola larga carne enterrada*—venison (*venado*) from the long-tailed deer cooked in one of Yucatán's famous underground ovens, known in Mayan as *píib*—caught my eye and led me to do a little sleuthing.

In fact, venison is so popular throughout the peninsula that several species of deer, including endemic ones like the Yucatán brown brocket deer (*Mazama pandora*), have been seriously overhunted, leading to government-applied hunting restrictions; scofflaws are subject to stiff fines or even jail time. Substitutions—and deceptions—therefore abound: often, when venison appears on restaurant menus,

a little arm-twisting will get waiters to reveal that "only today" is the venison actually beef, since the real thing "*no me llegó*" (didn't arrive). Because venison in Yucatán is so frequently shredded for its final use, it can be difficult to distinguish between the two meats. But closer inspection of the hefty chunks on display in the market—plus a free sample the vendor offered me—reassured me that the meat at Carnicería "El Tulipán" was indeed venison. Where it came from I may never know: thanks to those hunting restrictions coupled with Yucatecans' taste for venison, recent efforts to farm New Zealand red deer have begun but are only nascent—and not embraced. When I asked the vendor, "*¿Es criado?*" (Is it farmed?), he winked and whispered, "No, but let's just say I have my sources."

The vitrine of Taquería "La Pelusa" is packed with shanks of pit-smoked venison (right). Bones and visible parts of leg and hoof are left to "prove" it's really venison instead of beef. Trays of Salsa "Que no me olvides" (left rear) and finished Tsi'ik de venado (foreground) attract customers. [EC]

TSI'IK DE VENADO

MAYA "COBB SALAD" OF SHREDDED VENISON AND VEGETABLES

TO PREPARE AHEAD
Enriched Lard (p. 530)

FOR THE VENISON

1 gallon (4 L) water

½ cup (145 g) salt

½ cup (100 g) sugar

2 teaspoons (8 g) whole black peppercorns, coarsely crushed

10 whole allspice berries, coarsely crushed

2 pounds (1 kg) venison

FOR THE MARINADE

8 tablespoons (120 g) recado rojo (also known as "recado de achiote")

8 tablespoons (120 mL) Seville orange juice (substitute a mixture of 2 parts lime juice, 1 part grapefruit juice, and 1 part sweet orange juice)

2 tablespoons (28 g) Enriched Lard, melted

1 tablespoon (2 g) Mexican oregano flakes *plus* 1 teaspoon (3 g) cumin, lightly toasted together

1 teaspoon (12 g) whole black peppercorns

4 medium cloves garlic (1 oz./24 g), peeled and charred

1 tablespoon (18 g) sea salt

FOR GARNISHING AND WRAPPING

Large banana leaves

3 ounces (85 g) smoked bacon, thickly sliced (optional)

½ medium white onion (5 oz./137.5 g), thinly sliced and separated into rings

1 medium green bell pepper (6½ oz./185 g), seeded and thinly sliced into rings

Directly around the corner from Carnicería "El Tulipán" we found a tiny stall known as Taquería "La Pelusa"—really not much more than a rustic vitrine, a folding table, and a couple of stools—where Octaviano May and his entire family prepare memorable tacos of pit-smoked shredded venison that they cook themselves in their backyard. Part of the "memorable" aspect of these tacos comes from the salsa that they serve as an accompaniment, which they aptly name Salsa "Que no me olvides" ("Forget-me-not" sauce; recipe follows). The traditional preparation method for the venison is to roast it in a *píib*; the technique lends an ethereally smoky flavor to the meat. Smoking in a gas or charcoal grill using wood smoking chips can achieve a similar effect. The bacon is nontraditional and therefore optional, but it lends even more of the essential smokiness of Yucatecan food, and the fat is useful for lean game like venison.

Prepare-ahead note: The venison benefits from brining for 12–36 hours (see notes on brining on p. 527), although that step is optional; it also requires at least 30 minutes in the marinade. The venison can be cooked a day or two in advance; allow the meat to cool, then shred at room temperature (it is easier to shred if it has not been refrigerated), and refrigerate.

YIELD: 10 SERVINGS

BRINE THE VENISON

Combine the first 5 ingredients; stir until the salt and sugar are completely dissolved. Add the venison; refrigerate 12–36 hours. (As with other recipes in this book, the brining step is not traditional and therefore optional, but it does dramatically improve the flavor and texture of meats.)

PREPARE THE MARINADE

Dilute the *recado* with the juice; add the fat and stir to incorporate. Add more juice or *recado* to get the right consistency: thick, yet pourable, like barbecue sauce. Place the toasted oregano and cumin along with the remaining ingredients in a *tamul* or mortar and pestle (alternatively in a small food processor or blender), and grind until the garlic is thoroughly mashed and the mixture turns into a paste; add the paste to the *recado* mixture and stir to blend.

If you brined the meat, remove the venison from the brine, drain, rinse, and pat dry; discard the brining solution. Place the meat in a resealable plastic bag or a large baking dish; cover thoroughly on all sides with the marinade. (Your hands are the best tools for this job.) Marinate under refrigeration at least 30 minutes or up to 12 hours.

GARNISH AND WRAP THE MEAT

Arrange large pieces of banana leaf on a work surface, overlapping to avoid leaks. Place marinated meat in the center of the leaves and garnish the top with slices of optional bacon, onion, bell pepper, tomato, epazote, and bay or avocado leaves (in that order).

1 medium Roma tomato
(3½ oz./100 g), thinly sliced
across the width
1 bunch fresh epazote, separated
into leaves (substitute about
1 tsp. [0.125 g] dried epazote)
Bay or avocado leaves

FOR SERVING
Warm corn tortillas
Sliced avocado
Salsa "Que no me olvides"
(recipe follows)

Fold sides of banana leaves up and over, then tuck the ends, wrapping the meat as you would a package; tie with reserved ribs from the leaves or kitchen twine to secure. Allow meat to come to room temperature before cooking.

SMOKE MEAT AND FINISH
Preheat a gas or charcoal grill. Prepare mesquite wood smoking chips: if using charcoal, cover the chips with water and allow to soak for 30 minutes; if using gas, loosely wrap the chips in aluminum foil to form a small pouch. Locate the wrapped meat to one side of the heat source (a grilling basket will help contain it). Drain the chips and toss onto the hot coals of the charcoal grill; or, place the foil pouch under the grate of the gas grill as close to the heat source as possible. Close the lid and allow the venison to reach a temperature of 155°F–160°F (68°C–71°C). Allow the meat to cool to room temperature, then shred finely. Refrigerate until ready to serve.

TO SERVE
Mound a couple of heaping tablespoonfuls of the venison atop warm tortillas. Top with slices of avocado. Diners add their own Salsa "Que no me olvides" to taste. Since this taco is not served with lime wedges, diners should spoon plenty of the Seville orange juice from the salsa onto the meat.

[MC]

SALSA "QUE NO ME OLVIDES"

FIERY CHOPPED "FORGET-ME-NOT" SAUCE

FOR THE SALSA

1 cup (85 g) green cabbage, finely shredded

½ cup (60 g) radishes, halved and thinly sliced

½ cup (90 g) tomatoes (about 1 medium Roma), seeded, cut into medium dice, and drained

½ cup (85 g) red onion, cut into medium dice

2 medium chiles habaneros (½ oz./14 g total), or to taste, stems removed, leaving seeds intact; thinly slivered

1 cup (250 mL) Seville orange juice (substitute a mixture of 2 parts lime juice, 1 part grapefruit juice, and 1 part sweet orange juice, or all lime juice)

2 medium avocados (7½ oz./215 g), peeled, seeded, and cubed

¼ cup (15 g) cilantro, finely chopped

1 teaspoon (6 g) salt, or to taste

This sauce-qua-garnish is a fiery hybrid of Yucatán's *xni'pek* (dog's nose) salsa that features chopped onion, tomato, Seville orange juice, and habanero chiles; and the more conventional *salpicón* of shredded cabbage and slivered radishes used to prepare *tsi'ik*—Yucatán's ever-present chopped-meat-and-veg "Cobb salad." Peeking out here and there are also hearty chunks of avocado, the creamy fat of which seems to have a calming effect on the heat of the chiles.

PREPARE THE SALSA
Toss the first five ingredients together and refrigerate until ready to serve.

TO SERVE
Immediately before serving, add the remaining ingredients and toss to combine. Check seasonings.

[MC]

CHILE HABANERO

BOTANICAL: *Capsicum chinense*/Family Solanaceae | **ENGLISH:** habanero, Scotch bonnet | **MAYAN:** none

As important for regional pride as it is for income, the *chile habanero*—Yucatán's "mascot chile"—is grown by hundreds of small-scale producers throughout the peninsula, particularly in the zone immediately surrounding the state capital of Mérida. Yucatán is the most important source of *chile habanero* in Mexico, accounting for two-thirds of national output. In 2010, the chile was granted controlled denomination status as "*Chile habanero de la península de Yucatán.*" The demand for *chile habanero* exploded in the early twenty-first century: a large share of production is processed and exported to the United States and Japan as a paste, as a powder, and as dried peppers. Once ranked as the world's hottest chile, the habanero scores between 150,000 and 350,000 Scoville Heat Units. While several hybrids have recently stolen the title, the habanero is, if not the hottest chile in the world, then surely it is the hottest chile in Mexico. The habanero is revered among commercial salsa producers for its uniquely fresh/floral flavor; for more searing heat they rely on other species—remarkable considering how hot the chile is perceived to be by the uninitiated. Yucatecan cuisine is not considered complete without at least a few drops of a salsa containing the chile—or a few bites of a whole one. *Chile habanero* also appears in many Yucatecan foods beyond salsas, such as masa for tamales, bean dishes, or sautéed *chaya*. The habanero was first noted by the Spaniards in the Antilles, but in Yucatán it acquired the name "habanero" (one who or that which comes from Havana). It even reached the Eastern Hemisphere: in the eighteenth century, taxonomists erroneously concluded that it was of Asian origin and dubbed the species *Capsicum chinense*.

"Lights" vendor. [MC]

The jovial José Alejandro Gómez Rodríguez—owner of the *puesto* of all things beef known as El Divino Niño—told me that his beef comes from small production ranches within a radius of just 25 to 30 miles (40 to 50 km) of town. In the early colonial era, most of Yucatán was covered with grazing cattle, but today ranching is concentrated primarily in the area around Tizimín. The ranchers let their cows graze on what scrub may be available, and when the *sequía* (late winter drought) comes, cows just won't fatten, so they slaughter more than usual and sell the meat for a lower price—explaining the glut of beef (and customers) don José had on the day we visited.

Dangling from a rack at the corner of one of his butchers' tables was something I recognized as a "prepackaged" assortment of all the beef parts necessary for a famous regional dish, *mondongo k'aab-ik*—a rustic tripe stew fired up with local chiles. The large, pouch-like rumen (*toalla*, the gently textured "towel" tripe) was stuffed with a smaller bit of the reticulum (*colmena*, the "honeycomb" tripe) as well as a hefty pair of hooves (*patas*).

Noting my fascination with this offal goody bag, don José told me about a *puesto* that sells *to'bijoloch de bofe* (p. 31)—a tamale made of finely chopped beef lungs—and asked if I might be interested in a pair of the organs. He hauled them out of his small chest-type refrigerator and proudly splayed them on the table. Unfortunately for us, the tamales are so popular that they arrive at the market by 6:00 a.m. and sell out by 7:00 a.m., so we had to return the next day to enjoy them—and they were well worth the trip and the dawn's early rise.

(above) *After several hours of simmering, the marshmallow-tender* mondongo *at the Puesto "Ramón Araujo." Cook doña Soco Burgos Cetina uses three chile varieties for her* mondongo: *x'catik, chile de árbol, and habanero—clearly, her* mondongo *packs a punch. The tripe is served on a plate, the picante broth in a bowl, with garnishes of chopped habanero and chives on the side.* [MC]

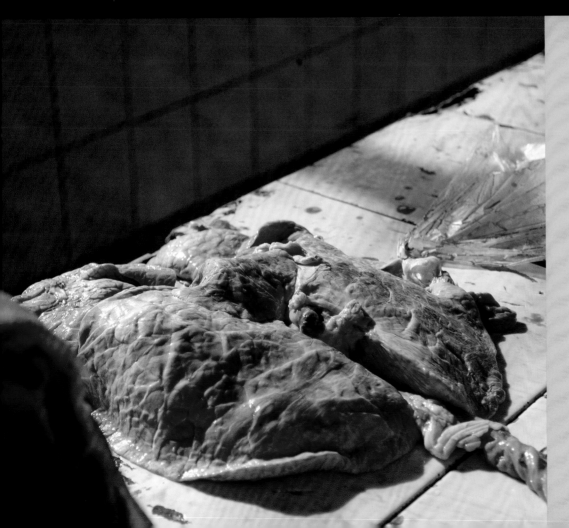

TO'BIJOLOCH DE BOFE/ BEEF LIGHT TAMALE

No, this isn't a "light tamale"; rather, "light" is a euphemism used in some English-speaking countries for the lungs of livestock. The English term dates to the medieval era and refers to "the light organs" (light in weight); it may be present in a common phrase "to knock someone's lights out," to render someone breathless. Lights are a frequent component in the Scottish stuffed-stomach sausage known as haggis, and they are broadly consumed in many countries of Europe (France, Hungary, Germany, Italy) and throughout Asia, in dishes famous and well loved. In Spanish-speaking countries and some regions of Mexico, lights are often included in *chanfaina*, a traditional organ meat stew with many variations. The more traditional *to'bijoloch* of Yucatán is a tamale filled with stewed or *piib*-smoked shredded pork and a sauce of achiote-tinged stock thickened with maize masa. This tamale substitutes the pork with a finely chopped picadillo of beef lungs, onion, garlic, and toasted ground squash seeds. Difficult to find in the United States, beef lungs are sometimes available at halal butchers.

(Left) "Lights" at El Divino Niño. [MC]

Humberto May Polanco was born in Izamal and has devoted his entire life to making tamales. He has been selling them in the market as well as on the streets of Izamal since he was a teenager—close to sixty years. His tamale known as to'bijoloch de bofe is a crowd pleaser, and his daily stock stacked carefully in a blue plastic bucket sells out within an hour. [MC]

TAQUITOS DE MORCILLA

TACOS OF BLOOD SAUSAGE, FRIED ONIONS, AND CHILES

TO PREPARE AHEAD

Enriched Lard (see p. 530, or substitute)

Blood sausage, known here as *morcilla*, is a perennial favorite throughout the Spanish diaspora. In Yucatán, every *chicharronería* prepares its own version of *morcilla*, usually chopped after frying and mixed with other meats and offal in the popular *chicharra surtida*. Many stalls—like the Puesto Ramón Araujo run by Armando Araujo Marín and his wife, Soco Burgos Cetina—also sell *morcilla* as its own stand-alone item, sautéed with sliced onions until the onions begin to caramelize. Recipes for preparing the actual sausage *morcilla* abound; most European versions include parsley in the blood mixture, but in Yucatán, cilantro and mint are the herbs of choice, lending these rich sausages a fragrant, light note. For this reason, I include those herbs in the sautéed mixture, which enhances that effect, especially important for commercial *morcilla*. *Morcilla* can be found at specialty markets or online. Yours will likely be precooked, but if fresh, poach the sausages in gently simmering water for 10 minutes or until a meat thermometer registers 165°F (74°C). Once fully cooked, the sausages are briefly sautéed, as per the following instructions.

Prepare-ahead note: The sauté may be prepared a few hours in advance and kept warm on the stovetop or in a slow oven. Reheat briefly and stir just before serving.

YIELD: 6—8 SERVINGS

[MC]

FOR THE TACOS

2 tablespoons (28 g) Enriched Lard (substitute vegetable oil)

1 pound (500 g) morcilla

1 medium white onion (10 oz./275 g), thinly sliced and separated into rings

2 whole chiles x'catik (2½ oz./70 g) total (substitute any blond chile such as Anaheim, Italian sweet, or banana pepper), seeded and cut into julienne

1 teaspoon (6 g) sea salt

1 tablespoon whole dried Mexican oregano *plus* ½ teaspoon (1 g) cumin seed, lightly toasted and ground together

½ teaspoon (2.5 g) ground black pepper

¼ cup (15 g) fresh mint leaves, coarsely chopped

¼ cup (15 g) fresh cilantro leaves, coarsely chopped

FOR SERVING

Warm corn tortillas

Habanero salsa or whole habaneros

PREPARE THE TACOS

Heat the lard in a large skillet until it is shimmering; add the whole sausages and sauté until lightly browned. Remove from the heat, transfer the sausages to a cutting board, and slice into thick rounds (dimensions don't matter, since the sausages will likely crumble during the next steps).

Heat the fat in the skillet until it is shimmering; add the onions and chiles, and cook, stirring frequently, until the onions are lightly caramelized, 6–8 minutes. Return the sliced sausages to the skillet and stir to incorporate; if the sausages do not naturally crumble, use a wooden spoon to break them up a bit. Add the seasonings, and cook, stirring frequently, 3–4 minutes to amalgamate flavors. Stir in the herbs; heat for 30 seconds, stirring constantly, and serve immediately.

TO SERVE

If your tortillas are thin, use two per taco. Top the warm tortillas with a heaping spoonful of the sautéed mixture and serve.

[MC]

COCHINITA NEGRA

SLOW-ROASTED PORK LEG IN CHARRED CHILE SAUCE

TO PREPARE AHEAD
Enriched Lard (see p. 530, or substitute)

Soco Burgos Cetina and her husband have had their *puesto* in the market since 1989 and have developed a very loyal following. I found doña Soco's pork recipe unusual because it is a riff on several beloved Yucatecan classics: Cochinita pibil, Pavo en relleno negro, and Lechón al horno. The first dish is an icon of Yucatecan gastronomy: traditionally, a small pig is marinated in achiote and Seville orange juice, then roasted in a *píib*. The next dish is known for its prodigious use of a charred-chile seasoning paste known as *recado negro*. The third dish is a suckling pig or pork leg with fat and skin that is roasted in a wood-burning oven, lending a lightly smoky taste. For Cochinita negra, the pork is first rubbed with the pitch black *recado negro*, then it is roasted in the residual heat of a baker's wood fire after all the bread baking for the day has been completed. I have adapted this recipe so that the pork roasts in a charcoal or gas grill over wood smoking chips rather than in a wood-burning oven. To finish off the roasted pork, a delicious *caldo* (stock) is made by simmering the pork in a liquid made with the chile paste and a few other flavorings—similar to the process for Pavo en relleno negro. Slightly thickened, the resulting graphite "gravy" is an essential component of the meal.

Known variously as *recado negro*, *recado para chilmole*, or simply *chilmole*, the charred-chile paste is available commercially beyond Mexico under several brand names.

FOR THE PORK

1 gallon (4 L) water

½ cup (145 g) salt

½ cup (100 g) sugar

2 teaspoons (8 g) whole black peppercorns, coarsely crushed

10 whole allspice berries, coarsely crushed

2 pounds (1 kg) pork rump or leg, with skin and fat intact

FOR THE MARINADE

8 tablespoons (120 g) recado negro

8 tablespoons (120 mL) Seville orange juice (substitute a mixture of 2 parts lime juice, 1 part grapefruit juice, and 1 part sweet orange juice)

2 tablespoons (28 g) Enriched Lard, melted (substitute vegetable oil)

1 tablespoon (2 g) whole dried Mexican oregano *plus* 1 teaspoon (3 g) cumin, lightly toasted together

1 teaspoon (12 g) whole black peppercorns

4 medium cloves garlic (1 oz./24 g), peeled and charred

1 tablespoon (18 g) sea salt

FOR THE STOCK

2 tablespoons (28 g) Enriched Lard

1 medium onion (10 oz./275 g), charred and finely chopped

4 medium cloves garlic (1 oz./24 g), charred and finely chopped

3 medium Roma tomatoes (10½ oz./300 g), charred and coarsely chopped

1 tablespoon (2 g) whole dried Mexican oregano, lightly toasted and crumbled

1 sprig fresh epazote (substitute 1 tsp. [0.125 g] dried, crumbled)

10 cups (2.5 L) water, divided

Prepare-ahead note: The optional brining step must be completed a day in advance. The entire dish may be prepared a day ahead and reheated.

YIELD: 8 SERVINGS

BRINE THE PORK

Combine the first 5 ingredients; stir until the salt and sugar are completely dissolved. Add the pork; refrigerate 12–36 hours. (The brining step is optional. See p. 527 for notes on brining.)

PREPARE THE MARINADE

Dilute the *recado* with the juice; add the fat and stir to incorporate. Add more juice or *recado* to get the right consistency: thick, yet pourable, like barbecue sauce. Place the toasted oregano and cumin along with the remaining ingredients in a *tamul* or mortar and pestle (alternatively in a small food processor or blender), and grind until the garlic is thoroughly mashed and the whole turns into a paste; add the spice mixture to the *recado* mixture and stir to blend.

Remove the pork from the brine, drain, rinse, and pat dry; discard the brining solution. Place the meat in a flameproof roasting pan; cover the meat thoroughly on all sides with the marinade. (Your hands are the best tools for this job.) Marinate under refrigeration at least 30 minutes or up to 12 hours.

ROAST THE MEAT

Preheat a gas or charcoal grill. Prepare mesquite wood smoking chips: if using charcoal, cover the chips with water and allow to soak for 30 minutes; if using gas, loosely wrap the chips in aluminum foil to form a small pouch. Place the roasting pan containing the meat to one side of the heat source. Drain the chips and toss onto the hot coals of the charcoal grill; or, place the foil pouch under the grate of the gas grill as close to the heat source as possible. Close the lid and allow the pork to reach a temperature of 110°F–120°F (43°C–49°C), adding more wood chips as necessary. The meat will not be fully cooked through; it will finish cooking on the stovetop. Remove the meat from the grill and reserve any juices that collected in the roasting pan.

PREPARE THE STOCK

While the meat is roasting, prepare the stock: heat the lard in a large stockpot until shimmering; add the onions and garlic and cook until translucent. Add the tomatoes and herbs and continue cooking another 5 minutes or until most of the liquid from the tomatoes has evaporated. Place the roasted pork and its juices into the stockpot containing the *sofrito*. Add 9 cups (2.25 L) water; bring to a boil, then reduce to a simmer. Place the remaining 1 cup (250 mL) water and the next three ingredients in the jar of a blender and process until thoroughly liquefied. Pour the contents of the blender through a fine-mesh sieve lined with cheesecloth into the stockpot; mash through and squeeze the cheesecloth to extract as much of the liquid as possible; discard any residue. Continue at a simmer until the pork reaches an internal temperature of 145°F

1 medium head garlic
(1¾ oz./50 g), charred and
separated into cloves
5 tablespoons (75 g) recado negro
2 tablespoons (24 g) powdered
chicken bouillon, or 2 bouillon
cubes
½ cup (67.5 g) masa harina

FOR SERVING
8 eggs, hard-boiled and quartered
Tacos: 36 corn tortillas
Tortas: 8 French rolls

(63°C). Remove the pork; when it is cool to the touch, pull it into large pieces; set aside and finish the stock.

FINISH THE SAUCE
Bring cooking liquid to a rapid boil and continue cooking another 8–10 minutes to reduce slightly. Mix 1 cup (250 mL) cooking liquid with the masa harina. Beat until well incorporated; transfer the mixture to the cooking liquid; return to a boil, reduce to a simmer, and whisk constantly until thoroughly incorporated. Continue to simmer another 10 minutes or until slightly thickened, whisking occasionally to prevent lumps. (*Note*: If lumps do form, use an immersion blender to smooth.)

TO SERVE
Doña Soco offered us three ways of ordering and eating the *cochinita*: as a plated dish (*plato, left foreground*); as a sandwich on French bread (*torta, rear center*); or as tacos (*right foreground*). Plate the dish by placing a mound of the pulled pork into a soup bowl; ladle on some of the stock, and top with the quartered boiled egg. To create a *torta*, slice a French roll in half, dip the cut sides into the cooking liquid, and place some of the pulled pork on the bread; garnish with sliced hard-boiled eggs. To create tacos, fill 3 or 4 tortillas with some of the shredded pork and roll into cylinders; spoon on some of the stock and top with sliced boiled eggs.

[MC]

PASTEL DE GALLETAS FRANCISCANO

FRANCISCAN ICEBOX PIE

FOR THE PIE

Approximately 20 tea biscuits or petits beurres

1 12-ounce (354 mL) can evaporated milk

¼ cup (62.5 mL) sweet sherry

1 14-ounce (396 g) can sweetened condensed milk

¼ cup (62.5 mL) freshly squeezed lime juice

Zest of 1 lime, finely grated

The market of Izamal kneels at the foot of an ancient Maya pyramid, the worn steps of which ascend to the sixteenth-century convent at the summit. The convent houses both nuns and monks of the Franciscan order. Therefore, it is not uncommon to see the faithful going about their daily business selling confections in the market, as they do in so many places in Mexico and have done for centuries, to raise money for their charitable works. During our visit, a couple of young monks were passing through the market selling flan and also a simple icebox pie they called *pastel de galletas* (cookie cake). Did the nuns make these desserts, in the great tradition of Mexico's convent sweets? No, they told me: the monks also make simple treats, mostly of the "no-bake" variety like this one. Times change.

Pastel de galletas franciscano is a heavenly hybrid resembling tiramisu, *pastel de tres leches*, and the icebox pies my mother used to make. The typical sweetened cookie used is thin and rectangular, like a tea biscuit or the French *petit beurre*.

YIELD: 8 SLICES

PREPARE THE PIE

Line the bottom of a 9-inch (20 cm) pie plate with one-third of the cookies, butted side to side and end to end; to fill the spaces around the edges, break cookies in halves or quarters. Try to cover the bottom of the pie pan, leaving few gaps.

Mix the evaporated milk with the sherry and set aside; mix the sweetened condensed milk with the juice and zest and set aside. Pour half of the evaporated milk over the first layer of cookies to cover. Arrange another layer of cookies on top of the first, and spread a thin layer of the condensed milk on top to cover. Repeat these steps until all of the ingredients are used, finishing with a layer of the sweetened condensed milk. Refrigerate at least 4 hours. Slice and serve chilled.

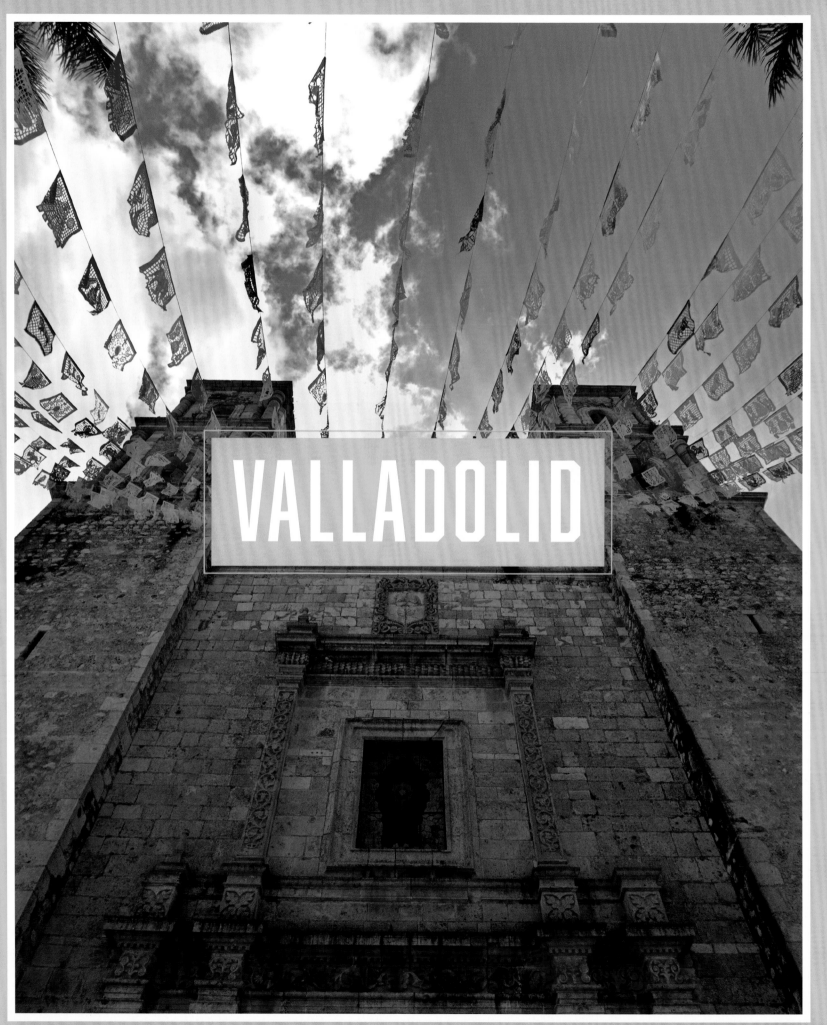

VALLADOLID

Mercado Municipal "Donato Bates Herrera." [EC]

Lᴀ sᴜʟᴛᴀɴᴀ ᴅᴇʟ ᴏʀɪᴇɴᴛᴇ—"Sultaness of the East"—is the sobriquet frequently applied to Valladolid, a town of about 45,000 inhabitants just 100 miles (162 km) east (*oriente* in Spanish) of Mérida. It is a common lunchtime stopover for tourists traveling from Cancún to the impressive archaeological site of Chichén Itzá. The romantic and somewhat aloof tone of the nickname is perhaps fitting: for years after its founding in 1543, and well into the nineteenth century, the people of Valladolid considered themselves the elite among Spanish gentry of the peninsula and were proud of their Iberian heritage. Principal streets were trimmed with mansions emblazoned with Castilian coats of arms above their doorways, and both pureblood Mayas and mestizos were restricted from the city center.

These facts positioned Valladolid at the crux of both regional and national struggles for the rights of native peoples. In 1546, a group of rebel Mayas—bent on revenge for a series of complaints, including their conscripted servitude and the tribute extracted from them by the Spanish Crown—rose up against hacienda owners, and although the violent revolt was quickly squelched, the conflict fanned the flames for further Maya uprisings, and would ultimately serve as a banner for indigenous rights. And, for more than sixty years starting in 1847, the infamous Guerra de las Castas (Caste War), which ignited in Valladolid, served to reshape the roles of both gentry and Mayas and ultimately built a foundation for Maya solidarity and pride.

The gastronomy of Valladolid mirrors its history. During the colonial period, the table of *vallisoletanos*—people from Valladolid—reflected their aspirational self-image and was replete with expensive prestige goods such as imported black pepper and sweet Spanish wines. In the modern market of Valladolid, it is still possible to find vintage recipes imported from Spain like *mechado*—meat larded with ham and cooked in a peppery broth dotted with capers, raisins, olives, and almonds. And today, many Maya foods, particularly tamales and other maize-based breads, take their rightful place at tables in the market stalls, too.

(above) Unlike the colossal market in Mérida—with its enigmatic cubbyholes and maze-like pathways—the much smaller Mercado Municipal "Donato Bates Herrera," just a block from the cenote of Zaci in the center of Valladolid, is bright, open, and logically organized. The main produce section is arranged in neat rows beneath an airy ceiling, and tidy eateries in small stalls rim the periphery. As is often the case in the markets of Mexico, vendors of prepared foods purchase most of their ingredients from their colleagues in the market. [EC] (below) Most of the vendors in Valladolid's municipal market are of Maya descent and wear traditional clothing. Many vendors are propios—those who grow their own produce and sell it in the market. [EC]

(above) A Maya ambulante *sells radishes and cilantro on a sidewalk outside the market.* [MR] *(below) According to William W. Dunmire in* Gardens of New Spain, *radishes (Raphanus sativus) were so popular in Spain that Columbus brought seeds to plant in the Antilles on his second American voyage in 1493. Radishes appear in many Yucatecan chopped salads and salsas, like Tsi'ik (p. 26).* [EC]

YUKATEK MAYAN/ MÀAYA T'ÀAN

The name they call themselves means simply "Mayan speech." The area the Mayas occupy is vast, including all of what is now considered the Yucatán Peninsula and extending south into several countries of Central America. Occupation of the region has been dated to between 13,000 and 11,000 BCE. The civilization reached its peak between 300 and 900 CE, known as the Classic period, and gradually diminished in power and importance thereafter and up to the arrival of the Europeans. The Mayas are credited with great works of art and architecture, fully developed writing and calendrical systems, and thriving market and trade networks. Since at least 1000 BCE, these networks supplied Honduras and Guatemala as well as central Mexico with salt, cacao, chicle, and many other coveted goods. The Mayan language is actually a language family composed of approximately twenty-eight distinct language groups; some 6 million indigenous people still speak forms of Mayan throughout the entire region, mostly in Guatemala, Belize, and Honduras. Mayan is still spoken by about 1.5 million people in Mexico; the largest language group is the Yukatek branch spoken in the Yucatán Peninsula. The traditional milpa system of farming continues virtually unchanged to the present day, and a substantial percentage of Yucatán's Maya population is still engaged in the practice. Government-subsidized programs foster traditional crafts like wood and stone carving, weaving of sisal products, and embroidery.

ACHIOTE

BOTANICAL: *Bixa orellana* L./Family Bixaceae | **ENGLISH:** annatto, lipstick tree, achiote | **MAYAN:** *kiwi'*

Recados—seasoning blends—are sometimes referred to as "the curries of Yucatán." Each *recado* (*xak'* in Mayan) is colored and flavored by its predominant ingredient; and each *recado* has its well-prescribed use in the gastronomy of Yucatán. *Recado rojo*, one of the most popular peninsular seasoning blends, is made with achiote, known in English as annatto. The prickly-looking achiote pod grows on a fruiting shrub or small tree that can reach 16½ to 33 feet (5 to 10 m) in height. Inside the pod are approximately fifty bright orange-to-red seeds. The seeds produce a potent dye, which in fact was used by the ancient Mayas as a paint, a clothing dye, and a colorant for the chocolate beverage.

Many people in Yucatán have achiote trees growing in their family orchards, since its use occurs almost daily in the peninsula. Once the pod is dry, it splits open, and the seeds are easily gathered; bags full of the seeds are sold in every market in Yucatán. According to food writer Harold McGee, the taste of achiote may be described as woody terpene humulone, which is also found in hops. For the *recado*, the seeds are finely ground with Mexican oregano (*Lippia graveolens*, p. 396), cumin seed, black pepper, and a few other ingredients. The paste is also broadly available commercially beyond Mexico.

(above) Not only food is sold in the market: since pre-Columbian times, useful kitchen tools like this hand-hewn limestone metate (ka' in Mayan), or grinding stone, have been plentiful. [EC]

(right) Seasonal native fruits: (left foreground) nance agrio (Botanical: Byrsonima bucidaefolia Standley/Family Malpighiaceae; English: sour murici; Mayan: sakpaj); (center foreground) saramuyo (Botanical: Annona squamosa L./ Family Annonaceae; English: sweetsop; Mayan: ts'almuy); (center right) guaya (Botanical: Talisia olivaeformis [Kunth] Radkl/Family Sapindaceae; English: honeyberry; Mayan: wayum). To the far left are bundles of the shell beans known as espelón (Vigna unguiculata [L.] Walp). [EC]

(far right) A vendor sells dulce de calabaza—squash cooked in sugar syrup. Holes allow the syrup to penetrate to the core. [MC]

(below) Convento de San Bernardino de Siena, founded in 1552. [DS]

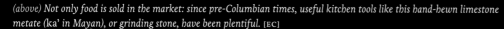

PIBILHUA DE LOMITOS

MAIZE BREAD SANDWICH OF STEWED PORK LOIN

TO PREPARE AHEAD

Enriched Lard (p. 530)

FOR BROWNING THE PORK

2 tablespoons (28 g) Enriched Lard

1 medium white onion
  (10 oz./275 g), peeled, charred,
  and cut to medium dice

8 medium cloves garlic
  (1½ oz./48 g), peeled and charred

2 pounds (1 kg) pork loin or leg,
  with some fat, cut into ¾-inch
  (2 cm) cubes

Lomitos de Valladolid is a classic dish of the pueblo, dating back at least 150 years. Cubed pork loin (*lomo* in Spanish) is slowly stewed in tomatoes, vinegar, and chiles—the ultimate mestizo combination; the meat is typically served atop a bed of puréed lima beans, but the innovation of Marciala Silva Luh, owner of the *puesto* "La Mudita," is to serve it as a sandwich on maize bread. *Pibilhua* in Mayan translates to "pit-baked" (*pibil*) "bread" (*hua* is also sometimes transcribed as *waaj*). The maize breads are crispy on the outside, soft and moist on the inside, and they have a lightly smoky flavor from being baked underground. To achieve a similar effect, ideally one would wrap the breads in banana leaves and cook them in a stovetop smoker or a charcoal grill to add the smoky flavor. Assuming that is too much work for most cooks, I'll provide instructions for frying them instead (although hopefully you'll experiment with the smoking!).

Prepare-ahead notes: The *lomitos* may be prepared a day or two in advance and reheated. The maize breads may be formed and refrigerated for a couple of hours; bring to room temperature and fry them immediately before serving.

YIELD: 8 SERVINGS OF TWO "SANDWICHES" PER PERSON

BROWN THE PORK

In a deep casserole or Dutch oven, heat the lard until shimmering; add the onions and whole garlic cloves and cook until the onions are translucent. Add the pork and sauté

[EC]

2 pounds (1 kg) Roma tomatoes,
    coarsely chopped

1 tablespoon (18 g) sea salt

6 whole chiles país, or 3 chiles de
    árbol (about 3 g total), toasted in
    a skillet until darkened

1 tablespoon (15 g) Recado rojo,
    dissolved in 2 tablespoons
    (30 mL) water

1 sprig fresh epazote (substitute
    1 tsp./0.125 g dried)

½ cup (125 mL) white vinegar

1 teaspoon (3 g) ground cayenne

FOR THE MAIZE AND BEAN BREADS

½ cup (112 g) Enriched Lard,
    chilled

1 tablespoon (12 g) baking powder

2 pounds (1 kg) fresh masa from
    nixtamal

½ cup (67.5 g) masa harina

1 medium clove garlic (¼ oz./6 g),
    peeled, charred, and minced

3 tablespoons (36 g) powdered
    chicken bouillon, dissolved in
    ½ cup (125 mL) hot water

1½ cups (250 g) fresh x'pelones or
    ibes (substitute fresh or frozen
    black-eyed peas or lima beans,
    cooked until just tender, not
    mushy, and drained)

Vegetable oil for frying

FOR SERVING

8 eggs, hard-boiled, peeled, and
    sliced

Habanero chile sauce or the chile
    sauce of your choice

over high heat, stirring frequently, until browned and onions are caramelized, about 5–6 minutes.

STEW THE PORK

Add the first five ingredients to the pork. Mash down the tomatoes periodically so that they break apart. Simmer uncovered over medium heat about 30 minutes, or until the tomatoes are completely rendered and reduced. Add the vinegar and continue cooking another 15 minutes, stirring constantly to avoid sticking, until most of the liquid has evaporated. The resulting sauce should thickly coat the pork pieces, and the bottom of the pot should be almost dry. Check the seasonings and add the cayenne; cover and keep warm until serving.

PREPARE THE MAIZE AND BEAN BREADS

Place the chilled lard and baking powder in the bowl of an electric mixer; beat on high speed until the lard turns fluffy and creamy, about 3 minutes.

Add the masa a bit at a time, beating after each addition until incorporated. Add the masa harina and garlic and beat on low to combine. With the motor still running, slowly add the bouillon mixture. Add enough to create a moist but not soggy dough: it should easily be formed into a ball without sticking to your fingers. Beat on high speed until thoroughly incorporated and the dough lightened, about 5 minutes. Remove the bowl from the mixer, add the whole beans, and knead with your hands to thoroughly incorporate. Cover the masa with a damp towel until ready to use.

Form the masa into 16 2½-ounce (75 g) balls. Working one at a time, cup your hands and roll the dough in the hollow of your palms, forming it into a smooth and elongated egg shape. Set aside and continue with remaining balls of masa.

Pour the vegetable oil into a deep skillet to a depth of 1½ inches (4 cm). Heat to 350°F (176°C). Add 3 to 4 of the maize breads at a time, being careful not to overcrowd. Fry until deep golden brown; flip and fry the other side. Drain on paper towels as you finish the rest.

TO SERVE

Use a sharp knife to split each maize bread down the center lengthwise. Place two of the breads per diner on individual serving plates, and spoon on a generous portion of the pork stew. Garnish with the sliced boiled egg. This is finger food in Valladolid, so be sure to offer plenty of napkins.

AREPITAS DE ALMIDÓN DE YUCA

CRISPY TAPIOCA FLOUR COOKIES

FOR THE AREPITAS

5 large egg whites, at room
  temperature
Pinch of sea salt
½ cup (125 mL) water
1⅓ cups (265 g) granulated sugar
½ cup (51 g) tapioca flour
½ teaspoon (1.5 g) ground canela
  (Mexican cinnamon; substitute
  zest of ½ large lime, finely
  grated)

Yuca (*Manihot esculenta*)—not to be confused with the decorative plant known as yucca—appears in many guises in the Valladolid market. Also known as cassava and manioc, yuca has been cultivated by the Yukatek Mayas since around 3000 BCE, and has sustained many peoples of the tropical Americas and the Caribbean for millennia; colonial chroniclers noted that the Arawak and Carib tribes of the Antilles made a flat-bread they called *casabe* that was made from pounded and grated yuca. Arepas—maize flatbreads—are typically associated with Venezuela and Colombia; they may also be made with grated yuca. Although low in protein, yuca is the third-largest source of carbohydrates in the world after rice and maize. Today, the starch (*almidón*) extracted from the tuber—known as tapioca starch or tapioca flour—is put to a wide range of purposes. The starch is an excellent thickener and has many uses in baking; it is also formed into pearls for the popular dessert pudding known as tapioca. In the Valladolid market, the crispy, light-as-air wafers known as *arepitas* (little arepas) are made of yuca flour and egg whites; as a result, they are gluten-free and almost completely fat-free—and cost just a few cents apiece. The starch is widely available, but if you are unable to locate it, purchase tapioca pearls and grind them twice: once in a food processor and again in a clean spice mill or coffee grinder to make the result as fine as possible. The market vendor who specialized in all things yuca used a pinch of *canela* (Mexican cinnamon) in his *arepitas*, but occasionally I use finely grated lime zest instead.

Prepare-ahead note: Arepitas de almidón de yuca keep well for a week or more in an airtight container.

YIELD: APPROXIMATELY 1 DOZEN

PREPARE THE AREPITAS

Preheat the oven to 250°F (121°C). Line two baking sheets with parchment. For convenience, place a stand mixer next to the stove where you will be making the sugar syrup. Beat the egg whites on low until they foam; add the salt; increase the speed to medium high and beat until soft peaks form. Turn the machine to very slow while you make the sugar syrup.

Choose a small saucepan equipped with a lid; combine the water and the sugar in the saucepan; place over high heat, swirling gently to dissolve the sugar; cover and continue to cook over high heat. Lift the lid after a minute or two: the sugar should be completely dissolved and the liquid clear. Remove the lid and insert a candy thermometer into the syrup: continue cooking on high heat until the syrup reaches the soft-ball stage, 238°F (114°C), 2–3 minutes.

Immediately turn the mixer to medium-high speed and continue beating as you slowly stream in the syrup. When all has been added, increase the speed to fast and beat for 6–8 minutes or until the meringue has cooled. Add the tapioca flour and *canela* (or lime zest if using) and continue beating until well incorporated, 1–2 minutes.

Form the wafers by spooning approximately ½ cup (106 g) of the meringue onto the prepared baking sheet; use a spatula to spread the meringue into a flat disk measuring about 5 inches (12.5 cm) in diameter.

Place the baking sheets in the preheated oven, locating one close to the top and one close to the bottom; bake for 20 minutes, then rotate the sheets. Bake another 20 minutes, then turn off the heat. Leave the wafers in the oven another 20 minutes. Remove and allow to cool to the touch; store in an airtight container.

All things yuca: Left, the yuca tuber; center background, a jícara gourd bowl holds (clockwise) yuca sweetened with refined sugar, buñuelos *(fritters) made from yuca, and yuca sweetened with the brown cone sugar known as* piloncillo; *right foreground,* Arepitas de almidón de yuca. [MC]

[MC]

[MC]

MARACUYÁ/GRANADILLA, PARCHA

BOTANICAL: *Passiflora edulis* f. *flavicarpa* Deg./Family Passifloraceae | **ENGLISH:** passion fruit | **MAYAN:** *poch'il*

A low stone wall that runs along the side of the Convento de San Bernardino de Siena is festooned with the trailing vines of *maracuyá*—passion fruit. There happened to be both flowers and fruits on the vines when we visited in early July; fruits are available primarily from May through June, and there were still bushel baskets full of them in the market. Surreal and exotic in appearance, the delicately fragrant flower attracts local bee and butterfly populations. Passion fruit is another Amazon basin native, but the vine dispersed naturally to Central America, Mexico, and the Caribbean. Spanish and Portuguese explorers carried it with them on their exploits, and now passion fruit can be found growing in Australia and New Zealand, Hawaii, Thailand, and many other subtropical regions; today, over five hundred cultivate types exist. There are two main varieties: one that produces a purple fruit, and the other, a yellow fruit, which is the variety found in the Yucatán Peninsula.

The ovoid fruit measures 1½ to 3 inches (4–7.5 cm) wide; its tough rind is smooth and waxy, and the Yucatecan variety appears as a pale yellow to pumpkin color. The rind itself is ⅛-inch (3 mm) thick and is attached to a ¼-inch (6 mm) layer of white pith inside. The cavity of the fruit is filled with an aromatic mass of pulpy juice suspending double-walled, membranous sacs filled with more juice and as many as 250 small, hard, dark brown or black seeds. The flavor of passion fruit is lightly sweet, slightly acidic, musky, and not unlike guava. Globally, passion fruit is used in pies, jellies, mousses, and even as a glaze for meats, but in Yucatán the primary use is for the preparation of *aguas frescas*—fruit juice mixed with water and sugar and served chilled. When the *agua fresca* is poured into small tubular bags and frozen, it becomes the popular hot-weather treat known as *bolis de maracuyá*; it can also be made into a refreshing sorbet.

Commercially produced sweet treats are colorful additions to every market, like these paletas (lollipops) and zunchos (a Yucatecan colloquialism for malvaviscos, or marshmallows, at far left). [EC]

2
—

SOUTHERN
HIGHLANDS

INTRODUCTION

WHEN YOU ENTER the Southern Highlands for the first time, you must downshift your perceptions from the everyday to the otherworldly. The starkly contrasting terrain ranges from tropical coastlines to soaring peaks dotted with high valley towns blanketed in mist. It is such fertile terrain that almost any species can be—and is—grown here, from New World tropical avocados to Old World temperate apples, from low-altitude Mexican cacao to high-altitude African coffee.

The names of the two states that compose the vast majority of the region—Chiapas and Oaxaca—come from Nahuatl words for exotic food plants that abound here. Chianpan translates loosely to "place of *chía*"—the oily seed (*Salvia hispanica*) now found in every health food store—and Huaxyacac means "nose (or center) of *guajes*" (*Leucaena leucocephala*, p. 95), a leguminous tree with edible seeds. Seeking to capitalize on these and other valuable resources—including gold—the Aztecs extended their empire to engulf most of

modern Oaxaca and parts of Chiapas, thereby dominating trade throughout the region. Their particular focus and the land they fought to control was the fertile Soconusco region (p. 79), rich in cacao. Soon their trade routes penetrated this otherwise remote region. One of these serves today as the Pan-American Highway, which slashes through the jungles of both states and across the border into Guatemala.

To be sure, the remoteness of the Southern Highlands from other regions of Mexico fostered the development of unique cultures, but geography also limited communication between the groups that settled there. Oaxaca can be subdivided into some eight discrete geological zones, and Chiapas, into seven. Occupying these zones are sixteen officially registered indigenous communities in Oaxaca; Chiapas counts fifty-six distinct language families.

The complexity of the ecosystems of the Southern Highlands, coupled with the exuberance of its cultures, has bred one of the most varied and rich gastronomies of the country. The cuisine of Oaxaca is legendary, but that of Chiapas is richly varied, too, though it is little known outside the region. Oaxaca is famous for its "seven moles," although in truth there are dozens more, each variation unique from pueblo to pueblo. Chiapas boasts one of the more plenteous efflorescences of tamales in the country—some tallies reach over one hundred varieties. Local specialties reflect local resources and cultural proclivities: in northern Chiapas, the Tzotziles prize river snails known as *xuti* and incorporate them in a fragrant broth scented with *momo* (*hoja santa*, *Piper auritum*); and in the Papaloapan subregion of Oaxaca, yuca is a staple among the Mazatecos and is used alone or in combination with maize to prepare tamales, tortillas, and other starchy fare. The infusion of other cultures had its impact on the region's cuisines, too: Spanish colonists discovered that the cool highlands of Chiapas proved to be the ideal environment for charcuterie, and thanks to the introduction of European dairy cows, both states now enjoy worldwide renown for fine cheeses as well as cured meats.

PHYSICAL ENVIRONMENT AND AGRICULTURE

The terrain of the Southern Highlands varies from towering volcanoes like Tacaná on the Chiapas-Guatemala border—at 13,428 feet (4,093 m) above sea level, it is the second-tallest peak in Central America—to breathtaking river gorges lined with steep, craggy slopes. Some of Mexico's major rivers run through the Southern Highlands toward deltas on either the Pacific or Gulf coasts, at times carving out deep ravines.

The Southern Highlands is the most biologically diverse region in Mexico. The Lacandón jungle in Chiapas contains as much as 25 percent of Mexico's species diversity; the state of Oaxaca preserves almost 50 percent of all species in Mexico. For this reason, the Southern Highlands is one of the most prolific food-producing regions in the country, and has been throughout history: archaeological studies of the Central Valley of Oaxaca demonstrate human habitation dating to about 11,000 years BCE in the Guilá Naquitz cave near the town of Mitla, where the earliest known evidence of domesticated food plants in the continent has been found.

Soconusco—a fertile strip of land in Chiapas wedged between the Pacific Ocean and the Sierra Madre de Chiapas—has soil enriched by volcanic ash and mountain runoff. Because of its rich terrain, pre-Columbian production of cacao, achiote, and other goods enjoyed large-scale operations. In recent years, tourism has flourished here, as coffee lovers travel the Ruta del Café to visit the many coffee-producing haciendas in the region.

The Central Valley of Oaxaca is the largest expanse of flat, arable land—roughly 965 square miles (2,500 sq. km)—in Mexico's otherwise rugged Southern Highlands. The valley is the drainage basin for several rivers, while other smaller valleys abut the larger valley. Most of the remainder of the state of Oaxaca is composed of jagged mountains. The largest agricultural production in the state occurs in the alluvium along the coast, which has the flattest terrain and the richest soils. The piedmont areas were originally covered with dense forest but have largely been cleared for agriculture; a majority of the populace of Oaxaca is engaged in agriculture, although most production is for auto-consumption. Staples of maize, beans, and squash are supplemented by cash crops like mangos, of which Oaxaca is one of the country's largest producers.

ETHNOLINGUISTIC GROUPS

Many people in Chiapas trace their lineage back to the ancient Mayas. The state is known for its spectacular and historically important Maya archaeological zones, such as Palenque, Yaxchilán, and Bonampak; much of the population still speaks some form of Mayan, and one-third of these do not speak Spanish. The most numerous Mayan language groups in Chiapas are Tzeltal, Tzotzil, Ch'ol, Tojolabal, Lancandon, and Mam.

Oaxaca has the highest percentage of speakers of indigenous languages of any state in Mexico; most speak forms of the Oto-Manguean language family, such as Zapotec or Mixtec. The Zapotecs established the first major settlement in Oaxaca in Monte Albán, which flourished from 500 BCE until 750 CE. The largest ethnolinguistic groups in Oaxaca today are Zapotec, Mixtec, Mazateco, and Mixe.

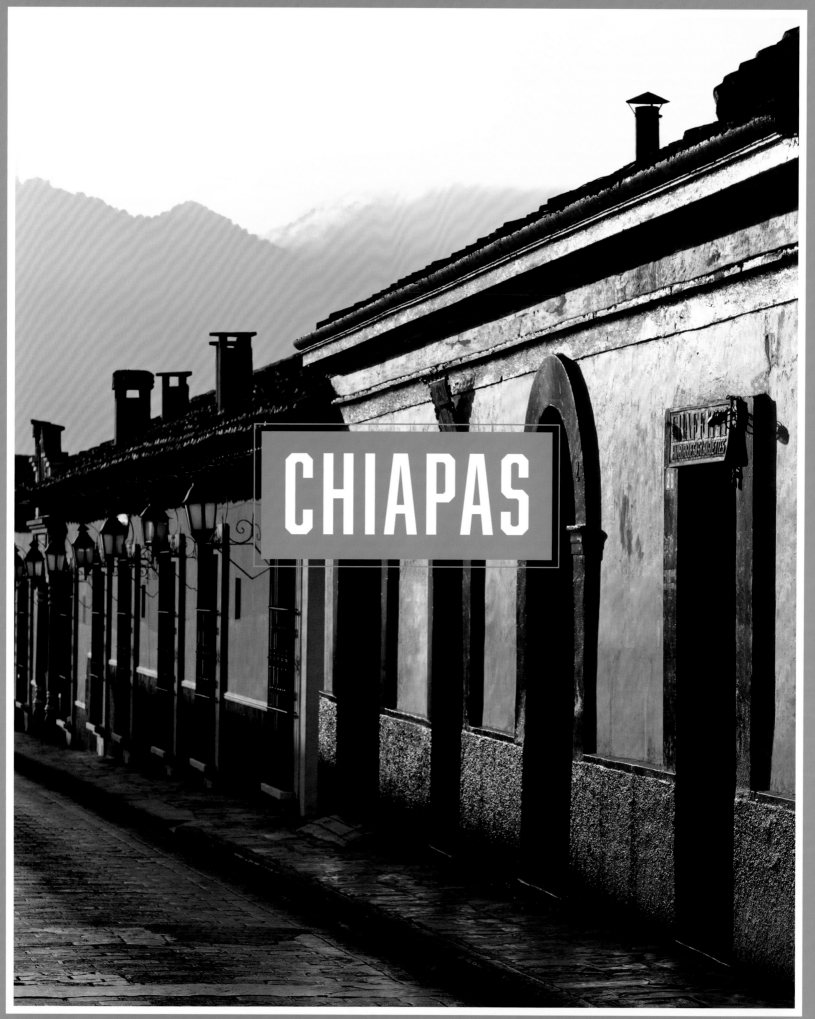

CHIAPAS

TUXTLA GUTIÉRREZ

E N ROUTE TO THE three pueblos we planned to visit in Chiapas—San Cristóbal de las Casas, Chiapa de Corzo, and Comitán de Domínguez—we paused overnight in Tuxtla Gutiérrez. To be sure, Tuxtla is wanting in terms of architectural wonders; the general fabric of the city is blandly modern.

Whatever Tuxtla may lack in history and architecture it more than makes up for in its gastronomy. Long a crossroads, Tuxtla Gutiérrez is a culinary cachepot of *cocina chiapaneca*. Traditional dishes from Pijijiapan on the southern coast to Palenque in the northern jungles are all found in Tuxtla's markets. It even boasts some marvelous seafood specialties from the Pacific as well as the Gulf coasts.

MERCADO MUNICIPAL "JUAN SABINES"
AND MERCADO "RAFAEL PASCACIO"

Although there are markets peppered throughout Tuxtla, the two main markets are located across the street from each other in the frantic downtown district: the large, clean, and modern Mercado Municipal "Juan Sabines" and the smaller Mercado "Rafael Pascacio."

Once inside the busy market "Juan Sabines," the pungent smell of salted dried shrimp pierced our noses. The shrimp is preserved at ports on the Pacific and Gulf coasts, then hauled inland. Vendors of the vividly pink-to-red-orange crustaceans mound them high in bins and tubs, and crowd virtually every stall just inside the entrance. In fact, there were so many vendors vigorously hawking the shrimp that we couldn't understand how their businesses could survive with so much competition. The only explanation must surely lie in how much of the salty, many-legged critters *tuxtlecos* consume. They are also plentiful in the market in San Cristóbal de las Casas, where they are consumed, not in market snacks, but in salads and other dishes at home.

EMPANADAS DE CAMARÓN SECO

DRIED SHRIMP TURNOVERS

TO PREPARE AHEAD

Enriched Lard (p. 530)

FOR THE FILLING

9 ounces (250 g) small salted dried shrimp (See notes above about size. This weight is the weight before cleaning; you will lose about 50%; you need about 4½ oz./125 g of cleaned shrimp for this recipe.)

3 tablespoons (42 g) Enriched Lard

1 cup (170 g) white onion, finely chopped

4 medium cloves garlic (1 oz./24 g), peeled and minced

¾ cup (140 g) green bell pepper, seeded and diced

1 sprig fresh epazote (substitute 1 tsp./1.5 g dried)

2 medium Roma tomatoes (7 oz./200 g), seeded and finely chopped

2 tablespoons (16 g) all-purpose flour

¼ cup (62.5 mL) milk

Two or three stalls in the center hall of Mercado "Rafael Pascacio" specialize in a variety of delicious empanadas, but the top seller is Empanadas de camarón seco. The pastry—even though made with masa—is surprisingly light, and every bite is rewarded with a satisfying *cruunch* from the salty shrimp inside. The dried shrimp sold in Chiapas vary in size from tiny (over 70 shrimp per pound) to small (51–60 shrimp per pound). Use the smallest ones you can find. If you only have access to larger ones, after cleaning them, break them into smaller pieces. Each shrimp (or piece) should be no more than about ¾ inch (2 cm) long. As they do in Tuxtla Gutiérrez, you may serve 4 empanadas to each diner as a main course, or 2 as an appetizer. Dried shrimp are available in Asian or Mexican markets or can be ordered online. Salted is preferred; if not, you will have to adjust the salt content of the filling.

Prepare-ahead note: The masa and filling may both be prepared in advance and refrigerated; bring to room temperature before assembling. Similarly, the empanadas may be completely assembled and frozen; allow to rest at room temperature for 30 minutes before frying. Serve immediately after frying. If time is an issue, finish the frying and keep them warm in the oven at a low temperature.

YIELD: APPROXIMATELY 2 DOZEN

PREPARE THE FILLING

Clean the shrimp: Remove the heads, tails, and any remaining legs; discard or save for making fish stock. There is no need to shell them; the crispy crunchiness is part of the

[MC]

FOR THE PASTRY DOUGH

½ cup (112 g) Enriched Lard,
  chilled
1 tablespoon (12 g) baking powder
2 pounds (1 kg) masa (see notes on
  p. 536)
½ cup (67.5 g) masa harina
1 medium clove garlic (¼ oz./6 g),
  peeled, charred, and minced
3 tablespoons (36 g) powdered
  chicken bouillon, dissolved in
  ½ cup (125 mL) hot water
Vegetable oil for frying

FOR SERVING
Salsa de chile de árbol (p. 531)
A *salpicón* of shredded cabbage,
  chopped radish, chopped red
  onion, and chopped cilantro
  dressed lightly with lime juice
  and salted to taste
Lime wedges

sensory appeal of the finished dish. (*Note*: Some recipes specifically call for the heads. If you will be saving them for another recipe, place them in an airtight container and freeze.) If necessary, break the shrimp into smaller pieces so that each piece is about ¾ inch (2 cm) long. Place the shrimp in a large bowl, and cover completely with cold water. Allow to soak for 10 minutes; drain thoroughly in a colander, then rinse again under cold running water. Transfer the shrimp to several layers of paper towels and blot dry with more paper towels; allow the shrimp to continue drying as you proceed.

Heat the lard in a large skillet until shimmering; add the next four ingredients and cook, stirring frequently, until the onions are translucent and the bell pepper is soft. Add the tomatoes and cook, stirring frequently, until all of the liquid from the tomatoes has evaporated. Add the shrimp, stir to incorporate, and continue stirring over low heat for about 2–3 minutes. Add the flour and cook 1–2 minutes, stirring constantly. Add the milk and stir until the mixture thickens, about 1 minute. Remove and discard the epazote; set the filling aside as you continue.

PREPARE THE PASTRY DOUGH

Place the chilled lard and the baking powder in the bowl of an electric mixer; beat on high speed until the lard turns fluffy and creamy, about 3 minutes.

Add the masa a bit at a time, beating after each addition until incorporated. Add the next two ingredients and beat on low to combine. With the motor still running, slowly add the bouillon mixture. Add enough to create a moist but not soggy dough: it should be easily formed into a ball without sticking to your fingers. Beat on high speed until thoroughly incorporated and the dough lightened, about 5 minutes. Cover with a damp towel until ready to use.

FORM AND FRY THE EMPANADAS

Form the pastry mixture into 24 balls, each weighing approximately 2 oz. (60 g). Working one at a time, place each ball on a large piece of plastic wrap; fold the plastic over the top of the ball; use a pie plate or other large, flat plate to press the ball into a tortilla measuring about 4 inches (10 cm) in diameter (you may also use a tortilla press for this step if you have one). Carefully peel away the plastic, and place 1 heaping tablespoon (20 g) of the shrimp mixture in a row down the middle; use the plastic to lift up one side of the dough and fold in half to form the empanada shape; seal tightly around the edges. Set each empanada aside as you finish the rest.

Just before serving, pour 2 inches (5 cm) of vegetable oil into a deep skillet. Heat to a temperature of 375°F (190°C). Working a few at a time, gently lower the empanadas into the oil and fry until golden brown, turning once, 1–2 minutes per side. Remove to paper towels to drain. Serve immediately or keep warm in a slow oven for 1–2 hours.

TO SERVE

As a main course, place 4 empanadas on individual serving plates; spoon the *salpicón* on the side of the plate and garnish with lime wedges. Diners spoon on Salsa de chile de árbol to taste. Serving instructions are the same for an appetizer portion of 2 empanadas per person.

TORTITAS DE CAMARÓN SECO

DRIED SHRIMP FRITTERS

FOR THE SALSA

3 cups (750 mL) chicken or vegetable stock or bouillon, divided

2 tablespoons (30 g) uncooked white rice

2 medium Roma tomatoes (7 oz./200 g)

¼ medium white onion (2½ oz./68.75 g)

1 medium clove garlic (¼ oz./6 g), peeled

1 tablespoon (15 g) recado rojo ("de achiote")

5 whole cloves

1 (1-inch/2.5 cm) *plus* 1 (3-inch/7.5 cm) stick canela (Mexican cinnamon)

1 tablespoon (15 mL) vegetable oil for frying

FOR THE SHRIMP FRITTERS

9 ounces (250 g) small salted dried shrimp (See notes above about size. This weight is the weight before cleaning; you will lose about 50%; you need about 4½ oz./125 g of cleaned shrimp for the recipe.)

6 eggs, separated

⅓ cup (40 g) all-purpose flour

Vegetable oil for frying

These puffy, salty, and crunchy fritters are popular along the Pacific coast and also in Tuxtla. They are not always available in the markets, but if you are fortunate enough to be present on a Sunday, look for women who travel inland from the coast and even from Oaxaca to sell Tortitas de camarón seco out of baskets. The special salsa bears a delicate hint of Spice Island flavors, beautifully complementing the hearty saltiness of the fritters.

Prepare-ahead note: Tortitas de camarón seco are best consumed immediately after frying, but you may prepare the salsa in advance, and also clean, soak, and dry the shrimp a day ahead and refrigerate.

YIELD: 6 SERVINGS (APPROXIMATELY 1 DOZEN TORTITAS)

PREPARE THE SALSA

Bring the stock or bouillon to a boil in a small saucepan; remove from the heat, add the rice, cover, and let soak for 30 minutes.

Working in batches as needed, place the next five ingredients *and* the 1-inch (2.5 cm) stick of canela in the jar of a blender along with the stock and the softened rice. Process until the mixture is thoroughly puréed and the spices well broken up, 2–3 minutes.

Pour the oil into a small skillet over medium-high heat. When the oil is shimmering, hold a fine-mesh sieve over the skillet and pour the contents of the blender jar through the sieve and into the hot oil all at once; the mixture should sputter and sizzle, so stand back. Use a rubber spatula to press through as much of the liquid in the sieve as possible; discard any residue. Add the remaining stick of canela, and stir to combine; bring the sauce to a boil, reduce the heat to simmer, and continue cooking, stirring frequently, until the sauce has deepened in color and has slightly thickened, 4–5 minutes. Check seasonings and add salt if necessary; set aside. Just before serving, reheat the sauce and remove the canela. You should have approximately 2½ cups (625 mL) of sauce.

PREPARE THE SHRIMP FRITTERS

Clean the shrimp: Remove the heads, tails, and any remaining legs; discard. There is no need to shell them. (*Note*: Use the discarded bits to make stock if you wish.) If necessary, break the shrimp into smaller pieces so that each piece is about ¾ inch (2 cm) long. Place the shrimp in a large bowl and cover completely with cold water. Allow to soak for 10 minutes; drain thoroughly in a colander, then rinse again under cold running water. Transfer the shrimp to several layers of paper towels and blot dry with more paper towels; allow the shrimp to continue drying as you proceed.

Thoroughly beat the egg yolks; in a separate bowl, beat the egg whites until they form soft peaks. Whisk the yolks into the whites (no need to worry about deflating the whites); add the flour and whisk until thoroughly incorporated. Add the shrimp and blend.

FOR SERVING

Plain cooked white rice or Arroz
de fiesta (p. 74), optional

Just before serving, pour 2 inches (5 cm) of vegetable oil into a deep skillet. Heat to a temperature of 375°F (190°C). Drop 1 heaping tablespoon (about 15 g) of the shrimp mixture into the oil to form a loose mound; immediately spoon another heaping tablespoon of the mixture on top of the first. (*Note*: Each portion should contain approximately 10 pieces of shrimp.) Repeat to form other fritters, being careful not to overcrowd (3–4 fritters is the maximum, depending on the size of your skillet.) Baste the tops of the fritters with oil until they inflate and lightly brown; flip to the other side and fry until browned. Transfer the fritters to paper towels to drain. Serve immediately.

TO SERVE

Place 2 fritters on individual serving plates accompanied by rice if you wish. Pour on a few spoonfuls of the tomato sauce.

TORTITAS DE MACABIL

FRIED MACHACA PATTIES

Every January, sport fishermen throng to the dramatic gorge of the Cañón del Sumidero near Chiapa de Corzo for a once-a-year tournament event: angling for the feisty *macabil*. Prized as a strong fighter, the neotropical freshwater *macabil* (*Brycon guatemalensis* Regan, 1908; Family: Characidae; English: machaca, macabi tetra) is found in the Río Grijalva, in the Pacific watershed south toward Honduras, and in the Atlantic watershed east toward Panama. It is in the class of bony fishes (toothy, too: it is related to the piranha); its pale pink, firm flesh is highly regarded throughout Chiapas. Continuing the Spanish tradition of sausage making so popular in the region, ground and seasoned *macabil* is stuffed into casings and poached or fried, a specialty of Tonalá near the Pacific coast known as *salchichas de macabil* (machaca hot dogs). Because the fish is so bony, and because its customary end use is for sausage, it is rare to find the whole fish in the market; instead, the flesh is scraped off the bones and ground immediately after the fish is caught, and then packed in plastic bags. If not destined for sausage, the ground meat is seasoned and formed into croquettes or patties and fried. The patties—Tortitas de macabil—are enormously popular in land-locked Tuxtla Gutiérrez; several stands in the Mercado Municipal "Juan Sabines" compete with their versions of the specialty. Olga Lilia Urbina, wife of the owner of "El Delfín del Lucio," shared her recipe with me.

[MC]

FOR THE TORTITAS

1 pound (500 g) macabil (substitute salmon, tuna, sea trout, Arctic char)

½ medium white onion (5 oz./137.5 g), coarsely chopped

1 medium clove garlic (¼ oz./6 g), peeled

1 medium chile jalapeño (1 oz./30 g), deveined, seeded, and coarsely chopped (*Note*: For a more picante version, leave veins and seeds intact.)

1 medium tomato (3½ oz./100 g), cored, seeded, and quartered

3 large sprigs fresh thyme, leaves only, chopped

1 tablespoon (15 g) recado rojo (achiote paste)

1 tablespoon (15 mL) fresh lime juice

1 teaspoon (6 g) sea salt

¼ teaspoon (1.25 g) freshly ground black pepper

2 tablespoons (10 g) *each* cilantro and parsley, leaves only, coarsely chopped

1 egg

Vegetable oil for frying

FOR SERVING

Shredded lettuce

Thinly sliced radishes

Thinly sliced cucumber

Lime wedges

Fresh corn tortillas or totopos

Salsa of your choice

Prepare-ahead note: The mixture for Tortitas de macabil should be made at least 1 hour prior to frying and serving. You may also form the cakes and freeze; partially defrost just before frying; serve immediately.

YIELD: 8 SERVINGS AS BOTANAS, OR 4 SERVINGS AS AN ENTRÉE OR MAIN COURSE

PREPARE AND FRY THE TORTITAS

Pass the fish through a meat grinder using the finest blade (grinding this way achieves the best texture, but if you don't have a grinder, pulse in a food processor until barely smooth). Place the remaining ingredients except for the oil in the jar of a blender and purée until just smooth; combine the purée with the ground fish and stir well to incorporate. Form a small patty and fry in a bit of oil to check for seasonings.

Form the fish mixture into 8 balls each weighing approximately 3 ounces (90 g). Place on a platter and refrigerate for 1 hour.

Pour 1 inch (2.5 cm) of vegetable oil into a large, deep skillet. Heat to a temperature of 350°F (176°C). Form the balls into cakes measuring approximately 3 inches (7.5 cm) in diameter and ½ inch (1.25 cm) thick. Gently lower the cakes into the oil. (To avoid lowering the temperature of the oil, add only 2–3 cakes at a time. Allow the temperature to return to 350°F/176°C before adding more.) Fry for 2–3 minutes, turn the cakes to the other side, and fry another 2–3 minutes or until the cakes are a deep golden brown overall. Transfer to paper towels to drain and continue with the rest of the *tortitas*. Serve immediately.

TO SERVE

In the market stalls of Tuxtla Gutiérrez, each *tortita* is sliced into 5–6 strips and arranged atop a bed of shredded lettuce; or, you may opt to leave the cakes whole. Decorate the side of the plate with radish and cucumber slices; serve lime wedges and tortillas or *totopos* on the side, and accompany with any of the salsas provided in this section on Chiapas.

SAN CRISTÓBAL DE LAS CASAS

WITH EXCRUCIATING SLUGGISHNESS, our bus inched its way from the stifling plateau of Tuxtla Gutiérrez, climbing slowly over serpentine roads through damp mountain forests and fleeting mists. The verdant valley in which San Cristóbal rests is like a chalice that holds a chilling, enchanted vapor, exorcised most mornings as soon as the sun slips over the crest of the bowl, awakening baroquely adorned buildings and green slopes that form a lush backdrop.

San Cristóbal de las Casas is still called its original name of Jovel by its Tzotzil-speaking inhabitants, but at times its ordered colonial-era street grid, refurbished cobblestone streets, and legions of coffeehouses crowded with expats and tourists threaten to drown out native voices. Ironically, the threat has served to strengthen indigenous identities: in

1988, on my first visit to San Cristóbal, our bus was briefly stopped on a steep mountain road by a band of Zapatistas, then just beginning their push for indigenous rights (with more bravado than bravery at that time). In 1994, the movement exploded with a major uprising in Chiapas, spearheaded by the evasive Subcomandante Marcos. Today, you will still be greeted by dozens of vendors selling Marcos dolls, complete with black face masks.

Politics aside, the graceful architecture, gently hilly streets, red tile roofs, and spectacular mountain setting led Mexican president Felipe Calderón in 2010 to call San Cristóbal "the most magical of the Pueblos Mágicos." Still, as you are enjoying your morning Chiapas coffee in a trendy café, it is important to recall that over one-third of the population is indigenous, speaking Tzeltal or Tzotzil as their first language, and remember to tread the cobblestone streets lightly and with great respect.

TZOTZIL/BATS'IL K'OP Tstos'il (nowadays more commonly written as Tzotzil) is the Castilian transcription of the word that means "strong"; the people call themselves *bats'il winik*, meaning "true people," and they call their own language *bats'il k'op*, which translates to "true word" or "true language." The Tzotzil are an indigenous Maya cultural group of central Chiapas in the Southern Highlands. Based on linguistic and archaeological data, scholars posit that the common ancestors of the contemporary Tzotzil and Tzeltal (p. 110) peoples entered the Los Altos region of Chiapas sometime between 750 and 500 BCE. According to indigenous histories reported to the Spanish chroniclers, immediately preceding the arrival of the Spanish, the Tzotzil were engaged in exporting quetzal feathers and amber to the Aztec capital of Tenochtitlán; they also produced salt from wells near Ixtapa on the Pacific coast, trading it throughout the Chiapas highlands, which they continued to do in the postcontact era. The Tzotzil became excellent shepherds shortly after Spanish contact. The municipalities with the largest Tzotzil populations are San Juan Chamula, San Cristóbal de las Casas, and Zinacantán.

A Tzotzil vendor travels daily from San Juan Chamula to the market of San Cristóbal de las Casas. Since the colonial era, the Tzotzil people—particularly the women—have been known for their skill as shepherds; the wool they gather from their long-haired sheep may be sold or used for their own clothing, as seen in the photo. Sheep raising for milk, meat, and wool accounts for more than one-third of Tzotzil income. [MR]

MERCADO PÚBLICO MUNICIPAL "JOSÉ CASTILLO TIELEMANS"

Like many days in this high mountain valley, our first day in San Cristóbal de las Casas began with a gray sky and a chilly mist. The narrow street we followed descended sharply and deposited us directly at the side entrance of the market, known as Mercado Público Municipal "José Castillo Tielemans" (named rather unromantically after a PRI (Partido Revolucionario Institucional) governor who presided from 1964 to 1970).

Inside, a steeply sloping walkway picked up where the street dead-ended; it was still wet and slippery from the morning's drizzle. We immediately sought something warm, and tucked ourselves beneath the canopied roof of "Cocina de doña Eva," soon packed with other chilled customers. Cheery young Daniela Rodas, the owner's daughter-in-law, tempted us with menu choices and shared recipes.

[MR]

[MR]

MOLE CHIAPANECO

SWEET AND SPICY MOLE FROM CHIAPAS

TO PREPARE AHEAD
Chocolate de mesa (p. 77), or
substitute

FOR THE MOLE PASTE

3 tablespoons (45 mL) vegetable
   oil, divided
3 medium Roma tomatoes
   (10½ oz./300 g), whole
3 medium tomatillos
   (10½ oz./300 g), paper removed,
   thoroughly washed and whole
1 medium white onion
   (10 oz./275 g), halved
1 medium clove garlic (¼ oz./6 g),
   peeled
¼ cup (50 g) peanuts
¼ cup (60 g) blanched almonds
¼ cup (60 g) raisins
1 tablespoon (10 g) sesame seeds
1 cup (225 g) Enriched Lard
3 chiles pasillas (1¼ oz./35 g),
   seeded
3 chiles guajillos (1 oz./25 g),
   seeded
7 ounces (200 g) chiles anchos,
   half with the stems removed,
   slit along the side, flattened,
   and seeds intact; the other half
   seeded
1 medium semiripe plantain
   (9 oz./250 g), peeled and thickly
   sliced on the diagonal
3½ ounces (100 g) pan francés de
   San Cristóbal (substitute challah,
   baguette, or Italian bread),
   thickly sliced
3½ ounces (100 g) pan de San
   Cristóbal (substitute tea biscuits)
1¾ ounces (50 g) animal crackers
2 corn tortillas (1 oz./30 g total)
4–6 cups (1–1.5 L) rich chicken
   stock, divided

Mole chiapaneco is featured at market stalls and *cocinas económicas* throughout the state, and it is a point of pride that it is *chiapaneco*—not like any other mole in the republic. And yet, the flavor differences compared to the famous *mole poblano* and the black mole of Oaxaca may seem subtle to the outsider. When I enquired what made it unique, the answers I received were as varied as the cooks who gave me their recipes: some swore by using only *chile ancho*; others called for two or three chile varieties; most agreed that Mole chiapaneco is sweeter than other moles in the country. But the most peculiar difference I noted had to do with the breads that were used: while several moles feature tortillas or bread as thickeners, I have never seen one that includes such a quantity and range of breads. First is the requisite *pan francés de San Cristóbal*, a lightly sweet egg bread; and then there is *pan de San Cristóbal*, the ubiquitous *canela*-scented, semisweet, dry cookie in a variety of shapes, not unlike commercial tea biscuits. But the most unusual bread found in the recipe for Mole chiapaneco—a recipe shared with me by María Leticia "Leti" Chong Ovalle, an experienced and knowledgeable local chef—must surely be animal crackers. This is not the culinary whim of one cook, mind you; it is an ingredient in several recipes I have run across. Leti's recipe yields an almost vulgar quantity of mole, but she put it to so many uses—as the filling and table sauce for a couple of tamale varieties, as a sauce for the evening's chicken, and as leftovers to freeze for another day—that I never bother to halve it, although you may choose to do so.

Prepare-ahead note: Mole chiapaneco may be prepared in advance and refrigerated for 2–3 days; it also freezes well for up to 6 months. Gently reheat and add more stock to achieve the desired consistency.

YIELD: APPROXIMATELY 10 CUPS (2.5 L)

PREPARE THE MOLE PASTE

Heat 2 tablespoons (30 mL) of the vegetable oil in a large, heavy skillet, preferably cast iron, over high heat. Add the next four ingredients and cook 15–20 minutes, turning occasionally, until the vegetables are thoroughly blackened. Transfer to a heatproof bowl and set aside.

Heat the remaining 1 tablespoon (15 mL) of the vegetable oil in a small, nonstick skillet. Add the next four ingredients and cook over medium-high heat, stirring constantly, until the raisins are inflated and the nuts and seeds are browned but not burned, 3–4 minutes; transfer to the bowl with the vegetables.

Melt the lard in a large, heavy skillet, preferably cast iron, over high heat. Working in batches as needed, fry the chiles until gently darkened; transfer to a large bowl lined with paper towels to drain. Fry the plantain until browned and transfer to a colander; fry the breads, animal crackers, and tortillas until browned; transfer to the colander and set aside.

Working in batches as needed, transfer the ingredients from the colander to the jar

FOR FINISHING THE MOLE

4 tablespoons (56 g) Enriched Lard
2 cups (500 mL) rich chicken
  stock, or more if needed
4 balls (3½ oz./100 g total)
  Chocolate de mesa (substitute
  Mexican table chocolate for
  beverages), chopped
2–4 tablespoons (24–48 g) sugar,
  or to taste (optional)

FOR SERVING

Chicken pieces from preparing
  the chicken stock, or simple
  boiled or baked chicken
Arroz de fiesta (p. 74)

of a blender; add up to 1 cup (250 mL) stock to each batch to keep the blades rotating. Process until thoroughly puréed; transfer the mixture to a large mixing bowl; repeat until all of the ingredients have been puréed.

Stir the mixture well to incorporate the different batches. Place a large, fine-mesh sieve over a large mixing bowl; working in batches as needed, pour the mixture into the sieve; use a rubber spatula to press through as much of the mixture as possible; discard any residue that won't pass through. Repeat until all of the mixture has been strained.

FINISH THE MOLE

Heat the lard in a large saucepan or stockpot until shimmering. Pour in all of the puréed mole mixture at once; it should sizzle and splatter, so stand back. Reduce heat to medium and cook, stirring constantly, until the mixture darkens and thickens, about 15–20 minutes. Add enough stock to result in a mixture that is thick yet pourable, rather like cream of wheat. Add the chocolate and stir until dissolved; check the seasonings and add the optional sugar if desired.

TO SERVE

Place chicken pieces or shredded chicken on individual serving plates and generously ladle on the mole. Accompany with Arroz de fiesta and a mixed green salad if desired. You may also use the mole to prepare Tamal untado (p. 82).

[MC]

ARROZ DE FIESTA

WHITE "PARTY" RICE WITH PEAS, CARROTS, AND CHICKEN GIBLETS

TO PREPARE AHEAD
Enriched Lard (p. 530)

FOR SAUTÉING THE RICE

3 tablespoons (42 g) Enriched Lard

2 cups (400 g) long-grain white rice, rinsed, thoroughly drained, and air-dried

½ medium white onion (5 oz./137.5 g), finely chopped

2 medium cloves garlic (½ oz./12 g), peeled and minced

¾ cup (100 g) carrot, cut to small dice

FOR SIMMERING AND STEAMING THE RICE

4 cups (1 L) rich chicken stock (preferably homemade with the accumulated fat reserved)

5¼ ounces (150 g) chicken giblets (or only livers if you prefer), cooked in boiling water for 10 minutes or until cooked through, then coarsely chopped

¾ cup (130 g) peas, fresh or frozen

Leti explained that in Chiapas, many foods have an "everyday" version and a "party" version. Simple tweaks can make a basic dish more fancy. Such is the case for Arroz de fiesta: standard issue white rice pilaf is enriched with chopped chicken giblets, peas, and carrots, and for best results Leti recommended using your own homemade (and very rich) chicken stock. In addition to the lard in which she fried the rice, she also scooped some extra fat from the top of her cauldron of chicken stock and added it to the rice at the same time she added the liquid. Of course you may opt for a lower-fat treatment if you use this as an everyday rice—but for a party, why not indulge?

Prepare-ahead note: Arroz de fiesta is best served immediately after preparing, although leftovers may be refrigerated 1–2 days, then steamed to reheat.

YIELD: 8–10 SERVINGS

SAUTÉ THE RICE

Choose a large skillet or saucepan with a tight-fitting lid. Heat the lard in the skillet until shimmering. Add the rice and cook over medium heat, stirring constantly, until it begins to turn opaque, 2–3 minutes (individual grains will appear whiter than others). Add the onions, garlic, and carrots and cook, stirring constantly, until the onions are translucent, 3–4 minutes. *Do not let the rice brown.*

SIMMER THE RICE

Add half of the stock to the skillet when the onions are translucent. *Do not stir.* To incorporate the liquid and the rice, give the skillet a vigorous but brief shake. Cook uncovered over medium heat, without stirring, until the liquid is mostly absorbed and you see small, percolating air holes appearing over the surface.

STEAM THE RICE AND FINISH

Add the remaining 2 cups (500 mL) of stock to the rice along with a spoonful of the reserved chicken fat, if using; add the giblets and peas, and shake the skillet to incorporate. *Do not stir.* Simmer until small air holes appear again. The rice should be quite dry, but there should still be a bit of liquid left. Wet a clean kitchen towel and wring it out. Spread it out on a work surface and place the lid from your pot or skillet right side up in the center of the towel. Gather the corners of the towel up toward the knob of the lid. Place the wrapped lid on the skillet and simmer the rice on the lowest heat for 3 minutes. Remove the skillet from the heat and allow the rice to steep, covered, for 20 minutes. Lift the lid, toss the rice lightly to incorporate all of the ingredients, and test for doneness. (If you prefer softer rice, add a bit of water, cover, and simmer 2 minutes more. Remove the pan from the heat and steep the rice for an additional 5 minutes.) Keep covered until serving.

(above) At the Museo del Cacao y Chocolatería Cultural in the center of San Cristóbal, a chunk of pure chocolate rests atop the massive slab from which it was prized. [MR] (below) A bag of dried cacao beans in the market. [MC]

CHOCOLATE DE MESA

SWEETENED FLAVORED CHOCOLATE FOR BEVERAGES AND COOKING

FOR THE CHOCOLATE PASTE

For roasting whole beans

1 pound (500 g) dried raw cacao
  beans

OR

For grinding beans or nibs

3 cups (13 oz./375 g) roasted peeled
  beans or cacao nibs

**FOR THE CHOCOLATE
BEVERAGE TABLET**

1 ounce (30 g) whole stick canela
  (Mexican cinnamon)

1 cup (200 g) sugar

Powdered cocoa for dusting

Since the time of the Olmecs (ca. 1500 BCE), who contrived ways to turn raw cacao beans into the miracle of chocolate, the purpose of the end product was almost exclusively to make an invigorating beverage. Not until the eighteenth century in France was chocolate concocted into the bonbons and other sweet treats we know today. To prepare the beverage, cacao beans are fermented, dried, roasted, and ground into a paste; the paste is flavored with additional ingredients, then formed into a dry, solid tablet or a ball—known as Chocolate de mesa—that can later be dissolved to make the chocolate beverage. In the pre-Columbian era, the tablet would have been dissolved in water; with the Spanish introduction of dairy cows, milk was soon substituted. With some minor postcontact changes and adaptations—namely the addition of *canela* and sugar—this is the same way chocolate has been processed for millennia. In some regions of Mexico, the chocolate paste is formed into flat tortillas, but in Chiapas its final form is the ball pictured above, common in the markets. Dissolve it in milk for the best hot chocolate you've ever drunk, or include it in the rich Mole chiapaneco (p. 72) or other dishes. Cacao beans are commercially available in a few formats: dried but raw, which require roasting; roasted and peeled whole beans; and roasted and peeled cracked beans known as nibs. Instructions for all forms are provided in this recipe.

Prepare-ahead note: Chocolate de mesa keeps well in cool, dry conditions for many months.

YIELD: APPROXIMATELY 2 DOZEN 1-OUNCE (25 G) PORTIONS

PREPARE THE CHOCOLATE PASTE

If you are working with peeled, roasted beans or nibs, skip to the next step. For dried, raw whole beans, use a large, heavy cast-iron skillet for this step. Heat the dry skillet on the highest heat for 5 minutes; add the beans. Very quickly the beans will begin to crack and pop; immediately flip and toss the beans in the skillet, or use a spatula to keep them in constant movement. Continue until they are fragrant and considerably blackened on all sides, about 5 minutes. Immediately transfer to a heatproof bowl and allow to cool.

Once the beans are cool, grasp one between thumb and forefinger and squeeze: the papery shell will crumble away. Continue until all of the beans are shelled. Some will likely break or crumble; just rescue the good parts as best you can and discard the rest. Accounting for loss, you should end up with about 3 cups (375 g) of peeled beans.

A small, heavy-duty food processor is recommended for this step. Fill the processor bowl with the roasted, shelled beans (or crushed nibs). Turn on the motor and be patient: the beans will immediately be broken into tiny bits; continue for another 5 minutes or so, until beans are turned into a fine powder. Eventually the powder will clump into a clayey mass. Continue processing; the end result will be a creamy, shiny black paste. The time required to finish depends on your processor: mine usually takes about 15–20 minutes. For a finer product, continue running the processor for several minutes after the paste develops until it turns from a paste to a liquid, like hot fudge sauce. You will need to tend the machine only occasionally to scrape down the sides of the bowl with a rubber spatula. Give your poor machine a rest every 5 minutes or so to cool down.

PREPARE THE CHOCOLATE BEVERAGE TABLET

In a cast-iron skillet or on a comal, toast the *canela* lightly; place it in a spice grinder or coffee grinder adapted for that purpose; grind until very fine; pass through a fine-mesh sieve and return any residue to the grinder; grind and sift again; discard any residue that won't pass through. Add 5 tablespoons (about 20 g) of the ground *canela* to the processor with the chocolate paste; add the sugar and process until the mixture is well incorporated and smooth.

Transfer the mixture to a mixing bowl and refrigerate until set but not hard, about 15–20 minutes. Line a baking sheet with waxed paper and dust liberally with the powdered cocoa. Using a round tablespoon measure or a large melon baller, drop scant 1-ounce (25 g) portions of the chilled mixture onto the waxed paper and roll quickly in the cocoa; shape into balls in the palms of your hands and roll again in the cocoa; set balls to one side as you continue. Repeat until you have used all of the mixture and have formed approximately 24 balls. Allow to dry at room temperature for about 1 hour. The balls will harden; they will also absorb the cocoa. To finish, roll the balls in the cocoa a final time, then store the balls in an airtight container in a cool, dry place until ready to use.

[MC]

CHOCOLATE
MEXICAN CHOCOLATE BEVERAGE

TO PREPARE AHEAD
Chocolate de mesa (p. 77)

FOR THE CHOCOLATE BEVERAGE
1 cup (250 mL) milk
1 ball Chocolate de mesa

Along with atole and steaming hot *café de olla*, chocolate is a popular beverage in Chiapas, especially on cold, damp mornings. Chocolate in many forms—cocoa powder, chocolate beverage "ball," raw cacao beans, powdered chocolate beverage mix—can be seen in every market of Chiapas. The state remains a prime center of cacao production and export. The head of foam on top of chocolate was highly prized in pre-Columbian Mesoamerica. It was achieved by pouring the liquid chocolate from one vessel to another to aerate it. To achieve this quintessential froth, use a wire whisk or small electric bar whisk.

YIELD: 1 SERVING

PREPARE THE CHOCOLATE BEVERAGE
Pour the milk into a small saucepan and bring to a boil; reduce to a simmer and add the Chocolate de mesa; stir until the chocolate has completely dissolved. Using a wire whisk or a small electric bar whisk, whisk the mixture until a light foam appears on the surface. Immediately pour the chocolate into a cup or mug and serve.

Fruit of all the kinds that the country produced were laid before him; he ate very little, but from time to time a liquor prepared from cocoa, and of an aphrodisiac nature, as we were told, was presented to him in golden cups. . . . I observed a number of jars, above fifty, brought in, filled with foaming chocolate, of which he took some . . .

BERNAL DÍAZ DEL CASTILLO IN THE COURT OF MONTEZUMA, 1519

SOCONUSCO Long home to the world's premier cacao, the Soconusco region of Chiapas is part of an extended lowland piedmont plain that runs along the Pacific Ocean from the Isthmus of Tehuantepec to the border of Guatemala. Its fertile alluvial and volcanic soils are ideal for nurturing fragile cacao trees. Before the arrival of Europeans, the Mayas, Aztecs, and other Mesoamerican groups fought over the region to dominate its riches. At the time of the conquest, the Aztecs controlled the prolific flow of cacao from the region they called Xoconochco into the great markets of Tenochtitlán, while the Mayas of Yucatán controlled the cacao trade from the somewhat less affluent center of Chontalpa in Tabasco. When the Spanish arrived to Xoconochco, they promptly conquered the territory for what they had come to realize was a highly valuable commodity among indigenous peoples, and changed the name to the more pronounceable (for them) Soconusco. The region later became a growing zone for several other important crops. After the introduction of coffee in the late nineteenth century, between 1890 and 1910 Soconusco became the largest producer of coffee in Mexico; it also remains a primary source of the cacao found in the markets of Chiapas. The Mayan ethnolinguistic group known as Mam has traditionally been associated with Soconusco.

COFFEE IN CHIAPAS Coffee can be seen and smelled everywhere in San Cristóbal de las Casas, from charming sidewalk coffee bars to aromatic shops that sell bags of whole beans or ground coffee brought from many regional plantations. It is plentiful in the municipal market, too, sold ground and packed simply in plastic bags with no marketing hype. In many food stalls, bubbling pots of *café de olla*—coffee sweetened with *panela* (see p. 538) and scented with *canela*—promise customers an eye-opening jolt.

Coffee is the most important agricultural product of Chiapas. The Arabica bean (*Coffea arabica*) was first introduced into the Soconusco region in 1875, and from 1895 until 1905, production grew 40 times. Traditional management methods—natural cultivation without chemical fertilizers or pesticides, hand harvesting by families—resulted in a high wholesale cost, which eventually led to a virtual collapse of the market in the early 1990s. But this near disaster opened the door to a new concept: by the mid-1990s, Chiapas coffee was "organic," which eased the acceptance of its higher market price. Today, Chiapas is a world leader in organic coffee production, and it is the largest producer of coffee in the country.

(above) A Tzotzil woman roasts coffee beans in Zinacantán, about 15 miles (25 km) northwest of San Cristóbal de las Casas. After grinding it, she'll sell some of the coffee locally within this small indigenous community of about 30,000 people, most of whom are Tzotziles; the rest of the coffee will be packaged simply and taken to the market in San Cristóbal. [MR]

Doña Mónica in her Sunday best. [MR]

TAMALES IN THE SUNDAY MARKET

Tamales are daily fare throughout Mexico, but on Sundays a bouquet of new offerings blooms and beckons. And Chiapas is one of several states thought to have the greatest quantity and variety of tamales.

Mónica Carballo Zepeda manages what appeared to be one of the most popular tamale stands in the market, and her enthusiasm as she rattled off the day's menu gave her perfect Spanish pronunciation a percussive energy. She was charming and generous with her recipes, and was pleased to hear that someone from the *extranjero* (outside Mexico) was taking an interest in the traditional tamales of Chiapas. Doña Mónica offered her customers squeeze bottles full of Salsa de chile de árbol and Salsa verde (p. 531) for dressing the tamales, although we abstained from the salsas for the perfectly self-contained Tamal untado (p. 82) and the Tamal de azafrán (p. 84).

TAMAL UNTADO "DE FIESTA"

"PARTY-STYLE" TAMALE WITH MOLE

TO PREPARE AHEAD
Masa para tamales (p. 530)
Mole chiapaneco (p. 72)

Untado in Spanish means "spread," and that is essentially how these tamales are formed: first a thin layer of masa is spread over the surface of a banana leaf, then a spoonful of Mole chiapaneco is spread on top of that. The Tamales untados that you will find in the market are most likely the "daily fare" versions, and therefore will only feature some shredded chicken in addition to the mole sauce. But the fancier "party style" also includes olives, almonds, prunes or raisins, and slices of plantain and boiled egg. I've included the party bits in this recipe; you may omit them if you wish.

Prepare-ahead note: The components for Tamal untado can be prepared well in advance and refrigerated or frozen until time to assemble. Similarly, the tamales themselves can be prepared well ahead of time and frozen; do not defrost, but steam for 1 hour and serve immediately.

YIELD: 1 DOZEN TAMALES

Banana leaves cut into 12 by
  16-inch (30 × 40 cm) rectangles

Masa chiapaneca

Mole chiapaneco *plus* 1 cup (125 g)
  of the chicken from its preparation, shredded

12 each of the following: pitted
  prunes (or 36 black raisins),
  blanched almonds, whole green
  olives (unpitted is the tradition),
  slices of plantain, slices of boiled
  egg (optional)

PREPARE THE TAMALES

Place the banana leaves on a flat work surface horizontally in front of you. Working one at a time, place approximately 3 heaping tablespoons (90 g) of the masa onto the leaf; use your wet fingertips to spread the masa side to side, leaving a 2-inch (5 cm) border around the edges (it does not have to be perfect).

Distribute approximately 3 heaping tablespoons (75 g) of the shredded chicken in a row down the middle of the masa, running lengthwise; spoon on 3 tablespoons (45 mL) of the mole sauce onto the chicken. Following in a straight row along the chicken, place the remaining ingredients, if using: one of the olives, a prune (or the raisins), an almond, one slice of plantain and one slice of boiled egg. These do not overlap, rather they form a little parade down the center so that each bite reveals something new.

Using the banana leaf, fold the long edge closest to you over the top so that the masa completely covers the fillings. Continue to fold and roll the banana leaf so that the long edge tucks under the tamale; use the sides of your hands to press the two ends of the tamale, and press lightly to compress. Tuck both loose flaps of the banana leaf under; press to form tightly, and set aside.

Add water to the bottom of a *vaporera* or stock pot fitted with a steaming basket; arrange the tamales flat at the bottom. Place the lid on tightly; bring the water to a boil, and steam for 1 hour, checking the water level halfway through the cooking and adding water as necessary.

TO SERVE

As noted above, these tamales do not really require any additional salsas, but you may spoon on some extra mole if you wish.

A tamal vendor on Sunday morning offers diners red-hot salsa from a squeeze bottle.

[MR]

TAMAL DE AZAFRÁN

SAFFRON TAMALE WITH CHICKEN AND RAISINS

TO PREPARE AHEAD

Your own rich chicken stock,
  reserving the chicken
Masa para tamales (p. 530)

FOR THE SAUCE

½ medium onion (5 oz./137.5 g)

1 medium clove garlic (¼ oz./6 g)

3 medium Roma tomatoes
  (10½ oz./300 g)

1 slice French bread (1 oz./28 g)

3½ ounces (100 g) pan de San
  Cristóbal (substitute tea biscuits)

1 small sprig fresh thyme

1 teaspoon (0.65 g) dried whole
  Mexican oregano

1 bay leaf

1 3-inch (7.5 cm) stick canela
  (Mexican cinnamon)

3 whole cloves

1 tablespoon (12 g) sugar

1 tablespoon (15 g) recado rojo
  ("de achiote"; see p. 45)

¾ cup (187.5 mL) rich chicken
  stock

2 tablespoons (30 mL) vegetable
  oil

2 generous pinches saffron

This elegant tamale is typical of Los Altos de Chiapas, especially San Cristóbal de las Casas. It is an exquisite tamale and a vivid representation of the mix of Spanish and indigenous cultures: a lightly sweetened sauce of Mesoamerican tomatoes is scented with *canela* and cloves and finished with two hefty pinches of Moorish saffron.

Prepare-ahead note: As with other tamales in this section, the components may be prepared in advance and refrigerated; bring to room temperature prior to using. Completed tamales may also be frozen for 3–4 months; before serving, steam the tamales for 1 hour.

YIELD: 1 DOZEN TAMALES

PREPARE THE SAUCE

Place all of the ingredients except the saffron in the jar of a blender (depending upon the size of your blender jar, you may need to work in batches). Purée until thoroughly liquefied.

Pour the vegetable oil into a large saucepan or skillet; heat until shimmering. Holding a fine-mesh sieve over the skillet, pour the contents of the blender jar into the hot oil: it should sizzle and splatter, so stand back. Use a rubber spatula to press as much of the mixture through the sieve as possible; discard anything that won't pass through.

Bring the sauce to a boil, reduce to a simmer; add the saffron, and continue cooking,

Tamales are sold at every turn in San Cristóbal on a Sunday. Their immense popularity yields great quantities: here, tamales de elote tierno—*fresh maize tamales still in their neat cornhusk wrappers—are sold out of a crate in the parking lot behind the market.*

[MR]

Banana leaves cut into 12 by
  16-inch (30 × 40 cm) rectangles
1 recipe Masa para tamales
1 cup (300 g) chicken from
  preparing the chicken stock,
  shredded
1 medium green bell pepper
  (6½ oz./185 g), seeded and cut
  into julienne strips
36 black raisins

stirring frequently, until the sauce has slightly darkened and thickened and the flavors have amalgamated, about 6–8 minutes.

FORM AND STEAM THE TAMALES

Place the banana leaves on a flat work surface horizontally in front of you. Working one at a time, place approximately 2 heaping tablespoons (60 g) of the masa onto the leaf; use your wet fingertips to spread the masa side to side, leaving a 3-inch (7.5 cm) border around the edge. (*Note*: This method is similar to the Tamal untado on page 82, but in this case the masa should be thicker.)

Distribute approximately 3 heaping tablespoons (75 g) of the shredded chicken in a row down the middle of the masa, running lengthwise. Place 1 strip of the bell pepper and 3 raisins running horizontally in the middle of the chicken; spoon 3 tablespoons (45 mL) of the tomato sauce onto the chicken.

Using the banana leaf, fold the long edge closest to you over the top so that the masa completely covers the fillings. Continue to fold and roll the banana leaf so that the long edge tucks under the tamale; use the sides of your hands to press the two ends of the tamale, and press lightly to compress. Tuck both loose flaps of the banana leaf under; press to form tightly, and set aside.

Add water to the bottom of a *vaporera* or stock pot fitted with a steaming basket; arrange the tamales flat at the bottom. Place the lid on tightly; bring the water to a boil, and steam for 1 hour, checking the water level halfway through the cooking and adding water as necessary.

TO SERVE

Place two tamales on individual serving plates; diners unwrap their own tamales and spoon on extra tomato sauce.

He carries tamales, and a few maize ears,
passing like a gigolo through a sea of lovers.

MATEO ROSAS DE OQUENDO, CA. 1598

THE SPECTRUM OF BEANS

The great variety of beans available in Chiapas is evident in the colorful bins and bags found in every market. There are more than twenty-five known varieties of beans in Chiapas, with fifteen wild species.

Among the Tzotziles and Tzeltales, beans are cooked simply with chile and salt, occasionally flavored with epazote or cilantro. Other additions include regional plants and herbs such as *hierba mora*, *hoja santa*, *chipilín*, or *guía de chayote* (see pp. 97, 129, 136, and 260). The common black bean (*Phaseolus vulgaris*) serves as the everyday bean in Chiapas, but many other varieties are also used interchangeably in recipes, especially in rural communities among indigenous populations. Specific varieties may be called for in certain dishes, and among them the *patashete*, *escumite*, and *bótil* appear most frequently.

A Tzotzil vendor bags patashete (red lima beans) in the tiny market of San Juan Chamula. [MR]

PATASHETE/PATAXETE/PATACHETE

BOTANICAL: *Phaseolus lunatus* L./Family Fabaceae
ENGLISH: lima bean

ESCUMITE/ESCOMITE/TEPARÍ

BOTANICAL: *Phaseolus acutifolius*/Family Fabaceae
ENGLISH: tepary bean

After the common bean (*Phaseolus vulgaris*), *P. lunatus*—or lima bean—is the most important of the genus. Its heritage can be traced to two distinct gene pools—one originating in the Andes and another in Mesoamerica—and both can be further divided into two subspecies, one wild (*P. lunatus silvester*) and one domesticated (*P. lunatus lunatus*). There is considerable diversity within the species, with a small-seed cultivar (1–2½ oz./24–70 g per 100 seeds) and a large-seed cultivar (2–10 oz./54–280 g per 100 seeds). Colors vary, too, ranging from white to red-purple, or yellow-brown to solid black, or with lighter spots or striations on any of the various colors. The characteristic lima bean form is most typically flattened and half-moon shaped. In Tuxtla Gutiérrez, the small, purple *patashete* is mixed with masa before forming it into thick cakes, known as *nacapitú*, that are baked in the oven. In the center of the state, a popular dish is *patashete con pepita*—lima beans cooked in a *pipián* of squash seeds, tomatoes, and onion. As with *bótil* (*P. coccineus*), the flowers of *patashete* are also consumed.

The tepary bean has been grown in Mesoamerica for millennia; archaeological remains found in Puebla date to five thousand years ago. The plant typically favors hotter, dryer growing zones, although wild forms are ecologically specialized: one variety grows alongside mesquite on the banks of streams, while another commingles with cactus and thorny shrubs in desert areas. Today, cultivated forms of *Phaseolus acutifolius* cover arid zones from Arizona and New Mexico to the southeastern United States, and as far south as the dry subtropical slope of the Pacific coast in Costa Rica. In fact, in Chiapas, the tepary bean is sometimes nicknamed *frijol costeño*—"coastal bean"—since it is generally grown in the lower, more arid subtropical region of the Pacific Coastal Plain that slopes downward from the Sierra Madre Occidental. Seed variability is less pronounced than that of the kidney bean, assuming two basic forms: one features a fairly small rounded black or white seed; the other is a larger-sized rhombohedral form with a softly faceted surface that may be white, gray, or greenish white; dark yellow, reddish brown or mahogany; coffee colored, black or purple mottled. A recipe for Frijol escumite con chipilín can be found on page 137.

BÓTIL/BOTI/CHOMBOROTE/AYOCOTE

BOTANICAL: *Phaseolus coccineus* L./Family Fabaceae | **ENGLISH:** scarlet runner bean

Well adapted to higher altitudes and cooler temperatures, *Phaseolus coccineus* was prized by early settlers of the Basin of Mexico, who cultivated it extensively and ensured its broad distribution throughout the Mesoamerican highlands. The pluriannual plant is easy to recognize by its long vine, which can extend up to 10 feet (3 m) in length, and by its large, crimson-colored seeds, which measure roughly ½ inch (1.5 cm) in length when dried, and up to ¾ inch (2 cm) in length when fresh. A shock of bright crimson, white, or two-toned edible flowers opens fifty days after sowing. The root may also be consumed as food as well as used medicinally. In central Mexico, *Phaseolus coccineus* is known by its Nahuatl-derived name, *ayocote*; it is called *bótil* in San Cristóbal de las Casas, but it is referred to as *chomborote* (sometimes *chamborote*) in San Juan Chamula. Some sources describe *bótil* as a black bean, and indeed any of the five domesticated species of *Phaseolus* have cultivars that can produce black seeds, but it is the crimson species that we found in the markets of Chiapas with the characteristics and nomenclatures described here.

FRIJOL BÓTIL REFRITO
PICANTE REFRIED SCARLET RUNNER BEANS

TO PREPARE AHEAD
Enriched Lard (p. 530)

Seasonal availability—and more particularly, price—can determine which beans cooks select for which dishes in Chiapas. In indigenous communities, particularly San Juan Chamula, dried black beans are available, but they are dramatically overshadowed by more colorful varieties. Therefore, while black may be the typical color used for *frijol refrito* or simple pot beans in the rest of Mexico, here it may just as well be made with red, brown, or purple beans. This recipe using scarlet runner beans is rich and packs a punch thanks to a handful of fried *chiles de Simojovel* (see p. 91); control the heat by reducing the quantity of chiles, if desired. The Tzeltal version of this dish is known as *chinculuaj* and is made with *chiles de árbol* and served wrapped in tortillas. Due to their zing, these refried beans are perhaps more appropriate as a *botana* served with maize chips than as a side dish.

Another variation of these beans using the caramelized onions but not the chiles was the accompaniment to the Costillitas fritas served by doña Josefina "Chepa" Zarco Juárez in the municipal market of San Cristóbal de las Casas, as well as by doña Maribel del Rosario in the "Primero de Mayo" market in Comitán de Domínguez. Both called the dish Frijoles de la olla; the recipe is in the "Market Fundamentals" chapter at the beginning of this book.

Freshly shelled bótil *beans in the municipal market, San Juan Chamula.* [MR]

FOR THE BEANS

1 pound (500 g) dried scarlet
  runner beans
10 cups (2.5 L) water
1 large sprig fresh epazote
  (substitute 1 Tbsp./4 g dried)

FOR THE ENRICHMENT

½ cup (112 g) Enriched Lard
⅓ cup (20 g) whole chiles de
  Simojovel (substitute chiles
  piquín)
½ medium white onion (137.5 g),
  chopped
4 medium cloves garlic
  (1 oz./24 g), peeled and chopped
1 tablespoon (2 g) dried whole
  Mexican oregano, lightly toasted
  and ground
½ teaspoon (2.5 g) black pepper,
  ground
1 teaspoon (6 g) sea salt, or to
  taste

FOR SERVING

Queso doble crema chiapaneco
  (substitute Cotija or queso
  fresco)
Totopos para botanas

Prepare-ahead note: Refried beans are better on the second day: reheat in a saucepan with a bit of water to achieve the desired consistency; stir frequently to avoid scorching; serve warm.

YIELD: 8–10 SERVINGS

PARBOIL THE BEANS

Place the beans in a large pot and cover them with the water; add the epazote and bring to a boil. Reduce to a simmer and cook uncovered for about 1½ to 2 hours, or until the beans are very tender and the cooking liquid has reduced: it should come barely to the top surface of the beans; add more water if necessary, or pour off any excess. Remove the epazote and discard. Use a potato masher to mash the beans until smooth; set aside.

PREPARE THE ENRICHMENT

Place the lard in a large saucepan and heat over medium-high heat until shimmering. Add the dried chiles and fry until slightly darkened, about 15–20 seconds. Immediately remove the chiles with a small sieve or finely slotted spoon; set aside. With the lard still on medium-high heat, add the chopped onion and garlic; stir constantly to prevent burning, and cook until the onions are just beginning to caramelize, 6–8 minutes. Add the oregano and pepper and stir to combine. Transfer the enrichment to the pot with the beans, and mash again with the potato masher to incorporate the onions with the beans; mash until there are no traces of whole beans. Add the fried chiles and salt and stir to combine.

TO SERVE

Mound warm beans on a serving platter and sprinkle with the crumbled cheese. Serve with *totopos* for dipping.

BOTANA DE FLOR DE BÓTIL

SAUTÉED SCARLET RUNNER BEAN FLOWERS

Rinse and pick through the flowers well, leaving any small stems attached. You should have about 200 g. of flowers. Plunge the flowers into boiling salted water and cook until just tender, 4–6 minutes; drain thoroughly and press to remove excess moisture. Meanwhile, slowly cook ½ c. chopped scallions in a skillet with 3 tablespoons olive oil or butter; add the drained flowers, stir to incorporate, and cook an additional 5 minutes until flavors amalgamate; add sea salt to taste and serve. For a picante variation, add 5–6 toasted, chopped *chiles de Simojovel* or dried *chiles piquín*, or a sprinkling of dried red chile flakes.

CHILE DE SIMOJOVEL/CHILE PIQUÍN /CHILE PEQUÍN

BOTANICAL: *Capsicum annuum* var. *aviculare* Dierb. syn.
C. annuum var. *glabriusculum* (Dunal) Heiser & Pickersgill/
Family Solanaceae | **ENGLISH:** bird pepper
TZELTAL: *'ich* | **TZOTZIL:** *ich*

A direct descendant of the world's first chile—progenitor of all of today's cultivated species—*C. annuum* var. *aviculare* originated in South America, whence it was distributed into Mesoamerica by birds, granting it its taxonomy as well as its common English name (Latin *avis* = "bird"). Through the eons, the chile has remained stubbornly wild: due to the berry's epicuticular waxy coating as well as a hard outer shell, which present a barrier to the penetration of humidity, germination is challenging, especially if forced by human hand. The acids found in birds' digestive tracts disrupt this barrier, thereby facilitating germination; folk wisdom avers that only if the chile passes through a bird's gut will it ever grow and bear fruit. People who gather *chile piquín* in the wild look for the plants beneath tall trees, near fences or telephone lines—anywhere birds might have the chance to perch for a while. In fact, some home gardeners try to get *chile piquín* to sprout by mixing seeds with a slurry of excrement from pet birds. There are two primary variations within the species: both are very small, only about ⅓ inch (0.8 cm) in diameter, ovoid to spherical; and both are green when young, orange to red when mature. However, the variation known commonly as *pequín* or *piquín* grows in more humid areas and has slightly larger, more elongated berries with a Scoville Heat Index of 50,000–100,000.

The variation commonly known as *chiltepín* can be found in dryer climates, is more rounded, and has a heat index of 30,000–50,000 Scoville units. Almost all consumption of the species in Mexico is from chiles gathered in the wild, generating cash income for the families who harvest them. Chiles may be consumed in their fresh form, either sprinkled atop foods, ground to make a salsa, or pickled (see Timpinchile, p. 128); they are also frequently dried and used whole (see Frijol bótil refrito, p. 89) or ground to a powder and added to foods. The dried *piquín* seen in Chiapas comes from the region around Simojovel de Allende, a small town of just over 10,000 inhabitants about 88 miles (143 km) northwest of San Cristóbal. Both the dried *chiltepín* and the *chile piquín* are available in Mexican markets north of the border or online.

FLOR DE BÓTIL

BOTANICAL: See p. 88

The brightly hued flower of the scarlet runner bean bursts open in late summer, and soon thereafter buckets full of them glow in the market. A vendor in San Cristóbal de las Casas told me that people often eat the fresh flowers garnished only with a little lime, chile, and salt, but she also gave me a simple recipe for cooked *flor de bótil* (opposite page). It makes for a lovely side dish sprinkled with crumbled *queso doble crema*; it may also be served as an appetizer with *totopos*. Scarlet runner beans are easy to grow and will delight you with their proliferation of colorful, edible flowers; heirloom varieties are widely available.

Scenes from the spacious charcuterie section of the municipal market in San Cristóbal de las Casas. Rows of fresh longaniza *and smoked chorizo hang side by side. A typical lunch, cocktail appetizer, or even evening meal in Chiapas often features plates of cold charcuterie from the markets.* [MC]

CHARCUTERIE OF CHIAPAS

To say that ham and other pork dishes are primordial to the Spanish diet would be an unfathomable understatement. The Iberian pig dates to the Neolithic Period: when Rome conquered the Iberian peninsula in 19 BCE, the conquerors happily found themselves in a land already well known for *jamón ibérico*, a product and process probably learned from the Celts. Needless to say, the first Spanish explorers to sail to the New World had salt pork and other cured meats on board. And when Christopher Columbus made his second American voyage in 1493, his ships were stocked not only with cured pork products, but also with eight domesticated pigs (most likely the species *Sus mediterraneus*) purchased in the Canary Islands. Corralled in Hispaniola, the pigs quickly multiplied and soon became feral. Their prolific progeny served as a mobile food source during the ensuing expeditions.

This new livestock adapted brilliantly to the cool climate and varied terrains of Chiapas, but it was in Los Altos de Chiapas, most notably the area around San Cristóbal de las Casas, that pork curing prospered after the Spanish shared their knowledge. Now the charcuterie of Chiapas is considered among the finest in the country. San Cristóbal itself as well as neighboring Teopisco are revered for their cured meat products.

A vendor patiently awaits an order. [MC]

[MR]

FOOD PLANTS OF CHIAPAS

The state of Chiapas is among the most biodiverse in the Americas. The total biodiversity of the state includes about 50,000 species; many of these are endemic, and several are in danger of extinction. The Lacandón Jungle in northeastern Chiapas contains roughly 25 percent of Mexico's total species diversity, most of which has not been researched.

For our market expeditions, I was introduced to Marina Entzin Espinosa, a young Tzotzil woman knowledgeable in regional gastronomy; and as we threaded our way through the maze of food stalls, she explained the ingredients we passed along the way, and recited traditional recipes for them.

[MR]

GUAJE BLANCO/GUASH/HUASH

BOTANICAL: *Leucaena glauca* B. Syn. *leucocephala* (Lam.)/Family/Fabaceae | **ENGLISH:** white leadtree
MIXE: *yail ba'ade* | **ZOQUE:** *pacapaca* | **TZELTAL:** *tol* | **TZOTZIL:** *olnob, paka'*

A native to southern Mexico, particularly the Yucatán Peninsula and the Isthmus of Tehuantepec, *guaje* (often pronounced *guash* or *huash* in Chiapas) is a tall, seed-bearing shade tree related to the mimosa. It is considered by many to be a highly invasive tree; through human intervention, it has spread to many other regions and is now found in the tropical zones of Africa, Hawaii, and Asia. The wood is often used to produce pulp for paper production, and the foliage and seedpods are used for fodder. Once a year, the tree displays shocks of tiny white flowers growing in clusters; following flowering, it produces seedpods that are 4½ to 10 inches (11 to 25 cm) long, pale green when young and a light brown color when they dry and fall from the tree. Each pod holds 15 to 30 seeds, which contain high quantities of Vitamin A and proteins (46%). The seeds are sometimes toasted and ground and used as a substitute for coffee. In Chiapas the seeds, which to me have a faint taste of garlic, are eaten as a snack with lime juice and chile powder, or are sprinkled onto other foods as a garnish.

SALSA DE TOMATE DEL MONTE

TAMARILLO TABLE SAUCE

When we made Marina's salsa recipe that evening, the result was sweet and hot with a flavor slightly reminiscent of apricot and a color to match. It was delicious as a *botana* with *totopos* for dipping, but we also served it alongside a plate of cold charcuterie and *butifarras* and spread it on the meats like mustard with wonderful results. Boil or roast the *tamarillos* until tender, 5–10 minutes, then slip the tough skins off the fruits and discard; scoop out and discard the seeds. Mash the pulp in a *molcajete* with ground *chiles de Simojovel* or *piquín* to taste and a pinch of salt, making sure to leave a rustic consistency. Finish by stirring in finely chopped white onion to taste.

[MR]

TOMATE DEL MONTE/TOMATE DE ÁRBOL/TAMARILLO

BOTANICAL: *Solanum betaceum*, syn. *Cyphomandra betacea*/Family Solanaceae
ENGLISH: tree tomato, tamarillo | **TZOTZIL:** *chichol*

This Andean native of the nightshade family spread naturally into Central America and now is seen as a wild species that grows in the cool, damp forests of the Chiapas high country. Its domestication and cultivation have been dated to the preconquest era. The fruit is ovoid with a smooth, tough skin; the variety found in Chiapas features a variegated color blending from a deep green-black to a vivid red-orange. Fruits measure 1½ to 4 inches (4 to 10 cm) in length. The flesh is lightly acidic and sweet, and the core is full of firm seeds larger than those of the common tomato. *Tamarillo* is increasingly available as an import from New Zealand through the same trade channels as the kiwifruit. Marina recited a simple recipe for *tamarillo* salsa.

HIERBA MORA GUISADA
SAUTÉED AMERICAN NIGHTSHADE WITH TAMARILLO

If you travel to Chiapas, you'll find these two ingredients plentifully. Or, though the taste won't be quite the same, substitute baby spinach leaves for the *hierba mora*. Prepare a *sofrito* using cooked, seeded, and chopped *tomate del monte* (*tamarillo*), scallions, and garlic. Blanch leaves of *hierba mora*, discard the water, and coarsely chop the leaves (skip the blanching step if using spinach). Add the chopped leaves to the *sofrito* and stir, seasoning with ground *chiles de Simojovel* or *piquín* and salt to taste; serve with tortillas or as a side dish.

[MR]

HIERBA MORA

BOTANICAL: *Solanum americanum*/Family Solanaceae | **ENGLISH:** American nightshade, glossy nightshade | **TZOTZIL:** *unen*

Care should be taken when consuming this leafy herb in the nightshade family: the plant contains toxic glycoalkaloids, natural toxins that evolved in certain plants for self-preservation. Nonetheless, it is a green that is eaten voraciously in many tropical regions of the world, and apparently toxicity depends considerably on local varieties and growing conditions. Botanists warn that if you are uncertain which strain the particular plant is, you should leave it alone, particularly the berries that the plants produce. Some scientific research indicates that cooking *hierba mora* at temperatures higher than 340°F (170°C) may destroy the toxins. *Hierba mora* is a large, bushy annual or perennial and can grow in height up to about 40 to 60 inches (1–1.5 m). The leaves vary greatly in size, up to 4 inches (10 cm) long and 3 inches (7 cm) wide. Berries are small (¼ to ⅓ inch/0.5 to 1 cm) and shiny black. Both Leti and Marina told me that in Zoque, Mam, and Tzeltal communities, *hierba mora* is often tossed into pots of beans. Marina shared another simple recipe with me.

[MR]

ARRAYÁN/AXOCOPAQUE

BOTANICAL: *Gaultheria acuminata* Schltdl. & Cham. syn. *Gaultheria chiapensis* Camp/Family Ericaceae
ENGLISH: acuminate wintergreen | **TZOTZIL:** *ojov*

The *Gaultheria* species is an evergreen shrub with spirally arranged leaves that taper to a sharp point—the botanical definition of "acuminate." The English name "wintergreen" applies to the entire *Gaultheria* species, and many plants fall within the category. *Arrayán* is in the Ericaceae family, commonly known as the heath or heather family, which includes azalea, rhododendron, cranberry, and huckleberry. *Arrayán* grows at elevations of 3,280–4,921 feet (1,000–1,500 m) above sea level and is distributed from central Mexico to Honduras. In Chiapas, the leaves and stems of *arrayán* are used in cooking, much as one might use bay leaves (which may be substituted), typically in pork dishes such as Cochito horneado (p. 139) and chicken dishes such as *olla tapada*; they are also used medicinally as an antiseptic, diuretic, and anti-inflammatory; flowers may be used for flavoring the chocolate beverage. Note that in other parts of Mexico, the name *arrayán* may refer to other plant species.

> *There is also an herb street, where may be obtained all sorts of roots and medicinal herbs that the country affords.*
>
> HERNÁN CORTÉS, 1520

One of the herb stalls at Central de Abastos in San Cristóbal is crammed with every imaginable dried and fresh herb, as well as dried chiles and various seasoning blends, like recado de achiote (p. 45). Here is where we found arrayán (p. 98), a dried leaf used as a seasoning in several dishes in Chiapas. The vendor animatedly described its earthy and unique flavor. [MR]

The outdoor area behind the market continues the flow of buying and selling. [MR]

A Tzotzil woman sells corn on the cob from a brazier on a street corner outside the market. [MR]

[MR]

MERCADO DE DULCES Y ARTESANÍAS

Just four blocks from San Cristóbal's Parque Central, I caught a heavy, almost sticky, sweet scent drifting from the Mercado de Dulces y Artesanías. Barely entering, we were welcomed by mountains of otherworldly treats to satisfy any sweet tooth; deeper inside are fantasies concocted of locally mined amber. But above all: the sweets!

Cerise, yellow, and orange cocadas are stacked in precarious towers (center), as are cones of gasnate, puff pastry cones filled with creamy turrón (in Chiapas often a catchall name for pastry cream or Italian meringue; bottom right corner). A pink bucket holds pink-sugar-dusted nuégados (center left) while an imposing fortress of empanizado de panela y cacahuate is layered like bricks (right). [MR]

EMPANIZADO DE PANELA Y CACAHUATE

BROWN SUGAR AND PEANUT BUTTER BARS

FOR THE PEANUT BUTTER BARS

Vegetable oil for the cake pan

3 cups (350 g) roasted, salted peanuts

2 cups (400 g) panela (see p. 538; substitute muscovado or dark brown sugar), grated and finely packed in the measuring cup

½ cup (125 mL) water

¼ teaspoon (0.75 g) ground canela (Mexican cinnamon)

In the Mercado de Dulces y Artesanías, stacks of drab brown Empanizado de panela y cacahuate compete side by side with more attention-getting offerings like preternaturally orange *cocadas* or fuchsia-tinged *nuégados*. This unprepossessing treat combines all the primal gastronomical elements we lust for: sugar, salt, and fat. In truth, these rich squares are virtually identical to halvah: just substitute peanuts for the sesame seeds, and syrup made with Mexican *panela* for the honey. (And as the treat's name would suggest, *panela*, rich unrefined sugar, is a primordial ingredient in the formula; purchase the best you can find.) The recipe for Empanizado de panela y cacahuate is almost ridiculously simple; the only difficult part is waiting the required time to eat it! But refrigeration for the specified time allows for the formation of sugar crystals, adding "mouth feel" to our list of gustatory lusts.

Prepare-ahead note: Empanizado de cacahuate requires 24–36 hours refrigeration time before serving. It keeps well in an airtight container under refrigeration for 2–3 weeks. Bring to room temperature before serving.

YIELD: 16 PIECES

PREPARE THE PEANUT BUTTER BARS

Thoroughly oil a 9-inch by 9-inch by 1½-inch (23 cm × 23 cm × 4 cm) cake pan; set aside. Place the peanuts in the bowl of a food processor; process until you achieve a smooth peanut butter, 4–5 minutes (you should still be able to see a bit of the texture

[MR]

of the peanuts); transfer to a cup measure: you should have 2 cups of peanut butter. Keep the peanut butter near the stove during the next step. In a large saucepan placed over high heat, melt the sugar in the water; add the *canela*, stir to blend, and heat the syrup until it reaches the soft-ball stage (240°F/115°C). Immediately add the peanut butter to the syrup and remove the pan from the heat source. Working quickly, beat the mixture vigorously with a wooden spoon until it is thoroughly blended and emulsified. Continue beating; as the mixture cools, after 2–3 minutes it will start to stiffen dramatically. At this stage you will no longer be able to beat the mixture, but keep it moving by stirring up from the bottom in a folding motion. After 1 minute more, pour the mixture into the prepared cake pan. Working with a rubber spatula, quickly press the mixture in place, spreading it from side to side and patting down the top surface to smooth. Let the mixture cool to room temperature. When cool, cut into 16 squares (4 across the pan and 4 down); cover the pan with plastic wrap and refrigerate for 24–36 hours.

NUÉGADOS

SUGARY GLAZED DOUGH BALLS

These could be thought of as "doughnut holes," since the recipe is similar, but they are actually formed purposely as a "positive" ball rather than being the "negative" shape left over from doughnut making. The name derives from the Latin *nux/nucis*, or nut, and by inference other fruits with a shell. In fact, other versions of the treat use nuts, dried fruits, and honey, which has led some to ponder a Moorish or possibly Jewish origin. But perhaps in this case the name simply refers to the nutlike shape. In the Fronteriza region of Chiapas, the little balls are dipped in a light glaze and stuck together in clumps of three or four, but in the center of the state they may be formed flat and elongated. A dusting of glowing *carmín*-tinted sugar guarantees that you can spot these little goodies from yards away. The sweet takes on many names depending on location: also look for *nuégano*, *muégado* (or *muégano* in Hidalgo), or *muégalo*.

Prepare-ahead note: *Nuégados* keep well at room temperature for 3–4 days.

YIELD: 1 DOZEN

FOR THE DOUGH
2 cups (250 g) all-purpose flour
2 teaspoons (8 g) baking powder
⅛ teaspoon (0.75 g) sea salt
½ cup (100 g) sugar
1 medium egg
½ cup (125 mL) milk
2 tablespoons (28 g) Enriched Lard (p. 530), melted

PREPARE THE DOUGH
In a small mixing bowl, combine the flour, baking powder, and salt. In the bowl of a stand mixer, combine the sugar and egg; beat until pale yellow and smooth, 3–4 minutes. Add the milk and lard and continue beating until thoroughly emulsified and smooth. Add the dry ingredients to the egg mixture; beat until just combined, 1–2 minutes. Wrap the dough in plastic wrap and allow to rest in the refrigerator for 30 minutes.

1 cup (130 g) powdered sugar
6 tablespoons (90 mL) milk
½ teaspoon (2.5 mL) Mexican
  vanilla extract

FOR DECORATING
1 cup (200 g) sugar
1 tablespoon (6 g) carmín (see
  p. 117; substitute powdered
  organic red food coloring)

FOR FRYING
Vegetable oil

[MR]

PREPARE THE GLAZE AND DECORATION

Meanwhile, in a small mixing bowl, combine the powdered sugar, milk, and vanilla extract, and stir vigorously until smooth. It should be a thin glaze rather than a frosting, with the consistency of syrup: add more milk if too thick, or thicken it slightly by adding more powdered sugar.

In a shallow bowl or small plate, mix the sugar with the powdered food coloring and set aside.

FORM THE NUÉGADOS AND FRY

On a lightly floured surface, roll the dough or flatten it with the floured palms of your hands to a thickness of about ½ inch (1.5 cm). Cut the dough into 2-inch by 2-inch (5-cm by 5-cm) squares by first cutting the strips top to bottom, then cutting side to side across the first strips. Weigh one square: it should weigh approximately 1.4 ounces (40 g). Form each square into a ball, and place it on waxed paper while you complete the remaining squares. Allow to rest for about 10 minutes while you heat the oil.

Pour 2 inches (5 cm) of vegetable oil into a large, deep skillet; heat to 375°F (190°C). Add 4–5 balls at a time, depending on the size of your skillet; flip to the other side and continue frying until golden. Transfer to paper towels to drain.

While still warm, dip the balls into the powdered sugar glaze and place them on waxed paper. After finishing four balls, stick them together in a pyramid shape with three at the bottom and one at the top (use more glaze if necessary so that they stick). Sprinkle the top ball with some of the tinted sugar. Set aside as you continue with the other balls. Store *nuégados* in an airtight container.

(above) At a dulcería just inside the Mercado de Dulces y Artesanías, the stall's eponymous Tía Marí entices customers with free samples. Here, the cherry-like nance *is preserved in* mistela— *a local adaptation of the Spanish fortified wine, in this case made from tropical fruits such as mango, tejocote, or ciruela. In the foreground is a stack of* dulce de chilacayote *(p. 114).* [MR]
(below) A parade of figures made of dulce de yema—*an egg-yolk-and-sugar confection descended from the Spanish* yemitas *and probably an earlier Moorish recipe.* [MR]

Templo Santo Domingo de Guzmán. [MR]

COMITÁN DE DOMÍNGUEZ

PERFECTLY MANICURED PLAZAS and uniquely ornamented churches seem to occupy every street corner of Comitán de Domínguez, leaving one to wonder why this mountain gem remains so far off the tourist radar. Perhaps overshadowed by its flashier sister, San Cristóbal de las Casas, the quietly elegant Comitán has been relegated to the supporting role of a pleasant day trip for tourists on the way to many important Maya sites on the western edge of the Guatemala border, just 50 miles (80 km) away.

From the steeply hilly San Cristóbal de las Casas, we traveled only about 57 miles (92 km) to Comitán, plunging 2,000 feet (610 m) along rollercoaster roads until we reached the high mountain plateau where this charming pueblo is nestled. Established as a Maya-Quiché site in the seventh century CE, in 1482 it was conquered by the Aztecs.

MERCADO PRIMERO DE MAYO

In the bustling heart of town, the "Primero de Mayo" market—inaugurated at the turn of the twentieth century—is the most unusual and best conserved market structure in the region. A stately corner entrance is penetrated by a steep stairway along which there are so many *ambulantes* (roving vendors) spilling down the steps hawking their wares that shoppers must boldly blaze a path upstream.

Inside, a graceful cast-iron colonnade supporting articulated wooden beams defines an O around a central atrium crowned with a skylight. The airy, bright, and open space is all about food, and most of the sit-down eateries line the periphery.

[MR]

[MR]

[TA]

TZELTAL/K'OP O WINIK ATEL

The people's name for themselves translates to "working men," and like the closely related Tzotziles, the name of their language means simply "true language." Along with the Tzotziles, the Tzeltal people migrated from Guatemala to the Altos de Chiapas region in the Southern Highlands sometime between 750 and 500 BCE; beginning in the thirteenth century, the two groups separated into different regions, and their languages began diversifying. During the colonial era, the Tzeltales were forced to pay tribute to the Spanish, to crank the *trapiche*—the mill that crushes sugarcane—to work in the amber mines near Simojovel, or to toil in the lumber mills and livestock haciendas of the Spanish. The Tzeltal people are the largest indigenous group in Chiapas. The traditional territory of the Tzeltal is to the northeast and southeast of San Cristóbal de las Casas. Agriculture is the predominant economic activity of the Tzeltales; crops include the traditional maize, beans, squash, tomatoes, and chiles, as well as yuca, *camote*, chayote, cotton, and coffee. Originally founded by Tzeltales, Comitán de Domínguez retains typical Tzeltal gastronomy in many dishes.

The warmly painted Comedor "Maribel del Rosario" is made even more inviting by the sunny disposition of the owner/cook, here seated peeling local peaches, which she will simmer in sugar syrup and pack in jars to sell in the market—a popular product throughout the region. Her husband serves as the comedor's jovial waiter, and she and her daughter share the daily cooking chores. Today's special: Costillitas fritas en salsa verde. [MR]

As throughout Mexico, the aguas frescas of Chiapas are made of mashed fruit, mostly local, that is sometimes strained, then mixed with water and sugar. The bounty of nature is the only limitation. Watermelon is a favorite, but also look for the more unusual chilacayote (p. 114), a variety of squash. [MR]

COSTILLITAS FRITAS EN SALSA VERDE

PORK RIBLET CONFIT WITH TOMATILLO SAUCE

TO PREPARE AHEAD
Enriched Lard (p. 530)
Salsa verde (p. 531)

The complex combination of flavors in these succulent, fatty riblets accompanied by simple Frijoles de la olla and Salsa verde belies the simplicity of this dish. Pork ribs are marinated for a couple of hours in lime juice and salt; once drained, they are plunged into boiling lard and cooked until tender and well browned. Doña Maribel served each of us six of the riblets side by side with a bed of red pot beans and rice, and ladled on a generous amount of the green sauce. Riblets are spare ribs that have been cut in half, with the curved center portion removed, resulting in a smaller, more uniform rib shape. This is the rib cut frequently used in Chinese barbecue recipes. Unless you have a meat saw, your butcher will have to prepare these for you.

Prepare-ahead note: The pork confit may be prepared several hours or a day in advance. Reheat quickly in lard immediately before serving. The Salsa verde may be made many days in advance and frozen, or a day ahead and refrigerated. Reheat prior to serving.

YIELD: 4 TO 6 SERVINGS, DEPENDING ON PORTION SIZE

[MC]

FOR THE PORK CONFIT

3½ pounds (1.5 kg) pork riblets
  (see notes above; for optional
  brining, see p. 527)
1 cup (250 mL) lime juice
3½ pounds (1.5 kg) Enriched Lard

FOR SERVING

Salsa verde
Frijoles de la olla (p. 530)
Steamed white rice or Arroz de
  fiesta (p. 74)
Salsa de chile de árbol (p. 531),
  optional
Simple salpicón of diced white
  onion, diced chile chamborote
  (substitute manzano, rocoto, or
  jalapeño chiles), and chopped
  cilantro tossed with lime juice
  and salt to taste

PREPARE THE PORK CONFIT

If you brined the riblets, remove them from the brine, rinse well, and drain; discard the brining solution. If the ribs are left in strips, cut between the bones to form individual riblets. Place the riblets in one layer in a large baking dish and cover with the lime juice. (If you did not brine the meat, sprinkle 1 teaspoon/6 g of salt over the riblets.) Refrigerate for 1 hour.

Remove the riblets from the juice and shake off the excess. Pat the ribs completely dry with paper towels. Place the lard in a large, deep stockpot or Dutch oven over high heat. When the lard has melted and reached a temperature of 350°F (176°C), carefully add the ribs a few at a time; they should be completely submerged in the lard. Maintaining the heat at the prescribed temperature, continue to fry the ribs until they are very well browned, about 6–8 minutes. (*Note*: Smaller riblets may take less time.) The internal temperature should read 145°F (63°C). Transfer the ribs to paper towels to drain as you continue frying the remaining riblets; sprinkle the riblets lightly with sea salt. Serve the riblets immediately or cover them with aluminum foil to keep them warm until serving time.

TO SERVE

Place 1 tablespoon (15 mL) vegetable oil in a medium saucepan, and heat until shimmering; add the Salsa verde all at once; it should sputter and sizzle, so stand back. Cook over medium-high heat for 5 minutes, stirring frequently, until slightly darkened and slightly thickened. Plate the ribs with accompanying beans and rice; ladle the hot Salsa verde over the ribs (some people request that the sauce go onto the beans and rice as well). Serve accompanied by the optional Salsa de chile de árbol, the *salpicón*, and warm tortillas if you wish.

VARIATION

Salsa de carne frita/Pork Riblet Confit with Tomato Sauce. This dish that we found in Zaachila, Oaxaca, is virtually identical to the above recipe, but uses Salsa de jitomate (p. 532) instead of the tomatillo sauce. Be sure to use plenty of chile and garlic in the tomato sauce.

[MR]

CHILACAYOTE/CHILACAYOTA

BOTANICAL: *Cucurbita ficifolia* Bouché/Family Cucurbitaceae
ENGLISH: fig leaf squash, fig leaf gourd, Malabar gourd | **TZOTZIL:** *mail*

Growing prolifically in mountainous regions at altitudes of 3,280–9,842 feet (1,000–3,000 m), this member of the squash family can be found throughout Latin America, from northern Mexico into South America; sixteenth-century explorers introduced the squash into parts of Europe and Asia, where it continues to proliferate. The extensive use of its Nahuatl-derived name, *tzilacayotli*, led early botanists to posit a Mexican origin of the species, but recent archaeological evidence points to an Andean birthplace. In Chiapas, *chilacayote* is grown during the rainy season; in neighboring Oaxaca, its growth may also extend into the dry period, and, in fact, from time to time the plant can behave as a perennial. It produces a rampant, spreading vine that trails for many meters along the ground or up fences or pergolas. Like others of the genus, the flowers, runners, fruits, and seeds are all consumed. Fruits are spherical to elliptical, with three color patterns: light or dark green with or without longitudinal white stripes extending toward the apex; minutely spotted white and green; or white to cream, with white flesh. The flesh is high in carbohydrates and lightly sweet. Small, young fruits are harvested and eaten much like zucchini; fruits that are left to mature can grow to the size of watermelons and are typically preserved in sugar syrup for the candied fruit treat known as *dulce de chilacayote* and also used for the preserved *conserva de chilacayote* (p. 519). In Chiapas, the seeds of *chilacayote* are cooked in *panela* and left to harden into bars for the snack known as *palanqueta*.

(above) Atole agrio *may appear in its natural pale yellow color (below), although to attract customers some vendors tint it a vivid magenta with the colorant known as* carmín *(p. 117).* [MR]

(below) A vendor doles out sumptuous portions of atole granillo *(with whole kernels of maize) in the center, and* agrio *at left, for which she has left the maize its natural color.* [MR]

ATOLE AGRIO

FERMENTED MAIZE PORRIDGE

Atole agrio—maize porridge that has been allowed to lightly ferment—is prepared in various parts of the country, often for feast days. In most parts of Chiapas, it is daily fare and a requisite accompaniment to tamales. Its faintly sweet-sour taste is a natural complement to the rich, savory tamales of the region; market vendors everywhere serve it in the tree-gourd bowls known as *jícaras* (or, just as often today, in Styrofoam cups). Throughout the state, *atole agrio* is traditionally prepared from *maíz negro*, black maize; the coloring of the maize lends a delicate lilac-to-purple cast to the finished *atole*. Since *maíz negro* is more expensive than white, some cooks use the white and tint the porridge with *carmín* (p. 117) to impart the customary color. In other parts of Chiapas, such as in Comitán de Domínguez, cooks occasionally unapologetically use yellow maize with no additional color. The fresh corn kernels are boiled and allowed to ferment for up to two days; the mixture is then ground, strained, diluted with water, and cooked to thicken into porridge; sugar is added to taste.

[MR]

[There were] colors as numerous as can be found in Spain, and as fine shades . . .

HERNÁN CORTÉS, 1520

CARMÍN   Powdered colorants are used frequently in Chiapas for tamales, sweet treats, even *atole*. A rainbow is available: blue, green, red, yellow. The most popular is red, known as *carmín*, which explodes in shocking pink bursts in *tamal de manjar* as well as atop *nuégados* (p. 105); the yellow is frequently used in egg-based breads to give them a rich yellow-orange color. Local cooks who use the colorants sold in the market won't tell you what they are made from (I suspect they are artificial colors), but the authentic and original are available, even in organic form. *Carmín* was originally produced from cochineal, the tiny scale insect that lives on the paddle cactus genus, *Opuntia*, native to tropical and subtropical America, but nowadays the red tints are more likely to consist of natural dyes from vegetables such as beets. The yellow is typically made from achiote (*Bixa orellana* L., annatto in English, p. 45).

A young boy in the market helps his mother sell small packets of powdered food coloring. [MR]

TAMAL DE BOLA

PORK RIBLET AND CHILE TAMALE

TO PREPARE AHEAD

Masa para tamales (p. 530), reserving the chicken bouillon

Descriptively named "ball tamale," the Tamal de bola acquires its spherical shape thanks to a whole pork back riblet buried inside, making eating the tamale a bit awkward: you first must scoop away some of the masa, then insert your fingers to pluck out the rib. Some diners pull the meat off the bone to mix with the rest of the ingredients; others simply gnaw on the bone either before or after devouring the flavorfully sauced masa. The tamales we enjoyed in the market featured a pickled jalapeño in the center, but Leti followed the traditional formula and placed several chiles de Simojovel inside the masa with the other fillings. Tamal de bola is popular and consumed throughout the state; nonetheless, Comitán de Domínguez claims it as its specialty. (*Note*: The riblets are inserted into the masa in their raw state; they cook perfectly during the steaming.)

Prepare-ahead note: The components for Tamal de bola may be prepared in advance and refrigerated or frozen; bring to room temperature before using. Similarly, the tamales can be prepared completely through steaming and subsequently frozen; to serve, do not defrost: place in a steamer and steam for 1 hour.

YIELD: 1 DOZEN TAMALES

FOR FORMING THE TAMALES

14 dried cornhusks

48 chiles de Simojovel (substitute dried chiles piquín or 12 pickled jalapeños)

FOR THE PORK

1 pound (500 g) pork back riblets (see note p. 328 for more information)

1 gallon (4 L) water

½ cup (145 g) sea salt

FOR THE SALSA

2 pounds (1 kg) medium Roma tomatoes

1 medium onion (10 oz./275 g), halved

2 medium cloves garlic (½ oz./12 g), peeled

1 chile guajillo, seeds and veins removed

1 tablespoon (15 g) recado rojo ("de achiote," p. 45)

¼ teaspoon (0.5 g) cumin seed

2 whole cloves

1 tablespoon (15 mL) vegetable oil

1 small sprig fresh thyme

½ teaspoon (3 g) sea salt

FOR THE MASA

1 recipe Masa para tamales

4½ ounces (125 g) chicharrón (pork cracklings)

PREPARE THE CORNHUSKS

Cut or tear very thin ribbons, following the grain, from two of the cornhusks. Set the strips aside to use as ties. Place the remaining cornhusks in a large stockpot and cover them completely with water. Place a heavy heatproof plate or bowl on top of the cornhusks to keep them submerged. Bring the water to a boil, reduce the heat, and simmer for 20 minutes. Remove the stockpot from the heat and allow the cornhusks to continue to soak and gradually come to room temperature, about 1 hour.

PREPARE THE PORK

Cut between each riblet to result in individual pieces with the bones intact, trimming away any large pieces of excess fat. Prepare a brine solution with the water and salt; when the salt is completely dissolved, add the pork riblets. Allow the riblets to soak at room temperature for 1 hour while you prepare the salsa.

PREPARE THE SALSA

Place the first four ingredients in a large stockpot; cover with water and bring to a boil. Cook until the onion and garlic are tender. Remove the vegetables and chile with a slotted spoon or wok strainer and set aside; reserve the cooking liquid.

Place the vegetables in the jar of a blender (depending on the size of your blender, you may need to do this step in batches). Add enough of the cooking liquid to keep the blades of the blender moving, about ½ cup (125 mL). Add the next three ingredients and purée: the resulting purée should be thick.

Pour the vegetable oil into a large skillet; heat until the oil is shimmering. Holding a fine-mesh sieve over the skillet, pour the puréed tomato mixture through it: it should sputter and sizzle, so stand back. Use a rubber spatula to press through as much of the contents of the sieve as possible; discard anything that won't pass through.

Add the sprig of thyme to the salsa, and cook over medium heat, stirring frequently, until the sauce intensifies in color and thickens slightly, 4–5 minutes. Add the salt and check the seasonings.

PREPARE THE MASA

As you prepare the masa, crumble the *chicharrón* into the jar of a blender; turn on the blender and process until the *chicharrón* is finely crumbled. Add the chicken stock or bouillon mixture prescribed in the recipe for the masa, and process until incorporated. Add this mixture to the masa as you mix it in the stand mixer. Cover the finished masa with a damp towel as you proceed.

FORM, WRAP, AND STEAM THE TAMALES

Drain the ribs, rinse lightly, and set aside. Prepare one tamale at a time: remove a cornhusk from the soaking liquid and pat dry. Place it on a work surface aligned vertically with the widest end toward you. Place 4 heaping tablespoons (120 g) of the masa in the center of the cornhusk; press one riblet into the center of the masa. Spoon on 2 tablespoons (30 mL) of the salsa to cover the riblet, and top with 4 chiles de Simojovel (alternatively you may use one slice of pickled jalapeño, drained).

Fold the left side of the cornhusk toward the center to cover the tamale; repeat with the right side of the cornhusk. Pinch the bottom flap closed and secure tightly with one of the ties; repeat with the top flap of the cornhusk. The tamale should be firmly compacted within the cornhusk.

Fill the bottom of a *vaporera* with water (alternatively you may use a large stockpot fitted with a steaming basket). Arrange the tamales flat inside the *vaporera* on top of the steaming platform, or inside a steaming basket located at the bottom of a stockpot. Place the lid on tightly; bring the water to a boil, and continue to boil for 1 hour. Halfway through the steaming time, check the water level and add more water if necessary.

TO SERVE
In Chiapas, diners usually receive 2 Tamales de bola. Plate them on individual serving plates, and accompany with the leftover salsa, warmed. Serve with Atole agrio (p. 116) if desired.

Bright pink Atole agrio *is the frequent accompaniment to any of the variety of regional tamales: left,* Tamal untado *(p. 82); right,* Tamal de bola. [MC]

PANELA/PILONCILLO/AZÚCAR MASCABADO

ENGLISH: muscovado sugar, molasses sugar, cone sugar

Pyramidal piles of *panela*—cones of dark, rich, unrefined sugar—welcome shoppers just inside the entrance of the municipal market. Rustically wrapped in dried sugarcane leaves rescued from the harvest, the cones are bundled in groups of four, weighing an arm-breaking 7 pounds (3.2 kg). The moment the vendor offered me a taste I was hooked: smoky, velvety, slow melting, trickling down the throat with the future promise of aged rum. Putting thoughts of the weight aside, I later made room in my shopping bag, and when back in Mérida, the treats I made with the *panela* recalled images of that particular bright, chilly morning in the market.

The short drive from the flat plain of Comitán de Domínguez to the plain of Tzimol passes through a mountain range famous in the region for its spectacular series of waterfalls, most particularly the one known as El Chiflón. Along the way, hundreds of acres of sugarcane fields are planted in flatter lands, and, in fact, sugar production is the chief industry of Tzimol. Many families are engaged in what remains a wholly artisanal craft here: sugarcane (see photo) is planted, harvested, stripped, and crushed, and the resulting nectar is cooked and molded all by hand, a highly labor-intensive practice that fueled the Caribbean slave trade during the colonial period. Even now, the process of transforming cane juice into dark brown blocks of sugar by artisanal methods is backbreaking and sweaty work, with many hours spent stoking the fires of the behemoth brick furnaces that bring cauldrons of the juice to a roiling boil before steaming batches of it are ladled into rows of weathered wooden molds.

A recipe for Empanizado de panela y cacahuate is on page 104. Other recipes that call for *panela* (known as *piloncillo* in some parts of Mexico) can be found throughout this book.

QUESOS CHIAPANECOS/CHEESES OF CHIAPAS

The cheese sections of the markets of Chiapas are always redolent of fermented milk—an olfactory advertisement that can be perceived from many feet away. The state's producers have acquired recognition for creating some of the finest cheeses in the country, and several of them have won international awards. Few *chiapaneco* dishes are not garnished with a sprinkle of the famous *queso doble crema*.

More than one million liters of milk are produced each day in Chiapas, and about 70 percent of that output will go into the production of artisanal cheeses. In the entire state, there are close to six hundred registered producers, most of them dedicated to *queso doble crema de Chiapas*, for which producers are seeking D.O.C. status (Denominación de Origen Controlada), a controlled production designation similar to that used for champagne in France and tequila in Jalisco. Cheese factories in Chiapas are typically small, with four to six employees, most of them family members. And half of these produce "farmstead cheese," meaning that they use milk from their own cows.

Cheese types include examples from other regions of Mexico—*asadero* and *quesillo*, for example—but the state has carved out its own niche with specialty cheeses like *queso de bola de Ocosingo* and *queso de cuadro doble crema*. Both are raw, fresh cow's milk cheeses, and both have been produced in Chiapas since the Porfiriato period.

Cheeses in the markets may come from any one of several towns: be sure to look for those from Ocosingo, Rayón, Venustiano Carranza, and Pijijiapan.

(above) Artisanal fresh cheeses from nearby Carranza are wrapped either in banana leaves or cornhusks. [MR]

[MR]

QUESO DE BOLA DE OCOSINGO

This is such a unique cheese that it has been granted a collective, controlled trademark. Rancho Laltic was the first to produce it in 1927; soon, other ranchers began producing it, too. *Queso de bola de Ocosingo* is actually three cheeses in one: the core is made of raw cow's milk double cream cheese, matured for twenty-one days; it is then covered in one and sometimes two layers of *queso descremado* (skimmed milk cheese) that is pulled into form. These layers dry into a firm, edible rind. The soft, creamy center is sharp and milky with a subtle herbal aroma; and because it is so salty, it is often used as an ingredient in dips or as an accompaniment to other foods. Or, it can be paired with a bold red wine or dark beer, both of which can stand up to the strong taste. The outer skin is often cut into strips and used as a filling for enchiladas or to make *chicharrones de queso* (crispy fried cheese "tostadas"). The lactography weblog host and Mexican cheese champion Carlos Yescas likens the cheese to Italian Caciocavallo. Made artisanally with the milk from small Holstein herds, *queso de bola de Ocosingo*—enormously popular throughout Chiapas—is virtually unknown outside the state. The bags in the basket in the photo hold fresh sweet *crema*.

QUESO DE CUADRO DOBLE CREMA

Like *queso de bola de Ocosingo*, this is a raw cow's milk double cream cheese; it is soft and creamy like goat cheese but with the flavor of a very sharp cheese. Unmistakable in the market, it is shaped like a brick and is about that size (*cuadro* means "square" and also "frame," referring to the mold used for forming the cheese); it is occasionally wrapped in bright yellow foil. Made only in Chiapas, primarily in Ocosingo and Rayón, *queso de cuadro doble crema* has won several awards in global competitions. *Queso de cuadro doble crema* frequently appears crumbled and dusted atop tamales, soups, and beans.

(above, right) Chiapas cheeses in the market: At far left is queso de cuadro doble crema, *formed in solid brick shapes. At center is* queso añejo enchilado, *an aged cheese that has been coated with a thin layer of chile powder.* [MR]

(above) Tire-sized rounds of quesillo, *the stringy Oaxaca-style cheese, mature in presses in the back room of an artisanal producer in Ocosingo. Individual packages of the string cheese are seen at left.* [MR] *(below) A market vendor produces artisanal chorizo in spherical shapes.* [MR]

As is true in San Cristóbal de las Casas and throughout much of the region, Comitán de Domínguez specializes in several forms of charcuterie. [MR]

Beef is salted and cured for the regional favorite, tasajo. [MC]

TASAJO

LIME-AND-SALT-CURED BEEF

In the era before refrigeration, meat was frequently cured to preserve it, and Tasajo—salt-cured beef—became a prominent item in the criollo kitchens of Mexico and South America. By the nineteenth century, it was produced in great quantities in Argentina and shipped "in bales like sole-leather" across the Atlantic on the infamous "Tasajo Trail" to cheaply feed slaves on sugar plantations in Cuba. The salting and drying process used in curing the meat perhaps not surprisingly resulted in meat so dry and leathery that it required labor-intensive soaking and shredding to render it edible. Tasajo as it is enjoyed today in Chiapas and in many parts of Mexico as well as in Cuba must still undergo the miraculous rebirth from "sole-leather" to masticable protein, and recipes for the transformation abound (see Pepita con tasajo, p. 134).

A market vendor in Comitán de Domínguez shared the following method of curing Tasajo with me. Her formula was simple: marinate thin strips of beef in lime juice, salt, and paprika for two or three days, then air-dry for a couple of days. Whether or not to use lime juice during the process of curing Tasajo remains a regional (and often

FOR THE TASAJO

2 pounds (1 kg) beefsteak (see notes above)

¼ cup (125 mL) freshly squeezed lime juice

1 teaspoon (5 g) paprika

¼ cup (125 g) coarse sea salt

Kitchen twine for tying

personal) choice, but most cooks I met in Chiapas do opt for it, and I like it, too: it provides a light, fresh foil for the rich, salty meat.

My vendor also had a special trick for air-drying the beef after the salting stage: as a first step, she bound two thin strips of the meat together with a tie from green *ixtle* (*Aechmea magdalenae*), an exotic flowering plant in the Bromeliaceae family native to southeastern Mexico and parts of Central America; *ixtle* fibers were used in pre-Columbian times to weave cloth for the peasant class and in the colonial era to stitch leather goods. The *ixtle* may be replaced with kitchen twine. After the salt cure, simply drape the bound meat over a plastic coat hanger or dowel rod—one strip to the front, one to the back, like pants—and allow the meat to dry.

Traditionally an economical dish, Tasajo is usually made with cheaper cuts like skirt steak, but for a tenderer result, use strip steak or sirloin, making sure that it has good marbling and hopefully even some fat around the outer edges.

Prepare-ahead note: The process of curing Tasajo takes approximately four days, with just about an hour of active time. Once dried, Tasajo can be kept for a couple of days at room temperature, weeks in the refrigerator, or months in the freezer.

YIELD: APPROXIMATELY 1¼ POUNDS (560 G)

PREPARE THE TASAJO

Cut the meat into sheets approximately ⅜ inch (1 cm) thick (depending on the cut you choose, you may wish to ask your butcher to complete this step). Slice the sheets into strips approximately 1½ inches (4 cm) wide and 10 inches (25 cm) long. Lay one strip on top of a second and use kitchen twine to tie together at one of the narrow ends. Place the bound meat strips in a large, nonreactive baking dish and pour on the lime juice; sprinkle on half of the paprika and salt; turn the meat to the other side and add the remaining paprika and salt. Refrigerate for 48 hours. After the first day, turn the meat to the other side, and return to refrigeration.

After 48 hours, remove the meat from the baking dish and arrange in one layer on a rack placed above a baking sheet lined with paper towels. Return to the refrigerator for an additional 24 hours. (This is the first step in the drying process: air will circulate around the meat, and any residual juices will be absorbed by the paper towels.)

Remove the meat from the refrigerator and drape the bundled strips over a plastic coat hanger or dowel rod in single file (do not overlap). Allow to air dry for 24 hours, remove the ties, then vacuum pack to freeze, store in resealable plastic bags to refrigerate, or use immediately in a recipe.

PALMITO/PALMA DE GUANO

BOTANICAL: *Sabal mexicana* Mart./Family Aracaceae
ENGLISH: Mexican palmetto, Texas palmetto, Rio Grande palmetto, heart of palm | **TZOTZIL:** *xan*

Sabal mexicana is a North American native tropical palm that is distributed in low coastal areas from Sinaloa to Chiapas and along the Gulf of Mexico from Tamaulipas to the Yucatán Peninsula. Mature palms can reach a height of 50 feet (15 m), with a trunk measuring up to 3 feet (1 m) in diameter and fan-shaped leaves spanning 3 feet (1 m) in width. Throughout much of the growing zone, the leaves are woven and used for roofing on structures known as *palapas*. The palm is also a food source: once the outer bark of the trunk is peeled away, the core, or heart, is left to dry for a couple of days, then it is cooked in water for about 10 minutes and is ready to consume. The heart of the palm, referred to in Chiapas as *palmito*, appears in various guises in *cocina chiapaneca*: it is a primary ingredient in a couple of popular pickles, and it is also baked underground for a dish called *shihuac*, which is served as a side dish along with a main course on the order of a vegetable accompaniment. It is also chopped and mixed with scrambled eggs.

Whole hearts of palm, known in Chiapas as palmitos. [MR]

PICLES/PICKLED HEARTS OF PALM GARNISH   Just around the corner from the vendor who sold giant cores of *palmito*—which looked ever so much like the legs from a piece of space-age furniture—I met the woman who operated Abarrotes "Jovita"—an ample stall that specialized in various pickled foods. Some were more conventional mixes of carrot/onion/chile; others were dominated by thick slices of *palmito*, a mixture known in the region simply as *palmitos* after its primary ingredient. She also shared with me her quick and easy recipe for Picles—the famous pickle of Comitán that is used as a garnish for tacos, eaten as a *botana*, or simply placed on the plate alongside the main course. (For the record, Picles is similar to the mixture known as *palmitos*, the most notable difference being that the ingredients of Picles are cut into smaller pieces to facilitate their use as a garnish for tacos.) Some cooks include chile jalapeño, others don't, and judging from what she told me, you can use just about any combination of vegetables you like, the one constant being hearts of palm. Cut hearts of palm across the width into rings; combine with sliced blanched carrots, onion rings, cauliflower, baby corn, and sliced jalapeños if you wish. Season pineapple or apple cider vinegar with salt, Mexican oregano, bay leaves, and a bit of sugar to taste; pack the vegetables into glass containers and pour in the vinegar to cover. Kept in the refrigerator, Picles will last for many months.

Center: Timpinchile *packed in lime juice; right:* pickled *palmitos.* [MC]

TIMPINCHILE/PICKLED PEPPERS

I purchased what must have been the family-sized jar of Picles (not cheap, by the way), and as I was leaving, my "pickle lady" practiced good salesmanship by giving me a small bonus jar of pickled *timpinchile* (*Capsicum annuum* L. var. *glabriusculum* [Dunal] Heiser & Pickersgill)—tiny *chiles* related to those we call *ají*, *piquín*, *chilpetín*, or a variety of other names, to refer to that sunward-striving chile descended from the earliest chiles that evolved in Central and South America. Those in my gift jar had been freshly harvested in the state's Central Depression, where Tuxtla Gutiérrez and Chiapa de Corzo are located. Only growing successfully in the wild, *timpinchile* fruits toward the end of the rainy season, from July through August, at which time voracious customers line up to purchase a year's supply. She packs the chiles in lime juice with a pinch of salt; after a few days, the chiles soften and exchange their flavor with the lime juice, with deliciously picante results. (See more about pickled chiles on p. 136.)

Tzotzil chile vendor. [MR]

CHAYOTE/CUEZA/ GUÍA DE CHAYOTE

BOTANICAL: *Sechium edule* (Jacq.) Sw.; *Sechium compositum*/ Family Cucurbitaceae | **ENGLISH:** chayote, vegetable pear
TZOTZIL: *ch'um* | **TZELTAL:** *ch'umate'*

Although the squash variety known as chayote has become a familiar item in recent years in the United States, it is unlikely that markets there will carry the *cueza*, the tuberized portions of the root of the chayote plant. But in its native habitat, the tubers and the tender young stems and leaves—known as *guía de chayote*—are eaten as well as the fruits. Wild forms of chayote are found in southern Mexico and Guatemala, suggesting the probability that it is native to the region. *Sechium compositum* is a species unique to Chiapas and Guatemala. In the 1700s, chayote was taken to Europe, the Antilles, and South America, and since the late nineteenth century it has been cultivated in the United States. In recent times, an infusion made from the *guía de chayote* has been studied for its potent cardiovascular properties. The *cueza* tuber may be used in stews or cooked in sugar syrup, but its most common use is for *cueza baldada*, a popular side dish in Comitán: slices of the tuber are dipped in egg batter, then fried and served with a lightly picante salsa. I made a *tortilla española* for breakfast one morning during our visit using the *cueza* instead of potatoes.

Cañón del Sumidero. [CPTM/FOTO: RICARDO ESPINOSA-REO]

CHIAPA DE CORZO

THE EAR-POPPING DESCENT of some 5,820 feet (1,609 m) from San Cristóbal de las Casas to Chiapa de Corzo takes us from the chilly pine-clad Altos de Chiapas to the hot, dry forests of the Central Depression. Cattle ranches punctuate our route, betraying the culprit behind the broad-stroke denuding of this 5,400-square-mile (13,985 sq. km) area, which miraculously still maintains a high level of biodiversity and endemism.

Our drive along the Pan-American Highway roughly follows a much older Maya trading route, later adopted by the Spanish as the Camino Real (Royal Road) from Mexico City to present-day Antigua, Guatemala, then an important colonial seat. Settlement in the area dates to prehistory and is important in the story of Mexico. A nearby archaeological zone, named Chiapa de Corzo after the pueblo, recently revealed the oldest-known pyramid tomb burial in Mesoamerica, dated to roughly 700 BCE. The ceremonial burial was clearly a royal one, indicated by precious belts of jadeite fashioned in the shapes of howler monkeys and crocodiles.

Church of Santo Domingo. [MC]

[MC]

MERCADO PÚBLICO MUNICIPAL, CHIAPA DE CORZO

The Mercado Público of Chiapa de Corzo rests atop a high bank overlooking the Río Grijalva, and until recently spilled over onto the surrounding streets that descend a few feet to water's edge. Popular food stalls and restaurants now line the shore, and it is from here that launches full of camera-bedecked tourists journey upriver through the breathtaking channel known as Cañón del Sumidero—also the site of an annual fishing tournament where anglers vie for the scrappy *macabil* (p. 66).

Flower stalls trim the market building every day, and on Sundays the adjacent park at the corner of the church of Santo Domingo fills with stalls offering the best regional fare. Specialties whose origins are attributed to Chiapa de Corzo—such as Cochito horneado (p. 139) and Pepita con tasajo (p. 134)—are the most popular items on the menu, and people often make the pilgrimage here to get "the real thing." Sundays are anticipated for the welcome arrival of several dishes not offered on other days of the week, such as Sopa de pan (p. 143).

CHIAPAS CATTLE

Of Mexico's thirty-two states, Chiapas ranks third in the production of dual-purpose cattle—those that yield both beef and milk. Conventional cattle ranching has typically been centered on the arid lowlands of the state, a situation that has resulted in considerable deforestation. Thankfully, recent efforts by small groups of innovative ranchers in the valleys of the Central Depression are converting to a more holistic management approach through careful land-use planning, rotational grazing, and diversified forage.

After so many years of living in Yucatán, where pork and poultry are the primary offerings on butchers' tables, I was surprised to see so much beef in Chiapas—and not just piled high in the butchers' market but also at the prepared food stalls, where beef dishes frequently top the menu and sell out before all others.

Dried beef variations on a theme: tasajo *(left; recipe on p. 125)* and cecina *(right) hang at Carnicería La Selecta, sold in the same locale in the Chiapa de Corzo municipal market since 1961.* [MR]

PEPITA CON TASAJO

LIME-AND-SALT-CURED BEEF IN CREAMY SQUASH SEED SAUCE

TO PREPARE AHEAD

Tasajo (p. 125), or substitute
Enriched Lard (p. 530)

Chiapa de Corzo hosts an annual festival that has been included in UNESCO's Intangible Cultural Heritage list. From January 4 until 22 each year, the festival La Fiesta Grande is celebrated with parades of traditional dancers known as "*parachicos*," who wear colorful serapes festooned with ribbons and wooden masks with blue-eyed European features. The special feast dish for La Fiesta Grande is called, appropriately, La Comida Grande, and consists of salt-cured beef (*tasajo*) revivified in a creamy *pipián* of squash seeds and tomatoes. The dish is so popular (and delicious!) that it is not reserved exclusively for this celebration, but is enjoyed year-round in the markets. In its more secular quotidian incarnation, it is known simply as Pepita con tasajo. Remarkably, the deep, musky flavor of the cured beef beautifully holds its own against the tangy richness of the *pipián*. In Chiapa de Corzo, market stall tables are stocked with jars of pickled *chile blanco*—the requisite accompaniment for the dish—and I have witnessed diners garnishing their Pepita con tasajo with as few as one or as many as half a dozen of them. A recipe for them follows, or use pickled wax or banana peppers or jalapeños instead if you wish.

Prepare-ahead note: The *tasajo* must be made several days in advance, or you may be able to purchase it at a Mexican *carnicería*. Pepita con tasajo improves with age and keeps well under refrigeration for 4–5 days; reheat gently, adding a bit of water to achieve the desired consistency.

YIELD: 8–10 SERVINGS

He sells foods, sauces . . .
of squash seeds.

BERNARDINO DE SAHAGÚN,
1540–1585

[MC]

FOR THE TASAJO

1 recipe Tasajo, approximately
  2 pounds (1 kg; or substitute
  commercial tasajo from a
  Mexican carnicería)
8 cups (2 L) water
½ medium white onion
  (5 oz./137.5 g), quartered
4 large cloves garlic (1 oz./24 g),
  peeled
2 bay leaves
½ teaspoon (2 g) black
  peppercorns
4 allspice berries
3 whole cloves
2 sprigs fresh thyme, or
  ½ teaspoon (0.5 g) dried

FOR THE PIPIÁN AND
FINISHING

½ cup (100 g) long-grain rice
3 cups (500 mL) water, divided
2 cups (250 g) hulled, raw green
  pumpkin seeds ("pepitas")
1 medium white onion
  (10 oz./275 g), quartered
3 medium Roma tomatoes
  (10½ oz./300 g), quartered
2 large cloves garlic (½ oz./12 g),
  peeled
2 tablespoons (32 g) recado rojo
  (achiote paste, p. 45)
1 tablespoon (16 g) Enriched Lard

FOR SERVING

Tortillas
Arroz de fiesta (p. 74)
Salsa de chile de árbol (p. 531),
  or the chile sauce of your choice
Lime wedges
Pickled wax or banana peppers or
  chiles jalapeño or peperoncini

PREPARE THE TASAJO

If you used string to tie your *tasajo*, remove it and discard; rinse the beef thoroughly under cold running water; cut the strips of *tasajo* into pieces measuring approximately 2 inches (5 cm) long. Transfer the *tasajo* to a large stockpot and add the remaining ingredients; bring to a boil, reduce to a simmer, and cook uncovered for 45 minutes to 1 hour, or until the beef is very tender. Remove the beef with a slotted spoon and set aside; discard the flavorings but reserve the cooking liquid.

PREPARE THE PIPIÁN AND FINISH

Place the rice in a medium saucepan with 1 cup of the water and add 1 cup (250 mL) of the cooking liquid from the *tasajo*. Bring to a boil, reduce to a simmer, and cover; cook until tender, 10–15 minutes. Remove the pan from the heat and set aside. (*Note*: The rice will probably still have liquid in the bottom of the pan, which is normal and should be reserved.)

Place a large cast-iron skillet or comal over high heat; after 5 minutes, add the pumpkin seeds. When they start to pop, keep the seeds in constant motion by tossing them in the skillet or using a wooden spoon to prevent them from scorching on the bottom. Toast the seeds for approximately 5 minutes or until pale golden and fragrant. Immediately transfer the seeds to a colander or bowl (if left in the skillet, they will continue to cook); allow to cool 10–15 minutes. Transfer the toasted seeds to the bowl of a food processor fitted with a metal blade; process until the seeds turn into a fine powder and begin sticking to the sides of the processor bowl. Use a spatula to push the powder back into the bowl, and process another minute; set aside.

Place the next four ingredients in the jar of a blender, and add 1 cup (250 mL) of the cooking liquid from the *tasajo*. Purée until smooth. Heat the lard in a large saucepan or Dutch oven until shimmering; add all of the tomato purée at once: it should sizzle and sputter, so stand back. Bring to a boil, reduce to a simmer, and stir frequently as it continues to cook.

Transfer the cooked rice and the ground pumpkin seeds to the jar of a blender; add 1 cup (250 mL) of the cooking liquid from the *tasajo*, and purée until smooth. Working in batches as needed, strain the rice/pumpkin seed mixture through a fine-mesh sieve into the pan containing the cooked tomato mixture; add 1 cup (250 mL) of the cooking liquid from the *tasajo* to the sieve and use a rubber spatula to press through as much liquid as possible. Pour any remaining rice/pumpkin seed mixture into the sieve and add 1 cup (250 mL) water; use the spatula to press through the liquid, and repeat with another 1 cup (250 mL) water, pressing through as much liquid as possible; discard any residue in the sieve.

Bring the liquid in the saucepan to a boil, then reduce to a simmer, stirring frequently; cook for approximately 5 minutes or until the mixture thickens to the consistency of thick batter. Add the *tasajo* and simmer 1–2 minutes to heat the beef and amalgamate the flavors.

TO SERVE

Ladle the beef and sauce into shallow plates or soup bowls. Accompany with tortillas and Arroz de fiesta (p. 74) if you wish. Diners add chile sauce, squeezes of lime juice, and pickled peppers to taste.

CHILE BLANCO

BOTANICAL: *Capsicum annuum*/Family Solanaceae
ENGLISH: blond chile/wax pepper

Several chile varieties sold in the markets of Chiapas are wild forms, gathered and sold by families. However, they may be sold side by side with cultivated varieties, so one can only trust that one's vendor is telling the truth when she says it is *silvestre* (wild), rather than just using good marketing tactics. The wild *chile blanco* species—found in the Fraylesca region, which corresponds roughly to the Central Depression—as well as its cultivated cousin, are cone shaped and pale yellow to green. Heat ranges from 5,000–10,000 on the Scoville scale. Their most frequent use is pickled, and the pickled *chile blanco* is the de rigueur accompaniment to Pepita con tasajo. The acid most commonly used for pickling chiles in Chiapas is lime juice.

CHIPILÍN

BOTANICAL: *Crotalaria longirostrata* Hook. & Arn./Family Fabaceae | **ENGLISH:** longbeak rattlebox | **TZOTZIL:** *ch'aben*

Chipilín is a native of southern Mexico, including Chiapas, Oaxaca, and Tabasco, and extends into Guatemala and other parts of Central America. It is a slender shrub or small tree, with stems that are often dark red and closely set alternate leaves. It is, in fact, the young shoots and leaves that are valued, cooked and eaten as "greens" or combined with beans, chopped meat, scrambled eggs, or used as an ingredient in tamales. Ricardo Muñoz Zurita describes *chipilín* as one of the many *quelites* (edible wild plants) of Mexico. In other parts of the world where it has been introduced, it is considered an invasive weed, and its growth is banned in Australia and Hawaii. It is not broadly available in the United States, although it may occasionally be found in farmers' markets and is sold frozen in some areas. The leaves are high in calcium, iron, thiamine, riboflavin, niacin, and ascorbic acid. The seeds and roots are toxic. There is no exact substitute, but pea shoots come close in flavor and form; watercress or purslane is also acceptable.

CHILE BLANCO EN ESCABECHE/PICKLED BLOND CHILES Use any small blond chile or Hungarian wax peppers. Wash thoroughly, slice off the caps and discard, and blanch the chiles in boiling water for 2 minutes. Drain, then pack several chiles in a jar with a tight-fitting lid. Mix sea salt to taste with enough lime juice to fill the jar; bring the juice mixture to a boil, and immediately pour over the chiles. Seal tightly, allow to rest at room temperature for 2–3 days, then refrigerate for 1 week before using. The canned market chiles are never refrigerated and may rest on the shelf for weeks or longer before being sold. Because lime juice may be many times more acidic than vinegar, it has been proven to be very effective against the development of a number of bacteria, but if you have any reservations about food safety, you may follow standard canning procedures instead.

FRIJOL ESCUMITE CON CHIPILÍN

TEPARY BEANS WITH LIME-AND-SALT-CURED BEEF AND WILD HERBS

TO PREPARE AHEAD
Tasajo (p. 125), or substitute

FOR THE BEANS AND
ENRICHMENT

1 pound (500 g) tasajo (substitute
  carne salada, cecina, jerky, or
  other salt-cured beef)
Ingredients for Frijol bótil refrito
  (p. 89), substituting tepary
  beans for the scarlet runner
  beans, omitting the chiles de
  Simojovel and salt
2 Roma tomatoes (7 oz./200 g),
  cored, seeded, and cut to
  medium dice
2 chiles jalapeño (1 oz./25 g each),
  chopped
½ pound (250 g) chipilín (substitute pea shoots, watercress, or
  purslane), leaves and soft stems
  only, coarsely chopped
Sea salt (optional)

Tepary beans, *chipilín*, and *tasajo* are consumed throughout the state: black beans cooked with *tasajo*, and tepary beans cooked with *chipilín* are common. However, I had never seen this particular combination anywhere but in Chiapa de Corzo, where a vendor offered it as the day's special; I suspect it may have been her inspiration. The herbal green note of the *chipilín* gracefully offsets the meaty beans and salty beef. As with many bean dishes in Chiapas, the accompaniment was Chirmol (recipe follows), adding yet another distinct layer of flavor.

Prepare-ahead note: Frijol escumite con chipilín improves with age; prepare the beans a day in advance and refrigerate.

YIELD: 8–10 SERVINGS

COOK THE BEANS AND PREPARE THE ENRICHMENT

Coarsely cut the *tasajo* into large cubes or chunks; cover the meat with cold water and allow to soak for 30 minutes; drain, cover with more cold water and soak another 30 minutes. Rinse with cold running water and drain. To cook the beans, follow the recipe for Frijol bótil refrito (p. 89). Cover the beans with the water as specified in the recipe, and add the meat. Bring to a boil and cook uncovered until the beans are

[MC]

tender, between 1½ and 2 hours. At all times, the beans should be covered with cooking liquid by about ½ inch (1.25 cm); add more boiling water during the cooking process if necessary. Prepare the enrichment as described in the recipe for Frijol bótil refrito using 3 tablespoons (42 g) Enriched Lard, the onions, garlic, oregano, and pepper, and the tomatoes and chiles specified in this recipe, but omitting the chiles de Simojovel and salt. When the tomatoes are soft and most of the cooking liquid has evaporated, add the enrichment to the beans; stir (do not mash) to incorporate. Add the *chipilín* and stir; cook an additional 20–30 minutes or until the greens are wilted and the flavors amalgamated. Check the seasonings, adding salt to taste: because the meat is salted, additional salt may not be necessary.

TO SERVE

Plate the beans and meat in deep soup bowls; garnish with more of the fresh greens if you wish; accompany with warm tortillas. Diners squeeze lime juice and top with Chirmol to taste.

CHIRMOL

COOKED FRESH TOMATO-CHILE TABLE SAUCE

This unusual salsa is part cooked, part fresh; it is quick and easy to prepare and is the requisite accompaniment for many of the bean dishes in Chiapas.

Prepare-ahead note: Chirmol can be prepared to the point just before adding the onions, chiles, and cilantro, and then refrigerated. When ready to serve, bring to room temperature and add the remaining ingredients.

YIELD: APPROXIMATELY 2 CUPS (500 ML)

FOR THE SALSA

4 medium Roma tomatoes
  (14 oz./400 g), quartered
1 medium clove garlic (¼ oz./6 g),
  peeled
½ cup (125 mL) water
½ teaspoon (3 g) sea salt
1 tablespoon (15 mL) vegetable oil
3 tablespoons (33 g) white onion,
  chopped
3 tablespoons (33 g) chile blanco
  (substitute Anaheim, sweet Italian), seeds and veins removed
  if you wish to control the heat,
  chopped
3 tablespoons (15 g) fresh cilantro
  leaves, coarsely chopped

PREPARE THE SALSA

Place the first four ingredients in the jar of a blender; process until thoroughly puréed. Heat the vegetable oil in a deep saucepan until shimmering; add the mixture all at once: it should sputter and sizzle, so stand back. Cook over medium heat, stirring frequently, for 6–8 minutes or until the salsa thickens slightly and deepens in color. Remove from the heat and allow to cool to room temperature. Before serving, stir in the chopped onions, chile, and cilantro; allow to rest 15 minutes to develop the flavors.

COCHITO HORNEADO

OVEN-ROASTED PIGLET IN ADOBO

The folks of Chiapa de Corzo will tell you that Cochito horneado is theirs—and even outsiders claim that the best examples are found here, explaining the throngs that descended on the Sunday market. Yet it would be difficult to pinpoint its exact birthplace, since so many variations of it exist throughout the state, with slightly different names, formulas, and cooking methods. The constants are pork (traditionally and for feast days a whole suckling pig is used, but nowadays cooks just as likely use a mix of cuts or cubed pork loin, which is the dish you will find in the markets) and an adobo—in Chiapas called affectionately "*recadito*"—of chile (always *ancho*, sometimes *guajillo*), vinegar, garlic, and spices. A couple of the most traditional recipes I have found also include leaves of *arrayán* (p. 98). Cooking methods also seem to distinguish the many physiognomies of this dish: a family-style version known as *asado coleto* is cooked on the stovetop, whereas Cochito horneado is baked in the oven—traditionally a brick bread-baking oven fired with wood. You might also find these same dishes in the

FOR THE RECADITO

6 chiles guajillos (1¾ oz./50 g)

5 chiles anchos (3½ oz./100 g)

3 medium Roma tomatoes
   (10½ oz./300 g), quartered

½ medium white onion
   (5 oz./137.5 g), quartered

4 medium cloves garlic
   (1 oz./24 g), peeled

½ cup (125 mL) pineapple or apple
   cider vinegar

1 tablespoon (12 g) panela, grated
   (see p. 120; substitute muscovado or dark brown sugar)

1½ teaspoons (9 g) sea salt

1 two-inch (5 cm) stick canela
   (Mexican cinnamon, about
   ¼ oz./5 g)

1 sprig fresh thyme

1 teaspoon (0.65 g) dried whole
   Mexican oregano

1 teaspoon (5 g) black peppercorns

3 allspice berries

2 whole cloves

FOR THE PORK

2 pounds (1 kg) pork, a mixture of
   cubed shoulder (known here as
   cabeza de lomo) or loin, leg, and
   slices of pork backbone (known
   here as espinazo), all with
   some fat

1 teaspoon (0.65 g) dried whole
   Mexican oregano

4 sprigs fresh thyme

3 arrayán leaves (substitute bay
   leaves)

FOR SERVING

Romaine or other lettuce, finely
   shredded

White onion, thinly sliced and
   separated into rings

Radishes, thinly sliced

Arroz de fiesta (p. 74)

Frijoles de la olla (p. 530), or plain
   cooked black beans

Salsa of your choice

markets labeled *cochito en adobo*, *cochito al horno*, *asado de puerco*, or simply *asado* or even *cochito*. While there may be minor variations among the different forms, the basics of pork cooked with chiles and spices remain the same. This easy recipe shared with me by María Leticia "Leti" Chong Ovalle is baked in a conventional oven.

PREPARE THE RECADITO

Remove the seeds and veins from the chiles; place them in a large saucepan; cover with water, bring to a boil, and cook until the chiles are tender and rehydrated, about 5 minutes. Remove chiles with a slotted spoon and reserve the cooking liquid.

Working in batches as needed, place the chiles with the remaining ingredients in the jar of a blender; add 1 cup of the chile cooking liquid, and process until thoroughly puréed; set aside.

MARINATE AND ROAST THE PORK

Place the pork pieces in a large casserole or Dutch oven fitted with a lid; pour the marinade over the pork, and use your fingers to rub and coat the meat completely. With a sharp knife, prick the pork all over so that the marinade can penetrate. Sprinkle the oregano and lay the thyme sprigs and *arrayán* or bay leaves on top of the pork; cover and refrigerate at least 2 hours or overnight.

Thirty minutes before roasting, bring the pork to room temperature. Preheat the oven to 300°F (150°C). Bake the pork for 45 minutes; lift the lid and spoon the marinade and juices over the meat to baste. Replace the lid, raise the oven temperature to 400°F (200°C), and continue baking another 45 minutes. Watch the level of the liquid; if it evaporates too much, add a bit of water. In the end, the liquid should have totally evaporated, leaving the meat coated with a caramelized and dark coating of the adobo.

TO SERVE

Plate pieces of the pork on individual serving plates; dress the lettuce with a light vinaigrette if desired and arrange on the side of the plate with the radish slices; place onion rings on top of the pork. Accompany with the rice and beans, if desired, either on the plate or in separate serving bowls. Diners add salsa to taste.

A vendor seemingly waves a magic wand to shoo flies from her table of carnes frías
(charcuterie). Cochito horneado *atop a blanket of lettuce fills a tin tub at right.* [MR]

CHILE MANZANO/CHILE CHAMBOROTE, ROCOTO, PERÓN, CANARIO

BOTANICAL: *Capsicum pubescens*/Family Solanaceae | **ENGLISH:** rocoto pepper | **TZOTZIL:** *k'anal ich, pujkan ich*

For a chile with so many colloquial names, it is perhaps not surprising that some difficulty may arise in its identification. In his comprehensive volume on Mexican chiles, Ricardo Muñoz Zurita identifies a different, near-extinct chile as the *chimborote*, but in our market excursions through Chiapas, the plentiful chile pictured above is the one vendors most consistently referred to as *chamborote* followed by *manzano*. *La Cocina familiar en el estado de Chiapas* (Family cooking in the state of Chiapas), published by CONACULTA, lists the two names as synonyms. The *pubescens* species of the large Capsicum genus intrigues me for several reasons: it is the only domesticated *Capsicum* species with no wild form, possibly suggesting that it was domesticated so long ago that the wild ancestor is now extinct; it was most likely domesticated in Bolivia approximately 6000 BCE, making it one of the oldest domesticated plants in the Americas; and it grows at high elevations within such a narrow temperature range that it is virtually isolated from other chile species and so does not readily cross-pollinate with them, resulting in very little diversity in pod shape, unlike other

Capsicum species. The plant and pod themselves are unique, too: the plant is characterized by ovate, hairy leaves (thus the taxonomy), and the pod is spherical to pear shaped, with black seeds clinging to the placenta. A recognizable node or "nipple" punctuates the crown of the chile just below the stem. It is green when young and matures to yellow, orange, or red. Botanist Charles Heiser noted that *pubescens* was the most common pepper among the Incas in Peru, just as it is today in modern Cusco. It was introduced into Central America and Mexico in the twentieth century. It is cultivated as a large cash crop only in certain areas of Peru, as well as around Pátzcuaro in Michoacán. It is well adapted to the terrain and climate of Los Altos de Chiapas, where it is typically grown in small family plots. The *chile manzano* is quite hot, ranging from 12,000 to 30,000 on the Scoville Heat Scale. It is eaten fresh, used as a plate garnish, or included in salsas. Varieties of it are available north of the border, known as "manzano," "rocoto," or occasionally as "apple pepper." While it will not have the same flavor, the *chile habanero* may be used as a substitute.

SOPA DE PAN

SPICED BREAD SOUP WITH VEGETABLES, RAISINS, AND PLANTAIN

TO PREPARE AHEAD
Enriched Lard (p. 530), or
substitute

FOR THE SOFRITO

1 tablespoon (14 g) Enriched Lard
(substitute vegetable or Spanish
olive oil)
½ medium white onion
(5 oz./137.5 g), chopped
2 medium cloves garlic (½ oz./8 g),
peeled and finely chopped
1 cup (140 g) red bell pepper, cut
to small dice
2 medium Roma tomatoes
(7 oz./200 g), seeded and
chopped

FOR THE VEGETABLES

2 small baking potatoes (1 lb./
500 g), peeled and sliced across
the width
2 medium carrots (7 oz./200 g),
peeled and sliced diagonally
across the width
8 ounces (225 g) green beans, ends
trimmed
2 medium zucchini (9 oz./250 g),
sliced diagonally across the
width

In Spain, bread and soup share such a primal bond that even the language expresses it: the first definition of *sopa* (soup) in the dictionary of the Real Academia Española is "Pedazo de pan empapado en cualquier líquido" (a piece of bread soaked in any kind of liquid). Spanish colonists brought their own versions of bread soup to Mexico, some no doubt delicious, others probably less so: watery vegetable broth soups were endured for Vigilia, or Lenten fasting, and similar concoctions were famously fed to the poor in Catholic convents. But who can resist dressing up something so beggarly in fancier clothes? Sopa de pan of Chiapas is composed of alternating layers of vegetables and fried bread—all soaked with poultry stock and flavored with spices from the Moluccas. What was traditionally a feast dish nowadays appears at special events and parties, but it is also available as daily fare in many restaurants in Chiapas. Only rarely does it appear in the markets, though, but in keeping with its "special" nature, it is offered in some stalls on Sundays—the day I luckily found it in Chiapa de Corzo. While the stock usually used for making Sopa de pan is made from chicken, the vendor I met in the market told me that her grandmother and mother used the turkey stock left over from making *guajolote en mole*. I loved the idea of rich turkey stock as a solid platform for the light sweetness of the other ingredients, so that is what I suggest here. Of course, you may use chicken stock if you prefer. Many recipes for Sopa de pan call for using stale baguettes or other French bread, but the *pan francés de San Cristóbal*—that is sold out of baskets by roving vendors in the markets and is the bread Leti used—was no mere French bread. Tinted yellow from eggs and quite dense, it was also lightly sweet, which became a leitmotif as we assembled the soup. For this recipe, I have suggested stale brioche or challah, although you may use regular French bread instead.

Prepare-ahead note: Sopa de pan is best served immediately after assembly. Prepare all of the components an hour or even a day ahead and assemble 10 minutes before serving.

YIELD: 8 SERVINGS

PREPARE THE SOFRITO
Heat the lard in a large skillet until shimmering. Add the onions, garlic, and bell pepper and cook, stirring frequently, until the onions are translucent, 3–4 minutes. Add the tomatoes and cook until they are softened, 4–5 minutes. Remove the skillet from the heat and set aside.

PARBOIL THE VEGETABLES
Bring a large saucepan of salted water to a boil. Add the potatoes and cook until barely tender, 4–5 minutes; remove with a slotted spoon and set aside. Add the carrots and green beans to the boiling water and cook 2–3 minutes until the vegetables are barely tender; add the zucchini and cook 1 minute to soften; immediately remove the saucepan from the heat and drain the vegetables; set aside.

8 cups (2 L) rich turkey stock (substitute rich chicken stock)

1 tablespoon (12 g) sugar

1 six-inch (15 cm) stick canela (Mexican cinnamon)

1 large pinch of saffron

2 sprigs fresh thyme

½ teaspoon (0.33 g) dried whole Mexican oregano, lightly toasted and crumbled

¼ cup (62.5 mL) Enriched Lard (substitute vegetable or Spanish olive oil)

4½ ounces (130 g) stale challah or brioche (substitute French bread or baguette), sliced into squares or rounds about ½ inch (1.25 cm) thick

1 large medium-ripe plantain, peeled and sliced diagonally across the width. (To peel, slice off both ends of the plantain; use a sharp knife to cut lengthwise along the ridges of the peel, then remove the peel.)

¾ cup (180 g) raisins

4 boiled eggs, peeled and quartered

ASSEMBLE THE SOUP

Preheat the oven to 400°F (200°C). In a stockpot, bring the stock to a boil, reduce to a simmer, and add the next five ingredients; simmer 5 minutes, cover, remove from the heat, and allow the stock to steep as you continue.

In a large ovenproof casserole or Dutch oven fitted with a lid, heat the lard until shimmering. (Traditionally a clay *cazuela* is used.) Working in batches as necessary, fry the slices of bread until golden brown on both sides; remove to paper towels to drain; continue until all of the bread has been fried. Add the slices of plantain to the hot fat, and fry until golden brown on both sides; transfer to a plate and set aside. Pour off most of the remaining fat from the casserole; use a paper towel to spread the remaining fat onto the sides of the casserole to prevent sticking when you bake the soup.

Place one-third of the fried bread on the bottom of the casserole to cover; distribute one-half of the sofrito, the potatoes, and the vegetables on top of the bread; follow with one-third of the fried plantains and ¼ cup (60 g) of the raisins. Use another one-third of the bread to create a second layer in the casserole; follow with the remaining sofrito, potatoes, and vegetables and another one-third of the plantains and ¼ cup (60 g) of the raisins. Finish by placing the remaining bread on top, and decorate with the remaining plantains, raisins, and the sliced boiled eggs. Return the stock to a boil; retrieve the thyme and the canela from the stock and discard. Pour the stock into the casserole to completely cover the ingredients. Place the lid on the casserole, and bake the soup for 20 minutes.

TO SERVE

Use a large serving spoon to "cut" the bread as you might a soufflé; transfer to individual serving bowls and spoon on some of the stock. An alternate, more casual method to using the casserole is to assemble the layers as described in individual bowls, then pour on the stock.

[MC]

NUCÚ/HORMIGA ARRIERA

BIOLOGICAL: *Atta fervens*/Family Formicidae
ENGLISH: leaf-cutter ant, parasol ant | **TZOTZIL:** *k'is, me'*

Leaf-cutter ants are such a dreaded pest in my garden that I would do anything I could to eradicate them—save eat them on a regular basis, as they do in Chiapas. During the rainy season (May to October), the ants emerge to mate, flying and filling the air with great dark clouds. After mating, the males die and the females begin creating their nests. It is the females—abdomens full of eggs—that are the delicacy. Although it might cause queasiness in some people, the ants are quite nutritious, with 42 percent high-quality protein and significant amounts of B vitamins, magnesium, and calcium. Sometimes referred to as "the caviar of Chiapas," leaf-cutter ants are a specialty of Chiapa de Corzo, and they are also consumed in Oaxaca, Guerrero, Veracruz, and Puebla, and south into parts of Central America. Typically toasted on a comal, the ants are served on tortillas with salt, a squeeze of lime juice, and a very picante chile sauce; they may also be accompanied by guacamole and fried *chiles de Simojovel*.

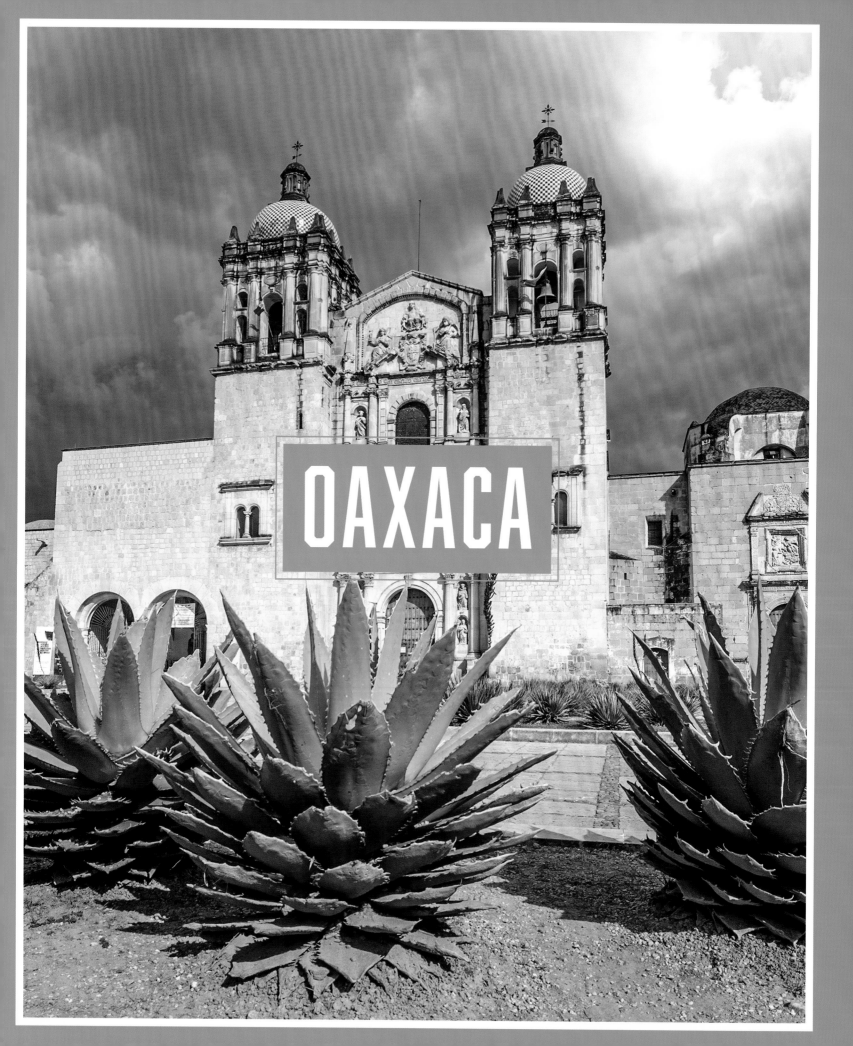

OAXACA

[MR]

OAXACA DE JUÁREZ

T HE ROILING CLOUDS in the skies above Oaxaca mirror the voluminous waves of undulating mountains below. The shifting chiaroscuro offers fleeting glimpses of pockets in the mountains—hidden valleys. It was in those scattered valleys that distinct indigenous groups settled thousands of years ago, their physical separation from one another aiding the evolution of unique cultures and gastronomies. Today, there are sixteen formally recognized indigenous groups in Oaxaca, the largest number in the country in one state; collectively, the native population is one of the largest in Mexico, second only to that of Yucatán.

The gastronomy of Oaxaca is legendary, from its famous "seven moles" to its rich chocolate. Perhaps unlike any other state in Mexico, the cuisine varies from pueblo to pueblo, resulting from the distinct microclimates formed by meandering sierras and those hidden valleys, microclimates that contain 50 percent of all species in Mexico. In fact, the state

(opposite page) Church of Santo Domingo de Guzmán

is composed of eight highly diverse regions—the Pacific Coast and the Isthmus of Tehuantepec, the Central Valleys, the Papaloapan region, the northern and southern Sierras, the Cañada and the Mixteca—each with its own traditions. From the Central Valleys comes a cornucopia of vegetables; from the lush Papaloapan region bordering Veracruz comes a seasonless supply of tropical fruits; and from the Isthmus and Pacific regions comes a bounty of seafood. These principal regions have been thoroughly documented by Diana Kennedy in her epic cookbook, *Oaxaca al Gusto*.

Human habitation of the region dates to about 11,000 BCE; by around 2000 BCE, agriculture had been well established in the Central Valleys—the region we will explore. Zapotec culture flourished here starting around 900 BCE. The crowning achievement of the Zapotecas was the city of Monte Albán, founded between 500 and 100 BCE. Large communities of Zapotec-speaking peoples still inhabit the Central Valleys.

Both Monte Albán and the city of Oaxaca de Juárez are today UNESCO World Heritage Sites. Basing ourselves in Oaxaca—the state's capital—we will tour markets in the city as well as markets in several nearby Zapotec pueblos.

ZAPOTEC/BE'ENA'A

The Zapotec name for themselves translates simply to "The People." The word "Zapotec" derives from the Nahuatl name that Aztec merchants and soldiers gave to the peoples—*tzapotécatl*, which translates roughly to "inhabitants of the place of *zapote*" (*tzapotl* = zapote; *calcatl* = inhabitant). Modern Zapotecas are descendants of an important pre-Columbian civilization that flourished in the Valley of Oaxaca, demonstrated by impressive archaeological remains that date back about twenty-five hundred years. Their ancient seat of power—Monte Albán—preserves dramatic pyramid-stepped buildings, ball courts, and magnificent tombs in which have been found finely worked gold jewelry. Monte Albán remained the largest city in the Southern Highlands until approximately 700 CE. Other Zapotec cities also show high levels of development, with sophisticated architecture, mural painting, writing, and engineering projects such as irrigation systems. The later city of Mitla survived until the arrival of the Spanish. Today, Zapotecas form the third-largest ethnolinguistic group in Mexico; the majority inhabits the state of Oaxaca. Several Zapotec communities in Oaxaca specialize in high-quality crafts: black pottery in San Bartolo Coyotepec, colorfully painted wooden figures in San Martín Tilcajete, and back-strap weaving in San Bartolo Yautepec.

A Zapotec vendor counts blandas. *This enormous Oaxacan tortilla can reach 12 inches (30 cm) in diameter.* [MC]

CENTRAL DE ABASTO "MARGARITA MAZA DE JUÁREZ"

The largest market in the state, Central de Abasto (supply center) is legendary for its labyrinth of endless aisles where getting lost is part of the experience. The entire market area covers almost 40 acres (16 hectares) and accommodates some ten thousand merchants and an equal number of shoppers. On the principal market day of Saturday, the number of visitors swells to over twenty-five thousand. The thrilling thing about Central de Abasto is that here can be found foods and ingredients from Oaxaca's eight regions, particularly a rainbow of chiles not found elsewhere.

Chile de agua (Capsicum annuum L.) is consumed broadly throughout the state, but its principal cultivation happens in the Central Valleys region, the only place in Mexico where it is commercially grown. Reaching up to 6 inches (15 cm) in length and tapering to a point, it is related to the Anaheim and the so-called blond chiles, although at 2,500–5,000 Scoville Heat Units it is considerably hotter. It may be used in salsas, cut into strips to garnish foods, or stuffed in ways similar to the much larger and milder chile poblano. In San Pablo Huixtepec, it is used as a shot glass for sipping mezcal. [MR]

CHILES OF OAXACA

According to one study, Oaxaca possesses 90 percent of the genetic diversity of chiles, represented in twenty-six unique varieties and scores of wild and semi-domesticated morphotypes. Small wonder, then, that chiles factor so prominently in the most renowned dishes of Oaxaca—specifically moles. In fact, all of the famed "seven moles of Oaxaca" feature one or more varieties of chiles, and while circumstances may demand substitutions, purists will aver that at least one specific chile lends the defining flavor to each mole. For example, the *chile chilcostle* is used for Mole amarillo (recipe on p. 179), and the *chilhuacle negro* for Chichilo (p. 197).

(above) *A few typical chiles of Oaxaca.* Left to right: chilcostle, chilhuacle rojo, chilhuacle negro, chilhuacle amarillo, costeño rojo, costeño amarillo, puya, *and* pasilla mixe *or* pasilla de Oaxaca. [MC] (below) *Bags of* chiles chilhuacles. *The typical colors of red, yellow, and black can be seen. They are further merchandised according to* primero *or* segundo—*referring to the first or second harvest. Those of the first harvest are larger and considered of better quality.* [MC]

TLAYUDAS

OAXACAN-STYLE "PIZZAS"

TO PREPARE AHEAD
Enriched Lard (p. 530)
Asiento Substitute (p. 153), unless
  purchased
Pasta de frijol (p. 154)

First-time visitors to Oaxaca reasonably express as much wonderment for the half-moon-shaped stuffed maize breads known as *tlayudas* as they do for mole. While *tlayudas* perhaps do not claim so dignified a history, they enjoy a starring role in the daily dining habits of *oaxaqueños*. I resort to the pizza comparison because so many others do, and it does seem to telescope the appearance and assembly method of this gargantuan—taco? A huge maize tortilla upward of 12 inches (30 cm) in diameter is first cooked on a comal until it just begins to crisp; it is then smeared with *asiento* and bean paste and topped with your choice of ingredients, folded, and cooked once more until it is browned and crispy overall. *Asiento* is the residue that sinks to the bottom of cauldrons during the process of rendering lard; a Mexican *carnicería* may be able to provide it, but if not, I offer instructions for how to prepare a substitute. Because transferring such a large tortilla to the comal can be unwieldy in any but the most expert hands, it will be easier for you to bake it in the oven. As with pizza, the variety of toppings is infinite and open to interpretation, but I have suggested some of the most common ones. Order a *sencilla* and you'll get a *tlayuda* with only vegetables and cheese and no meat. We observed the assembly process at the Comedor "Chonita."

FOR THE TLAYUDAS

1 cup (250 g) masa from nixtamal
  (substitute masa prepared from
  masa harina according to the
  package instructions)
2 tablespoons (32 g) Enriched Lard
½ teaspoon (3 g) sea salt
½ cup (125 mL) asiento (substitute;
  see below)
½ cup (125 mL) Pasta de frijol

Prepare-ahead note: Have all of the components on hand and serve immediately after assembly and cooking.

YIELD: 2 TLAYUDAS, 2–4 SERVINGS

PREPARE THE TLAYUDAS

Preheat the oven to 425°F (218°C). Knead the masa with the lard and salt; divide the masa into two equal balls. Place one ball between two large pieces of plastic wrap; press or roll the ball to form a circle measuring 10–12 inches (25–30 cm) in diameter. Carefully peel away the top piece of plastic; invert a lightly oiled baking sheet on top of the tortilla and gently lift and flip the tortilla from the bottom so that it is resting

Stacks of tlayudas tostadas. *Similar to other tostadas, Oaxaca's behemoths are used for* botanas: *broken-off bits are gobbled with cheese or dipped into salsas.*

[MC]

For a more authentic flavor, use a grilling rack as seen in the photo, and briefly toast the tlayuda *over hot coals.* [MR, MC]

FOR THE TOPPINGS

Grilled Cecina (p. 397), or sautéed
  crumbled chorizo, or shredded
  grilled chicken, or grilled
  arrachera
Shredded lettuce or cabbage
White onions cut in half moons
  (quartered, then sliced)
Sliced tomatoes
Sliced avocado or spoonfuls of
  guacamole
Queso de Oaxaca, pulled into
  strands (substitute grated
  mozzarella or Monterey Jack)
Sea salt to taste

FOR SERVING

Salsa de chile de árbol (p. 531),
  or Salsa verde (p. 531), or Salsa
  de chile pasilla (p. 173), or Salsa
  de chintestle (p. 175)

on top of the baking sheet; carefully peel away the remaining layer of plastic. Finish shaping and flattening the tortilla on the baking sheet; it should be slightly thicker than a standard tortilla. Bake for 10–12 minutes or until the tortilla begins to dry around the edges. Allow the tortilla to cool on the baking sheet for 5 minutes; remove and place it between pieces of waxed paper until you are ready to finish, up to 2 hours.

ADD THE TOPPINGS AND FINISH

On the top side of one tortilla, spread approximately ¼ cup (62.5 mL) of the *asiento* (or substitute; see below) to cover side to side; repeat with ¼ cup (62.5 mL) of the Pasta de frijol. Arrange the remaining ingredients over one-half of the tortilla, starting with the meat (if using), followed by the lettuce or cabbage, onions, tomatoes, avocados or guacamole, and cheese; sprinkle with sea salt to taste. Fold the *tlayuda* in half and transfer to a preheated comal or large skillet. Cook until the tortilla is well browned and crispy; flip to the other side and repeat. Serve immediately.

TO SERVE

Plate one *tlayuda* for a hungry person, or cut in half to serve two. Diners open the *tlayuda* and add salsas to taste.

Asiento Substitute: Some of the mills you will see around town—even chocolate mills—put their grinding machines to double duty preparing this ready substitute for *asiento*. Process 2¼ ounces (65 g) *chicharrón* in a food processor until it becomes the texture of coarse meal; add ¼ cup (64 g) Enriched Lard and process until creamy. *Yield: Approximately ½ cup (125 g)*

PASTA DE FRIJOL
BLACK BEAN PURÉE

This ubiquitous black bean paste appears in everything from sandwiches to the Tamal de frijol (p. 177) and Tlayudas (preceding page). Its consistency depends on its end use: for the Tamal de frijol, more cooking liquid is drained from the beans, and once puréed, they are cooked to become a stiff paste much like refried beans; for Tlayudas, more cooking liquid is reserved and the consistency is like thick pancake batter. Follow the recipe for Frijoles de la olla on page 530 using black beans and substituting 2–3 avocado leaves, lightly toasted and ground, for the epazote. Cook the beans as instructed in the master recipe, but reserve more of the cooking liquid; prepare the enrichment omitting the chiles, and add to the pot of beans 30 minutes prior to the end of the cooking time. When the beans are very tender, use a blender, food processor, or handheld immersion blender to purée thoroughly. If you require a thicker paste, heat a bit of vegetable oil or lard in a large skillet, add the purée, and cook over medium heat, stirring frequently, until the liquid has evaporated and the beans are stiff; for a thinner purée, add only enough extra water as necessary to create a batter-like consistency.

Hoja de aguacate (Persea drymifolia)—*avocado leaves—are used plentifully in the region and lend a delicate anise flavor to beans, tamales, and other foods. They are available dried in many places.* [MC]

(above) Oaxaca has achieved a reputation as the "land of chocolate," even though most of the cacao you will find here comes from either Tabasco or Chiapas. And it is used plentifully. As you meander through the corridors of the market, from time to time you will be embraced by the sweet aroma of chocolate that wafts out of the many molinos, or chocolate mills. Although hand-ground chocolate—chocolate de metate—is still a point of pride for some, most people rely on commercial mills for grinding the chocolate paste that serves for beverages and moles. Customers specify the exact formula in a ratio of cacao beans:almonds:canela:sugar, to get just the flavor balance they desire. A recipe for the chocolate beverage can be found on page 79. [MR]

(below, left) Chocolate mill. [MR]   (below, right) Vendors happily offer samples of their "house blend." [MC]

[MR]

[MR]

A popular local saying is that if you visit Oaxaca and eat chapulines (Sphenarium purpurascens)—grasshoppers—you will return one day. Oaxaqueños take them very seriously as a foodstuff and select them fastidiously according to size, age, and specific variety. While they are only produced naturally during a three-month window, they are so popular year-round that they are even bred commercially. They may be dusted with chile and eaten as is, ground into salsas, or toasted and eaten on a fresh tortilla. As in other parts of Mexico, the maguey worm (gusano de maguey, see p. 378) finds its place in the pantry of Oaxaca, too, and is consumed in similar ways to the grasshoppers. It is also famously found at the bottom of some bottles of mezcal (p. 191), arguably the state spirit of Oaxaca. Another common use of the worms is grinding them with salt and chile to make sal de gusano, a seasoning that may be a stand-in for table salt, or more typically is dusted on top of orange slices and sucked between sips of mezcal.

[MR]

[MC]

Sal De Gusano

Mercado "20 de noviembre." [MR]

MERCADO "20 DE NOVIEMBRE" AND MERCADO "BENITO JUÁREZ"

Located at the corner of a bustling intersection, these two markets complement each other. "Benito Juárez" features a little bit of everything: a wide range of local produce, as well as religious artifacts and supplies for folk religion, cowboy hats, juice and sorbet stands, local handicrafts (especially the carved wooden fantasy creatures known as *alebrijes*), bags, shoes, as well as *comedores*. The "20 de noviembre" market is mostly devoted to prepared food stalls, in particular the incomparable *pasillo de humo*—smoke hall.

In this chaotic passageway where smoke hangs like a curtain, you participate in the creation of your meal, selecting all the components and paying for each one separately.

Make your first stop at a stand that sells a variety of uncooked meats—*cecina*, *tasajo*, chorizo, *milanesa*. After making your selection, you vie for a seat at a table, and the meats are whisked away to one in a lineup of grills crowned with smokestacks.

The cook grills the meat for you, all the while arduously encouraging the flames with handwoven reed fans.

Meanwhile, waiters arrive at your table with an assortment of garnishes—grilled onions and chiles, guacamole, salsas. Choose an assortment, and pay. Next, order your drinks from the beverage waiter and pay. Finally, the tortilla lady arrives and you purchase the quantity required by your group. Now it's time to sit back, relax, and savor some of the most delicious tacos you'll ever enjoy.

CECINA ENCHILADA

BEEF IN SMOKY CHILE ADOBO

FOR THE ADOBO

6 chiles guajillos (about ¾ oz./18 g)

3 chiles anchos (about 1¼ oz./33 g)

1 chile pasilla de Oaxaca (about
½ oz./14 g.; substitute 2 chiles
chipotles in adobo)

4 tablespoons (60 g) recado rojo
(also known as recado de achiote
or pasta de achiote, p. 45)

½ medium white onion
(5 oz./137.5 g), coarsely chopped

4 medium cloves garlic
(1 oz./24 g), peeled

1 teaspoon (6 g) cumin seed *plus*
1 tablespoon (2 g) dried whole
Mexican oregano, lightly toasted
and ground together

½ teaspoon (1.5 g) canela (Mexican
cinnamon), ground

½ teaspoon (2.5 g) black pepper,
ground

¼ cup (62.5 mL) pineapple vinegar
(substitute cider vinegar)

2 tablespoons (30 mL) vegetable
oil

1 teaspoon (6 g) sea salt (*Note:*
If using cured cecina, omit
the salt.)

2 pounds (1 kg) cecina (substitute
beef or pork milanesa, or thin
cuts of lean meat pounded to no
more than ¼ inch/6 mm thick)

For best flavor, this dish ideally begins with the lightly cured meat known as Cecina (recipe on p. 397); you may be able to locate it at a Mexican *carnicería*. If not, you can just as easily start with very thin slices (*milanesa*) of beef (you may also use pork). Have your butcher cut these for you, or start with thicker slices and pound them between pieces of waxed paper. The finished pieces should be no more than about ¼ inch (6 mm) thick. To make a festive party, grill the Cecina enchilada along with plain *milanesa*, plus a few chorizos at the same time as the requisite scallions and chiles. Serve all together with the accompaniments suggested below.

Prepare-ahead note: The Cecina enchilada should marinate under refrigeration for at least 8 hours. Once grilled, it should be served immediately.

YIELD: 6–8 SERVINGS

PREPARE THE ADOBO

Remove and discard the seeds and veins from the chiles. Briefly toast the chiles on a hot comal or in a cast-iron skillet over high heat until fragrant and just beginning to blister. Transfer the chiles to a heatproof bowl and cover them with boiling water. Allow the chiles to soak for 20 minutes; remove the chiles from the soaking liquid with a slotted spoon and reserve the liquid. Working in batches as needed, place the chiles and the remaining ingredients except for the meat in the jar of a blender; process until thoroughly puréed, adding just enough of the soaking liquid to keep the blades moving.

Place the meat in a shallow baking dish and cover thoroughly with the adobo. Refrigerate at least 8 hours or overnight.

Cecina enchilada (left) *with grilled* milanesa, *onions, and* chiles de agua.

[MR]

Young bulb onions or scallions,
  with the greens
Chiles de agua (substitute
  Anaheim, banana pepper, or
  jalapeño), whole
Guacamole or slices of avocado
Salsas of your choice
Lime wedges
Warm maize tortillas

TO PREPARE AHEAD

Pan de yema (p. 187), or substitute
Enriched Lard (p. 530)
Chocolate de mesa (p. 77), or
  substitute

FOR THE BEANS

1 pound (500 g) alubias (substitute
  any medium to large white bean
  such as navy, Great Northern, or
  cannellini)
4 quarts (4 L) water
1 medium white onion
  (10 oz./275 g), peeled, divided
3 medium cloves garlic
  (¾ oz./18 g), peeled

GRILL THE MEATS AND ACCOMPANIMENTS

As noted above, grill other meats at the same time if desired. Preheat a charcoal or gas grill; when the coals are hot, toss some soaked and drained mesquite wood smoking chips onto the coals or place a loose foil pouch containing dry chips close to the burner elements of the gas grill. Place the onions and chiles in a grilling basket located above the heat source; grill the meat 3–4 minutes per side or until springy to the touch (beef should register 140–150°F/60–65°C, and pork should reach 145°F/63°C on a meat thermometer). Serve immediately.

TO SERVE

Diners slice or tear off with their fingers pieces of the meat to fashion tacos with tortillas, garnishes, and salsas to taste.

COLORADITO DE FRIJOL BLANCO Y CAMARÓN

"LITTLE RED" MOLE WITH WHITE BEANS AND DRIED SHRIMP

One of the most popular eateries in Mercado 20 de noviembre is Comedor "María Teresa," owned and operated by María Teresa Gutiérrez. *Coloradito* is a cousin to the family of Oaxacan moles. Although this dish appears only infrequently—usually just during Lent when the chicken is swapped out for white beans and dried shrimp—other *comedor* owners know about doña María's version and speak of it with a tinge of envy. Rightly so. The subtle sweetness of the mole poised vertiginously against the salty crunch of the shrimp and the butteriness of the beans is the stuff of dreams. Information about dried shrimp can be found on page 62; use small to medium shrimp for this dish. Most Oaxacan cooks—and doña María is no exception—state that the centerpiece chile of choice is the *chilcostle*, and the bread should be *pan de yema*. But not wanting to allow petty realities to intervene where good food is concerned, they will also resort to the *chile guajillo* and French bread when the preferred ingredients are not available.

Prepare-ahead note: Coloradito con frijol blanco y camarón improves with age; prepare a day in advance, refrigerate, and reheat just before serving. You may also prepare the mole paste a day in advance, refrigerate, and finish the beans on the day you plan to serve.

YIELD: 8–10 SERVINGS

PREPARE THE BEANS

Rinse and pick through the beans; drain thoroughly and transfer to a large stockpot or Dutch oven. Cover the beans with the water; coarsely chop half of the onion and add

1 teaspoon (0.65 g) whole dry
   Mexican oregano, lightly toasted

¼ teaspoon (4 g) black
   peppercorns

⅛ teaspoon (0.25 g) whole cloves

1 three-inch (5 cm) stick canela
   (Mexican cinnamon)

4 ounces (115 g, about 8 pieces)
   chiles anchos, stems removed
   and seeded

2 ounces (57 g, about 6 pieces)
   chiles chilcostles (substitute an
   equal weight of chiles guajillos),
   stems removed and seeded

3 medium Roma tomatoes
   (10½ oz./300 g)

5 medium cloves garlic
   (1¼ oz./30 g), peeled

½ cup (100 g) sesame seeds

4 tablespoons (56 g) Enriched
   Lard, divided

1½ ounces (40 g) stale Pan de
   yema (substitute brioche or
   French bread), sliced

1 small plantain (10½ oz./300 g),
   peeled and sliced into thick
   rounds

1½ teaspoons (9 g) sea salt

FOR FINISHING THE BEANS

½ pound (250 g) medium dried
   shrimp

4 cups (1 L) rich chicken stock

2 balls Chocolate de mesa
   (1½ oz./45 g total; substitute
   ½ tablet commercial Mexican
   drinking chocolate)

1 large dried avocado leaf

2 teaspoons (8 g) sugar

FOR SERVING

White rice

Warm maize tortillas

it, along with the garlic cloves, to the beans. Place the beans over high heat and bring to a boil; reduce to a simmer and continue cooking for 1½ to 2 hours until the beans are just tender (this will depend on your beans). During the cooking process, add boiling water to the pot to keep the beans covered by at least 1 inch (2.5 cm). When the beans are tender, cover and remove from the heat.

PREPARE THE MOLE PASTE

While the beans are cooking, place the first four ingredients in a spice mill or coffee grinder adapted to the purpose; grind until fine and pass through a fine-mesh sieve, discarding any coarse residue; set aside. In a large, heavy skillet, preferably cast iron, toast the chiles over high heat until blistered, blackened in patches, and fragrant; transfer the chiles to a heatproof bowl and cover with boiling water; allow the chiles to soak for 30 minutes as you proceed. In the same hot skillet, char the tomatoes, the remaining half onion, and the garlic until blackened in patches; transfer to a heatproof bowl. Add the sesame seeds to the skillet and quickly toast them, tossing constantly, until lightly browned; transfer the sesame seeds to the bowl with the tomatoes. In the same hot skillet, melt 2 tablespoons (28 g) of the lard until shimmering; add the bread and plantain and cook until browned; transfer the bread and plantain to the bowl containing the tomatoes. Add the ground spices to the hot fat and cook over medium heat, stirring constantly, until just fragrant; transfer the spices as well as any melted lard to the bowl with the other ingredients; set aside.

Remove the chiles from the soaking liquid with a slotted spoon, and transfer them to the jar of a blender; reserve the soaking liquid. Working in batches as needed, add the tomatoes and all of the other ingredients from the bowl and process until thoroughly liquefied. Add some of the soaking liquid just to keep the blades turning; add the salt and process to combine. Pass the purée through a fine-mesh sieve placed over a large mixing bowl; use a rubber spatula or wooden spoon to press as much of the mixture through as possible; add a bit more of the chile soaking liquid as needed to pass the mixture through; discard any residue.

Melt the remaining 2 tablespoons (28 g) of the lard in a heavy skillet until shimmering; pour all of the chile/tomato mixture into the skillet at once: it should sizzle and splatter, so stand back. Cook over medium heat, stirring constantly, for 6–8 minutes or until slightly thickened; remove from the heat and set aside.

FINISH THE BEANS

Remove the legs, heads, and tails from the shrimp; cover with cold water, allow to soak for 10 minutes, then drain and rinse thoroughly; add the shrimp to the pot with the beans. Add the mole paste and the remaining ingredients and stir to combine; bring to a simmer and continue cooking over low heat another 15–20 minutes to melt the chocolate and amalgamate flavors; check for seasonings.

TO SERVE

Plate the mole in shallow serving bowls; accompany with rice and tortillas if desired.

NIEVE DE MEZCAL

EGGLESS MEZCAL ICE CREAM WITH ORANGE AND CHILE

FOR THE NIEVE

2 cups (500 mL) whipping cream

1 cup (250 mL) milk

1 cup (250 mL) freshly squeezed
orange juice

1 cup (250 mL) light corn syrup

½ cup (100 g) sugar

1 teaspoon (1 g) finely grated
orange rind

½ teaspoon (3 g) sal de gusano
(substitute ⅛ tsp. (0.75 g) *each*
sea salt and cayenne)

¼ cup (62.5 mL) *plus* 3 tablespoons
(45 mL) mezcal

I have made a couple of enhancements to the basic recipe recited to me by the owner of Nieves "Chonita" in Mercado "Benito Juárez": in honor of the Oaxacan custom of sucking sweet orange wedges with a bit of *sal de gusano* before, during, and after sips of mezcal, I have added orange juice and the "worm salt" to the formula. If you have difficulty locating it north of the border, you may substitute cayenne and sea salt. Choose a *joven* or *reposado mezcal* that isn't too smoky.

YIELD: APPROXIMATELY 1½ QUARTS (1.5 L)

PREPARE THE ICE CREAM

Combine the first seven ingredients in a saucepan. Heat over high heat until the mixture reaches the boil; cool to room temperature, then chill at least 2 hours or overnight. Immediately before freezing, stir in ¼ cup (62.5 mL) of the mezcal; process in an ice cream maker according to the manufacturer's instructions; at the end of freezing, fold in the remaining mezcal. Transfer the ice cream to an airtight container and freeze at least 4 hours before serving.

Sorbets at Nieves "Chonita" in Mercado "Benito Juárez." Left to right: nieve de maracuyá (passion fruit sorbet) and Nieve de mezcal. [MR]

Church of Preciosa Sangre de Cristo. [MC]

TEOTITLÁN DEL VALLE

JUST AS WE pulled up outside the home of Reyna Mendoza—a member of a respected family of local cooks—the huge wooden gate of the house just across the street swung open, and a squat man struggled to coax outside two burly oxen that were hitched at the shoulders with a ponderous-looking yoke. It's a common sight here: even though Teotitlán del Valle enjoys worldwide renown as a weaving village, many people—even those families involved in the art—still plant and till their own crop fields, producing a variety of foods destined primarily for their own tables.

According to reports by Fray Francisco de Burgoa, Teotitlán was founded in 1465 as a Zapotec village. It remains predominantly Zapotec, and a visit to the lively Sunday market affords the opportunity of listening to the rich tonal cadences of that language almost exclusively, interrupted by just a smattering of Spanish for business transactions. Women carry armloads of flowers or baskets full of chayote and squash blossoms and *quelites*; greetings are gracious, as one person extends both hands prayerfully and the other gently accepts and presses the hands between their own.

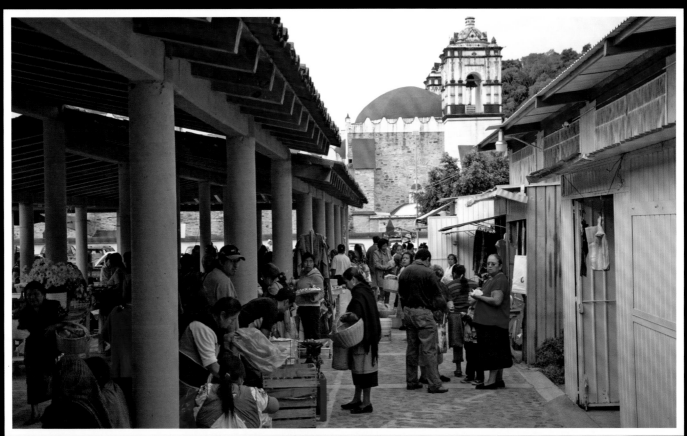

[MR]

MERCADO MUNICIPAL

As in so many Mexican pueblos, the market of Teotitlán del Valle nestles just to one side of the church. It is one of the most colorful markets in the region, and it attracts people from many nearby towns. We followed Reyna as she floated through the tranquil aisles, identifying unique ingredients and offering us tastings of several prepared foods. The Sunday market is active starting at around 9:00 a.m., dramatically emptying out by about 11:00 a.m., and virtually asleep on Mondays, so we rushed to purchase some things we knew we wouldn't find the next day for our cooking.

(below) The ideal preshopping breakfast at the market—hot chocolate and a concha.

(below) Guías de calabaza, *squash vines.*

[MR]

[MC]

The wispy herb between the radishes and the chayote is known as chepiche. [MC]

CHEPICHE/PIPITZA, TEPICHA

BOTANICAL: *Porophyllum tagetoides* (Ard.) DC./Family Asteraceae | **ENGLISH:** pepicha, pipicha

This native Mexican *quelite* is considered an intrusive weed in many states, but it is particularly prized in the cuisine and traditional medicine of Oaxaca. The perennial grows tall and wispy like tarragon to a height of about 10 to 20 inches (25 to 50 cm). *Chepiche* blooms from August through December, producing hermaphroditic purple tubular flowers. Wispy, thin blue-green leaves resemble pine needles and grow to a length of 1¾ inches (4.5 cm). The edible leaves have a strong flavor of mint, cilantro, dill, and marjoram, a mixture of which can serve as a substitute. *Chepiche* may be used in white rice, as well as in *sopa de guías* and Caldo de chepil (p. 171). In market *comedores*, it often appears in a bowl alongside other garnishes so that you can pluck off a few leaves to sprinkle onto mole or meats.

[MC]

CHEPIL

BOTANICAL: *Crotalaria* spp./Family Fabaceae
ENGLISH: Longbeak Rattlebox

The *Crotalaria* genus is expressed by many species in southern Mexico, and *chepil* is closely related to *chipilín* of Chiapas. Although the names are sometimes used interchangeably, the species most commonly found in Oaxaca is probably *C. pumila*, while that of Chiapas is *C. longirostrata*. *Chepil* is a primary ingredient for soups, and as with *chipilín* in Chiapas, the leaves of *chepil* are also mixed with masa for a unique tamale.

[MR]

[MR]

CALDO DE CHEPIL

SUMMER SOUP OF SQUASH VINES AND BLOSSOMS, ZUCCHINI, AND WILD HERBS

FOR THE VEGETABLE STOCK

2 cups (500 mL) guía de calabaza, cut into 2-inch (5 cm) lengths including the leaves (*Note:* Use only the tenderest part of the stalks; strip and peel away the tough fibers from the sides; substitute watercress or purslane.)

6 cups (1.5 L) water

4 small zucchini (about 10½ oz./300 g), cut lengthwise into thick wedges

2 cups (500 mL) chepil leaves (substitute baby spinach, chopped)

8–10 squash blossoms, petals only

¼ cup (125 mL) chepiche leaves (substitute a mixture of any or all of the following to the specified quantity: fresh mint, cilantro, marjoram, dill, coarsely chopped)

Back in her cheerful open-air kitchen, Reyna proceeded to show me how to make this remarkably easy soup. The only challenge outside of Mexico will be sourcing some of the ingredients, although I have suggested substitutions. You may occasionally find the squash vines in farmers' markets, or you may be growing some yourself in your backyard garden. The vines are indeed an important component of the dish, which is often called *sopa de guías* (*guía* means both "guide" and "squash vine"). Reyna also called it *sopa de chepil* or *espesado de chepil*, since it is thickened (*espesado*) at the end with ground fresh maize kernels. Some recipes call for onion and garlic, but I believe that the brightness of the herbs stands out more without them; you may include them at the beginning of the cooking process if you wish. Reyna added no salt, making this a truly humble dish, but I suggest it as a serving option.

Prepare-ahead note: Caldo de chepil is best served on the day it is prepared.

YIELD: 6–8 SERVINGS

PREPARE THE VEGETABLE STOCK

Thoroughly rinse and drain the squash vines, blossoms, and herbs. Bring the water to a boil in a large stockpot. When rapidly boiling, add the squash vines; reduce the heat to a simmer and continue cooking another 5 minutes. Add the remaining ingredients and simmer an additional 10 minutes or until the zucchini is tender.

[MC]

FOR THICKENING

1 cup (250 g) fresh field corn ker-
    nels (look in farmers' markets
    for the starchier corn and try to
    avoid the sweet summer variety)
½ cup (125 mL) water
1 teaspoon (6 g) sea salt (optional)

FOR SERVING

Sea salt to taste
Salsa de chile de árbol (p. 531), or
    Salsa de chile pasilla (p. 173), or
    Salsa de chintestle (p. 175)
Lime wedges

THICKEN THE SOUP

Place the corn kernels in the jar of a blender with the water, and process until smooth. Pour the mixture into the stockpot with the vegetables and stir; return the soup to a simmer, and continue cooking another 5 minutes, stirring occasionally, or until the soup slightly thickens. Add the salt, if using, and check for seasonings.

TO SERVE

Ladle the soup into serving bowls and garnish with more fresh herbs if you wish. Diners add salt, salsa, and squeezes of lime juice to taste.

[MR]

Reyna Mendoza plucking leaves of chepil. [MC]

SALSA DE CHILE PASILLA DE OAXACA

OAXACAN CHILE PASILLA TABLE SAUCE

FOR THE SALSA

½ pound (250 g) tomatillos, husks
  removed and rinsed

2 large chiles pasillas de Oaxaca
  (about ¾ oz./18 g total; substitute 1 standard chile pasilla
  and 2 chiles chipotles in adobo,
  drained)

2 medium cloves garlic
  (½ oz./12 g), peeled and coarsely
  chopped

½ teaspoon (3 g) sea salt

[MR]

To accompany the soup, Reyna made two quick salsas that are widely used in the markets as a garnish for tamales and other foods. They are also wonderful dipping salsas served with *totopos*.

Prepare-ahead note: Salsa de chile pasilla and Salsa de chintestle keep well under refrigeration for about 1 week.

YIELD: ABOUT 1 CUP (250 ML)

PREPARE THE SALSA

On a comal or in a large cast-iron skillet over medium-high heat, slowly roast the tomatillos until softened and browned in patches, 10–15 minutes; transfer half of them to the jar of a blender, and the other half to a bowl. On the same comal or skillet over high heat, toast the dried chiles until fragrant, inflated, and slightly darkened. Transfer the chiles to a bowl filled with cold water and allow them to soak for 10 minutes; tear the chiles into pieces and remove the seeds and veins; transfer the chile pieces to the blender and discard the soaking liquid and seeds. Add the garlic to the blender, and process until thoroughly liquefied. Add the remaining tomatillos and pulse to blend, leaving a rustic texture. Add the salt and check for seasonings. Allow the salsa to rest at room temperature for 15 minutes to amalgamate the flavors. After refrigeration, bring to room temperature and stir before serving.

Roasting miltomates. [MC]

MILTOMATE/TOMATE MILPERO, TOMATITO

BOTANICAL: *Physalis ixocarpa* Brot./Family Solanaceae | **ENGLISH:** none | **P'URHÉPECHA:** *tómari juki*

By now many people beyond Mexico are familiar with the tomatillo, or husk tomato, a member of the gooseberry family. This particular variety, however, is much smaller, only about ¾ inch (2 cm) in diameter. It is called *milpero* because it is the species commonly planted in the milpa among maize, beans, squash, and other foods; it is not cultivated on a broad scale, making it more expensive than the larger tomatillo (*P. philadelphica*). Expensive or not, it is preferred by many people because of its more intense, earthy, sweet-sour taste. *Miltomate* grows on small, scraggly bushes that can spread like a weed, which is most likely how it was originally dispersed. It is a Mexican native and was traditionally used in herbal medicine; today it is prized for salsas, green moles, or pozole.

SALSA DE CHINTESTLE

SMOKY CHILE TABLE SAUCE

The multipurpose seasoning paste known as Chintestle (recipe follows) is quite salty due to the content of dried shrimp; be sure to taste this salsa for salt before adding any at the end. Reyna used the tiny tomatillos she called *miltomates* (p. 174), but standard tomatillos will work as well.

TO PREPARE AHEAD
Chintestle (below)

FOR THE SALSA
½ pound (250 g) miltomates, husks removed and rinsed (substitute tomatillos)
1 tablespoon (16 g) Chintestle
¼ cup (125 mL) water
Sea salt to taste

PREPARE THE SALSA
On a comal or in a large cast-iron skillet over medium-high heat, slowly roast the *miltomates* or tomatillos until softened and browned in patches, 10–15 minutes; transfer to a bowl. Place the Chintestle and water in a *molcajete*, blender, or small food processor and crush or process to blend; add the tomatillos and crush or pulse to blend, leaving a rustic texture. Check for seasonings and add salt if desired. Allow the salsa to rest at room temperature for 15 minutes to amalgamate the flavors. After refrigeration, bring to room temperature and stir before serving.

CHINTESTLE/CHILTEXTLI

PICANTE-SMOKY SEASONING PASTE/SPREAD

[MR]

After we purchased several delicious tamales from Guillermina López Sosa (recipes for which follow; she can be seen in the photo to the left), she rewarded me with a bonus pack of Chintestle—the uniquely Oaxacan seasoning paste that she prepares at her home for selling in the market. Although there are many versions of Chintestle, varying with the whim of the cook and the particular region of the state, the paste typically includes plenty of garlic and the smoky *chiles pasillas de Oaxaca* or another regional chile. Doña Guillermina's trick was to add pungent dried shrimp to counterbalance the sweetness of the chiles, lending it an almost Asian flavor profile. The versatile paste may be used in salsas or diluted with vinegar, orange juice, or even water to make a marinade for meats (like pork for the dish known as *pizotl en chiltextli*). A taxi driver told us that it's also delicious simply spread on a crispy *tlayuda tostada* or a tortilla. You will get a much smoother and finer paste like that of doña Guillermina by grinding the ingredients on a *metate*, but a blender may be used instead.

Prepare-ahead note: Chintestle lasts several weeks in the refrigerator and indefinitely in the freezer. Doña Guillermina divided the paste into 3-tablespoon (48 g) portions and packaged each in small plastic bags.

YIELD: APPROXIMATELY 1 CUP (250 ML)

FOR THE SEASONING PASTE

15 large chiles pasillas de Oaxaca
   (about 5¼ oz./150 g; substitute
   12 standard chiles pasillas and
   3 chiles chipotles in adobo,
   drained)
1 large head garlic (1¾ oz./50 g)
3¼ oz. (90 g) salted dried shrimp
1 oz. (30 g) sesame seeds, toasted
   and ground

PREPARE THE PASTE

Remove and discard the stems from the dried chiles; slit the chiles open, shake out the seeds, and reserve them. On a comal or in a cast-iron skillet over moderate heat, briefly toast the seeds until fragrant and just beginning to color; transfer the seeds to a spice mill or coffee grinder adapted for the purpose; grind the seeds until very fine and set aside. On the comal over high heat, toast the chiles until fragrant and slightly darkened; transfer the chiles to a heatproof bowl and cover them with boiling water; allow the chiles to soak for 30 minutes (no need to soak the chipotle if using). Drain the chiles and reserve the soaking liquid.

Separate the garlic into cloves and peel the cloves; char the cloves on a skewer in an open flame, or toast them on a comal or in a cast-iron skillet until mostly blackened. Thoroughly rinse the whole shrimp (heads, legs, and all), drain them, and transfer them to the jar of a blender along with the chiles, ground sesame seeds, and garlic. Process until very smooth, adding some of the soaking liquid a few drops at a time to keep the blades in motion. The finished consistency should be a thick paste, not watery. Store as described above.

TO SERVE

Serve all of the tamales with Salsa de chile de árbol (p. 531), Salsa de chile pasilla de Oaxaca (p. 173), or Salsa de chintestle (p. 175).

Doña Guillermina's tamales, left to right: Tamal de chepil, Tamal de frijol, Tamal de mole amarillo. [MC]

TAMAL DE CHEPIL

TAMALE WITH WILD GREENS

A similar tamale appears in Chiapas using the closely related *chipilín*. Follow the recipe for Masa para tamales on page 530; after beating the masa with the flavorings and lard, knead in 1 cup (45 g) *chepil* leaves (substitute chopped watercress leaves, pea shoots, or baby spinach). Follow the instructions for forming tamales in cornhusks and for steaming on page 526.

TAMAL DE FRIJOL

TAMALE WITH BLACK BEAN PASTE AND AVOCADO LEAVES

Of course this recipe works best with fresh avocado leaves, but dried can be used effectively, although they may be too tough to eat; nonetheless, they will rehydrate a bit during cooking and will impart some flavor to the tamale. Prepare the recipe for Pasta de frijol on page 154 to create a thick, spreadable paste. Follow the recipe for Masa para tamales on page 530, and for preparing and filling cornhusks on page 526. Form 2 tablespoons (60 g) of masa into a thick tortilla in the palm of your hand; top with 1 tablespoon (14 g) of the bean paste and fold the tortilla closed to form an empanada; seal the edges and locate the empanada inside one cornhusk toward the wide end. Place one large avocado leaf on top of the masa, fold the cornhusk sides to cover, and steam as instructed on page 526.

Vendor with bundles of hoja de milpa *and a basket full of* hierba santa *(hoja santa).* [MC]

TAMAL DE MOLE AMARILLO

TAMALE WITH CHICKEN AND YELLOW MOLE

Make use of leftover Mole amarillo for this tamale. Although the typical wrapper is *hoja de milpa* (the fresh leaf from a cornstalk, not the dried cornhusk) you may substitute a 5-inch by 4-inch (12 cm × 10 cm) piece of banana leaf instead. Follow the recipe for Masa para tamales on page 530 and for Mole amarillo on page 179. When the mole is completed, remove the chicken from the sauce and shred it. Working with a large *hoja de milpa*, thinly spread 2 tablespoons (60 g) of the prepared masa onto the widest end, top with 2 tablespoons (50 g) of chicken and 2 tablespoons (30 mL) of the mole sauce. Roll the tamale from the widest end to the halfway point of the leaf, fold on the diagonal, and continue rolling side to side to the tip of the leaf to enclose the ends. Steam as per instructions on page 526.

(*above*) *A cook at the Puesto "Soyla y Elisa" flips an empanada of Mole amarillo. A snippet of* hierba santa *(hoja santa) peeks out one side.* [MC] (*below*) *To prepare an empanada of Mole amarillo, briefly cook both sides of a large raw maize tortilla; top with a leaf of* hierba santa *(hoja santa), some shredded chicken, and a spoonful of the mole sauce. Some customers also request* quesillo. *Fold in half and cook on both sides until browned in patches.* [MC]

MOLE AMARILLO

CHICKEN AND VEGETABLE STEW IN YELLOW CHILE SAUCE

[MC]

Sauces of chiles (*chilmole*: *chilli* = chile + *molli* = sauce in Nahuatl) were meticulously documented by the colonial chroniclers, particularly by Bernardino de Sahagún in *Historia general de las cosas de Nueva España*. Mole amarillo was described as consisting of tomatoes and yellow chiles. Because Sahagún began his history less than two decades after the conquest of Teotihuacan, we might reasonably assume that moles predate contact and are in fact ancient. Like the other famed "seven moles of Oaxaca," this one evolved to include several Old World ingredients, perhaps the most important being the spices. Recipes for Mole amarillo vary: some include chicken, some beef; some use the regional herb *pitiona* (p. 199) as a flavoring, others use *hierba santa* (hoja santa). Chiles vary, too: many traditional recipes I have found call for the *chilcostle*—logical, since its Nahuatl name means "yellow chile" (*chilli* = chile + *coztic* = yellow)—perhaps the one Sahagún referred to. Reyna used the *chilcostle* as well as *chilhuacles rojos* and *amarillos*. And in the end, to achieve a brighter color, she also added some *guajillo*—the much milder, sweeter chile you will likely have to use as a substitute and to which Oaxacan cooks resort when they can't find the other chiles. Diana Kennedy's *mole amarillo* includes the small maize dumplings known as *chochoyotes*, but none of the market versions we encountered featured them. In any case, while the dumplings are lovely, the potatoes provide enough starch for my diet. A subtle if important flavor component of Reyna's mole was the touch of anise from *hierba santa*. Since the fresh herb will not likely be available beyond Mexico, I have suggested a couple of tricks. Besides being plated as shown in the photo, Mole amarillo may also be used as a filling for tamales and empanadas.

FOR BRINING THE CHICKEN

16 cups (4 L) water

½ cup (145 g) sea salt

1 large chicken (about 6½
  lbs./3 kg), cut into serving
  pieces, or an assortment of
  your favorite pieces

FOR THE CHILE PASTE

5 chiles chilcostles, 2 chiles
  chilhuacles rojos, 2 chiles
  chilhuacles amarillos (about
  2½ oz./75 g total; substitute an
  equal weight of chiles guajillos)

1 tablespoon (2 g) dried whole
  Mexican oregano

½ teaspoon (1 g) cumin seed

½ teaspoon (2 g) black
  peppercorns

6 whole cloves

FOR THE STOCK

12 cups (3 L) water

1 medium white onion
  (10 oz./275 g), quartered

6 medium cloves garlic
  (1½ oz./36 g), peeled

2 teaspoons (12 g) sea salt

[MC]

Weighing ejotes—green beans—at the market for the mole. [MR]

Prepare-ahead note: Mole amarillo benefits from an overnight rest in the refrigerator. If you do that, to avoid overcooking the vegetables, omit them in the step described below; on the day you plan to serve, cook them in a pot of boiling water, drain, and plate them with the chicken immediately.

YIELD: 8 SERVINGS

BRINE THE CHICKEN

Combine the water and salt and stir until the salt is thoroughly dissolved. Add the chicken and refrigerate for 1–4 hours. (This brining step is optional. See notes about brining in the "Market Fundamentals" chapter, p. 527.)

PREPARE THE CHILE PASTE

Remove the stems from the chiles and discard. Slit the chiles open and rescue the seeds. On a gently heated comal or in a cast-iron skillet, toast the seeds for a few minutes, moving them constantly, until just beginning to color; remove and set aside. With the heat on high, toast the oregano and cumin seed until fragrant and barely beginning to smoke; transfer the chile seeds, oregano, cumin seed, peppercorns, and cloves to a spice mill or coffee grinder adapted for the purpose; grind until very fine and set aside. With the heat still on high, toast the chiles on the comal until fragrant and slightly darkened in patches but not burned; transfer the chiles to a heatproof bowl and cover them with boiling water. Allow the chiles to soak for 30 minutes as you proceed.

PREPARE THE STOCK

Remove the chicken from the brining solution and discard the brine. Place the chicken in a large stockpot and add the next four ingredients. Bring to a simmer, skimming as necessary, and continue cooking for 20 minutes; with heat on medium high, add the potatoes and chayote and continue cooking another 15 minutes; add the green beans

1 pound (500 g) whole new
  potatoes or small, waxy potatoes
  cut in half
1 pound (500 g) chayote, peeled
  under running water if the
  skin is tough, and cut into large
  cubes about the size of the
  potatoes
½ pound (250 g) green beans, tips
  and strings removed

FOR THICKENING

1 medium Roma tomato
  (3½ oz./100 g), quartered
1 medium tomatillo
  (3½ oz./100 g), quartered
½ medium white onion
  (5 oz./137.5 g), coarsely chopped
2 medium cloves garlic
  (½ oz./12 g), peeled
6 large leaves fresh hierba
  santa (hoja santa; about
  1½ ounces/48 g, thick center
  stems removed. For a substitute,
  see notes below.)
1½ cups (375 g) maize masa, either
  from nixtamal or prepared from
  masa harina according to the
  package instructions
2 teaspoons (8 g) sugar

FOR SERVING

Sea salt
Jalapeños en escabeche (pickled
  jalapeños)
Warm maize tortillas

Reyna ground the chiles, seeds, and hierba santa on a metate, resulting in a smooth, creamy paste. You can achieve a similar texture using a blender and then straining the mixture through a fine-mesh sieve.

and cook another 6–7 minutes. The chicken and vegetables should be tender and the green beans still a bit al dente. Transfer the chicken and vegetables to a platter and set aside; strain the stock. You will need only 8 cups (2 L) of stock for the sauce; drain off any extra and reserve for another use.

THICKEN AND FINISH

Drain the chiles and reserve the soaking liquid. Place the ground chile seeds and spices along with the chiles, the tomato and tomatillo, onion and garlic, and the *hierba santa* in the jar of a blender; process until smooth, adding just enough of the reserved soaking liquid to keep the blades turning freely. Pour the mixture through a fine-mesh sieve placed over a bowl; use a rubber spatula to press out as much of the mixture as possible, adding stock from the stockpot as needed to pass the mixture through; set aside.

Place the masa and 3 cups (750 mL) of the stock in the blender jar and process until thoroughly liquefied; add the mixture to the strained purée; add the sugar and stir to combine. With the stock at a simmer, pour in the mixture stirring constantly; return to a simmer and stir frequently for 8–10 minutes until slightly thickened. Use an immersion blender or whisk if needed to remove any lumps. Serve immediately.

TO SERVE

Plate the chicken and vegetables and sprinkle with sea salt to taste; spoon on a generous portion of the sauce. Diners add strips of jalapeño to taste and warm tortillas if desired.

Note: If you do not have access to fresh *hierba santa*, you can achieve a similar flavor by adding 1 teaspoon (2 g) aniseed when you grind the spices and chile seeds. Alternatively, add 4–5 leaves dried *hierba santa* to the chiles when you cover them with boiling water; proceed as instructed.

[MR]

Church of La Asunción de Nuestra Señora.

TLACOLULA DE MATAMOROS

I N STARK CONTRAST to the pert orderliness and open airiness of the Municipal Market of Teotitlán del Valle, the Sunday market in Tlacolula—just 7½ miles (12 km) away—is a rambling riot of colorful chaos, marvelous in its own way. It brings to mind what medieval European markets or the ancient markets of Mexico must have been like.

[MR]

MERCADO MUNICIPAL "MARTÍN GONZÁLEZ"/MERCADO DOMINGUERO

The market of Tlacolula de Matamoros is one of the oldest continuously operating markets in the country and among the largest in Oaxaca's Central Valleys region. Here, instead of women clutching bouquets of flowers and whispering their orders as in Teotitlán, traditionally dressed Zapotecas clutch docile turkeys or chickens to their breast, men boisterously hawk the products they are selling, and customers scramble for seats at crowded *comedores*. With plastic and cloth tarps defining provisional stalls, the Sunday market absorbs surrounding streets and swells from the daily 24,500 square feet (2,276 sq. m) to almost double its size, making getting lost ridiculously easy. One member of our party wandered off to check out the market's famed breads, and we spent the next two hours looking for him!

[MR]

[MR]

[MR]

One of the Tlacolula market's many claims to fame is the vast hall dedicated to *barbacoa*. Here, the pit-roasted meat is often goat and sometimes mutton. Order a *roja* and you'll receive a bowl with the meat swimming in a rich red consomé; order a *blanca* and the meat arrives shredded on a tortilla for fashioning a taco. Or, if you'd rather make your own *barbacoa*, whole carcasses are available, with coats of oily wool still clinging to the bones as witness to the meat's authenticity. A recipe for *barbacoa* can be found on page 363.

PAN DE YEMA

RICH BUTTERY EGG BUNS

These brioche-like breads can be found in many places in the Central Valleys region, but perhaps nowhere as plentifully as in Tlacolula, and many families here are devoted to their preparation. Precarious pyramids of them fill a broad aisle running through the heart of the market, and periodically men carrying long planks on their heads laden with breads fresh from the oven arrive to restock supplies. The flavors we found in the market ranged from vanilla to anise or *canela*, and I provide instructions for all three. Most were garnished with a dusting of sesame seeds, but during holiday festivities, such as the Day of the Dead, they may be sprinkled with sugar and decorated with figures. The texture of Pan de yema lends itself brilliantly to toast served with a spoonful of jam, but perhaps most perfectly for dunking in a bowlful of steaming Oaxacan *chocolate*. This recipe makes use of a stand mixer, but you may do all the same steps by hand.

[MR]

FOR THE STARTER

½ cup (125 mL) milk

2¼ teaspoons (¼ oz./1 package)
   active dry yeast

1 pound 6 ounces (625 g, approximately 5 cups) all-purpose flour,
   divided, plus additional for
   kneading

FOR THE DOUGH AND
FINISHING

4 tablespoons (48 g) sugar

2 teaspoons (12 g) sea salt

4 tablespoons (60 mL) water

2 teaspoons (4 g) aniseed *or*
   2 teaspoons (6 g) ground
   canela (Mexican cinnamon) *or*
   2 teaspoons (10 mL) Mexican
   vanilla extract

3 eggs *plus* 4 egg yolks, at room
   temperature, divided

1½ cups (750 mL) unsalted butter,
   melted

¼ cup (62.5 mL) milk

2–3 tablespoons (20–30 g) sesame
   seeds

Prepare-ahead note: Pan de yema keeps well at room temperature for a couple of days, in the refrigerator for about a week, or in the freezer for a couple of months. The bread is best revivified by toasting or reheating.

YIELD: 3 ONE-POUND LOAVES OR 1 DOZEN BUNS

PREPARE THE STARTER

In a small saucepan, heat the milk until bubbles appear around the edges; remove the milk from the heat and allow it to cool to tepid. In a small mixing bowl, dissolve the yeast in the milk; add 1 cup (4¼ oz./125 g) of the flour and stir to incorporate into a loose mass. Cover and allow the starter to rest at room temperature for 2 hours.

PREPARE THE DOUGH AND FINISH

In a small mixing bowl, dissolve the sugar and salt in the water; add your choice of aniseed, *canela*, or vanilla, and stir to combine; set aside. In the mixing bowl of a heavy-duty stand mixer fitted with the flat paddle-type blade, place 8½ ounces (250 g, about 2 cups) of the flour and the three whole eggs; beat until the dough pulls away from the sides of the bowl. Add the flavored water, the melted butter, and 3 of the egg yolks and beat to achieve a very thick batter. Add the remaining flour a bit at a time, beating after each addition. Continue until all the flour has been incorporated; add the starter and resume beating; beat for about 10 minutes, adding a bit more flour as needed until the dough is no longer tacky to the touch. Turn onto a lightly floured work surface and knead 3–4 minutes to achieve some elasticity, adding a bit more flour as needed to prevent stickiness. Transfer the dough to a large buttered bowl, cover, and allow it to rise at room temperature for 2 hours or until doubled in volume. Punch down the dough, turn it upside down, cover again, and refrigerate for 2 hours or overnight.

One hour before baking, remove the dough from the refrigerator; allow it to rest at room temperature for 20–30 minutes. Preheat the oven to 400°F (200°C). Turn the dough onto a lightly floured surface. *For loaves:* Divide the dough into thirds and shape into balls, tucking under and pinching the dough on the bottom to create a tight seam; place the balls seam side down on a buttered baking sheet and cover them loosely with a clean towel; allow to rest for 30 minutes. *For buns:* Proceed as above, dividing the dough into 12 balls.

Beat the remaining egg yolk with ¼ cup (62.5 mL) milk. Using a very sharp knife or razor blade, cut a ¼-inch (6 mm)-deep slash side to side in the tops of the breads. Glaze each bread with some of the egg-milk mixture and sprinkle with some sesame seeds. Place the breads in the oven, and with a spray bottle filled with water, lightly mist the breads just before closing the oven door. Bake for approximately 25 minutes or until golden brown. Remove from the oven and allow the breads to cool at least 30 minutes before serving.

HIGADITO

CHICKEN AND SCRAMBLED EGGS IN CONSOMMÉ

FOR THE CONSOMMÉ
½ large chicken (about
   3 lbs./1.5 kg)
10 cups (2.5 L) water

[MC]

This unusual specialty of Tlacolula can be found in most market *comedores*. The process is somewhere between making egg-drop soup and clarifying stock for consommé: a thin thread of eggs beaten with a bit of shredded chicken is slowly streamed into simmering stock, then spoons are used to gather the eggs toward the center of the pot, creating the "raft" typical of consommés. The result is a congealed mound of scrambled eggs floating in a perfectly clear broth, which I've been told is the true test of the cook's skill in this dish. The name is a mystery: *higadito* in Spanish means "little liver," but this dish has nothing to do with liver whatsoever, except that some people consider it a hangover remedy.

Prepare-ahead note: To remove the fat from the stock, prepare it a day in advance and refrigerate overnight. Skim the fat off the top the next day. *Higadito* is best served immediately after finishing. Have the stock ready in advance and stir in the eggs just before serving.

YIELD: 6–8 SERVINGS

PREPARE THE CONSOMMÉ

Place the chicken in a stockpot and cover with the water; bring to a simmer, skimming to remove any accumulated foam, and continue over medium heat until the chicken is tender, 25–30 minutes. Remove the chicken to a platter, allow to cool, then finely shred the meat; refrigerate it until time to finish the soup. Cool the stock, then refrigerate overnight; just before finishing, skim off the accumulated fat.

FOR THE EGGS

1 teaspoon (5 g) cumin seed,
  lightly toasted
4 medium cloves garlic
  (1 oz./24 g), peeled
½ medium white onion
  (5 oz./137.5 g), finely chopped
8 large eggs, well beaten
3 medium Roma tomatoes
  (10½ oz./300 g), seeded and cut
  to small dice
2 teaspoons (12 g) sea salt

FOR SERVING

Salsa de chile de árbol (p. 531)

PREPARE THE EGGS

In a blender or mortar and pestle, finely grind the cumin seed with the garlic until you achieve a smooth paste. Transfer the garlic paste with the chopped onion to the stock and bring to a boil; boil for 2 minutes. Combine the eggs, chicken, and tomatoes; with the stock at a boil, slowly stream in the egg mixture, immediately reduce the heat to simmer, and use a wooden spoon to *gently* scrape the bottom of the pot to prevent sticking. As the eggs cook and congeal, use two spoons inserted between the gathering of eggs in the middle and the sides of the pot to delicately encourage the eggs toward the center of the pot. Continue with this motion until all of the eggs have been unified and form a soft yet solid mass. Add the salt, stir gently, and check for seasonings. *Note*: If the broth remains cloudy, mash 1–2 cloves garlic to a fine paste and stir in just before serving.

TO SERVE

Using a spoon, gently cut away some of the eggs and place them in the center of a soup bowl; ladle on some of the clear broth. Diners add Salsa de chile de árbol to taste.

VARIATION

Higadito de fandango/Party Chicken and Scrambled Eggs in Consommé: Reyna shared this party version with me, and it looks very festive, indeed! Prepare the soup as instructed, but instead of adding the tomatoes to the eggs, garnish the finished dish with a few slices of tomato. Cut the top off of one small tomato and remove the seeds; fill the hollow with Salsa de chile de árbol; place the filled tomato in the center of the mound of eggs in the bowl.

[MR]

Artisanal mezcal with bags of sal de gusano *(p. 156) at left.* [MR]

MEZCAL

There are many beverages made from Mexico's native agave plants: pulque and *aguamiel* (p. 365), mezcal and tequila among them. *Mezcal* is a generic term for distillates produced from a variety of species of agave; tequila is a type of mezcal that can only be produced from certain species in certain regions, specifically, blue agave (*Agave tequilana*) in the state of Jalisco (and the town of Tequila, p. 452) being the most prominent. Although seven states can legally produce mezcal, Oaxaca dominates the market with 80–90 percent of all production. To make either one, the bulbous base of the plant known as the *piña*, shorn of its spiny leaves, is cooked to extract its flavorful juice that is later distilled. For tequila, modern commercial production achieves this in giant pressure cookers; for mezcal, the *piña* is slowly roasted in an underground oven, lending a smoky note to the finished product. The area surrounding

Tlacolula is known for mezcal production, and agave fields stretch for miles toward the horizon. Regional markets boast scores of brands of local mezcal, many of them not found outside Mexico—some not even available beyond Oaxaca. Some of the best of these are not even labeled, so experiment and try to find a hidden gem. Erick Hernández of the Destilería Tlacolula has gained an international reputation for his artisanal mezcal branded Ilegal, which supposedly started as bootlegged hooch smuggled from Mexico to Guatemala.

TEJATE/FOAMY CHOCOLATE-MAIZE BEVERAGE

Just as the Spanish recorded beverages of chocolate and maize when they arrived in Oaxaca in 1521, visitors to any of Oaxaca's markets today will notice voluminous clay pots filled with a mysterious liquid capped with a chalky-looking, sludgy foam. This is *tejate*, or *cu'ubb* in Zapotec—a beverage that probably dates to at least four thousand years ago. Its preparation occurs throughout the state, but it is particularly associated with Tlacolula. Vendors of *tejate* prepare mountains of a special masa at home, then bring it to the market, where they mix it with water. The mixing process—done by hand—is laborious and intended to aerate the liquid to produce the requisite foam. It is scooped out with a *jícara* and poured into another *jícara* for serving (or just as commonly today, into plastic or Styrofoam cups). Recipes vary: maize may be toasted and ground to a flour (the Nahuatl name translates to "flour water" [*textli* = flour; *atl* = water]), or boiled with ash and ground to a paste to produce what in Oaxaca is known as *nicuanextle*. Other ingredients include red or white cacao beans that have been fermented and roasted; *rosita* (*Quararibea funebris*), also known as cacao flower but not related to cacao; *corozo*, an edible seed or fruit from any one of a variety of palms, or sometimes peanuts; *pistles* or *pixtli*, the seeds of the *mamey* fruit (*Pouteria sapota*), the chemical compounds of which lend a light almond flavor; and sugar to taste. All are ground on a metate or at a commercial mill, then combined into a thick dough. Once mixed with water, the fats from the cacao and the solids from the flowers float to the surface to create the soft, creamy foam. The experience of drinking it as well as the taste are reminiscent of iced mochaccino.

(above, left) Pistles, *seeds of the mamey fruit.* [MC] *(above, right)* Corozo, *the seeds of any one of a variety of palms.* [MC] *(below)* Rosita, or flor de cacao (Quararibea funebris). [MC]

VILLA DE ZAACHILA

MANY SMALL PUEBLOS with excellent and dynamic markets are within a few minutes' drive of Oaxaca de Juárez; the Villa de Zaachila is just 8½ miles (14 km) to the southwest and is well worth the visit, especially on Thursdays for the big Mercado de Plaza. Zaachila is also noted for its historical and archaeological importance. After the decline of Monte Albán sometime in the eleventh century, Zaachila rose to power and controlled much of the Central Valleys region until the arrival of the Spanish, who were impressed by the city's beautifully decorated temples.

[MR]

MERCADO PÚBLICO MUNICIPAL "ALAR II"

Go to the market any day but Thursday, and you are guaranteed an easy seat at one of the popular *comedores*. We befriended the affable María de Jesús Mases Luis at Comedor "Itzel," who generously shared recipes with us. She did, however, whisper them so that her neighboring competitors could not learn her secrets! I can't say with certainty that Estofado (p. 200) and Chichilo (p. 197) are specialties of Zaachila—as doña María boasted—but I can say that of all the markets we visited, we never saw them elsewhere.

CHICHILO

BEEF SHORT RIB MOLE WITH VEGETABLES AND OAXACAN HERBS

TO PREPARE AHEAD
Enriched Lard (p. 530)

FOR THE STOCK

3 tablespoons (42 g) Enriched Lard

4 pounds (2 kg) beef short ribs,
   cut into individual ribs

1 medium white onion
   (10 oz./275 g), quartered

8 medium cloves garlic
   (2 oz./48 g), peeled

½ teaspoon (1 g) cumin seed,
   lightly toasted

1 tablespoon (18 g) coarse sea salt

12 cups (3 L) water

FOR THE CHILE PASTE

10–12 chiles chilhuacles negros
   (about 4 oz./125 g total; substitute an equal weight of chiles
   guajillos)

3 chiles mulatos (about 1½ oz./45 g
   total)

1 chile pasilla (about ½ oz./14 g)

1 four-inch (10 cm) stick canela
   (Mexican cinnamon)

6 allspice berries

½ teaspoon (2 g) black
   peppercorns

2 maize tortillas

1 medium white onion
   (10 oz./275 g), quartered

8 medium cloves garlic
   (2 oz./48 g), peeled

6 medium tomatoes zarazones
   (1⅓ lbs./600 g. See notes above;
   substitute 3 each medium Roma
   tomatoes and tomatillos to the
   same total weight.)

2 tablespoons (28 g) Enriched Lard

Although considered one of the most important of the "seven moles of Oaxaca," Chichilo is lesser known outside the region; perhaps its intensity is off-putting to some. According to Diana Kennedy in *The Art of Mexican Cooking*, Chichilo is traditionally made with the *chile chilhuacle negro*, but because of its rarity and expense, many people substitute charred *chiles guajillos*. Doña María's recipe calls for *tomates sarazones*—vine tomatoes just ripening from green to red, a trick that lends the dish its characteristic tartness. A mixture of red tomatoes and tomatillos can achieve the same end. Other recipes for Chichilo call for pork or chicken instead of or in addition to beef, or a combination of all three meats. While some versions specify avocado leaves or *hierba de conejo* (*Tridax coronopifolia*) as a key herbal flavoring, doña María's recipe used *pitiona* (p. 199), which provides a citrusy fresh/floral contrast to the meaty stew. To substitute, a combination of more common herbs can result in the same basic flavor profile.

Prepare-ahead note: Chichilo benefits from an overnight rest in the refrigerator. If you do that, to avoid overcooking the vegetables, omit them in the step described below; on the day you plan to serve the dish, cook them in a pot of boiling water, drain, and add them to the mole immediately before serving.

YIELD: 8–10 SERVINGS

PREPARE THE STOCK

In a large stockpot or Dutch oven, heat the lard until shimmering; working in batches as needed, sauté the beef ribs until well browned; transfer to a platter as you continue.

On a comal, in a cast-iron skillet, or over an open flame, char the onion until blackened in patches. Char the garlic, and in a mortar and pestle, blender, or small food processor, grind the garlic with the cumin seed and salt to achieve a smooth paste. Return the beef ribs to the stockpot, add the onion, cover with the water, and add the garlic paste. Bring to a boil, reduce to a simmer, and continue cooking, uncovered, until the beef is tender, from 1 to 2 hours, depending on the quality of your beef, adding a bit more water as needed.

PREPARE THE CHILE PASTE

While the beef is simmering, remove the stems from the chiles and discard. Slit the chiles open and rescue the seeds. On a gently heated comal or in a cast-iron skillet, toast the seeds a few minutes, moving them constantly, until fragrant and deep golden. Transfer the seeds to a spice mill or coffee grinder adapted for the purpose, and add the *canela*, allspice, and peppercorns; grind the ingredients until very fine and set aside. With the heat on high, toast the tortillas on the comal until blackened in patches; set aside. Toast the chiles until fragrant and slightly darkened in patches (if using *guajillos*, toast until very dark); transfer the chiles to a heatproof bowl and cover them with boiling water. Allow the chiles to soak for 30 minutes as you proceed.

1 pound (500 g) whole new
potatoes or small, waxy potatoes
cut in half

1 pound (500 g) chayote, peeled
under running water if the
skin is tough, and cut into large
cubes about the size of the
potatoes

½ pound (250 g) green beans, tips
and strings removed

¼ cup (15 g) fresh pitiona, coarsely
chopped (substitute dried
pitiona, crumbled; *or* 3 Tbsp./15 g
each fresh mint, chopped,
and chopped lemon verbena
or minced lemongrass; *plus*
1 Tbsp./2 g dried whole Mexican
oregano, lightly toasted and
crumbled)

½ cup (125 g) maize masa either
from nixtamal or prepared from
masa harina according to the
package instructions

1 cup (250 mL) beef stock from
above preparation

FOR SERVING

Lime wedges

Slivered fresh chiles de agua
(substitute any blond chile such
as Anaheim or jalapeño)

White onion cut in half moons
(quartered, then thinly sliced)

Warm maize tortillas

With the comal or cast-iron skillet over high heat, char the onion, garlic, tomatoes (and tomatillos, if using) until blackened in patches and slightly soft. Drain the chiles, reserving the soaking liquid; working in two batches or as needed, place the chiles, ground spices, tortillas, tomatoes (and tomatillos, if using) in a blender along with 1 cup (250 mL) of the chile soaking liquid per batch, and process until very smooth. Strain the mixture through a fine-mesh sieve placed over a large bowl; use a rubber spatula to press through as much of the liquid as possible; any residue should be thick and dry; discard the residue.

In a large, deep saucepan or stockpot, heat the lard until shimmering; pour in all of the strained chile mixture at once: it should sputter and splatter, so stand back. Cook over medium heat, stirring frequently, until reduced by one-third and darkened in color, about 15 minutes; set aside.

THICKEN AND FINISH

When the beef is tender, add the potatoes and chayote to the stockpot and continue cooking another 15 minutes; add the green beans and cook another 6–7 minutes. The potatoes and chayote should be tender and the green beans still a bit al dente. Remove the meat and vegetables to a platter, strain the cooking liquid, and skim off any excess fat. Return the cooking liquid to the stockpot; you should have about 8 cups (2 L) of the stock; drain off any extra and put to another use. Pour the chile mixture into the stockpot and stir to combine; bring to a boil, reduce to a simmer, add the herbs, and continue simmering over low heat as you finish.

Combine the masa with the stock and mash with a fork or potato masher until thoroughly incorporated. With the stockpot at a simmer, pour in the masa mixture, whisking constantly; return to a simmer and stir frequently for 4–5 minutes until slightly thickened; the consistency should be like a cream soup, not batter-like; remove any lumps with a whisk or handheld immersion blender. Return the beef and vegetables to the stockpot and simmer over medium heat another 6–8 minutes to amalgamate flavors.

TO SERVE

Place ribs in individual serving bowls along with vegetables and plenty of the sauce. Accompany with warm tortillas. Diners add squeezes of lime juice, onions, and chiles to taste.

PITIONA/HIERBA NEGRA, PRONTO ALIVIO

BOTANICAL: *Lippia alba* (Mill.) N.E. Br. ex Britton & P. Wilson/Family Verbenaceae
ENGLISH: bushy matgrass, bushy lippia, Oaxaca lemon verbena

Many Oaxacan families have *pitiona* growing on their patios, which is where I first encountered it. In the markets, it appears fresh only on certain days (depending on the reliability of the vendor's supply from home); sometimes in dried form; and occasionally as living plants sold in the company of flowers and other garden ornamentals. *Pitiona* is a tropical American native, ranging from southern Texas into Mexico, Central and South America, and the Caribbean. The multibranched shrub can reach 5 feet (1.5 m) in height; leaves measure ⅜ to 1¹⁄₁₆ inch (1–3 cm) in length and ⅜ to ¾ inch (1–2 cm) in width. The plant's roughly textured leaves are clustered in opposing fashion or in threes.

Flowers with white, pink, or light-purple corollas form on stems measuring ¾ inch (2 cm) in length. Closely related to Mexican oregano and in the same family as lemon verbena, *pitiona* shares several of the flavor compounds of both. Essential oils like piperitone (mint), limonene (lemon zest), geranial (lemongrass), and linalool (cinnamon and mint) give *pitiona* its unique flavor and point to substitutions. *Pitiona* is used in Oaxacan moles, and may be used medicinally for its analgesic, somatic, and sedative properties; it is also being investigated for its antifungal activity as an alternative to synthetic fungicides.

ESTOFADO

CREAMY ANDALUSIAN-STYLE MOLE WITH CHICKEN

TO PREPARE AHEAD
Enriched Lard (p. 530)

FOR BRINING THE CHICKEN
16 cups (4 L) water
½ cup (145 g) sea salt
1 large chicken (about 5½ lbs./
   2.5 kg), cut into serving pieces,
   or an assortment of your
   favorite pieces

FOR THE STOCK
10 cups (2.5 L) water, or just
   enough to cover the chicken
1 medium white onion
   (10 oz./275 g), peeled and
   quartered
6 medium cloves garlic
   (1½ oz./36 g), peeled
2 bay leaves
2 large sprigs fresh thyme
2 teaspoons (12 g) sea salt
¼ teaspoon (0.33 g) black
   peppercorns

FOR THE MOLE PASTE
1 six-inch (15 cm) stick canela
   (Mexican cinnamon)
6 allspice berries
4 whole cloves
1 tablespoon (2 g) dried whole
   Mexican oregano

Doña María's mess of flavoring ingredients. [MR]

[MC]

Creating an English description for this dish was challenging: *estofado* translates literally to "stew," but that doesn't quite capture it. It's rather more like a mole, yet it contains no chiles as so many of them do. Instead, it acquires its flavor from a ground paste featuring Moorish/Andalusian sesame seeds, olives, capers, and almonds, and Asian spices like cloves and cinnamon. And, in medieval Moorish fashion, it is thickened with bread. A strip or two of the requisite pickled chiles brings the delicately sweet, satiny sauce back to Mexico. Doña María's method was streamlined and quite interesting: she prepared all of the ingredients for the mole paste ahead of time quite quickly, and dumped them all together in a large bowl. She took the bowl to a commercial mill, where she had everything ground to a fine paste; you can achieve adequate results with a blender. Doña María's Estofado has a subtle yet noticeable finish of Asian spice. Even though I follow her recipe to the letter, mine never does, so I have taken to adding a bit of ground spices at the end; I list those as optional.

Prepare-ahead note: Estofado may be prepared a day in advance and refrigerated; reheat gently to avoid overcooking the chicken.

YIELD: 8 SERVINGS

BRINE THE CHICKEN
Combine the water and salt and stir until the salt is thoroughly dissolved. Add the chicken and refrigerate for 1–4 hours. (The brining step is optional. See notes about brining in the "Market Fundamentals" chapter, p. 527.)

PREPARE THE STOCK
Remove the chicken from the brining solution and discard the brine. Place the chicken

¼ cup (40 g) sesame seeds

3 medium Roma tomatoes
(10½ oz./300 g)

3 medium tomatillos
(10½ oz./300 g)

6 tablespoons (90 mL) Enriched
Lard, divided (substitute
vegetable oil)

1 large, stale bolillo (2¼ oz./65 g;
substitute French or Italian
bread), sliced into thick rounds

1 medium onion (10 oz./275 g),
sliced

1 large head garlic (1¾ oz./50 g),
separated into cloves and peeled

1 medium bunch parsley
(2¼ oz./65 g)

10 almonds

10 medium pitted green olives

1 tablespoon (12 g) capers, drained

2 tablespoons (20 g) black raisins

FOR FINISHING

1 tablespoon (12 g) sugar

¼ teaspoon (1 g) ground cloves,
optional

¼ teaspoon (1.5 g) ground canela,
optional

16 almonds, blanched

16 medium green olives, whole,
pitted, or stuffed with pimiento

2 tablespoons (24 g) capers,
drained

2 tablespoons (20 g) black raisins

FOR SERVING

Slices of pickled jalapeño, or
Picles (p. 127)

Plain white rice or bolillos

in a large stockpot and add all of the ingredients for the stock. Bring to a simmer and continue cooking for 30–40 minutes or until the chicken is tender. Transfer the chicken to a platter and set aside; strain the stock through a fine-mesh sieve, discarding the contents of the sieve. Set aside 6 cups (1.5 L) of the stock; reserve the rest for another use.

PREPARE THE MOLE PASTE

On a comal or dry cast-iron skillet, briefly toast the first four ingredients until fragrant; transfer to a small bowl to cool. In the same skillet, briefly toast the sesame seeds until pale golden. Place the seeds and the spices in a spice mill or coffee grinder adapted to the purpose, and grind until fine; transfer to a large mixing bowl.

In a large saucepan, cover the tomatoes and tomatillos with water. Bring to a boil, reduce to a simmer and cook 10–15 minutes or until tender but not disintegrating. Using a slotted spoon, transfer the tomatoes and tomatillos to the large mixing bowl with the spices; reserve the cooking liquid.

In a large, heavy skillet, heat 3 tablespoons (45 g) of the lard until shimmering. Working in batches as needed, and in the following order, fry the bread until browned, the onion and garlic until softened, the parsley until wilted, and the remaining ingredients until fragrant. As you finish each batch, transfer all of the ingredients along with any residual lard to the mixing bowl.

Working in batches as needed, purée the ingredients from the mixing bowl in a blender, adding 1 cup (250 mL) of the tomato cooking liquid a bit at a time to keep the blades moving. With a fine-mesh sieve placed over a large mixing bowl, strain the contents of the blender; using a rubber spatula, push through as much of the mixture as possible and add another 1 cup (250 mL) of the tomato cooking liquid a bit at a time to help pass the mixture through. Depending on your stamina, when you finish you may have as much as one-quarter of the paste left; discard the residue.

Heat the remaining 3 tablespoons (45 mL) of the lard in a large skillet until shimmering; pour in the strained mixture all at once: it should sputter and sizzle, so stand back. Cook over medium heat, stirring frequently, until thickened, about 12–15 minutes. The consistency should be like thick cake batter.

FINISH THE SAUCE

Bring 6 cups (1.5 L) of the strained stock to a boil and stir in the mole paste. Over high heat, boil the mixture until thickened (this may take anywhere from 15 to 30 minutes). The consistency should be like thin pancake batter. Add the remaining ingredients and check for seasonings. Transfer the chicken to the sauce and simmer another 3–4 minutes to heat through.

TO SERVE

Plate one piece of chicken per diner and spoon on about 1 cup (250 mL) of the sauce, making sure to distribute the olives, capers, raisins, and almonds evenly. Top each piece of chicken with a slice or two of the pickled chiles. Diners use rice or bread to sop up the aromatic sauce.

[MR]

VILLA DE ETLA

Etla is an unprepossessing town with an unremarkable history, or perhaps it only seems that way, since most of its records have been lost or destroyed. But on Wednesdays—the principal market day—the tiny pueblo of around seven thousand people is enlivened by many thousands more, as people from nearby villages as well as throngs of tourists come to exchange goods or to just marvel at them.

MERCADO MUNICIPAL "PORFIRIO DÍAZ"

A significant percentage of the population in the area surrounding Etla is engaged in agriculture and the management of pasture-fed cattle. Not surprisingly, then, the region has become famous for its cheeses—most produced artisanally—and the market showcases the best of them. In turn, market *comedores* offer a variety of cheesy specialties.

THE CHEESES OF OAXACA

Spheres of compactly wound, taut string cheese resembling balls of cream-colored yarn are a common sight throughout Oaxaca. Known variously as *queso Oaxaca*, *quesillo*, or *queso de hebra* (*hebra* means "thread" or "string"), it is arguably the most popular and famous cheese in the country. Its mild flavor and stringy meltability, much like mozzarella, make it a natural for many uses. Although other cheeses may be employed, *queso Oaxaca* is the de rigueur cheese for quesadillas, practically a Mexican staple. While some claim that Franciscan monks introduced the cheese to the region during the colonial era, food historian Rachel Laudan posits that Italians brought it in the mid-twentieth century as the popularity of pizza surged worldwide. In fact, *queso Oaxaca* is produced in the *pasta filata* style similar to mozzarella: fresh curd from cow's milk gets a hot water bath while it is pulled and stretched like taffy to give it its elastic properties.

An artisanal producer we visited in Reyes Etla, the center of regional production, expressed the difficulties of maintaining high standards. Many competitors' cheeses, she said, from Puebla and other states are made with powdered milk, which deleteriously alters the taste. Furthermore, it takes a full liter of milk to make a ball of cheese that weighs just 8 ounces (250 g), which might explain why so many producers resort to the cheaper substitutions.

SALSA DE QUESO

FRIED CHEESE IN TOMATO SAUCE

TO PREPARE AHEAD
Salsa de jitomate (p. 532)

FOR THE CHEESE
1 tablespoon (15 mL) vegetable oil
8 ounces (225 g) queso fresco
(substitute Monterey Jack), cut
into long bars
1 cup (250 mL) Salsa de jitomate
(p. 532)
1 sprig fresh epazote (substitute
parsley or cilantro)

FOR SERVING
Warm maize tortillas or bolillos
(substitute French or Italian
bread)

Rather than a sauce made of cheese, as the name might suggest, this dish featured two hefty hunks of *queso fresco* that were fried until just oozing, then drowned in a lightly picante tomato sauce. Another version we sampled while in Oaxaca used *queso Oaxaca* and salsa verde (p. 531). Both were delicious. The latter was served to us at breakfast, while the former made a hearty lunch with plenty of *bolillos* for tucking away bits of cheese and for sopping up the flavorful sauce. It is also a great appetizer served with beer or cocktails. Consuela Matadamas of the Comedor "La Fonda" demonstrated the easy preparation method.

YIELD: 1 SERVING AS A MEAL OR 4 SERVINGS AS A SHARED APPETIZER

PREPARE THE CHEESE
In a large nonstick skillet, heat the vegetable oil until shimmering; add the cheese and fry until the cheese begins to soften and lightly brown, about 3–4 minutes, then turn to the other side. Continue to fry an additional 2–3 minutes; pour on the Salsa de jitomate and add the epazote. Bring to a simmer and continue heating until the cheese is very soft to the touch, another 3–4 minutes.

TO SERVE
Use a spatula to carefully transfer the cheese to a serving plate, then pour on all of the salsa. Eat with warm tortillas or bread.

Queso fresco—*"fresh cheese"*—is a salty cow's-milk cheese molded in wooden or reed rings. [MR]

[MC]

ENFRIJOLADAS/ENTOMATADAS

EASY BEAN OR TOMATO "ENCHILADAS"

TO PREPARE AHEAD
Pasta de frijol (p. 154)
Salsa de jitomate (p. 532)

FOR THE "ENCHILADAS"
For the enfrijoladas
1 cup (250 mL) Pasta de frijol, diluted with a bit of water to achieve the consistency of pancake batter
1 tablespoon vegetable oil
3 fresh maize tortillas

For the entomatadas
1 cup (250 mL) Salsa de jitomate
1 tablespoon vegetable oil
3 fresh maize tortillas

FOR SERVING
White onion, thinly sliced and separated into rings
Queso fresco, queso añejo, or Cotija (substitute ricotta, feta, or parmesan), crumbled or grated
Fresh cilantro leaves, coarsely chopped
Salsa verde (p. 531)
Salsa de chile de árbol (p. 531)

One might call these "faux enchiladas." Rather than tortillas bathed in chile sauce like an enchilada, these make use of a bean purée or tomato sauce; and, rather than being rolled, they are simply folded in half on the order of a taco. While they may sometimes feature fillings of chicken, beef, beans, or cheese, they are just as likely to be served simply, as we had them at Comedor "La Fonda." Have either the bean purée or the tomato sauce at the ready, and these dishes can be assembled in mere moments. Both are perfect foils for a hearty topping of tangy cheese. Either may be accompanied by a slice of grilled Cecina (p. 397), chorizo, or chicken for a more substantial meal.

YIELD: 1 SERVING OF EACH FLAVOR

PREPARE THE "ENCHILADAS"
In a large, shallow skillet, heat the bean purée or the tomato sauce, and maintain at a simmer as you continue.

In a separate skillet, heat the vegetable oil until shimmering. Heat a tortilla on one side for just a few seconds until it starts to curl; flip to the other side and heat another few seconds. Using tongs, dip the tortilla in the purée or sauce, and flip to the other side to coat completely. Use the tongs to fold it in half, then transfer to a serving plate. Repeat with the remaining tortillas.

TO SERVE
Spoon on the rest of the purée or sauce, then garnish with onion rings, cheese, and cilantro. Diners add table salsas to taste.

[MC]

[MC]

(above) *The Wednesday market at Etla is so crowded that vendors spill onto stairways and into passageways. One woman sells beautifully decorated breads of* hojaldra *(flaky pastry); at the foot of the stairs another woman sells* agua de chilacayote—*a beverage made of the cooked squash and flavored with* piloncillo *and* canela—*out of a large clay tub.* [ALL PHOTOS BY MR]

THE
GULF
COAST

INTRODUCTION

SEA-LEVEL SWAMPS and marshy coastal floodplains rimmed by the occasional brown sandy shore belie the fact that the Gulf Coast region has been the setting for many important cultural firsts in Mexico. It was here that the Olmecs established what archaeologists have come to consider the first great civilization of Mesoamerica, one that influenced all that were to follow. While cacao and vanilla may have originated beyond the region, it was along the Gulf Coast where both were first cultivated and produced in quantities sufficient for lucrative trade. And in 1519, it was here that the Spanish established Veracruz, the first European city in Mexico. Subsequently, Veracruz became the first great port in the region, the earliest point of entry for a steady flood of colonizers, European immigrants, and African slaves.

During the colonial era, the road between the port of Veracruz and the Spanish capital in Mexico City became a principal trade route of the new colony. Mexican mines and vast tracts of cactus-peppered landscape provided the two most valuable exports of New Spain: silver and red cochineal dye. Other New World products—such as cacao, vanilla, chiles, and myriad others—soon became highly sought after in Europe, and exports soared. Goods flowed both ways in this new trans-Atlantic trade, and the Spanish presence in Mexico assured a ready market for such European products as wheat, rice, and other food plants, as well as sheep, cows, goats, horses, and other livestock. Trade with the Caribbean brought sugarcane and pineapple. Walled cities and turreted fortresses can still be spotted throughout the Gulf region, vestiges of the defenses against frequent pirate attacks waged to seize a seemingly endless flow of valuable cargo. Citizens of Veracruz fought for and eventually gained control of virtually the entire Gulf coastline in order to ensure their port's monopoly.

Much of what we think of as modern Mexican identity was shaped in the Gulf region, for it was here where the first significant *mestizaje*—miscegenation—of indigenous peoples with European and African cultures occurred. The first African Maroon settlement in the New World was established in central Veracruz state in the sixteenth century. Just as newcomers intermarried with indigenous Huastecas, Totonacas, and other Gulf Coast groups, gastronomical marriages took place as native maize, beans, squash, and chiles found their way into European recipes alongside recently arrived Old World ingredients to engender what became some of Mexico's first fusion dishes.

PHYSICAL ENVIRONMENT AND AGRICULTURE

The Mexican portion of the Gulf of Mexico coastline spans 1,743 miles (2,805 km) and forms a natural boundary for the states of Tamaulipas, Veracruz, Tabasco, Campeche, Yucatán, and Quintana Roo (in this book, the last three are considered part of the Yucatán Peninsula). The land that rims the Gulf Coast is characterized by uniformly low-lying terrain, which includes marshes, swamps, and many long, narrow barrier islands, as well as stretches of sandy beach. The coast presents a range of habitats, including submerged vegetation and over 5 million acres of wetlands; there are over thirty major estuarine watersheds in the Gulf of Mexico. Inland, the coastline gives way to piedmont as the land rises to meet the Sierra Madre Oriental and several other smaller ranges; Veracruz is home to Mexico's tallest peak, the Pico de Orizaba, a dormant volcano that reaches 18,491 feet (5,636 m) above sea level.

The dramatically varied landscape—from sea-level swamps to snowcapped peaks—creates a diverse ecology. Fishing is a major industry, with major catches in red snapper, amberjack, swordfish, and grouper as well as shrimp, crabs, and oysters; the states that line the coast are known nationwide for their fine seafood dishes. Farther inland, the piedmont is adorned with cactus species and pastureland, while evergreen tropical forests dominate the more mountainous regions. It is in the piedmont where most agricultural production occurs, with coffee, vanilla, cacao, sugarcane, tobacco, bananas, and coconuts representing important yields; local farmers still depend on the cultivation of maize and beans as well as other traditional Mesoamerican crops. Veracruz grows half of the country's citrus fruit, with the most variety, including limes, oranges, tangerines, mandarins, and grapefruit; it is also the country's leading producer of the Manila mango. Tabasco has extensive areas of natural grasslands, lending itself to widespread meat production, including cattle, pigs, sheep, goats, and domestic fowl.

ETHNOLINGUISTIC GROUPS

Generally considered to be Mesoamerica's first major civilization, the Olmecs originally occupied much of the Gulf Coast region, particularly the states of Veracruz and Tabasco, starting some three thousand years ago. The civilization reached its height around 800 BCE, and by 300 CE, the Mayas had achieved dominion over the region. Incursions from the north brought the Huastecas, Chichimecas, and Otomíes; the Totonacas resided in the north-central area of Veracruz.

Today, three important ethnolinguistic areas subdivide the Gulf Coast region. La Huasteca includes parts of the Gulf states of Tamaulipas and Veracruz, as well as a few adjoining inland states. The region was first inhabited by the Huastec peoples, who still occupy the region, although Nahuas now form the largest block of the indigenous population.

Totonacapan, today much smaller than it was during the pre-Columbian era, defines a region of land that overlaps Veracruz and Puebla. For hundreds of years, the Totonacas have been connected to the growing and production of vanilla (p. 275).

Chontalpa (p. 226) is an area of northwestern Tabasco occupied traditionally by a large percentage of Chontal Mayas; other groups in Chontalpa are Ch'ol, Tzeltal (p. 110), Zapoteca, Nahua, and Tzotzil (p. 69). Chontalpa has traditionally been linked with the cultivation of cacao and the production of chocolate (p. 77).

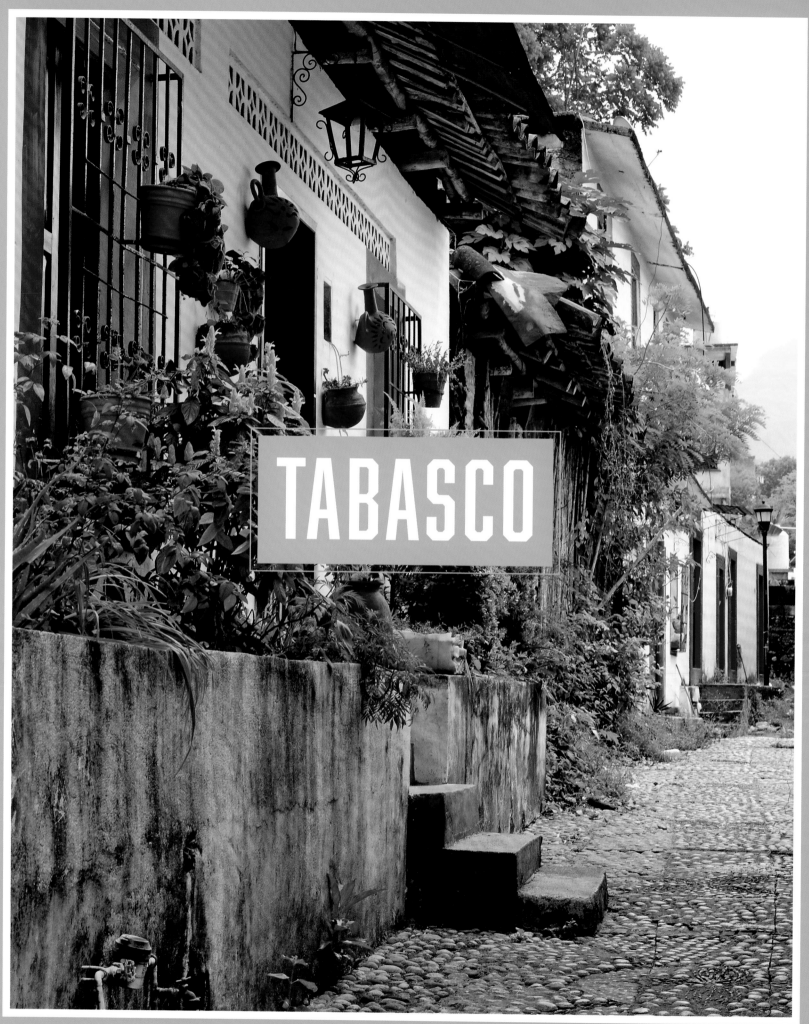

TABASCO

VILLAHERMOSA

Knowing that some of the world's best chocolate lay just a couple of states to the west of my home in Mérida propelled me on a quest that took me to Villahermosa for the first time many years ago. I wanted to use it in my cooking classes, and at the same time I was exploring an itinerary for a culinary expedition along the Cacao Route for my students. While I didn't find the Holy Grail of chocolate in Villahermosa, about an hour north of our base in the city I chanced upon a little hacienda producing an organic version of the prized Criollo variety of *Theobroma cacao*. At 80 percent pure cocoa, this variety hooked me at the first bite, and I continue to source my chocolate there.

An expansive flat green canopy envelops Villahermosa, and that gives it the nickname "Emerald of the Southeast." No matter where you go in the city, you are reminded of the precarious symbiosis of the natural and urban landscapes as an irregular network of roads whisks past flood-prone wetlands, marshes, and lagoons commingled with modern shopping malls and high-rise hotels. And, popping up every now and then above the green are replicas of the colossal basalt heads—their hollow eyes seeming to peer backward in time—that are the hallmarks of the ancient Olmec civilization and that are now the mascots of modern Tabasco.

Hernán Cortés landed here in 1519, establishing at the marshy mouth of the Grijalva River one of the earliest European settlements in mainland America. The harsh tropical monsoon climate and unforgiving landscape drove Cortés westward in search of the legendary gold of Tenochtitlan; the colonists who remained behind eventually moved the settlement farther up river to its present position, and Santa María de Victoria was rechristened Villa Hermosa. The town remained a sleepy backwater until the 1970s, when massive offshore oil deposits were discovered and reversed the state capital's fortunes.

Traditional agriculture has always proven challenging in these sodden soils, but the Olmecs triumphed and also made use of the plentiful marine resources found here. The same is true today, and seafood still plays a leading role in the gastronomy: the "living fossil" fish *pejelagarto* (p. 216) was an important food source and symbol for the ancient peoples of the region, and it continues in popularity today. Just beyond the city limits, groves of sugarcane, bananas, and coconut yield important commercial crops, and closer to the Gulf Coast can still be found many hectares of cacao plantations, just as there were millennia ago, their earthy sweet aroma if not quite reaching Villahermosa, at least beckoning the overnight visitor to a decadent day trip.

Mercado Municipal "José María Pino Suárez"

The first public market in Villahermosa was inaugurated on November 24, 1849, with the name "Gregorio Méndez." It was known for its spotless *puestos* lined with gleaming white tiles. By the turn of the twentieth century, it was renamed Mercado Municipal "José María Pino Suárez" after a Mexican statesman and hero of the revolution. Inaugurated in 1961, the current building, like its predecessor, features high ceilings and expansive banks of openings for air circulation in this hot, humid environment.

Mercado Municipal "José María Pino Suárez," ca. 1900.

The admiral showed to some of the Indians there cinnamon and pepper, and they recognized it, it is said, and by signs told him that in the neighborhood there was much of it.

JOURNAL OF CHRISTOPHER COLUMBUS, NOVEMBER 4, 1492

[MC]

PIMIENTA DE TABASCO/PIMIENTA GORDA, PIMIENTA DULCE, PIMIENTA DE JAMAICA

BOTANICAL: *Pimenta dioica* (L.) Merr./Family Myrtaceae | **ENGLISH:** allspice, Jamaica pepper
NAHUATL: *xocoxóchitl* | **TOTONAC:** *ukún, ukúm* | **MAYAN (YUKATEK):** *nukuch pool, boox pool*

That allspice has so many indigenous names shines light on its prolific use throughout Mesoamerica in pre-Columbian times. The dried berry and the fresh leaf were used in cooking, but the spice's primary use was to flavor the chocolate beverage. *Pimienta de Tabasco*—the only common pantry spice native to the New World—acquired the name "allspice" as early as 1621 when the English described it as having a taste of cinnamon, nutmeg, and cloves combined. Native to southern Mexico and Guatemala, with its natural reach extending into the Greater Antilles, allspice is the dried berry of a large evergreen shade tree that can grow to heights of 23 to 33 feet (7–10 m). The dried berries look like black peppercorns but are twice as large, measuring about ¼ inch (6 mm) in diameter. During his first American expedition, Christopher Columbus spotted allspice in Jamaica, where he mistook it for black pepper (*Piper nigrum*). During the seventeenth century, Dutch and English tradesmen commercialized allspice on a global scale. Since the nineteenth century, the states of Chiapas, Tabasco, and Veracruz have been the primary growers in Mexico, although today Jamaica supersedes all other producers. Allspice is used in many dishes in Mexico, including moles and in pickling formulas, and in Yucatán it is found in several of the regional spice blends known as *recados*.

PEJELAGARTO

TAXONOMIC: *Atractosteus tropicus* T. N. Gill/Family Lepisosteidae | **ENGLISH:** tropical gar

A local saying goes, "If you are talking about *pejelagarto*, you are talking about Tabasco." In fact, the prehistoric-looking fish is such a symbol of the state that its image can be found on everything from carved wooden key rings to coffee mugs. Beyond tourist memorabilia, it has long been a powerful icon among the region's indigenous peoples. In Chontal communities, it is considered an aphrodisiac. In a Chontal tale, a disobedient young man puts on the Lord's cape and unwittingly unleashes fierce storms; only the saliva of the *pejelagarto* constrains him. Among the Huastec, *d'hipak* refers both to maize and to *pejelagarto*, which is thought to have flesh of maize. D'hipak is the deity who must defeat hunger (death) and is the Alpha and Omega of the cosmology, forming the symbol of the first day of their calendar. *Pejelagarto* is described by some as a "living fossil," since its basic physiology has not evolved since it appeared during the Cretaceous period some 100 million years ago. Its elongated form, dramatically pointed snout, and razor-sharp teeth grant it its Spanish name (*lagarto* = alligator). Found in freshwater rivers, lakes, and swampy areas from southern Mexico to Costa Rica, *pejelagarto* is a carnivore that eats smaller fish and even small waterfowl;

in the wild it may reach lengths of over 4 feet (1.25 m) and weigh 45 pounds (20 kg) or more. *Pejelagarto* flesh is white, fine-grained, and soft, somewhat dry, with a delicate flavor; the flesh is laced with many small bones, which can pose a challenge to eating. The scales are diamond-shaped and interlocking, and the skin is so tough that it is sometimes dried and used in place of leather. Substitutes for *pejelagarto* include other freshwater fish such as catfish or trout.

Pejelagarto is most typically consumed roasted (*asado*) and served with chile, salt, and lime juice, folded into a tortilla doused with *mojo de ajo*. Along the side of the road extending about 11 miles (18 km) north of Villahermosa toward Nacajuca can be seen rustic shelters made of wood and thatch where the fish are impaled on long sticks and grilled; piles of both fresh and roasted fish may be found in the markets of Villahermosa. The roasted fish may also be subsequently shredded and fried with other ingredients, then used as a filling for tamales or empanadas. The indigenous Chontal dish *chirmol* features the fish cooked in a distinctive creamy sauce of ground squash seeds and charred tortillas. It is also included in Tortillas gruesas hechas a mano (p. 222) and Pejelagarto en verde (p. 218).

[MC]

(below) After cutting a slit in the tough skin and peeling it away, a waiter deftly separates the delicate flesh from the carcass.

[MC]

PEJELAGARTO EN VERDE

TROPICAL GAR IN HERB SAUCE

FOR THE HERB PURÉE

3 medium tomatillos
(10½ oz./300 g), husks removed
and rinsed

1 medium plantain (9 oz./250 g),
peeled and cubed

2 cups (500 g) chaya (substitute
spinach or kale), chopped

½ cup (30 g) chile amashito leaves
(substitute parsley), chopped

½ cup (30 g) chipilín leaves
(substitute watercress leaves or
pea shoots), chopped

½ cup (250 mL) cilantro, chopped

1 medium green bell pepper
(6½ oz./185 g), seeded and
coarsely chopped

½ white onion (5 oz./137.5 g),
coarsely chopped

2 medium cloves garlic
(½ oz./12 g), peeled and chopped

FOR THE FISH AND SAUCE

8 cups (2 L) water

8 black peppercorns

4 whole allspice berries

2 bay leaves

2 teaspoons (12 g) sea salt

3 pounds (1.5 kg) whole pejelagarto (substitute whole trout or
other freshwater white-fleshed
fish, or catfish steaks, or 6
steaks of any of the above)

½ cup (4½ oz./125 g) masa

FOR SERVING

White rice

Warm maize tortillas

Salsa verde (p. 531)

If not the most attractive dish in the world, Pejelagarto en verde certainly is dramatic, as the snarling, toothy grin of the *pejelagarto* lurches out of a swamp-green puddle of herbed sauce. Traditional recipes call for the inclusion of ingredients not widely available beyond the region—*chaya* (p. 260), *chipilín* (p. 136), and leaves of the *chile amashito* plant (p. 236). I offer acceptable substitutes, and the subtly sweet flavor is worth the minor changes. I'm not sure why the leaves of *amashito* are used, since in scientific tests quantities of capsaicin are virtually undetectable in the plants themselves; perhaps it is the slightly bitter taste that they impart. For this reason, I substitute parsley. Substitutions for the other ingredients are listed below. For the most dramatic effect, use a whole fish, but excellent flavor can still be achieved with more easily manageable fish steaks.

Prepare-ahead note: The herb purée may be made a few hours in advance and refrigerated. Pejelagarto en verde is best served immediately after preparing.

YIELD: 6 SERVINGS

PREPARE THE HERB PURÉE

In a medium saucepan, cover the tomatillos and plantain with water and bring to a boil; continue cooking until both are tender, about 10 minutes. Remove with a slotted spoon and reserve the cooking liquid. Place the tomatillo and plantain along with the remaining ingredients in the bowl of a food processor; add a scant ½ cup (125 mL) of the cooking liquid, and process until thoroughly puréed. Add a bit more of the liquid as needed to create a thick, homogeneous paste. Set aside or refrigerate until time to use it.

PREPARE THE FISH AND SAUCE

Place the water and next four ingredients in a large stockpot; bring to a boil, reduce to a simmer, and add the fish. With the heat on low, continue to simmer for about 10 minutes or until the fish is gently firm to the touch. Remove the fish and strain the cooking liquid through a fine-mesh sieve. Return the cooking liquid to the stockpot and add the herb purée and the masa. Use a potato masher or immersion blender to remove lumps. Continue cooking over medium heat, stirring frequently, until the mixture thickens slightly, about 5–6 minutes. Return the fish to the sauce and simmer an additional 8–10 minutes to amalgamate flavors and to finish cooking the fish. Serve immediately.

TO SERVE

Place the whole fish on a suitably sized platter; bathe with more of the herb sauce. Alternatively, plate individual steaks and spoon on some of the sauce. Serve with white rice and tortillas. Diners add Salsa verde to taste.

*María Hernández Pérez of Restaurante "Astrea" in the market
presents an aptly shaped platter of Pejelagarto en verde.* [MR]

[MC]

TIANGUIS "UNIÓN DE LOS CAMPESINOS"

What originated as a typical *tianguis* with billowing canvas canopies sheltering individual vendors has evolved into a hybrid somewhere between an open-air *tianguis* and a formal market building. Rows of cement blocks define the parameters of the space, while spindly steel columns support an expansive corrugated steel roof. It is one of the most popular markets in town. The overall impression is of one enormous room, in the center of which are throngs of people clinging to civility while wiping their brows and clamoring for prepared foods; around the periphery lies a ragtag labyrinth of produce stands.

(above) Two popular treats in the market: A wooden canoe emblematic of Tabasco is filled with orejitas de mico—small halved papayas cooked in honey or sugar syrup. The name derives from the resemblance of the fruit to the ears of a small monkey. The vendor pours pozole con cacahuate—a sweet beverage made with nixtamal-ized maize and ground peanuts. The two treats are frequently consumed together. [MR] (below, left) Cooks in the market pat out huge disks of masa to form Tortillas gruesas hechas a mano (recipe follows). Each giant pie contains one or more of a wide variety of fillings, including pejelagarto asado. [MR] (below, right) A cook wrestles with heavy griddles where Tortillas gruesas hechas a mano in a range of flavors are sizzling. [MR]

TORTILLAS GRUESAS HECHAS A MANO (CON PEJELAGARTO)

THICK TORTILLA (FILLED WITH TROPICAL GAR)

By far the most popular stall in the market was the Tortillería "La Güera" (Blondie) located squarely in the center of the chaos. Lines of hungry customers clogged the narrow aisles and snaked their way past juice stands and produce in other sections of the market to order quantities of the handmade (*hecha a mano*) thick tortilla (*tortilla gruesa*) to take home or eat on the fly. The attraction of "La Güera" is these huge (about 12 inches/30 cm in diameter), fat tortillas that incorporate an almost limitless list of fillings directly in the masa: *chicharrón*, *salsa mexicana*, *longaniza*, *pejelagarto*. You can mix and match, too. The temptation was to order one of each, but we restricted ourselves to just two: the *salsa mexicana* with *chicharrón*, and the *pejelagarto*. Both recipes call for "Tabascan parsley," or *culantro* (p. 233), but since that may be difficult to find, I suggest a combination of cilantro leaves and ground coriander to simulate *culantro*'s intense flavor. These make wonderful appetizers or cocktail snacks.

[MC]

2 tablespoons (30 mL) vegetable
  oil

½ cup (137.5 g) white onion,
  chopped

2 medium cloves garlic
  (½ oz./12 g), peeled and chopped

½ pound (250 g) pejelagarto (substitute trout, catfish, or other
  mild white-fleshed fish), grilled,
  skinned, boned, and shredded
  (finished weight). (*Note*: The fish
  may be oven roasted, but it is
  best grilled on a gas or charcoal
  grill with smoke provided by
  mesquite wood chips.)

¼ cup (15 g) *culantro*, coarsely
  chopped (substitute an equal
  measure of fresh cilantro leaves
  plus ¼ teaspoon/0.5 g ground
  coriander)

½ teaspoon (3 g) sea salt

⅛ teaspoon (0.625 g) freshly
  ground black pepper

FOR THE TORTILLAS

½ pound (250 g) masa (see notes
  on p. 525)

¼ cup (56 g) Enriched Lard (see
  notes on p. 530)

½ teaspoon (3 g) sea salt

½ medium green bell pepper
  (3¼ oz./90 g), seeded and cut
  lengthwise into julienne strips

FOR SERVING

The chile sauce of your choice

Prepare-ahead note: You may make the fried fish mixture a day in advance and refrigerate. Tortillas gruesas hechas a mano are best served immediately after cooking, although leftovers can be revived by quickly reheating in a bit of lard or oil.

YIELD: 6 SERVINGS (1 LARGE TORTILLA)

PREPARE THE FISH

Heat the vegetable oil in a large skillet; add the onions and garlic and cook, stirring frequently, until the onions are translucent. Add the fish and stir to combine; add the remaining ingredients, stir, and cook until all moisture has evaporated. Check for seasonings and set aside.

PREPARE THE TORTILLA

In a large mixing bowl, combine the masa with the lard (your hands are the best tools for this job). Add the fish and salt and mix to thoroughly combine; check for seasonings.

Have ready a 12-inch (30 cm)-diameter nonstick skillet. Extend a sheet of plastic wrap over a plate larger than the skillet. Place the masa mixture on the plastic and pat out to form a thick round. (The disk will be about ½ inch/1.25 cm thick.) Place the skillet upside down over the plate and carefully invert the plate and skillet together so that the masa falls into the skillet; peel away the plastic. Press six of the bell pepper strips into the top of the masa radiating out from the center. Place the skillet over medium heat, and cook the tortilla until well browned on the bottom, about 4–5 minutes. Place a plate over the skillet and invert; slide the tortilla back into the skillet and continue cooking another 4–5 minutes or until well browned. Using a small, sharp knife, cut a tiny slit in the surface to see if the masa is cooked through and firm; if not, continue cooking another minute or two. Transfer the tortilla to a cutting board and allow to cool for 5 minutes; cut the tortilla into six wedges, leaving the pepper strips in the center of each slice. Serve immediately.

VARIATION

Tortillas gruesas hechas a mano (con salsa mexicana)/Thick Tortilla (Filled with Rustic Tomato Sauce): One day in advance, prepare your own *salsa mexicana* with seeded and diced tomatoes, chopped onion, chopped *chile serrano*, chopped *culantro* (or the substitute suggested above), lime juice, and a pinch of salt. On the day of making the tortilla, drain the salsa and combine 1 cup (200 g) of it with the prepared masa. Form the tortilla as described above; slice 2 medium *chiles serranos* (20 g total) across the width, and arrange 12 of the pieces on top so that each wedge of the finished tortilla will have 2 chile pieces. Cook and serve as described above. For another variation, mix ½ cup (22 g) of crumbled *chicharrón* with the masa and salsa.

[MR]

COMALCALCO

THE UNPREPOSSESSING TOWN of Comalcalco just 45 miles (60 km) north of Villahermosa belies its ancient importance as a major Maya trade center. Because of its key location in the Chontalpa region (p. 226), archaeologists believe that the center must have been involved in the trade of cacao. Since it was and remains the westernmost outpost of the expansive Maya region, Comalcalco probably also served as a significant gateway for Maya merchants to the Aztecs of the Central Highlands. The ancient city of Comalcalco, now an important archaeological zone, lies just a few kilometers from the modern town; it is unique in that it is the only major city of Mesoamerica to be constructed of bricks rather than limestone. Today, Comalcalco is a tourist destination and stopover for the popular Ruta del Cacao (p. 226). Cacao is still a major product in the municipality, with Comalcalco accounting for some 20 percent of Tabasco's output.

MERCADO "27 DE OCTUBRE"

Mercado "27 de octubre" has been in the same location since the town was founded in 1820; the most recent incarnation of the building was inaugurated in 1974. While the Villahermosa market is much larger, I was thrilled by this market's variety of unique plants, ingredients, and prepared foods not found in the metropolis, most of them brought to market daily from outlying pueblos by indigenous vendors. The market receives its mysterious name from the date in 1838 when the remains of Agustín de Iturbide—complicated hero of the independence, president, emperor—were transferred to Mexico City and interred in the cathedral there.

*Cacao blossoms and a nascent cacao pod at Hacienda Cacaotera
Jesús María in Comalcalco.* [MC]

One hundred leagues from this city is a
province called Chontalpa, which is very rich
in a fruit named cacao, which is very valuable
in this country of New Spain.

BISHOP JUAN IZQUIERDO TO PHILIP II, 1599

CHONTALPA REGION

AT THE TIME OF European contact, the
Chontalpa region in the northwestern
quadrant of the modern state of Tabasco was the
dominant player in Mesoamerica's production
and commercialization of cacao, rivaled only by
the Soconusco region in southern Chiapas. The
Chontal Mayas who inhabited the area took
advantage of its sea-level elevations, tangled
river network, and alluvial plains to develop an
extensive canoe-borne trade route that traced
the Yucatán Peninsula and reached as far south
as commercial centers in Honduras. Trade
marched overland, too, and even entered the
Central Mexican Highlands. The commodity—
and coin—that stoked this highly lucrative trade
apparatus was cacao. Today, Tabasco accounts
for 70 percent of the national production of
cacao, and Comalcalco—a Late Classic (600–
900 CE) Chontal Maya trade node—remains
a principal supplier. La Ruta del Cacao (Cacao
Route) links several important nineteenth-
century cacao haciendas where visitors can
experience the production of chocolate, from
the cacao fruit to bars and beverages.

Top left to bottom right: malanga, camote, *yuca, and* makal. [MC]

MAYA ROOT VEGETABLES

While widespread catch phrases like "the three sisters" popularize the importance of the synergistic Mesoamerican crops of maize, beans, and squash, in fact the typical pre-Columbian Mexican milpa probably contained close to one hundred unique species. Among those were a variety of root vegetables that contributed essential nutrients, carbohydrates, and fiber to the diet.

Culinary uses are the same as those for other starchy root vegetables: they may be boiled and mashed, sliced and fried, or, because of their high starch content, they may be used in ways similar to—and substituted for—wheat flour.

MALANGA/MACAL, YAUTÍA

BOTANICAL: *Xanthosoma sagittifolium* (L.) Schott/
Family Araceae | **ENGLISH:** new cocoyam, tannia, yautia
MAYAN: *makal* | **TOTONAC:** *shashaca-titlaque, pisis*

CAMOTE

BOTANICAL: *Ipomoea batatas* (L.) Poir./Family Convolvulaceae
ENGLISH: sweet potato | **MAYAN:** *is, xmóorado iis*

YUCA

BOTANICAL: *Manihot esculenta* Crantz/
Family Euphorbaceae | **ENGLISH:** yuca, cassava
MAYAN: *ts'íim* | **TOTONAC:** *kgoxkgewi*

MAKAL/MACAL

BOTANICAL: *Xanthosoma yucatanense* Engl./Family Araceae
ENGLISH: elephant ear | **MAYAN:** *kukut makal, xmaca*

TORREJITAS DE YUCA

SWEET YUCA PANCAKES

FOR THE PANCAKES

1 pound (500 g) yuca

2 eggs

½ cup (125 mL) sugar

2 ounces (½ stick/56 g) butter, softened

2 tablespoons (16 g) all-purpose flour

1 teaspoon (2 g) cornstarch

1 teaspoon (4 g) baking powder

½ teaspoon (1.5 g) ground canela (Mexican cinnamon)

⅛ teaspoon (0.75 g) sea salt

Vegetable oil for frying

The puzzlement of what to do with stale leftover bread has led to culinary innovation since bread was invented. In the United States, French toast is one manifestation, as is bread pudding; France has *pain perdu* and Spain its *torrijas*. By now, this sweet treat has spread throughout Mexico and Central and South America and may be called *torrijas* or *torrejas*. In the case of Tabasco, it is called "little *torrejas*" and substitutes cheaper and more plentiful yuca for the bread, retaining only the taste, appearance, and name of the original. Instead of refreshing stale bread in a milk-and-egg mixture, a small pancake of sweetened yuca is formed and fried. It may be eaten as is, sprinkled with sugar and canela, or bathed in sugar syrup or honey on the order of pancakes or French toast. Thanks to an abundance of yuca throughout the Gulf region, Torrejitas de yuca may also be found in Veracruz.

Prepare-ahead note: The yuca mixture may be prepared in advance and refrigerated overnight; bring to room temperature before frying. In the market, Torrejitas de yuca are served at room temperature, but they are best consumed immediately after frying.

YIELD: 6—8 SERVINGS

PREPARE THE PANCAKES

Peel the yuca and cut it into fist-sized pieces; cut each piece in half lengthwise and remove the coarse fiber that runs through the center. To avoid discoloration, place each peeled piece in a bowl of cold water as you continue working. Thoroughly drain the yuca and finely grate it into a large mixing bowl. Add the remaining ingredients except for the vegetable oil, and beat with a wooden spoon to combine.

[MC]

Honey or pancake syrup
(optional)

Heat ½ inch (1.25 cm) vegetable oil in a large skillet until shimmering. Spoon approximately 2 heaping tablespoons (42 g) of the yuca mixture into the hot oil; repeat until you have formed 3–4 pancakes. Cook approximately 2 minutes or until browned on the bottom, then flip to the other side. Transfer pancakes to paper towels to drain, and serve immediately.

VARIATION

Torrejitas de plátano verde/Sweet Plantain Pancakes: This is another little cake that is very typical of this banana-rich region. Replace the yuca with an equal weight of peeled underripe plantains. Serving suggestions are the same.

[MR]

BANANAS IN TABASCO

Just about anywhere you go in Tabasco you are likely to see gently fluttering banana trees (*Musa × paradisiaca* L./Family Musaceae), their fragile leaves shredded to fringe by Gulf winds. They grow along roadsides and stand like columns beside regal estates and rustic huts alike. But their most dramatic appearance is in the acres and acres of commercial banana plantations that trim the shoulders of highways and extend to the horizon, their clustered fruits gathered into neon blue plastic bags to protect them from fungi, insects, and bruising.

Tabasco is second only to Chiapas in production of bananas, accounting for 25 percent of national yield. Mexico's largest banana export company, San Carlos Tropical Exports, is based in Tabasco. There are eight varieties of banana grown in Mexico; in Tabasco the principal varieties are Cavendish Gigante, Tabasco, and Macho (or plantain);

the two most consumed varieties beyond Mexico are the Cavendish and Tabasco. All banana species are divided into two main categories: dessert bananas (sweet, consumed as hand fruits), and cooking bananas (starchy plantains, known in Spanish as *plátano macho*). Plantains factor prominently in the cuisine of Tabasco.

Bananas are thought to have originated in southern Asia. In the fifteenth century, Portuguese navigators and slave traders introduced bananas to the Canary Islands, and from there to Brazil and the Antilles. Bananas reached Mexico for the first time in 1554, when Vasco de Quiroga—first bishop of Michoacán—brought saplings from Santo Domingo. Today, Mexico is the world's tenth-largest exporter of bananas; 80 percent of banana imports to the United States are from Mexico.

IXGUÁ

SWEET MAIZE CAKE

Described as a savory corn cake from Tabasco by Diana Kennedy in *My Mexico: A Culinary Odyssey*, Ixguá also comes in a sweet version, like this one we spotted in Comalcalco. Similar to its cousin, it is made of fresh corn recently cut from the cob. It is also sometimes made with yuca, and its Mayan name suggests yet another recipe, since it translates to "sweet potato bread" (*íis* = sweet potato, *waaj* = bread). The texture is dense, more like cheese than bread; the large, thick slabs sold in the market are meant to be sliced and shared.

Prepare-ahead note: Ixguá keeps up to one week under refrigeration.

YIELD: APPROXIMATELY 10 SERVINGS

FOR THE CAKE

Banana leaves (substitute parchment paper)

6 cups (1 kg) fresh maize kernels (preferably field corn, about 8 medium ears)

1 stick (4 oz./113 g) butter, softened

¾ cup (150 g) sugar

1 egg, beaten

½ teaspoon (2.5 mL) Mexican vanilla extract

¼ teaspoon (0.75 g) ground canela (Mexican cinnamon)

⅛ teaspoon (0.75 g) sea salt

¾ cup (115 g) raisins

PREPARE THE CAKE

Preheat the oven to 350°F (179°C). Prepare a 9 by 5 by 3-inch (23 × 13 × 8 cm) loaf pan: Line the pan with banana leaves, making sure to allow ample leaves extending up the sides and over the top for covering.

Place the corn kernels in the bowl of a food processor, and process until thoroughly puréed and smooth. In a large mixing bowl, use an electric mixer to cream the butter and sugar until pale yellow; add the beaten egg and continue to beat until well blended. Add the corn purée and the next three ingredients and beat to combine. Fold in the raisins; pour the mixture into the prepared loaf pan. Cover the top with the leaf extensions.

Bake the Ixguá for 45 minutes; open the leaf extensions to reveal the cake; carefully place a plate over the top and invert to remove the bread. The bottom should be golden brown. Slide the cake back into the pan, cover the top with the leaves and continue baking another 45 minutes or until the top is golden brown. Unmold the bread, remove the leaves, and allow to cool to room temperature.

TO SERVE
In Tabasco, slices are consumed with the fingers. Although not traditional, slice and serve plated with fresh strawberries or other fruit.

Penchuque is a large, thick tortilla that may be eaten plain with a meal, much like a standard tortilla, but it is more commonly dressed with refried beans, coconut, or chicharrón. *We enjoyed ours simply, with a bite of* chicharrón *alternating with a bite of the tortilla.* [MR]

Above foreground: Chinín. In the background are bundles of dried cornhusks used for wrapping tamales. [MR]

CHINÍN/CHININI, CHININE, AGUACATILLO, AGUACATE DEL MONTE

BOTANICAL: *Persea schiedeana* Nees/Family Lauraceae | **ENGLISH:** wild avocado | **MAYAN:** *oon, koyó, koyokté*
NAHUATL: *pahua* | **TZELTAL:** *iw, tsits* | **TOTONAC:** *lhx'pu*

While it is not likely that you will find this wild avocado as the basis for guacamole, it is common in the markets to see people peeling them, cutting away a thin slice, and popping it onto a tortilla to eat with salt and chile, taco-style. The *chinín* is thought to be the ancestor of modern avocado varieties. The flesh tastes similar to the domesticated avocado, slightly buttery but a bit sweeter; easily removable fibers run through the pulp and can be eaten, but many people choose to pick them out. *Chinín* fruits range in size and shape from that of the common avocado, to large, crook-necked specimens like those seen in the photo. Color runs from pale to dark green, brownish purple, or black, depending on variety and ripeness. Like some other avocado species and much like leaves of the bay laurel, which is a relative, leaves of the *chinín* tree may be used in cooking, particularly to flavor beans and tamales; the leaves bear a slight taste of anise. *Chinín* trees are small to medium sized, growing to 13 to 50 feet (4–15 m). Wild avocado is a typical cloud forest species appearing at elevations of 2,625 to 5,250 feet (800–1,600 m).

[MR]

[MR]

HOJA DE TO'/HOJA BLANCA, HOJA BLANCA DE TÓ, PLATANILLO

BOTANICAL: *Calathea lutea* (Aubl.) E. Mey. ex Schult./
Family Marantaceae | **ENGLISH:** cigar calathea,
Mexican cigar plant, Havana cigar | **MAYAN:** *to'*

This large-leaf tropical plant is put to many uses in its native habitat, reflected in its taxonomy and common names. The Mayan word *to'* translates to "wrapper" or "container," and indeed an impermeable waxy coating on the underside of the leaf makes it suitable for fashioning waterproof baskets or roofs for makeshift shelters. The leaf is frequently used to wrap tamales and other foods, in Tabasco particularly for *barbacoa* and a popular pork dish known as *mone de cerdo*. In one market stall, we saw it used as a wrapper for fresh cheeses. Native to broad swaths of Central America and northern South America, the Antilles, and southeastern Mexico, *Calathea lutea* grows in humid forests in swampy zones or along riverbanks at low or medium altitudes. The plant is an evergreen perennial species that reproduces by means of rhizomes. Reaching heights of 6½ to 13 feet (2–4 m), *Calathea lutea* is defined by 12 to 40-inch-long (30–100 cm) ovate leaves that come to an abrupt point; 4 to 12-inch (10–30 cm) flowers are actually spirally arranged bracts that are initially yellow and, with time, turn a reddish-brown or bronze color. In many places *Calathea lutea* is prized as an ornamental for both its handsome foliage and its long-lasting blooms.

PEREJIL/PEREJIL RANCHERO, PEREJIL DE TABASCO, CILANTRÓN, CULANTRO

BOTANICAL: *Eryngium foetidum* L./Family Apiaceae
ENGLISH: Tabascan parsley, Mexican coriander, serrated
coriander, saw-tooth coriander, long coriander

In Tabasco, some cooks say that if you truly love someone, you will use *perejil* in their soup or stew instead of cilantro or parsley. In fact, *Eryngium foetidum* tastes rather like a combination of the two herbs, although it is considerably more pungent than either. The Latin *foetidum* means "stink" or "bad odor." Thank heavens for taxonomies, or we would be hopelessly lost amid the myriad nomenclatures for this aromatic herb. In fact, *perejil* in Spanish translates to "parsley," but in Tabasco the word may be used to refer to both herbs, most particularly to *Eryngium foetidum*. In the United Kingdom, "coriander" is the preferred term for the leaves of the plant we call "cilantro" (*Coriandrum sativum*), but in the United States we reserve the word "coriander" for the seeds. In vintage cookbooks, *culantro* and cilantro are often used interchangeably (and confusingly), even though the former is a New World native, while the latter is an Old World specimen, probably originating in western Asia and southern Europe, where it grows wild. *Eryngium foetidum* is a biennial herb with long, serrated, and oblanceolate (with the pointed end at the base) leaves forming a basal rosette; it can grow up to 12 inches (30 cm) in length, with leaves reaching 1½ inches (4 cm) in width. The herb is a native to the tropical Americas and the Antilles, but in recent times it was taken to Southeast Asia, where it remains very popular in many dishes such as the Vietnamese noodle soup, *pho*.

DULCE DE COCO Y PIÑA

CHEWY COCONUT AND PINEAPPLE BARS

FOR THE BARS

1 cup (200 g) pineapple, finely crushed and thoroughly drained

1 cup (75 g) unsweetened flaked coconut

½ teaspoon (2.5 mL) Mexican vanilla extract

¼ teaspoon (1.5 g) sea salt

1 cone (250 g) piloncillo, grated (substitute 1 cup/256 g muscovado or dark brown sugar)

4 tablespoons (60 mL) corn syrup

8 tablespoons (112 g) salted butter, melted

These dark brown slabs attracted our attention primarily because of the leaves that separated them to prevent their sticking together. Our vendor told us that the leaves were *almendro de la India*, or "Indian almond" (*Terminalia catappa* L.), an introduced species now found in many regions of Mexico but particularly along the Gulf Coast and in the Yucatán Peninsula. Plentiful coconut and pineapple of the region form a happy marriage in this addictive, chewy treat, bound by *piloncillo*—unrefined sugar—cooked to the point of caramelization.

Prepare-ahead note: Dulce de coco y piña keeps well in an airtight container for about one week.

YIELD: 1 DOZEN BARS

PREPARE THE BARS

Combine the first four ingredients in a mixing bowl and set aside. Butter a 9 by 13-inch (23 × 33 cm) sheet pan and set aside.

In a large saucepan, preferably copper, combine the *piloncillo* or brown sugar with the corn syrup; with the saucepan over high heat, maintain vigilance as the sugar begins to melt; swirl the pan frequently to dissolve the sugar. Continue cooking and swirling over high heat until a candy thermometer reaches the hard-ball stage at 265°F (129°C) and syrup is a dark brown color. Remove from the heat source and very slowly and cautiously drizzle in the melted butter, stirring constantly. Add the pineapple-coconut mixture and continue to stir for about 5 minutes or until the mixture stiffens and cools slightly. Turn into the prepared sheet pan and spread to cover completely. When cool, slice into 12 equal bars. Store in an airtight container with the bars separated by waxed paper to prevent their sticking together.

[MC]

MARAÑÓN/ANACARDO, NUEZ DE LA INDIA

BOTANICAL: *Anacardium occidentale* L./Family Anacardiaceae
ENGLISH: cashew apple, cashew

Because cashew nuts are expensive, few people in Mexico other than the wealthy have experience with them, much less know that they come from the *marañón*, pictured above. Instead, this pseudo-fruit is enjoyed as a hand fruit, or more typically juiced and used to make *aguas frescas*; in some places, it is cooked with sugar to make a conserve or dried on the order of prunes. The actual fruit—the cashew nut itself—grows inside a hard outer shell, which appears on the tree first and later develops the fleshy, pear-shaped peduncle or receptacle, considered by botanists to be a "false fruit," known as the cashew apple. An oil inside the seed is highly caustic, requiring special technology to extract it and reach the nut, making it a labor-intensive and expensive exercise, such that not every country where *marañón* grows capitalizes on the valuable cashew. In Mexico and many other growing regions, the hard nut is twisted off and discarded, and the cashew apple consumed. A native of Amazonia, the tree was dispersed by the Portuguese in the sixteenth century, taken first to Mozambique and India and later to other tropical zones around the globe, including southeastern Mexico, where significant production is found today in Tabasco and Campeche. Its Spanish name, *nuez de la India* (Indian nut), derives from the fact that until recent times, the greatest production of the cashew nut occurred in India; today, Vietnam is the world's leading producer. The cashew apple has a thin, fragile skin and is highly perishable, making it difficult to transport; the flesh is sweet and juicy, quite tannic and fibrous; the taste is vaguely reminiscent of peaches. It ranges in color from bright yellow to red-orange, and may be 2 to 4½ inches (5–11.25 cm) in length. The bushy, low-branched, spreading tree may reach heights and widths of 35 feet (10.5 m). *Marañón* is related to mangos and poison ivy; those who exhibit allergies to either or to tree nuts should avoid consuming *marañón*.

[MC]

Achiote (Bixa orellana, p. 45) is a pungent seed used as a flavoring and coloring in various states of the republic, although most prolifically in the Gulf Coast and Yucatán Peninsula. In Yucatán, it is ground with garlic, salt, and herbs like oregano and bound with water, Seville orange juice, or vinegar to form a paste known as recado de achiote or recado rojo. In Tabasco, however, the seed is soaked in water, ground, and strained to form an intensely pungent paste known as pasta de achiote. It is so concentrated that a little goes a long way; for this reason it is sold in tiny cubes. Similar to its use in Yucatán, it is used to color and impart an earthy flavor to various stews and soups such as Cazuela de mariscos (p. 237) as well as meats, tamales, and other foods.

CHILE AMASHITO/CHILTEPÍN

BOTANICAL: *Capsicum annuum var. aviculare* Dierb. syn. *C. annuum var. glabriusculum* (Dunal) Heiser & Pickersgill/Family Solanacea | **ENGLISH:** bird pepper
NAHUATL: *cilchilli* | **TOTONAC:** *laktsupín*
CHONTAL: *amash, amax, mash* | **MAYAN (YUKATEK):** *maax iik*

Descendants of this ancient chile (*Capsicum annuum* L.) can be found throughout the Mexican republic, assuming different names from region to region. (See, for example, *chile de Simojovel*, p. 91.) As the *chile habanero* is the "mascot chile" in Yucatán, the diminutive *amashito* is the chile of choice for most *tabasqueños*. It is incorporated into everything from simple salsas to thick moles and the maize beverage pozole; it is also served whole as an accompaniment to many foods. Hardly any meal is served without *salsa de chile amashito*, which is prepared by grinding the whole chiles (sometimes roasted) with vinegar or lime juice and a pinch of salt. The taste is described as smoky, with hints of citrus and almond. The chile ranges from 30,000 to 50,000 Scoville Heat Units, making it several times hotter than the serrano, which weighs in at a meager 10,000 to 30,000. Nonetheless, the *chile serrano* may be used as a substitute.

[MR]

CAZUELA DE MARISCOS

GRATINÉED SEAFOOD STEW

FOR THE CHILE PURÉE

2 chiles guajillos (about
  ½ oz./13 g), seeds and veins
  removed

1 tablespoon (30 g) chile amashito
  (substitute chile piquín), or to
  taste, lightly toasted

3 medium Roma tomatoes
  (10½ oz./300 g), charred

1 medium white onion
  (10 oz./275 g), peeled and
  charred

6 medium cloves garlic
  (1½ oz./24 g), peeled and charred

1 teaspoon (7 g) pasta de achiote
  (see p. 236; substitute 1 table-
  spoon/16 g commercial recado
  de achiote)

While combining seafood and cheese may be sacrilegious in some cultures, in Mexico there are happily no such restraints, as witnessed in this hearty stew finished with gratinéed *quesillo* cheese on top. Because of its inclusion of the beloved *chile amashito*, the stew packs quite a zing, but heat can be controlled by the amount used. I list all of the seafood varieties our stew included, but you may use the mix that suits your fancy. David Álvarez, cook and owner of Puesto "Marisquería Álvarez," shared the recipe with me.

Prepare-ahead note: You may prepare the chile purée a few hours or a day in advance and refrigerate until time to use it. The stew is best consumed immediately after finishing.

YIELD: 6—8 SERVINGS

PREPARE THE CHILE PURÉE

In a heavy skillet, toast the *guajillos* until fragrant and just beginning to darken; remove the chiles from the heat and cover them with hot water. Allow the chiles to soak for 10 minutes. Drain the chiles, reserving the soaking liquid, and transfer them to the jar of a blender. Working in batches as needed, purée the remaining ingredients with the chiles until very smooth, adding ½ cup (125 mL) of the soaking liquid or a bit more to keep the blades moving. Set aside or refrigerate until ready to use.

[MC]

FOR THE STEW

2 tablespoons (30 mL) Spanish
  olive oil
8 cups (2 L) fish stock (substitute
  bottled clam juice or shrimp
  bouillon)
1 sprig fresh thyme (substitute
  ½ tsp./.5 g dried whole thyme)
3 pounds (1.5 kg) assorted seafood
  (raw shrimp, cooked octopus or
  squid, cubed whitefish fillets,
  clams, lump crabmeat or legs or
  claws)
2 tablespoons (30 mL) fresh lime
  juice

FOR SERVING

Queso quesillo (also known
  as queso Oaxaca; substitute
  mozzarella), grated
Chopped white onion
Chopped cilantro
Lime wedges
French bread or tortillas

PREPARE THE STEW

In a large stockpot, heat the olive oil until shimmering. Pour in the chile purée all at once; it should sputter and sizzle, so stand back. Cook over low heat for 5–6 minutes or until slightly darkened. Pour in the fish stock and stir to combine; add the thyme and bring to a boil. Cook for 3–4 minutes to amalgamate flavors; reduce the heat to simmer and add the seafood. Cook on low heat for 4–5 minutes or until the shrimp and fish fillets are cooked through. Add the lime juice and serve immediately.

TO SERVE

Ladle the stew into individual heatproof bowls or ramekins. Sprinkle on about 2 tablespoons (25 g) of the cheese and place under a broiler; gratinée until the cheese is bubbling and just beginning to brown. Diners add onion, cilantro, and squeezes of lime juice to taste.

A fisherman with his haul of
cangrejos *(crabs).* [MR]

TAPIJULAPA

DRIVING ALMOST DUE south from Villahermosa, we are saluted by legions of commercial palm-oil palms that stand at attention along the highway, strictly positioned in well-disciplined rows. Eventually, the soggy sponge of alluvial flatlands dotted with bobbing white cranes heaves upward and reaches a height of 2,952 feet (900 m) above sea level at the peak known as El Madrigal—the highest point in Tabasco—today veiled in mist. We have now entered the State Reserve of the Sierra de Tabasco, a range that is part of the Sierra Madre del Sur, which extends well into Chiapas. Fifty miles (80 km) later, we arrive at Tapijulapa, a dreamy mountain jewel that propels the frenzied modernity of Villahermosa from our minds.

Settlement of Tapijulapa dates to sometime in the fifth or sixth century CE, when Zoques from northern Chiapas migrated to the region; there is still a strong Zoque influence here. Registered as a Pueblo Mágico in 2010, the town is enjoyed for its tranquil cobblestoned streets, whitewashed houses with brick-red trim and red tiled roofs, and pots of flowering plants that grace every façade.

Produce and other goods are strewn casually along the street, forming an ad hoc market. Vendors arrive at dawn, and most of the selling is completed by 10:00 a.m. [MR]

MERCADO MUNICIPAL DE TAPIJULAPA

Although streets are not restricted to traffic, there is so little of it that everyone walks fearlessly in the middle of the road. In fact, the municipal market occupies a couple of blocks of a cobbled street, located at the foot of a building where poultry and other meats are sold. Peek through the open doors of any one of a number of homes, and you will see artisans crafting all kinds of goods from wicker.

(above) A young vendor offers totopostes, *large, crispy maize tostadas that measure upward of 15 inches (38 cm) in diameter. Some were sprinkled with sesame seeds; others were almost black from the inclusion of mashed beans in the masa. They are consumed as is or fashioned into Pishul.* [MR] *(below) Chayotes, chard, and spring onions in the Tapijulapa market.* [MR]

PISHUL

GIANT TOSTADA "SALAD"

The original Zoque version of this dish simply features a large *totoposte* smeared with refried beans and sprinkled with a handful of *chiles amashitos* (p. 236). Doubtlessly influenced by the popularity of pizza—even in this remote mountain enclave—the list of ingredients has now swelled to include shredded pork or chicken, shredded lettuce, onion rings, slices of tomato, crumbled *queso fresco*, chopped cilantro, and a generous anointing of Mexican *crema*; *salsa de chile amashito* is served on the side. We tried cutting the tostada into wedges à la pizza, but it was so crispy that it broke apart hopelessly, leaving us to scoop up the commingled contents and pile them onto our plates, eating it with a fork rather like a Cobb salad. You may create something similar to Pishul by forming individual servings atop a single tostada. Or for those with skills at making tortillas, make your own whopping *totoposte* by forming a 15-inch (38 cm) round of maize masa, the same thickness as a standard tortilla; cook on a comal, then fry in a bit of hot oil until crispy. Toppings are suggested above, but use your imagination—always with the primordial base of refried black beans.

[MR]

EMPANADAS DE CALABAZA (CON CHAYA)

SQUASH TURNOVER PASTRY (WITH "TREE SPINACH" FILLING)

Like several foods in this diminutive town, the empanadas we had were ironically supersized: a full 8 inches (20 cm) long. The unusual thing about these empanadas, other than their scale, is that they are made with a pastry dough into which roasted squash has been kneaded. This adds a delicately sweet flavor that sets off the filling, in this case the nutty, leafy green vegetable known as *chaya* (p. 260), or refried beans.

Prepare-ahead note: The empanadas may be assembled and fried a couple of hours in advance; reheat on a comal or skillet immediately before serving.

YIELD: 1 DOZEN

FOR THE FILLING

6 cups (48 oz./1.37 kg) chaya (substitute kale or chard), cut into chiffonade ribbons

2 tablespoons (30 mL) vegetable oil

½ medium white onion (5 oz./137.5 g), finely chopped

2 medium cloves garlic (½ oz./12 g), peeled and finely chopped

1 medium Roma tomato (3½ oz./100 g), seeded and finely chopped

1 teaspoon (10 g) chile amashito, finely chopped (substitute 1 medium chile serrano, seeded and finely chopped)

½ teaspoon (0.325 g) dried whole Mexican oregano, lightly toasted and ground

½ teaspoon (3 g) sea salt

¼ teaspoon (1.25 g) freshly ground black pepper

FOR THE DOUGH

1 pound (500 g) winter squash such as butternut, Hubbard, or pumpkin, seeds removed

One-half recipe for the empanada pastry dough found on page 63

FOR FRYING THE EMPANADAS

Vegetable oil for frying

Local calabaza criolla *is a key component of the pastry dough for these empanadas (foreground). The* totoposte *(right) acquires its earthy color from black beans.* [MC]

PREPARE THE FILLING

Parboil the *chaya* in salted water for 15 minutes; drain into a fine-mesh sieve and press firmly to extract as much liquid as possible; set aside.

In a large skillet, heat the vegetable oil until shimmering; add the onions and garlic and cook over medium heat until the onions are translucent, 4–5 minutes. Add the tomato and *chaya* and continue cooking over medium heat until all of the moisture has evaporated and the mixture has become quite dry. Add the remaining ingredients, stir, and cook an additional 2 minutes to amalgamate flavors. Remove from the heat and allow the mixture to cool thoroughly.

PREPARE THE DOUGH

Preheat the oven to 350°F (179°C). Place the squash on a baking sheet and cover loosely with aluminum foil. Bake until the squash is very tender, about 1 hour, depending on the size. Allow to cool, then remove the rind; purée the flesh in a blender or food processor, and set aside. Follow the instructions for preparing one-half recipe of the pastry dough found on page 63. Knead the masa thoroughly with the puréed squash. Cover with a damp towel until you are ready to use it.

FORM AND FRY THE EMPANADAS

Follow the instructions on page 63 for forming and frying the empanadas. For these, divide the pastry dough into 12 equal balls, each weighing about 4 oz. (120 g); flatten the dough into a circle measuring approximately 8 inches (20 cm) in diameter. Fill and fry as directed, using about 2 heaping tablespoons (35 g) of the filling for each empanada. Serve with the chile sauce of your choice.

VARIATION

Empanadas de calabaza (con frijol)/Squash Turnover Pastry (with Bean Filling): Proceed as instructed above, using approximately 1½ cups (360 g) refried black beans for the filling.

TAMAL DE MASA COLADA

STRAINED MASA TAMALE WITH CHICKEN AND CHILES

TO PREPARE AHEAD
Enriched Lard (page 530)

FOR THE SAUCE

5 chiles pasillas (about 1½ oz./45 g)

3 chiles guajillos (about ¾ oz./20 g)

3 chiles anchos (about 1 oz./33 g)

1 medium Roma tomato
  (3½ oz./100 g), charred

½ medium white onion
  (5 oz./137.5 g), charred

3 medium cloves garlic
  (¾ oz./18 g), peeled and charred

1 teaspoon (6 g) sea salt

2 tablespoons (30 mL) vegetable
  oil

Several versions of this delicate tamale may be found throughout the Yucatán Peninsula and Gulf Coast region. In Yucatán, it is sometimes called *tamal de boda* because its exquisite fineness makes it an appropriate delicacy for weddings; and in Veracruz, it is known as *tamal de cuchara* because it is so tender that it may be eaten with a spoon. In Tabasco, as its name implies, Tamal de masa colada acquires its delicateness from the fact that the standard maize masa is strained (*colada*) to creamy perfection to remove all fine bits of pericarp and germ that may remain from the kernels. Further, the strained masa is diluted and cooked much like *atole* until it thickens; it is then spooned or poured onto a piece of banana leaf before being filled, wrapped, and steamed, such that the finished tamale has actually been cooked twice. In Yucatán, it is most typically filled with pork and an achiote-tinged, maize-thickened "gravy"; in Tabasco, the fillings were shredded chicken and a three-chile sauce. With the additional step of straining, this tamale is somewhat more labor intensive than most, but you will surely agree that its refined, pudding-like quality is worth the effort.

Prepare-ahead note: Tamal de masa colada may be made well ahead of time and frozen; to reheat, steam 1 hour prior to serving.

YIELD: 1 DOZEN TAMALES

PREPARE THE SAUCE

Remove the stems, veins, and seeds from the chiles; toast them on a comal or in a heavy skillet until they are fragrant and just beginning to darken. Transfer the chiles to a heatproof bowl and cover with boiling water; allow them to soak for 20 minutes, then drain, reserving the soaking liquid.

[MC]

2 medium cloves garlic
   (½ oz./12 g), peeled

4 cups (1 L) chicken stock or
   bouillon

4 cups (1 kg) masa (see p. 530)

1 cup (250 mL) water

1 teaspoon (6 g) salt, or to taste
   (optional)

½ cup (112 g) Enriched Lard,
   melted

FOR GARNISHING, WRAPPING,
AND FINISHING

12 pieces banana leaves, cut to
   approximately 10 by 16 inches
   (25 × 40 cm)

About 1 cup (300 g) cooked,
   shredded chicken

FOR SERVING

Salsa de jitomate (p. 532)

Place the chiles and the next four ingredients in a blender; add ½ cup (125 mL) of the soaking liquid and process until you achieve a smooth purée, adding more of the liquid as necessary to keep the blades moving freely. Pour the purée through a fine-mesh sieve into a mixing bowl, and with a rubber spatula, press through as much of the purée as possible; discard any dry residue that remains in the sieve.

Heat the vegetable oil in a large, heavy skillet until shimmering; pour in all of the chile purée at once; it should sputter and sizzle, so stand back. Cook over medium heat, stirring frequently, until the mixture is slightly thickened and darkened in color, about 5–6 minutes. Remove from the heat and set aside.

PREPARE THE MASA

In a medium saucepan, simmer the garlic in the stock until soft, about 15 minutes. Remove the pan from the heat; using a handheld immersion blender or a standard blender, process until the garlic is thoroughly puréed. Combine the stock with the masa in the saucepan. Working with a potato masher or the immersion blender again, mix thoroughly to remove any lumps.

Pass the masa mixture through a fine-mesh sieve placed over a clean saucepan. Using a rubber spatula, mash the contents of the sieve, pressing through as much liquid as you can. After you have pressed through about half of the liquid, add the cup (250 mL) of water to the sieve and continue to press through; discard any residue. Check seasonings, adding salt, depending on the saltiness of your stock.

Bring the liquid to a boil, stirring constantly. As it reaches the boil, it will begin to thicken dramatically. (Use an immersion blender again if lumps form.) Using a wooden spoon, beat vigorously as you gradually drizzle in the lard. Reduce the heat to low; continue cooking and beating another 8–10 minutes, or until the mixture is stiff, thick, and satiny, resembling polenta. The masa will start pulling away from the pan and will hold its shape when dropped from a spoon; remove from the heat.

GARNISH, WRAP, AND FINISH

Arrange the prepared banana leaves on a work surface horizontally before you. When the masa has thickened, immediately pack some of it into a ½-cup (120 g) dry measure and turn onto one of the banana leaf sections. Center about 1 heaping tablespoon (25 g) of the shredded chicken on top of the masa, then spoon on 1 tablespoon (15 mL) of the chile sauce. Fold the bottom edge of the banana leaf over the tamale; repeat with the top edge. Use your hands to firmly compress the tamale on the sides and shape it into a rectangle. Fold the left edge of the leaf under the tamale and tuck tightly; repeat with the right edge. Repeat with the remaining leaves, masa, and fillings. Set aside until you have completed all of the tamales.

Arrange the tamales in a *vaporera* (see p. 539) and steam for 1½ hours. Remove the tamales from the steamer and allow them to cool at least 15 minutes before serving.

TO SERVE

The tradition in Tabasco is to open the leaves, leaving the tamale in its place and eating it with a spoon. Diners add Salsa de jitomate to taste.

VERACRUZ

FARO

VENUSTIANO
CARRANZA

Port of Veracruz, nineteenth century.

HEROICA VERACRUZ

T**HE DOMINANT PHYSICAL FEATURE** of Heroica Veracruz is its expansive port. Directions are given referencing it, and *veracruzanos* often use the term *el puerto* (the port) to differentiate the city from the state. Tourists throng the *malecón* to watch the frequent military parades and marching bands (this is the home of the Mexican navy, and the national naval academy is on an adjacent peninsula) or simply to take photos in front of the kaleidoscopic 3-D Veracruz sign. Towering cranes lift containers onto and off of a steady armada of cargo ships.

During the three-hundred-year colonial era, Veracruz was the principal port of Mexico. Fired by rumors of gold, the Spanish conquistador Hernán Cortés launched an expedition from Cuba to the Gulf port in 1519 and arrived on Good Friday. In honor of the holy day (and always with an eye on more profane matters) he dubbed it Villa Rica de la Vera Cruz (Rich Town of the True Cross). In short order, he and his soldiers had drafted a city council, and Vera Cruz soon received the mainland's first coat of arms, granted by Carlos V. But the lure of riches proved too strong, and by November Cortés had left the sweltering coastal plain and marched overland to enter the Valley of Mexico to begin the conquest of the Aztec capital of Tenochtitlan. This history, combined with its natural location, made Veracruz a communication hub that linked the Central Highlands with the rest of the world, a role it continues to play into the twenty-first century.

The port also had its nefarious side. The riches loaded onto ships bound for Spain became a frequent target for pirate attacks. And, it was a tragic gateway for thousands of slaves brought from Africa to work in the lucrative sugar-cane fields: at one point, Veracruz had more slaves than any other state in Mexico. The term *tercera raíz* (third race) has arisen to explain the African presence in Veracruz alongside Spanish and indigenous peoples. A positive impact of these heinous circumstances was felt in the gastronomy. African staples like yams and black-eyed peas were soon appearing in regional recipes; and curiously, New World foods like yuca, *malanga*, peanuts, and sweet potatoes that had been taken to West Africa by early explorers eventually made the round-trip journey back home, pausing briefly in the Antilles. These foods, combined with plentiful seafood, lead many people to say that the cuisine of Veracruz is more closely akin to Afro-Caribbean gastronomy than to that of the rest of Mexico. Spanish-inspired dishes like *huachinango a la veracruzana*—red snapper with olives and capers—and indigenous foods like Zacahuil (p. 284)—an enormous roasted tamale—round out the menu.

Live jaibas *(blue crab,* Callinectes sapidus Rathbun*) are kept immobile by palm-leaf ties.* [MR]

Fishermen often pray at this shrine of the Virgin of Guadalupe to ensure safety—and a good haul—while on the open seas. [MR]

MERCADO "PESCADERÍA PLAZA DEL MAR"

Housed for many years in the city's historic center near the port, the Pescadería Plaza del Mar was relocated (in fact forcibly; many vendors fought the move) in 2007 about ten minutes outside the urban core. Trucks arrive with fresh fish loaded on shaved ice early every morning, and men with ice-filled wheelbarrows and huge plastic crates distribute it to the vendors, all of whom line the periphery of what seems to be a veritable gallery of seafood. Vendors sing "¡Hay hueva! ¡Hay hueva!" (Fish roe for sale!) and "¿Qué va a llevar?" (What will you be taking with you today?). Sprinkled here and there amid the displays of fish, and upstairs, too, are *comedores* whose proprietors buy the fish and prepare some of the best seafood dishes you are ever likely to taste.

[MR]

CHILPACHOLE DE JAIBA

BLUE CRAB AND CHILE STEW

Apart from the famed and ubiquitous *huachinango a la veracruzana* (Veracruz-style red snapper), Chilpachole de jaiba must surely be the state's most iconic seafood dish. The name derives from Nahuatl: *chilli* = chile + *patzolli* = mashed and softened between the fingers. Plentiful blue crabs from the Gulf are simmered in a picante broth of tomatoes and *chiles chipotles*; the broth is slightly thickened at the end of cooking with a bit of maize masa. By all accounts, fresh epazote is essential for this dish, but you may have no choice but to opt for the substitutions I note below. This same recipe also serves for shrimp (preferably whole, shells intact), or a mixture of the two. This and the following recipes were shared with me by Socorro Cruz, the owner of "Coctelería 'El Coquito.'" She and her entire family work together to make this one of the most popular eateries in the market.

Prepare-ahead note: You may prepare the broth a day in advance and refrigerate; reheat, add the crabs and/or shrimp, and thicken immediately before serving.

YIELD: 6 SERVINGS

FOR THE BROTH

3 dried chiles chipotles, stems,
  veins, and seeds removed
4 medium Roma tomatoes
  (14 oz./400 g), charred and
  peeled
½ medium white onion
  (5 oz./137.5 g), charred
4 medium cloves garlic
  (1 oz./24 g), peeled and charred
3 tablespoons Enriched Lard
  (see notes on p. 530; substitute
  Spanish olive oil)
12 cups (3 L) fish stock (substitute
  bottled clam juice or shrimp
  bouillon)
1 three-inch (7.5 cm) stick canela
  (Mexican cinnamon)
4 allspice berries
3 large sprigs fresh epazote
  (substitute 1 large sprig each of
  parsley and cilantro)
Sea salt to taste

FOR THE SEAFOOD AND FINISHING

6–12 blue crabs (Allow 1–2 crabs
  per serving, depending on size.
  Blue crabs weigh on average
  5½ oz./155 g, but of course sizes
  can vary. As noted above, you
  may substitute an equal weight
  of whole shrimp, or combine
  the two.)
½ cup (125 g) maize masa

FOR SERVING

Lime wedges
Warm tortillas, French rolls,
  or other bread

PREPARE THE BROTH

On a comal or in a heavy skillet, lightly toast the chiles until fragrant and slightly darkened; transfer to a bowl and cover with hot water; allow to soak for 20 minutes, then drain, reserving the soaking liquid.

Place the drained chiles and the next three ingredients in the jar of a blender, and process until thoroughly puréed, adding just enough of the soaking liquid to keep the blades moving freely. In a large skillet, heat the lard until shimmering; pour in the purée all at once: it should sputter and sizzle, so stand back. Cook over medium heat until slightly thickened and darkened, about 4–5 minutes.

In a large stockpot, bring the fish stock or bouillon to a boil; reduce to a simmer; add the tomato purée and the remaining ingredients. Continue cooking at a simmer for 5–6 minutes to amalgamate flavors. Check seasonings, adding salt to taste (depending on your stock, you may not need to add salt).

PREPARE THE SEAFOOD AND FINISH

Clean the crabs: Using metal tongs, turn the crab onto its back; with an icepick or sharp, thin knife, pierce the shell at the top point of the triangle, known as the "apron." Pull away the apron and discard. Pull away and discard the sponge-like gills located on either side of the legs; cut the crabs in half lengthwise and rinse under cold running water to remove the innards. (Further instructions for how to clean blue crabs can be found in other books or online.)

With the stock at a simmer, add the crabs; continue cooking for 8–10 minutes. Ladle about 2 cups (500 mL) of the stock into a heatproof bowl; add the masa and mash with a fork or potato masher until the ingredients are thoroughly combined. Pour the masa mixture into the stockpot and stir or whisk quickly to avoid lumps. Simmer an additional 5–6 minutes, stirring frequently, until slightly thickened.

TO SERVE

Place one or two crabs in a deep plate or individual serving bowl; ladle in some of the stock. Diners add squeezes of lime juice to taste. Bread or tortillas are used for sopping up the flavorful stock.

CAMARONES AL AJILLO

SHRIMP WITH GARLIC AND CHILE

FOR THE SHRIMP

½ cup (125 mL) Spanish olive oil
10 medium cloves garlic
  (2 oz./60 g), peeled and thinly
  slivered
5 chiles guajillos (about 1¼ oz./
  33 g), stems, seeds, and veins
  removed and cut across the
  width into thin rounds
1½ pounds (680 g) large or jumbo
  whole shrimp (Allow about
  4 oz./115 g per person, or the
  quantity you desire.)
½ teaspoon (3 g) sea salt

FOR SERVING

The rice of your choice (plain
  white rice is typical)
A simple salad of shredded
  lettuce, sliced tomato, onion
  rings, and avocado slices
Lime wedges
Warm maize tortillas

The name is simply a contraction of two Spanish words: *ajo* = garlic, and *guajillo*, a particular kind of chile. The *al ajillo* style is so ubiquitous in Mexico that there is probably no species of creature in the wide ocean that has not been treated to this cooking method: thin slices of garlic and *chile guajillo* are sautéed in olive oil, to which mixture the seafood is added for quick cooking. The garlic-chile oil that is left over is used to garnish the plated seafood. This is a great dish that can be prepared in twenty minutes or less.

YIELD: 6 SERVINGS

PREPARE THE SHRIMP

In a large skillet, heat the olive oil until shimmering; add the garlic and chiles and cook, stirring frequently, until the garlic is translucent. Add the shrimp, stir to cover with the olive oil, and cook an additional 3–5 minutes (depending on the size of your shrimp) or until the shrimp are pink and opaque. Take care not to overcook. Sprinkle on the salt and serve immediately.

TO SERVE

Plate the shrimp and spoon on some of the garlic-oil-chile mixture to garnish. Serve with rice and salad if desired, along with lime wedges and warm tortillas.

[MC]

ARROZ A LA TUMBADA

MIXED SEAFOOD AND RICE IN CHILE BROTH

FOR THE CHILE BROTH

2 dried chiles chipotles, stems, veins, and seeds removed

3 chiles anchos (about 1 oz./33 g), stems, veins, and seeds removed

4 medium Roma tomatoes (14 oz./400 g), charred and peeled

½ medium white onion (5 oz./137.5 g)

4 medium cloves garlic (1 oz./24 g), peeled

3 tablespoons Enriched Lard (substitute Spanish olive oil)

10 cups (2.5 L) fish stock (substitute bottled clam juice or shrimp bouillon)

1 sprig fresh epazote (substitute flat-leaf parsley or cilantro)

Many people accurately describe this dish as being something like paella, but soupier. The colorful legend of its invention dates to the early twentieth century: A crew of fishermen spent many days on the high seas, successfully filling their boat. As was typical of the era, provisions onboard included coffee, salt, lard, rice, and water crackers. When the crew finally returned to shore one late afternoon, as per custom one of the men was charged with preparing a meal using the ship's provisions as well as a selection of the seafood that had been caught. The man voted to the task remains nameless for the history books, but it is a refrain in the story that he—like all the others—was something less than an experienced cook. He took some of the rice and heated it in a tin that contained some residue of lard; when he saw that it was cooking very quickly, he threw in a mixture of seafood, followed by a generous quantity of water and some salt. He then occupied himself with helping the other crew members unload more of the haul and prepare it for sale. When he suddenly remembered the rice cooking on the wood fire, he rushed over and added more water to keep it from burning. Trying to avoid another similar occurrence, he removed the cooking utensil from the fire and set it aside. After the work on the boat had been completed, the crew members started clamoring for their supper. Our unwitting cook checked the pot and saw that the rice had not absorbed all of the liquid. No matter, the crew said, we'll eat it anyway. And of course they loved it. When asked what his secret was, our cook replied that the dish must be *tumbada*—laid down or set aside—in other words, removed from the fire and allowed to rest. Obviously, the dish has experienced some embellishments since the story ended. You may use any combination of mollusks, shellfish, or fish you like, although ours at "El Coquito" included blue crab, shrimp, and octopus.

Prepare-ahead note: The chile broth for Arroz a la tumbada may be prepared a day in advance and refrigerated. Half an hour before serving, reheat the broth and prepare the rice; add the seafood moments before serving.

YIELD: 6–8 SERVINGS

PREPARE THE CHILE BROTH

On a comal or in a heavy skillet, lightly toast the chiles until fragrant and slightly darkened; transfer to a bowl and cover with hot water; allow to soak for 20 minutes, then drain, reserving the soaking liquid.

Place the drained chiles and the next three ingredients in the jar of a blender, and process until thoroughly puréed, adding just enough of the soaking liquid to keep the blades moving freely. In a large skillet, heat the lard until shimmering; pour in the purée all at once: it should sputter and sizzle, so stand back. Cook over medium heat until slightly thickened and darkened, about 4–5 minutes.

In a large stockpot, bring the fish stock or bouillon to a boil; reduce to a simmer; add the tomato purée and the epazote. Continue cooking at a simmer 5–6 minutes to

FOR THE RICE AND SEAFOOD

3 tablespoons Enriched Lard
   (substitute Spanish olive oil)
2 cups (14 oz./400 g) long-grain
   white rice, rinsed and thoroughly air-dried
½ medium white onion
   (5 oz./137.5 g), chopped
4 medium cloves garlic
   (1 oz./24 g), peeled and finely
   chopped
2 pounds (1 kg) mixed seafood
   (any combination of clams or
   mussels, shrimp, crab, cubed
   whitefish, cooked octopus, or
   squid)

FOR SERVING

Frijoles de la olla (p. 530), optional
Warm maize tortillas
Lime wedges

[MR]

amalgamate flavors. Check seasonings, adding salt to taste (depending on your stock, you may not need to add salt).

PREPARE THE RICE AND SEAFOOD

In a deep clay *cazuela*, casserole, or stockpot, heat the lard until shimmering. Reduce the heat to medium, add the rice, and stir to coat with the fat; continue cooking over medium heat until the rice turns opaque, about 3–4 minutes. Add the onions and garlic, stir, and continue cooking and stirring until the onions are transparent, about 3–4 minutes. Pour in the chile broth and bring to a boil; reduce the heat and simmer for about 15–20 minutes or until the rice is just tender. Add the seafood in stages (crab first, followed by shrimp and whitefish; add mollusks and cephalopods moments before finishing) and simmer until the seafood is just cooked and heated through.

TO SERVE

In many places in Veracruz, the clay *cazuela* used for cooking is brought to the table, and diners help themselves. Alternatively, scoop some of the rice into individual serving bowls or deep plates; distribute pieces of the seafood evenly, and ladle on a generous portion of the broth. Serve black beans in a separate bowl on the side if desired, along with the warm tortillas. Diners add squeezes of lime juice to taste.

RÓBALO ENCHILPAYADO

SNOOK IN PICANTE AÏOLI SAUCE

FOR THE AÏOLI

6 medium cloves garlic
  (1½ oz./36 g), peeled

2 teaspoons (10 mL) *plus* 3 tablespoons (45 mL) fresh lime juice,
  divided

⅛ teaspoon (0.85 g) sea salt

2 egg whites

1⅓ cups (330 mL) neutral vegetable oil (canola, safflower)

2 tablespoons (30 mL) cold water

1 teaspoon (7 g) chiles chilpayas
  (substitute 1 chile habanero,
  seeds and veins removed)

The tiny *chile piquín*, known by so many names in the different regions of Mexico, is here known as *chile chilpaya* in its fresh, green form. It lends quite a zing to this creamy egg-white aïoli, so best add in stages, tasting as you go along. Fishing restrictions in some parts of the United States may require looking for a substitute for the snook, such as sea trout, whiting, rock sole, or cobia. Alternatively, the sauce is served with a wide variety of seafood in Veracruz (octopus and shrimp, among others), and you may elect to do the same.

Prepare-ahead note: The aïoli may be made a day in advance and refrigerated. Poach the fish and finish the sauce immediately before serving.

YIELD: 6 SERVINGS

PREPARE THE AÏOLI

Place the garlic, 2 teaspoons (10 mL) lime juice, and the salt in the jar of a blender. Process 2–3 seconds to break up the garlic; stop the motor, push the garlic down toward the blade with a spatula, and repeat. The garlic does not have to be finely chopped to continue.

[MC]

(above) Róbalo (Centropomus *spp.* Lacépède, 1802) in the market. A native of the Americas found in rivers and estuaries as well as in the Atlantic, the Caribbean, and the Gulf of Mexico, róbalo *(also robalo or snook) is easily spotted thanks to a dark gray stripe that runs along the side of the fish from head to tail. Flesh is white and mild tasting with a tender, flaky texture.* [MR] *(below) The Cruz family. Socorro is in the light blue shirt at right.* [MR]

2 cups (500 mL) fish stock
(substitute bottled clam juice or
shrimp bouillon)

2 bay leaves

4 black peppercorns

2 pounds (1 kg) skinless snook fillets (6 fillets of about 5 oz./160 g
each; substitutes: see above)

4 tablespoons (60 mL) heavy
cream

FOR SERVING

White rice

Salad of shredded lettuce, sliced
tomatoes, onion rings, and
avocado slices (optional)

Add the egg whites to the blender jar. Process for 1 minute, scraping down the sides of the jar periodically as needed. Process an additional 1½ minutes until the emulsion turns white and creamy and bits of garlic are no longer visible. With the motor running, through the feedhole of the blender lid, slowly drizzle about one-quarter of the oil in a thin stream, aiming for the center where the blade is. Scrape down the jar and repeat two more times. When you get to the last quarter of the oil, drizzle in the remaining lime juice and the rest of the oil simultaneously. If you go slowly, your emulsion should hold together; if it separates, transfer half of it to a small bowl; add one more egg white to the mixture in the blender and process until it becomes creamy, then return the emulsion you removed. Process until smooth.

With the motor off, pour the water into the blender jar and stir. (Because the emulsion is thick and oily, the water will sit on top unless stirred to mix.) Once the water is incorporated, purée on high until the mixture becomes light and fluffy, about 30 seconds. Add the chiles and process until bits of them are no longer visible. Transfer the aïoli to an airtight container, and refrigerate until ready to use.

PREPARE THE FISH AND FINISH

In a broad, shallow skillet, heat the first three ingredients until just simmering. With the heat on low, add the fish fillets and poach gently, turning once if necessary, until springy when pressed with your finger, about 4–5 minutes, depending on the thickness of your fillets. Transfer to a warm platter and reserve the poaching liquid.

In a small saucepan, heat ½ cup (125 mL) of the poaching liquid over low heat until simmering; stir in the cream and the aïoli and whisk to combine thoroughly. Keep warm until time to serve.

TO SERVE

Arrange the fish fillets on individual serving plates and spoon on some of the sauce. Accompany with rice and salad if desired.

[MR]

MERCADO "HIDALGO"

Inaugurated in 1923, Mercado "Hidalgo" underwent a major overhaul in 2016, turning it into Mexico's first and only market with "green technology": a battery of 448 solar panels powers the air conditioners located in the area where meats, chicken, and fish are sold.

(above) A couple selling cruceta (Acanthocereus tetragonus *[L.] Hummelinck*). In the same family as the nopal cactus (p. 418), cruceta is so named for the form of its cross-shaped vertical trunk and branches. Culinary uses are the same as for the nopal, or it may be prepared and sold in adobo. [MR] *(below)* A market vendor sorts leaves of hoja santa. [MR]

They have a small tree with soft branches containing much sap, whose leaves they eat as a salad, tasting like cabbage and good with plenty of fat bacon. The Indians plant it wherever they make their homes, and then have the leaves for gathering the whole year.

FRAY DIEGO DE LANDA, 1566

[MC]

[MC]

HOJA SANTA/HIERBA SANTA, MOMO, ACUYO

BOTANICAL: *Piper auritum* Kunth/Family Piperaceae
ENGLISH: Mexican pepperleaf, root beer plant
MAYAN: *x'makulan* | **NAHUATL:** *axihuitl* | **TOTONAC:** *jina, jinaj*

Hoja santa is part of the large botanical family that includes black pepper. Native to tropical Mesoamerica, the plant is a large bush that may grow as much as 6 feet (1.8 m) in height. Ear-shaped leaves may reach 12 inches (30 cm) or more in length. Large specimens of the plant may be seen along roadsides throughout southeastern Mexico, and many people locate the plants next to the house in order to protect the floppy, fragile leaves from strong winds. A high content of the essential oil safrole is found in the leaves, giving them a delicate aroma and flavor that has been compared to sassafras, anise, black pepper, or nutmeg. In its native region, *hoja santa* is used prolifically in the cuisine, particularly in Tabasco and Veracruz. Most commonly, the pliable leaves are used as wrappers for fish or tamales; in Oaxaca they are ground with other ingredients in the preparation of *mole verde*. In traditional medicine, the leaves may be used as an analgesic, or to treat asthma, stomach ailments, or bronchitis.

CHAYA

BOTANICAL: *Cnidoscolus acontifolius* (Mill.) I. M. Johnst., *C. chayamansa* McVaugh/Family Euphorbiaceae
ENGLISH: tree spinach, cabbage star
MAYAN: *chaay, chay, chaykeken*

Among the indigenous populations throughout its native region of distribution, *chaya* is often the principal source of the nutrients found in green leafy vegetables. With high levels of protein, Vitamin C, calcium, and other vitamins and minerals, *chaya* is two to three times more nutritious than chard or spinach. Believed to have originated in the Yucatán Peninsula, *chaya* spread to eastern Mexico and Central America; it is also cultivated from northern Mexico to Guatemala and today even in parts of tropical Africa and the southern United States. In the same family as poinsettia, *chaya* is a large shrub or small tree that can grow to 20 feet (6 m) in height. Leaves that resemble the maple leaf feature three to five lobes and can reach 4–12 inches (10–30 cm) in length. Very fine, almost invisible stinging hairs can make the wild plant difficult to handle, although the cultivated variety, *C. chayamansa*, has few if any of the hairs; when stems or branches are broken, the plant releases a milky latex that can irritate the skin. In addition, *chaya* contains toxic cyanogenic glycosides that convert to cyanide upon tissue damage, but a few minutes of cooking over high heat destroys the chemical. *Chaya* is widely consumed in southeastern Mexico. It may be chopped and mixed with scrambled eggs, or with maize masa to form small tamales; in Yucatán, leaves may be used as wrappers for tamales or for ground meat in the Lebanese community for a dish on the order of stuffed grape leaves. In Tabasco, it is puréed to make a cream soup, or simply chopped and added to broth along with maize masa dumplings that include the chopped leaves. In Veracruz, it is chopped and added to *puchero vaquero*, a stew featuring salt-dried beef. *Chaya* may be found year-round in the markets, although it is more abundant during the rainy months of June through November.

In the Puesto "Tacos el Huastequito," a pot of fresh pápalo is placed alongside pickled onions and salsas, and served with tacos of carne enchilada and cecina. The delicate herbaceousness of the leaves gracefully counterbalances the heartiness of the meats. [MC]

PÁPALO/PAPALOQUELITE

BOTANICAL: *Porophyllum ruderale* (Jacq.) Cass./Family Asteraceae | **ENGLISH:** pore leaf, Bolivian coriander, summer cilantro | **NAHUATL:** *papaloquilitl* | **TOTONAC:** *chapawat*

Another of Mexico's pantheon of *quelites*, pápalo is a tropical and subtropical annual native to the Americas. In much of its range it is considered a weed. The name derives from the Nahuatl: *papalotl* = butterfly + *quilitl* = wild edible plant. Mature plants may reach heights of 5 feet (1.5 m) and a diameter of 3 feet (1 m). Small, oval, blue-green leaves measure between 1 and 2½ inches (2.5–6 cm) in length. Described as tasting like a combination of cilantro, arugula, and rue (alluding to a likely substitution), the leaves of *pápalo* are used fresh, not cooked, mixed with salsas, or used as a garnish. In many markets, the fresh herb is kept close at hand so that diners may pinch off leaves to scatter on top of tacos and other foods. In traditional medicine, it has been used to treat liver problems; recent studies suggest that it may help reduce cholesterol and high blood pressure.

[MC]

COATEPEC

Less than half an hour south of the state capital of Xalapa, in the shadows of the volcanic peaks of the Sierra Madre Occidental, at 4,100 feet (1,250 m) above sea level, Coatepec is often shrouded in fog or drenched in rain.

The entire region surrounding Xalapa, Xico, and Coatepec is dense with lush vegetation and is a prime growing zone for coffee as well as mango and sugarcane. Coatepec vies with its two neighbors for the title "coffee capital of Mexico," although that title should have been conferred a few decades ago on Chiapas, today the country's largest producer and exporter of coffee (p. 80). Still, residents cling to the banner and boast that their coffee is of superior quality. In fact, coffee growing in Mexico got its start in Coatepec, when in the late eighteenth century the first

plants were brought from Cuba and the Dominican Republic; some eighty years later, coffee had become a major economic activity in Veracruz. Coatepec hosts an annual coffee festival each May. Originally a Totonac settlement, Franciscans built the first church and established a Spanish village in the 1500s. Andalusian-style houses with beautiful interior gardens garnered the town the distinction of a Pueblo Mágico in 2006, and 370 buildings of historic value lent the town Mexico's prestigious distinction as a National Historic Heritage site.

Herbal remedy "pharmacy" in the market. [MR]

MERCADO "MIGUEL REBOLLEDO"

As in Tabasco, we found the most unique ingredients in smaller, more remote pueblos like Coatepec. In the Mercado "Miguel Rebolledo," we located several rare plants that we had not seen elsewhere.

There are trees that they call Iczotl; they are thick, the bark is black or auburn, like the bark of a palm, and they have leaves almost like palm leaves; it is a flabby tree with a tender pith, it has very white flowers, almost like those of the palm; but it doesn't produce any fruit. They used them to place in front of their sacred altars.

BERNARDINO DE SAHAGÚN, 1540–1585

[MR]

XONEQUI/CHONEQUI, CHONEGUI

BOTANICAL: *Ipomoea dumosa* (Benth.) L. O. Williams/
Family Convolvulaceae | **ENGLISH:** jalap
NAHUATL: *xonequelite*

Another in the long list of Mexico's *quelites*, *xonequi* is rare to find in the market, appearing only occasionally when a vendor happens to gather it in the wild or harvests some from a backyard plot. The Nahuatl name derives from *xonacatl* (onion) and *quilitl* (wild edible plant). Other species in the genus include sweet potato and morning glory, the latter a known psychoactive; the closely related *I. purga* has been used for centuries as a purgative and vermifuge. Another variety has spines and is called *cilantro del monte* (wild cilantro). Considered endemic to Veracruz, *Ipomoea dumosa* is a perennial climber or creeper with stems that can reach 6½ to 15 feet (2–5 m) in length. Heart-shaped leaves that come to a sharp point are meaty and have a faint taste of cilantro. Red-to-purple or pink-to-purple flowers appear in December through January. Culinary uses include cooking the leaves with black beans instead of using epazote, in which case the dish is known simply as *xonequi*, and often kneading chopped leaves with masa to make small dumplings that are cooked along with the beans.

[MR]

IZOTE/ESPADÍN, COYOL, PALMITA

BOTANICAL: *Yucca* sp./Family Asparagaceae
ENGLISH: tree yucca, St. Peter's palm
NAHUATL: *iczotl* or *ixotl* | **TEENEK (HUASTECO):** *k'oyol*

A dominant and haunting image visible in many places throughout the country is the spectral *izote*—one of some fifty species in the Yucca genus (not to be confused with yuca, p. 227). When yuccas are in bloom, ghostly bunches of delicate pale white, almost translucent flowers cluster together and seem to float several feet above the plant. In the sandy soils of the southern United States, they are sometimes referred to as "ghosts in the graveyard" due to their ethereal appearance and the belief that they tend to sprout in cemeteries. Its dramatic foliage has made yucca a popular ornamental plant for gardeners; it can grow to 32 feet (10 m) in height. Yucca is indigenous to hot, arid regions of the Americas and into the Caribbean. Many parts of the plant are edible, including the flowers, seeds, and fruits (in spite of Sahagún's erroneous statement). The flower, known as *flor de izote* in Spanish, is produced by several Yucca species; flowering occurs generally in the summer months and occasionally into September. Indigenous peoples of

Mexico have consumed *flor de izote* since precontact times; it is traditionally gathered before sunrise, when still very young. The flower may be included in tamales, mixed with scrambled eggs, added to soups, and, most commonly today, dipped in a batter of frothed egg whites and flour and fried, similar to *flor de calabaza*, squash blossom. The flavor has been described as a cross between asparagus and artichoke; I would add to that description a breath of floral perfume. Beyond the culinary, in indigenous communities the plant is also used for firewood or forage for cattle; in industry, the fibers are used in textiles or to make kraft paper.

[MR]

CHILEATOLE DE FLOR DE IZOTE

PORK SPINE CHOPS IN CHILE BROTH WITH YUCCA FLOWERS

FOR THE MEAT STOCK

3 pounds (1.5 kg) pork spine chops, preferably brined (See notes on page 527. Substitute bone-in pork rib chops with some fat. You may also substitute an equivalent weight of chicken pieces.)

2 tablespoons (30 mL) Enriched Lard (substitute vegetable oil)

12 cups (3 L) water

2 teaspoons (12 g) sea salt

1 sprig fresh epazote (substitute ½ tsp./0.75 g dried, crumbled)

Looking something like the set for a tableau vivant, the generous proscenium arch of Puesto "Alacena 16" neatly framed the warm kitchen managed by sisters Ángeles and Marta Rodríguez Martínez. Both puttered about the space silently (Ángeles is rather hard of hearing), managing to stay out of each other's way as they jointly contributed to the day's cooking, each knowing her sister's movements like clockwork. Ángeles wasn't sure how long they had been in this location—somewhere between thirty-five and forty years, she thought—continuing their mother's work. We had seen several big shocks of *flor de izote* at a nearby stall in the market and were eager to have a dish incorporating it. When we enquired, the sisters told us that their customers typically expect *flor de izote* on the weekends, when plentiful supplies are brought in from the *monte*, so they had nothing prepared. But since it was there on this weekday, we asked, might they not make an exception? A few minutes later, we had purchased a huge stalk of the blooms, and Ángeles busied herself with removing the flowers one by one, pulling the petals away from the stigma. It soon became apparent that our lunch was going to take a long time, so we all pitched in to help. The sisters already had a big pot of *chileatole* on the stovetop, so it would be a simple matter of adding the flowers moments before serving. *Chileatole* is clearly of pre-Columbian origin: a simple maize gruel flavored with chile and salt or perhaps honey. Today it may be found in many guises in central-eastern states, and particularly in Veracruz. A green version may include epazote, leaves of squash and chayote vines, and *chile serrano* with corncobs and kernels. Red or green, it is almost always thickened with a bit of maize masa. For the *flor de izote*, a substitute that resembles the flowers both in form and flavor is baby artichokes, fresh or frozen; or if you have access to fresh squash blossoms, you may use those instead.

[MR]

[MC]

FOR THE SOFRITO

4 chiles guajillos (about 1 oz./26 g), stems, veins, and seeds removed

4 chiles anchos (about 1⅓ oz./ 36 g), stems, veins, and seeds removed

2 chiles secos (about 0.4 oz./12 g), stems, veins, and seeds removed (substitute dried, smoked chile chipotle, stems, veins, and seeds removed and lightly toasted)

3 medium Roma tomatoes (10½ oz./300 g), charred and quartered

1 medium white onion (10 oz./275 g), charred and coarsely chopped

6 medium cloves garlic (1½ oz./36 g), charred and coarsely chopped

2 tablespoons (32 g) Enriched Lard (substitute vegetable oil)

FOR FINISHING

1 cup (250 g) masa

3 cups (approximately 390 g) flor de izote (Substitute fresh or frozen baby artichokes, trimmed and halved or quartered, depending on their size. If available, you may also substitute *flor de calabaza*.)

FOR SERVING

Warm maize tortillas

Lime wedges

Several cooks in the region told us that the *chile seco* is a smoked chipotle that has also been lightly toasted. These are commonly sold in the market, but lacking those, you can simply toast the chile yourself.

Prepare-ahead note: The entire dish except for the flowers may be prepared in advance and refrigerated; reheat and add the flowers immediately before serving.

YIELD: 6–8 SERVINGS

PREPARE THE MEAT STOCK

If you brined the meat, drain it and discard the brining solution; thoroughly dry the meat on paper towels. In a large stockpot or Dutch oven, heat the lard until shimmering. Working in batches as needed, sauté the meat until well browned on both sides; transfer to a platter as you finish the rest. Return the meat to the pot and add the remaining ingredients; bring to a boil, reduce to a simmer, and continue cooking 15–20 minutes as you proceed.

PREPARE THE SOFRITO

Place the chiles in a saucepan and cover with water; bring to a boil, reduce to a simmer, and cook 5 minutes. Transfer the chiles to the jar of a blender and reserve the cooking liquid. Working in batches as needed, place the next three ingredients in the blender jar and process until thoroughly puréed, adding just enough of the cooking liquid to keep the blades moving freely. In a large, deep skillet, heat the lard until shimmering; pour in all of the chile purée at once; it should sputter and sizzle, so stand back. Reduce the heat to medium and continue cooking, stirring frequently, until the mixture thickens and darkens slightly, about 6–8 minutes.

THICKEN AND FINISH

Add the *sofrito* to the stock and stir to combine. Transfer about 2 cups (500 mL) of the stock to a heatproof mixing bowl; add the masa and mash to thoroughly incorporate (a potato masher or large fork works well). With the heat on medium, return the masa mixture to the pot and stir to combine. (If necessary, push the meat to one side and use an immersion blender to remove any lumps.) Add the *flor de izote* and continue cooking at a simmer for 15–20 minutes or until the flowers are just tender.

TO SERVE

Ladle some of the meat, stock, and flowers into individual serving bowls. Serve with warm tortillas; diners add squeezes of lime juice to taste.

XICO

THE SHORT 9-MILE (15 km) drive from the state capital of Xalapa to Xico (HE-ko) meanders through expansive orchards of mango. In mango season, scores of roadside vendors offer the fruit—principally the Manila variety—and tempt customers with crates full of mangos arranged in meticulous golden rows, all stacked one on top of the other. Xico lies at about 4,210 feet (1,283 m) above sea level, and the higher we climbed, the vegetation morphed from lush tropical jungle to dense forest. Pine and palm commingled with fruit trees. Soon, the mango plantations gave way to vast stretches of banana trees. Clusters of coffee plants nestled at the foot of each banana tree, whose fragile, flopping leaves shield the delicate coffee plants from the harsh rays of the sun. During an annual fair in July, the principal street is adorned with a "rug" made of colored sawdust and flowers. And, Mole xiqueño (p. 270) is famous nationwide, even appearing as a branded product in supermarkets throughout the country.

Cabbages and kings of Mexican entertainment. [MR]

MERCADO MUNICIPAL

The O-shaped configuration of Xico's tiny Mercado Municipal means that you can see just about everything for sale the moment you enter; you can "do" the market in just a few minutes—that is, unless you make pit stops to sample the many versions of Mole xiqueño, each vendor naturally touting the superiority of her own.

MOLE XIQUEÑO

[MR]

It was María Eugenia Tlaxcalteco Colot who eventually won us over with her charm and graciousness—not to mention the fact that her mole was exceptional. We sampled her *enmoladas*—rather like enchiladas dipped in the sauce—and I purchased a kilo of the paste to take home. Naysayers argue that Mole xiqueño is simply a copy of *mole poblano*, and indeed the city of Puebla is just a 2-hour drive away, so the connection is plausible. However, one taste will shatter that myth. Mole xiqueño is definitely sweeter than *mole poblano*, but most notable is its fruitiness. Doña María Eugenia's mole contained not only the more customary raisins, but also prunes, apples, and plantain, making "fruitiness" the top note.

Prepare-ahead note: The mole paste may be prepared several days or even weeks in advance and refrigerated or frozen; add the stock and finish the dish immediately before serving.

YIELD: 2 POUNDS (1 KG) MOLE PASTE, ENOUGH FOR ABOUT 24 SERVINGS OF THE FINISHED SAUCE

TO PREPARE AHEAD
Chocolate de mesa (p. 77, or substitute)

FOR THE MOLE PASTE

—*The spices*

2 teaspoons (1.3 g) dried whole Mexican oregano

1 three-inch (7.5 cm) stick canela (Mexican cinnamon)

1 teaspoon (3 g) aniseed

1 teaspoon (5 g) black peppercorns

4 whole cloves

—*The chiles*

15 chiles mulatos (6⅓ oz./180 g)

10 chiles pasillas (about 3 oz./90 g)

5 chiles anchos (about 1½ oz./55 g)

—*The nuts*

2 tablespoons (about 0.6 to 0.7 oz./18 to 20 g) each walnuts, almonds, pine nuts, squash seeds (pepitas), and peanuts, and 2 tablespoons sesame seeds (about ½ oz./15 g)

PREPARE THE MOLE PASTE

Working in batches as needed, place the spices in a spice grinder or coffee mill adapted to the purpose; grind until very fine, and set aside.

Remove the stems, seeds, and veins from the chiles. Working with a comal or large, heavy, dry skillet, preferably cast iron, lightly toast the chiles until fragrant and just beginning to darken; transfer the chiles to a heatproof bowl and cover with boiling water; allow the chiles to soak for 20 minutes.

In the same skillet or comal over medium heat, toast the nuts until just beginning to brown; transfer them to a large mixing bowl.

Place the tomato, onion, and garlic in the dry skillet over high heat, and char until blackened in patches; transfer to the bowl with the nuts.

Heat half of the lard in the skillet until shimmering; add the next four ingredients and cook, stirring frequently, until the raisins are plump and the apple is lightly browned. Add the reserved spices and heat, stirring constantly, until fragrant, 2–3 minutes. Transfer the fruit and spices to the mixing bowl with the other ingredients.

In the same skillet or comal, toast the bread and tortillas until golden; transfer to the mixing bowl.

Drain the chiles, reserving the soaking liquid; transfer the chiles to the bowl of a food processor. Working in batches as needed, add all of the ingredients from the mixing bowl along with 1 cup (250 mL) of the soaking liquid, and process until thoroughly puréed. Transfer the purée to a fine-mesh sieve placed over a large mixing bowl; with a rubber spatula, press through as much of the purée as possible, discarding any residue (this process may take 15–20 minutes).

In a large, heavy skillet or stockpot, heat the remaining lard until shimmering; pour in all of the purée at once: it should sputter and sizzle, so stand back. Add the sweeteners and stir until thoroughly dissolved. Continue cooking over medium heat, stirring

—The fruits and vegetables

1 medium Roma tomato
   (3½ oz./100 g)

1 medium white onion
   (10 oz./275 g), peeled

4 medium cloves garlic
   (1 oz./24 g), peeled

½ cup (128 g) Enriched Lard
   (substitute vegetable oil),
   divided

1 small ripe plantain (8 oz./225 g),
   peeled and thickly sliced

1 medium sweet apple
   (8 oz./220 g), peeled, cored, and
   cubed

6 pitted prunes (2 oz./55 g)

2 tablespoons (1 oz./30 g) black
   raisins

—The thickeners

1 stale French roll, sliced, or
   3 thick slices of Italian bread
   (2 oz./50 g)

2 stale maize tortillas

—The sweeteners

2 oz. (57 g) Chocolate de mesa
   (substitute Mexican drinking
   chocolate)

2 tablespoons (30 g) sugar

FOR FINISHING THE MOLE

Rich chicken or turkey stock
Sea salt to taste

frequently, until the mixture darkens and thickens, about 30 minutes. Refrigerate, freeze, or finish as per the following instructions.

FINISH THE MOLE

To finish the mole sauce, you will dilute the prepared paste with chicken or turkey stock. The proportions of paste to stock will vary according to the thickness of your paste, but a reliable ratio is two parts paste to three parts stock. Heat the paste in a saucepan and add the stock, stirring to dissolve. Cook, stirring frequently, until slightly thickened; the consistency should be like thick pancake batter. Check seasonings and add salt to taste.

TO SERVE

You may use the finished mole sauce to prepare *enmoladas*, as did doña María Eugenia, or as a sauce for poached chicken. For the *enmoladas*, heat the sauce in a shallow, broad skillet; using tongs, dip one side of a fresh maize tortilla in the sauce and turn to the other side; transfer the dipped tortilla to a serving plate and use the tongs to fold it in half and in half again to form a triangle shape; repeat with more tortillas (servings are typically 4 tortillas per person). For the chicken, poach whole bone-in chicken breasts or other pieces; plate, and spoon on some of the sauce. Garnishes vary, but for the chicken it would be typical to sprinkle on some toasted sesame seeds; both the *enmoladas* and the chicken require white onion rings; and for the *enmoladas*, spoon on some Mexican *crema* and sprinkle on some crumbled *queso fresco*, Cotija, or feta.

Enmoladas *with* cecina. [MR]

Chiles jalapeños (Capsicum annum) *abound in the region surrounding Xalapa (ha-LAH-pah) for which the chile is named.* [MC]

[MR]

TORTITAS DE VENA

SPICY JALAPEÑO SEED PANCAKES

In this land of the *chile jalapeño*, it is perhaps not surprising to encounter it in many guises. Second only to the pickled chile, the most common is chile relleno—the chile stripped of seeds and veins (*vena*) and stuffed with cheese, shredded chicken, or picadillo, then dipped in batter and fried (p. 514). But what to do with the seeds? Waste not, want not: they are ground and mixed with the same batter that is used to cover the chiles rellenos, such that you get two snacks at the same time. María de Socorro Costeño Yoba of Comidas y Antojitos "La Providencia" shared the recipe with us. These little pancakes are salty and quite picante, making them an excellent accompaniment for beer or cocktails.

Prepare-ahead note: You may prepare the batter for Tortitas de vena an hour or two in advance; they are best served immediately after frying.

YIELD: 1 DOZEN PANCAKES

FOR THE BATTER

4 medium chiles jalapeños
  (5 oz./140 g)
3 large eggs *plus* 3 egg whites, at
  room temperature, separated
¾ cup (90 g) all-purpose flour
1 teaspoon (6 g) baking powder
½ cup (125 g) masa
½ teaspoon (0.325 g) dried whole
  Mexican oregano, lightly toasted
  and ground
¼ teaspoon (1.25 g) ground black
  pepper
1½ teaspoons (9 g) sea salt
Vegetable oil for frying

FOR SERVING

Salsa de jitomate (p. 532)
Warm maize tortillas

PREPARE THE BATTER

Remove the seeds and veins from the chiles and prepare the chiles as chiles rellenos or put them to another use. Place the seeds and veins and the 3 egg yolks in the jar of a blender and process until thoroughly puréed; set aside. In a large mixing bowl, beat the 6 egg whites until they form stiff but not dry peaks; set aside.

Combine the remaining ingredients (except the oil) in a large mixing bowl; pour in the egg-chile mixture from the blender and beat and mash to combine (the mixture will be dry and crumbly). Transfer approximately one-third of the egg whites into the bowl with the egg-flour mixture, and use a handheld mixer to combine, adding a little more of the egg whites if too dry. The resulting mixture will be the consistency of very thick cake batter. Transfer this mixture to the remaining egg whites, and use a rubber spatula to fold gently to incorporate.

Pour 1 inch (2.5 cm) of oil into a large skillet; heat to 350°F (176°C). Working in batches as needed, spoon in about 2 heaping tablespoons (28 g) of the batter, using a spatula to flatten the batter into a pancake. Fry until lightly browned on the bottom; turn over and fry until golden. Transfer the finished pancakes to paper towels to drain.

TO SERVE

Both chiles rellenos and the Tortitas de vena are customarily served atop tortillas and eaten taco-style; diners add spoonfuls of salsa to taste.

Doña María prepares the chiles rellenos (back) *and Tortitas de vena* (front) *in advance and reheats them on a comal immediately before serving.* [MC]

[MR]

PAPANTLA

ENTERING PAPANTLA, I fully expected the air to grow thick with the sweet scent of vanilla. While my fantasy was not fulfilled, we didn't have to travel far to find it lingering in this corner or floating out of that doorway whichever way we turned. Papantla is considered the home of vanilla, and from well-merchandised shops to ragtag market stalls, vanilla is plentiful throughout the town and beyond.

A decoction of vanilla beans steeped in water causes the urine to flow admirably . . . they warm and strengthen the stomach; diminish flatulence; cook the humours and attenuate them; give strength and vigor to the mind; heal female troubles; and are said to be good against cold poisons and the bites of venomous animals.

"THE NATURAL HISTORY OF NEW SPAIN," FRANCISCO HERNÁNDEZ, 1570–1577

Indigenous drawing of vanilla plant, Florentine Codex, ca. 1577.

VAINILLA

BOTANICAL: *Vanilla planifolia*/Family Orchidaceae
ENGLISH: vanilla | **TOTONAC:** *xanat*
NAHUATL: *cuauhmecaexotl* (plant); *ixtlilxochitl* (flower)
MAYAN: *siis bik*

Vanilla is the protagonist in a many-thousand-year history that is integrally connected to the humid coastal plains of Veracruz. Indigenous peoples of prehistory traced the perfumed air of their tropical rainforests to the pod-like fruits of a particular orchid; they crushed the pods with copal and burned them together as incense in temple offerings. Later, the Olmecs employed vanilla medicinally and perhaps as a flavoring for food. The Mayas probably first used it as a flavoring for the chocolate beverage. Thereafter, the Totonacas came to inhabit vast stretches of the modern state of Veracruz and were possibly the first to domesticate vanilla. Much later, the Aztecs (Mexicas) adopted it along with several other flavorings for their beloved chocolate beverage,

[MR]

and demanded the pod as tribute from the Totonacas. When the Spanish conquistador Hernán Cortés reached the Valley of Mexico in 1519, he observed its use among the Aztecs. Vanilla pods are produced when an orchid is pollinated; flowers live only up to twenty-four hours, leaving a brief window of opportunity for pollination. Because the only natural pollinators are bees and birds native to the region, Mexico—and Papantla more particularly—retained a virtual monopoly on vanilla production for more than three hundred years after the arrival of the Spanish. It was not until 1841 when a twelve-year-old enslaved boy named Edmond Albius, who lived on the Indian Ocean island of Île Bourbon (today Réunion), discovered that the flowers could be pollinated by hand, thereby unwittingly opening the door for large-scale global production and commercialization of the fruit. While vanilla was long synonymous with Mexico, today Indonesia is responsible for the vast majority

of Bourbon vanilla, the variety produced from Mexico's *Vanilla planifolia*. The term "*planifolia*" refers to the orchid's distinctive flat leaves. The Nahuatl *ixtlilxochitl* means "black flower"; the Spanish *vainilla* is the diminutive of *vaina* (sheath) and is transcribed into English as "vanilla." Fruits are ⅓-inch (8.5 mm) thick and 6 to 9 inches (15–23 cm) long and are usually referred to as "vanilla beans," although they are not beans at all. Vanilla is one of the most laborious agricultural products in the world: after harvesting, the fruits, which resemble large green beans, go through an elaborate ritual of curing and drying, including rests in the sun, rests in the shade, and hand massaging, to dehydrate and release and concentrate essential oils. The entire process—from pollination to finished bean ready for commercial use—takes approximately one and a half years, explaining why real, quality vanilla is so expensive.

Curing vanilla beans at Eco Park Xanath. [MC]

TOTONAC/TUTUNAKÚJ

The meaning of the name for the language and the people in Totonac is "three hearts," believed by some scholars to refer to the three principal cities of Cempoala, El Tajín, and Teayo. Together with Tepehua, the Totonac language composes an isolated language family—one not known to be related to any other language group. The Nahuas defined the region occupied by the Totonacas as Totonacapan, an area that extends from Papantla in the north of modern-day Veracruz to Cempoala in the south. Today, Totonacas may also be found in the states of Hidalgo and Puebla. The Totonac peoples are considered one of the possible builders of El Tajín. When the Totonacas came under the control of the Aztec Triple Alliance and were forced to render tribute, including vanilla, they became resentful and eventually sided with the invading Spanish to help overthrow Tenochtitlan. The Totonacas still participate in the production of vanilla, but tourism—such as that attracted by the Voladores as well as by a growing number of eco-parks—is becoming an important part of the economy.

The ceremonial "flight" of the famous Voladores (flyers) of Papantla. The cultural tradition had its beginnings in agricultural fertility rituals, and those who practiced it were often vanilla growers. The commerce in vanilla was thoroughly entrenched in Papantla as early as 1743. Vanilla is still a highly important aspect of Totonac culture, religion, and economy. [LP]

Vanilla beans are woven and stitched together to form a variety of fragrant shapes. [MR]

MERCADO MUNICIPAL "MIGUEL HIDALGO"

Early mornings, until about noon or 1:00 p.m., the entrance to the Mercado Municipal "Miguel Hidalgo" is clogged by white-clad vendors of tamales and the ravenous fans who buy them. The market, which was inaugurated in 1964, perches on a gentle incline in hilly Papantla, and entering the dark space, you must step down to access the stalls that sell everything from produce and clothing to cooking utensils and, of course, vanilla.

(above, left) A Totonac woman pauses in front of the market. [MC] *(above, right) A vendor carries* atole morado—*a deep purple gruel made from corn of the same color.* [MC] *(below) Tamale vendors.* [MR]

PULACLES

BEAN AND VEGETABLE TAMALES

The *tamales corrientes*, which feature pork, were surely the top sellers at the tamale stands outside the market. But second in line were these flavorful vegetable tamales. A version of this tamale may be found in nearby Puebla, but our understanding is that those do not feature the *pipián*—a creamy squash seed sauce—which in my estimation gives these tamales the hearty "meatiness" that made them so popular. With a couple of simple tweaks, this may easily become a vegetarian tamale.

Prepare-ahead note: Like most tamales, Pulacles may be made well in advance and frozen; to reheat, do not defrost, but steam for 1 hour before serving.

YIELD: 1 DOZEN TAMALES

TO PREPARE AHEAD

Banana leaves cut into 12 by
16-inch (30 × 40 cm) rectangles
Masa para tamales (p. 530. *Note*:
To make vegetarian tamales,
substitute vegetable oil for
the lard.)

FOR THE FILLING

2 tablespoons (30 mL) vegetable
oil
¼ cup (42 g) white onion, finely
chopped
1 medium clove garlic (¼ oz./6 g),
peeled and finely chopped
2 medium (about 70 g) chiles
jalapeños, seeded and finely
chopped, or to taste
1 medium Roma tomato
(3½ oz./100 g), charred and
peeled
½ cup (125 mL) water
1 teaspoon (6 g) sea salt
½ cup (60 g) pepitas (green
pumpkin or squash seeds),
lightly toasted and ground
½ cup (65 g) each zucchini and
chayote, cubed and parboiled
until barely tender
½ cup (116 g) cooked black beans,
drained
¼ cup (23 g) fresh hoja santa
leaves, finely chopped (substitute dried, crumbled)
¼ cup (15 g) cilantro, finely
chopped

FOR THE TAMALES

Banana leaves prepared as noted
above
1 recipe Masa para tamales

FOR SERVING

Salsa de jitomate (p. 532)

PREPARE THE FILLING

Heat the vegetable oil in a large skillet until shimmering; add the onions and garlic and cook over medium heat until the onions are translucent. Add the chiles and stir to combine.

Place the next three ingredients in the jar of a blender, and process until thoroughly puréed. Pour the purée into the skillet and stir; add the ground squash seeds and continue cooking over medium heat, stirring constantly, until the mixture thickens slightly. Add the remaining ingredients, stir to combine, and cook another 2–3 minutes to amalgamate flavors.

FORM AND STEAM THE TAMALES

Place the banana leaves on a flat work surface horizontally in front of you. Working one at a time, place approximately ½ cup (125 g) of the masa onto the leaf; use your wet fingertips to press the masa side to side, forming an elongated oval and leaving a 3-inch (7.5 cm) border around the edge.

Distribute approximately 3 heaping tablespoons (90 g) of the filling in a row down the middle of the masa, running lengthwise.

Using the banana leaf, fold the long edge closest to you over the top so that the masa completely covers the filling. Peel away the banana leaf, and repeat the same motion on the opposite side. Once more lift the edge closest to you to cover the masa, and continue to fold and roll the banana leaf so that the long edge tucks under the tamale; use the sides of your hands to press the two ends of the tamale, and press lightly to make the tamale more compact. Tuck both loose flaps of the banana leaf under; press to form tightly, and set aside.

Add water to the bottom of a *vaporera* or stock pot fitted with a steaming basket; arrange the tamales flat at the bottom. Place the lid on tightly; bring the water to a boil, and steam for 1 hour, checking the water level halfway through the cooking and adding water as necessary.

TO SERVE

Place two tamales on individual serving plates; diners unwrap their own tamales and spoon on tomato sauce.

[MR]

(below) Tamal corriente—*also known as* tamal de cuchara *because it is eaten with a spoon—has a close relative in Yucatán known as* tamal colado. *In this case, a thick atole is poured onto a section of banana leaf and a tomato/chile chipotle sauce spooned in. A chunk of raw pork is placed on top, and the whole is wrapped and steamed. The masa does not thicken considerably, which explains why it must be eaten with a spoon.*

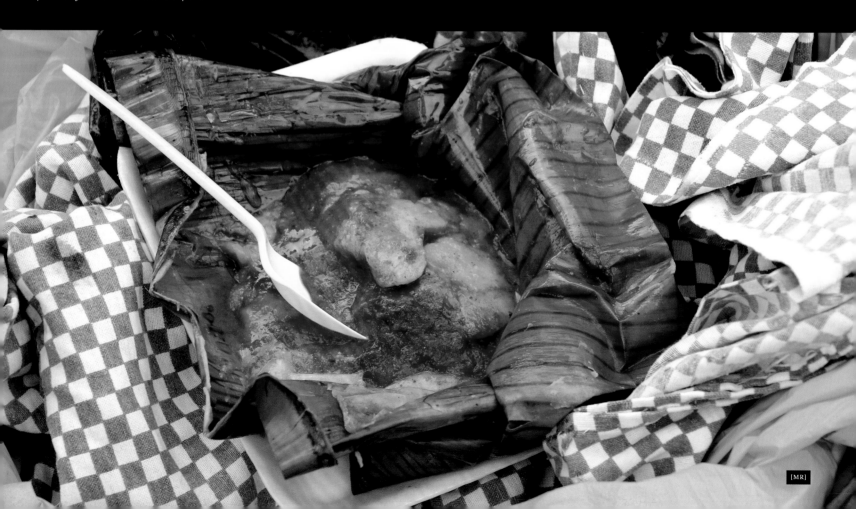

[MR]

[MR]

MERCADO "BENITO JUÁREZ"

Considering how small Papantla is, we found it somewhat surprising that it sustains a couple of rather large public markets. I suppose it is a testament to the fact that many residents continue to shop in traditional ways rather than at supermarkets. The claim to fame of "Benito Juárez" is its spacious upstairs area devoted to *comedores* specializing in Zacahuil, a popular—and famous—regional tamale. Customers order Zacahuil all week long, but if you go on a weekend, prepare to vie for a seat at the counter.

ZACAHUIL

PORK AND HOMINY PUDDING "TAMALE"

TO PREPARE AHEAD

Enriched Lard (p. 530), or
substitute

[MC]

The Huasteca region that occupies part of northern Veracruz is notable for the Zacahuil—which by most accounts is the world's largest tamale. Indeed, it can reach an
impressive size of as much as 6½ feet (2 m) long and 2 feet (60 cm) wide, tipping the
scale at around 65 pounds (30 kg) and serving anywhere from fifty to one hundred
people. The tamale has a long heritage of ritualistic purpose, and still does, although
today it is a more quotidian affair. When prepared in the traditional manner, a wooden
wheelbarrow is lined with banana leaves (the prefix *zaca* in Nahuatl means "to transport something in a cart") and filled with coarsely crushed *nixtamal*; deep inside are
buried a whole turkey, shanks of pork, and a chile sauce. Once wrapped and tied, the
finished tamale looks something like a shrouded corpse; it is wheeled to a large brick
oven, sealed inside, and cooked for 10–12 hours. As for Tamales corrientes (p. 282), the
masa doesn't fully set, so it is served by spooning it onto plates along with pieces of
the shredded meat, which is why I describe it as a pudding. So great is the popularity of Zacahuil that market cooks have adapted the recipe to be able to cook it in a
large stewpot on the stovetop or in a conventional oven. As the owner of the Puesto
"El Paso de las Damas," Valentina Olarte Zalazar, explained to us, the *nixtamal* for this
tamale should be *martajado* or *quebrado*, that is, coarsely crushed rather than finely
ground. Equivalent results may be achieved by briefly pulsing cooked hominy in a
food processor.

Prepare-ahead note: The chile sauce for Zacahuil may be made a day in advance and
refrigerated until time to use it.

YIELD: 8–10 SERVINGS

FOR THE SAUCE

10 chiles anchos (about
   3½ oz./110 g)
6 chiles guajillos (about
   1½ oz./40 g)
4 chiles pasillas (about 1⅓ oz./36 g)
1 medium Roma tomato
   (3½ oz./100 g), charred
½ medium white onion (137.5 g),
   charred
6 medium cloves garlic
   (1½ oz./24 g), peeled and charred
1 teaspoon (3 g) sea salt
2 tablespoons (30 mL) Enriched
   Lard (substitute vegetable oil)

FOR THE TAMALE

8 cups (860 g) cooked hominy,
   drained
1 cup (135 g) masa harina
½ cup (250 mL) Enriched Lard
2 cups (500 mL) rich chicken
   stock (substitute chicken
   bouillon)
2 pounds (1 kg) pork leg, preferably brined (see notes on p. 527)
Banana leaves

FOR SERVING

Verduras en escabeche (p. 480), or
   canned, pickled jalapeños

PREPARE THE SAUCE

Remove the stems, seeds, and veins from the chiles; lightly toast them on a comal or in a heavy skillet until they are fragrant and just beginning to darken; transfer the chiles to a heatproof bowl and cover them with boiling water; allow the chiles to soak for 20 minutes.

Drain the chiles, reserving the soaking liquid; transfer the chiles to the jar of a blender with the next four ingredients and process until thoroughly puréed. Pass the chile mixture through a fine-mesh sieve placed over a large mixing bowl; use a rubber spatula to press as much of the mixture through as possible. Heat the lard in a large, heavy skillet over medium heat until shimmering; pour in the chile mixture all at once: it should sputter and sizzle, so stand back. Cook over moderate heat, stirring frequently, until the sauce thickens and darkens slightly, about 5–6 minutes. Remove the sauce from the heat and set aside.

PREPARE THE TAMALE

Place the hominy in the bowl of a food processor; pulse five or six times until the hominy is broken up into the size of small lentils, but not puréed. Add the next three ingredients, plus 1 cup (250 mL) of the reserved chile soaking liquid, and pulse again just until combined; set aside.

Preheat the oven to 350°F (179°C). If you brined the pork, drain it and discard the brining solution. Remove the spines (if any) from the banana leaves and discard; cut the pork into large chunks about 6 inches (15 cm) cubed. (Alternatively you may cut it into 1-inch/2.5 cm cubes for more convenient if less traditional serving.) Use the banana leaves to line a large ovenproof casserole or Dutch oven fitted with a lid, leaving stretches of the leaves hanging over the edges of the pot. Pour in half of the masa mixture; place the pork chunks on top of the masa and pour on the tomato/chile sauce to cover. Pour in the remaining masa mixture. Fold over the banana leaves to cover, and put the lid in place. Bake for 2 hours; at the end of baking time, lift the lid and check the masa: it should be somewhat firm on the outside. If not, return it to the oven for an additional 30 minutes or until firm.

TO SERVE

Spoon the masa into deep serving plates or individual serving bowls. Shred the whole pork and arrange strips of it on top; if you cubed the pork, arrange pieces of it on top. Diners add Verduras en escabeche or pickled chiles to taste.

MOLOTES

PORK-FILLED MAIZE FRITTERS

TO PREPARE AHEAD
Enriched Lard (p. 530)

Molotes assume an almost infinite variety of forms and fillings, depending on where you find them. Sometimes they are based on tortillas, other times they take the shape of empanadas, and here we found them in an elongated oval shape, not unlike their cousins, *pol'kanes*, in the Yucatán Peninsula. The most common filling is mashed potatoes and/or cheese, but the ones we enjoyed at the Taquería y Cocina Económica "Reyes" were filled with pork picadillo. Topped with shredded lettuce and plated with beans, these little appetizers became a full and satisfying meal.

Prepare-ahead note: The picadillo may be prepared a day in advance and refrigerated; reheat immediately before using in the dish.

YIELD: APPROXIMATELY 3 DOZEN

[MC]

FOR THE PICADILLO

2 tablespoons (32 g) Enriched Lard
  (substitute vegetable oil)
½ medium white onion
  (5 oz./137.5 g), finely chopped
4 medium cloves garlic
  (1 oz./24 g), peeled and finely
  chopped
1 medium Roma tomato
  (3½ oz./100 g), seeded and
  chopped
1 pound (500 g) ground pork
1 teaspoon (6 g) sea salt
1 teaspoon (0.65 g) dried whole
  Mexican oregano, lightly toasted
  and ground
½ teaspoon (1 g) ground cumin
½ teaspoon (2.5 g) freshly ground
  black pepper

FOR THE FRITTERS

½ cup (112 g) Enriched Lard,
  chilled (*Note*: You may substitute
  vegetable oil, although it will
  not chill well.)
1 tablespoon (12 g) baking powder
2 pounds (1 kg) masa, preferably
  from nixtamal
½ cup (67.5 g) masa harina
1 medium clove garlic (¼ oz./6 g),
  peeled, charred, and minced
3 tablespoons (36 g) powdered
  chicken bouillon, dissolved in
  ½ cup (125 mL) hot water
Vegetable oil for frying

FOR SERVING

Shredded lettuce (optional)
Salsa de jitomate (p. 532) or Salsa
  verde (p. 531)
Frijoles de la olla (p. 530; optional)

PREPARE THE PICADILLO

Heat the fat in a large skillet until shimmering; add the onions and garlic and cook over medium heat, stirring frequently, until the onions are translucent. Add the tomato and continue cooking until it is soft. Add the pork, use a spatula to break it into smaller pieces, and continue to cook until the meat is cooked through. Add the remaining ingredients and stir to combine; set aside.

PREPARE THE FRITTERS

Place the chilled lard and the baking powder in the bowl of an electric mixer; beat on high speed until the lard turns fluffy and creamy, about 3 minutes. Add the masa a bit at a time, beating after each addition until incorporated. Add the next two ingredients and beat on low to combine. With the motor still running, slowly add the bouillon mixture. Add enough to create a moist but not soggy dough: it should easily be formed into a ball without sticking to your fingers. Beat on high speed until thoroughly incorporated and the dough lightened, about 5 minutes. Cover with a damp towel until ready to use.

Form the masa into approximately thirty-two 1¼-ounce (35 g) balls. Pat one ball into a 1½-inch (3.75 cm) tortilla in the palm of your hand. Top the tortilla with a scant 1 teaspoon (about 6 g) of the picadillo in a straight row down the center. Fold the tortilla in half, creating an empanada shape; tightly seal the edges. Cupping your hands and rolling the dough in the hollow of your palms, form it into a smooth and elongated egg shape. Set aside and continue with the remaining balls of masa.

Pour the oil into a deep skillet to a depth of 1½ inches (4 cm). Heat to 350°F (176°C). Add 3–4 of the Molotes at a time, being careful not to overcrowd. Fry until deep golden brown; flip and fry the other side. Drain on paper towels as you finish the rest.

TO SERVE

You may serve these as appetizers, allowing 2–3 pieces per person. For a plated meal, plate 5–6 of the Molotes, top with shredded lettuce and some sauce, and accompany with beans.

4
—

CENTRAL
HIGHLANDS

Guanajuato City. [MR]

INTRODUCTION

Some of the most indelible icons of Mexico, in whatever sphere—political leaders like Emiliano Zapata, artists like Diego Rivera and Frida Kahlo, and, of course, foods like *mole poblano* and *chiles en nogada*—come from the Central Highlands.

This has historically been the most populated region in Mesoamerica: the Valley of Mexico had one of the largest concentrations of people in the world at the time of European contact, and still does, due in large part to the lure of its agricultural and mineral wealth. As a result, much of the drama of Mexican history was enacted in the Central Highlands. Here, Spanish battalions fought fierce Aztec armies, eventually seizing the rich lands. Three centuries later, native peoples fought arm in arm with criollos to oust Spanish rule and forge Mexican independence, and later

still, Napoleon III's troops saw their expansionist dreams defeated. The gastronomy of the Central Highlands bears the *sazón* of its piquant history, for it was here perhaps more than anywhere else in the country where indigenous and Old World techniques and ingredients met and married to create what today we recognize as some of the pinnacles of Mexican gastronomy.

Indigenous foods form the foundation. Cactus fruits and pads, maguey roots and leaves, seeds, sugar-rich mesquite pods, insects that live on desert plants, and small animals composed the diet of the earliest inhabitants of the Central Highlands—seminomadic tribes described collectively as Chichimecas. These were also the people who most likely developed the method of pit cooking known in the region today as *barbacoa* (p. 362). By about 6500 BCE, early maize and squash cultivation had occurred in the valleys of the Balsas and Tehuacán Rivers. All of these foods continue to factor prominently in the cuisine of the Central Highlands, and most can still be found in the markets.

Among the first New World foods tasted by the Spanish were those shared with them in the palatial halls of Moctezuma, ruler of the mighty Aztec Triple Alliance in Tenochtitlan. Hernán Cortés and his retinue kept meticulous diaries of the menus they savored there. One banquet featured over three hundred dishes of foods completely foreign to them: chocolate, pulque, turkey, maize, chiles, chia, amaranth, tomatoes, cactus fruits, and a tantalizing assortment of wild greens known in Nahuatl as *quilitl* were just a few of the things they recorded. The conquerors also wrote with breathless wonderment of the hundreds of other comestibles they saw in the impressive market of Tlatelolco, by all reports more sumptuous than anything in Spain.

The three hundred years of Spanish rule between the conquest and Mexican independence witnessed the flowering of a wholly new cuisine as indigenous techniques and ingredients fused with those brought from the Old World. *Mole poblano*—legendarily elaborated in the late seventeenth century in the convent of Santa Rosa in Puebla—is arguably the most archetypal example: the medieval European technique of thickening and flavoring a sauce with bread, nuts, and Asian spices like cinnamon and cloves married New World chiles and chocolate to engender this classic sauce.

PHYSICAL ENVIRONMENT AND AGRICULTURE

The Central Highlands region is actually a high-altitude plateau averaging 6,600 feet (2,011 m) that stretches from Zacatecas south to the Trans-Mexican Volcanic Belt (Eje Volcánico Transversal). Squeezed between the Sierra Madre Occidental and Sierra Madre Oriental, the region is pocked with valleys originally formed by lakes, many of them situated near volcanoes. Popocatépetl and Iztaccíhuatl in the Valley of Mexico are the country's two most iconic volcanoes; the former is active. Many lakes still dot the Valley of Mexico in the Estado de México. One of these lake-valleys was the location of the towering Aztec city of Tenochtitlan, built on an ever-extending island painstakingly reclaimed from lakebed silt by Aztec engineers. Today, the megalopolis of Mexico City occupies the same site.

The terrain of the Central Highlands varies from vast expanses of *matorral* (scrubland) to subtropical dry forests and temperate coniferous forests on the slopes; rich alluvial soils are favorable for a range of crops. A single valley in Hidalgo produces more than half of Mexico's green chiles. The warm temperatures of Morelos nurture fields of sugarcane, maize, tomatoes, onions, and rice, as well as poinsettias and other ornamental plants; Morelos is the largest grower of roses in Mexico. The gently rolling hills of the Bajío—a subregion that includes parts of the states of Aguascalientes, Guanajuato, and Querétaro—allow for extensive mechanized agriculture, making its farmland among the most productive in the country. Wine has been produced in Aguascalientes since the colonial era, and the pueblo of Calvillo is known as "the guava capital of the world." Elsewhere in the region, the land produces apples, quinces, limes and *tejocote* (*Crataegus mexicana*), as well as edible fruits of cactus plants such as *tuna* (*Opuntia ficus-indica*, p. 326), *garambullo* (*Myrtillocactus geometrizans*, p. 335), and *xoconostle* (*Opuntia matudae* syn. *O. joconostle*, p. 353).

ETHNOLINGUISTIC GROUPS

Many of the region's indigenous groups identify themselves as Nahua—descendants of the Aztecs, a modern term given to the Nahuatl-speaking tribe known as the Mexica. That's because most of the Central Highlands were at one time part of the Aztec Empire, also known as the Aztec Triple Alliance, which was at its peak when the Spanish arrived. Although the empire lasted not quite one hundred years—from 1428 CE until 1521 CE—their lake kingdom of Tenochtitlan radiated power and influence outward toward the four cardinal points.

The Toltecs (800 CE–1000 CE) preceded the Aztecs, and legends of their culture profoundly influenced many that followed. Their magnificent capital was Tula (p. 343), in the modern state of Hidalgo. Lesser-known groups of the Central Highlands also played vital roles in the history of Mexico, and preceded the Aztecs and Toltecs by centuries.

The predominant cultural groups of the Central Highlands today are Nahua, Otomí, Huastec, Totonac, and Chichimeca Jonaz.

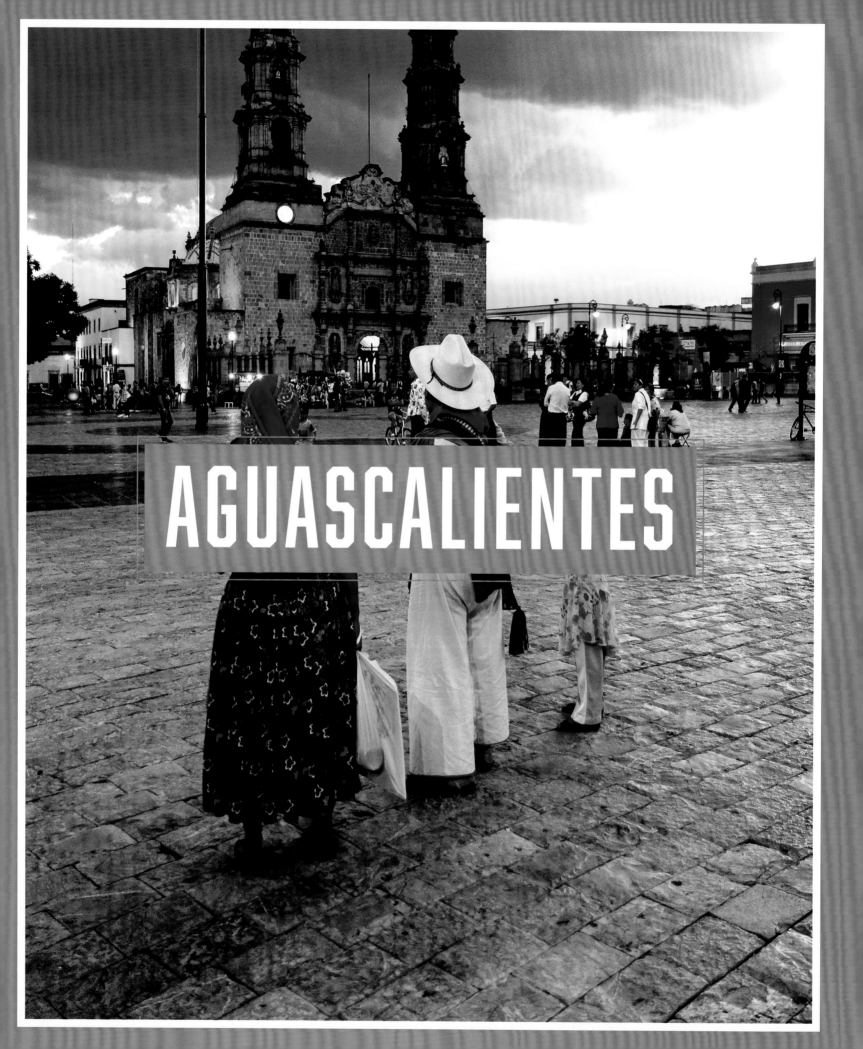

AGUASCALIENTES

AGUASCALIENTES (CITY)

I TREASURE A CACHE of romantic impressions of Mexico's history, many of them no doubt polished beyond recognition like a pearl within my psyche. Not least of these is that of the Silver Road (Ruta de la Plata) that stretched almost a thousand miles south from San Juan Pueblo near Santa Fe, New Mexico, to the Valley of Mexico. Officially, and perhaps even more romantically, known as Camino Real de Tierra Adentro (Royal Road of Inner Lands), it was originally a dusty trail worn through the arid highlands by nomadic Chichimeca tribes; during the colonial era, the road was formalized and used by an endless caravan of wagons herded by muleteers to carry a wealth of precious minerals and other goods from north to south, through the great Chihuahuan Desert to Zacatecas, Aguascalientes, Guanajuato, and finally, Mexico City. Perhaps along the way, drivers had a chance to enjoy a soak in one of the region's many thermal springs that gave Aguascalientes (hot waters) its name. Due to its central location, Aguascalientes became a key commercial hub; the old road cuts straight through the historic center of the capital, past the gargantuan wholesale market (Central de Abastos Agropecuario, p. 294), and north to connect to Highway 45 leading to Zacatecas. Today, the Camino Real de Tierra Adentro is on the UNESCO World Heritage list.

By far the most important load transported along the road was food for provisioning the miners who had settled in the region to exploit seemingly endless mother lodes of silver. Foodstuffs were basic at best: meat, chiles, seeds, and spices. The capital of Aguascalientes was founded in 1575, and shortly thereafter the surrounding region was developed with vineyards; the royal road became the primary conduit for the export of grapes and other fruits. Table grapes and winemaking remain key industries in the state. By the eighteenth century, businesses emerged that fulfilled important, if not to say necessary, roles: noteworthy were the scores of corner shops that sold pulque to the parched muleteers and miners, run almost exclusively by women.

Two main valleys make up the semiarid scrubland of Aguascalientes: the valley of Aguascalientes, which is where the capital of the same name is located, and Huajúcar, the fertile setting for Calvillo, known for its prolific production of guavas (p. 302). Our approach to the capital from the southwest gently lowered us from higher terrain, with occasional glimpses of the valley below. My romantic visions were kept in check as images of pulque shops were supplanted by careering kilometers of superhighway lined with gleaming bunkers that house two major Nissan factories. Although Aguascalientes is the third-smallest state in the country, it remains a vital player in the commerce and history of Mexico, more than its diminutive size might suggest.

The old Mercado de San Marcos, ca. 1891.

(opposite page) Huichol campesinos stand before the inspiring cathedral of Aguascalientes, the Basílica de la Virgen de la Asunción.

Smaller merchants stake their claim amid the frenetic movement of the warehouse. Here, a lone ambulante watches over his modest stock of free-range eggs and dried rattlesnake. [LP]

CENTRAL DE ABASTOS AGROPECUARIO

Beginning early every morning and extending well into the afternoon, tons of produce arrive and are dispatched from the great Central de Abastos Agropecuario, the city's central warehouse. The market lies alongside the old Camino Real de Tierra Adentro, now Avenida Independencia. Although there are several important brick-and-mortar markets in Aguascalientes, a plethora of *tianguis* assures that this city of just under one million residents never goes hungry.

[LP]

TIANGUIS DE LA PURÍSIMA "LA PURI"

Rambling from street to street surrounding the neo-Gothic Templo de la Purísima Concepción, the popular *tianguis* nicknamed "La Puri" is saturated with inexpensive clothing and electronic goods interrupted sporadically by food stalls. The best of these occupy spots with enviable views of the church.

VOLCÁN/MOLTEN CHEESE TOSTADA This is a decadent way to make use of leftover meats—Carnitas (p. 477), *carne asada*, grilled chicken, or fried liver (the way we ordered ours)—although you could just as handily use sautéed mushrooms or *huitlacoche*. Have tostadas ready by frying maize tortillas in 1 inch (2.5 cm) of vegetable oil until lightly browned and crisp; set aside on paper towels to drain. Thinly slice a white onion and separate it into rings; fry the onions in a bit of vegetable oil until they are just beginning to caramelize; set aside. Meanwhile, coarsely chop the meat; form a 2-tablespoon (18-g) ball of *queso asadero* (or fresh mozzarella, Muenster, or provolone) and push your finger into the center to create a well. Fill the well with the meat and press the cheese closed. Lightly brush a nonstick skillet with vegetable oil; fry the cheese ball, turning frequently, until melted but not runny. Use a spatula both to lift and flip the ball and to press it closed if gaps open. Transfer the fried cheese to the tostada and top with some of the fried onions. Serve with lime wedges and a *salpicón* of chopped white onion and cilantro.

A rainbow display of maize and bean varieties, as well as raw cone sugar, rice, and cal. [MC]

TIANGUIS "LAS FLORES"

Trailers hiding shelves full of dried beans and vendors armed with umbrellas and tables whoosh onto a narrow street early in the morning, and before you know it, the tianguis "Las Flores" is in full swing.

TAMALES DORADOS

CRISPY FRIED TAMALES

FOR THE TAMALES

2 tamales per diner

Vegetable oil for frying

FOR SERVING

Enchiladas mineras (p. 315), optional

Potato-and-carrot medley from the enchiladas recipe

Shredded iceberg lettuce

White onion, thinly sliced and separated into rings

Mexican crema (substitute crème fraîche, plain yogurt, or sour cream)

Queso fresco or Cotija (substitute Monterey Jack, feta, Muenster), crumbled

Salsa verde (p. 531), Salsa de chile de árbol (p. 531), or the chile sauce of your choice

The *familia* Corona Martínez at *tianguis* "Las Flores" has hit upon a couple of attractive breakfast offerings for brisk mornings: *enchiladas hidrocálidas*, and Tamales dorados. The former is the local interpretation of the Enchiladas mineras that we found in Guanajuato (and the *enchiladas placeras* in Pátzcuaro), while the latter is an addictive way of repurposing leftover tamales by deep-frying them. Both were served buried beneath the sautéed potato-and-carrot medley typical of the enchiladas, a blanket of shredded lettuce, and a squirt of *crema*. The señora served your choice of red or green tamales—the red prepared with ground beef, *chile guajillo*, and cumin, and the green composed of *rajas* and *salsa verde*. For hearty appetites, serve two tamales and two Enchiladas mineras per diner.

Prepare-ahead note: The tamales may be prepared several weeks or months in advance and frozen. Allow to defrost thoroughly prior to frying.

FRY THE TAMALES

Pour 2 inches (5 cm) of oil into a wok or a deep skillet and heat to 350°F (176°C). Working a few at a time, remove the wrappers from the tamales and fry them in the hot oil until lightly browned, 2–3 minutes per side. As you finish the rest, keep the browned tamales warm by pushing them out of the way onto the sides of the wok. If desired, use the wok to prepare the Enchiladas mineras at the same time, frying the tortillas on the side of the wok. Just before serving, quickly reheat the potatoes and carrots in the shallowest part of the hot oil and transfer to the serving plate with a slotted spoon.

TO SERVE

Plate two tamales per diner. Arrange the enchiladas, if serving, to one side of the tamales. Top with some of the potatoes and carrots, the shredded lettuce and onion rings, and finish with a spoonful or two of *crema* and some of the crumbled cheese. Diners add salsas to taste.

[MC]

[MC]

CALVILLO

LOCATED NEAR THE junction of the three states of Aguascalientes, Jalisco, and Zacatecas, the broad, fertile valley of Huajúcar cradles the little *Pueblo Mágico* of Calvillo, which, along with the state of Michoacán, produces three-quarters of the country's guavas. The 32-mile (52.5 km) drive from the capital of Aguascalientes to the town traces a trail through rugged hills covered with scraggly vegetation and populated with looming anthropomorphic Joshua trees, soon softened by rolling acres of guava trees.

The guava orchards of Aguascalientes represent about 75 percent of the agricultural area of the state, and Calvillo produces some 100,000 tons of the fruit annually. No wonder, then, that Calvillo is known as the "Guava Capital of the World." Bags, bushels, and bins full of guavas can be found on every street corner in peak season, and bakeries throughout the town entice visitors with sweet treats made with the fruit. Thanks to the valley's mild climate, several varieties of the fruit are plentiful year-round, but the highest yield comes in December, which is celebrated with the annual Feria Nacional de la Guayaba (National Guava Fair).

(bottom, left) A street cart laden with guavas. [LP] *(bottom, right) An* ambulante *tends his wares of bright purple guaje (Leucaena glauca), asparagus, nopalitos, and several bags of guavas.* [ALL PHOTOS BY LP]

MERCADO "GUEL JIMÉNEZ"

Located across the street from the magnificent Parroquia del Señor del Salitre (Lord of Saltpeter) church, which boasts the second-largest cupola in Latin America, the Mercado "Guel Jiménez" offers a representative sampling of regional ingredients and prepared foods with a particular emphasis on guavas.

GUAYABA/GUAYAVA

BOTANICAL: *Psidium guajava* L./Family Myrtaceae | **ENGLISH:** guava
NAHUATL: *chalchocotl, xalxocotl, xoxocotl* | **HUICHOL:** *vayeeváxi*

The musky aroma of ripe guava evoking sweet floral decay is not appealing to everyone, and yet it is one of the most popular tropical fruits in the world, consumed in a wide variety of ways. It is eaten as a hand fruit, but more common is to remove the seeds and slice it to serve as a dessert or in a salad. Recipes abound for pies, cakes, puddings, ice cream and sherbet, jams and jellies, chutney and relish. One of the most common uses of *guayaba* in Latin America is in the confection of *ate* (p. 306)—a fruit paste made by cooking the pulp with an equal weight of sugar. Guava fruits grow on a small evergreen tree that can reach 33 feet (10 m) in height; dense foliage clusters on broadly spreading branches. The tree is easy to recognize because of the thin, smooth copper-colored bark that flakes off, revealing the live greenish wood beneath. Fruits may be round, pear-shaped, or ovoid, and measure 2 to 4 inches (5–10 cm) long from tip to base, with 4 or 5 protruding floral remnants (sepals) at the apex. When ripe, the skin is thin and light yellow, frequently tinged with pink. Just beneath the skin is a layer of somewhat grainy flesh, ⅛ to ½ inch (3–12.5 mm) thick, colored white or yellowish, light

or dark pink, or near red; the flesh is juicy, ranging from lightly acidic to sweet. While some guava varieties may be nearly seedless, most have a core in the center of the flesh filled with several hundred very hard, yellowish seeds. The origin of guava is thought to be southern Mexico stretching into Central America; by 1526 it had been introduced to the West Indies, and now it can be found growing in many tropical zones around the globe. Mexico remains one of the world's leading producers. Throughout the tropics, the leaves, bark, roots, and immature fruits of *guayaba* are used as herbal remedies for gastroenteritis and dysentery, or to treat oral ulcers and inflamed gums among other maladies.

The largest landowner and guava producer in the region is Saúl Landeros Cardona. His Rancho San Isidro el Chiquihuitero orchard within the municipal district of Calvillo encompasses 62 acres (25 hectares) where more than five thousand guava trees are cultivated. The subsidiary "Frut [*sic*] Land Grupo" experiments with new uses for the fruit and employs local labor to produce guava confections— from *ate* and cookies to teas and liquors. All of them are sold in the Mercado "Guel Jiménez" in Calvillo.

(below, right) During peak season, guavas are air-dried in quantity, then used later in jellies or pastes.

[LP]

[MC]

EMPANADITAS DE GUAYABA

GUAVA MARMALADE PASTRIES

FOR THE MARMALADE

2 pounds (1 kg) guavas

1 cup (250 mL) water

2 cups (400 g) sugar

Don Saúl & Co. bake dozens of these fresh every morning for selling in Calvillo markets. You may use your favorite piecrust dough for the pastry, but working with commercially packaged puff pastry makes these treats come together very quickly. The buttery pastry is the perfect foil for the exotic sweetness of the marmalade. This recipe produces approximately 3 cups (750 mL) of the marmalade, but you will need only about half that amount. You may scale down the recipe if you wish, but I have never done so because it does require quite a bit of vigilance on the stove, such that a smaller quantity doesn't really make sense. Besides, I like to store the extra in jars to have with my morning toast.

Prepare-ahead note: Make the marmalade for Empanaditas a day or two in advance and refrigerate. The finished pastries keep well for 3–4 days.

YIELD: APPROXIMATELY 2 DOZEN

PREPARE THE MARMALADE

Trim off the sepals at the apex of each fruit; slice the guavas in half and scoop out the seeds and the pulpy core; transfer the seeds and pulp to the jar of a blender and add the water; set aside for 30 minutes. Lightly pulse the blender just enough to liquefy the pulp but not pulverize the seeds; pour the purée through a fine-mesh sieve into a large, heavy saucepan and press through as much of the pulp as possible; discard the seeds and any residue.

Chop the guavas (medium dice is a good guide) and transfer them to the saucepan with the purée; add the sugar and stir to combine. Place the saucepan over high heat; when the mixture reaches a boil, reduce the heat to medium and continue cooking,

[MC]

FOR THE PASTRY DOUGH

1½ pounds (680 g) homemade,
    refrigerated, or frozen slab puff
    pastry
Flour for dusting
Softened butter, as needed
1 large egg, well beaten
Sugar for sprinkling (optional)

[MC]

stirring constantly and using a potato masher to break up the fruit until it has disintegrated and the mixture thickens and reaches 220°F (104°C) on a candy thermometer, about 20–25 minutes. Remove the marmalade from the heat and allow it to cool thoroughly, or refrigerate until time to use.

FINISH THE PASTRIES

Preheat the oven to 400°F (204°C). Divide the dough into thirds; work with one-third at a time and keep the rest wrapped in plastic under refrigeration. Place the dough on a lightly floured surface; dust it with a bit of flour and roll it out to a thickness of ⅛ inch (3 mm). Use a 4-inch (10 cm)-diameter circular cookie cutter or other round form to cut the dough into disks. Each third of dough should yield 8 disks. Use a smear of softened butter to reunite any scraps, layering them and rolling out and cutting as before. Working one at a time, place a dough circle on a piece of waxed paper (this step is rather messy, and the waxed paper will keep your counter and each empanada clean). Arrange a scant 1 tablespoon (about 12–13 mL) of the marmalade in the center of the circle. Lightly brush around the circumference of the circle with the beaten egg. Use the waxed paper to help lift and fold the circle in half; press around the ridge of the filling to remove any air bubbles; use a fork to tightly crimp and seal the edges of the Empanaditas; prick the surface a couple of times with a sharp knife or fork. Continue until all of the Empanaditas have been filled.

BAKE AND FINISH

Arrange the Empanaditas on a baking sheet lined with parchment paper or a silicone baking mat and brush with some of the beaten egg; sprinkle a bit of sugar on top if desired. Bake until golden brown, about 40 minutes. Remove to a cooling rack. Serve while still warm or store in an airtight container in a cool, dry place.

COPITAS

GUAVA PASTE AND MILK CANDY CONFECTIONS

FOR THE GUAVA PASTE

2 pounds (1 kg) guavas

3 cups (750 mL) water, divided

Vegetable oil

Approximately 1½ pounds (750 g) sugar (You will measure it precisely at the moment of assembly.)

[LP]

Another of Frut Land Grupo's delectable products, these "little cups" (*copitas*) are sugary dreams of soft *ate* (guava paste) rolled up and topped with a golden nugget of creamy milk candy and a pecan half. Surely this treat was invented just for me. I provide the recipe for the guava paste here for those who like an adventure in cooking, but you may purchase commercial paste instead—now widely available—many of which are quite good. Wrap leftovers of the guava paste in waxed paper and keep refrigerated; bring to room temperature, slice, and serve with any kind of cheese for a wonderful afternoon snack or after-dinner treat.

Prepare-ahead note: The guava paste must be made at least 24 hours in advance in order to set. Make the milk candy on the day you plan to finish the candies. Copitas keep well for 2–3 weeks in a cool, dry environment in an airtight container.

YIELD: APPROXIMATELY 4 DOZEN

PREPARE THE GUAVA PASTE

Trim off the sepals at the apex of each fruit; slice the guavas in half (no need to peel them). Using a soupspoon or melon baller, scoop out the fleshy, seedy core; transfer the seeds and pulp to the jar of a blender and add 1 cup (250 mL) of the water; set aside for 30 minutes.

Coarsely chop the guavas and place in a large saucepan with the remaining water. Bring the water to a boil, reduce to a simmer, and cook until the guavas are very tender, 10–15 minutes. Drain the guavas and allow them to cool.

Prepare a 10-inch by 15-inch (25 cm × 38 cm) baking sheet: rub it with a few drops of vegetable oil and line it with waxed paper (the oil will help the paper adhere to the sheet); rub the top of the paper with a bit of oil, too; set aside. Lightly pulse the blender containing the guava cores just enough to liquefy the pulp but not pulverize the seeds; pour the purée through a fine-mesh sieve held over the bowl of a food processor. Press through as much of the pulp as possible, being sure to scrape off the bottom of the sieve from time to time; discard the seeds and any residue in the sieve. Transfer the

FOR FINISHING THE CANDIES

Milk candy mixture for Huesos
    (p. 473, adding 1 tsp./5 mL
    Mexican vanilla extract when
    you add the butter), warm and
    soft immediately after making it
Softened butter
48 pecan halves
48 No. 5 paper or foil candy
    cups (1¼ inches × ¾ inch/
    32 mm × 19 mm)

cooked guavas to the food processor and process until finely puréed. Weigh or measure the mixture, and then weigh or measure an equal amount of sugar (you should have approximately 3 cups or 750 g of the purée).

Pour the guava purée into a tall, narrow, heavy saucepan (copper works best for this) and add the sugar. Place over high heat and stir until the sugar is completely dissolved; reduce the heat to simmer and continue cooking, stirring very frequently, for about 1 hour. Signs that it is ready are that the mixture will reduce by about one-half; it will turn a deep amber color; when you stir with a wooden spoon, the bottom of the pan will be revealed for a couple of seconds; and when you press some of the purée with the spoon against the sides of the pan and then pull away, it will form thick strands. Remove from the heat, and beat the mixture with a wooden spoon until it cools slightly and thickens to a stiff paste, about 10 minutes. Pour the paste into the baking sheet and use a rubber spatula to spread it evenly from side to side. Place the paste in a cool place and allow to set for at least 24 hours.

ASSEMBLE THE CANDIES

Invert the baking sheet over a large sheet of waxed paper to unmold the guava paste; carefully peel away the paper that is on top. Slice the paste into 48 strips measuring about 3 inches long by ¾ inch wide (7.5 cm × 2 cm. *Note*: If using commercial paste, the strips should be sliced to be about ¼ inch/6.3 mm thick). Roll one strip into a very tight spiral, compressing as you roll; press and mash the loose end so that it stays tightly closed, then place it at the bottom of one of the candy cups. Butter a large sheet of waxed paper; when the milk candy is cool and firm but not hard, spoon 48 mounds of about 1 heaping teaspoon (15 g) each onto the waxed paper; allow the mounds to set thoroughly, 1–3 hours depending on your climate conditions, enough that you are able to pick them up and shape them. Butter your hands well; form one mound of the paste into a ball, place the ball atop the guava paste in one of the cups, then flatten the ball into a thick disk. Top the milk candy with a pecan half. Repeat until all of the candies have been formed. Store in an airtight container.

Copitas and Empanaditas de guayaba in the Mercado "Guel Jiménez." [MC]

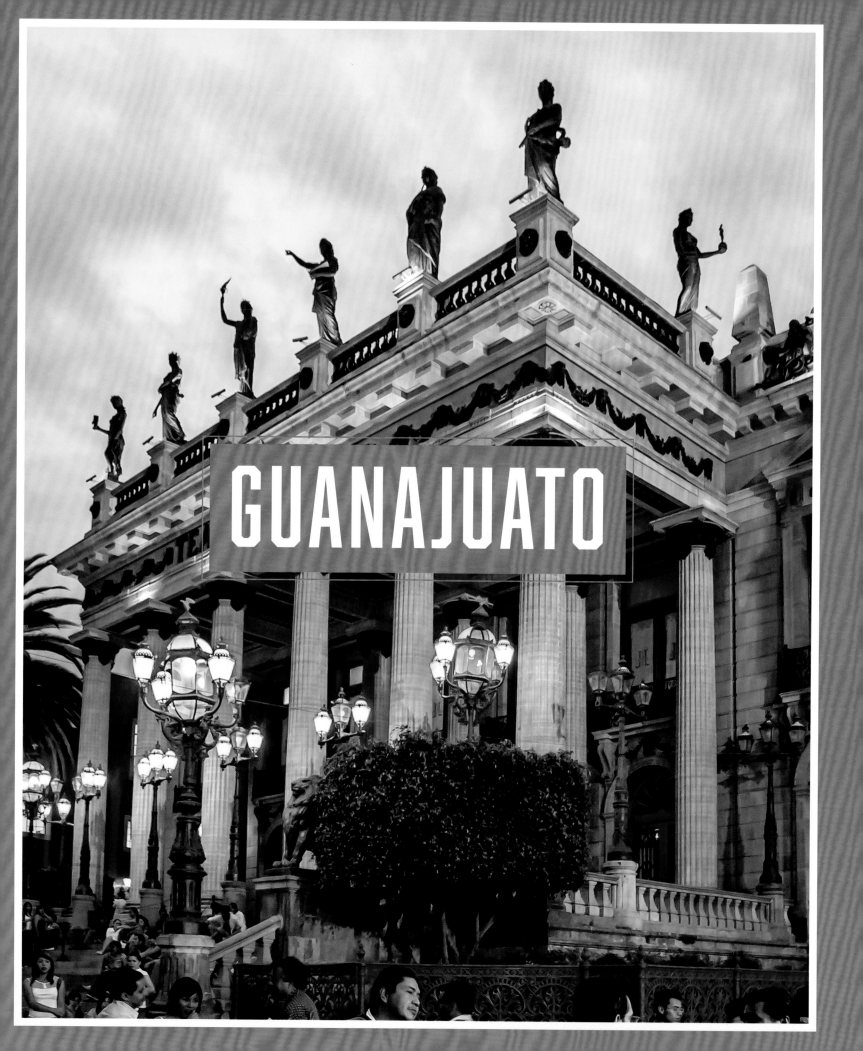

GUANAJUATO

[MR]

GUANAJUATO (CITY)

Guanajuato appeals equally to nature and culture lovers. Dusty ghost towns surviving from the silver boom are crowded with more cactus than tourists, and clutter hauntingly beautiful, stony valleys pocked by erosion. Two of Mexico's most celebrated muralists are linked to the state. Diego Rivera was born here (his early home is now a museum), and David Siqueiros grew up in Irapuato—also famous for its strawberries. The state capital, Guanajuato, is a place where one wants to dress smartly. Tailored topiary bays that grace the main square, genteel plazas enjoyed by businesspeople and their dates, sophisticated theater-goers spilling out of the Teatro Juárez on a cool evening, or crowds of intelligentsia celebrating the annual International Cervantes Festival—all seem to demand a comportment and attire that lend elegance to the scene rather than detract from it.

Cosmopolitans have been at home in Guanajuato for close to three hundred years. By the eighteenth century, Guanajuato had become the world's largest silver extraction center, and the impressive neoclassical and Italianate buildings like the Teatro Juárez, Mercado Hidalgo, and the Alhóndiga de Granaditas bear testament to that wealth.

(opposite page) Teatro Juárez

[MR]

MERCADO HIDALGO

The impressive Mercado Hidalgo—the municipal market of Guanajuato—is one of the most beautiful market buildings in all of Mexico, if not the world. The soaring iron structure faced with a pink limestone Beaux Arts façade was originally planned as a railroad station. The market was inaugurated on September 16, 1910, by President Porfirio Díaz in honor of the centennial celebrations of Mexican independence.

The structure is laid out in a T form; thirty-four windows admit light on all sides, and three entrances mark each end of the T. Through the left door is a large space occupied by vendors of prepared foods, and on the right side is the spacious produce market. Since Guanajuato was historically a mining town, with little or no farmland nearby, virtually all produce was and still is imported from the neighboring towns of Irapuato, San Francisco del Rincón, Celaya, San Miguel de Allende, and Silao.

[MR]

(above) The soaring iron structure of Mercado Hidalgo dates to the early twentieth century.

[MR]

[MC]

(above, left) **Customer at CarnitaSam.** [MC] *(below)* *Serving Gorditas de carnitas with a healthy salad of* nopalitos, onion, tomatoes, and chile at CarnitaSam. [ALL PHOTOS BY MC]

GORDITAS DE CARNITAS

THICK MAIZE PANCAKES FILLED WITH PORK CONFIT AND CACTUS SALAD

TO PREPARE AHEAD

Masa para tamales (p. 530)
Carnitas (p. 477)
Ensalada de nopales (p. 390)

FOR THE MASA

3½ ounces (100 g) pork cracklings
   (*chicharrón*: purchase from a
   Mexican butcher or *chicharronería* to avoid the packaged kind,
   which can be rancid)
1 recipe Masa para tamales

FOR THE FILLINGS

½ recipe Carnitas
½ recipe Ensalada de nopales

FOR SERVING

Ensalada de pepino and Salsa
   mexicana de Guanajuato
   (recipes follow)

[MC]

You may have to fight for a spot at the counter of Puesto "CarnitaSam." The reason for its popularity is the owner's "invention"—a confluence of three tasty dishes in one: Gorditas, Carnitas, and Ensalada de nopales. Their Gorditas are prepared in the traditional *guanajuatense* manner—with *migajas* mixed into the dough. *Migajas* translates to "crumbs" or "leftovers"; in this dish they refer to *asiento*—the Spanish word for the tiny bits of crispy meat and fat that sink to the bottom of the cauldron in which lard is rendered. Lacking *asiento*, you may use crushed pork cracklings to give a similar texture and meaty taste. In addition to the *nopalito* salad used to accompany the Carnitas that were stuffed inside the gordita, another couple of exciting garnishes were offered as side salads or salsas: one, a mixture of cucumber, pineapple, and jicama; the other, a fresh spin on the everyday *salsa mexicana* made fiercely hot with two kinds of chile. The taste and texture contrast among the varied ingredients was thrilling. The cucumber salad could serve as a side dish for just about any main course.

Prepare-ahead note: Prepare the Carnitas a day in advance and refrigerate. While the Ensalada de nopales and the Ensalada de pepino may also be prepared a day in advance and refrigerated, they are best made on the day of serving. Reheat the Carnitas gently in a bit of lard or vegetable oil, and bring the salads to room temperature if refrigerated.

PREPARE THE MASA AND FINISH THE GORDITAS

Place the *chicharrón* in the bowl of a food processor, and pulse several times until the *chicharrón* is broken up into very small bits and roughly resembles the texture of uncooked rice; it should still have some texture and not be a powder. Knead the *chicharrón* with the masa, then form and cook the Gorditas as instructed on page 411, omitting the flavored cheese; fill with the Carnitas and reheat the Gordita as described, adding the salad garnishes immediately before serving. Diners add Salsa mexicana de Guanajuato to taste.

SALSA MEXICANA DE GUANAJUATO

FIERY CHOPPED TOMATO AND CHILE SAUCE FROM GUANAJUATO

FOR THE SALSA

4 medium Roma tomatoes
   (14 oz./400 g), seeded, very
   finely chopped, and placed in a
   fine-mesh sieve to drain

½ medium white onion
   (5 oz./137.5 g), peeled and very
   finely chopped

2 medium chiles serranos
   (approximately 7 oz./20 g total),
   very finely chopped

4 medium chiles de árbol
   (approximately 0.15 oz./4 g
   total), stems removed, lightly
   toasted on a comal or in a heavy
   skillet, and ground in a spice
   grinder or coffee mill

2 tablespoons (10 g) cilantro,
   finely chopped

½ teaspoon (3 g) sea salt

2 tablespoons (30 mL) white
   vinegar

This version of "*salsa mexicana*" or "*pico de gallo*" was quite different from any of the many variations I have sampled. The tomatoes and onions were chopped extremely finely, and rather than being dressed with lime juice, they were doused with white vinegar. The salsa was also quite fiery, since it included not only finely chopped *chiles serranos* but also toasted and ground *chiles de árbol*. The result is one of the best *pico de gallo*-type salsas that I have ever tasted, but it is definitely not for the heat-shy.

Prepare-ahead note: Salsa mexicana de Guanajuato keeps well under refrigeration for about 1 week.

PREPARE THE SALSA

Combine all of the ingredients in a mixing bowl and toss to combine. Refrigerate; bring to room temperature before serving.

An inventive method for preventing an avalanche of chiles. On the left, chiles pasillas; *on the right*; chiles guajillos. [MC]

ENSALADA DE PEPINO

CUCUMBER, PINEAPPLE, AND JICAMA SALAD

FOR THE SALAD

1 medium cucumber (7 oz./198 g),
  peeled, seeded, and thinly sliced

1 small pineapple (14 oz./400 g),
  peeled, cored, and cut into large
  dice

1 small jicama (10½ oz./300 g),
  peeled and cut into thin julienne
  strips

1 medium red onion (10 oz./275 g),
  peeled, and cut into half-moons
  (cut the onion into quarters,
  thinly slice each quarter top
  to bottom, then separate the
  sections into small "half-moon"
  shapes)

1 seven-ounce (198 g) can pickled
  jalapeños (*en escabeche*; they may
  be sliced for nachos or strips),
  drained

3 medium fresh jalapeños
  (3¼ oz./92.5 g total), stems
  removed and thinly sliced across
  the width

½ medium bell pepper
  (3¼ oz./92.5 g) *each*: red, yellow,
  and green, seeded and cut into
  thin julienne strips

½ cup (125 mL) pineapple vinegar
  (substitute apple cider vinegar)

½ cup (30 g) cilantro, coarsely
  chopped

½ teaspoon (3 g) sea salt

Prepare-ahead note: Ensalada de pepino keeps well under refrigeration for a day or two.

PREPARE THE SALAD

Place the first seven ingredients in a large mixing bowl; toss to combine. Pour on the vinegar and toss; add the cilantro and salt immediately before serving, and toss to combine.

ENCHILADAS MINERAS

GUANAJUATO-STYLE ENCHILADAS WITH CHICKEN, POTATOES, AND CARROTS

You will find this theme-and-variation dish in several states of Mexico, each time with a new detail or nuance so that state residents can give it a special name and claim it as their own. People from Guanajuato will tell you that Enchiladas mineras ("miners' enchiladas") is their signature dish; folks in Querétaro will swear that *enchiladas queretanas* is their dish and theirs alone, while in Michoacán they rave about *enchiladas placeras*. The basic format of tortillas bathed in *chile guajillo* sauce, fried, and served with potatoes and carrots, along with some kind of meat, never falters. Variations include whether the potato-carrot medley goes inside or outside of the enchiladas; what kind of meat is served (sautéed chicken, chorizo, beef fillet, or *cecina* are some options); and the size of the serving (the *enchiladas placeras* in Pátzcuaro are gargantuan!). Evangelina Palma Cancino, owner of the Puesto "Doña Silvia" in the prepared food area alongside

[MR]

FOR THE SALSA

12 chiles guajillos (about
    4¼ oz./120 g total), stems, seeds,
    and veins removed
½ medium white onion
    (5 oz./137.5 g), peeled and
    coarsely chopped
4 medium cloves garlic
    (1 oz./24 g), peeled
2 tablespoons (24 g) sugar
1 tablespoon (15 mL) white
    vinegar
1½ teaspoons (9 g) sea salt
1 teaspoon (0.65 g) dried whole
    Mexican oregano *plus* ½ tea-
    spoon (1 g) cumin seed, lightly
    toasted together and ground
4 tablespoons (60 mL) vegetable
    oil, divided

FOR THE CHICKEN

1 gallon (4 L) water
½ cup (145 g) sea salt
6 chicken pieces (your favorite
    parts; doña Evangelina used a
    single thigh for each customer;
    for a heartier serving, I like
    whole legs—drumsticks and
    thighs joined)

FOR THE VEGETABLES

Water for boiling vegetables
1 teaspoon (6 g) sea salt
1 pound (500 g) baking potatoes,
    peeled and cut into large dice
1 pound (500 g) carrots, peeled
    and cut into large dice

Mercado Hidalgo led us through the simple steps. The only trick is to have all the components together well before serving. I timed her, and she fed us just 6 minutes after starting to work on the dish. Naturally, such speed is important if you are serving a steady stream of hungry customers throughout the day. Interestingly, doña Evangelina used a wok for the frying; when you understand the process, it makes perfect sense, because all of the components can be fried and tended separately—but at the same time.

Prepare-ahead note: The chiles need to soak overnight. As mentioned, prepare all of the other components a day or two in advance, or earlier on the day you plan to serve. With a little practice, you can plate Enchiladas mineras as fast as doña Evangelina did.

YIELD: 6 SERVINGS

PREPARE THE SALSA DE CHILE DE GUAJILLO

Cover the chiles with boiling water and allow them to soak overnight.

Remove the chiles from the water, reserving the soaking liquid; place the chiles in the jar of a blender; pour 2 cups (500 mL) of the chile soaking liquid into the blender; add the remaining ingredients except for the vegetable oil, and process until thoroughly puréed.

In a medium saucepan, heat 2 tablespoons (30 mL) of the oil until shimmering; pour in all of the chile purée at once: it should sputter and sizzle, so stand back. Bring to a boil, reduce to a simmer, and continue cooking, stirring frequently, until the mixture thickens slightly, 4–5 minutes; the consistency should be like pancake batter—as doña Evangelina said, "not too thin, not too thick." You should have about 3 cups (750 mL) of sauce. Set aside or refrigerate until you are ready to assemble the dish.

(*Note*: This *chile guajillo* sauce serves for a few more recipes throughout this book.)

PREPARE THE CHICKEN

Pour the water into a stockpot, add the salt, and stir to dissolve; add the chicken pieces and refrigerate for 3–4 hours as you do other steps. (The brining step is optional; see p. 527 for notes on brining.)

At the end of the brining time, drain and rinse the chicken; discard the brining solution. Pat the chicken thoroughly dry with paper towels. Heat the remaining 2 tablespoons (30 mL) of oil in a large skillet or wok until shimmering. Working in batches as needed, add the chicken pieces in one layer and fry on all sides until well browned; reduce the heat and cook the chicken to an internal temperature of 165°F (74°C). (If you did not brine, lightly salt the chicken at this point.) Transfer the chicken to a platter and set aside or refrigerate until you are ready to assemble the dish.

PREPARE THE VEGETABLES

Fill a pot with water and add the salt. Bring the water to a boil; plunge the vegetables into the boiling water. Continue to cook over high heat until the potatoes and carrots are just tender, 5–6 minutes. Drain and set aside, or refrigerate until you are ready to assemble the dish.

Vegetable oil for frying

12–18 day-old maize tortillas
  (*Note*: The tortillas should be
  somewhat dry or they may fall
  apart during cooking; air-dry
  fresh tortillas overnight. Tortilla
  sizes vary throughout Mexico;
  common sizes range from
  4 to 6 inches/10–15 cm. For the
  smaller size, serve 3 enchiladas
  per person; for larger tortillas,
  serve 2 enchiladas per person.)

8 ounces (225 g) queso Oaxaca
  (substitute fresh mozzarella),
  grated

Frying all of the components at the same time. [MR]

ASSEMBLE THE ENCHILADAS AND SERVE

As you see in the photo, all of the main components are in the wok at the same time. Timing for this step is critical, so study the procedure carefully before you begin; have all of the finishing garnishes ready. You will be plating one serving at a time; have a large plate or platter at hand for the first lucky diner.

Bring the chicken and vegetables to room temperature and reheat the chile sauce in a broad, shallow skillet; keep it warm as you are working. Preheat a wok or a large skillet with sloping sides over high heat. Pour 1 tablespoon or 2 (15–30 mL) of vegetable oil into the wok and heat until shimmering; swirl the wok to coat the sides with the oil. Reheat one piece of chicken on one side of the wok; add a large spoonful or two of the vegetables; use a wok strainer or spatula to turn the chicken and vegetables, cooking them until they are heated through and the vegetables are lightly browned. Move the chicken and vegetables to one side to create room for the enchiladas. Working quickly with one tortilla at a time, dip the tortilla into the chile sauce to thoroughly coat it, front and back. Place the tortilla on the side of the wok (avoid placing it in the puddle of fat at the bottom, since this can weaken it); sauce another tortilla, and another (if using the smaller tortillas as described above). After about 15 seconds, turn the first tortilla to the other side; repeat with more tortillas. When the first tortilla is browned on both sides, sprinkle about 1 heaping tablespoon (12.5 g) of the *queso Oaxaca* in a row down the middle; use tongs to quickly fold the tortilla in half (these enchiladas are folded, not rolled). Cook for another few seconds to allow the cheese to melt as you finish the other enchiladas.

FOR SERVING

Mexican crema (substitute crème
  fraîche, plain yogurt, or sour
  cream)
Queso Cotija (substitute feta),
  crumbled
Iceberg lettuce, shredded
Roma tomatoes, thinly sliced
White onion, thinly sliced and
  separated into rings
Pickled jalapeños ("nacho" style
  or strips), drained

[MR]

TO SERVE

Place the enchiladas in the center of a large platter or plate and spoon on a bit more of
the chile sauce; drizzle on a bit of *crema* and sprinkle on some of the crumbled Cotija
cheese. Arrange the sautéed vegetables around the edge; place the fried chicken to one
side. Top the whole plate with a generous amount of shredded lettuce, some tomato
slices, onion rings, and jalapeño pieces. Repeat for the other servings.

*Doña Evangelina served the shredded lettuce and other garnishes piled on top of the chicken, vegetables, and
enchiladas. In the photo, the components have been separated so that you can see how everything looks.* [MC]

GUACAMAYA

SANDWICH OF PORK CRACKLINGS, AVOCADO, AND BOILED EGG

FOR THE SANDWICH

1 bolillo (Mexican roll or crispy
 French bread or sourdough roll)
½ medium avocado (about
 5¼ oz./150 g), peeled, seeded,
 and sliced
1 hard-boiled egg, peeled
Sea salt to taste
Large pieces of chicharrón
Salsa mexicana de Guanajuato (or
 the tomato salsa of your choice)
½ lime

Imagine the crispiness of a crusty roll filled with *chicharrón*, balanced with the creamy smoothness of avocado and boiled egg—perked up with a squeeze of lime and a dollop of tomato salsa—and you'll surely understand why this is one of the state's most popular snack foods. The city of León claims it as its own, but the Guacamaya really knows no borders. There is no "recipe" per se, so I list the ingredients and assembly instructions. The real key to this sandwich is to choose a flavorful roll with a very crispy crust and a soft center. *Guacamaya* translates to "macaw." Some people say it got the name because of how colorful the sandwich is—like the bird—but our vendor said it is called that because of the "squaaaawk" sound produced when your teeth crunch down through the crispy crust and the *chicharrón* with every bite.

YIELD: 1 SANDWICH

PREPARE THE SANDWICH

Slice the roll in half lengthwise, leaving one of the long sides semiattached. Pinch out some of the bread in the center of the roll to create a hollow (discard or put to another use). Place the sliced avocado in the hollow, and mash and smear it to cover the bread. Place the boiled egg on top of the avocado, and with a knife, slice it into rough quarters, mashing it into the avocado and making sure to distribute both evenly. Sprinkle with sea salt to taste. Insert several pieces of *chicharrón* into the sandwich; close the sandwich, then mash lightly to compress and break the *chicharrón*. Finally, carefully open the sandwich to add the tomato sauce and a squeeze of lime juice. Serve.

Crunchy bolillos *for Guacamayas.* [MR]

(above) *A refreshing and healthful palate cleanser: pomegranate seeds with lime.* [MR] (below) *Irapuato in the state's south-central region is known nationally for its production of strawberries.* [MC]

The city of Guanajuato is famous for its Museo de las Momias—the mummy museum. Following a cholera outbreak in the nineteenth century, bodies buried in graveyards surrounding the city became naturally mummified due to the lack of groundwater and the presence of nitrates and alum. Many of these are on display in the museum, which is at the top of a hill swarming with tour buses and taxis. Forms of the mummies are popular in folk art, tourist trinkets, and even candy, as seen in the photo. This type of pulled, hard ribbon candy made with piloncillo is known as charamusca and comes in a wide variety of shapes—from candy canes to the mummy couple seen in the photo— all available in the market. [MR]

DOLORES HIDALGO

THE SURNAME HIDALGO appears frequently in the Central Highlands. Mexicans revere the name, although they abbreviate the full name of the honored bearer. Don Miguel Gregorio Antonio Ignacio Hidalgo y Costilla Gallaga Mandarte y Villaseñor (1753–1811) was a Jesuit priest and the man credited for spearheading the fight for Mexican independence. In his service at the church in Dolores, near Guanajuato, he was appalled by the conditions of poverty and injustice that he saw being inflicted upon his flock. He dedicated his life to humanitarian acts, as well as reading philosophy and political tracts, fueling himself with ideas about the recent successful freedom fights in France and the United States.

On Sunday, September 16, 1810, amid growing tensions between indigenous peoples and the Spanish ruling class, Hidalgo rang the bell in the tower of his parish church—Nuestra Señora de Dolores (Our Lady of Sorrows)—summoning his parishioners to morning Mass. Those in attendance heard the now-famous "Grito de Dolores" ("shout" or "cry" of Dolores) in which Hidalgo brazenly denounced local authorities. Hidalgo was executed less than a year later, but independence was eventually won on September 27, 1821. And today—in murals, school lessons, and annual celebrations—the kindly Creole Padre Hidalgo is remembered as the father of Mexican independence.

MERCADO MUNICIPAL "HIDALGO"

Before we could enter the dining halls of the Mercado Municipal "Hidalgo," piles of tasty-looking gorditas being sold in stacks just outside tempted us. The unique feature of these gorditas, made with maíz quebrado *(p. 410), is that they were dipped in a piquant* chile guajillo *sauce before being cooked on the comal, imparting yet another layer of flavor.* [MR]

GORDITAS DE DOLORES HIDALGO

THICK MAIZE PANCAKES FROM DOLORES HIDALGO

Prepare the Salsa de chile guajillo found on page 316; prepare the Gorditas de maíz quebrado, as explained on page 410; slice open the Gorditas, dip the entire pancake in the sauce, and fry both sides in a little bit of lard (or vegetable oil) on a hot comal, griddle, or cast-iron skillet. Fill with any of the recommended fillings found throughout this book, and reheat as per the instructions on page 410.

NOPALITOS CON PAPAS

CACTUS PADDLE STRIPS WITH FRIED POTATOES AND ONIONS

FOR THE FILLING

2 tablespoons (30 mL) vegetable oil

2 medium baking potatoes (10½ oz./300 g), peeled, cooked until barely tender, drained, and cut into large dice

1 medium white onion (10 oz./275 g), peeled, thinly sliced, and separated into rings

1 cup (108 g) nopalitos, sliced and precooked as per the instructions on page 390 (substitute packaged, thoroughly drained and patted dry)

1 teaspoon (6 g) sea salt

½ teaspoon (0.325 g) dried whole Mexican oregano, lightly toasted and crumbled

This was [is?] a particularly noteworthy filling; as you'll see, it would lend itself as a filling for many other foods in this book, but it is also a lovely stand-alone vegetable side dish.

Prepare-ahead note: Nopalitos con papas may be prepared several days in advance and reheated; store in an airtight container in the refrigerator.

PREPARE THE FILLING

Heat the vegetable oil in a large skillet until shimmering; add the potatoes and onions, and cook over medium heat, stirring frequently, until the potatoes are browned and the onions are beginning to caramelize, 5–6 minutes. Add the remaining ingredients, stir to combine and heat through, and check for seasonings.

VARIATION

Chorizo con papas/Spicy Sausage with Potatoes and Onions: This is a classic combination you will find throughout Mexico as a filling for tacos, Gorditas, and many other foods; it can also be added to scrambled eggs. Substitute the *nopalitos* for an equal weight of Mexican chorizos (3.8 oz./108 g). Skin the sausages and coarsely chop the meat; add to the potatoes and onions cooking in the skillet; stir to brown lightly and use a wooden spoon to crumble the chorizo as it cooks. Omit the salt and oregano.

[MR]

An assortment of peeled tunas (prickly pears) outside the market. The colors are known regionally by unique names: pelona (red), amarilla (yellow), reina (green), and cardona (purple). Their sweetness makes them a popular hand fruit, although they are loaded with rather crunchy (albeit edible) seeds. Tunas are also used to make the popular queso de tuna, a caramel-like candy made with the fruit cooked in sugar. [MR]

[MC]

TUNA/HIGO CHUMBO

BOTANICAL: *Opuntia* spp./Family Cactaceae
ENGLISH: prickly pear cactus | **NAHUATL:** *nochtli*
OTOMÍ (Hñähñu): *kähä* (sweet tuna), *ixkähä*
(sour tuna or *xoconostle*)

For a complete description of the *Opuntia* species and tunas, see page 353.

(top) *A block from Mercado Municipal "Hidalgo," prepared-food* comedores *and produce stalls share space in the Mercado Independencia.* [MR] *(bottom) Irma Erdola of "Fonda Irma" displayed six different* guisados *in lovely clay* cazuelas. *Here she serves* bistec en salsa verde. [MR]

MERCADO INDEPENDENCIA

CALDO DE PUERCO

PORK RIBLETS WITH TOMATOES, POTATOES, AND RED POBLANO CHILES

TO PREPARE AHEAD
Enriched Lard (p. 530)

Piles of bright red *chiles poblanos* were in both markets and even on street corners in Dolores Hidalgo. This stew features a quantity of them in long, wide strips. While the more common green poblano turns a deep red, almost burgundy to black as it matures, a slight genetic variation yields these, which are a vibrant red at their peak. This may pose a bit of a challenge for cooks who can't find red poblanos: you could opt for maintaining the flavor of the stew but changing its aesthetic by using green poblanos; or you could keep the monochromatic aesthetic but alter the flavor by using red bell peppers that have been charred, peeled, seeded, and sliced, or large, canned pimientos.

Pork riblets are spare ribs that have been cut in half, with the curved center portion removed, resulting in a smaller, more uniform rib shape. This is the rib cut frequently used in Chinese barbecue recipes. Unless you have a meat saw, your butcher will have to prepare these for you.

Prepare-ahead note: Like many stews, Caldo de puerco benefits from an overnight rest in the refrigerator; prepare a day or two in advance and reheat just before serving.

YIELD: 6–8 SERVINGS

[MC]

FOR THE RIBLETS

½ cup (145 g) sea salt

1 gallon (4 L) water

3½ pounds (1.5 kg) pork riblets

FOR THE STEW

½ medium red onion (5 oz./137.5 g)

3 medium Roma tomatoes
(10½ oz./300 g)

2 medium cloves garlic
(½ oz./12 g), peeled

1 medium chile jalapeño
(¼ oz./35 g), preferably red, stem
removed and seeded (substitute
1 medium chile chipotle in
adobo, ⅓ oz./10 g, drained)

2 tablespoons Enriched Lard

8 cups (2 L) water, divided

2 medium baking potatoes
(13½ oz./380 g) peeled, halved,
and thickly sliced

3 medium red chiles poblanos
(1¼ lbs./555 g total; substitute
red bell peppers), charred,
peeled, seeded, and cut into
wide strips top to bottom, or
canned red pimientos (*Note*: If
using canned pimientos, there
is no need to char or peel them;
simply cut into long, wide
strips.)

2 teaspoons (12 g) sea salt, or
to taste

FOR SERVING

The rice of your choice

Frijoles de la olla (p. 530. *Note*:
Doña Irma made her frijoles de
la olla with the delectable flor de
junio beans, a pale violet bean
with cream-colored striations;
lacking those, use pintos.)

Warm maize tortillas

Salpicón of chopped white onion
and cilantro

Lime wedges

Salsa de molcajete (p. 533)

PREPARE THE RIBLETS

Dissolve the salt in the water; add the ribs and refrigerate for 3–4 hours. (The brining step is optional; see notes on brining in the "Market Fundamentals" chapter on p. 527.)

Remove the riblets from the brine and rinse thoroughly; discard the brining solution. Pat the riblets thoroughly dry with paper towels.

PREPARE THE STEW AND FINISH

Place the first four ingredients in the jar of a blender; add 1 cup (250 mL) of the water. Process until thoroughly liquefied; set aside.

Heat the lard in a large skillet or medium stockpot until shimmering; add the riblets a few at a time to brown; transfer the browned riblets to a platter until you have completed all of them.

Return the riblets to the skillet and pour in all of the tomato liquid from the blender; it should sputter and sizzle, so stand back. Add the rest of the water and stir to combine. Layer the potato slices and strips of *chile poblano* on top of the meat; shake the pan to cover the chiles with some of the liquid. Cook over medium heat for 15–20 minutes or until the potatoes are tender and the riblets reach an internal temperature of 145°F (63°C). Add the salt and check for seasonings.

TO SERVE

See notes on page 333 for reheating and serving. Slice the riblets into individual ribs, or leave 2–3 attached as preferred; plate with the rice and beans and tortillas if desired; diners sprinkle on the *salpicón* and add squeezes of lime juice and salsa to taste.

An enviable mound of fresh chiles in Dolores Hidalgo. The red ones at left are red chiles poblanos *(see recipe on preceding page); at center front are bags of fresh green* chiles guajillos; *on the far right are* chiles de chorro. *All are varieties of the* Capsicum annuum *species.* [MR]

CHILE DE CHORRO

BOTANICAL: *Capsicum annuum* L./Family Solanaceae | **ENGLISH:** yellow poblano pepper
NAHUATL: *chilli* | **OTOMÍ (HÑÄHÑU):** *ñ'i*

The *chile de chorro*—a variety of *chile poblano*—is popular throughout Guanajuato; it is grown only in the northern reaches of the state and essentially evolved by means of seed selection in the hands of campesinos. According to botanists, it is separated from the more common poblano by only two genes. It is longer and narrower than the common poblano and is a pale yellow-green color; it is also considerably more picante. The plant that produces *chiles de chorro* can grow to 24 to 32 inches (60–80 cm) in height; fruits measure 5 to 6¼ inches (12–16 cm) in length, and 2½ to 3¼ inches (6–8 cm) in width, making this one of the largest chiles in the world. *Chorro* in Spanish means "stream" or "jet" and refers to the fact that these chiles are grown on a very small scale in family plots and are therefore watered one plant at a time by hand from a hose or bucket. A popular dish in Guanajuato, *chile de chorro relleno*, features a chile filled with fresh cheese, onion, and cilantro; doused with an herbed vinaigrette and tomato sauce; and baked. The more common poblano may be used as a substitute to prepare a similar dish.

PICADILLO

PORK-AND-BEEF-MEATBALL STEW WITH POTATOES, CARROTS, AND ZUCCHINI

FOR THE MEATBALLS

2 tablespoons (30 mL)
  vegetable oil

¼ medium white onion
  (2½ oz./68.25 g), finely chopped

1 medium clove garlic (¼ oz./6 g),
  peeled and finely chopped

1 teaspoon (0.65 g) dried whole
  Mexican oregano *plus* ½ teaspoon (1 g) cumin seed, lightly
  toasted together and ground

½ teaspoon (2.5 g) black pepper,
  ground

1 teaspoon (6 g) sea salt

¼ cup (15 g) parsley, finely
  chopped

1 pound (500 g) *each* ground pork
  and ground beef

½ cup (60 g) breadcrumbs

1 medium chile chipotle in adobo
  (⅓ oz./10 g), with some adobo,
  minced

1 egg, beaten

Picadillo usually refers to a mincemeat mixture that is cooked and served atop a bed of rice. But doña Irma's Picadillo was a hearty meatball stew with vegetables. It had only the lightest hint of chile for a pleasantly warming effect—welcome on a chilly, gray day.

Prepare-ahead note: Like many stews, Picadillo benefits from an overnight rest in the refrigerator; prepare a day or two in advance and reheat just before serving.

YIELD: 8 SERVINGS

PREPARE THE MEATBALLS

Heat the vegetable oil in a skillet until shimmering; add the onions and garlic and cook over low heat until the onions are translucent, 3–4 minutes; add the ground oregano and cumin, black pepper and salt, and continue to cook for 1 minute; add the parsley, stir, and cook for 30 seconds. Transfer the onion-garlic mixture with the oil to a large mixing bowl. Add the meats to the mixing bowl; add the breadcrumbs and mix to combine. Add the minced chile to the beaten eggs, beat again to combine, and pour into the meat mixture; use your hands to knead and combine thoroughly. Fry a small patty to check for seasonings.

Form the meat mixture into 24 balls weighing approximately 1½ ounce (45 g) each; place the finished balls on a large platter as you proceed; refrigerate the meatballs as you prepare the rest of the stew.

[MC]

FOR THE STEW

½ medium red onion (5 oz./137.5 g)

3 medium Roma tomatoes
(10½ oz./300 g)

2 medium cloves garlic
(½ oz./12 g), peeled

1 medium chile chipotle in adobo
(⅓ oz./10 g), drained

2 tablespoons (30 mL)
vegetable oil

8 cups (2 L) water, divided

2 medium carrots (7 oz./200 g),
peeled and sliced on the
diagonal

2 medium baking potatoes
(13½ oz./380 g) peeled and cut
into large dice

2 medium zucchini (1 lb./454 g
total), halved lengthwise, seeded
if seeds are large and dry, halved
crosswise, then cut into strips
lengthwise

2 teaspoons (12 g) sea salt, or
to taste

FOR SERVING

The rice of your choice

Frijoles de la olla (p. 530; also
see Caldo de puerco, p. 328, for
recommended bean varieties)

Fresh sprigs of parsley

Warm maize tortillas

Lime wedges

Salsa de molcajete (p. 533)

Garnishes for the guisados *at doña Irma's* fonda: *top left, chiles serranos,* which can be sliced or eaten whole; *center, salsa de molcajete;* and *top right, a salpicón* of onion and chopped cilantro, along with lime wedges. [MC]

PREPARE THE STEW AND FINISH

Place the first four ingredients into the jar of a blender; add 1 cup (250 mL) of the water. Process until thoroughly liquefied. Heat the oil in a large skillet or medium stockpot until shimmering; pour in all of the tomato mixture at once: it should sputter and sizzle, so stand back. Add the rest of the water; bring to a boil, reduce to a simmer, and continue cooking another 8–10 minutes until the liquid reduces slightly. Gently lower the meatballs into the simmering liquid one at a time; shake the pan a bit to cover the meatballs with the liquid. When all of the meatballs have been added, add the vegetables and the salt. Shake the pan again to cover the vegetables. Continue cooking another 6–8 minutes or until the vegetables are tender; the meatballs will rise to the surface when they are fully cooked.

TO SERVE

See notes on page 333 for reheating and serving. Scoop some rice onto a plate; spoon on three meatballs per person and some cooking liquid along with some of the vegetables; ladle on some beans to one side if you wish. Garnish with fresh parsley; diners add tortillas, squeezes of lime juice, and salsa to taste.

There are restaurateurs that furnish food and drink at a certain price.

HERNÁN CORTÉS, 1520

[MR]

As you can see from the photo, doña Irma reheated the components of each dish immediately before serving. Pour a bit of vegetable oil into a skillet and heat until shimmering; add the meat of whatever kind first, followed by a portion of the vegetables. Heat on high heat for 1–2 minutes or until heated through. Use a large spoon or ladle to add some of the cooking liquid to the skillet; heat until boiling and serve immediately. It should be noted that Caldo de puerco, Picadillo, and Chuletas en chile pasilla were not served in bowls like soup; rather, they were served on plates with rice to sop up the couple of spoonfuls of cooking liquid that doña Irma poured on. On the far right is a large clay *cazuela* that holds Chuletas en chile pasilla (recipe follows).

CHULETAS EN CHILE PASILLA

PORK CHOPS SIMMERED IN TOMATILLO AND PASILLA SAUCE

TO PREPARE AHEAD
Enriched Lard (p. 530)

FOR THE PORK CHOPS
½ cup (145 g) sea salt
1 gallon (4 L) water
3½ pounds (1.5 kg) pork chuletas
(See above for description; for
the thin chops, you should plan
on two chops per serving. You
may also use smoked pork chops
for this recipe.)

FOR THE PASILLA SAUCE
3 ounces (85 g) chiles pasillas
(about 6–8 chiles), stems, seeds,
and veins removed
5 medium tomatillos (1 lb./500 g),
husks removed and rinsed
½ medium white onion
(5 oz./137.5 g)
2 medium cloves garlic (½ oz./12 g)
1 teaspoon (0.65 g) dried whole
Mexican oregano, lightly toasted
and crumbled
4 tablespoons (56 g) Enriched Lard
6 cups (1.5 L) chicken stock or
bouillon

For one reason or another (possibly thriftiness), the pork chops known as *chuletas* throughout Mexico are generally extremely thin, usually no more than ½ inch (1.25 cm) thick. If you can find those or have your butcher cut them for you, you'll have a more typical dish, but you may also use standard thick-cut pork chops if you prefer (or pound thicker ones to be thinner). Because *chuletas* are so thin, they cook very quickly, and they are extremely forgiving of overcooking (which is why they can simmer for such a long time in the chile sauce); thicker chops, on the other hand, need to be monitored closely so that they do not go above the recommended finishing temperature of 145°F (63°C).

Prepare-ahead note: The *chuletas* are best served on the day they are prepared. Use any leftover *pasilla* sauce to cook more *chuletas* on another day.

YIELD: 6–8 SERVINGS

PREPARE THE PORK CHOPS
Dissolve the salt in the water; add the chops and refrigerate for 3–4 hours. (If using smoked pork chops, omit this step. As with other recipes in this book, the brining step is optional.)

Remove the chops from the brine and rinse thoroughly; discard the brining solution. Pat the chops thoroughly dry with paper towels.

PREPARE THE PASILLA SAUCE
Do not toast the chiles (doña Irma was emphatic about this). Instead, cover them with boiling water and allow them to soak for a couple of hours until the water is cool to the touch.

While the chiles are soaking, bring a medium saucepan full of water to a boil; add the tomatillos and boil them for 5–6 minutes or until tender when pierced with a sharp knife.

Transfer the chiles to the jar of a blender, and reserve the soaking liquid. Transfer the tomatillos to the blender jar with the chiles and add the onions, garlic, and oregano; add 1 cup of the reserved chile soaking liquid to the jar and process until thoroughly liquefied.

SAUTÉ THE PORK CHOPS AND FINISH
Place the lard in a large, deep skillet and heat until shimmering. Sauté the pork chops a few at a time until browned, 2–3 minutes per side; transfer browned chops to a platter while you finish the rest. (Smoked pork chops may require less browning time.) Working with the same skillet in which you sautéed the pork chops, turn the heat to high; when almost smoking, pour in the chile sauce all at once: it should sputter and sizzle, so stand back. Bring the chile liquid to a boil; pour in all of the chicken stock and stir to incorporate; return the liquid to a boil. Add the pork chops to the sauce, reduce to

FOR SERVING

The rice of your choice

Frijoles de la olla (see Caldo de
  puerco, p. 328, for recommended
  bean varieties)

Warm maize tortillas

Lime wedges

Salsa de molcajete (p. 533)

a simmer, and continue cooking over medium heat for another 10–12 minutes, or until the chops are cooked through and the sauce slightly thickened.

TO SERVE

See notes on page 333 for reheating and serving. Plate two thin chops (or one thick chop) per person; place rice and beans on one side of the plate, and ladle some of the *pasilla* sauce over the meat and rice. Diners add tortillas, squeezes of lime, and salsa to taste.

> *It is a spiny plant similar in certain ways to the prickly pear cactus; it puts out many hexangular branches full of spines ordered at intervals in the form of stars, but one sticks out longer than the others, and near its base are fruits resembling blackberries in color, taste, form, and size. The juice of the berries cures rheum or other eye infirmities, especially when mixed with human milk.*

FRANCISCO HERNÁNDEZ, *HISTORIA DE LAS PLANTAS DE NUEVA ESPAÑA*, 1574–1577

[MC]

GARAMBULLO: GARBANCILLO, PADRE NUESTRO

BOTANICAL: *Myrtillocactus geometrizans* (Mart. ex Pfeiff.) Console/Family Cactaceae | **ENGLISH:** blue candle, whortleberry cactus, garambulla cactus, blue myrtle cactus | **NAHUATL:** *basto* | **OTOMÍ (HÑÄHÑU):** *biti-xoba*

The columnar cactus that produces the berry known in Spanish as *garambullo* is a characteristic sight in the semi-deserts of the Central and Northern Highlands. The cactus can reach heights of 15 feet (4.5 m). It has a well-defined trunk from which grow numerous branches in a blue-green color; these branches form other branches and eventually take the shape of candelabra. The branches have 5 or 6 rounded "ribs" or ridges, with evenly spaced, sharp spines; it is between and among these spines that the flowers and fruits are produced. The white flowers—known as *claveles de garambullo*, or whortleberry carnations—are consumed as a vegetable in some rural areas; they are prepared much like

flor de calabaza (p. 351), battered and fried, or chopped and mixed with scrambled eggs. Fruits are 5⁄16 to ¾ inch (1–2 cm) in diameter. Flowers appear from March through June, and fruits from May through July; cultivated specimens may produce in other seasons. The fruits are consumed fresh or dried like raisins. They have a sweet taste not unlike blueberries, which in fact they resemble. Fruits may also be used in marmalades, *aguas frescas*, and compotes, as well as in sorbet and ice cream; in many localities fruits are used to prepare a sweet wine. The quickly growing cactus is sometimes used as a natural fence, or as a silo for dried corn, thus impeding goats, cows, and other hungry animals.

Some famous nieves of Dolores Hidalgo, left to right: Garambullo, Aguacate, Mantecado, and Pétalos (made with the petals of roses or other flowers). [MR]

NIEVES

No trip to Dolores Hidalgo is complete without indulging in a few fantastical flavors of *nieves*. Although *nieve* translates literally to "snow," in everyday parlance it is an umbrella word for two classes of frosty foods: juice-based frozen treats, like sorbets, and milk- or cream-based ones.

Every day of the year, from 8:00 a.m. until 10:00 p.m., the *neveros*—makers and sellers of *nieves*—surround the main square, selling their wares from portable carts or wagons. Since the square is just a couple of blocks from the markets, it's common practice to fill up on something hearty in a *comedor*, then extend the market experience with a *nieve*. Many of the folks that prepare and sell *nieves* in Dolores Hidalgo have been in the business for several generations. It's a welcome and familiar sight to see the

vendors reaching out to you with a tiny wooden paddle balancing a clump of the flavor of your choice as a sample.

The offerings at Helados Aguilar—one of the most popular *neveros* in town—include a few unique flavors. Here is a list of a few of them: Tequila, *cerveza* (beer) with lime, *chicharrón* (pork cracklings), *camarones* (shrimp in frozen Clamato), *aguacate* (avocado), *garambullo*, mole, *carnitas*, and *pipián*.

The owner's niece Patricia Aguilar kindly shared several of her family's recipes.

NIEVE DE GARAMBULLO

BLUE CANDLE BERRY ICE

The markets of Dolores Hidalgo were flooded with *garambullo* when we visited. They aren't always available, though, so Patricia told us that when they aren't to be had, she makes a very similar flavor using three berries: blueberries, blackberries, and raspberries. Even when she has *garambullo*, she may toss in some of the other more plentiful berries as extenders. You may use any berry combination you like. The raspberry-flavored Chambord liqueur is my touch, and therefore optional.

YIELD: 1 QUART (1 L)

FOR THE SIMPLE SYRUP

1½ cups (300 g) sugar

1½ cups (375 mL) water

2½-inch (1.25 cm)-wide strips lime rind

FOR THE BERRIES

3 cups (390 g) garambullos (substitute assorted berries such as those mentioned above)

½ cup (125 mL) water

3 tablespoons (45 mL) Chambord liqueur (optional)

PREPARE THE SIMPLE SYRUP

Place the sugar, water, and rind in a small saucepan and bring to a boil. As the mixture heats, swirl the pan to dissolve the sugar. Cook about 1 minute or until the sugar has completely dissolved and the liquid is clear. Remove from the heat, cover, and allow to steep for 30 minutes as you proceed.

PREPARE THE BERRIES

Working in batches as necessary, place about half of the berries in a blender and reserve the rest; add half of the water and process 1 minute to thoroughly liquefy. Pour the liquid through a fine-mesh sieve into a large mixing bowl. Repeat, using the remaining berries, water, and liqueur if using.

Retrieve the lime rind from the simple syrup and discard; combine the puréed berries with the simple syrup in a heatproof bowl. Cover, and refrigerate at least 4 hours or preferably overnight.

FREEZE AND FINISH

Process in an ice cream freezer according to the manufacturer's directions. Place the finished ice in a covered container and freeze for 2–3 hours before serving.

NIEVE DE TEQUILA

TEQUILA ICE WITH FRESH GRAPEFRUIT AND ORANGE CHUNKS

FOR THE SIMPLE SYRUP

½ cup (100 g) sugar

1 cup (250 mL) water

½ cup (125 mL) *each* freshly
squeezed orange and grapefruit
juice

½ cup (125 mL) tequila (try to use
a reposado tequila)

2 tablespoons (30 mL) triple sec

FOR THE FRUIT

1 cup (200 g) *each* fresh orange
and grapefruit sections, peeled,
seeds and all traces of skin and
pith removed

[MR]

I won't say you could get drunk on this potent ice (maybe on an empty stomach you
could feel a bit of a buzz), but when you taste it, you'll have no question that it's made
with plenty of tequila. The small bits of fresh orange and grapefruit balance the tequila
and keep it from being too boozy, not to mention add a pleasant textural contrast.

YIELD: 1 QUART (1 L)

PREPARE THE SIMPLE SYRUP

Place the sugar and water in a small saucepan and bring to a boil. As the mixture heats,
swirl the pan to dissolve the sugar. Cook about 1 minute or until the sugar has completely dissolved and the liquid is clear. Remove from the heat and add the juices and
tequila; cover and allow to cool completely; stir in the triple sec. Cover, and refrigerate
at least 4 hours or preferably overnight.

PREPARE THE FRUIT

Coarsely chop the orange and grapefruit sections; pour any accumulated juices into the
bowl containing the tequila mixture. Chill the fruits thoroughly before using.

FREEZE AND FINISH

Process the tequila mixture in an ice cream freezer according to manufacturer's directions. About 1 minute prior to finishing, add the chopped fruits; continue processing
until thoroughly combined. Place the finished ice in a covered container and freeze
for 2–3 hours before serving.

DAIRY-BASED NIEVES

NIEVE DE MANTECADO

VANILLA FROZEN CUSTARD WITH NUTS AND CANDIED FRUITS

Mantecado is the Aguilar's top seller: not surprising when you experience the creamy sweet vanilla base contrasting with the crunchy, savory nuts. The dictionary of the Real Academia Española defines *mantecado* as a kind of bun or bread roll enriched with lard, or *manteca*—hence the name. *Mantecado* may also appear as the name of a very short sugar cookie, or even a kind of rich pound cake. Some recipes for the ice cream call for *nata*—rather like clotted cream; others include butter. Although clotted cream can now be had rather easily, I've opted for the butter—the Aguilar's choice—which in any case imparts a wonderful flavor and the right color for the dessert. The novelty of the Aguilar recipe is that it includes candied fruits and nuts: chopped raisins and the candied cactus known as *acitrón* (p. 419), as well as salted pecans and pine nuts. Since *acitrón* may not be available, I suggest a substitution of candied pineapple.

YIELD: 1 QUART (1 L)

[MC]

FOR THE FROZEN CUSTARD BASE

1 cup (250 mL) milk

1 Mexican vanilla bean, split lengthwise

1 can (14 oz./397 g) sweetened condensed milk

2 cups (500 mL) whipping cream

¼ cup (56 g) unsalted butter

¼ teaspoon (1.25 mL) salt

5 large egg yolks

1 tablespoon (15 mL) pure Mexican vanilla extract

FOR FREEZING AND FINISHING

1 tablespoon (14 g) butter

¼ cup (30 g) pine nuts

¼ cup (27 g) pecans, chopped

Salt to taste

¼ cup (33 g) acitrón, cut into small dice (substitute candied pineapple)

¼ cup (35 g) raisins, chopped

PREPARE THE FROZEN CUSTARD BASE

Pour the milk into a small saucepan fitted with a lid. Bring to a boil, add the vanilla bean, remove from the heat, cover, and allow to steep for 30 minutes. Retrieve the two halves of the bean and scrape off the seeds with a sharp knife; return the bean halves to the pan.

Add the next four ingredients to the pan with the milk and vanilla and heat over medium heat until small bubbles appear around the edge of the pan. Meanwhile, place the egg yolks in a large heatproof mixing bowl. Using a whisk, beat the yolks until light and fluffy. Still beating, slowly stream a ladleful (about 1 cup/250 mL) of the warm milk mixture into the beaten eggs. Beat thoroughly; repeat 2–3 times, adding more ladlefuls of hot milk, until the eggs are heated through. Very slowly stream the hot egg mixture back into the saucepan, whisking constantly. With the heat on medium-low, constantly stir the mixture with a wooden spoon 2–3 minutes or until the mixture is thick enough to coat the spoon. A candy thermometer should read 180°F (82°C). *Do not allow to boil*, or the eggs may scramble.

Immediately remove the pan from the heat source to stop cooking, and transfer the custard back into the heatproof bowl. Allow the custard to cool; cover and refrigerate several hours until thoroughly chilled, preferably overnight.

FREEZE AND FINISH

While the frozen custard base is chilling in the refrigerator, melt the butter in a small skillet until the foam subsides; add the pine nuts and pecans and toss to lightly coat the nuts with the butter (they should brown only very lightly); sprinkle on salt to taste and transfer to a small bowl.

Retrieve the vanilla bean and discard or save for another use. Add the vanilla extract and stir to combine thoroughly. Process the chilled custard in an electric ice cream maker according to manufacturer's directions. Just before removing the ice cream from the machine, add the chopped fruits and nuts and continue to process for 1 minute. Place the finished ice cream in a covered container and freeze for 2–3 hours before serving.

NIEVE DE AGUACATE

AVOCADO FROZEN CUSTARD

FOR THE CUSTARD BASE
1½ cups (375 mL) milk
1½ cups (375 mL) whipping cream
½ cup (100 g) sugar
¼ cup (62.5 mL) light corn syrup
¼ teaspoon (1.25 mL) salt
5 large egg yolks

FOR FINISHING
3 large ripe avocados (about
   1½ lbs./750 g total)
1 tablespoon (15 mL) freshly
   squeezed lime juice
3 tablespoons (45 mL) Midori
   liqueur (optional)

According to Davidson's *Oxford Companion to Food*, many Spaniards in the colonial era ate avocados with sugar; the trend persists in several countries throughout the tropics where avocados grow—although not as frequently in Mexico. The earthy avocado combined with sweetened milk is a natural. The *familia* Aguilar has been making this flavor since the business started in 1969 (the founding father claims to have created it). The bright green, melon-flavored Midori liqueur is my touch, and therefore optional.

Prepare-ahead note: Nieve de aguacate freezes well for a day or two but loses its distinctive fresh avocado flavor thereafter.

YIELD: 1 QUART (1 L)

PREPARE THE CUSTARD BASE
Place the first five ingredients in a large saucepan and stir to combine. Heat over medium heat until the sugar is dissolved and small bubbles appear around the edge of the pan. Meanwhile, place the egg yolks in a large heatproof mixing bowl. Using a whisk or handheld mixer, beat the yolks until light and fluffy. Still beating, slowly stream a ladleful (about 1 cup/250 mL) of the milk mixture into the beaten eggs. Continue beating and repeat 4–5 times, adding more ladlefuls of hot milk, until the eggs are heated through. Very slowly stream the hot egg mixture back into the saucepan, beating constantly. With the heat on medium-low, constantly stir the mixture with a wooden spoon about 2–3 minutes or until the mixture reaches 180°F (82°C) on a candy thermometer. *Do not allow to boil*, or the eggs may scramble. Immediately remove the pan from the heat source to stop cooking, and return the custard to the heatproof bowl. Allow the custard to cool; cover and refrigerate at least 2 hours or until no longer warm.

FINISH AND FREEZE
Cut the avocados in half; remove the seeds, scoop out the flesh, and coarsely chop them. Immediately drizzle the lime juice on them to prevent discoloring.

Pour about 2 cups (500 mL) of the custard base into the jar of a blender; add the chopped avocados, and the liqueur if using, and process until thoroughly liquefied. Pour the avocado mixture into the bowl with the remaining custard, stir to combine, and refrigerate until thoroughly chilled, preferably overnight.

Process the custard in an electric ice cream maker according to manufacturer's directions. Place the finished ice cream in a covered container and freeze for 2–3 hours before serving. The ice cream is best left at room temperature for 10–15 minutes before serving to slightly soften it.

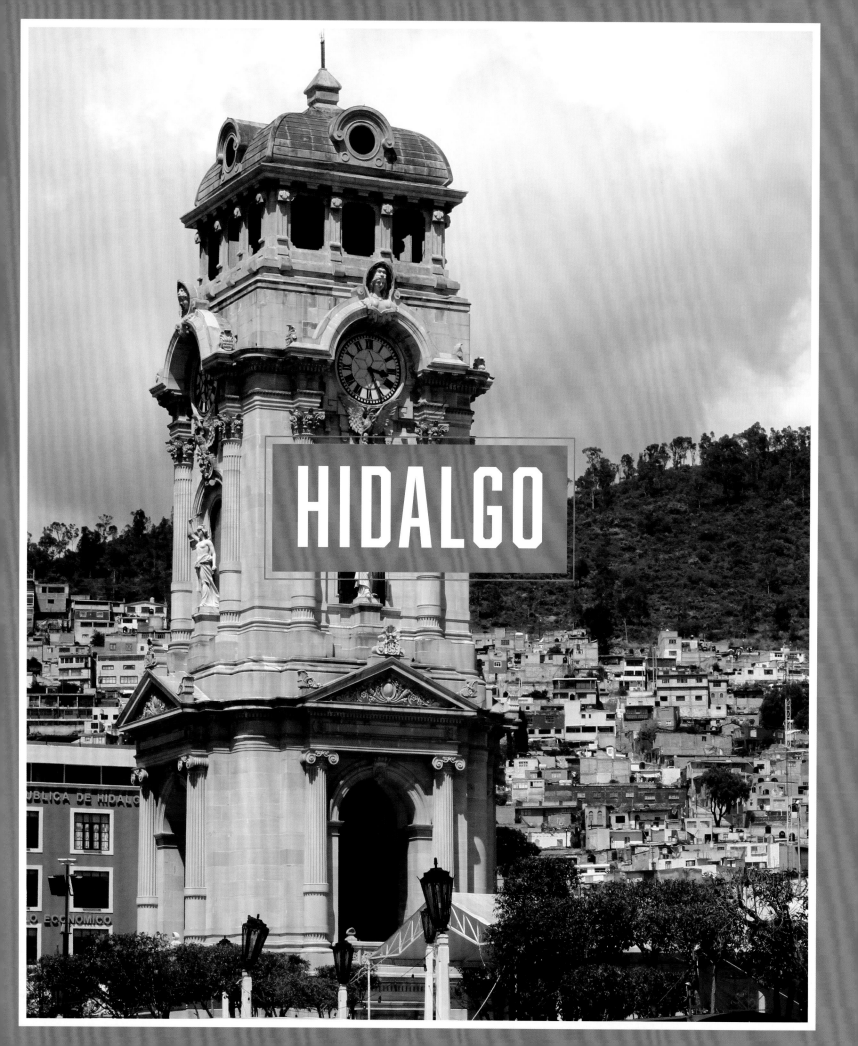

HIDALGO

PACHUCA DE SOTO

THE STATE CAPITAL of Hidalgo—Pachuca de Soto—stands as a bastion of progress, its neoclassical *cantera* stone buildings barely holding the surrounding wilderness at bay. Just beyond, wind-worn stone outcroppings tower above rocky landscapes skewered with spiky gray-green maguey plants and mesquite trees, painting a rugged backdrop. In fact, many movies have been filmed throughout the state, exploiting the natural setting as the stage set for dramas about the Mexican "Wild West." Residents burnish the image by boasting that their home is the birthplace of *barbacoa*, *charrería* (horsemanship), Mexico's mining industry, and soccer in the Americas. Plenty of other *hidalguenses* also chime in that Hidalgo has long been the source of the best pulque in the country. Gargantuan servings, maguey worms, and meat pocket pastries round out the menu.

The earliest settlers in the region made brilliant and extensive use of desert resources like maguey; the Spanish lust for precious metals and their introduction of horses and cattle impacted but did not supplant local traditions and economy. Although the fortunes of Pachuca have waxed and waned with the vicissitudes of the mineral industry, it was once the center of one of the richest mining regions in Mexico. In 1552, the first veins were discovered; by the mid-twentieth century it was estimated that one billion ounces of silver and five million ounces of gold had been mined. As new extraction methods were developed, the wealth of Pachuca radiated outward to nurture many other mining towns, some of which we will visit.

THE MEZQUITAL VALLEY AND THE OTOMÍES

The drive from Tequisquiapan, Querétaro, to Pachuca meanders through the magical and historical Mezquital Valley. This arid valley in southwestern Hidalgo has accommodated a large population of Otomíes since the Classic era (200–600 CE); they are still the dominant ethnicity in the region.

The site of Tula, capital of the Toltec civilization near modern Pachuca de Soto. The Toltecs, a highly influential Mesoamerican culture that occupied the Mezquital Valley starting in about 900 CE, were involved in the cultivation of maguey for a variety of purposes, including the extraction of aguamiel and the fermentation of pulque (p. 365). [CPTM/FOTO: RICARDO ESPINOSA-REO]

(opposite page) Mining revenues financed the 130-foot (40 m) tall Monumental Clock, which was inaugurated in 1910. [DCC]

Mercado de Barreteros, 1922.

MERCADO DE BARRETEROS

Of the nine markets in Pachuca, the Mercado de Barreteros is the oldest built market, opened to the public in the 1920s. (A *barretero* is a man who uses a pick to dig out minerals in a mine.)

[He sells] pointed tamales . . . with shelled beans mashed . . .

Tlacoyos are prepared by the score at Puesto "Joany" in the mark

TLACOYOS

THICK MAIZE CAKES FILLED WITH PURÉED PEAS

Historians of Mexican gastronomy generally concur that Tlacoyos are among the oldest surviving maize preparations in Mexico. In the sixteenth century, Bernardo de Sahagún and several other Spanish chroniclers described a panoply of maize breads displayed in the *tianguis* of Tenochtitlan: thick and thin, of different shapes, filled and unfilled, sauced and plain. One in particular was described as being pointed, elongated, and thick; some, he notes, were filled with mashed beans. Perhaps Sahagún was describing what today is called a *tlacoyo*. The word is probably a bastardization of the Nahuatl *tlatlaolli*, which means simply "masa of ground maize kernels." These small football-shaped snacks are extremely popular in the Central Highlands: in Mexico City, they are typically made of blue corn masa and are filled with cooked, mashed beans. One of several beans may be used, such as fava, lima, or navy beans; in other places, fillings may vary to employ cheese or meat such as *chicharrón prensado* (p. 397) instead. The states immediately surrounding Mexico City claim their own versions: that of Hidalgo is filled with a creamy purée of cooked *alverjones* (dried peas), and is served with a ladleful of *salsa verde*, a splash of *crema*, and some crumbled cheese. They may also be topped with Ensalada de nopales (p. 390)—or with nothing. Tlacoyos may be made and filled essentially as the recipe for Gorditas (p. 410), substituting the flavored cheese for the filling of your choice, shaping them in the characteristic elongated oval, and cooking as described.

TO SERVE

Place Tlacoyos on individual serving plates, and pour warm *salsa verde* over each. Drizzle on some Mexican *crema* or crème fraîche and sprinkle with crumbled Cotija or feta cheese, to taste. Some people also garnish with rings of sliced white onion or strips of *nopalitos*, although that was not something we saw in the *comedores* in Pachuca.

[MR]

HUITLACOCHE/CUITLACOCHE, HONGO DE MAÍZ

FUNGIC: *Ustilago maydis* (DC) Corda/Family Ustilaginaceae
ENGLISH: corn smut, maize smut, blister/boil smut (of maize) | **NAHUATL:** *cujtlacochi*

The English name of *huitlacoche* betrays the contempt felt among farmers in the United States and other English-speaking countries for this fungal parasite—which, by the way, is delicious. The fungus grows worldwide, although Mexico is the only country in which it is broadly consumed. Even though great efforts are made to eradicate it in farmland beyond Mexico, here it is considered a delicacy and is incorporated into many dishes. A parasitic fungus that grows on cobs of maize and also of its ancestor, known as *teocintle*, *huitlacoche* belongs to a group of macroscopic fungi colloquially called *carbones* (charcoals) or *tizones* (charred logs). The fungus spends part of its life inside the infected plant; spores are produced outside and can spread to other maize plants. Actually it can affect any part of the plant it touches, but the growth most commonly forms on the cobs and appears as black and gray blisters—hence another of its English names. The fungus grows on and among the individual grains of maize, such that when it is harvested,

some grains often stay attached; these become a recognizable feature of dishes prepared with *huitlacoche*. In fact, some recipes that include it also call for additional maize kernels. *Huitlacoche* is consumed throughout Mexico, but it is particularly prized and used more frequently in the Central Highlands. It is harvested by hand from July through September and sold fresh; nowadays it may also be dried or canned. It is unclear whether the fungus was consumed in ancient times or, like today's view, was considered a pest that threatened a good harvest. What is clear, however, is that only in the twentieth century did it become considered an ingredient of the haute cuisine of Mexico. Modern chefs may include it in crêpes, rather like truffles, or use it in lasagna or even desserts; in more humble cuisine, it is typically sautéed with onion, garlic, chile, and epazote and used as a filling for many of the maize breads found in this book, most particularly quesadillas.

QUESADILLAS

CHEESE-FILLED TURNOVERS

TO PREPARE AHEAD

Enriched Lard (p. 530)

Tortillas (unless purchased; the tortillas should be medium in size, about 6 inches/15 cm in diameter)

Quesadillas with three fillings, left to right: Alambre, Huitlacoche guisado, Hongos guisados. Salsas are: left, Salsa de xoconostle (p. 352); right, Salsa verde (p. 531). A mound of fresh maize masa in the background awaits transformation into Quesadillas. [MR]

Although the name is the diminutive of *quesada* ("cheesed," originally a type of cheesecake from Cantabria)—and although in its purest form the Mexican quesadilla contains little more than cheese—today, as with so many foods of Mexico, the hearty snack is wide open to interpretation. Different regions of the republic have their preferences for fillings—from meat or chicken to mushrooms, squash blossoms, or *huitlacoche*; most also contain some strips of stringy *queso Oaxaca*. Preparation methods vary, too: traditionally the quesadilla consists of an uncooked maize tortilla that is filled, folded, and sealed closed before being fried in hot oil; today it is just as common to place the fillings on a precooked tortilla and reheat the package on a comal or griddle—the way we saw them prepared in Pachuca. Tradition aside, the Pachuca method is easier for entertaining, since the tortillas may be prepared in quantity in advance (or even purchased, if of excellent quality), filled, and reheated immediately before serving. In the Central Highlands, quesadillas are often prepared with blue maize tortillas, and if you have access to them, give them a try. I offer the three fillings we enjoyed at the "La Güera" stall—Alambre, Huitlacoche guisado, and Hongos guisados—but there are many other *guisados* throughout this book that may also serve. By the same token, these *guisados* may be used as fillings for other snacks, such as Gorditas.

Prepare-ahead note: Prepare all the *guisados* up to one day in advance; reheat before serving. Assemble the Quesadillas just moments before cooking on the comal.

YIELD: 1 DOZEN

Enriched Lard, melted

1 dozen fresh maize tortillas
(preferably handmade)

2 cups (448 g) guisado of your
choice (recipes follow), warmed

12 ounces (340 g) queso Oaxaca
(substitute fresh mozzarella),
pulled into strings

FOR SERVING

Salsa verde (p. 531), and Salsa de
xoconostle (p. 352) or Salsa de
chile mora (p. 354)

Lime wedges

FOR THE ALAMBRE

1 chile chipotle in adobo, drained

½ cup (250 mL) white vinegar

4 tablespoons (60 mL) Spanish
olive oil, divided

1 teaspoon (6 g) sea salt

1 pound (500 g) beef tenderloin,
cut into 1½-inch (4 cm) cubes

1 medium white onion
(10 oz./275 g), cut into eighths

3 medium bell peppers (about
6½ oz./185 g each), in assorted
colors (red, yellow, green),
seeded and cut into eighths

PREPARE THE QUESADILLAS

Brush approximately 1 teaspoon (5 mL) of the melted lard onto a hot comal, griddle, or heavy skillet (preferably cast iron). Place one tortilla on the hot surface and cook over medium heat for about 30 seconds or until lightly browned; flip to the other side and cook until just browned. Remove from the comal, and immediately spoon 2 tablespoons (28 g) of the warm *guisado* onto the center of the tortilla; drape approximately 1 ounce (28 g) of the string cheese over the *guisado*. Fold the tortilla in half to cover the ingredients, and set aside as you prepare the rest.

Immediately before serving, brush the comal or griddle with more lard. Working in batches, heat the Quesadillas over medium heat until they are browned and the cheese is melted, 1–2 minutes per side. Serve immediately.

TO SERVE

Plate one or two Quesadillas per person; diners add their own salsas and squeezes of lime juice to taste.

ALAMBRE

BEEF BROCHETTE FILLING FOR QUESADILLAS

Alambre translates as "wire," and in Mexico the word is also used to signify a kebab or brochette. You may indeed thread the ingredients onto a skewer before grilling, but since everything will be coarsely chopped at the end, it is just as easy to place the meat and vegetables in a grilling basket. You can also coarsely chop the raw ingredients and sauté them on the order of stir-fry instead of grilling them, but for best flavor, cook on a gas or charcoal grill with lots of smoke.

YIELD: ABOUT 2 CUPS (650 G)

PREPARE THE ALAMBRE

Place the chile in the jar of a blender and add the vinegar, 2 tablespoons (30 mL) of the oil and the salt; process until thoroughly liquefied. Place the cubed meat in a nonreactive baking dish and pour on the vinegar mixture; refrigerate for 1 hour. Meanwhile, prepare a gas or charcoal grill.

Remove the meat from the marinade; discard any leftover marinade. Thread the cubes of meat alternating with pieces of the onion and the bell pepper onto a skewer. (Or, as noted above, you may place everything together in a grilling basket.) Grill until some char marks appear; the meat should still be quite rare. Remove from the heat and allow to cool.

Very coarsely chop the meat and vegetables. Immediately before serving, heat the remaining oil on a comal, a griddle, or in a heavy skillet (preferably cast iron) until shimmering. Add the meat and vegetables and stir until the meat is cooked to the desired doneness and the mixture is heated through. Serve immediately.

HUITLACOCHE GUISADO

SAUTÉED MAIZE FUNGUS

FOR THE HUITLACOCHE

⅓ cup (85 mL) Spanish olive oil

1 cup (175 g) fresh corn kernels
(2–3 large ears of corn)

½ medium white onion
(5 oz./137.5 g), charred (optional)
and finely chopped

2 medium cloves garlic (½ oz./12 g
total), charred (optional) and
finely chopped

2 medium chiles serranos (about
½ oz./14 g total), charred, peeled,
seeded, and finely chopped

1½ pounds (750 g) fresh huitlacoche, coarsely chopped if in
large pieces (substitute canned
huitlacoche, drained in a fine-
mesh sieve for 20 minutes)

1 teaspoon (6 g) sea salt, or to
taste

2 tablespoons (10 g) fresh
epazote leaves, chopped
(substitute 1 tsp./1.5 g dried
epazote, crumbled)

Well-prepared *huitlacoche* is like nothing else on earth: musky like the best marriage of mushrooms and truffles. I suppose some people have a problem with the texture, which at times can be slimy. But that happens most typically only if it is canned or frozen, or if it has matured too much. The issue of "too wet" *huitlacoche* may be somewhat mitigated by simply cooking it as follows but uncovered until it is quite dry; truly fresh *huitlacoche* doesn't present the same problem. Of course the fresh is infinitely superior in texture and flavor, but if you can only find canned, don't let that stop you from experimenting with this exotic dish. If you are able to locate fresh *huitlacoche*, it will most likely already have been removed from the cob. But should you be lucky enough to find it intact, just use a very sharp knife held close to the cob to slice it off along with any attached kernels. It isn't typical to char the onion and garlic for this dish, but one vendor we met did so, and the resulting smokiness beautifully complements the earthiness of the fungus; I list the charring as optional.

YIELD: 6–8 SERVINGS

PREPARE THE HUITLACOCHE

Heat the oil in a large, nonstick skillet until shimmering; add the corn kernels and cook over medium heat, stirring constantly to avoid sticking; cook until the kernels are pale golden, about 2–3 minutes. Add the onion, garlic, and chiles, and continue cooking over medium heat, stirring frequently, another 2–3 minutes or until the onions are translucent. Add the *huitlacoche* and salt and stir to incorporate; cover the skillet and cook, stirring frequently, until the *huitlacoche* has lightly browned and softened and any moisture has evaporated from the bottom of the skillet, 15–20 minutes. (*Note*: If using canned *huitlacoche*, add only ½ tsp./3 g salt and do not cover.) Add the epazote and check for seasonings; serve immediately or keep warm until using in a Quesadilla or other dish.

HONGOS GUISADOS

SAUTÉED MUSHROOMS

The thick pine and broadleaf forests of the Central Highlands produce a multitude of mushrooms during the rainy summer season and into fall. You may see any or all of these in the markets, as well as plain old white button or oyster mushrooms. A combination works well for this dish. For deepest flavor, be sure to include in the mix an intensely funky mushroom, such as shitake.

YIELD: 6–8 SERVINGS

Follow the preceding recipe for Huitlacoche guisado, using just 3 tablespoons (45 mL) Spanish olive oil, omitting the corn kernels and the *huitlacoche*, and using 1½ pounds (750 g) mixed fresh mushrooms, trimmed and very coarsely chopped. Over high heat, sauté the mushrooms in the oil until browned, 4–5 minutes; add the onions, garlic, and chiles, cover, and proceed as instructed. At the end of the cooking time, uncover and cook over high heat to evaporate all moisture. Finish with the salt and epazote.

FLOR DE CALABAZA CON RAJAS
SAUTÉED SQUASH BLOSSOMS AND CHILE POBLANO STRIPS

This vegetarian medley is lovely enough to serve as a side dish. Also try it as the filling for Tlacoyos (p. 346) or simple tacos; use leftovers in scrambled eggs. *Rajas* are thin strips of chile, most commonly the poblano. The skin of poblanos is quite thick and tough, so it must be removed by charring it; the process also gently cooks and softens

In the Mercado de Gastronomía of Mineral del Chico, Hidalgo, we spotted these humongous Quesadillas. Half Flor de calabaza con rajas, half Huitlacoche guisado (p. 350)—both with plenty of stringy, melted Oaxaca cheese. The "super-sized" quesadilla occupies the entire plate. [MR]

FOR THE POBLANO STRIPS

2 large chiles poblanos
  (6 oz./170 g each)

FOR THE SOFRITO

2 tablespoons (30 mL) Spanish
  olive oil
1 cup (170 g) white onion,
  chopped
2 medium cloves garlic
  (½ oz./12 g), finely chopped
1 medium chile serrano
  (⅓ oz./10 g), seeded and finely
  chopped
½ pound (250 g) squash blossoms,
  stems removed, rinsed, and
  thoroughly dried; coarsely
  chopped
1 sprig fresh epazote, leaves
  only, finely chopped (substitute
  ½ tsp./0.75 g dried epazote,
  crumbled)
1 teaspoon (6 g) sea salt

the chile. *Rajas* are widely available in cans, but of course the fresh will be more flavorful—and more rewarding to prepare. Beyond Mexico, squash blossoms are increasingly available seasonally in farmer's markets.

Prepare-ahead note: You may prepare the *rajas* a day or two in advance and refrigerate. Complete the filling an hour or two before you plan to finish the Quesadillas.

YIELD: 6–8 SERVINGS

PREPARE THE POBLANO STRIPS

Char the poblanos over a gas flame, in a grill, or in a searingly hot cast-iron skillet; they should be well blackened over all; any uncharred patches will not release their skin (the top stem area is particularly stubborn, but persist). Place the charred chiles in a resealable plastic bag, and seal tightly closed. After 10 minutes, carefully open the bag; working with one chile at a time, hold the chile under cold running water and rub off as much of the blackened skin as you can. Cut a slit in the chile lengthwise along one side; pry it open and remove the stem, all seeds, and veins; discard. Slice the chile into ½-inch by 3-inch (1.25 cm × 7.5 cm) strips; repeat with the remaining chiles.

PREPARE THE SOFRITO AND FINISH

Heat the oil in a large skillet until shimmering; add the onion, garlic, and *chile serrano* and cook over medium heat, stirring constantly, until the onions are translucent. Add the previously prepared *rajas* (if using canned, drain first and measure 1 cup/188 g); stir to incorporate and heat through; cook, stirring frequently, for 2–3 minutes. Add the squash blossoms and stir, turning the blossoms under the other ingredients so that they heat through and wilt. Reduce heat to low, and continue cooking, stirring constantly, for 2–3 minutes or until the blossoms are completely softened. Add the epazote and salt; stir and check for seasonings. Use at once, or keep warm for up to 1 hour.

SALSA DE XOCONOSTLE

HOT-SOUR PRICKLY PEAR SAUCE

The marriage of the citrusy-sour *xoconostle* with the smoky and picante *chile mora* creates a vibrant salsa that is excellent with seafood or grilled meats, or used as a counterbalance for anything with an earthy taste, such as Hongos guisados or Huitlacoche guisado (p. 350).

Prepare-ahead note: Salsa de xoconostle keeps well under refrigeration for up to 1 week. Bring to room temperature before serving.

YIELD: APPROXIMATELY 1 CUP (250 ML)

A pink tub of xoconostle *nestles among other locally grown products: pomegranates, pecans, and bundles of lemongrass.* [MC]

XOCONOSTLE/JOCONOSTLE, SOCONOSTLE, TUNA ÁCIDA

BOTANICAL: *Opuntia* spp./Family Cactaceae | **ENGLISH:** acidic prickly pear | **NAHUATL:** *xococnochtli*

Two ubiquitous fruits are produced by the useful *Opuntia* cactus species: *tuna* (prickly pear) and *xoconostle* (acidic prickly pear, pronounced show-coe-KNOWST-lay). The *tuna* (p. 326) is lightly tart and sweet, while the *xoconostle* is acidic and sour. In fact, the name in Nahuatl describes it: *xococ* = acid, sour; *nochtli* = *tuna*, the prickly pear fruit. *Xoconostles* are composed of a thin outer wall or skin that is somewhat difficult to peel; a thick inner wall, which is edible; and seeds arranged in the center of the fruit around a dry, fibrous core. Fruits vary in size according to maturity, but average about 1¾ inches (4.5 cm) wide by 2⁵⁄₁₆ inches (6 cm) long. Color gradates from fuchsia to pale yellow-green; the surface has a dull, waxy appearance. *Opuntia* is distributed throughout arid and semiarid zones of the Americas, with a high concentration in the Central Highlands of Mexico; *xoconostles* are cultivated primarily in the states of Hidalgo, Querétaro, San Luis Potosí, and México; they may also be gathered in the wild. The *xoconostle* species is quite genetically diverse and demonstrates at least twenty-five unique accessions (an identifier given to DNA sequences). *Xoconostle* as well as other products of the *Opuntia* species (e.g., *nopalitos*, p. 418) have been studied for health benefits and are high in antioxidants; fruits are also a rich source of soluble and insoluble dietary fiber. Peeled and seeded before consuming, *xoconostle* is used in salsas, stews such as *mole de olla*, in preserves and marmalade, in fruit drinks, or as a snack when salted and dried. Fresh *xoconostle* is increasingly available in specialty markets, but you may also use dried and rehydrate it.

FOR THE SALSA

6–8 medium xoconostles
(1 lb./500 g)

4 chiles moras (about ½ oz./15 g
total; substitute an equal weight
of chile morita or 1–2 chiles
chipotles), stems, seeds, and
veins removed, slit open and
flattened

¼ medium white onion
(2½ oz./68.75 g), peeled

2 medium cloves garlic
(½ oz./12 g), peeled

¼ teaspoon (1.5 g) coarse sea salt

PREPARE THE SALSA

Place a comal or heavy cast-iron skillet over high heat; add all ingredients except for the salt, and roast, turning frequently, until the chiles are darkened and fragrant and the other ingredients exhibit some overall darkening and char marks. Transfer the ingredients to a heatproof bowl and allow all but the chiles to cool. Place the chiles in 2 cups (500 mL) boiling water, and continue at a boil for 10 minutes; drain and discard the water. Peel the *xoconostles*; slice them in half and use a spoon to scoop out the seeds. (*Note*: For dried, unflavored *xoconostle*, rehydrate 4 oz./115 g of them in hot water for 1 hour to soften; drain, and proceed with the recipe.) Transfer all of the ingredients to the bowl of a food processor. Pulse a few times until the ingredients are well mashed but not completely puréed: the mixture should have some texture. (Alternatively, you achieve a more rustic texture by grinding the ingredients in a *molcajete* or mortar and pestle; grind the chiles, onion, garlic, and salt first, and add the *xoconostles* at the end.) Check seasonings; store in an airtight container.

SALSA DE CHILE MORA

SMOKY-SWEET CHILE SAUCE

Salsas of *chile mora* are very common in Hidalgo—where Sahagún served as missionary for a period in his career—and the first one we tasted was so exquisite that we immediately went on a quest for the chief ingredient (not difficult to find, in fact just a few stalls away from the one where we were eating the salsa). Lacking *moras*, you may use the more broadly available chipotles or *moritas* with equal success.

Prepare-ahead note: Salsa de chile mora keeps well refrigerated for up to 2 weeks; serve at room temperature.

YIELD: 2 CUPS (500 ML)

FOR THE SALSA

4 cups (1 L) water

8 ounces (225 g) chile mora
(substitute dried chipotle or
chile morita)

2 medium cloves garlic (½ oz./12 g)

1 teaspoon (6 g) sea salt

PREPARE THE SALSA

Bring the water to a boil in a medium saucepan; remove from the heat and add the chiles. Allow the water to cool to room temperature. Remove the chiles with a slotted spoon and reserve the soaking liquid. Cut or pull off the stems of the chiles and discard; place the chiles in the jar of a blender along with the garlic, salt, and 1½ cups (375 mL) of the reserved water. Process until thoroughly liquefied and there are no signs of whole pieces of the garlic. Store in an airtight container.

CHILE MORA/CHIPOTLE MORA, CHILE RAYADO

BOTANICAL: *Capsicum annuum*/Family Solanaceae | **ENGLISH:** none

Similar to the chipotle, the *chile mora* is also produced by smoke-drying a red jalapeño to preserve it. In this case, the jalapeño used is a slightly smaller variety than that for the chipotle, and the smoke-drying takes place for a shorter period of time, leaving the flesh still pliable and berry-colored (*mora* means "berry" in Spanish). The lightly sweet berry taste is more pronounced than that of the chipotle, too, due to the preservation technique. The visual difference between the two makes them easy to distinguish: the chipotle is a rich brown, the color of cappuccino, and looks very dry and dusty; the *chile mora* retains the deep red-to-purple tones, looks moist, and is less deeply wrinkled than the chipotle. While *chile mora* may not be easy to source, another chile in the same family—the *chile morita*—is broadly available. Also a small jalapeño when fresh, the *morita* is allowed to dry on the bush, and like the *mora*, is smoked for less time than the chipotle. As is true for most dried chiles, the sugar content becomes concentrated, contributing to the "berry" or "cherry" flavors that many people perceive. As you'll read throughout this book, the names for the same ingredients change dramatically from one place to the next, often making it difficult to pinpoint exact varieties. The vendor from whom I purchased the chiles in the photo called them *chiles moras*, while another vendor across the aisle called them *chiles rayados*. A rare jalapeño variety cultivated exclusively in Hidalgo, the *chile rayado* is bright red and covered with thin white veins. It may be sold fresh or smoked like the *chile mora*.

Chiles chipotles *have a dry, papery appearance compared to the* chile mora. [MC]

He sells . . . sauce of smoked chile.

BERNARDINO DE SAHAGÚN, 1540

HUASCA DE OCAMPO

RESIDENTS OF Huasca de Ocampo, suffering the effects of dwindling revenues from the town's traditional mining economy, have reinvented themselves and reversed the town's fortunes by exploiting its natural beauty and historical riches. Flyers publicizing zip-lining over the region's many gorges can be seen everywhere, and the town's official website presents a colorful cartoon animation of hot-air balloons drifting above lakes, hills, and valleys. Most visitors come for a weekend retreat from Mexico City, although Huasca de Ocampo—the first Pueblo Mágico to be named when the program launched in 2001—is now piquing international interest.

The narrow streets in the center of town are lined with colorfully painted limestone houses capped with pitched red tile or laminate roofs. Leaving town toward the east, the landscape opens to a valley where wealthy mining families built sprawling haciendas—now tourist attractions. The dramatic terrain surrounding them has been used as the setting for several movies, such as *Old Gringo* and *The Mask of Zorro*.

PORTALES/HUASCA DE OCAMPO

There is no official market building in Huasca de Ocampo. Instead, at times it seems that the entire town is a market: vendors cluster beneath the porticoes (*portales*) that trim the main square; and even on side streets, open doors and pleasant aromas invite you inside to try baked goods, fresh tortillas, or *pastes* (p. 382), the famed Cornwallian "empanada."

Barbacoa de carnero is one of the most beloved and well-known dishes in Mexico. And it is taken very seriously—almost as seriously as soccer. In fact, *barbacoa* is *the* food to eat while watching a soccer match on television. Many states proffer their own recipe as "the original," but *barbacoa* is most typically associated with the state of Hidalgo. Literally tons of *barbacoa* are prepared overnight in towns like Acatlán and Tulancingo and rushed to customers for breakfast in Mexico City, just an hour and a half to the

southwest. The sides of the highway between the city and Pachuca are littered with open-air restaurants that offer up heaping helpings of the delectation. *Chilangos* (as folks from Mexico City are known) rabidly voice their *barbacoa* preferences according to provenance, or meat, or a particular cook. And, for better or worse, commercially packaged *barbacoa* in the freezer section of many national supermarkets is boldly labeled "Barbacoa de Hidalgo."

Vendors of barbacoa are always recognizable in the markets by the rumpled sheath of maguey leaves that springs out of the container. The leaves were used during the cooking process, and now they serve to keep the meat warm and flavorful—and to promote the product as "the real thing." [MR]

In Hidalgo, *barbacoa* typically consists of mutton that is covered with maguey leaves (p. 365) and slow-roasted in a super-heated pit. Beyond that basic formula, we are drowned in a maelstrom of variations. The pit may be dug out of the earth, or formed below grade with brick and cement, or just cement. Or the cooking may happen in a traditional oven or in a pressure cooker. The meat may be lamb instead of mutton, or it may be beef, or goat, or even turkey or chicken. Seasonings vary, too: from something as simple as salt to complex adobos of dried chiles, cloves, oregano, marjoram, and other herbs and spices. Some cooks pour pulque into the pot; some don't. Mesquite wood may be used for the fire, or *encino* (holm oak), or whatever firewood may be available. And instead of maguey leaves, the meat may be covered in banana leaves or the bark of banana trees.

With so many variants, what exactly is *barbacoa*? To strip it to its essentials, *barbacoa* is some kind of meat (most commonly of the *Ovis* genus) that is seasoned, covered with a vegetal wrapper, steamed for several hours (traditionally in an underground oven), pulled, and served atop tortillas, with its own juices in a bowl on the side—the coveted *consomé*. But that lowly description hardly does justice to the magic of *barbacoa* as it is prepared in the hands of experienced cooks—who are usually devoted exclusively to *barbacoa*—each of whom adds his own unique *sazón*.

Most market *comedores* of the region offer *barbacoa* to their customers, but unlike many other market foods, the rather elaborate process of making *barbacoa* requires that it be done off premises. To understand the process, we spent the day with a famous local *barbacoa* master just a mile or so from the Huasca market. Don Viviano Escorza Aguilar prepares *barbacoa* only once a week, on Saturday. At 7:00 a.m. on Sunday morning, the feeding frenzy begins, and all 66 pounds (30 k) of his melt-in-your mouth *barbacoa* is sold out within a couple of hours.

[MC]

(above, left) An adolescent sheep weighing about 66 pounds (30 kg) was slaughtered on Saturday morning and hung until late afternoon to thoroughly drain all blood, and also to dry and briefly cure the meat. [MR] *(above, right) The most laborious part of the process is to slowly roast 12 pencas (maguey leaves) one at a time over the flame in the barbacoa pit to soften them. They will be used to line the cooking pit as well as to cover the meat.* [MC] *(below, left) In the kitchen, don Viviano adds garbanzos to the other ingredients in the giant pot for the consomé.* [MR] *(below, right) The huge pot holds potatoes, garbanzos, a fistful of whole garlic cloves, slivered onions, and a potent guajillo chile sauce. With some water and the captured juices from the meat, the whole morphs into the fabulous consomé—to some people the best part of eating barbacoa.* [MR]

(above) The pot of future consomé is carefully lowered into the white-hot pit. The hole measures about 26 inches (65 cm) deep by about 24 inches (60 cm) in diameter. Lined with bricks, the pit retains heat from a wood fire that has raged all morning. [MR] (below, left) Now the softened pencas are arranged around the hole in a characteristic flower pattern, tucked neatly between the pit walls and the pot of consomé. [MR] (below, right) A rack is placed atop the pot; the meat will be arranged on top of the rack. [MC]

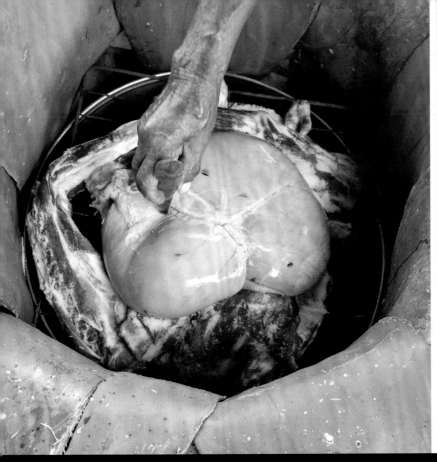

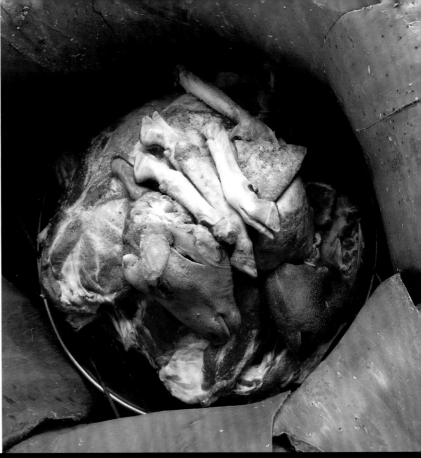

(above, left) Pieces of meat are arranged on top of the rack, with a liberal sprinkling of salt on each piece. Next is placed the panza—stomach—of the animal that has been filled with viscera and more of the guajillo sauce. Don Viviano pierces the pouch to allow steam to escape and keep it from rupturing during cooking. [MR] (above, right) A final layer of meat is arranged on top of the panza. Head and hooves go last. [MR] (below, left) The preparations are almost completed. A steel disk is lowered over the pit to cover it completely, and shovelfuls of ash from last week's fire are piled on to seal the pit. [MR] (below, right) Finally, a smoldering log and charcoal are arranged on top to create a fiery heat source from above. An animal the size prepared by don Viviano the day we visited will take about 4 hours to cook; a larger sheep can take up to 8 hours. The meat may be left in the pit until time to sell it, up to 7 or 8 hours. [MR]

Although he never crossed the Atlantic, the Franco-Flemish editor and engraver Theodor de Bry (1528–1598) wrote and illustrated many books about the New World based on explorers' accounts. This is De Bry's rendition of a barbacoa. *In today's* barbacoa, *the vestigial rack that holds the meats may still be wood but is just as likely to be a repurposed metal oven rack.*

BARBACOA: HISTORY AND ETYMOLOGY Along with words like "canoe," "hurricane," "papaya," "maize," "tobacco," and many others, *barbacoa* passed through Spanish into the English language from the Taino people of the Caribbean. Unlike today's "Texas barbecue," the Taino *barbacoa* had nothing to do with a flavor or a specific food, or even a cooking process. Instead, it was a wooden structure with many uses. According to *The Modern Taino Dictionary*, a *barbacoa* was a tall, four-legged platform, made of green sticks or the bark of a royal palm, used in the process of roasting, drying, or smoking meat. It also served as a cot. Gonzalo Fernández de Oviedo y Valdés, historiographer to the Spanish Crown during the conquest of the Indies, further described the *barbacoa* as a tall rack for storing corn out of the reach of vermin and humidity, or where native boys could perch to watch over the crop fields. When used for cooking, the green, young wood and the height of the platform above the flames prevented the structure from catching fire; it also meant that meats and fish were most likely smoked or slowly dried, rather than roasted.

Culinary scholars and experts in Mexican cuisine Cristina Barros and Marco Buenrostro speculate that the art of pit-cooked *barbacoa* was developed by the Chichimecas, seminomadic tribes that extended throughout northern Mexico. In the pre-Columbian era, meats like turkey, peccary, or iguana as well as fish may originally have been roasted in this manner. Old World goats and sheep did not arrive in Mexico until European contact; however, the *borrego cimarrón* (*Ovis canadensis*, bighorn sheep) occupied large swaths of North America, extending into the Chichimeca home of northern Mexico, and may at some time have been included in the primal *barbacoa de carnero*.

BARBACOA DE CARNERO

SLOW-ROASTED LAMB AU JUS

FOR THE MARINADE AND THE LAMB

6 chiles guajillos (approximately 2½ oz./75 g), stems removed and seeded

4 cups (1 L) boiling water

2 tablespoons (30 mL) vegetable oil

¼ cup (62.5 mL) pineapple or apple cider vinegar

1 medium white onion (10 oz./275 g), peeled and charred

4 medium cloves garlic (1 oz./24 g), peeled and charred

2 sprigs fresh epazote, leaves only (substitute 1 tsp. dried epazote, crumbled)

1 teaspoon (0.65 g) dried whole Mexican oregano, lightly toasted and crumbled

2 teaspoons (12 g) sea salt

1 bone-in leg of lamb or mutton (approximately 6 pounds/ 2.75 kg), trimmed of fat

Banana leaves (substitute parchment paper)

Dissecting don Viviano's technique can suggest some alternatives for creating *barbacoa* in the home setting: instead of the maguey leaves, we'll use more easy-to-access banana leaves to add the herbaceous flavor to the meat; for the smokiness captured in the pit, we'll give the meat a light hit of smoke either in a stovetop smoker or on a gas or charcoal grill; and to finish, we'll jerry-rig a pot filled with water that will slowly steam the meat in a conventional oven and produce the flavorful and coveted *consomé*. This recipe comes pretty close to the original in flavor.

Prepare-ahead note: This slow-roasting method takes about 4 hours, so plan accordingly. Marinate and smoke the meat a day in advance, and refrigerate the meat until the next day. Make the preparations for the *consomé* and complete the roast in the oven on the day you plan to serve.

YIELD: 6–8 SERVINGS

MARINATE AND SMOKE THE LAMB

Place the chiles in the boiling water; remove from the heat and allow to cool to room temperature. Transfer the chiles to the jar of a blender with a slotted spoon, and reserve the soaking liquid. Pour 2 cups (500 mL) of the liquid into the blender jar with the chiles, and add the next seven ingredients. Process until thoroughly liquefied.

Tacos of Barbacoa de carnero. [MR]

FOR THE CONSOMÉ

6 cups (1.5 L) water

2 cups (500 g) garbanzos,
   parboiled until just tender

2 cups (500 g) potatoes, peeled,
   cut into 1-inch (2.5 cm) cubes,
   and parboiled until just tender

1 medium white onion
   (10 oz./275 g), cut into half-
   moons (quartered, then each
   quarter sliced into half-moon
   shapes and separated into
   sections)

6 medium cloves garlic
   (1½ oz./36 g), peeled

2 sprigs fresh epazote (substitute
   1 tsp. dried epazote, crumbled)

FOR SERVING

Warm maize tortillas

Lime wedges

Salsa verde (p. 531) or the salsas of
   your choice

Place the lamb in a baking dish large enough to hold it comfortably; pour the chile marinade over the lamb to cover it completely. Refrigerate at least 2 hours or overnight.

After the marinating period, remove the lamb from the marinade and shake off any excess; reserve the marinade. Place 2 or 3 large banana leaves on a work surface, the edges overlapping a bit to prevent leaks. Place the lamb in the middle of the leaves, fold the leaves over, and wrap to completely cover the meat. (*Note*: If using parchment, place 5–6 whole bay leaves on top of the meat before wrapping.)

Smoke the wrapped lamb for 30 minutes in a stovetop smoker or in a gas or charcoal grill using mesquite wood smoking chips. (Full instructions for both methods are found in *Yucatán*, pp. 537–538, or in online resources.) The smoking step is optional, but adds great flavor.

PREPARE THE CONSOMÉ AND ROAST THE LAMB

Remove all but one rack from your oven, and position the remaining rack at the lowest level; preheat the oven to 285°F (140°C). In a 4-quart (4 L) stockpot, pour the reserved chile soaking water and the reserved marinade, and add the ingredients for the *consomé*. Locate a cake rack or other type of heatproof rack on top of the stockpot. Open the bottom part of the banana leaves from the lamb to expose the meat, leaving the rest of the meat wrapped (this is to provide a place where the juices can drip out to collect in the stockpot). Place this half-wrapped lamb on the rack atop the stockpot, cover the top of the lamb with heavy-duty aluminum foil, extending over the sides of the pot and crimped tightly to the edges of the rack to seal openings and prevent steam from escaping from the stockpot during roasting. Place this whole contraption into the oven. Bake for approximately 4 hours, or until a meat thermometer reaches approximately 175°F (80°C).

TO SERVE

Pull the meat off the bone and tear into large pieces (see photo on p. 363). Place the meat atop warm tortillas; diners add squeezes of lime juice and their favorite salsas to taste. Serve the *consomé* on the side in individual soup bowls.

*Honey is also extracted from the plant called maguey, which is superior to sweet
or new wine; from the same plant they extract sugar and wine, which they also sell.*

HERNÁN CORTÉS, 1520

[CPTM/FOTO: RICARDO ESPINOSA-REO]

AGUAMIEL AND PULQUE

While both of these uniquely Mexican beverages are produced in several states in the Central Highlands, the greatest production of the pulque maguey occurs in Hidalgo. Simply explained, *aguamiel* (honey water) is the sweet, herbaceous nectar extracted from any one of several species of agave; pulque is produced by allowing the *aguamiel* to ferment overnight or for as long as ten days. With an alcohol content ranging from 4 percent to 8 percent, pulque is comparable to most beers. As in ancient times, sale of pulque in the markets is often prohibited, although many vendors work around the system by keeping their stash well out of sight and by moving around a lot. Nonetheless, pulque is frequently employed in many foods served in the markets, including *barbacoa*, or in breads (p. 368) and even some sweets.

(left) Pulque fresh from the maguey plantations in Hidalgo was rushed by train to pulquerías in Mexico City. (right) Pulquería "La Flor Pura" in the neighborhood of Tacubaya, Mexico City, 1880s.

(left) An Otomí woman selling an assortment of Pan de pulque—pulque bread. [MR] *(right) Market stalls, bakeries, tortillerías, and comedores line streets of the tiny pueblo of Huasca de Ocampo. Tempting aromas emanate from doorways and corridors. Panadería "Doña Sol" is renowned for its pan de pulque.* [MR]

In precontact times, the mildly intoxicating effects of pulque made it suitable for a variety of mystical ceremonies, including the rites of human sacrifice. While the Mayas apparently tolerated a culture of imbibing, even drunkenness, the sale and administration of pulque were strictly controlled in Aztec society: it was the drink of priests and warriors. Immediately following the conquest, pulque lost its sacred status and was enjoyed by natives as well as the Spanish colonialists. After Mexican independence in 1821, the production and consumption of pulque exploded, and soon there emerged the phenomenon of the *pulquería*—bars where pulque was served. By the early twentieth century, there were some one thousand *pulquerías* in Mexico City alone.

Starting in the 1860s, great plantations of the maguey grown for pulque proliferated in many areas, but most were in Hidalgo and Tlaxcala. Due to its rapid fermentation, pulque was typically produced at the hacienda near the maguey plants and consumed locally; but for larger production, it had to be rushed by train to market each morning, most of it destined for the *pulquerías* in Mexico City.

As the pulque industry gradually diminished during the course of the twentieth century, the land formerly used for maguey was employed for other crops. Nonetheless, pulque remains an ongoing pleasure among locals wherever it is produced—annual pulque fairs are held in many communities of Hidalgo as well as nationally—and recent advances in packaging techniques mean that several brands of pulque are now available beyond Mexico.

Soledad Villa ("doña Sol") welcomes visitors to her bakeshop, which has been in operation in the same location near the market porticoes since 1982. [MR]

PAN DE PULQUE

PULQUE BREAD

TO PREPARE AHEAD

Enriched Lard (p. 530)

[MR]

Although pulque dates back a millennia or two, bread leavened with the fermented beverage happened only in the hands of Spanish-trained Indian bakers a few generations after Columbus had brought grains of wheat to the New World on his second American voyage. The natural fermentation of pulque from *aguamiel* occurs spontaneously as an interaction among several yeast strains (e.g., *Saccharomyces carbajali*), bacteria (e.g., *Lactobacillus* sp.), and sugars (mostly sucrose and glucose); these interactions describe essentially the same process as that used for making bread rise. Unlike commercial yeasts, however, pulque is a very slow leavener: it can take anywhere from 4 to 7 hours or more for the dough to double in volume. Prepare the dough in the morning, and bake in the afternoon or evening. Until quite recently, pulque has not been available beyond the maguey-growing regions of Mexico. But now, new canning technologies have made the beverage increasingly available in select outlets; you will appreciate the light sweetness and gently herbaceous quality that the pulque lends to the bread. Some of the newly available canned pulques are flavored. Feel free to experiment! However, these flavorings may affect the leavening effects of the pulque; if you have any doubts, you may add up to 1 tablespoon (16 g) of active dry yeast to the mixture at the same time you add the pulque (this will naturally affect the rising time). Lacking pulque, use a sweet, malty beer. In Querétaro and Hidalgo, Pan de pulque is formed into any of a variety of fanciful shapes: *doblados* (folded), *papayas* (elongated), *conchas* (round with shell-shaped flavored sugar toppings). This recipe offers instructions for the *doblados* ("folded" into a shape resembling a pig's face), but you may make simple balls or any shape you like working with 3 ounces (83 g) of the dough.

Prepare-ahead note: As mentioned above, allow several hours for the rising; the dough can be made in about 15 minutes, and the baking takes just 15–20 minutes. Pan de pulque keeps for about 3–4 days in an airtight container; leftovers make great toast.

FOR THE DOUGH

1 cup (200 g) granulated sugar, divided

½ cup (100 g) piloncillo, grated (substitute an equal quantity of dark brown sugar or muscovado)

1 cup (250 mL) pulque (substitute sweet, malty beer)

4 cups (500 g) all-purpose flour, plus additional for kneading

1 teaspoon (6 g) sea salt

1 teaspoon (3 g) ground canela (Mexican cinnamon)

½ teaspoon (1.5 g) ground anise

9 ounces (250 g) Enriched Lard

2 large eggs, lightly beaten

PREPARE THE DOUGH

Add 1 tablespoon of the granulated sugar and all of the *piloncillo* or muscovado to the pulque and stir until dissolved. Allow to rest for 1 hour.

Sift the dry ingredients together and set aside. In the bowl of a stand mixer fitted with the dough hook, beat the lard until lightened in color and fluffy; add the eggs and continue beating until loosely incorporated. Add the pulque mixture and continue to beat slowly as you gradually add the dry ingredients. Once the dry ingredients have been added, beat on high for 2–3 minutes to begin the kneading process.

Turn the dough out onto a floured surface, and knead 3–4 minutes or until elastic, sprinkling more flour onto the work surface as needed to keep the dough from sticking. Place the dough in a large bowl greased with butter or more lard, and allow to rise in a warm place for several hours or until doubled in size. (As noted above, this can take as few as 4 or as many as 7 or 8 hours, depending on your cooking environment and climatic conditions.)

FORM THE BREADS AND BAKE

Grease two large baking sheets with lard or vegetable oil. Turn the risen bread onto a floured work surface and knead briefly, about 30 seconds. Cut the dough into 12 pieces weighing about 3 ounces (83 g) each. Knead one ball briefly, then flatten into a circle measuring about 4 inches (10 cm) in diameter. Using a sharp knife, cut two slits on the top of the circle spaced 1 inch (2.5 cm) apart. Form the resulting flaps into points. Fold the center part between the two points down to cover two-thirds of the circle to form the "snout"; use your fingers to press two small indentations for the nostrils. Then fold down the two pointed flaps to form the "ears." (See the adjacent photo for finished results.) Proceed with the remaining dough. Allow to rise in a very warm place (near the preheating oven if possible) for 3 hours. (*Note*: After rising and baking, the darling pig faces lose quite a bit of detail, so don't be too disappointed!)

Preheat the oven to 425°F (220°C); sprinkle the breads lightly with the remaining granulated sugar, and bake approximately 15 minutes or until risen and golden brown.

[MC]

(above) Around the corner from the bakery, vendors of prepared foods set up shop beneath the porticoes of the main square, serving a tempting array of offerings. Ana María Magos shared recipes with us as she hectically waited on customers. Large clay *cazuelas* held *Huitlacoche con calabaza*, *Requesón guisado*, *Mole verde*, rich mole for *Mole con queso*, *Verdolagas con carne de puerco*, and many more *guisados* used for filling maize-based snacks. [MC] (below) Tacos of *Huitlacoche con calabaza* (left) and *Requesón guisado* (right). [MC]

GUISADOS PARA TACOS, QUESADILLAS Y GORDITAS

FILLINGS FOR MEXICAN MAIZE SNACKS

Use these fillings for tacos, as explained below, but many of them can also be used to fill Quesadillas and Gorditas. Recipes yield enough filling for 1 dozen pieces. Once you try a few, you'll quickly realize that many of these *guisados* can also serve as stand-alone stews or side dishes.

To prepare tacos, lightly heat fresh maize tortillas before adding the fillings. Brush a comal or griddle with melted lard or vegetable oil; heat one maize tortilla quickly for 8–10 seconds per side. Remove the tortilla from the comal and immediately fill with your choice of *guisado*. Fold in half, then reheat again briefly on both sides. Serve immediately with your favorite salsas. The call to do this as a party is loud and clear: prepare several of the following *guisados* (or others in this book); keep them warm in chafing dishes (or better yet, clay *cazuelas* as pictured in the photo) arranged on a buffet; heat the tortillas using a portable cooktop, and assemble and heat the tacos to order.

HUITLACOCHE CON CALABAZA

MAIZE FUNGUS WITH ZUCCHINI FILLING

Follow the instructions on page 350 for Huitlacoche guisado, replacing the corn kernels with an equal amount of medium-diced zucchini.

REQUESÓN GUISADO

RICOTTA WITH HERBS AND SERRANO CHILE FILLING

2 cups (500 mL) requesón
  (substitute ricotta cheese)
½ cup (85 g) white onion, minced
¼ cup (15 g) *each* fresh cilantro
  and epazote leaves, chopped
  (substitute flat-leaf parsley for
  the epazote)
2 medium chiles serranos (about
  ⅓ oz./10 g each), finely chopped

Mix all ingredients and store in an airtight container.

Left, *Mole con queso*; right, *Mole verde.* [MC]

MOLE VERDE

GREEN MOLE WITH SHREDDED CHICKEN FILLING

Doña Ana María and all of the operators of *comedores* in the Huasca market arrive at the *portales* around 8 a.m., and they wind down sometime around 9 p.m., a rhythm that repeats seven days a week year-round. Somehow during their "rest" period, they are able to make more food for the next day's customers. Obviously, some shortcuts are taken. Given today's harried pace, I don't mind a few shortcuts myself—as long as they are delicious. The señora gave me her wonderful secret for a fast and flavorful *mole verde*.

Prepare-ahead note: Prepare the Salsa verde a day or more in advance and refrigerate or freeze as per the instructions; cook chicken pieces of your choice and shred as much as a day in advance, or use leftovers.

TO PREPARE AHEAD
Salsa verde (p. 531)

FOR THE MOLE VERDE
1 tablespoon (15 mL) vegetable oil
1 recipe Salsa verde
¾ cup (93.75 g) pepitas (green pumpkin seeds), lightly toasted over high heat in a heavy skillet until some of the seeds are barely golden, and ground to a fine powder in a food processor
¼ teaspoon (0.5 g) ground cumin
2 cups (600 g) cooked, shredded chicken

PREPARE THE MOLE
Heat the vegetable oil in a large saucepan; when shimmering, add all of the Salsa verde at once: it will sputter and sizzle, so stand back. Add the ground squash seeds and cumin, and cook over medium heat, stirring frequently, for 4–5 minutes or until slightly thickened. Add the shredded chicken and stir to combine. Continue to cook another 2–3 minutes to amalgamate the flavors.

MOLE CON QUESO

MOLE WITH CREAM CHEESE FILLING

TO PREPARE AHEAD
Mole xiqueño paste (p. 270) or
Mole chiapaneco paste (p. 72)

FOR THE TACOS

1½ cups (325 mL) mole paste

½ cup (125 mL) rich chicken stock or bouillon

1 eight-ounce (225 g) package double cream cheese, at room temperature

Doña Ana María's version used *mole poblano* (I suspect purchased from another vendor). It was essentially the mole paste, very thick, thinned only with a little stock. Use the very similar paste for Mole chiapaneco or Mole xiqueño for this recipe. The cheese she used was *queso doble crema*; use double cream cheese if available, or standard cream cheese.

PREPARE THE TACOS

Dilute the paste with the chicken stock; cook over medium heat for 3–4 minutes until the mixture re-thickens. Prepare a tortilla as explained above. Spread 2 heaping table-spoons (about 30 g) of the mole in the center of the tortilla; top with 1 heaping table-spoon of the cheese (about 18 g). Fold the tortilla closed and finish as described above.

Entertainments in the market are an enduring tradition. Roving musicians stroll through the market corridors; enjoy the entertainment while you eat in exchange for a (voluntary) small tip. The day's playlist was an assortment of lively ranchera *tunes.* [MC]

TINGA DE POLLO

SHREDDED CHICKEN IN CHIPOTLE-TOMATO SAUCE FILLING

TO PREPARE AHEAD

Salsa de jitomate (p. 532)

FOR THE TINGA

1 recipe Salsa de jitomate

½ teaspoon (1 g) ground cumin

1 chile chipotle in adobo (10 g), drained

2 tablespoons (30 mL) vegetable oil or lard

½ cup (137.5 g) white onion, chopped

2 cups (600 g) cooked, shredded chicken (*Note:* For more flavor, grill the chicken on a gas or charcoal grill; shred while still warm.)

PREPARE THE TINGA

Pour half of the tomato sauce into the jar of a blender; add the ground cumin and the chile; process until thoroughly liquefied; set aside. Heat the vegetable oil in a large skillet. Add the onions and cook over medium heat until translucent, 3–4 minutes. Add the shredded chicken and stir to incorporate. Pour all of the tomato mixture from the blender into the skillet at once; it should sputter and sizzle, so stand back. Add the remaining tomato sauce and continue to cook over medium heat, stirring occasionally, 6–8 minutes or until most of the liquid has evaporated. The mixture should be quite dry.

Tinga de pollo. [MR]

VERDOLAGAS CON CARNE DE PUERCO

PORK WITH TOMATOES AND PURSLANE

Follow the recipe for Costillas con verdolagas on page 401, but substitute 1 pound (500 g) coarsely chopped (not ground) pork meat for the chops. Proceed as directed.

CALDO DE ALVERJÓN

PEA SOUP WITH CACTUS PADDLE STRIPS

FOR THE SOUP

1 medium chile guajillo
(⅓ oz./11 g), stems, seeds, and
veins removed

½ pound (250 g) whole dried peas

10 cups (2.5 L) water, divided

2 teaspoons (12 g) sea salt

1 sprig fresh epazote (substitute
½ tsp./0.75 g dried epazote,
crumbled)

3 ounces (85 g) smoked slab bacon

2 tablespoons (30 mL) Spanish
olive oil

½ medium white onion
(5 oz./137.5 g), chopped

2 medium cloves garlic
(½ oz./12 g), peeled and chopped

2 medium Roma tomatoes
(7 oz./200 g), quartered

8 ounces (250 g) fresh nopal
paddles, spines removed and
sliced into strips measuring
approximately 2 inches by
¼ inch (5 cm × 63 mm; substitute canned nopalitos, drained)

It can be quite chilly in this mountain town, so hearty soups and stews are always welcome. At the *puesto* "Doña Mar," Margarita Fernández maintains many pots at the simmer, and her offerings change daily. She has been in this same corner location—right next to Ana María Magos—since 1970. The *alverjones* (dried peas) doña Mar used were pale yellow, but any dried whole pea will work. This soup is also delicious with garbanzos or cannellini beans. The secret is to simmer the soup slowly for another 30 minutes to 1 hour after the peas are barely tender to reduce the stock slightly and intensify the flavors.

Prepare-ahead note: Like many soups and stews, the flavor only improves with an overnight rest in the refrigerator. Prepare a day in advance if you wish and reheat just before serving.

YIELD: 8 SERVINGS

PREPARE THE SOUP

Cover the *guajillo* with boiling water, and allow it to soak for 30 minutes as you proceed.

Rinse and pick through the peas; drain, and transfer the peas to a medium stockpot. Cover the peas with 9 cups (2.25 L) of the water; add the salt, the epazote, and the bacon, and bring the water to a boil. Reduce to a simmer, and continue simmering as you proceed.

In a medium skillet, heat the olive oil until shimmering; add the onions and garlic and cook, stirring frequently, until the onions are translucent, 3–4 minutes. Transfer the mixture to the stockpot with the peas.

Place the remaining 1 cup (250 mL) water in the jar of a blender; add the tomatoes; drain the *guajillo* and add it to the blender jar. Process until thoroughly liquefied. Pour the mixture into the stockpot with the peas and stir to incorporate.

Continue to simmer the soup until the peas are tender, about 1½ to 2 hours. Add the *nopalitos*; reduce the heat to low and continue to simmer another 30 minutes to 1 hour to amalgamate the flavors and reduce the liquid slightly.

Serve immediately with French bread or warm tortillas, or refrigerate and reheat the next day, as noted above.

[MC]

[MR]

The lively and enthusiastic Gerardo, son of the eponymous owner of *puesto* "Doña Mar," was full of many surprises during our visit, and this one was the clear winner. Throughout the rainy season, many delicacies of the *cerro* (mountains) are gathered by local Otomí campesinos and brought to market. Mushrooms of all varieties were in full display, and the first morning we ate at the market, Gerardo presented us with a large carton full of freshly dug blue mushrooms. Sautéed simply in a bit of oil and served on blue maize tortillas—there can be no finer or more memorable meal, earthy in flavor and elemental in character.

Sautéed wild blue mushrooms on a blue maize tortilla [MR]

CALDO DE HONGOS

WILD MUSHROOM SOUP

FOR THE SOUP

¼ cup (125 mL) plus 2 tablespoons
  (30 mL) Spanish olive oil,
  divided
1 pound (500 g) assorted mushrooms, washed, dried thoroughly, and cut into large dice
  (If using button mushrooms,
  slice instead of dice to retain
  the shape.)
2 teaspoons (12 g) sea salt
½ medium white onion
  (5 oz./137.5 g), chopped
2 medium cloves garlic
  (½ oz./12 g), peeled and chopped
10 cups (2.5 L) water, divided
2 sprigs fresh epazote, leaves only
  (substitute 1 tsp./1.5 g dried
  epazote, crumbled)
2 medium Roma tomatoes
  (7 oz./200 g), quartered
1 chile chipotle in adobo (10 g),
  including a bit of the adobo

[MC]

Blue mushrooms were only the first of a streaming rainbow of wild mushroom colors. All eventually found their way into this simple yet lusty soup. Use any assortment of mushrooms you like, but for best flavor, be sure to include a couple of "strong"-tasting ones, like shitake.

Prepare-ahead note: This soup may be prepared a day in advance and reheated, but the fresh mushroom flavor is best enjoyed on the day it is cooked.

YIELD: 8 SERVINGS

SAUTÉ THE MUSHROOMS

Sauté small batches of the mushrooms at a time so that they brown rather than steam: Heat the ¼ cup (125 mL) of the oil in a large, heavy skillet over high heat until almost smoking; add about one-quarter of the mushrooms. Toss or stir constantly to keep the mushrooms in movement. When they are nicely colored, transfer the mushrooms to a plate or bowl, sprinkle with a pinch of the salt, and repeat this process with the remaining mushrooms.

Heat the remaining 2 tablespoons (30 mL) of the olive oil in a medium stockpot; add the onions and garlic, and cook over medium heat, stirring frequently, until the onions are translucent. Pour 5 cups of the water into the stockpot, and add the sautéed mushrooms and the epazote. Bring to a boil, then reduce to a simmer as you continue. Add the remaining water and keep at a simmer.

Place the tomatoes in the jar of a blender with the *chile chipotle*. Ladle about 1 cup (250 mL) of the cooking liquid into the blender; process until completely liquefied. Pour the mixture into the stockpot, return to a simmer, and continue simmering over low heat for another 30 minutes.

Serve with French bread or warm tortillas.

(bottom, left) Pretty in pink, but too squirmy. [MR] *(bottom, right) Movement thankfully stops once they hit the comal.* [ALL PHOTOS BY MR]

CHINICUILES/TOASTED MAGUEY WORMS

Not to worry, I won't be providing a recipe for this specialty of Hidalgo! But should you ever have the chance to visit around August, be on the lookout for them. That's the season when this destructive pest—the larvae of the moth *Hypopta agavis*—bores its way into the maguey core and roots, feeding on the plant's flesh. People rid themselves of the pest by gathering great quantities of them and wolfing them down—either raw or toasted. Gerardo at *puesto* "Doña Mar" presented us with a container full of the squiggling critters. I steered clear of the live ones (they were squirming too much), but the toasted ones, tucked discreetly inside a fresh, warm blue maize tortilla—and with a sanctifying anointment of lime juice—had a texture and flavor not unlike toasted walnuts. This is one of the caterpillar species that you'll also find at the bottom of some bottles of mezcal.

REAL DEL MONTE

THE UNIQUE CULINARY specialty of Real del Monte gives one a double take at first: *pastes* (pronounced "PAH-stess," from the English "pasties," are little stuffed pastry pockets, a vestige of the long-standing Cornwallian presence in the town. Today, Real del Monte hosts the annual Festival Internacional del Paste; during the eighth annual event in 2016, chefs concocted what was proclaimed to be the "world's largest *paste*," measuring 16 feet (5 m) long and tipping the scales at almost 200 pounds (91 kg). The town even boasts a *paste* museum.

At one of the highest inhabited elevations of Mexico—around 8,900 feet (2,700 m)—Real del Monte is quite cool year-round and is often blanketed with mists and fog. Perhaps the climate made it the perfect territory for English immigrants.

In the early 1800s, as mining revenues diminished, a wealthy local miner imported Cornish mining technology, hiring British mining companies to bring in steam-powered machinery and other modern extraction techniques to revive the sagging sector. In addition to the introduction of British technology, by 1825 a few hundred Cornish miners arrived, too, escaping worse economic hardships in their native land. Eventually, miners' wives prepared *pastes*, a portable meal to accompany their husbands into the mines.

(Local folklore says that miners sometimes pilfered their valuable finds and sneaked them out of the mines inside the *pastes*.)

Other Cornish traces remain in Real del Monte, too: Methodism, for one, and plenty of Cornish surnames. To amuse themselves, the miners also brought tennis, rugby, cricket, and golf, but the most notable introduction—after *pastes*, that is—must surely be soccer, or "*fútbol*" as it is called in Mexico. The British mining concern Compañía Real del Monte y Pachuca established the first Mexican soccer team in 1901, and the first official game took place in Real del Monte that same year.

[MR]

MERCADO CAMERINO MENDOZA

The imposing Mercado Camerino Mendoza looks like a temple of food. Soaring ceilings and stair-stepped clusters of arched windows create an airy and open space, the perfect place to revere a pantheon of regional products. A few prepared foods are offered inside, but most are found on adjacent streets.

(above) Grapes, guavas, socks, and umbrellas are all within easy reach.

PASTES
Y
EMPAÑADAS

PASTES
Y

On their home turf of Cornwall, *pastes* are humbly filled with ground beef and potatoes. But in their adopted Mexican homeland, they may just as well feature lamb or chorizo, mole or fruit preserves, or even *arroz con leche*. Thanks to the silver mines in Hidalgo, today *pastes* can be found in markets and on virtually every street corner in Real del Monte, as well as in Pachuca and Huasca de Ocampo. (Some die-hard fans believe that because the *paste* has become so commercialized in Real del Monte, better versions of it can today be found in Huasca—and indeed we found some marvelous recipes for it there.)

So which flavor do you want? And how do bakers know which is which? The sausage Paste is identified with a small ball of dough poised on top; mole verde is marked with a single squash seed; and mole rojo is garnished with a sprinkling of sesame seeds. Choose your own markers for your favorite flavors to avoid confusion. [MR]

PASTES

FILLED PASTRY TURNOVERS

It isn't surprising that so many bakers of *pastes* also make empanadas. The forms and processes are similar, although the fillings and crusts may differ. Filling options for *pastes* are legion; feel free to experiment and try some of the *guisados* found elsewhere in this book, such as Mole verde (p. 372), Tinga de pollo (p. 374), or Requesón guisado (p. 371). The dough recipe yields 1 dozen Pastes; the same is true for the fillings.

Prepare-ahead note: Like many baked goods, Pastes are most delicious while still warm. Serve immediately after baking; alternatively, store in an airtight container in the refrigerator for up to 2 days and reheat just before serving.

YIELD: 1 DOZEN

TO PREPARE AHEAD
Enriched Lard (See notes on
  p. 530)

FOR THE FILLINGS
Papas con carne de cerdo/
Pork and potatoes with green chile
8 ounces (225 g) lean ground pork
1 cup (170 g) white onion, finely
  chopped
1 medium clove garlic (6 g), finely
  chopped
2 medium chiles serranos (about
  10 g each), finely chopped
2 tablespoons (8 g) parsley, finely
  chopped

PREPARE THE FILLINGS
Papas con carne de cerdo
Place all the ingredients in a large mixing bowl, and use your hands to knead and incorporate the ingredients. Check seasonings by frying a small amount. The filling is used raw, so refrigerate until time to fill the Pastes.

1 medium baking potato
  (7 oz./190 g), boiled until just
  tender, peeled, and cut into
  medium dice
1 teaspoon (6 g) sea salt
½ teaspoon (2.5 g) ground black
  pepper

ZARZAMORA CON QUESO/
BLACKBERRY PRESERVES WITH
DOUBLE CREAM CHEESE
1 quart (500 g) blackberries
  (substitute other types of
  berries, or a mix)
2 cups (400 g) granulated sugar
1 tablespoon (15 mL) lemon juice
Pinch of salt
¼ cup (62.5 mL) water
1 eight-ounce package (225 g)
  double cream cheese (substitute
  standard cream cheese)

FOR THE DOUGH
4 cups (500 g) all-purpose flour
1 teaspoon (6 g) sea salt
1 cup (250 g) Enriched Lard,
  chilled
2 eggs, well beaten
Approximately 5 tablespoons
  (75 mL) ice water

Zarzamora con queso
Place the first five ingredients in a medium saucepan over high heat; cook until the sugar is dissolved, 2–3 minutes. Bring to a boil, reduce heat to low, and simmer for 12–15 minutes until the berries have disintegrated and the syrup reaches the soft-ball stage (a candy thermometer should read 223°F–235°F/106°C–113°C). Allow to cool, then refrigerate to set, at least 1 hour. Meanwhile, slice the cream cheese into twelve ⅔-ounce (18 g) pieces; refrigerate until time to fill the Pastes.

PREPARE THE DOUGH
Place the flour and salt in the bowl of a food processor and pulse 2–3 times to incorporate. Add the chilled lard, and pulse until the mixture resembles coarse meal. Mix in the two eggs. Stream in the ice water a tablespoon at a time, adding enough to hold the dough mass together; the dough should be firm and not sticky.

FILL, FORM, AND BAKE THE PASTES
Form the dough into 12 balls, each weighing about 2½ ounces (75 g). Working on a floured surface, with a floured rolling pin, roll out one of the balls into a circle measuring about 6 inches (15 cm) in diameter. Place 3 heaping tablespoons (about 84 g) of the filling of your choice in the center of the circle; spread it roughly over the circle, avoiding the edges. Fold the dough circle in half, and press the edges tightly to seal. Now, make the characteristic braid pattern: Use one finger to fold the edge of the dough toward the top of the pastry; use a finger of the other hand to twist/tuck/fold the adjoining dough underneath. Repeat, until the entire curved edge is "braided" in this way.

Members of the extended Villa family divide the tasks: one rolls the dough, the other fills and folds the pastry. [MR]

QUERÉTARO

Querétaro aqueduct, ca. 1910.

SANTIAGO DE QUERÉTARO

WHETHER OR NOT the state of Querétaro harbors the geographic center of the country (a monument in Tequisquiapan claims to pinpoint the exact spot), it is often thought of as the spiritual heart of Mexico. The state is richly endowed with several natural, historical, and cultural treasures. The calcareous soils and steeply fluctuating temperatures within the Querétaro semidesert have proven fruitful for wine grapes, and the vast expanses of scrub provide a happy home for the European goats, sheep, and cows whose milk is today turned into award-winning cheeses. Mexico's most beloved heroine, Josefa Ortiz de Domínguez, known as "La Corregidora," lived here and played a pivotal role as an insurgent in the Mexican War of Independence. The historic center of the state capital, Santiago de Querétaro, and the Sierra Gorda

Biosphere Reserve enjoy UNESCO designations as World Heritage Sites; and two of the towns we will visit—Tequisquiapan and Bernal—are Pueblos Mágicos.

Standing in the imposing European-style squares of Santiago de Querétaro, or strolling through its flower-bedecked alleyways, it is easy to forget that the state today plays a key role in the country's economy. Querétaro is located within Mexico's Bajío—an agriculturally rich plain ranging from 5,500 to 7,000 feet (1,675 to 2,134 m) above sea level, a region that also includes Guanajuato and parts of Aguascalientes and Jalisco. During the colonial era, Querétaro's prime location made it the breadbasket for the nearby mining towns of Guanajuato and Zacatecas.

By the seventeenth century, Santiago de Querétaro shared in the wealth generated by the booming mining industry, and grand buildings and public works were erected in the fashionable Baroque style, transmogrified in the hands of indigenous builders. The dramatic aqueduct—one of the most impressive engineering feats of colonial Mexico, and the symbol of the city—was built in the 1730s and served as the city's main source of drinking water, supplying public and private fountains until the 1940s. In the twenty-first century, the Bajío has become the most economically prosperous area in the country, and Querétaro is frequently described as having the highest quality of life in Mexico.

Of the many markets in Santiago de Querétaro, we visited two: Mercado Escobedo and Mercado de la Cruz. Both offer representative samplings of regional gastronomy.

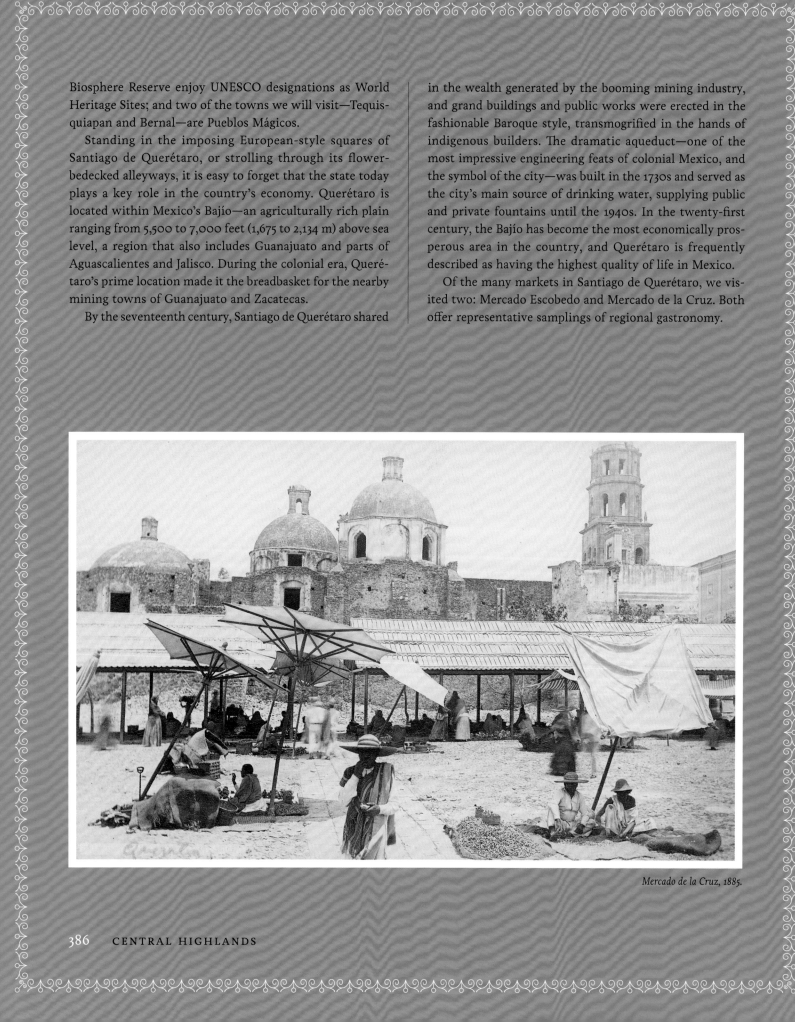

Mercado de la Cruz, 1885.

Early morning at Mercado Escobedo. Proprietors Jesús Mendoza Reyes (foreground) and Isabel Robles (background) of "Tamales El Poblano" offer an assortment of typical Central Mexican tamales; left to right: Tamal verde, Tamal con rajas y queso asadero, Tamal rojo. [MR]

MERCADO ESCOBEDO

TAMAL VERDE

TOMATILLO AND PORK TAMALE

TO PREPARE AHEAD
Salsa verde (p. 531)
Masa para tamales (p. 530)

FOR THE PORK

8 ounces (250 g) pork, preferably
  bone-in with some fat, cut into
  a few large cubes
¼ medium white onion
  (2½ oz./68.75 g), finely chopped
1 medium clove garlic (¼ oz./6 g),
  peeled and finely chopped
1 cup (250 mL) water
½ teaspoon (3 g) sea salt

FOR THE TAMALES

2 tablespoons (30 mL)
  vegetable oil
½ recipe (2 cups/500 mL) Salsa
  verde
2 pounds (1 kg) Masa para tamales
15 cornhusks, softened as
  described on page 526
15 cornhusk strips for tying,
  as described on page 526

[MC]

Often *tamales verdes* feature chicken, but at "Tamales El Poblano" they used pork. You may use either one.

Prepare-ahead note: Prepare the Salsa verde a few days in advance—or even weeks ahead and freeze—and this tamale will come together very quickly.

YIELD: 15 TAMALES

PREPARE THE PORK

Place all the ingredients in a skillet; bring to a boil, reduce to a simmer, and continue cooking until the water completely evaporates and the pork is cooked, 10–12 minutes. Remove from the heat and allow to cool. Finely shred the pork, mixing it with any accumulated fat, as well as with the onions and garlic. Set aside as you proceed.

FORM THE TAMALES AND FINISH

Heat the vegetable oil in a saucepan until shimmering; pour in all of the Salsa verde at once: it should sputter and sizzle, so stand back. Cook, stirring frequently, for 4–5 minutes or until the sauce is slightly thickened; set aside.

Prepare cornhusks for tamales as described on page 526. Flatten the masa in the husk; add approximately 2 tablespoons (50 g) of the shredded pork and spoon on 2 tablespoons (30 mL) of the cooked sauce; fold the masa empanada-style, close the husks, tie, and steam for 1 hour as instructed on page 526.

TAMAL ROJO

GUAJILLO CHILE AND CHEESE TAMALE

TO PREPARE AHEAD
Masa para tamales (p. 530)

FOR THE SALSA
10 chiles guajillos (2½ oz./65 g)
2 cups (500 mL) boiling water
¼ white onion (2½ oz./68.75 g),
    chopped
1 medium clove garlic (¼ oz./6 g),
    peeled and chopped
½ teaspoon (3 g) sea salt
2 tablespoons (30 mL)
    vegetable oil

FOR THE TAMALES
2 pounds (1 kg) Masa para tamales
15 cornhusks, softened as
    described on page 526
15 cornhusk strips for tying,
    as described on page 526
4 ounces (125 g) queso asadero
    (substitute Muenster or
    provolone), thinly sliced into
    15 long strips

The simple, quick sauce of *chile guajillo* can also be used as a dip or salsa for tacos. The sauce is mixed with the masa to thoroughly permeate the tamale with color and flavor. Unlike many *tamales rojos*, this featured no pork but instead included strips of cheese. You may substitute cooked, shredded pork if you like, as directed in the preceding recipe.

YIELD: 15 TAMALES

PREPARE THE SALSA
Remove the stems from the chiles; place the chiles in a heatproof bowl and cover with the boiling water; allow to stand until cool to the touch. Transfer the chiles and 1 cup (250 mL) of the soaking liquid to the jar of a blender; discard the remaining water. Add the remaining ingredients except for the vegetable oil and process until thoroughly puréed. Heat the vegetable oil in a saucepan until shimmering; add all of the chile purée to the saucepan at once: it should sputter and sizzle, so stand back. Cook over medium heat, stirring constantly, until slightly thickened and reduced, 3–4 minutes; remove from heat and allow to cool.

FORM THE TAMALES AND FINISH
Place the masa in a large mixing bowl; pour on the chile sauce and use your hands to knead until the masa and sauce are thoroughly incorporated. Prepare cornhusks for tamales as described on page 526. Flatten the masa in the husk; add 1 slice of the cheese, fold the masa empanada-style, close the husks, tie, and steam the tamales for 1 hour, as instructed on page 526.

[MC]

[MR]

In the first hall of the Mercado Escobedo, two women (friendly competitors) flanked an aisle that led to another part of the market. Both women were selling virtually identical versions of homemade Ensalada de nopales, and Nopales en chile negro. I felt bad ordering from one and not the other, but the ebullient personality of Alicia Resendiz immediately won us over. (Be prepared for similarly awkward circumstances when you visit the market: go hungry, because if you are nagged by guilt as we were, you'll order food from the adjacent vendor, too.) Many diners ordered the salad plated and ate it with a fork, accompanied by what she called *tlayudas de maíz quebrado*: large crispy tostadas made with coarsely crushed field corn. Both dishes could also be served atop a tortilla for a taco (which is how we had them) or as a filling for Gorditas (p. 410), or other maize-based snacks. Regardless of the serving method, both were blessed with a hefty dousing of *crema* and a dusting of crumbled *queso añejo*. This salad is deliciously picante; control the heat if you wish by using fewer *chiles serranos* and *manzanos*.

ENSALADA DE NOPALES

MIXED SALAD WITH CACTUS PADDLES, TOMATOES, CHILES, AND BELL PEPPER

FOR THE SALAD

1 pound (500 g) nopales (cactus paddles; substitute canned nopalitos, drained weight)

2 tablespoons (30 mL) vegetable oil

2 teaspoons (12 g) sea salt, divided

½ *each* medium red and white onion (5 oz./137.5 g each), cut into half-moons (cut into quarters, then thinly slice the quarters and separate into sections)

½ *each* medium yellow, red, and green bell pepper (3¼ oz./92.5 g each), seeded and sliced into julienne strips

2 medium chiles manzanos (substitute chiles rocotos, 1½ oz./40 g each), seeded and sliced into julienne strips

3 medium chiles serranos (⅓ oz./10 g each), seeded and sliced into julienne strips

4 medium Roma tomatoes (14 oz./400 g), seeded and cut into large dice

1 cup (60 g) cilantro, coarsely chopped

¼ cup (62.5 mL) white vinegar

Prepare-ahead note: Like all salads, this one is best served on the day it is prepared. Leftovers will keep under refrigeration for 2–3 days.

YIELD: 8–10 SERVINGS

PREPARE THE SALAD

If possible, purchase nopales that have already been cleaned of the spines (many Mexican markets sell them that way). (*Note*: If you can only find spiny nopales, lay them flat on a cutting board, and holding a very sharp knife parallel to the cutting surface, place

Tlayudas de maíz quebrado. [MR]

[MC]

FOR SERVING

Tortillas or tostadas

Mexican crema (substitute crème fraîche, plain yogurt, or sour cream)

Queso añejo, crumbled (substitute Romano, feta, or Parmesan, grated)

Alicia Resendiz. [MR]

the knife on the nopal and move the knife away from you as you slice/scrape away the spines. Try to leave as much of the outer skin as possible; check to see if there are any bumps, especially around the edges, which may still harbor small spines; remove them with a paring knife or potato peeler. Trim away the base where the paddle was connected to the plant, and trim about ¼ inch/6 mm from the sides.) Rinse under cold water, and pat completely dry. Cut the nopales into strips measuring approximately ½ inch by 2½ inches (1.25 cm × 6.3 cm).

(*Note*: Nopales tend to be filled with mucilage, much like okra. The next step will help eliminate it.) Pour the oil into a large skillet; heat the oil until it is shimmering. Add the nopales and 1 teaspoon (6 g) of the salt and cook over low heat, stirring frequently, 3–4 minutes, until heated through. Cover, and continue cooking over low heat for 15–20 minutes or until all of the mucilage and liquid have completely evaporated. Remove the nopales from the heat and allow to cool thoroughly. (If using packaged *nopalitos*, thoroughly drain them and skip the cooking step.)

Place the nopales, onions, bell peppers, chiles, tomatoes, and cilantro in a large mixing bowl. Toss briefly to combine; add the vinegar and the remaining 1 teaspoon (6 g) salt and toss to combine.

TO SERVE

As noted above, plate as you would a salad, or use as a topping on tostadas, or on tortillas to serve as tacos. Drizzle on some cream and sprinkle with cheese.

NOPALES EN CHILE NEGRO

CACTUS PADDLE AND CHILE PASILLA SALAD

FOR THE NOPAL MIXTURE

2 pounds (1 kg) nopales (cactus paddles; substitute canned nopalitos, drained weight)

10 chiles pasillas (4¼ oz./120 g)

4 cups (1 L) boiling water

4 medium cloves garlic (1 oz./24 g), peeled and charred

1 medium white onion (10 oz./275 g), peeled, charred, and quartered

½ teaspoon (0.32 g) dried whole Mexican oregano, lightly toasted and ground

1 teaspoon (6 g) sea salt

1 tablespoon (15 mL) vegetable oil

½ cup (125 mL) white vinegar, divided

¼ cup (15 g) cilantro, chopped

This very Mexican mixture is delicious served in the ways described above, but it is also excellent as a side dish for seafood, grilled meats, or chicken.

Prepare-ahead note: Nopales en chile negro keeps well under refrigeration for 3–4 days. Bring to room temperature before serving.

YIELD: 6–8 SERVINGS

PREPARE THE NOPAL MIXTURE

Clean the nopales, cut them into strips, and cook as described in the preceding recipe; leave them in the skillet in which they cooked, and set aside as you proceed. (If using packaged *nopalitos*, skip the cooking step.)

Slit the chiles open along one side; remove the cap, seeds, and veins. Preheat a comal, griddle, or large, heavy skillet (preferably cast iron). Flatten the chiles and place them on the heated comal. Cook, turning once, until the chiles are fragrant and gently darkened, about 2–3 minutes. Transfer the chiles to a heatproof bowl and cover them with the boiling water; allow them to soak for 30 minutes; reserve the soaking liquid. When the chiles are cool to the touch, cut 4 of them in half across the width, then cut each half lengthwise into thin strips measuring about ¼ inch (6 mm) wide and set aside; leave the remaining chiles whole.

Place the whole chiles in the jar of a blender; add the garlic, onion, oregano, salt, and 1 cup (250 mL) of the soaking liquid. Process until thoroughly liquefied.

Making sure that all of the liquid has evaporated from the skillet containing the nopales, pour in the vegetable oil. Heat over high heat until the oil is shimmering. (If using packaged *nopalitos*, thoroughly drain them and add them now.) Add all of the mixture from the blender jar at once: it should sputter and sizzle, so stand back. Add the reserved chile strips and ¼ cup (62.5 mL) of the vinegar, reduce the heat, and cook at a simmer, stirring frequently, for 4–5 minutes until the mixture thickens and reduces. Remove from the heat and allow to cool thoroughly.

Transfer to a serving bowl or platter; add the cilantro and remaining vinegar and toss to combine. Serve as instructed for Ensalada de nopales, above.

CACAHUATES ESPAÑOLES/SPICY PEANUT SNACK

One particular aisle in the market was devoted to ready-to-eat *botanas*, or cocktail snacks. Some items caused a bit of whiplash, such as the bull penis *botana* seen in the photo below. Although we passed on that, we did order these spicy peanuts loaded with toasted *chile de árbol*. Heat a tablespoonful or two of vegetable oil in a large, heavy skillet until shimmering. Add 12–15 whole *chiles de árbol* and toast over high heat, turning them constantly, until they are darkened and fragrant, 2–3 minutes. Reduce the heat to medium, add about 1 pound (500 g) raw peanuts, and continue to roast, tossing and stirring constantly, until some of the peanuts have browned, 3–4 minutes. Add salt to taste, toss to incorporate, and immediately transfer to a serving bowl. Snackers add squeezes of lime juice to taste.

(above) Cacahuates españoles. [MR] *(below) Botana de viril with whole jalapeños is marketed as having Viagra-like effects.* [MR]

(top) Señora Alicia García at Mercado de la Cruz reigns over a vivid assortment of fruits: pitahayas, zarzamora (wild blackberries), nance (p. 46), pomegranate, and garambullo (p. 335). In her hand is a bottle of aguamiel (p. 365). [MR] *(bottom) Alicia's pomegranates (Punica granatum), guanábana (Annona muricata), and pitahaya (Hylocereus undatus), a cactus fruit.* [MR]

MERCADO DE LA CRUZ

The Otomíes of Querétaro planted figs alongside indigenous plants in family orchards shortly after the Spanish introduced fig trees to Mexico in the 1530s. Querétaro remains a significant producer of the fruit. Here, figs are often consumed fresh, but just as frequently they are preserved in sugar, a technique attributed to the Moors and brought to the New World by the Spanish. Today, almost any fruit imaginable is candied, such as the prickly pear, or *tuna*.

ORÉGANO

BOTANICAL: *Lippia* spp./Family Verbenaceae | **ENGLISH:** Mexican oregano | **MAYAN:** varies by region

"Oregano" is the common name for any one of more than sixty plant species used worldwide as a flavoring in food. Since the mid-1800s, hundreds of taxonomic names have been given to members of the genera, and considerable confusion still exists due to their broad expression. Part of this confusion persists because the name "oregano" describes plants from two completely different families: Lamiaceae (represented primarily by the *Origanum* genus) and Verbenaceae (represented primarily by the *Lippia* genus). *Origanum* is an Old World plant, and what we use when we make Italian tomato sauce; *Lippia* is a New World plant, native to Mexico, where it is both cultivated and gathered in the wild, and used in a wide array of foods. Today, all varieties of oregano represent the largest selling herb in the world, with some 10,000 tons produced annually. Species of both the *Origanum* and *Lippia* genera have a similar aroma (which probably explains why the Spanish explorers applied the old word to the unfamiliar species they encountered in Mexico), although the *Lippia* varieties have a more pungent taste due to the higher content of essential oils. *Origanum* generally has a smaller leaf than *Lippia*, and it is used both fresh and dried, whereas the Mexican oregano is typically used in its dried state. To further complicate the story, several different species exist within both genera. In Mexico, *L. graveolens* is found in Yucatán, while in most of the rest of Mexico you may find *L. berlandieri*, *L. palmeri*, or *L. origanoides* as well as several others. As Diana Kennedy recommends in *From My Mexican Kitchen*, look for local oregano varieties each time you visit a pueblo market, since they will all likely be different. For cooks in the United States or Canada, look for "Mexican oregano," which is by now widely available. European or "Italian" oregano (*Origanum*) is not a suitable substitute.

CECINA/SALT-CURED DRIED BEEF

Along with Tasajo (p. 125), Cecina is another form of dried beef that is plentiful throughout the country. Traditionally, Cecina is salted and then "cooked" in sunlight, but you may simply dry it in your kitchen. Follow the instructions for Tasajo, using thin *milanesa* cuts of beef tenderloin (your butcher can do this for you); omit the lime juice and the tying method; after the refrigeration step, simply drape a whole sheet of the salted meat on a plastic coat hanger as though it were a towel or pair of pants. If you live near a Mexican butcher, you may be able to find Cecina already prepared. Cecina is often fried in lard and served with simple pot beans.

CHICHARRÓN PRENSADO/ PRESSED PORK BELLY CONFIT

I feel endless fascination with and reverence for the creativity applied to pig meat throughout the Spanish diaspora. *Chicharrón prensado* has to be one of the more baroque expressions. The cooking process is quite similar to that for Carnitas (p. 477). Fatty pork pieces are fried, drained, and pressed in a special device to form the cylindrical shapes seen in the photo at left. *Chicharrón prensado* may be consumed as is in a taco, but more typically it is prepared as a *guisado*—chopped and cooked with other ingredients— and then used as the filling for Gorditas (p. 410), Tlacoyos (p. 346), or almost any maize masa snack found in this book. *Chicharrón prensado* may be available beyond Mexico in some specialty stores or Mexican *carnicerías*; short of having the real thing, you may use *carnitas* for any recipe in this book that suggests *chicharrón prensado*. The flavor isn't quite the same: real *chicharrón prensado* has a taste rather like ham or other cured meat, since it is processed using Prague powder, saltpeter, or other nitrates/nitrites for preservation prior to the frying step.

TEQUISQUIAPAN

JUST UNDER AN hour from Santiago de Querétaro, and a little over two hours from Mexico City, Tequisquiapan (teh-kees-key-AH-pahn) has become a weekend magnet for stressed-out city workers. A grid of loosely woven colonial streets placed against a magical desert backdrop seems to melt away jangled nerves. A vibrant culinary scene is an attractive draw, too, especially for oeno- and turophiles who make it base camp for the famed Ruta del Queso y Vino that trails through the arid terrain. The town also hosts the National Cheese and Wine Fair each June. The ageless thermal mineral springs found in the town, known in Spanish as *balnearios*—discovered and enjoyed by the precontact Otomí-Chichimeca peoples of the region—offer world-weary aficionados a relaxing and restorative retreat between tipples.

The banks of the San Juan River, where the earliest indigenous peoples of the region originally settled, today provide fertile soils for walnut, peach, apricot, pomegranate, guava, and fig trees. The municipality also produces voluminous quantities of green *chile chilaca*, which, when dried, is commonly known as *pasilla*—essential in many Mexican dishes; it is known as *chile negro* in Querétaro and a few other places.

An ambulante in the Tequisquiapan market. Ambulantes—or roving vendors—have played a pivotal role in the Mexican market since precontact times. Rather than pay rent for a stall, they typically spread their wares on the floor of the interior or exterior spaces of the market. This Otomí woman is selling (counterclockwise from top) huitlacoche *and* tunas, *squash, spinach, squash blossoms, piles of nopales, more* tunas, *and a big bag of* verdolaga *(p. 400).* [MR]

There is another herb that they also eat cooked, and it is called itzmiquílitl (verdolaga).
It is vining. It has thick stems and the leaves are round and flat.

BERNARDINO DE SAHAGÚN, 1575–1577

[MR]

VERDOLAGA

BOTANICAL: *Portulaca oleracea* L./Family Portulacaceae | **ENGLISH:** purslane, little hogweed, wild portulaca, pigweed
OTOMÍ: *tzutcani* | **NAHUATL:** *itzmiquílitl*

One of the most popular *quelites* in Mexico is *verdolaga*, or purslane. It is a fleshy, trailing herb, sometimes climbing on thick stems that range from 2 inches (5 cm) to 16 inches (40 cm) in length; waxy leaves average about 1 inch (3 cm) in length and ½ inch (1.5 cm) in width, and are ovoid and cradle-like. Small yellow hermaphroditic flowers appear periodically and produce seed-bearing fruits. Even though it is considered a dreadfully invasive and aggressive weed in many places, it is an absolutely delicious plant that is growing in popularity beyond Mexico, largely due to its remarkable health benefits: *verdolaga* is antibacterial; it has the highest content of antioxidants and omega-3 fatty acids of any plant studied to date; and in alternative medicine it is used as a diuretic and to treat kidney, bladder, and liver problems. Due to its rapid proliferation, it can be found in many places around the globe, making its origin difficult to identify, although some botanists suggest it is North Africa through Iran and the Indian subcontinent. Evidence has been found to indicate a North American presence well before the arrival of Europeans. While it grows in almost every state of Mexico, it is most appreciated in the Central Highlands, where it may be cooked with potatoes or eggs, or most popularly with pork (p. 401). Stems, leaves, and flowers are edible and have a slightly salty, tangy, acidic flavor, and a delicate crunch while being quite mucilaginous. There are over forty different varieties of purslane, some gathered in the wild, or it may be cultivated. It is now cultivated in the United States and may be found at farmers' markets or even some supermarkets.

COSTILLAS CON VERDOLAGAS

PORK RIBLETS WITH PURSLANE AND TOMATOES

Women who work in the markets are always very generous with their recipes; they recite and I take frantic notes as they keep working. Nothing beats getting down in the trenches, though, so in my culinary expeditions I always take time to link up with local cooks who invite me into their kitchens. One such charming lady was Gudelia "Gude" Rojo Almaraz. She was born in Tequisquiapan, got married and had children there, and while her eyes sparkle when she talks about visiting other places, she has never left and doesn't really plan to. A few days in tranquil Tequisquiapan explained the reason for her rootedness. Gude is well versed in the cooking of the region, and in fact works as a private cook and housekeeper. This marvelous dish is one of several she taught me; it makes only rare appearances in market stalls, she told me, so I felt lucky to have stumbled upon it one day. In the market, the cooks used pork riblets (p. 328), but Gude used thin-cut pork chops; you may also use thick-cut bone-in pork chops or even cubed pork loin. Costillas con verdolagas usually features tomatillos, but Gude used red tomatoes, which I thought allowed the pleasant sourness of the purslane—not to mention the earthy green color of the plant—to stand out. You may use whichever you prefer. Serve with simple pot beans (Frijoles de la olla, p. 530) or the beans or rice of your choice.

Prepare-ahead note: Costillas con verdolagas is best served on the day it is prepared.

YIELD: 6 SERVINGS

[MC]

FOR THE PORK

17 cups (4.25 L) water

½ cup (145 g) *plus* 1 teaspoon (6 g) sea salt

1 pound (500 g) pork riblets with some fat, or other cuts as noted above

½ medium white onion (5 oz./137.5 g), peeled, thickly sliced, and separated into rings

FOR THE PURSLANE

3 cups (110 g) verdolaga (purslane)

¼ medium white onion (2½ oz./68.75 g), thickly sliced

2 medium cloves garlic (½ oz./12 g), peeled

2 cups (500 mL) water

½ teaspoon (3 g) sea salt

½ teaspoon (2 g) bicarbonate of soda

FOR THE TOMATO SAUCE

1 medium chile mora (0.4 oz./11 g; substitute chile morita)

3 medium Roma tomatoes (10½ oz./300 g), charred

2 medium cloves garlic (½ oz./12 g), peeled and charred

1 teaspoon (2 g) ground cumin

TO PREPARE AHEAD

Enriched Lard (see notes on p. 530)

PREPARE THE PORK

Pour 16 cups (4 L) of the water into a stockpot; add ½ cup (145 g) of the salt and stir until the salt completely dissolves; add the pork and refrigerate 2–3 hours. (The brining step is optional. See notes on brining on p. 527.)

At the end of the brining time, drain the pork and discard the brine solution. Place the pork in a large, shallow skillet; add the remaining 1 cup (250 mL) water, 1 teaspoon (6 g) sea salt, and the onion rings. Bring the water to a boil, and continue to cook over high heat until the liquid has completely evaporated. Reduce heat to medium and continue to cook, stirring frequently, until the meat is browned and the onions caramelized, 6–8 minutes. Remove from the heat, cover, and allow to rest as you continue.

PARBOIL THE PURSLANE

Rinse and drain the purslane; remove any tough stems and pinch off any flowers that may be going to seed. Place the purslane in a large saucepan and add the remaining ingredients. Bring to a boil, cover, reduce to a simmer, and cook for 4 minutes. Remove from the heat and allow to rest for 10 minutes.

PREPARE THE TOMATO SAUCE AND FINISH

Remove and discard the stem, seeds, and veins from the chile; toast the chile on a hot comal or skillet until fragrant. Transfer the chile to a heatproof bowl and cover with boiling water; allow to rest for 30 minutes, then drain, reserving the soaking liquid. Place the drained chile along with the remaining ingredients and 1 cup (250 mL) of the soaking liquid in the jar of a blender, and process until thoroughly puréed; set aside.

Drain the purslane and add it to the skillet with the meat. Pour on the tomato purée and stir to combine; continue to simmer another 1–2 minutes to amalgamate the flavors and reduce the sauce slightly. Check for seasonings, and serve.

HUEVOS EN CHILE NEGRO

SCRAMBLED EGGS IN CHILE PASILLA SAUCE

Morning menu boards in the market stalls hawk *huevos al gusto* (eggs cooked your way); be sure to ask for this one when you get a chance. It's a typical morning meal for many families in Tequisquiapan, and Gude prepared it for us one day. Pasilla chiles are only slightly picante with a rating of just 1,000–2,000 Scoville Heat Units. Still, serve this with a cup of *café de olla* for an eye-opening welcome to the day.

YIELD: 6 SERVINGS

(left) Mounds of chile pasilla *known in Querétaro as* chile negro (left), *and* chile guajillo (right). *Many kilos of chiles are packed in tight layers in burlap bags, compressed, and then "unmolded" to form towering columns (rear).* [MR] *(right) The gracefully elongated* chile catarina, *similar to the* cascabel, *is common throughout the Bajío.* [MC]

FOR THE CHILES
10 chiles negros (pasillas), about
   3½ oz./100 g total weight
4 cups (1 L) boiling water
2 tablespoons (28 g) Enriched Lard
½ medium white onion
   (5 oz./137.5 g), thinly sliced and
   separated into rings

FOR THE EGGS
1 tablespoon (15 mL) vegetable oil
12 eggs, well beaten
1 teaspoon (6 g) sea salt, or to
   taste

FOR SERVING
Frijoles de la olla (p. 530; optional)

PREPARE THE CHILES
Toast the whole chiles in a heavy skillet (preferably cast iron) until slightly darkened and fragrant; transfer to a heatproof bowl and pour in the boiling water. Allow the chiles to soak for 30 minutes.

Meanwhile, heat the lard in a medium skillet until shimmering; add the sliced onions and cook, stirring constantly, until the onions are caramelized. Transfer the onion/lard mixture to the jar of a blender. Remove the chiles from the water, reserving the soaking liquid, and cut off and discard the stems; place the chiles in the blender containing the onions and add 2 cups (500 mL) of the soaking liquid; discard the rest. Process until thoroughly liquefied; set aside.

COOK THE EGGS AND FINISH
In a large, nonstick skillet, heat the oil until shimmering. Add the eggs and cook over medium heat until the edges are set. Using a spatula, lift up the edges to allow the liquid eggs to flow underneath and cover the bottom of the skillet. Repeat this action until the eggs are cooked through and lightly browned in parts.

Pour in the chile-onion mixture, and stir to combine. Cook over medium heat until the liquid is reduced by half, 4–5 minutes. Add the salt, check seasonings, and serve immediately.

TO SERVE
This is a delicious accompaniment to the eggs, but is optional: Fry ¼ medium white onion (2½ oz./68.75 g), chopped, in 2 tablespoons (28 g) Enriched Lard until the onions caramelize, 4–5 minutes. Add 2 cups (500 mL) of Frijoles de la olla with their cooking liquid, and stir to combine. Add salt to taste and plate alongside the eggs.

Otomí women in Tequisquiapan.

OTOMÍ/HÑÄHÑU (MEZQUITAL OTOMÍ)

The word "Otomí" comes from the Nahuatl *otomitl*, which, according to the Nahuatl dictionary, means a disrespectful or bad-tempered person. The name they call themselves (Hñähñu) translates roughly to "speaks well." The Otomíes (or Otomís), a cultural group considered "Chichimeca" by the Spaniards, were peoples believed by some scholars to be among the earliest inhabitants of the Central Highlands, specifically the Valley of Mexico—future home of the Mexica ("Aztecs," p. 537). Sedentary farmers with some hunting/gathering activity, the Otomíes coexisted with other peoples of the area, but over the decades were eventually driven north-northeast by other invading tribes. When the Nahuas arrived and established the Aztec Empire, the Otomíes became their tributaries, but they were mostly ignored, since the Aztecs viewed their land as desolate and unproductive. The Spanish forced them to work in the mines along with other Chichimeca groups. Today, several Otomí groups occupy the Mezquital Valley and La Huasteca region in Hidalgo, and Sierra Gorda in Querétaro. Most speakers are concentrated in the Central Highlands. In Querétaro and Hidalgo, the cuisine of the Otomíes remains linked to many desert foods such as *tunas* (prickly pears), nopales (cactus pads), maguey (in the form of *aguamiel* and pulque, p. 365), and certain insects that prey on desert plants. Many Otomíes have also become shepherds and employ the meat in the popular dish *barbacoa* (p. 363), the preparation of which likely evolved among several Chichimeca groups in their desert environment.

[MR]

TEQUESQUITE

"Tequisquiapan" in Nahuatl means "place of *tequesquite*," which in turn translates to "efflorescent stone" (*tetl* = stone + *quixquitl* = efflorescent). *Tequesquite* is a mineral salt that has been used throughout Mesoamerica for centuries as a leavening agent and flavoring. In times of *sequía*, or drought, the mineral salt effloresces, or "blooms," in thin layers atop the banks of lakes, rivers, and even damp hollows as waters recede and evaporation occurs more rapidly. Chemically, it is an alkaline formation composed of several minerals, principally sodium bicarbonate and sodium chloride, but it also contains potassium carbonate, sodium sulfate, and various clay compounds. It is these minerals that give the local thermal springs their purported medicinal value, and regional wines their unique bouquet and taste. Several traditional centers for the production of *tequesquite* are scattered throughout Mexico (one is a town in Jalisco called simply El Tequesquite), and Tequisquiapan remains one of the most important. *Tequesquite* is still a key ingredient in many Mexican dishes, although many modern cooks use baking powder instead to achieve any desired leavening effects.

While several large-scale enterprises are producing wines, like Freixenet, and cheeses like the popular Quesos VAI, the truly exciting thing about the Cheese and Wine Route in the area surrounding Tequisquiapan is that a handful of young entrepreneurs have discovered the quality

Sheep at Quesos VAI on the Cheese and Wine Route. Sheep and goat breeding are important activities in Tequisquiapan. Querétaro hosted the World Sheep and Wool Congress in 2007. El Gavillero y Shangrila ranch in Tequisquiapan is home to over six hundred head of the prized Katahdin breed. Sheep's milk is increasingly being used to produce world-class cheeses. [MR]

of the soil and growing environment, and have launched artisanally made products that are of superior quality and are gaining attention in international markets.

Javier Pérez Rocha Malcher, owner of Rancho Santa Marina, took over the family farm that had produced asparagus for a generation and converted it into a sheep ranch that today produces seven types of cheese using primarily sheep's milk and some goat's milk. Of those, four are made in the French style (Perail, Chabichou, Crottin, and Piramide), two in the Italian technique similar to Pecorino, and one Greek-style cheese like feta. His buttery, dreamy cheeses have won several national awards. Cheeses of Rancho Santa Marina are sold in some local markets as well as in specialty markets in Mexico City.

[MR]

Cheeses of Rancho Santa Marina. [MR]

THE QUERÉTARO SEMIDESERT

THE DRIVE NORTH from Tequisquiapan takes us past sheep ranches and vine-yards, through the southernmost outskirts of the Querétaro semidesert, and toward a land of mirage and mysticism. The broad, arid belt of the *semidesierto quere-tano* traverses the state east to west, occupying roughly its middle third; the region is important both ecologically and culturally.

The Querétaro semidesert, which varies in elevation from about 5,600 feet (1,705 m) to 6,900 feet (2,100 m), is on the watch list of many conservationist groups: several endemic species, such as the Lamb's Tail Cactus (*Echinocereus schmollii*), among others, appear on the red list of threatened species. Ecotravel to the region has become important, and modern-day pilgrims come here, too—those who wish to absorb the "sacred energy" of the Bernal monolith, which stands like a sentinel at the semidesert's southern edge.

BERNAL

EACH YEAR AT the vernal equinox, thousands of visitors fill the small town of San Sebastián Bernal to "recharge" in the magnetic field they believe emanates from the mammoth stone monolith known as the Peña de Bernal. Good vibrations or otherwise, the stone is the tallest freestanding rock in the world.

Rising 1,421 feet (433 m) above the surrounding ground, the Peña de Bernal was formed some 8.7 million years ago as the lava dome of a volcano pushed its way upward, breaking away surrounding rock and soil, some time after the dome had mostly solidified. The pale pink stone seems to sparkle due to a high content of silica quartz, which perhaps explains why the Otomí-Chichimeca peoples of the region as well as the throngs of spirit-seeking tourists believe the giant rock holds special powers.

The town is so tiny, and the monolith so huge, that it crops up in every vista—even crowning the Mercado de Comida. A former bullfighting and rodeo ring, the market's space-age design seems comfortable in the otherworldly setting.

Because the population of Bernal swells with visitors (most of them from other parts of Mexico) on weekends, the market is hopping only on Saturdays and Sundays; other days of the week, when vendors have to rely on the small population of the town, offerings may be sparse.

The culinary claim to fame of Bernal is the gordita. In fact, as the proclaimed "capital of gorditas," Bernal hosts the "Feria de la Gordita" every year on November 20. Hundreds of women from Querétaro as well as neighboring states come to strut their creations, and perhaps thanks to their inventiveness, the gordita has evolved to almost infinite expression, as you can see from the list below.

[MC]

GORDITAS

THICK MAIZE PANCAKES WITH FILLINGS

TO PREPARE AHEAD

Enriched Lard (see notes on p. 530)

[MC]

*He sells tamales . . .
of broken, cracked
grains of maize.*

BERNARDINO DE
SAHAGÚN, 1575–1577

We saw these little fat ("*gordita*") maize pancakes in almost every color but the more typical white or yellow: black, blue, red. One unique characteristic of gorditas from Bernal is that they are almost all made with *maíz quebrado* (broken maize)—traditionally dried field corn that has been broken or damaged in the process of scraping it from the cob, and nowadays produced commercially for both animal and human consumption—that is *nixtamal*-ized and ground into masa. This adds not only a visual texture but also a pleasant crunchiness. I've suggested an alternate way of achieving the texture. At the *puesto* "Doña Lupita," owned by Imelda Uribe and run by her daughter, Lupita, gorditas took on even one more twist: her gorditas were marketed as *gorditas de queso adobado* (cheese flavored with a chile adobo). Fresh *panela* cheese is kneaded with a purée of *chile guajillo*; the crumbly mixture is then stuffed inside a ball of raw masa before being flattened into a gordita and cooked on a comal. As the cheese melts, the intense orange/red of the chile stains the outer layer of the gordita. Gilding the lily, Lupita then slits open a cooked gordita and, as tradition dictates, shoves in yet another filling, or *guisado*—your choice, and the sky is the limit. The *puesto* "Doña Coco," across the aisle from "Doña Lupita," is quite famous throughout town with a small branch or two in the center of the pueblo, and offered equally delicious dishes. Between the two of them, the list of offerings was tantalizing if somewhat overwhelming. Following is the list of *guisados* on offer that day; several of these can be found elsewhere in this book; recipes for some of the others are given below. Make several *guisados* and host a "Gordita" party. For a special pleasure, add two *guisados* per gordita as we did.

Barbacoa (p. 363); Rajas con crema; Nopales en penca; Huitlacoche guisado (p. 350); Papas con chorizo (p. 325); Carne deshebrado en salsa chipotle; Chicharrón prensado en salsa pasilla; *chicharrón en salsa roja*; Tortas de camarón; and Frijoles de la olla (p. 530).

Prepare-ahead note: As they do in the markets, you may make the Gorditas filled with the cheese a couple of hours in advance; you'll be reheating them after you add the second filling.

YIELD: 15 GORDITAS

FOR THE FLAVORED CHEESE

6 chiles guajillos (about
  1½ oz./40 g total), stems, seeds,
  and veins removed
¼ pound (250 g) panela cheese
  (substitute fresh mozzarella
  or Monterey Jack), at room
  temperature

FOR THE MASA

1 cup (225 g) Enriched Lard,
  chilled, plus more at room
  temperature for frying
1 tablespoon (12 g) baking powder
2 pounds (1 kg) masa
1 cup (110 g) coarse cornmeal
1 teaspoon (6 g) salt

FOR FILLING

The guisados of your choice

FOR SERVING

The salsas of your choice
Lime wedges

PREPARE THE FLAVORED CHEESE

Lightly toast the chiles on a hot comal or griddle or in a cast-iron skillet until fragrant, 2–3 minutes. Remove the chiles from the comal and immediately cover them with boiling water. Allow the chiles to soak for 30 minutes; drain the chiles and discard the soaking water.

Transfer the chiles to the bowl of a food processor; process until the chiles are thoroughly mashed. Add the cheese and pulse 3–4 times, or until the chiles and cheese are roughly incorporated. The mixture will be crumbly. Cover and set aside.

PREPARE THE MASA

Place the lard and baking powder in the bowl of a stand mixer, and beat on high speed until the lard is fluffy and aerated, 3–4 minutes. Add fist-sized balls of masa to the lard a few at a time, beating between each addition; continue until all of the masa has been added. Add the cornmeal and salt, and beat on high speed for 2 minutes to incorporate the ingredients and lighten the dough. Keep the dough covered until you are ready to use it.

FORM AND FRY THE GORDITAS

Form the masa into 15 balls, each weighing about 2½ ounces (75 g); place the balls on a tray and keep them covered as you work with one Gordita at a time. Press one of the balls in your palm to form a flat disk, or thick tortilla, measuring about 3 inches (7.5 cm) in diameter. Place a heaping tablespoon (about 12 g) of the flavored cheese on the center of the tortilla; fold the tortilla in half like an empanada; seal tightly closed around the edges. Reshape the empanada into a ball, taking care not to let any of the cheese poke through (if it does, seal again or patch with a bit more masa). Now flatten the ball into a thick tortilla, measuring about 4½ inches (11.5 cm) in diameter. (*Note*: You may use your hands, a rolling pin, or a tortilla press for this action.) Repeat this step only when you are ready to fry; fry 2–3 of the Gorditas at a time.

Preheat a comal, griddle, or large cast-iron skillet on the highest heat; brush the surface with a bit of lard. Place one Gordita in the center of the comal (add up to two more close to the first one; the center is the hottest part of the comal); brush the tops of the Gorditas with a bit of lard. Cook until the edges of the Gordita appear a bit dry, with signs of cracking; use a spatula to lift the Gordita and check the bottom side: it should have patches of brown overall. Flip to the other side, brush with a bit of lard, and cook until browned (the second side takes less time; the time required depends on the temperature of your comal). Continue until all the Gorditas have been fried; keep them warm in a low oven or on a metal baking sheet covered with aluminum foil until you are ready to fill and serve.

FILL THE GORDITAS AND SERVE

Carefully slit open one edge of a Gordita; pry it open and fill with approximately 2 tablespoons (30 g) of the *guisado* of your choice. Reheat as per the instructions above, brushing the Gorditas with a bit of lard on both sides during cooking. Serve immediately with the salsas of your choice and a squeeze of lime.

GUISADOS PARA GORDITAS

FILLINGS FOR GORDITAS

Nowadays, there is no single "traditional" filling, and to my mind, the best Gorditas I have had feature things that never would have occurred to me—such as the Tortas de camarón (p. 414). Experiment, invent, mix and match. And, as mentioned, be daring and combine a couple of complementary (or contrasting) fillings in the same Gordita.

Prepare-ahead note: All of these *guisados* may be prepared a day in advance and refrigerated. Reheat prior to using in a Gordita. If you will be using the filling immediately after preparing it, cover, and keep it warm over low heat as you fill all of the Gorditas.

RAJAS CON CREMA

POBLANO STRIPS IN CRÈME FRAÎCHE

FOR THE POBLANO STRIPS

1 tablespoon (15 mL) vegetable oil
½ medium white onion
  (5 oz./137.5 g), cut into
  half-moons
1 medium clove garlic (¼ oz./6 g),
  peeled and finely chopped
6 chiles poblanos (about
  5 oz./140 g total), charred,
  peeled, seeded, and cut into
  strips (see instructions on p. 352;
  substitute canned rajas, drained)
¾ cup (187.5 mL) Mexican crema
  (substitute crème fraîche or
  plain yogurt)
¼ cup (62.5 mL) milk
½ teaspoon (3 g) sea salt
¼ teaspoon (0.325 g) dried whole
  Mexican oregano, crumbled

PREPARE THE POBLANO STRIPS
Heat the vegetable oil in a large skillet until shimmering; add the onions and garlic and cook over low heat, stirring constantly, until the onions are translucent, 3–4 minutes. Add the remaining ingredients and stir to combine. Continue cooking over low heat, stirring frequently, another 2–3 minutes or until the liquid is bubbling and reduced somewhat.

[MC]

CARNE DESHEBRADA EN SALSA CHIPOTLE

SHREDDED PORK CONFIT IN CHIPOTLE SAUCE

This was the five-star winner at our table. It seems a bit labor-intensive, but remember that our vendor would have already had the Carnitas on hand. Make them a day or so in advance and serve them as Carnitas, then repurpose the leftovers to make this awesome dish another day. We had our Gorditas double-filled: this *guisado* and Nopales en penca (p. 415). It was almost too much pleasure to bear.

TO PREPARE AHEAD
Carnitas (p. 477)

FOR THE SHREDDED PORK CONFIT
1 Roma tomato (3½ oz./100 g), quartered
½ medium white onion (5 oz./137.5 g)
3 chiles chipotles in adobo (1 oz./30 g), drained
1 medium clove garlic (¼ oz./6 g), peeled
½ cup (125 mL) water
½ teaspoon (3 g) sea salt
¼ teaspoon (0.325 g) dried whole Mexican oregano, crumbled
1 tablespoon (15 mL) vegetable oil
2 cups (448 g) Carnitas, finely shredded

PREPARE THE SHREDDED PORK CONFIT
Place the first seven ingredients in the jar of a blender; process until thoroughly liquefied; set aside.

Heat the vegetable oil in a large skillet until shimmering; pour all of the chipotle–tomato sauce into the skillet at once; it should sputter and sizzle, so stand back. Add the shredded pork and stir to combine. Bring the liquid to a boil, reduce to a simmer, and continue to cook another 4–5 minutes, stirring frequently, until the liquid has thickened and reduced slightly.

CHICHARRÓN PRENSADO EN SALSA PASILLA

PRESSED PORK BELLY CONFIT IN CHILE PASILLA SAUCE

If you are lucky enough to live near a Mexican butcher, you'll probably find Chicharrón prensado (p. 397); if not, substitute Carnitas, making the Carnitas on one day, and employing it in this dish on another.

FOR THE PRESSED PORK BELLY
2 cups water (500 mL)
6 chiles pasillas (about 2 oz./54 g total), seeds and veins removed
1 Roma tomato (3½ oz./100 g), quartered
½ medium white onion (5 oz./137.5 g)
1 medium clove garlic (¼ oz./6 g), peeled
½ teaspoon (3 g) sea salt
¼ teaspoon (0.325 g) dried whole Mexican oregano, crumbled
1 tablespoon (15 mL) vegetable oil
2 cups (450 g) chicharrón prensado, chopped (substitute Carnitas, p. 477)

PREPARE THE PRESSED PORK BELLY
Bring the water to a boil in a medium saucepan; add the chiles and return to a boil; remove from the heat, cover, and allow to soak for 30 minutes.

Remove the chiles from the water and transfer them to the jar of a blender; add 1 cup of the soaking liquid to the blender. Add the next five ingredients to the blender and process until thoroughly liquefied.

Heat the vegetable oil in a large skillet until shimmering; pour the contents of the blender into the skillet all at once: it should sputter and sizzle, so stand back. Add the chopped pork, and stir to incorporate. Bring the liquid to a boil, reduce to a simmer, and continue to cook another 4–5 minutes, stirring frequently, until the liquid has thickened and reduced slightly.

TORTAS DE CAMARÓN

DRIED SHRIMP FRITTERS IN TOMATO SAUCE

TO PREPARE AHEAD

Tortitas de camarón seco (p. 64), with its accompanying sauce

---

FOR THE SHRIMP FRITTERS

1 tablespoon (15 mL) vegetable oil

PREPARE THE SHRIMP FRITTERS

Prepare the sauce as described, cover, and set aside.

Prepare the fritters as described, but make them smaller by using just 1 tablespoon (15 g) of the shrimp mixture when you fry them. Set the fritters aside to drain on paper towels.

Heat the vegetable oil in a large skillet until shimmering; pour all of the tomato sauce into the skillet at once; it should sputter and sizzle, so stand back. Gently lower the fritters into the sauce a few at a time; shake the skillet so that the sauce covers them without breaking them. When all of the fritters have been added, continue to simmer over low heat for 2–3 minutes to incorporate flavors. When you fill the Gorditas, use 1–2 fritters and some of the sauce for each one.

Continuing north, the vast belt of semidesert culminates in its most arid expression just before butting into the great ranges of the Sierra Gorda, a massive barricade that serves as the first line of defense in the encroachment of Gulf Coast humidity toward the desert.

Agriculture here is sparse: maize, beans, fava beans, and peas occupy several acres, but these are mostly for auto-consumption. A meager 568 acres (230 hectares) are irrigated and support larger yields of zucchini, tomatoes, cucumber, and chiles, as well as maize and beans. One particular resource of this seemingly desolate region deserves special mention: cactus.

In this beautifully bleak area, cactus grows prolifically. While cactus grows in most states of Mexico (somewhat surprisingly, the largest production of prickly pear cactus, or nopal, occurs in the land surrounding Mexico City), according to Botanic Gardens Conservation International, Querétaro is home to a particularly diverse range of cactus and succulent species. Two remarkable botanical gardens in Cadereyta exhibit hundreds of species and thousands of specimens.

It could be said that cactus has helped shape what might be thought of as a "semidesert cuisine:" nopales, or cactus paddles, are common, but more unusual is the regional favorite, *biznaga* (p. 419) and its fruits, known as *borrachitas*

An Otomí-Chichimeca woman in the market of Tolimán in the semidesert slices nopalitos. [MC]

(little female drunks), consumed in various ways, as well as its candied core known as *acitrón* (p. 419). A delectable dish popular in both Querétaro and Hidalgo, Nopal en penca consists of a large cactus paddle hollowed out and filled with more cactus paddles cut into strips as well as onions and chile. It is typically roasted slowly atop the smoldering embers of a wood fire.

Enormous nopal paddles known as "verdulero" growing along the roadside. We gingerly removed one and used it to make Nopal en penca (below). [MR]

NOPAL EN PENCA

ROASTED CACTUS PADDLE FILLED WITH NOPALITOS AND CHICKEN

Making good use of the huge cactus paddle we had found on our road trip, Gude Rojo walked us through the steps of making this wonderfully simple and delicious dish, exactly as we had seen it in the Bernal market. Her father had taught her how to make it, and he had learned the preparation from his father. Gude's grandfather was a simple man who survived as best he could, with a little farming, a little hunting, selling whatever he produced or found that people would pay money for. On his frequent excursions into the *cerro* (mountains) he would scavenge—as we did—in order to have something to eat. The bag he took with him had only an onion, a couple of chiles, some herbs and salt, and a knife. The rest—as he told Gude—the *cerro* would provide. In its simplest and purest indigenous form, then, Nopal en penca is basically just cactus, with a few flavorings. Today's meat-eating public, however, has called for the addition of the meat or seafood of choice; we decided to use chicken. The *penca* that we found (*penca* is a general term used to refer to large leaves from the maguey as well as the nopal) was large enough to hold an entire chicken, cut into eight pieces. The instructions here are for using chicken; use any meat you like, or use only the vegetables. Since you will most likely not have easy access to a large nopal paddle, I have given instructions at the end of the recipe for how to use several smaller paddles instead—and wanting those, using only strips of *nopalitos*. Wrapping the whole package and roasting it in a gas or charcoal grill will give an authentically smoky flavor, but you may also wrap it in banana leaves and aluminum foil and bake it in the oven—something a lot of the market vendors do.

Prepare-ahead note: Nopal en penca can be kept warm for several hours before serving, wrapped in foil and placed in a low oven.

YIELD: 8 SERVINGS

FOR THE CACTUS PADDLE

1 large cactus paddle (approximately 12–14 inches/30.5–35.5 cm in diameter. *Note*: If you do not have access to a large paddle, substitute 4–5 smaller ones, or see alternate method below.)

FOR THE FILLING

1 medium chicken (about 4 lbs./1.8 kg), preferably brined, cut into 8 serving pieces

1 teaspoon (6 g) sea salt (up to 1 tsp./6 g more if the chicken was not brined)

2 tablespoons (8 g) parsley, finely chopped

4 cups (432 g) nopalitos, cut into large dice (see p. 390 for preparation instructions; substitute canned nopalitos, thoroughly drained)

2 medium Roma tomatoes (7 oz./200 g), seeded and cut into medium dice

2 medium cloves garlic (½ oz./12 g), peeled and finely chopped

½ medium white onion (5 oz./137.5 g), thinly sliced and separated into rings

2 chiles serranos (½ oz./14 g), seeded and finely chopped

1 tablespoon (2 g) dried whole Mexican oregano, lightly toasted and crumbled

3 sprigs fresh thyme (substitute ¾ tsp./0.75 g dried)

2 sprigs fresh marjoram (substitute 2 tsp./1 g dried)

4 bay leaves

[MR]

PREPARE THE CHICKEN AND CACTUS PADDLE

Sprinkle the chicken with the salt and parsley, and set aside. Prepare a gas or charcoal grill (for this step you may use a gas burner on the stovetop). Lay the paddle directly over the flame or on the hottest part of your grill. Check after 3–4 minutes; it should demonstrate scorch marks and some of the spines should be burned and loose. Use a very sharp knife to scrape/slice away the spines. Flip to the other side, and repeat. The paddle should be well scorched and considerably softened.

With a long, sharp knife, on the side opposite where the paddle was connected to the plant, cut a slit that reaches the halfway point of the diameter of the paddle. Using the knife as well as your hands, pry the paddle open; scrape and scoop out as much of the mucilage as possible; discard the mucilage. It tends to be a very messy, stringy job, so is best done outdoors, or at least held over a large wastebasket.

FILL THE CACTUS PADDLE AND ROAST

Shove the chicken pieces as deeply as possible into the closed end of the paddle. Pile the *nopalitos* on top of and all around the chicken, distributing them evenly over the interior of the paddle. Spread the next four ingredients on top of the *nopalitos*; sprinkle with the oregano and top the pile with the herbs.

The next trick is to tie the nopal paddle tightly closed. In the *cerro*, people use natural fibers like *ixtle* (p. 126); at home, they may just as easily use wire. Lacking either one, Gude improvised with paper-coated metal twist-ties (avoid plastic, which may melt and release toxins during roasting). Whatever method you choose, use a large needle or nail to perforate holes through the top and out the bottom of the edges of the nopal, keeping the holes at least 1 inch (2.5 cm) from the edge to prevent tearing.

Lime wedges
The chile sauce of your choice
Warm maize tortillas (optional)

Space the holes about 3–4 inches (7.5–10 cm) apart. Use the wire, fiber, or twist-ties to thread through the holes one at a time, knot, and seal closed.

Wrap the nopal tightly in aluminum foil; place close to the heat source of the grill, lower the lid, and roast for 1 hour. Remove from the grill, remove the foil and recycle; remove the ties. Plate the nopal on a large serving platter. Serving is done at the table by using a large spoon to scoop out the vegetables, and a serving fork for spearing the chicken pieces. Each diner receives 1 piece of chicken and a large scoop of the vegetables. Diners may use fresh tortillas to assemble their own tacos if desired, and top with squeezes of lime juice and the salsa of their choice.

Alternate method: If using several smaller paddles instead of a single large one: Proceed to roast 4–6 paddles and scrape off the spines as instructed above. Use a very sharp knife to slit each paddle around the edges, cutting it completely in half, top to bottom and around the sides, and separate into two pieces; scrape off any mucilage as instructed. Line a baking dish or casserole with large sheets of aluminum foil that extend well beyond the dish, and then line the foil with large pieces of banana leaf (optional). Arrange one layer of paddles, cut sides up, followed by the remaining ingredients as instructed, then top with the final layer of paddles, cut sides down. If you cannot locate whole paddles, use an extra quantity of *nopalito* strips. Close the banana leaves, crimp the foil tightly to seal, and bake in a preheated oven at 350°F (176°C) for 1 hour. You may also roast the entire package on a gas or charcoal grill rather than in the oven. Serving instructions are the same.

VARIATIONS

Use chorizo, Cecina (p. 397), or cubed beef or pork riblets instead of the chicken, or omit the meats altogether for a vegetarian option.

(left) Slicing open the cactus paddle before filling and roasting. [MR] *(right) Ingredients for Nopal en penca, clockwise from bottom: a small plate of dried oregano, diced nopalitos, garlic cloves and sliced onion, chicken with chopped parsley, diced tomatoes, chopped serrano, and a bunch of "hierbas de olor"—thyme, bay leaves, marjoram.* [MR]

There are trees in this land they call nopalli, which means tunal, or tree with tunas; it is a monstrous tree, the trunk is composed of leaves and the branches are made of these same leaves; the leaves are broad and thick, having juice and are viscous; the same leaves have many thorns. . . . The leaves of this tree are eaten raw and cooked.

BERNARDINO DE SAHAGÚN, 1575–1577

[MR]

NOPAL

BOTANICAL: *Opuntia* spp./Family Cactaceae | **ENGLISH:** prickly pear cactus, paddle cactus
NAHUATL: *nopalli* | **OTOMÍ (HÑÄHÑU):** *xät'ä*

Colonial chroniclers reported seeing many cactus varieties in the New World, but perhaps none with such fascination as the prickly pear cactus. The plant is known botanically as *Opuntia*, and among speakers of Nahuatl as *nopal* or *nopalli*; the fruit of the plant is known in Nahuatl as *nochtli* and in Spanish as *tuna*, originally an Antillean word.

Cacti are native to North and South America and the West Indies; many species are endemic to Mexico. Domesticated thousands of years ago, they are one of only a few plants that serve as food for humans as well as for animals, that are used medicinally, and that can be grown industrially for commercialization. They are remarkably tolerant of a wide range of growing conditions and soils, and are resistant to drought and to temperatures as high as 131°F (55°C).

The large Cactaceae family has some 122 genera and approximately 1,800 species, almost all of which are characterized by spiny protuberances. Forms vary dramatically, from epiphytic trailing vines that climb over other plants or structures, to barrel-shaped or tall columnar species, and the well-known cactus paddles called nopales—*Opuntia ficus-indica*—the most common species worldwide. Many of these varieties produce edible fruits that have been consumed in Mexico for thousands of years. The *Opuntia* genus produces not only the mucilaginous paddles but also a sweet-tart fruit known generally as "cactus pear" or "prickly pear" and as *tuna* in Mexico; a sour species is called *xoconostle* (p. 353). The fruit may be confected into candies, jams, or jellies, or its juice may be fermented to produce a mildly alcoholic beverage called *colonche*. The paddles, known in Mexico as *nopalitos* when prepared for eating, are consumed as a fresh vegetable and also as a processed food, including dried and pickled forms. In Mexico, nopal is the fifth most important vegetable in volume of production, after tomatoes, potatoes, chiles, and onions. The demand is highest in the Central Highlands, where its production is also highest. *Opuntia* is gathered in the wild, as well as being cultivated in small family plots, or even in vast commercial orchards.

BIZNAGA/BIZNAGA GIGANTE, BIZNAGA BURRA, BIZNAGA DE LANA, BIZNAGA DULCE, ACITRÓN

BOTANICAL: *Echinocactus platyacanthus* Link & Otto/Family/Cactaceae | **ENGLISH:** giant barrel cactus, candy barrel cactus
NAHUATL: *huitznáhuac, teocomitl* | **OTOMÍ (HÑÄHÑU):** *däxpe*

Colloquially (and humorously) known here as *asiento de suegra* (mother-in-law's seat), the giant barrel cactus is a dramatic resident of the central Mexican landscape, distributed through the states of Coahuila, Nuevo León, Tamaulipas, Guanajuato, San Luis Potosí, Zacatecas, Querétaro, Puebla, and Oaxaca. Many species are endemic to Mexico, and therefore subject to special protection. Actually, there are at least four species in the genera *Echinocactus* and *Ferocactus* that are known as *biznaga*; all are used in similar ways. The cactus is generally spherical, or it may take the form of a distended cylinder; it can reach heights of 6½ feet (2 m) and widths of 5 feet (1.5 m); the body is subdivided by deep "ribs" or ridges; along the edges of these ribs grow strong spines that are yellow with tinges of pink when young, or grayish when older. Barrel cactus produces yellow flowers at the crown; bees and wasps are pollinators. Flowers eventually give way to fuzzy finger-shaped fruits known as *borrachitas* (little female drunks); the fruits are preserved in sugar syrup or honey and sold as a snack in the markets. Additionally, the core of the cactus is cooked in sugar and dried until the pulp crystalizes, and is known as *acitrón* (p. 472), which is a key ingredient in the meat filling for the Puebla classic, *chiles en nogada*; it is also one of the candied fruits used atop the holiday bread known as *rosca de reyes*, and appears alongside raisins and chopped nuts in the ice cream known as Mantecado (p. 339, a specialty of Dolores Hidalgo, Guanajuato). *Biznaga* is still gathered in the wild, and efforts to cultivate it for commercial use are nascent, the challenge being the many years the plant takes to mature. In any case, *acitrón* is difficult to locate outside of Mexico; a suitable substitute is candied pineapple.

Borrachitas *are the fruits of the giant barrel cactus, biznaga,* typically cooked in sugar syrup or honey. At rear is another cactus fruit, garambullo (p. 335). [MC]

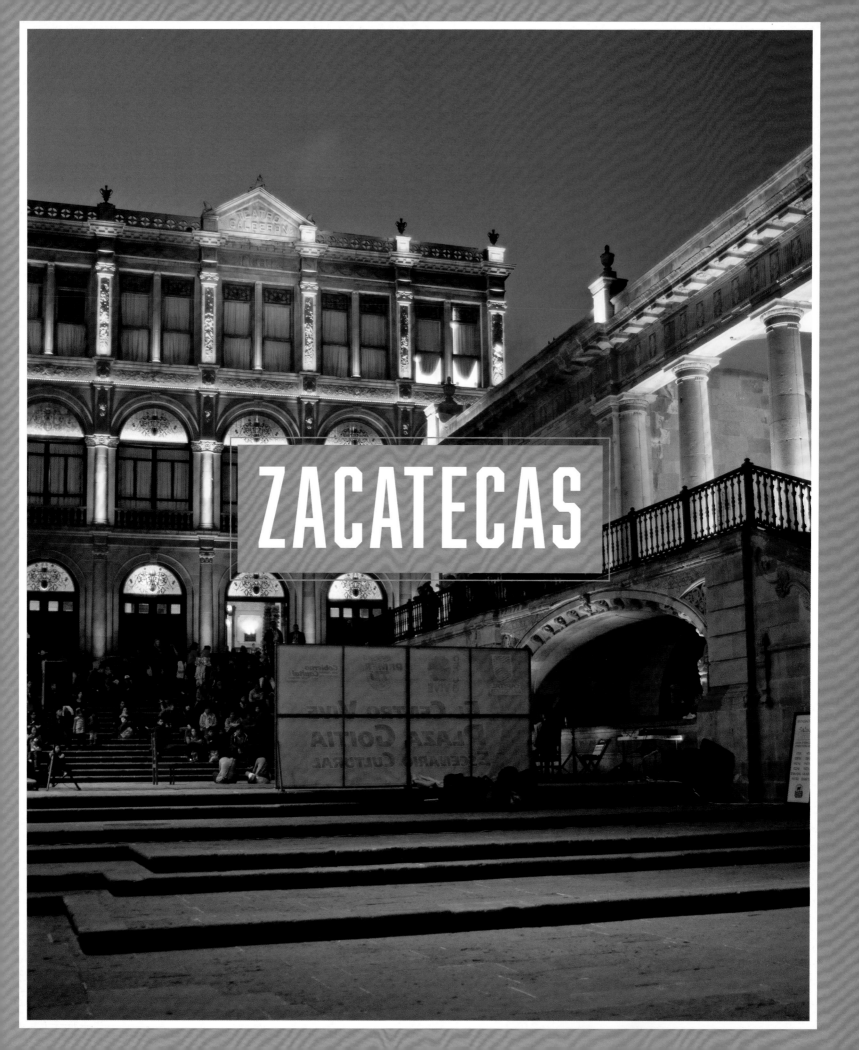

ZACATECAS

ZACATECAS (CITY)

THE NORTHERNMOST REACH of our expedition took us to the rugged state of Zacatecas and its elegant capital of the same name. The first stop we made—even before the markets—was the *teleférico*, a Swiss-Canadian-engineered cable car that swoops you high above the city to the peak of Cerro de la Bufa, where lies the entrance to the old Mina El Edén silver mine, now a museum. Our aim was not so much to relive the daily drudgery of the miners who worked in this prosperous silver town, as it was simply to soak in the panoramic views from the cabin spread out before us in 360 degrees. The street plan of Zacatecas as seen from above was a jigsaw puzzle with streets dead-ending at one refined neoclassical building or another, only to pick back up again on the other side. Lay that plan atop an unrelentingly undulating topography, and you get a city that is visually dramatic, easy to get lost in, and great exercise.

PANCHO VILLA AND HIS DIVISIÓN DEL NORTE

We had coincidentally arrived in Zacatecas on the day when Mexicans everywhere celebrate Día de la Revolución—the day that marks the first shots of the Mexican Revolution. Listening to the tinny sounds of marching bands and fireworks ringing up the slopes of La Bufa from the valley where the historic center of the city is located, we thought it fitting to visit the small museum at the crest of the hill called La Toma de Zacatecas (the taking of Zacatecas), which portrays the history of the largest and bloodiest battle of the revolution. With those sounds, it was easy to imagine the day in 1914 when Pancho Villa commandeered his División del Norte to fight Federalist forces, storming up and down between La Bufa and El Grillo, a hill on the other side of the valley, to take control of the city—a strategic location due to its recently installed telegraph lines, a railway, and great wealth.

Whatever route you take to Zacatecas, the vistas along the way are guaranteed to be spectacular, sandwiched as it is between the great ranges of the Sierra Madre Occidental and the Sierra Madre Oriental. The capital clings to the piedmont at 8,010 feet (2,440 m) above sea level, making it one of the highest cities in Mexico. The small Sierra Zacatecas range cuts through the state east to west and forms a neat boundary between the Central and the Northern Highlands. During the colonial era, Zacatecas was the final outpost of "civilization" before one headed north into the heart of Chichimec territory and the vast Chihuahuan Desert. But the Spanish felt obliged to do so for many reasons: the northern lands proved fertile for growing wheat, the only grain blessed for the production of communion wafers; on that same note, there were souls to be saved; and after 1546 when a major silver mine was found in the territory, there ensued a feverish quest that soon led to the opening of over five thousand mines stretching even farther north into the inhospitable terrain. By the seventeenth century, a flood of wealth streamed south into Mexico City along the Camino Real de Tierra Adentro.

The hostile landscape immediately surrounding the capital proved challenging for agriculture, and most goods had to be hauled in from other areas: along with precious minerals, the Camino Real served as the highway for the yearly importation of over six thousand wagonloads of basic provisions throughout the seventeenth century. The table of miners and their families was basic at best: they often consumed little more than tortillas with a bit of *quelites* and chile. According to CONACULTA's *La cocina familiar en el estado de Zacatecas*, taverns along the royal road served what today we would call *antojitos*—simple snacks like *garnachas*, pickled pigs' feet tostadas, tamales, chiles

(opposite page) Zacatecas by night. The historic center, encompassing 272 acres (110 hectares), is now a UNESCO World Heritage Site. At right is the old González Ortega market (1886), today a gallery of craft shops. [LP]

rellenos, and sometimes heartier fare like grilled meats, stews of *quelites*, or *pipián*. When food was scarce, cooks made use of desert resources, preparing them with recipes modified from those brought from Spain and more robustly utilized in the populous south. Mexican food columnist Karen Hursh Graber states that this resulted in a kind of "minimalist" cuisine with greatly streamlined ingredient lists. She further explains that just as Zacatecas straddles the cusp between north and south, so does its cuisine.

Today, mining is still an important activity in Zacatecas: the state accounts for more than 21 percent of the country's gold output and 53 percent of its silver output, thanks to which Mexico is considered the world's largest producer of silver. Although much of the state is desertlike, irrigation has made it agriculturally rich: Zacatecas is Mexico's top producer of dry beans and is a major producer of chiles, guavas, and nopal; peaches, plums, grapes, and apricots rank high in production; and Zacatecas is Mexico's prime producer of pine nuts.

In addition to a more conventional sign, Carnicería Panchito in "El Laberinto" attracts customers with a scale model of the butcher shop itself. [MC]

MERCADO GENARO CODINA "EL LABERINTO"

Stone-trimmed arches and vaulted ceilings form the refined cloister-like halls of Mercado Genaro Codina, a fitting setting for the veneration of local meats and produce. Named after the fireworks fabricator and harpist who composed the "Marcha de Zacatecas," which is considered to be the second national anthem of Mexico, the market was constructed in 1810 for its original purpose as a grain exchange. In other incarnations, it was a tobacco factory, a school for señoritas, and finally in 1906 it became the city's main meat market. Soon thereafter the market began selling all kinds of comestibles, a function it continues to the present.

Jugos "Los Chachis" and several other juice stands greet visitors at one entrance with a steady parade of "morning-after" beverages. [MC]

MERCADO "ARROYO DE LA PLATA"

Steps from the Mercado Genaro Codina lies the less saintly Mercado "Arroyo de la Plata" (Silver Stream). A jumble of stalls displays everything from offerings to Santa Muerte to more mundane plastic goods from China. For the immediately hungry, a smattering of *comedores* offers full meals for breakfast and lunch.

POLLA

ORANGE JUICE AND SHERRY "EYE-OPENER"

The hair-of-the-dog remedy of choice at Jugos "Los Chachis" is this wonder-working tonic: equal parts fresh orange juice and sweet sherry (Tres Coronas was the brand), finished with two tiny quail eggs cracked on top. Or, you can order the same thing with *rompope* (an eggnog-like beverage) instead of the orange juice; blended with milk, the beverage changes here to *ponche*. The Spanish *polla* translates to "chick," referring either to the bird or the girl; and in some streets it may refer vulgarly to the male member.

The owner pours Tres Coronas from an industrial-sized jug. [MC]

A generous glass of Polla is in the foreground. [MC]

ASADO DE BODA

PORK LOIN AND CHILE STEW

TO PREPARE AHEAD

Chocolate de mesa (p. 77), or
   substitute
Enriched Lard (see notes on
   p. 530), or substitute

FOR THE ADOBO

8 chiles guajillos (2 oz./50 g), seeds
   and veins removed
8 chiles anchos (2⅔ oz./88 g),
   seeds and veins removed
1 three-inch (7.5 cm) stick canela
   (Mexican cinnamon)
½ teaspoon (2 g) coriander seeds
½ teaspoon (2 g) black
   peppercorns
8 allspice berries
4 whole cloves
½ medium white onion
   (5 oz./137.5 g), coarsely chopped
3 medium cloves garlic
   (¾ oz./18 g), peeled and coarsely
   chopped
1 thick slice stale French or Italian
   bread, about 1 ounce (28 g)
3 cups (750 mL) water, divided

In the northern states of Coahuila, Durango, and Zacatecas, for decades wedding parties on ranches have been fed with the hearty Asado de boda (wedding roast). The tradition continues today, although the dish has become so popular that it is also served for other special occasions or even daily at many restaurants. When history is sketchy in the kitchen, everyone jumps in to claim her recipe as "the original." Such is the case for Asado de boda, which *zacatecanos* proudly claim as their own and link to their history: the legend they refer to is that Pancho Villa ordered a dish of pork and chiles after celebrating a major victory in Zacatecas during the Mexican Revolution. Thereafter, as a point of patriotic pride (and perhaps to become heroes by association), young bridegrooms would order it for the family of the bride, and soon the wedding connection was permanent. The adobo for Asado de boda bears a striking resemblance to many moles, although its preparation is considerably simpler, as can be seen from this adaptation of the version we had at Puesto "Danny."

Prepare-ahead note: Like many stews, Asado de boda benefits from an overnight rest in the refrigerator. Prepare a day in advance and refrigerate, skim off any accumulated fat, and reheat just before serving, adding a bit more liquid if necessary.

YIELD: 8–10 SERVINGS

PREPARE THE ADOBO

Cover the chiles with boiling water and allow to soak for 20 minutes.

   Place all of the spices (the next five ingredients) in a spice grinder or coffee mill adapted for the purpose; grind until fine and transfer to the jar of a blender.

   Remove the chiles from the soaking liquid and transfer them to the blender along with the onion, garlic, and bread; discard the soaking liquid. Add 1½ cups (375 mL) of the water and process until thoroughly liquefied. Pour the mixture through a fine-mesh sieve placed over a large mixing bowl. Using a rubber spatula, press and mash the mixture to extract as much as possible through the sieve, adding the remaining water a bit at a time to help the mixture pass through. Discard any residue left in the sieve. Set the strained mixture aside.

PREPARE THE PORK AND FINISH

Cut the pork into 1-inch (2.5 cm) cubes. In a large pot or Dutch oven, heat the lard or oil until shimmering; add the pork a few pieces at a time and sauté until well browned; transfer the browned pork to a platter as you finish the rest. Return the pork to the pot and add the bay leaves, marjoram, thyme, and orange rind. Pour in the chile mixture, add the water, and stir to combine. Bring to a boil, reduce to a simmer and continue cooking until the pork is tender, about 30 minutes. Add more water as needed to keep the mixture at a consistency that thickly coats a spoon as well as the individual cubes of pork. When the pork is thoroughly cooked, add the remaining ingredients, stir until

FOR THE PORK AND FINISHING

3½ pounds (1.5 kg) pork loin, with a thin layer of fat
¼ cup (62.5 mL) Enriched Lard (substitute vegetable oil)
2 medium bay leaves
1 medium sprig *each* marjoram and thyme
Rind of 1 sweet orange
1½ cups (375 mL) water
½ cup (125 mL) white vinegar
1½ tablespoons (27 g) sea salt, or to taste
1 tablespoon (12 g) sugar, or to taste
1 ball (3¼ oz./90 g) Chocolate de mesa (substitute the same weight of commercial Mexican drinking chocolate in tablet form)

FOR SERVING

½ medium white onion (5 oz./137.5 g), thinly sliced and separated into rings
Slices of queso ranchero or other fresh cheese
Arroz de fiesta (p. 74), or plain white rice, optional
Frijoles de la olla (p. 530), optional
Warm tortillas

the chocolate dissolves, and simmer an additional 10 minutes to amalgamate flavors; check for seasonings and serve.

TO SERVE
Place a few spoonfuls of Asado de boda on individual serving plates and garnish with onion rings and a slice of cheese. Accompany with rice, beans, and tortillas if desired.

[LP]

CARNE DE PUERCO CON NOPALITOS

PORK IN SPICY TOMATILLO SAUCE WITH CACTUS STRIPS

TO PREPARE AHEAD

Enriched Lard (see notes on
p. 530), or substitute
Salsa verde (p. 531)

[MC]

Aside from Ensalada de nopales (p. 390), this is one of the few dishes I can think of that makes such generous use of the cactus pads known as nopales—plentiful in Zacatecas. Volume-wise, they stand head-to-head with the pork in this dish, and you can eat with a clear conscience, since according to many sources, they are loaded with health benefits (immune-response boosters, high in fiber, help regulate blood sugar levels) and are extremely low in calories.

Prepare-ahead note: Having the Salsa verde at hand makes this dish come together quickly. Carne de puerco con nopalitos benefits from an overnight rest in the refrigerator, although it does not freeze well. Reheat gently just before serving.

YIELD: 6–8 SERVINGS

PREPARE THE STEW

Clean, slice, and cook the *nopalitos* as per the instructions on page 390; set aside.

In a large stockpot or Dutch oven, heat the lard or oil until shimmering; add the pork a few pieces at a time and cook, turning frequently. Sprinkle with some of the cumin and continue cooking until the meat is browned and the cumin fragrant; transfer the cooked pork to a platter and repeat until all of the pork is browned and seasoned with all of the cumin.

1 pound (500 g) nopales (cactus paddles; substitute canned nopalitos, drained weight)

3 tablespoons (48 g) Enriched Lard (substitute vegetable oil)

2 pounds (1 kg) pork loin, cubed, or pork riblets, or a combination

1 teaspoon (2 g) ground cumin

2 cups (500 mL) water

4 cups (1 L) Salsa verde (1 recipe)

FOR SERVING

White rice or the rice of your choice, optional

Frijoles de la olla (p. 530), optional

Salpicón of chopped white onion and cilantro, dressed with a bit of lime juice

Lime wedges

Return the pork to the pot; pour in the water; bring to a boil, reduce to a simmer, cover, and continue cooking until the meat is tender, about 45 minutes. Toward the end of cooking, check frequently to make sure that all of the water has not evaporated; if so, add a bit more. You should have a scant ¼ cup (62.5 mL) left at the end.

Add the Salsa verde and the cooked *nopalitos* to the pot, stir to combine, and continue cooking at a simmer another 10–15 minutes to amalgamate flavors.

TO SERVE

You may either serve Carne de puerco con nopalitos as a stew in deep serving bowls, or plated with rice and beans. Diners add the *salpicón* garnish and squeezes of lime juice to taste.

Occupants of the pantheon of Puesto "Danny": a cow clock, a frog bank, and a plaster statue of Jesus. [LP]

5

PACIFIC
REGION

Lake Chapala.

INTRODUCTION

THE FAMOUS LA QUEBRADA cliff divers on the Acapulco coast offer a daring demonstration of the split personality of the region's topography: skyward-reaching mountains and earth-hugging ocean. Such a dichotomous setting makes for breathtaking beach resorts, and there are dozens of incomparably alluring ones strung along the Pacific coast: Acapulco, Ixtapa, and Zihuatanejo in Guerrero; Puerto Vallarta in Jalisco; Punta Mita in Nayarit; Mazatlán in Sinaloa.

In fact, all of the states that line the Pacific on Mexico's central-western edge are similarly composed, with altitudes ranging from zero to 650 feet (200 m) above sea level along the coastal plain, and dizzying heights of 14,000 feet (4,300 m) or more farther inland. The multifarious topography has helped forge the Pacific region's history, culture, and gastronomy.

While the jagged mountains may supply thrills for voyeuristic tourists, it is actually the flatlands defined by the ranges—piedmont at sea level and arid to semiarid plateaus at higher elevations—that have historically produced the *carnitas*, pozole, and tequila that have become indelibly linked to the Mexican table and spirit.

PHYSICAL ENVIRONMENT AND AGRICULTURE

The region along Mexico's central-western coast represents some of the oldest settled land in the country, with occupation dating to 15,000 years ago. The Balsas River is one of the longest in Mexico, originating in Puebla and snaking its way through Jalisco and Guerrero before finally emptying into the Pacific near Lázaro Cárdenas in Michoacán. The Balsas River basin—at 44,828 square miles (116,000 sq. km) one of Mesoamerica's largest—is believed to have been an early site for the domestication of maize, dating to some 9,200 years ago. Lake Chapala in Jalisco is the country's largest lake, and the state provides 15 percent of the surface freshwater in Mexico. Freshwater fish, such as *pescado blanco* (whitefish) and *charal* (p. 495), are ubiquitous in the cuisine. Commercial fishing in the Pacific brings in shark, sea bass, lobster, clams, tuna, and octopus, as well as red snapper, grouper, and shrimp; sailfish and marlin are popular in sport fishing but can be found in markets, too.

During the colonial era, the high plains surrounding Guadalajara in Jalisco and the Tierra Caliente piedmont of the Sierra Madre Occidental in Michoacán both became major centers of agriculture and ranching. The cowboy culture on the ranches eventually engendered the musical style known as *ranchera*, and soon followed the stylized performers known as mariachis and their iconic hit song-and-dance, "Jarabe tapatío," better known as "The Mexican Hat Dance." Of course, ranching had its culinary impact, too: Jalisco and Michoacán are leaders in Mexico's production of dual-purpose cows, and the region yields one-fifth of the country's goat meat—the primordial substance of Jalisco's famed *birria* (p. 440). Pork is important, too: Jalisco and Sonora are Mexico's top pig producers, accounting for 45 percent of the market share. Pork figures prominently in many variations of the region's ubiquitous hominy stew, pozole (p. 443), and the crispy pork "little meats" known as *carnitas* are Michoacán's culinary claim to fame.

The Trans-Mexican Volcanic Belt slashes through the region and is peppered with extinct, dormant, and active volcanoes. In the shadow of the Volcán de Tequila, a shallow valley is filled with black soil where the blue agave (*Agave tequilana*) found the ideal terroir for the production of top-shelf tequila; redder, mineral-rich soils in Jalisco's high plains are also fruitful.

Tierra Caliente, or the lowlands along the coast, is characterized by hotter temperatures and lower rainfall. A major supplier of beans, the Tierra Caliente also produces lemons, limes, oranges, mangos, guavas, tamarinds, watermelons, and cantaloupes. Michoacán is the world's largest producer of avocados.

The physical environment of the Pacific region has also played a vital role in Mexico's history. With the conquest of the Aztec Triple Alliance in the Central Highlands behind them, the Spaniards turned their gaze westward. In 1521, when they first arrived in P'urhépecha (Tarascan) lands in the modern states of Michoacán and Jalisco, the ruler gave Spanish emissaries gifts of gold. The P'urhépechas were well known for their skills in metalworking (p. 482), fashioning tools of copper and ornaments of gold and silver. The dream of more mineral wealth attracted the attention of Hernán Cortés and the infamous Nuño de Guzmán; large swaths of modern-day Michoacán and Jalisco soon fell under their power.

But it was not only gold that lured the Spaniards to the west. Columbus's dream of a western passage to Asia was still very much part of their plan, and the natural harbor at Acapulco enabled the building of ships to handle a burgeoning overseas trade. Spices, silk, ivory, porcelain, lacquerware, and other valuable commodities from Asia were mostly purchased with silver mined in Mexico and Bolivia.

By 1565, the Manila Galleons (also called La Nao de China)—a fleet of huge mercantile ships—made the four-month journey across the Pacific from Acapulco to China and Manila, and back again. Once in Acapulco, the cargo was unloaded and hauled overland for some twelve days along the rough and dangerous Acapulco Trail to Mexico City, or on to Veracruz, from where it sailed to Spain. The prospect of lucrative overseas trade made the Acapulco Trail one of the busiest colonial routes in Mexico.

ETHNOLINGUISTIC GROUPS

The majority of the modern state of Michoacán and the eastern third of Jalisco were part of the Tarascan State and are still inhabited by indigenous P'urhépecha (p. 482). The P'urhépecha (or Tarascan) State emerged in the thirteenth century and eventually came to rival the Aztec Triple Alliance.

The flow of goods through the Tarascan Empire occurred primarily as a result of tributes demanded by the ruling dynasties. The goods that appear most frequently on tribute lists from the sixteenth century are cotton cloth and clothing; domestic servants and slaves; weapons and metal objects of copper, bronze, silver, and gold; gourds; and animal skins, as well as foodstuffs such as maize, tropical fruits, cacao, salt, beans, chiles, turkeys, rabbits, honey, and pulque. While most of these goods were consumed by elites, certain tribute goods, such as obsidian tools, fine pottery, and metal artifacts, were eventually traded in the markets.

Modern P'urhépechas have a strong sense of identity, and in 1993 they united to create a people's flag. In it, a symbolic crest is centered on a field of four colors that represent the four regions of Michoacán where they reside. Nahua and Otomí peoples also inhabit the state, as do smaller numbers of Mazahuas.

Eight out of every one thousand people in Jalisco speak an indigenous language—higher than the national average of six per one thousand; 14 percent of all native speakers do not speak Spanish. Dominant groups are Huichols and Nahuas, followed by P'urhépechas and Mixtecs. The largest concentrations of native speakers can be found in Mezquitic, Zapopan, and Guadalajara.

Mariachis in the Plaza de Armas, Guadalajara, ca. 1930–1950.

GUADALAJARA

T HE STATE-SPONSORED SLOGAN for Jalisco is "Jalisco is Mexico," and everything from its terrain to its culture would seem to lend credence to the claim. Geographically speaking, it includes all five of Mexico's ecosystems and encompasses such topographical landmarks as the Central Plateau and the Trans-Mexican Volcanic Belt, the Sierra Madre Occidental and the Sierra Madre del Sur. The variety and beauty of its terrain attracts millions of visitors annually, and many thousands of expats have settled in the resort town of Lake Chapala and along the mountain-clad beaches of Puerto Vallarta on the Pacific coast. Culturally, too, it is home to many definers of Mexican identity and pride: mariachi and *ranchera* music; *birria*, a spicy roast-meat dish revered nationwide; and perhaps the best-known Mexican export of all: tequila.

Guadalajara, the state capital and second-largest metropolitan area in the country, has its share of historic sites, but today it is often referred to as the "Silicon Valley" of Mexico due to its proliferation of high-tech industries. The physical city reflects its galloping history, with tailored buildings from the colonial era rubbing elbows (at times rather uncomfortably) with modern brutalist blockbusters. But *tapatíos*, as people from Guadalajara are known, seem blasé about the blur of history that has forged their city as they stroll amicably along pedestrian-only boulevards or lick ice cream in the sun-bleached plaza that spreads before the magnificent Hospicio Cabañas, full of spectacular murals depicting much of that history painted by native son José Clemente Orozco. The Huichol (p. 447) and Nahua (p. 291) peoples are the dominant indigenous groups of Jalisco.

(opposite page) Catedral Basílica de la Asunción de María Santísima and the Plaza de Armas. [LP]

MERCADO SAN JUAN DE DIOS ("LIBERTAD")

In so many colonial towns and cities throughout Mexico, marketplaces were situated on the grounds of or adjacent to churches. Such was the case for Mercado Libertad—popularly known as Mercado San Juan de Dios—originally a *tianguis* in the neighborhood of San Juan de Dios, which surrounds the eponymous church. The modern building on the same site, inaugurated in 1958, invades the colonial grid; its stark façade is relieved inside by architect Alejandro Zohn's clever reference to the billowing canvases of the old *tianguis*, each canopy brightened by skylights in the shape of four-pointed stars.

In fact, the cast-concrete roof covers what market officials say is the largest roofed market building in Latin America. Its 450,000 square feet (40,000 sq. m) host a flood of some 2,800 vendors daily, opening at 7:00 a.m. and closing at 8:00 p.m. every day year-round.

The three-story building displays fresh fruits and vegetables on the main floor, batteries of comedores *on the second floor, and everything from crafts to imported electronics on the top floor.* [LP]

(above) Vista of the produce section as seen from the second-floor balcony. [MC] *(below)* Comedores on the second floor hawk sushi and other Asian dishes. Fish dishes such as Caldo michi *(next page)* are also popular. Portuguese traders brought Asian slaves to Mexico as early as the sixteenth century; a tidal wave of Japanese immigration to Mexico occurred in the 1800s. During World War II, Japanese residents were relocated to inland cities like Guadalajara, where their participation in the culture is still important. [LP]

CALDO MICHI

CATFISH AND VEGETABLE SOUP

FOR THE FISH-STOCK BASE

2 pounds (1 kg) whole catfish

8 cups (2 L) water

4 tablespoons (48 g) powdered
   shrimp bouillon, or 4 cubes

FOR THE SOFRITO

3 tablespoons (45 mL) olive oil

½ medium white onion
   (5 oz./137.5 g), sliced half-moon
   style

3 medium cloves garlic
   (¾ oz./18 g), peeled and finely
   chopped

2 medium Roma tomatoes
   (7 oz./200 g), seeded and cut
   into medium dice

2 medium tomatillos (7 oz./200 g),
   husks removed, rinsed, and cut
   into medium dice

1 teaspoon (0.65 g) whole dried
   Mexican oregano, lightly toasted
   and crumbled

½ teaspoon (2.5 g) freshly ground
   black pepper

FOR THE SOUP

½ pound (250 g) carrots, peeled
   and cut into thick rounds

½ pound (250 g) zucchini, cut into
   large cubes

½ pound (250 g) chayote, cut into
   large cubes

½ pound (250 g) baking potatoes,
   peeled and cut into large cubes

¼ cup (15 g) *total* coarsely chopped
   cilantro and fresh basil leaves

4 jalapeños en escabeche (pickled
   jalapeños), sliced into rounds (or
   use 10–12 pickled chiles labeled
   "nachos")

1 tablespoon (15 mL) of the
   vinegar from the chiles

This light fish broth (*michin* is the Nahuatl word for "fish") crowded with vegetables and sparked with a faint zing of chile is another specialty of Jalisco; variations of Caldo michi can also be found in Michoacán and Guanajuato. Caldo michi typically employs only freshwater fish, such as catfish or tilapia. Many restaurants advertise that their catfish was caught in Lake Chapala (although who's to tell if it really came from one of the many aquaculture farms that are near the shore?). Traditional recipes for Caldo michi often call for the addition of *ciruela* (*Spondias purpurea*) or *arrayán* (Myrtaceae family, p. 439), both small fruits that impart a sour or tart flavor. Since neither is likely to be readily available beyond Mexico, I substitute tomatillos and a splash of vinegar.

Prepare-ahead note: You may prepare the fish-stock base a day or so in advance and refrigerate; finish on the day you plan to serve. The fish should simmer in the stock no more than 10 or 15 minutes, so add it just before serving. Caldo michi is best served immediately after preparing.

YIELD: 6 SERVINGS

PREPARE THE FISH STOCK BASE

Clean the fish, removing and discarding the skin, tail, and fins. Slice off the head (or heads if using several small fish) and reserve; cut the fish in half lengthwise, then slice the fish across the girth into arc-shaped steaks about 1 inch (2.5 cm) thick; set aside. (*Note*: Smaller fish may not require halving. You may also cut the fish into fillets if you prefer.)

In a large stockpot, cover the head(s) with the water and add the bouillon. Bring to a boil, skimming off any foam that accumulates, then reduce to a simmer. Continue at a simmer for 30 minutes; remove the head(s) and discard; set the stock aside. (*Note*: If you wish, and are not squeamish about such things, remove the meat from the head and add to the soup immediately before serving.)

PREPARE THE SOFRITO

Heat the olive oil in a large skillet; add the onions and garlic and cook over medium heat until the onions are translucent and just at the verge of caramelizing. Add the tomatoes and tomatillos, and cook until they are softened, about 6–8 minutes. Add the oregano and pepper, stir, remove the *sofrito* from the heat, and set aside.

PREPARE THE SOUP

Add all of the vegetables to the fish-stock base; bring to a boil, reduce to a simmer, and cook for 5 minutes. Add the fish steaks or fillets, return to a simmer and cook for another 8–10 minutes or until the vegetables and fish are tender. Stir in the last three ingredients and simmer for 1 minute to amalgamate flavors. Check seasonings and serve immediately.

TO SERVE

Place fish in individual serving bowls and ladle on some of the stock and vegetables. Diners add squeezes of lime juice and fresh herbs to taste.

ARRAYÁN/GUAYABILLO

BOTANICAL: *Eugenia spp./Psidium spp./Mosiera spp.*/Family Myrtaceae | **ENGLISH:** none

Not to be confused with the *arrayán* found in Chiapas (*Gaultheria acuminata* in the Ericacea family, p. 98), in some regions of the country the name is also applied to several species of tree that produce small edible fruits or berries, all related to the guava. Native to the subtropical and tropical Americas, all of the species produce trees that can reach 32 feet (10 m) in height and are covered with thin, shiny leaves that measure an average of 2 inches long by ¾ inches wide (5 cm × 2 cm). They produce numerous fragrant flowers, making the tree a popular ornamental in gardens and on streets. After flowering, small seed-bearing fruits appear, measuring from ⅓ to ¾ inches (10 mm to 2 cm) in diameter, and may express colors from red to yellowish-green, deep maroon to black. They may be sweet or sweet-sour. According to Ricardo Muñoz Zurita, *arrayán* lends a unique taste to *atole* in the Estado de México. In Nayarit and Jalisco, it is coated with sugar, dried, and eaten like a candy. It is also sometimes used to provide a tart taste to Caldo michi in Jalisco (p. 438).

BIRRIA TATEMADA

OVEN-ROASTED GOAT

FOR THE MEAT

1 gallon (4 L) water

½ cup (145 g) sea salt

3 pounds (1.5 kg) goat meat, leg, shoulder, rump, or a mix, left in whole pieces, preferably with some bone

Banana leaves (optional)

FOR THE ADOBO

1.3 ounces (38 g) chiles chilacates (about 6 chiles; substitute 2 chiles anchos and 4 chiles guajillos or to the weight specified)

1 chile chipotle in adobo (⅓ oz./10 g), drained

½ medium white onion (5 oz./137.5 g), coarsely chopped

6 medium cloves garlic (1½ oz./36 g), peeled and coarsely chopped

1 tablespoon (2 g) whole dried Mexican oregano *plus* 1 teaspoon (2 g) cumin seed, lightly toasted and ground together

10 allspice berries *plus* 3 whole cloves, ground together

½ cup pineapple or apple cider vinegar

According to the dictionary of the Real Academia Española, *birria* translates to "person or thing of little value or importance." *Tatemado(a)* signifies "roasted or toasted," from the Nahuatl word *tlatemati*, meaning "burned." The dictionary also lists a synonym for *birria*: *barbacoa*. But describe *birria tatemada* as "an unimportant, burned thing just like *barbacoa*" to any self-respecting *jalisciense* and you are inviting a heated argument if not a match of fisticuffs. While recipes for *birria* can be found in several states, it is most typically identified with Jalisco—particularly Guadalajara—and *tapatíos* take it very seriously. But get them to pinpoint specifics (Is it made with goat, lamb, veal, beef, or chicken?) and to distinguish it from *barbacoa* (Is it pit-roasted or oven-baked? Is it served dry as a taco or in a bowl with its consommé?), and you will likely hit a wall. My tastes are flexible enough that I say "yes" to all of the above—and, in fact, all of the above is what you will find in Jalisco. There are some fine points, however: in Guadalajara, *birria* most frequently refers to a yearling goat (*chivo*). Elsewhere in the state, the younger kid will be labeled simply *cabrito*; other meats will be called *birria de* (*ternera* = veal; *res* = beef; *pollo* = chicken, and so on ad infinitum). *Birria* may be wrapped in maguey leaves and cooked in a pit like *barbacoa*, but the most common method today is to oven roast the meat, with or without the leaves. Birria tatemada is in a class by itself. Claudia Gutiérrez of Puesto "El Palenque" shared this two-step technique with me. The meat is first steamed until meltingly tender; then it is rubbed with adobo and roasted in the oven until a dark brown, caramelized crust forms on top. As suggested here, you may try other meats besides goat.

Prepare-ahead note: Birria tatemada is best served on the day it is prepared. Leftovers may be gently reheated in the oven, a microwave, or in a bit of oil in a skillet.

YIELD: 8–10 SERVINGS

PREPARE THE MEAT

Mix the water with the salt until thoroughly dissolved; cover the meat with the brine and refrigerate 4 to 6 hours. Remove the meat from the brine and discard the brine solution. (See p. 527 for notes on brining.)

Prepare a steamer or large *vaporera*. If using banana leaves, loosely wrap the meat with them. Add water to the bottom of the steamer and place the meat in the top portion. Cover tightly with the lid, bring the water to a boil, and continue to steam over high heat for 3½ to 4 hours, adding more water as needed, or until the meat is very tender. Remove the lid and allow the contents to cool.

PREPARE THE ADOBO

Remove the seeds and veins from the dried chiles and toast them on a comal or in a heavy skillet until fragrant and just beginning to swell. Transfer the chiles to a heat-proof bowl and cover with boiling water; soak for 15 minutes, then drain, discarding

FOR THE SAUCE

2 pounds (1 kg) Roma tomatoes

4 cups (1 L) water

3 medium cloves garlic
  (¾ oz./18 g), peeled and coarsely
  chopped

1 teaspoon (6 g) sea salt

½ teaspoon (2.5 g) ground black
  pepper

⅛ teaspoon (0.25 g) *each* ground
  cloves, marjoram, thyme, and
  cumin

FOR SERVING

Warm maize tortillas

Salsa de chile de árbol (p. 531),
  made with chile de árbol de
  Yahualica (p. 442) if available

Scallions, white and green parts,
  sliced into thin rounds

Lime wedges

the water. Place the chiles with the remaining ingredients in the jar of a blender; process until the mixture is thoroughly puréed and smooth.

Preheat the oven to 400°F (204°C). Remove the meat from the steamer and reserve the accumulated juices. Once the meat is cool to the touch, break it up into large pieces. Arrange the pieces in one layer on the bottom of a large baking dish. Pour the adobo onto the meat, and use your fingers to massage the meat and cover it on all sides with the adobo.

Bake the meat for 30 to 45 minutes, or until the top is very well browned and caramelized.

PREPARE THE SAUCE

Boil the tomatoes in the water until tender when pierced with a small knife. Transfer the tomatoes to the jar of a blender, and working in batches as needed, add the water and the remaining ingredients and process until thoroughly liquefied.

Pour the tomato mixture into a large saucepan and add the reserved juices from the meat. Bring to a boil, reduce to a simmer, and continue cooking until the sauce darkens slightly, 5–6 minutes. Remove from the heat and keep warm until time to serve.

TO SERVE

You may prepare tacos of the *birria*, topping tortillas with some of the meat; diners add the tomato and chile sauces, scallions, and lime juice to taste. Or, place some of the meat in a shallow serving bowl and ladle on a hefty dousing of the tomato sauce; diners add chile sauce, scallions, and lime juice to taste.

[MC]

CAPRA AEGAGRUS HIRCUS: THE DOMESTICATED GOAT

The Spanish goats brought to Mexico in the sixteenth century fared well in the arid and semi-arid Northern Highlands, which is where much production is still focused today, particularly in the Comarca Lagunera region of Coahuila and Durango; neighboring Zacatecas is also a leading producer. Low-income families own 73 percent of the ten million goats in Mexico, which are bred for milk, meat, and hides. Most cheese in Mexico is made from cow's milk, although some producers are beginning to make inroads in the production of goat's- and sheep's-milk cheeses (p. 405). Goat's milk is frequently used in Mexican sweets such as *cajeta* and *jamoncillo*.

Chile chilacate *is frequently specified for Jalisco's birrias; it is also the chile of choice for* chilaquiles. *According to Ricardo Muñoz Zurita, in its green form, the* chile chilacate *is called Anaheim or the New Mexico chile pepper. Dried, it has a lightly sweet, slightly smoky taste, and like all chiles in the "blond" family, they can range from about 1,000 to 10,000 Scoville Heat Units, so testing a small section before use is advised. Like most of Mexico's most frequently used chiles,* chile chilacate *is the* Capsicum annuum *species.* Chile ancho *may be used as a substitute.* [MC]

CHILE CHILACATE

Chile chilacate is frequently specified for Jalisco's *birrias*; it is also the chile of choice for *chilaquiles*. According to Ricardo Muñoz Zurita, in its green form, the *chile chilacate* is called Anaheim or the New Mexico chile pepper. It has a lightly sweet, slightly smoky taste, and like all chiles in the "blond" family, they can range from about 1,000 to 10,000 Scoville Heat Units, so testing a small section before use may be advised for the heat-shy. Like the majority of Mexico's most popular chiles, *chile chilacate* is the *Capsicum annuum* species. *Chile ancho* may be used as a substitute.

CHILE DE ÁRBOL DE YAHUALICA

Yahualica, a small town about 78 miles (125 km) northeast of Guadalajara, is best known for producing this popular local chile. While it is a type of *árbol* chile, *jaliscienses* boast about its superior flavor. It does possess a somewhat nutty taste, and the heat is similar to the more common *chile de árbol*, somewhere between 15,000 and 30,000 Scoville Heat Units. It is the requisite chile for the hot salsa served with *birria*.

POZOLE

PORK-AND-HOMINY STEW

FOR THE WHITE POZOLE

2 pounds (1 kg) white hominy
(your own prepared *nixtamal* or
canned hominy), drained

20 cups (5 L) water, divided

1 large head garlic (1¾ oz./50 g),
separated into cloves, peeled,
and thinly slivered

2 pounds (1 kg) pork leg, shoulder,
or butt, preferably with bone

1 large white onion (10 oz./275 g),
coarsely chopped

1 tablespoon (2 g) whole dried
Mexican oregano *plus* ½ teaspoon (1 g) cumin seed, lightly
toasted and ground together

2 bay leaves

1 tablespoon (18 g) sea salt

FOR THE GREEN POZOLE

3 medium tomatillos
(10½ oz./300 g), husks removed
and rinsed

½ white onion (5 oz./137.5 g),
peeled and coarsely chopped

1 medium clove garlic (¼ oz./6 g),
peeled and coarsely chopped

¼ cup (15 g) cilantro, chopped

2 medium chiles serranos (20 g),
seeded

½ teaspoon (3 g) sea salt

*José, doña María Félix's son, shreds the pork
immediately before serving the pozole.* [LP]

Pozole most certainly has pre-Hispanic roots (anthropologists and archaeologists maintain it originally featured the flesh of sacrificial victims), and by now can be found (with pork or chicken) in just about every state in the republic and beyond, each claiming its own recipe. Although pozole may assume many expressions, the most common versions are white (*blanco*, simply pork or chicken and its stock with the corn), green (*verde*, with tomatillos, fresh green chiles, and cilantro), or red (*rojo*, with a variety of dried red chiles). María Félix Gámez of Fonda "Virgen" shared this clever recipe with me that allows you to meet diners' demands by turning *pozole blanco* into *rojo* or *verde* with a few simple adjustments. She starts by making *pozole blanco*, then has the other ingredients ready to add the moment someone at the crowded counter asks for *verde* or *rojo*. This makes great sense for dinner parties, too. Since recipes abound for how to make *nixtamal* from dried field maize, this recipe simply calls for cooked hominy. Make it from scratch using excellent *maíz pozolero*, or use canned, drained hominy.

Prepare-ahead note: The entire dish may be made a day or two in advance and reheated. Coarsely shred the meat while still warm, but do not add it to the stew until the moment of serving.

YIELD: 10–12 SERVINGS

PREPARE THE WHITE POZOLE

Place the hominy in a large stockpot and cover with 10 cups (2.5 L) of the water; add the garlic. Bring to a boil, reduce to a simmer, and continue cooking until the hominy is very tender, 30 minutes to 4 hours, depending on the kind of hominy you are using. During the cooking process, add more boiling water as needed to keep the hominy just covered. In a separate stockpot, cover the meat with the remaining water; add the onion and spices (hold salt until the end) and bring to a boil; reduce to a simmer, skimming off any foam that accumulates. Continue at a simmer until the meat is very tender, about 1 hour. Transfer the meat to a platter to cool, reserving the stock; remove the bay leaves and discard; add the salt to the stock and check for seasonings. When the meat is cool enough to handle, coarsely shred it; cover with foil to keep it warm until time to serve. Pour the reserved stock into the pot with the hominy, bring it to a boil, reduce to a simmer, and continue cooking another 30 minutes to amalgamate flavors. Serve immediately as Pozole blanco, or continue with the instructions to serve Pozole verde or Pozole rojo.

PREPARE THE GREEN POZOLE

In a medium saucepan, cover the tomatillos with water, bring to a boil, reduce to a simmer, and continue cooking until they are tender when pierced with a sharp knife, about 10 minutes. Remove the tomatillos with a slotted spoon, reserving the cooking liquid, and transfer them to the jar of a blender. Add ¾ cup (187.5 mL) of the soaking liquid and the remaining ingredients. Process until thoroughly liquefied. You should

FOR THE RED POZOLE

3 chiles guajillos (¾ oz./20 g),
   seeds and veins removed
2 chiles chilacates (½ oz./14 g;
   substitute chiles anchos), seeds
   and veins removed
1 chile chipotle in adobo
   (⅓ oz./10 g), drained
½ white onion (5 oz./137.5 g),
   peeled and coarsely chopped
2 medium cloves garlic
   (½ oz./12 g), peeled and coarsely
   chopped
½ teaspoon (3 g) sea salt
2 tablespoons vegetable oil

FOR SERVING

Sliced radishes
Shredded green cabbage
Chopped white onion
Chopped cilantro
Crispy tortilla chips
Ground chile powder (or grind
   your own chile de árbol)

[MC]

have about 2 cups (500 mL) of the tomatillo mixture. *To prepare individual servings of Pozole verde*: When time to serve, heat one serving (about 1½ cups [375 mL]) of the pozole in a small saucepan. Add approximately ¼ cup (62.5 mL) of the tomatillo mixture, or to taste, and stir; continue simmering another 2–3 minutes to amalgamate flavors. Serve.

PREPARE THE RED POZOLE

Place the dried chiles in a heatproof bowl and cover with boiling water; allow the chiles to soak for 30 minutes; remove the chiles with a slotted spoon, reserving the soaking liquid, and transfer them to the jar of a blender. Pour in 1½ cups (375 mL) of the soaking liquid and add the remaining ingredients except the vegetable oil. Process until thoroughly liquefied; strain the mixture through a fine-mesh sieve into a mixing bowl, pressing through as much of the liquid as possible; discard any residue. Heat the vegetable oil in a large skillet until shimmering; pour in all of the chile mixture at once: it should sputter and sizzle, so stand back. Reduce heat to a simmer and continue cooking another 6–8 minutes or until the mixture has deepened in color and slightly thickened; set aside. You should have about 2 cups (500 mL) of the chile mixture. *To prepare individual servings of Pozole rojo*: When time to serve, heat one serving (about 1½ cups [375 mL]) of the pozole in a small saucepan. Add approximately ¼ cup (62.5 mL) of the chile mixture, or to taste, and stir; continue simmering another 2–3 minutes to amalgamate flavors. Serve.

TO SERVE

Ladle the Pozole into individual serving bowls and top with some of the shredded meat. Diners add garnishes to taste.

TORTA AHOGADA

PORK SANDWICH "DROWNED" IN CHILE AND TOMATO SAUCES

TO PREPARE AHEAD

Salsa de chile de árbol (p. 531)

Carnitas (p. 477)

Salsa de jitomate (p. 532)

FOR THE TORTA AHOGADA

½ sourdough baguette, cut in half lengthwise

4 tablespoons (56 g) refried beans (canned, reheated; or prepare Frijoles de la olla, p. 530, then mash and fry in a bit of lard or vegetable oil)

2 tablespoons (30 mL) Salsa de chile de árbol

½ cup (112 g) Carnitas

1 cup (250 mL) Salsa de jitomate, heated

¼ medium white onion (2½ oz./68.75 g), thinly sliced, separated into rings, and soaked in 2 tablespoons (30 mL) lime juice for 30 minutes

FOR SERVING

Additional Salsa de chile de árbol

Lime wedges

Torta ahogada (literally "drowned sandwich") is another icon of Jalisco's gastronomy, particularly of Guadalajara. As legend would have it, one Sr. Ignacio Saldaña "El Güerito" (Little Blond Guy) invented the sandwich in the early twentieth century when one day he returned home from work, hungry, and found little to eat in the house. He improvised a sandwich for himself with a roll of crusty bread, some refried beans, leftover *carnitas*, and a tomato sauce that his wife had prepared for another use. He smeared the bread with some of the beans, filled it with the meat, doused it with some of his favorite chile sauce, then poured on a generous helping of the tomato sauce. And with minor variations, that is how Torta ahogada is still prepared today. The bread of choice is known in Jalisco as *birote*; it resembles the common Mexican *bolillo*, but it is firmer inside and out and has a crunchier crust. This, obviously, is useful in keeping the sandwich from falling apart once it has soaked up the sauces. The sponge for *birote* is allowed to ferment up to 7 hours, giving the bread a slightly sour taste. Use a broad, sourdough baguette to approximate the flavor and texture. The recipe shared with me by Claudia Gutiérrez of Puesto "El Palenque" is not so much a "recipe" as it is a set of assembly instructions.

Prepare-ahead note: The entire dish may be made a day or two in advance and reheated. Coarsely shred the meat while still warm, but do not add it to the stew until the moment of serving.

YIELD: 1 SANDWICH

PREPARE THE TORTA AHOGADA

Spread the beans on the cut side of one of the halves of bread. Pour the Salsa de chile de árbol on the other half and allow it to soak in for a few seconds. Arrange the meat on top of the side of bread with the salsa, close with the other half, and place the sandwich on a large, deep plate. Pour on the tomato sauce to cover the sandwich completely, then top with the pickled onions. Serve immediately. Diners may add more chile sauce and squeezes of lime juice if they like.

[MC]

Basílica de Nuestra Señora de Zapopan.

ZAPOPAN

WHAT BEGAN AS A major corn-producing village of Zapotec, Maya, and Nahua settlers is today one of the largest municipalities in Mexico, contributing to the swelling population of greater metropolitan Guadalajara. Several excellent markets attract visitors from outlying areas, but perhaps the greatest draw is the basilica, which houses a museum of the Huichol people and the statue of Nuestra Señora de Zapopan. The figure is made of *pasta de caña de maíz*—pieces of cornstalk smoothed and adhered together by glue extracted from the bulb of a type of orchid (*Sobralia citrina*).

HUICHOL/WIXÁRITARI, WIXÁRIKA

Wixáritari—what the Huichol people call them-selves—means simply "the people"; Wixárika is their name for their language. There has been so much assimilation of indigenous peoples in Zacatecas that few identify themselves as such; however, the Huichol is the largest group in the state with about one thousand speakers. In fact, UNESCO has classified Huichol as a "vulner-able" language. The Huichol occupy zones pri-marily in the Zacatecas desert and in the Sierra Madre Occidental extending into the states of Nayarit, Jalisco, and Durango. The Huichol are particularly identified with the consumption of peyote (*Lophophora williamsii*), a small, spine-less cactus with hallucinogenic properties. They ingest it as part of a pre-Columbian religious ceremony known as *hikuri*. In their faith, the visions induced by the cactus enable them to communicate with the spirit world. The Hui-chol are also known for their fantastical crafts: wooden figures covered with beeswax and pine resin, then ornately decorated either with col-orful yarn or beads; the graphic representations symbolize their conceptions of the cosmos. [TA]

After whetting your appetite poring over the icy bins of seafood in Mercado del Mar, pause for a moment at one of the many stalls and restaurants that serve dishes ranging from ceviche to fish-head soup. [MC]

MERCADO DEL MAR

Not quite surpassing in size Mexico City's behemoth seafood market La Nueva Viga, Mercado del Mar in Zapopan is nonetheless of staggering proportions. Premiering in 1930 on one side of Guadalajara's San Juan de Dios market, it was originally operated almost exclusively by Asian merchants. During the 1940s, as transportation modes expanded, *tapatíos* were soon able to enjoy seafood from the Pacific coast on the same day it was caught. Fish comes not only from Jalisco, but also from the Mexican states of Colima, Nayarit, and Sinaloa. As the taste for fresh seafood grew beyond the days of Lent, the market grew, too, and by 1981 it moved to a new, larger location in Zapopan. Today, the market houses over seventy wholesale and retail vendors that operate every day year-round.

(above) Work at Mercado del Mar begins early. Vendors haul huge crates of crushed ice to chill down their catch, in this case Pacific oysters from Nayarit (Crassostrea corteziensis). [LP]
(below, left) A merchant weighs lisa (Mugil cephalus L. 1758). [LP] (below, right) Langostino de río (giant freshwater prawns, Macrobrachium rosenbergii [De Man, 1879]). [LP]

MARLÍN AHUMADO GUISADO

SMOKED MARLIN TOSTADAS

The Pacific black marlin (*Istiompax indica*) is much prized in sport fishing, and in Mexican waters it is most plentiful off the coast of Puerto Vallarta in western Jalisco. We saw none of the fresh fish in Mercado del Mar, but *marlín ahumado* (smoked marlin) was offered—shrink-wrapped—by practically every vendor. It is savored as is, in tacos with plenty of shredded cabbage and mayonnaise. But what we saw most commonly was a *guisado* (stew or casserole) of the fish cooked in tomato sauce and chiles and served atop crispy tostadas. Smoke your own marlin or purchase commercial, or use any type of smoked fish such as swordfish or Arctic char. It must be firm-fleshed or it may disintegrate during cooking.

To prepare ahead: You may make the sauce for the fish a day or two ahead and refrigerate or freeze; reheat and add the fish immediately before serving.

YIELD: 8–10 SERVINGS OF 2 TACOS EACH

[MC]

FOR THE TOMATO SAUCE

3 chiles guajillos (¾ oz./20 g), seeds and veins removed

2 pounds (1 kg) medium Roma tomatoes

1 chile chipotle in adobo (⅓ oz./10 g), drained

1 tablespoon (2 g) whole dried Mexican oregano, lightly toasted and ground

FOR THE SOFRITO

2 tablespoons (15 mL) olive oil

2 tablespoons (16 g) butter

½ medium white onion (5 oz./137.5 g), peeled and finely chopped

3 medium cloves garlic (¾ oz./18 g), peeled and finely chopped

1 medium red bell pepper (6½ oz./185 g), seeded and cut to small dice

2 pounds (1 kg) smoked marlin, cut into ½-inch (1.25 cm) cubes

2 tablespoons (30 g) capers, drained

20 medium green pimiento-stuffed olives, sliced

½ teaspoon (3 g) sea salt

½ teaspoon (2.5 g) freshly ground black pepper

¼ cup (20 g) cilantro, chopped

FOR SERVING

Tostadas (preferably homemade)

Shredded green cabbage

Lime wedges

PREPARE THE TOMATO SAUCE

Place the *chiles guajillos* in a heatproof bowl and cover them completely with boiling water; allow the chiles to soak for 20–30 minutes as you proceed.

On a comal or griddle, in a cast-iron skillet, or directly in a flame, char the tomatoes until the skin is blistered and blackened. Working in batches as needed, transfer them to the jar of a blender. Remove the *chiles guajillos* from the water and add them to the blender, reserving the soaking liquid. Add the *chile chipotle* and oregano and about 1 cup (250 mL) of the soaking liquid to the blender. Process until thoroughly puréed, adding a bit more of the soaking liquid as needed to keep the blades of the blender moving. Set aside.

PREPARE THE SOFRITO

In a large, deep skillet, heat the oil and butter together until the butter is melted and the fats are shimmering. Add the onion, garlic, and bell pepper and cook over low heat until the onions are translucent and the pepper tender, about 6–7 minutes. Add the next three ingredients and stir to combine, cooking 1–2 minutes until the fish is heated through. Pour on the tomato sauce from the blender and bring to a simmer; add the salt and pepper and continue cooking another 4–5 minutes to amalgamate flavors. Check seasonings and just before serving stir in the cilantro.

TO SERVE

You may either assemble the tostadas yourself or allow guests to do it. Top each tostada with a couple of spoonfuls of the fish mixture followed by some of the shredded cabbage. Diners add squeezes of lime juice to taste.

A worker known as a jimador uses the long, sharp, spade-like tool called a jima or coa de jima to lop off the pointed leaves of the agave. The bulbous body that remains is called a piña (for its resemblance to a pineapple), and it is the piña that is cooked and crushed to extract the juice that will ultimately become tequila.

TEQUILA

THE DRIVE FROM Zapopan to Tequila is lined with grain silos, technology parks, and no-tell motels—then suddenly, after a brief clearing, we saw acres and acres of blue agave, the plant used in the distillation of the world-famous elixir that bears the same name as the town.

Actually, the town and the alcoholic beverage are inextricably linked, as are the history of pulque (p. 365), mezcal (p. 191), and tequila. For at least two thousand years, pulque had been fermented from the juice of several agave species. When the Spanish arrived in the sixteenth century, they sought ways to soften its unfamiliar, vegetal taste. They discovered that if they cooked the agave pulp, it resulted in a sweeter brew, which, when fermented, they called "mezcal wine." The blue agave (*Agave tequilana* Weber) surrounding the village of Tequila was considered to yield a better flavor than that from other regions, and soon the popularity of this "mezcal wine from Tequila" spread to Guadalajara and nearby silver-mining towns like San Luis Potosí and Aguascalientes. Later experiments led to distillation of this "wine" to a beverage with a higher alcohol content. In 1656, the governor of Nueva Galicia granted a charter to the village to produce and sell the brew, which soon came to be known simply as tequila. It also gradually distinguished itself from mezcal by its production method: for tequila, the bodies of the blue agave (known as *piñas*) are steamed or cooked in giant pressure cookers before extracting the juice to be twice distilled, whereas for mezcal, the *piñas* of a variety of agave species are roasted in underground charcoal-fired ovens before the juice is extracted and distilled, lending mezcal its characteristically smoky taste. Since 1974, tequila's production methods and growing region have been strictly controlled, and the name is tightly regulated by a Denominación de Origen Controlada, much like champagne or cognac.

Not surprisingly, the town attracts many tourists who come to soak in the colonial charm, but who are mostly keen to soak up what has become one of the world's favorite spirits.

[MC]

The white sail-like canopies of the municipal market of Tequila float in a V formation to one side of the church of Nuestra Señora de la Purísima Concepción. Tucked temptingly beneath the canopies is the Mercado de Comidas "Cleofas Mota," the inviting, sunlit dining hall of which can be seen below.

[LP]

CARNE AL TEQUILA

SAUTÉED BEEF FLAMBÉED WITH TEQUILA

FOR THE MARINADES

¼ cup (62.5 mL) Spanish olive oil

4 medium cloves garlic
 (1 oz./24 g), peeled and coarsely
 chopped

1½ pounds (690 g) beef tenderloin

4 tablespoons (60 g) achiote paste

2 tablespoons (30 mL) Maggi
 Seasoning Sauce

¾ cup (187.5 mL) lime juice

For sautéing

¼ cup (62.5 mL) tequila reposado
 or añejo

3 tablespoons (45 mL) vegetable oil

Tourist gimmick or not, a lot of foods in Tequila are prepared with tequila. Occasionally it is used as a marinade or in a salsa, but most frequently it is employed to flame foods just at the end of cooking. We found a few such dishes in the Mercado de Comidas "Cleofas Mota," but this was our favorite. Another veteran ingredient we encountered was Maggi sauce—here known as Jugo de Maggi (Maggi juice). The layering of the two contrasting flavors—crisp herbal and savory umami—virtuosically framed the beefiness of the steak. For assured tenderness, use the tenderloin, but I have also made this recipe with less-expensive skirt or flank steak with good results, in which case the meats should never pass the "medium" stage.

Prepare-ahead note: The marinade can be made several days in advance and refrigerated. The meat needs to rest in the marinade up to 2 hours. Sauté and flame meat immediately before serving.

YIELD: 6 FOUR-OUNCE (115 G) SERVINGS

PREPARE THE MARINADES

Place the oil and garlic in the jar of a blender, and process until the garlic is completely liquefied.

FOR SERVING

Salpicón of shredded cabbage,
   julienned radishes, chopped
   red onion, and cilantro lightly
   dressed with lime juice
Refried beans (for instructions,
   see p. 89) and/or guacamole
White rice (optional)
The chile sauce of your choice
Warm tortillas
Lime wedges

Slice beef loin across the grain into 6 equal rounds, each weighing about 4 ounces (115 g). (*Note*: Ideally, the rounds would measure about ¾ inch (2 cm) thick, but this will depend on the loin you purchase.) Place each steak between two pieces of waxed paper, and using a wooden mallet or rolling pin, pound the steaks to a thickness of about ½ inch (1.25 cm). Place the steaks in a large baking dish and brush both sides of each steak with the olive oil–garlic mixture; set aside.

Place the next three ingredients in the jar of the blender and process until completely liquefied. Pour the marinade over the steaks, making sure each piece of the meat is well covered. Refrigerate a minimum of 1 hour and no more than 2 hours.

SAUTÉ THE MEAT

Bring the beef to room temperature. Heat the tequila until warm and set aside. Heat the oil in a large skillet until shimmering. Remove the meat from the marinade, and shake off any excess. With the heat on medium-high, sauté the meat, turning once, about 2–3 minutes per side or until the meat reaches the desired internal temperature (recommended 140°F–145°F/60°C–63°C for medium rare). Immediately pour on the tequila and ignite it, taking care to stand back. Wait about 5 seconds, then shake the skillet gently until the flames die out. Transfer the meat to a warm platter and pour on any liquid accumulated in the skillet.

TO SERVE

Place steaks on individual serving plates; garnish with the *salpicón*, refried beans, and guacamole, and accompany with white rice if you wish. Diners cut slices of meat and roll into warm tortillas, adding chile sauce and squeezes of lime juice to taste.

CAMARONES ZARANDEADOS

SWEET-AND-SPICY GRILLED SHRIMP

The verb *zarandear* is defined as "to toss" or "to shake." The similar *zarandar* means "to move something quickly and dexterously" or simply "to pass something through a *zaranda*" (sieve). In popular usage, however, the word *zaranda* has come to refer to an object that can only be referred to in English by means of several words, something like "a foldable grill or rack for barbecuing." And that's how these tasty crustaceans are cooked: placed in one layer on a portable grilling rack or basket, then flipped quickly from top to bottom over glowing coals until the shrimp are a bright pink-orange and delectably smoky. Like many seafood dishes in Jalisco, Camarones zarandeados is also popular in the Pacific states of Nayarit and Sinaloa. For the most dramatic results, use whole jumbo or colossal shrimp with the shells, heads, and tails on. All the Camarones zarandeados we found were served with a dipping sauce that for all intents and purposes resembled Thousand Island dressing, although the cooks were never able (or willing) to identify it. For a fancy occasion, make your own.

FOR THE ADOBO

1 chile chipotle in adobo
(⅓ oz./10 g), drained

3 tablespoons (45 mL) mayonnaise

3 medium cloves garlic
(¾ oz./18 g), peeled and minced

2 tablespoons (30 mL) Worcester-
shire sauce

2 tablespoons (30 mL) Salsa Valentina (substitute your favorite red
chile sauce), or to taste

1 tablespoon (12 g) powdered
shrimp bouillon

1 tablespoon (16 g) muscovado
sugar (substitute dark brown
sugar)

1 tablespoon (15 mL) soy sauce

FOR THE SHRIMP

2 pounds (1 kg) jumbo (21–25) or
colossal (12–15) whole shrimp

Vegetable oil

4 tablespoons (60 mL) melted
butter

FOR SERVING

Chopped cilantro

White rice

Mixed green salad with thinly
sliced tomatoes and red onions
cut in half-moons

Slices of avocado

Lime wedges

Thousand Island dressing

Prepare-ahead note: Prepare the adobo at least 1 hour in advance and allow it to rest at room temperature to develop flavor. Camarones zarandeados must be served immediately after grilling.

YIELD: APPROXIMATELY 6 SERVINGS

PREPARE THE ADOBO

Place all the ingredients in a blender jar and process until thoroughly puréed, adding just enough water to keep the blades moving. The resulting mixture should be a thick yet pourable sauce. Leave at room temperature for half an hour to amalgamate flavors.

PREPARE THE SHRIMP

Preheat a charcoal grill. (*Note*: If using a gas grill, prepare an aluminum foil package of mesquite wood smoking chips to place directly on the heat source.) Working one at a time, lay each shrimp on a flat work surface. Using a very sharp knife, carefully slice through the curved (back) part of the shrimp starting just below the head and stopping just above the tail. Open the shrimp and rinse it under cold water, removing any visible black "veins." Pat each shrimp dry with paper towels and set aside.

Thoroughly brush the grilling basket or rack with vegetable oil to prevent sticking. Arrange the shrimp, "butterflied," with the shell side down, in one layer on the rack. Brush the top side of each shrimp with some of the adobo, then flip to the other side and repeat. Flip the rack over again so that the shell side of the shrimp is facing down. Above coals that are mostly ash and very smoky, place the rack above the heat; blow or fan to generate more smoke. Check the bottom of the shrimp after about 3–4 minutes: they should be brightly colored with some grill marks appearing. Brush the top (meat) side of the shrimp with the melted butter, and flip the rack to the other side. Lower and raise the rack as needed to moderate cooking and smoke. Shrimp cook quickly, so constant vigilance is required.

TO SERVE

Plate 4–6 shrimp per person, depending on the size of the shrimp and whether they are to be served as an appetizer or main course; sprinkle the shrimp with some of the cilantro. Accompany with rice, salad, and avocado if desired. Diners add squeezes of lime juice to taste or dip the shrimp in the dressing.

CHICHARRÓN DE PESCADO

FRIED FISH "CRACKLINGS"

At last—the satisfying crispiness of pork cracklings without quite so much guilt! Popular in Peru but now found in several Pacific states of Mexico, these little "fingers" were designed to resemble shards of *chicharrón*, but the final reveal is of tender white fish. Tilapia is often used, but any lean, firm-fleshed white fish will do, such as cod, flounder, or catfish. (Truth be told, there is so much flavor in the crust that even the much-maligned "insipid" tilapia suits the bill perfectly and is less expensive than many other species.) The Maggi Sauce may seem a bit out of place here, but it provides the essential umami taste to fool you into thinking that these crispy bits are meat. Another trick is to fry the fish long enough so that the crust is just this side of being burned; that adds more meaty flavor and a crispier texture like *chicharrón*. These may be served as a main course, but it is probably more appropriate to serve them as a *botana* with beer or cocktails. Make extra because they go fast.

FOR THE SALSA VERDE DE CHILE SERRANO

6 large chiles serranos (about
  2 oz./60 g total), caps removed
1 medium clove garlic (¼ oz./6 g),
  peeled and coarsely chopped
¼ cup (67.5 mL) white vinegar
¼ teaspoon (1.5 g) sea salt

FOR THE MARINADE

1 tablespoon (15 mL) lime juice
3 medium cloves garlic
  (¾ oz./18 g), peeled and minced
3 tablespoons (45 mL) Maggi
  Seasoning Sauce
3 tablespoons (45 mL) soy sauce
2 large eggs, well beaten

FOR THE COATING

⅓ cup (40 g) cornmeal
⅓ cup (43 g) cornstarch
1 tablespoon (7 g) chile ancho
  powder
⅓ cup (135 g) all-purpose flour

FOR THE FISH

2 pounds (1 kg) white fish fillets
Vegetable oil for frying

FOR SERVING

Thin slices of tomato, cucumber,
  and avocado
Warm tortillas
Lime wedges
Salsa verde de chile serrano

Prepare-ahead note: Make the marinade a day or two in advance and refrigerate. Chicharrón de pescado must be served immediately after frying.

YIELD: 6–8 SERVINGS

PREPARE THE SALSA VERDE DE CHILE SERRANO

Place all of the ingredients in the jar of a blender and process until thoroughly liquefied. Pour into a serving bowl and allow the salsa to rest at room temperature until time to serve.

PREPARE THE MARINADE

Mix all of the ingredients together and either use immediately or refrigerate overnight. Whisk to mix again just before using.

PREPARE THE COATING

Mix the first three ingredients together and spread on a large, flat plate or baking dish. Place the flour on another plate or baking dish and set both aside.

PREPARE TO FRY THE FISH

Cut the fish fillets into "fingers" about 1 inch wide by 3 inches long (2.5 cm × 7.5 cm). Heat the oil in a large skillet to a temperature of 375°F (190°C). Working with a few pieces at a time, roll the fish in the flour to coat thoroughly; working quickly, dip the fish pieces in the marinade and immediately roll them in the cornmeal mixture. Transfer the fish carefully to the hot oil. Fry the fish, turning once or twice, until deep brown, about 3–4 minutes. Transfer to paper towels to drain. Repeat with the remaining fish.

TO SERVE

Line the plate garnishes listed above around the rim of a large serving platter and arrange the fish in the center. Diners make their own tacos using the fish, garnishes, some of the hot sauce, and squeezes of lime juice to taste.

Tacos de barbacoa
Jugos Tortas
Licuados
Desayunos

(above) Oranges for juice are kept cleverly at hand in the market in Tlaquepaque. [LP] (below) A makeshift shrine in Tlaquepaque blesses a random selection of produce. [LP]

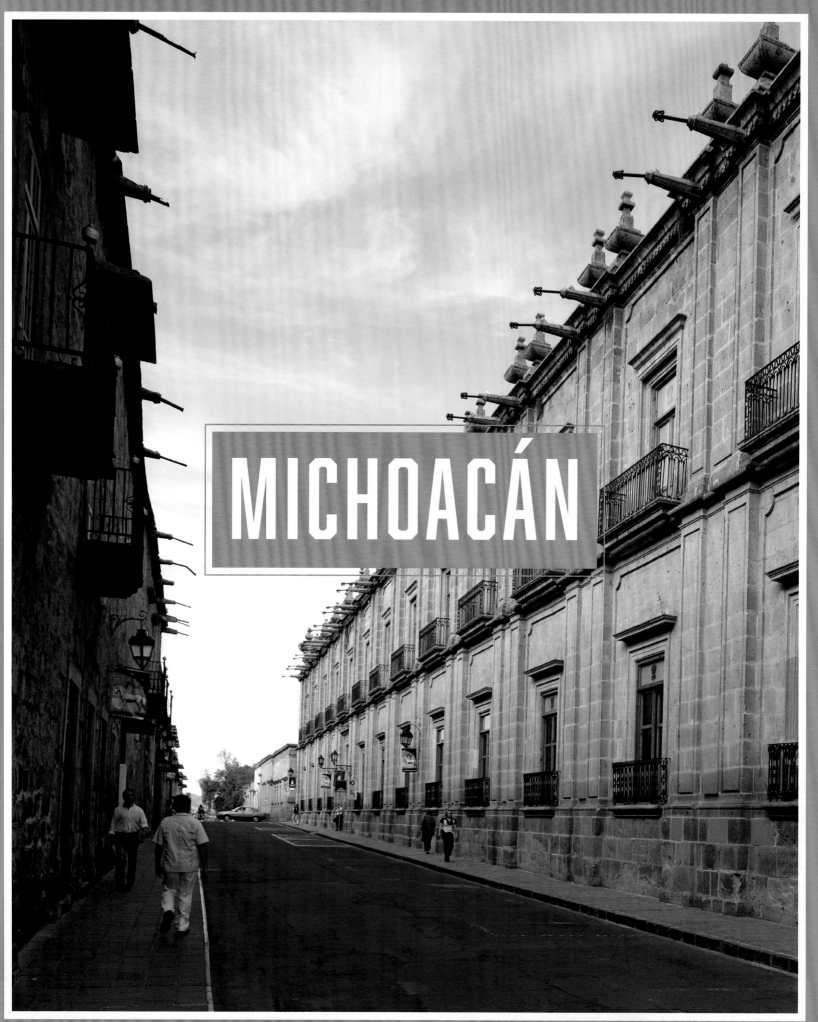

MICHOACÁN

MORELIA

ORELIA RESTS ON A broad plateau in an open valley cradled by several trun-cated mountain ranges: arriving to the city, you travel down the hills, then up again to make a grand entrance at the level of the city. The overall impression is that Morelia is a theater-in-the-round, a glittering stage perched gracefully above the surrounding countryside. The gridded street plan telescopes views of the hills just beyond.

Majestic boulevards, urban squares filled with lush gardens, arcades anchored by imposing towers, and cupolas covered with colorful Talavera tiles energize the otherwise sober buildings of Morelia, built with local pink granite in a style that is referred to as "Baroque Moreliano." It is the quiet dignity, the measured use of architectural elements, and the exceptional mastery of design in this Spanish colonial city that inspired UNESCO to designate Morelia as a World Heritage Site in 1991. Its markets are repositories of regional gastronomy, and the city serves as a convenient hub for exploring markets in nearby mining towns.

In the early sixteenth century, fifty noble families settled the city—then called Valladolid—but the population remained predominantly indigenous; the indigenous population is still significant today. In the late sixteenth century, the Colegio de San Nicolás Obispo—one of the oldest institutions of higher learning in Mexico—was transferred from Pátzcuaro to Valladolid, thus establishing the city as an intellectual center. The intelligentsia made the city a pivotal player in Mexico's fight for independence in the nineteenth century. Two of the leading figures in the struggle were Miguel Hidalgo and José María Morelos. In honor of the latter hero—who was a Valladolid native—the city's name was changed to Morelia in 1828.

Fresh leaves from cornstalks are used to wrap Corundas—the iconic multifaceted tamale of the P'urhépechas. [LP]

A vendor fashions simple wood-and-reed armatures for floral arrangements. [MC]

MERCADO DE SAN JUAN

The nondescript modern façade and gleaming white tile floors inside Mercado de San Juan—also known as "Mercado Revolución"—belie the fact that the market has been in the same location, albeit in different forms, since precontact times. Indigenous vendors who painstakingly weave armatures for funeral wreaths or deftly whip corn leaves into shape for the multifaceted tamales known as *corundas* (p. 463) testify to the tenacity of tradition.

CORUNDAS

P'URHÉPECHA TRIANGULAR TAMALES

We watched, mesmerized, as Graciela Gómez—owner of the Puesto "Corundas Chelas"—spooned clumps of masa onto the wide end of a cornstalk leaf, then whipped around the slender length of the leaf to cover the masa, once more and then again and again, up and over and around and below, until only the point of the leaf was left, and the little tamale finally settled into a triangular shape. Another common form of the Corunda is a polyhedron—six facets with five points; P'urhépecha women deftly make these using only half of a leaf, resulting in a very small Corunda. Corundas are a popular breakfast item throughout the state, and large steamers were full of them when we arrived at the market—half empty by the time we left (there were many hungry customers besides us). The name is a Spanish transcription of the P'urhépecha word for "tamale": *k'urhunda*. One colonial chronicler called Corundas *panecillos del palacio* (palace buns) because it was believed that they were served to the P'urhépecha leaders known as *caltzontzin* during nuptial banquets. And because they are traditionally made of masa prepared of maize softened in a solution of wood ash instead of *cal*, they are also sometimes called *tamales de ceniza* (ash tamales). Simple Corundas may have no fillings at all and acquire their savoriness from a piquant red or green sauce. Some Corundas are filled with cheese and are served with Mexican *crema*. Made with black beans, they are known as *chakikurindas*. It is also increasingly common among indigenous groups to fill them with pork or chicken, a recipe historically reserved for festivals or special occasions.

[LP]

(above) A towering mound of dried herbs. [MC] *(below)* Tamarind pods. Tamarind (Tamarindus indica *L.)*, *an African native introduced to Mexico in the sixteenth century, is used to prepare aguas frescas; the sweet-sour pulp inside may be covered with powdered chile and eaten as a snack or confected into candy.* [MC]

UCHEPOS DE NATA

SWEET FRESH MAIZE TAMALES WITH CLOTTED CREAM

FOR THE UCHEPOS

12–15 large ears field corn
  (You will need 6 cups [920 g]
  of kernels.)
1 cup (250 mL) nata (substitute
  clotted cream)
½ cup (128 g) sugar
1 tablespoon (12 g) baking powder
½ teaspoon (1.5 g) ground canela
  (Mexican cinnamon)
¼ teaspoon (1.5 g) sea salt

When you go on a quest for these, note that the word may be incorrectly spelled *huchepos* with the redundant silent *h*. It is a P'urhépecha word that simply means "tamale of fresh maize" (to distinguish it from tamales made of *nixtamal*-ized maize). Traditionally, Uchepos were only made in late summer when fresh maize was ready to harvest, but modern irrigation and more frequent harvests result in a steadier supply. Since some novices to Mexican cuisine may feel intimidated to attempt other tamales made from "exotic" *nixtamal*-ized maize masa, banana leaves, or dried cornhusks, I hope that Uchepos will encourage them to experiment, since almost everyone will have access to fresh corn on the cob. Look for large ears of unshucked field corn (not sweet corn) at your farmers' market. Follow the instructions below to shuck them yourself, reserving the husks for the wrappers. Uchepos may be sweet or savory; the savory ones we tried were filled with pork. Isabel García Venegas of the Puesto "Huchepos (Chabe) Lita" served both with a fiery red sauce of *chile de árbol* and some Mexican *crema*; some people also serve them with *queso fresco*. My favorites are the sweet ones, and while the hot sauce provides a wonderful counterpoint, truth be told these are so delicate that I prefer them just with *crema*—or with nothing at all. This recipe employing *nata* (essentially the same as English clotted cream) is based on one shared with me by Cynthia Martínez Becerril, owner of the popular restaurant San Miguelito in Morelia.

Prepare-ahead note: Uchepos freeze brilliantly. Reheat for 15–30 minutes in a steamer (depending on quantity) or for about 2 minutes in a microwave.

YIELD: 18 TAMALES

PREPARE THE UCHEPOS

Working with a large, sharp knife, cut away the base (stem end) of one of the cobs, about 1 inch (2.5 cm) above the point where the leaves join the base (this will allow you to easily remove and separate the husks). Carefully peel away the husks one at a time and place them in a pot full of cold water; continue with the remaining ears of maize. (If the husks are stubborn and don't want to come away from the base easily, trim away a bit more of the base. And, as you remove more and more husks, it will be more difficult to find the next one in line, rather like a roll of tape! Look toward the tip of the ear to find the next one, and carefully peel it away.) Slice away the kernels from each cob; you should have approximately 6 cups (920 g); freeze or cook any extra for another use. Pick out any stray corn silk and discard.

Place the kernels in the bowl of a food processor, and process until the kernels are thoroughly puréed, about 2–3 minutes, scraping down the bowl as necessary.

In a large mixing bowl, use an electric mixer to beat the remaining ingredients until light, creamy, and aerated, 2–3 minutes. Transfer the ground corn from the food processor to the *nata*-sugar mixture and use a wooden spoon to mix and beat until thoroughly incorporated; the mixture will be slushy, something like cooked oatmeal.

Remove a large husk from the pot of water, and pat it dry. Place it on a worktable

FOR SERVING
Salsa verde (p. 531) or Salsa de
 chile de árbol (p. 531)
Mexican *crema* (substitute crème
 fraîche, plain yogurt, or sour
 cream)

in front of you, with the square (base) end closest to you and the pointed tip opposite. Spoon on approximately 6 tablespoons (125 g) of the mixture in a mound running vertically along the center of the husk, leaving space on all sides, especially toward the pointed end. Fold the left side of the husk over to cover the mixture; repeat with the right side. Fold the tip (the pointed end farthest away from you) down to cover about one-third of the tamale. (*Note:* The square end is not sealed, so make sure the mixture is not squeezing out at this stage; it will expand during steaming.) Set aside; repeat with the remaining husks and maize mixture.

Arrange the Uchepos upright, with the open ends at the top, in the top chamber of a *vaporera* or steamer, taking care not to overcrowd them. Steam for 1 hour; allow the tamales to cool at least 15 minutes before serving.

TO SERVE
Plate 2–3 Uchepos per person. Diners add salsas and/or *crema* to taste.

Fresh field maize with corn silk at rear. Apart from uses in traditional medicine, the corn silk is burned to ash along with the papery shells of cacao beans. Together they are ground and added to atole *made from dried maize that has not been* nixtamal-ized. *The resulting black porridge is known as* atole negro, *a specialty of Uruapan.* [MC]

Chile chocolate, *a deep red-to-brown chile, is a variety of the* chile habanero (Capsicum chinense, *p. 29). The Scoville Heat Index is considerably higher for this chile than for the habanero.* [MC]

MERCADO INDEPENDENCIA

A few blocks south of Mercado de San Juan, past the looming aqueduct, the low-slung building of Mercado Independencia is almost completely obscured behind a chaotic *tianguis* where an irrational clutter of dried fish and shoes and wild mushrooms threatens to disrupt the ordered streets of this most rational of cities.

Michoacán is distinctive for its expansive system of waterways comprising rivers, streams, and lakes. Lago de Pátzcuaro is one of Mexico's largest lakes, with a basin of volcanic stone that covers approximately 49 square miles (126.9 sq. km). The surrounding wetlands shelter some two hundred species of birds—some of which are endemic—as well as many fish species such as trout and charales (p. 495), salamanders, and frogs (left). Frogs are particularly prized in Uruapan, where several restaurants are dedicated to their preparation. Favorites include caldo de ranas (frog soup) and empanizado de ranas (breaded fried frogs). Both are believed to be hangover remedies. The volleyball team of Uruapan is named after the amphibian.

[MC]

GAZPACHO MORELIANO

CHOPPED FRUIT SALAD WITH LIME, CHILE, AND CHEESE

Throughout the state, signs announcing "gazpacho" pop up everywhere, with a particular concentration in Morelia. You will be quick to realize that this gazpacho has nothing to do with the Andalusian chilled soup, rather it is a layered fruit salad served in a parfait glass (or plastic takeaway cup) accompanied by a long spoon. The fruits used are subject to whim and taste, but Sara Valdez of Puesto "Frutería Sarita" told

[LP]

Jicama, peeled

Pineapple, peeled and cored

Mango, peeled and seeded

White onion (optional)

Limes

Fresh orange juice

Mexican crema (substitute crème fraîche, plain yogurt, or sour cream)

Queso Cotija or ranchero (substitute feta or Monterey Jack), crumbled or grated

Powdered chile (cayenne, chile de árbol, piquín)

Salsa Valentina (see notes above) or Salsa de chile de árbol (p. 531)

us that the most traditional combination includes just three primary components: jicama, mango, and pineapple. Many times it also includes chopped onion; doña Sara didn't use it, but I like it, and so include it in this recipe as an optional ingredient. The fruits (as well as the jicama) are expertly diced, then layered in the glass with Mexican *crema*, orange juice, and a squeeze of lime juice, and topped with another spoonful of *crema* and some crumbled *queso ranchero* (*fresco*) or Cotija. Invariably the salad is finished off—either by the vendor or the diner—with a splash of Salsa Valentina, a commercially available red hot sauce that is hugely popular throughout the country. I am not ashamed to admit that I really like Salsa Valentina, so try it if you wish (it is readily available beyond Mexico). But if you are a purist and prefer to make everything from scratch, use the Salsa de chile de árbol. I do not list quantities here, only the components and assembly instructions; adjust quantities for your number of diners.

PREPARE THE GAZPACHO

Cut the first three ingredients into small dice; combine in a large mixing bowl. Finely chop the onion, if using, and set aside.

Fill a tall parfait or Tom Collins glass halfway with some of the fruit salad mixture; add a tablespoon or so of the chopped onion if using, and two or three tablespoons of the *crema*. Fill the glass to the top with more fruit; pour orange juice into the glass to reach almost to the top; squeeze on the juice of 1 lime. Top with more *crema* and some of the cheese, and a sprinkle of powdered chile; you may pour on some of the Salsa Valentina or other chile sauce for your diners, or allow them to add their own to taste.

[LP]

[MC]

Within the peripheral tianguis area near the market's entrance, a P'urhépecha man was selling wild mushrooms known colloquially as trompos de puerco (pig's top, i.e., the spinning kind), referring humorously to the cones of meat known as carne al pastor, which they do indeed resemble; they are also known in some places as orejas de puerco (pig's ears). In English, they are usually called "lobster mushrooms." Actually, the taxonomy (Hypomyces lactifluorum) describes not a mushroom—the fruiting body of a fungus—but rather a type of fungus that survives as a parasite on the surface of a few mushroom genera, particularly Lactarius, Lactifluus, and Russula. The fungus is an earthy rust-red color, like cooked lobster shells, giving it the English name; at maturity, the fungus completely covers the mushroom, rendering it virtually unrecognizable. Trompos de puerco and many other wild mushroom varieties grow in several regions of Mexico in the rainy season; they are not commercially cultivated but are instead still gathered by hand in the forests. At a gastronomy event in Morelia, I enjoyed a chicken breast stuffed with trompos de puerco—a delicious if untraditional dish. Wild mushrooms are important in the gastronomy of the Mazahua ethnolinguistic group.

[LP]

Some of the highlights at Mercado de Dulces y Artesanías: front left, higos cubiertos *(candied figs);* center left in the basket, queso de tuna *(prickly pear paste);* packages on lower shelf, ates *(a variety of fruit "barks" or pastes);* front right, limones con coco *(candied whole lime peels filled with sweetened coconut).* [LP]

MERCADO DE DULCES
Y ARTESANÍAS

O n the stately boulevard that ushers visitors into Morelia from east and west—a couple of blocks from the main square and just past the cathedral—is the unabashedly hedonistic Mercado de Dulces y Artesanías "Valentín Gómez Farías." Here you will find an unedited representation of some of Michoacán's most famous sweets, for which it has gained a nationwide reputation. My teeth ached just to look at it all!

Frutas cubiertas (candied fruits). The assortment includes chilacayote *(p. 114, the white pieces with black seeds);* tunas *(pink-orange round pieces in the foreground); and the oval shape at the top,* acitrón *(p. 419, the candied pulp of the barrel cactus known as* biznaga*).* [MC]

HUESOS DE LECHE

PEACH-PIT-SHAPED MILK CANDIES

I'm an utter fool for any sort of milk candy, so Huesos de leche easily won my heart. *Huesos* in Spanish means "bones," but it also refers to the stones or pits found in fruits like olives, apricots, and peaches. I have yet to locate the clever molds for these peach-pit shapes, but any candy mold will do—abstract ones or holiday themes. Choose flexible silicone for ease of removing the finished candies. The recipe is essentially the same as for *jamoncillo*—a genre of candies usually made with milk and sometimes seeds or nuts and appearing in a variety of shapes, from squares or extruded "macaroni" shapes to petite "cushions" tufted with pecan or walnut halves. The twist with these Huesos (other than their shape) is that they are flavored: the sign on the box in the lower center of the photo lists three flavors: *canela* (Mexican cinnamon), *vainilla* (vanilla), and *guayaba* (guava). The recipes for the first two are virtually identical; the latter takes some quantity adjustments, so I provide a variation of the master recipe below. Lacking fresh guavas, many decent guava purées and pulps are now widely available in vacuum packs or frozen.

[LP]

FOR THE CANDIES
Butter for the molds
1 can (12 oz./354 mL) evaporated
  milk
3 cups (600 g) sugar
4 tablespoons (56 g) butter

FOR THE FLAVORINGS
2 teaspoons (6 g) canela (Mexican
  cinnamon), ground, *or* 1 tablespoon (15 mL) Mexican vanilla
  extract

Prepare-ahead note: Huesos de leche keep well for about 2 weeks in a cool, dry environment in an airtight container.

YIELD: 2–3 DOZEN, DEPENDING ON THE SIZE OF YOUR MOLDS

PREPARE THE CANDIES
Very lightly butter the candy molds (alternatively, you may use a sheet pan and later cut the candy into squares). Combine the milk and sugar in a medium-sized, heavy saucepan, preferably copper. Bring the mixture to a boil, stirring constantly to dissolve the sugar. Reduce heat and continue cooking at a simmer, stirring frequently and taking care that the mixture does not boil over, until the mixture deepens slightly in color and thickens, about 15 minutes; a candy thermometer should reach the soft-ball stage, 235°F (118°C). Remove from the heat source, add the butter and your choice of flavorings, and use a handheld electric mixer or wooden spoon to beat vigorously until the mixture cools slightly and displays tracks from the beater, about 10 minutes. Immediately spoon the mixture into the candy molds, pressing down to fill each one completely. Allow the candies to cool and solidify at room temperature overnight. (*Note*: Depending on your climate, the candies may stubbornly refuse to set; if so, leave them in the refrigerator for an hour or two and bring to room temperature before serving.) Unmold and store in an airtight container.

VARIATION
For the guava flavor, replace 2 cups (500 mL) of the milk with the same quantity of fresh or frozen guava pulp (strained of seeds). If using sweetened guava paste, replace 2 cups (500 mL) of the milk with the same quantity of the paste, puréed with the remaining milk, and eliminate 1 cup (200 g) of the sugar. Proceed with the rest of the recipe.

Not only candies attract customers with intense colors in the market. Brightly painted wooden rattles, musical instruments, tops, and other toys also vie for attention. [LP]

(top) Prepared food puestos *line the streets surrounding the main square of Quiroga. The top seller is* carnitas. *(bottom, right) Tortillas are warmed on a portable stove.*
[MC, LP]

QUIROGA

CARNITAS ARE SO identified with the state of Michoacán that wherever else you may find them in Mexico (and you will find them everywhere, even as far away as Yucatán), they will always be tagged *carnitas estilo Michoacán.*

Carnitas are sold in market *puestos* but are usually prepared off-premises due to the dangers of the hot fat; they are also sold in freestanding shops or stalls. The little town of Quiroga is considered by many to be the hotbed of great Carnitas—possibly just because they are so plentiful here. It's customary among local residents on the way to Pátzcuaro from Morelia to stop in Quiroga for a Carnitas breakfast—and that's just what we did. The main square is host to the morning food market every day, and people set up colorful umbrellas or carts from which to sell their wares. Vendors tempt customers by offering plenty of free samples.

CARNITAS

CHOPPED PORK CONFIT

TO PREPARE AHEAD
Enriched Lard (p. 530)

Simply described, Carnitas are pieces of pork (typically coarsely chopped just before serving; "little meats" is the translation) that have been slowly cooked in their own fat—in this case, pork lard—confit-style. The most basic recipe for Carnitas includes just four ingredients: pork, lard, water, and salt. The way Carnitas are made in Quiroga, and the recipe shared with me by Blanca Vidales Vega—renowned *maestra de carnitas* in Ziracuarétiro, between Uruapan and Pátzcuaro—is this very simple way. Blanca, whom I met at a festival of traditional *michoacana* gastronomy in Morelia, starts out by heating lard in a huge copper *cazo*, or pot; those made in Santa Clara del Cobre (p. 501) are common. In her *comedor*, she uses 55 pounds (25 kg) of lard and 33 pounds (15 kg) of pork. The ratio of lard to meat, therefore, is almost two to one. When the lard is hot, Blanca carefully lowers large pieces of *cabeza de lomo* (shoulder/butt) into the roiling vat; once it's browned, after just a few minutes, she adds three large *costillares* (rib racks). After 15 minutes, she carefully streams in a quart (liter) of salted water. The *buches* (pork stomachs) immediately follow, and the cooking continues another 45 minutes. Finally, she places sheets of *cuero* (skin) atop the meats to hold the steam in and to add one more layer of flavor and texture. Another 1½–2 hours of cooking, and the Carnitas are ready to serve. The first item out of the *cazo* is the *cuero*—which she now calls *sancochado*, parboiled. The meltingly tender skin is coarsely chopped and served on tortillas as the prelude to the meats. Even more traditional for Carnitas is to add organ meats, ears, and other pig parts so as not to waste anything after a slaughter. In some places in Mexico, Carnitas are still made in this traditional way, with offal and other bits in the mix; asking for *surtido* (assorted) assures that you'll get a little bit of everything. But less adventurous modern tastes among her customers have led Blanca to include

[LP]

FOR MARINATING THE PORK

2 cups (500 mL) milk

1 teaspoon (6 g) sea salt

4 medium cloves garlic
(1 oz./24 g), peeled and mashed

2 bay leaves

1 tablespoon (2 g) whole dried
Mexican oregano *plus* 1 teaspoon
(2 g) cumin seed, lightly toasted
and ground together

3 pounds (1.5 kg) pork pieces (Use
a mix of butt, leg, and back ribs
totaling the specified weight.
A modest layer of fat improves
flavor. *Note:* Some home recipes
call for cutting the meat into
pieces, but don't; it should
remain in large, whole pieces.)

FOR FRYING THE CARNITAS

3 cups (375 mL) water, divided

5 pounds (2.25 kg) Enriched Lard

6 ounces (175 g) pork skin (Look
for this in a Mexican carnicería;
a standard butcher can prepare
it, too, but you may need to
order it in advance. It should be
cleaned of bristle and completely
stripped of all fat, and be in one
or two large sheets.)

1 cup (250 mL) pineapple juice

1 teaspoon (6 g) sea salt

only "better" cuts of meat in her Carnitas. The chopped-meat tacos are served with a gorgeous garnish of chiles and vegetables that have been pickled in pineapple vinegar.

Perhaps in an effort to add more flavor, or to adapt recipes for the home kitchen, or both, a deluge of more baroque Carnitas recipes has surged in recent years; these suggest the addition of evaporated or sweetened condensed milk, Coca-Cola, brown sugar, orange wedges, lime juice, garlic, herbs—even chile—either individually or all together. All probably work well in one way or another. And I understand the reasoning behind most of them: the sugars from the Coca-Cola, brown sugar, and orange help the meats to brown and caramelize at the end of cooking to create a delectable crust; the garlic, herbs, and chile add flavor; and the milk probably has a couple of effects—to tenderize the meat (milk's lactic acids help denature meat proteins) as well as to add some caramelization from the milk's natural sugar content.

I have adapted Blanca's simple recipe to include just a couple of the newer ideas: I marinate the meat in herbed milk first (a trick used in many cultures to tenderize meat; milk-braised pork is a tradition in Italy); and at the end I add a small amount of pineapple juice rather than orange to help with the caramelization (pineapple's bromelain enzyme also has a tenderizing effect).

Blanca and others swear by their copper pots, but the only truly important thing is that your heavy pot be quite deep; the lard should only come halfway up to the top after adding the meats. This is essential, because when you stream in the water, some fierce bubbling will happen, and you want to prevent the hot fat from overflowing. The Enriched Lard is important for good flavor. A candy thermometer is useful for monitoring the temperature of the fat: the temperature should hover at around 200°F (93°C) through the entire cooking time in order to dissolve collagen and further tenderize the meat. A mix of meats (as well as the soft skin) is recommended: when these are all chopped together, the flavor is richer and more complex—and more like real Carnitas.

Prepare-ahead note: Carnitas is best served immediately after cooking. If you do have leftovers, however, they can be adequately resurrected by gently reheating them in a bit of lard or vegetable oil in a skillet, but it is not recommended to prepare them a day in advance.

YIELD: APPROXIMATELY 10 SERVINGS

MARINATE THE PORK

Dissolve the salt in the milk; add the garlic and herbs and stir to combine. If your pork has fat of any thickness, use a sharp knife or razor blade to score it liberally in a hatch-mark pattern. Place the pork pieces in a large baking dish or bowl and cover with the milk mixture. Turn the pieces to coat completely. Refrigerate 8–12 hours, turning the pork at least two times during the marinating process.

FRY THE CARNITAS AND FINISH

At the end of the marinating time, remove the pork from the milk, reserving the milk; rinse the pork thoroughly under cold water and pat the meat completely dry with

(left) A bubbling cauldron of lard and carnitas—this one with some viscera. [MR] *(right) Perfectly browned* carnitas: *in the mixture are skin, ribs, and fatty rump that has been scored to ensure even cooking.* Carnitas *are coarsely chopped on special boards just before serving.* [MC]

FOR SERVING
Warm tortillas
Lime wedges
Guacamole and/or Salsa verde
  (p. 531)
Verduras en escabeche (p. 480)
Your favorite red chile table
  salsa such as Salsa de molcajete
  (p. 533)

paper towels. Mix the reserved milk with 2 cups (500 mL) of the water; pour through a fine-mesh sieve to remove the bay leaves and garlic; discard the bay leaves and garlic; set the milk solution aside; retrieve the ribs and skin and set aside.

Heat the lard over high heat until it reaches a boil (this will depend on the burner of your stovetop; if weak, the lard may only shimmer rather than actually roil); continue cooking on high heat for 8–10 minutes or until the lard darkens slightly. You will add the ribs and skin later, so set these aside. Carefully lower half of the meat into the lard a piece at a time; it will fiercely sizzle and pop, so stand back. Add the remaining meat and reduce the heat to a simmer; place the candy thermometer into the oil and monitor the heat carefully until the end of cooking time; it should stay at around 200°F (93°C) the entire time; adjust as necessary. Use a large wooden spoon to turn the meat occasionally to prevent sticking.

After 30 minutes, add the ribs. Carefully pour the milk mixture into the pot (to do this, place a large wooden spoon into the fat, and allow the liquid to dribble down the handle of the spoon; as the lard cools, you can add the liquid more quickly). Return to a boil, then adjust the heat as necessary; continue cooking for 1 hour until there is no sign of the liquid at the top of the pot.

When the liquid has completely evaporated, arrange the pork skin on top of the meat; mix the remaining 1 cup (250 mL) of the water with the pineapple juice and salt; stir to dissolve the salt thoroughly. As described above, slowly stream the liquid into the pot. Continue cooking for 1 hour or until the liquid has evaporated. Move the meats occasionally so that they brown evenly. Transfer the skin and meats to a heatproof platter, and allow them to cool to the touch; reserve the lard for another use.

TO SERVE
Coarsely chop the pork skin and set aside; break the meats apart with your fingers, then coarsely chop; mix all the meats together with the skin. Serve with warm tortillas and the suggested accompaniments, which diners add to taste.

VERDURAS EN ESCABECHE

PICKLED VEGETABLE GARNISH

FOR THE VEGETABLE PICKLE

- 1 large carrot (7 oz./200 g), peeled and thinly sliced across the width
- ½ medium white onion (5 oz./137.5 g), peeled, thinly sliced, and separated into rings
- 4 medium chiles perón (5½ oz./160 g total; substitute half the weight of chiles habaneros), seeds and stems removed, and thinly sliced across the width
- 6 medium cloves garlic (1½ oz./36 g), peeled
- 1 tablespoon (2 g) whole dried Mexican oregano, lightly toasted and crumbled
- 1 teaspoon (4 g) black peppercorns
- 5 allspice berries
- 3 bay leaves
- 2 sprigs fresh thyme (substitute ¼ tsp./0.25 g dried, crumbled)
- 2 sprigs fresh marjoram (substitute ¼ tsp./0.25 g dried, crumbled)
- 1 teaspoon (3 g) sea salt
- 3 cups (750 mL) pineapple vinegar (see notes above; substitute apple cider vinegar)

Doña Blanca explains that this is the requisite accompaniment for Carnitas—and it is certainly omnipresent in Quiroga. It is very easy to assemble, although it does take several days to thoroughly "cook" the vegetables in the vinegar and be ready to eat. Pineapple vinegar is increasingly available, but if you can't find it, you can easily make it yourself; recipes are plentiful online, and Diana Kennedy offers an easy recipe in *The Essential Cuisines of Mexico*. If all else fails, you may substitute apple cider vinegar. (Some people use plain white vinegar, but it does not achieve the flavor we're aiming for.) Local cooks use the chile they call *perón*, which is the regional variety of what is also known as *chile manzano* or *rocoto*. If you can't locate them, use a lesser quantity of habanero.

Prepare-ahead note: Verduras en escabeche needs to macerate for 5 days prior to serving. It will keep well indefinitely in the refrigerator.

YIELD: 4 CUPS (1 L)

PREPARE THE PICKLE

Combine the vegetables, spices, and herbs in a large, nonreactive mixing bowl or glass or ceramic storage jar. Pour the vinegar over the vegetables; it should just come to the top of them; add less or more vinegar according to your storage container, the size of the vegetables, etc. Cover and allow to macerate at room temperature for 5 days, then refrigerate. Bring to room temperature before serving.

[LP]

PÁTZCUARO

THE FORESTED MOUNTAIN ROAD that winds from Quiroga to Pátzcuaro first passes through several quaint villages—one renowned for its handcrafted wooden furniture—and finally past tailored rows of luxurious walled vacation homes blessed with lake views. The walls prevented us from seeing the lake at first, but just after a sharp curve—there it was!

Lago de Pátzcuaro achieved fame in the mid-twentieth century for its picturesque islands and fishermen with their iconic "butterfly" nets in shallow launches slipping silently across the water. Devastation of the ecosystem has tragically marred that innocent image, but the little town of Pátzcuaro with its tile-roofed, two-tone adobe buildings still has a strong romantic allure and remains a popular tourist destination—and, the lake is slowly recovering.

It was the lake and its rich aquatic life that originally attracted nomadic Chichimeca groups, who founded a city here in the early fourteenth century. In time, P'urhépecha-speaking groups coalesced to form what the Spanish would later erroneously call the Tarascos, or "Tarascan State." It is the P'urhépecha-speaking descendants of the Tarascans who still occupy the region surrounding the lake.

P'URHÉPECHA/PURÉPECHA

The P'urhépecha Empire, more commonly known as Tarasco or the Tarascan State, grew to prominence during the late post-Classic period (early 1300s to 1521 CE); its rise to power corresponded to the rise of the Aztec (Mexica) Triple Alliance. The two realms abutted one another on the western edge of modern-day Estado de México. The Aztec realm occupied the Valley of Mexico, and its dominance extended well beyond; the P'urhépecha Empire, on the other hand, was essentially confined to most of the modern state of Michoacán, encroaching into parts of Jalisco and Guanajuato. The two were rather fierce enemies, although the Aztecs never conquered the P'urhépecha, a fact that could explain why the name for the people given by the Aztecs in Nahuatl—Michoaque, "people of the land of fish"—is not applied to the cultural group, although it formed the basis for the word Michoacán. The capital city of the P'urhépecha was originally established in Pátzcuaro but was soon transferred to Tzintzuntzan, while Pátzcuaro remained a retreat and lake resort for nobles. The Aztecs admired (or envied) the marvelous abilities of the P'urhépecha as metalsmiths, a trade that continues today in the copper workshops of Santa Clara del Cobre (p. 501). The P'urhépecha language, spoken by nearly 200,000 people in Michoacán, is a small language family that shows no relationship to other Mesoamerican languages. Michoacán is known for its richly varied cuisine, much of it in the P'urhépecha tradition. Two tamales—*corundas* (p. 463) and *uche-pos* (p. 465)—are both P'urhépecha names and recipes. And the dish known as *atápakua* is a hallmark of P'urhépecha gastronomy; it may contain *huitlacoche* or squash or fish or meat, but the unifying element is that the stew is always thickened with maize masa. [TA]

MERCADO MUNICIPAL/ PÁTZCUARO

We arrived in Pátzcuaro early in the morning, and our hunger pangs led us directly to the market, wedged in the corner of a tangled network of streets clogged with taxis. We spotted wonderfully exotic ingredients as we snaked our way through the market's meandering passageways, shaded from the fierce sun at this high altitude beneath rippling gauze and canvas sails—reminiscent of those fishermen's nets.

[LP]

(above) Guasanas—fresh garbanzos (Cicer arietinum *L., in English known as chickpeas) steamed and lightly salted; you eat them like Japanese edamame, squeezing the pod and popping the soft bean into your mouth. At left are cups of nance (Byrsonima crassifolia)—here known as changungas; a smattering of hot fuchsia pomegranate seeds commingle with the garbanzos. [MC]*

(below) Quiote is the tall, flowering stalk of the agave pulquero (Agave salmiana), which can reach 10 feet (3 m) in height. Once it flowers, the stalk is removed to extract aguamiel, *which is subsequently fermented to create pulque (p. 365). The disks above are slices of the quiote stalk that have been cooked and soaked in honey. The taste is pleasant, but as can be discerned from the photo, the texture is extremely fibrous. The trick to eating it is to chew and suck vigorously to extract all the sweet nectar, then spit out the fibers.* [LP]

Purplish-red maize is plentiful in all of the markets of Michoacán. [MC]

POZOLE ROJO BATIDO

CREAMY RED HOMINY STEW WITH BEEF AND PORK

FOR THE NIXTAMAL

2 pounds (1 kg) dried red field
  corn

1 gallon (4 L) water

2 tablespoons (20 g) calcium
  hydroxide (available as a
  pickling supply in supermarkets)

The delicately pinkish and smoothly creamy Pozole batido is a specialty of Pátzcuaro. Many foods in Mexico seem to pay homage to the tricolor Mexican flag (or is it the other way around?) and pozole is no exception: its red, white, and green versions are now quite famous, even in the United States. The red *pozole rojo* is most commonly made with dried white field corn and acquires its vivid color from dried red chiles such as *ancho* or *guajillo*. The version we found at the *comedor* "Pozole doña Caro" in the municipal market of Pátzcuaro, however, included no chile and instead used the dried red or purplish corn that we had seen in many local markets; the diner adds the delicious chile flavor (and heat) via salsas or chopped chiles to taste once the pozole is served. Another point of difference with regard to other pozoles is that this one is vigorously stirred—*batido*, or beaten—at the end of cooking, an action that strips away outer layers of starch on the kernels of maize, causing the cooking liquid to thicken, much like the process of making risotto. A huge wooden spoon—almost like an oar—is widely used throughout Michoacán for this and other purposes. The pork and beef are finely shredded, and combined with the creamy stock, the result is a hearty, thick stew wonderful for chilly days by the lake. Note that while traditional pozole recipes call for removing the pointy germ at the tip of the kernel, allowing it to split open or "flower," this is increasingly optional, and the step was skipped by doña Carolina, one assumes because of the huge quantities—27 pounds/12 kilos of uncooked corn—that she prepares every day to sell in her *comedor*.

Prepare-ahead note: As do most recipes for pozole, this one requires that you *nixtamal-ize* the corn—that is, cook it briefly with calcium hydroxide ("slaked lime," or *cal* in Spanish), then drain and rinse; the resulting corn is called *nixtamal* in Mexico, and is quite similar to that which is known as hominy in the United States. Much has been written on the benefits of this process. The corn is soaked in water overnight, then cooked with the *cal*. The entire process takes about 15 hours (including the overnight soak), so plan accordingly; cooking with the rest of the ingredients takes an additional 2–3 hours. The finished pozole benefits from a rest in the refrigerator; prepare the stew a day or two in advance and reheat just before serving.

YIELD: 10–12 SERVINGS

Doña Carolina uses one of the enormous wooden spoons typical of Michoacán to scoop out the last bites of Pozole rojo batido. It sells out daily by 1:00 or 2:00 p.m.—and we arrived just in time. [LP]

PREPARE THE NIXTAMAL

Rinse and pick through the dried corn, discarding any small stones or broken pieces. Put the corn in a large stainless-steel stockpot and cover the corn with water; place the lid on the pot and allow the corn to soak 12 hours or overnight. (*Note*: Since you will use the same pot later for cooking the corn with the calcium hydroxide, it is strongly recommended that you use stainless steel; other materials are likely to be damaged by the *cal*.)

Drain the corn into a large stainless-steel colander. Pour the 1 gallon (4 L) of water into the stockpot; bring to a boil and add the calcium hydroxide; use a stainless-steel

1 gallon (4 L) water

½ cup (145 g) sea salt

3 pounds (1.5 kg) pork ribs (meaty, with plenty of fat)

2 pounds (1 kg) bone-in beef shank (*Note*: I specify shank because that is the cut used by doña Caro, most likely because it is an extremely inexpensive cut of meat. However, it can be very tough and even difficult to shred at times; if you prefer, substitute another bone-in cut, such as round steak or arm pot roast.)

FOR THE STEW

1 gallon (4 L) water, *plus* more as it evaporates during cooking

6 medium cloves garlic (36 g), peeled

1 teaspoon (0.5 g) whole dried Mexican oregano, lightly toasted and crumbled

1 tablespoon (18 g) sea salt, or to taste

[MC]

spoon to stir and dissolve the *cal*. Transfer the corn to the *cal* solution in the stockpot, and bring the solution to a boil; cook over high heat for 15 minutes. Remove the pot from the heat, cover, and allow the corn to soak in the *cal* solution for 2 hours.

PREPARE THE MEATS

While the corn is being cooked and soaked, pour the water into a large bowl or stockpot; add the salt and stir to dissolve thoroughly. Add the pork to the brine and refrigerate for 3 hours. (The brining step is optional; see notes on p. 527.)

FINISH THE STEW

Place the stockpot containing the *cal*-treated corn in the sink and flood the corn with fresh, cold water. Immerse your hands in the water and massage or knead the corn, grasping it with your fists, and rubbing it between your palms to remove the papery outer layer, known as the pericarp; the water will turn yellowish. Hold a lid or plate slightly ajar over the top of the pot, and drain off most of the water; add more, and continue the kneading/flushing process until the water runs almost clear.

Drain the corn into a large stainless-steel colander; flush with water and vigorously turn the corn with your hands to remove all traces of the *cal*; continue until the water runs clear. Thoroughly wash the stainless steel stockpot in which the corn soaked; transfer the *nixtamal*-ized maize to the stockpot.

Pour the 1 gallon (4 L) of water over the corn in the stockpot; bring to a boil and

3 chiles perón (approximately
   4¼ oz./120 g total; substitute
   chiles manzanos or rocotos),
   seeded and cut into medium
   dice (*Note*: For more intense
   flavor and heat, you may
   substitute the Salsa tarasca
   on p. 489, if you wish.)
Dried red chile powder (Use
   commercial or make your own
   by removing the seeds and veins
   from chiles de árbol, lightly
   toasting and finely grinding
   them.)
Chopped red onion
Shredded cabbage
Thinly sliced radishes
Lime wedges

cook over high heat uncovered for 1 hour. Skim off any foam that rises to the surface. Keep the corn covered with water; as it evaporates during cooking, add more to cover. (Use boiling water to avoid interrupting the cooking process.) During the process of cooking the stew to completion, you may need to add an extra 12 to 18 cups (3–4.5 L) of water in order to maintain the same level as when you started.

About 20 minutes before the corn has cooked the full hour, drain and rinse the pork, and discard the brine. Place the pork and beef in a stockpot other than the one holding the corn; cover the meats completely with water; bring the water to a boil, skimming off any foam that accumulates on the surface. Continue to cook over high heat for another 15–20 minutes or until the foam disappears, skimming constantly. (Be very vigilant about skimming off the foam, since it can ruin the aesthetic of the dish as it clings to the individual kernels of maize.) Remove the meats, transfer them to the pot containing the corn, and discard the water in which the meats cooked.

Add the garlic and oregano to the corn. Return the pot to a boil, and continue cooking over high heat for 1 hour or until the maize is tender. Remove the pot from the heat and transfer the meats to a platter to cool. When cool to the touch, finely shred the meats. Add the shredded meats to the stockpot with the corn, pouring in more hot water as necessary, and bring to a boil. (*Note*: The cooking liquid should reach about 1 inch/2.5 cm above the corn and meats.) Continue cooking over high heat; using a large wooden spoon, stir the corn vigorously for 15–20 minutes, or until the liquid thickens; the meats will further disintegrate, which is normal. (This stirring or beating takes a strong arm and lots of patience: to avoid tedium and fatigue, switch arms, change the way you stir from a circular motion to a folding action, etc.) Add the salt, stir to incorporate, and check for seasonings.

TO SERVE

Ladle the pozole into individual serving bowls. Diners add chile and/or chile powder, onion, cabbage, radishes, and squeezes of lime juice to taste. Or instead of the chopped chile, serve it with Salsa tarasca, p. 489.

SALSA TARASCA

CHILE DE ÁRBOL AND CRISPY TORTILLA STRIP GARNISH FOR SOUPS
AND POZOLE

FOR THE GARNISH

1 tablespoon (12 g) sesame seeds
4–5 chiles de árbol (¼ oz./7 g
 total)
5–6 maize tortillas (2¼ oz./65.25 g
 total)
Vegetable oil for frying
Sea salt to taste

What looks a bit like breakfast cereal is actually a crispy/fiery salsa qua garnish concocted by cooks in the *puesto* "Estelita" in Morelia specifically for serving with pozole. This clever garnish combines a couple of the elements required for soups and pozoles: crunch and heat. When you're frying the chiles, fry a few extra and serve them whole in a bowl by themselves.

Prepare-ahead note: Because this garnish contains no fresh ingredients, it keeps well at room temperature in a dry environment for 3–4 days.

Lightly toast the sesame seeds in a dry skillet and transfer them to a serving bowl. Remove the stems from the chiles. Cut the tortillas in quarters, then cut each quarter into strips measuring about ½ inch (1.25 cm) wide. Heat the vegetable oil to 350°F (176°C); add the chiles and fry until darkened, about 30 seconds; remove with a slotted spoon and set aside. Fry the tortilla strips in batches until lightly golden and the sizzling subsides, about 1 minute. Transfer to paper towels to drain; sprinkle with salt to taste and transfer the strips to the bowl with the sesame seeds. Allow the cooking oil to cool, then measure ½ cup (125 mL); pour the oil into the jar of a blender; add the chiles, and process until thoroughly liquefied. Pour the oil-chile mixture over the tortilla strips and toss to combine. Check seasonings and add salt as needed.

[LP]

[MC]

ANISILLO/ANÍS DEL CAMPO, HIERBA ANÍS

BOTANICAL: *Tagetes micrantha* (Cav.) DC./Family Asteraceae
ENGLISH: wild anise, licorice marigold
P'URHÉPECHA: *pusuti, putsuta*

A strong scent of anise wafts from this bushy herb as you brush by it in its environment, and the scent becomes even more pronounced if the body of the plant is squeezed; a greenish liquid in the plant is extracted and tastes like strong anise. *Anisillo* originated in Mexico and southwestern United States in temperate and semiarid zones; it grows in semidesert scrubland, pastureland, and mixed oak/pine mountain forests between 6,528 and 9,450 feet (1,900–2,880 m) above sea level. The plant can reach heights of 20 inches (50 cm). Threadlike leaves are divided into individual sheets, in groups of three to nine clusters. Tiny white and yellow flowers are found at the head of thin stems. In numerous states of Mexico, *anisillo* is used medicinally for the treatment of various digestive problems. Culinarily, it may be used as a substitute for anise, and is a primary flavoring agent for Atole de grano (below).

ATOLE DE GRANO

FRESH CORN AND WILD ANISE SOUP

FOR THE INFUSION

2 cups (500 mL) water
3 medium bunches anisillo
(¾ oz./20 g total; substitute an
equal weight of *hoja santa*, or
1 Tbsp./6 g aniseed)

*Doña María meticulously dices
chiles perón.* [MC]

Mornings and evenings can be quite chilly in Pátzcuaro, so warm foods like this are welcome. This is traditionally prepared with *anisillo*—wild anise. It gives the *atole* its characteristic flavor as well as its bright green color. The herb is ground on a metate until thoroughly mashed, mixed with the water used for the atole, and strained. Sometimes when there is no *anisillo* to be found, people use leaves of *hoja santa* (p. 260), which imparts a flavor and color close to the original. Since both ingredients will be difficult for most people to locate, I've adapted the recipe to substitute aniseed for a similar flavor; I further suggest some (totally optional) organic food coloring to get the customary color given by the *anisillo*. The *atole* is also typically flavored with *chile verde*—any one of several may be used, including the jalapeño—but nowadays most vendors delete the chile in the mixture, serving it instead on the side.

PREPARE THE INFUSION

Bring the water to a boil; add the *anisillo*, *hoja santa*, or the aniseed; remove from the heat and cover. Allow to steep for 15 minutes as you continue.

FOR THE ATOLE

9 pounds (4 kg) fresh corn cobs (approximately 12 ears, weight before husking; 6 lbs./2.7 kg weight after husking. You will need about 5 cups/875 g of corn kernels. *Note*: Look for field corn at a farmers' market, and by all means avoid sweet corn.)

16 cups (4 L) water, divided

1 cup (250 g) masa, prepared with nixtamal or with masa harina

A few drops organic green food coloring (optional)

FOR SERVING

5–6 chiles perón (substitute yellow manzano or rocoto chiles), stems and seeds removed, and cut into medium dice

The hot sauce of your choice

Lime wedges

Salt

Pour the water and the herbs into the jar of a blender; process until thoroughly liquefied; set aside. (*Note*: If using aniseed, skip the blender step.)

PREPARE THE ATOLE

Cut 3 of the cobs into 4–5 equal pieces and set aside; slice off the grains from the remaining cobs. Place the corn cobs and kernels in a large stockpot; add 12 cups (3 L) of the water; bring to a boil; reduce to a simmer and cook for 10–15 minutes or until the corn is al dente.

Dissolve the masa with the remaining 4 cups (1 L) of water; pour the mixture through a fine-mesh sieve into the stockpot and stir to incorporate. Bring the liquid to a boil; reduce to a simmer and cook, stirring constantly to avoid sticking, approximately 5 minutes or until the mixture thickens.

Pour the reserved herb infusion through a fine-mesh sieve held over the stockpot, discarding the contents of the sieve. Add the food coloring, if using; stir the *atole* to incorporate the ingredients, and cook another 3–4 minutes to re-thicken. Serve immediately.

(left) Manzano, rocoto, perón, chamborote—*just a few of the regional names for the* Capsicum pubescens *(see page 142).* [LP] *(right) Anise-flavored Atole de grano is scooped from a large clay pot decorated in the typical style of Pátzcuaro. María de la Luz Urtiz Domínguez serves it every morning and evening in the Plaza Gertrudis Bocanegra.* [MC]

(*above*) Chile-encrusted queso ranchero enchilado. [LP] (*below*) *Rounds of* queso Cotija. *The Cotija cheese you have eaten—certainly if purchased in the United States—is most likely "queso tipo Cotija," cheese produced in the style of Cotija. Cristina Potters explains that the far western Jalmich region of Michoacán, bordering on Jalisco, has been designated the origin of genuine Cotija—the name of the largest town in the region—a product that emerged shortly after the Spanish brought dairy cattle to Mexico. It is traditionally made with fresh whole raw cow's milk mixed with natural rennet from the stomachs of ruminants. Production only happens from June through November—the rainy season—and cheeses are aged a minimum of 3 months. Cotija may be more moist or drier, depending on the time it is aged. It is easy to crumble or grate and has been compared to Parmesan and feta, with the same tangy-salty taste. It is consumed in a variety of ways: look for it crumbled atop refried beans or enchiladas; or rub grilled corn cobs with lime juice and sprinkle on some finely crumbled cheese.* [MC]

CHONGOS ZAMORANOS

SWEETENED CURDS AND WHEY WITH MEXICAN CINNAMON AND VANILLA

[LP]

Chongos are a divisive treat: people either love them or hate them. For those who love them, Chongos often bring back blissful childhood memories. Chongos were legendarily invented in the convents of the northwestern city of Zamora—supposedly when a nun forgot about some milk she had left on the stove. To make Chongos, milk is curdled in a manner much like that of cheese making; the clotted curds are then sweetened with sugar and flavored with sticks of *canela*. The curds are typically served with some of the sweetened whey in a bowl, but in the markets (look for them in the cheese stalls) they are sold in plastic cups and eaten with a spoon or fingers. If you like anything resembling *cajeta* or sweetened condensed milk, you will love Chongos. They are so popular in Mexico that they even come in cans. The commercial production of them in home kitchens as a cottage industry is so common that PROFECO—Mexico's consumer advocacy association—published a detailed recipe for Chongos on their website, with thorough food-safety tips. The following recipe is adapted from it; at the end of the recipe, it calls for canning the Chongos in a 22-ounce (650 mL) sterilized jar, but for my own use, I just put them in a glass container with a lid and leave them in the refrigerator; they keep well for about 1 week, which is all they last at my house. They're delicious chilled but perhaps best eaten at room temperature, so plan ahead for your sugar craving.

YIELD: 10–12 SERVINGS

FOR THE CHONGOS

¼ cup (62.5 mL) water (distilled, filtered, and/or nonchlorinated)

¼ teaspoon (0.75 mL) liquid calcium chloride

8 cups (2 L) whole milk

Slightly more than ½ teaspoon, or ½ teaspoon *plus* ⅛ teaspoon (3 mL) liquid rennet

1 tablespoon (15 mL) Mexican vanilla extract

1 cup (256 g) muscovado sugar (substitute dark brown sugar or grated piloncillo)

4 three-inch (7.5 cm) sticks canela, broken into long, thin strips

PREPARE THE CHONGOS

Pour the water into a glass measuring cup or clean jar; add the calcium chloride and stir to combine; set aside.

Pour the milk into a large saucepan and heat until bubbles appear around the edges, taking care not to let the milk boil (for best results, use an instant-read digital or candy thermometer and bring the milk to 120°F/49°C). Turn off the heat but leave the saucepan on the burner. Slowly pour in the calcium chloride solution as you stir the milk. Add the rennet, stir just to incorporate, and stop all stirring. Allow the milk mixture to rest until it is firm and resembles tofu; this will take anywhere from 1 to 3 hours, depending on your rennet. With your thermometer, test the mixture from time to time, and turn on the heat if necessary in order to maintain the temperature somewhere between 100°F and 120°F (38°C–49°C; in a warm kitchen, reheating may not be necessary). Slip a long, narrow knife into the curds to the bottom of the pan; if it comes out clean, you are ready for the next step; if not, wait another few minutes.

With the same long knife, insert it from the top to the bottom, and cut the curds into 1-inch (3 cm) squares all the way through; allow the curds to rest another 10 minutes.

Sprinkle the vanilla over the entire surface of the curds, followed by the sugar; insert the *canela* pieces into the slits that you cut. Turn the heat to low and gently simmer for 1 hour. (*Note*: Some of the curds will remain in the squares you cut, others may disintegrate into smaller pieces. This will not affect the finished product.) Remove and discard the *canela* sticks and allow the curds to cool. Break up the curds with a spoon, and empty into a storage container along with the whey; cover and refrigerate.

TO SERVE

Serve at room temperature or chilled; spoon into serving bowls with some of the whey. If you wish, garnish with sliced strawberries or other fruit, raisins, or toasted walnuts or pecans.

[MC]

A common sight throughout the market of Pátzcuaro are mounds of the tiny, dried fish known as charales. [LP]

CHARAL/CHARAL PRIETO

ICHTHYOLOGICAL: *Chirostoma attenuatum* Meek/Family Atherinopsidae | **ENGLISH:** slender silverside

The *Chirostoma* genus has approximately twenty-three species, all found in freshwater bodies throughout Mexico, all similar in appearance, and varying mostly by size. *C. attenuatum* known as *charal* is endemic to the Lerma River basin—the second-longest river in Mexico—and specifically to two lakes in the basin, Pátzcuaro and Zirahuen. *Charales* are very small, only about 2½ to 4¾ inches (6–12 cm) in length. The fish have two dorsal fins; scales are silvery, giving the fish its English name. In the first stages of life, *charales* consume the smallest sizes of zooplankton; when adults, they may be considered carnivorous, since they eat larger zooplankton as well as insect larvae. *Charales* are preyed upon by the *pescado blanco*—which is a larger species of the *Chirostoma* genus, reaching lengths of up to 16 inches (40 cm). Both species are fished commercially. *Charales* may be consumed fresh, but the most common way you will see them is salted and dried; they are separated into piles according to size, as seen in the photo. *Pescado blanco* is more generally consumed fresh. The Lerma River basin as well as lakes Pátzcuaro and Zirahuen have become badly polluted due to runoff as well as the fact that until recently waste treatment facilities were not adequately updated for growing populations, and many smaller communities around the lake had none at all. *C. attenuatum* is considered vulnerable, although fishing goes on unabated. In recent years, government programs in San Jerónimo Purenchécuaro on the northern end of the lake and in a few other communities have revived some shoreline wetlands, and *charales* are returning. In addition, scientists from the US Environmental Protection Agency have conducted chemical analyses of the fish found in these wetlands and determined them to be free of toxins. Because they are near the bottom of the food chain, these small fish are not as likely to be contaminated by heavy metals as are larger fish. Dried *charales* may be fried with no breading or coated with flour prior to frying; they may also be covered with chile powder and eaten whole as a snack, or fried with garlic and served with Salsa verde (p. 531). Bunches of quick-fried *charales* are common fillings for tacos, with Salsa de molcajete (p. 533) and squeezes of lime juice used as garnishes.

The romantic image of butterfly-shaped fishing nets on Lake Pátzcuaro is almost a thing of the past. While some older generations in remote communities may still fish this way, more typically the nets only appear occasionally for special holidays or touristic events.

A large platter of fried charales *with the requisite Salsa de molcajete, at right.* [MC]

CHARALES FRITOS

FRIED "SLENDER SILVERSIDE" FISH

Rosalba Morales Bartolo is a P'urhépecha cook from San Jerónimo Purenchécuaro who was honored by the state of Michoacán for her work in rescuing traditional methods of cleaning and preparing *charales*. In recent years, the fish acquired a bad reputation due to the pollution of Pátzcuaro, but now a handful of indigenous people, including Rosalba, are working to restore the ancient practice of their ancestors and subsequently preserve the local economy. First, the fish Rosalba purchases come only from the *humedales*—wetlands that surround the lake—that are undergoing meticulous cleaning and protection thanks to progressive government programs. Furthermore, while completely gutting and scaling the tiny fish is a laborious task that many people are neglecting to do properly these days, Rosalba thoroughly cleans them in the manner she was taught by her mother and grandmother; it takes 20 minutes for every 4½ pounds (2 kg) of fish. After cleaning them, she spreads them out in the sun on *petates* (see photo p. 498) and sprinkles them lightly with salt, leaving them to dry for about 6 hours. The *charales* you will find in huge piles in the market of Pátzcuaro are similarly dried. Rosalba's best-selling Charales fritos are lightly coated in flour—organic wheat that a local mill grinds for her—then plopped into sizzling oil. She avoids any other herbs or spices so that the natural flavor of the fish comes through.

6 ounces (170 g) dried charales
  (See notes above about
  substitutions.)
Juice of 1 medium lime
2 cups (250 g) organic whole
  wheat flour
Vegetable oil for frying

Charales are popular throughout Mexico, and since they are salted and dried, they travel and store well; they surge in popularity during Lent. You may find dried *charales* in small packages in Mexican markets. Similarly, look in Korean or other Asian markets for dried sprats, sardines, or anchovies. Depending on your region, you may substitute small fresh sprats or smelts, cleaned, heads removed or not according to taste. Should you have trouble locating any of the above, I offer a variation below using fresh trout with its skin, cut into very thin strips. (It is not such a stretch, after all, since Rosalba also prepares many dishes of local trout—including fried—in her *comedor*.) Of course, nothing is quite the same as biting into the crunchy body of the whole little fish, head, tail, and all! Whatever the case, you will appreciate the simplicity of these fish tacos accompanied by the potent Salsa de molcajete and a hearty squeeze of lime juice.

Prepare-ahead note: To ensure the fish are hot when you serve them, as traditional cooks in Michoacán do, you may fry the fish lightly once and leave on paper towels for up to 3–4 hours, then fry them again for a few seconds immediately before serving.

YIELD: 6–8 SERVINGS

PREPARE THE FRIED FISH

Place the *charales* in a large bowl and cover them completely with cold water. Add the lime juice to the water and stir; let the fish rest for 10 minutes, stirring occasionally, then drain; rinse thoroughly under cold water and drain again. Spread the fish on paper towels and lightly pat them dry.

Spread the flour in a large, deep platter; add the fish and toss to thoroughly coat them with the flour. Pour 1½ inches (4 cm) of the oil into a large, deep skillet; heat to a temperature of 350°F (176°C). Working in batches, transfer a big handful of the flour-coated fish to a colander and shake off any excess flour into the platter containing

Fried and chile-coated charales *are available as snacks to buy before you take a launch out into Lago de Pátzcuaro en route to one of the lake's six islands.* [MC]

Rolls of petates in the market. Petates *are all-purpose mats that may be used for sleeping or napping, or for drying seeds, chiles, fish— what have you. In other parts of Mexico, they may be woven of palm leaves, but in Pátzcuaro, petates are made of chuspata—a reed in the Juncaceae family that grows along the banks of the lake. It has been used since precontact times by indigenous peoples for weaving a variety of utilitarian goods.* [LP]

the remaining fish. Carefully transfer the fish from the colander to the oil; use a wok strainer or slotted spoon to move and turn them; add another big handful and stir. Bring the temperature back to 350°F (176°C) and fry, turning occasionally, until the fish are lightly browned, 1–2 minutes; transfer to paper towels to drain; repeat until all of the fish have been fried. Check for seasonings and sprinkle lightly with salt if desired. Serve immediately or see notes above about reheating the fish.

TO SERVE
Assemble tacos for your diners by heaping approximately ½ ounce (14 g) of the fried fish on a warm tortilla. Alternatively, arrange the fish on a large, heated platter so that diners may assemble their own tacos, adding salsa and squeezes of lime juice to taste.

VARIATION
Trucha frita/Fried Trout: Work with 1 pound (500 g) trout fillets with the skin intact. Cut the fillets into very thin strips, measuring about 2 inches long by ½ inch wide (5 cm × 1.25 cm). Instead of soaking the fish strips in water, cover them with the juice of 2 medium limes and allow the fish to rest at room temperature for 10 minutes; drain and pat dry. Mix 1 teaspoon (6 g) sea salt and ½ teaspoon (2.5 g) ground black pepper with the flour and proceed with the recipe. After frying, check for seasonings and sprinkle lightly with salt if desired. Serving suggestions are the same. Follow this variation if you will be using fresh smelts or sprats (see above).

NIEVE DE PASTA
ALMOND PASTE ICE CREAM

Whether found inside the market or immediately outside, sorbets and ice creams of exotic flavors are a continuation of market grazing. Wonderfully creamy Nieve de pasta has become a tourist attraction of Pátzcuaro, and Nevería La Pacanda, which has been making and selling ice creams and sorbets here since 1905, claims ownership of the recipe. Vendors whispered the basics of the recipe to me: almonds, walnuts, and raisins are liquefied with whole, raw milk, which is then mixed with evaporated and sweetened condensed milks—*tres leches*, as they called it. The mixture is poured into a large copper kettle and stirred with a wooden paddle for an hour or two over medium heat as the milks gradually darken and thicken. It is a process that reminds me of *dulce de leche* or *cajeta*, and like those sweet treats, this must be stirred almost constantly to prevent scorching. The long simmering in effect pasteurizes the milk, so for best flavor, use raw milk if you can find it; if not, whole pasteurized milk will do. Huge copper kettles from Santa Clara del Cobre are used at the *nevería*'s artisanal production kitchen; it is recommended to use a large copper saucepan if you have one, since it will help prevent the mixture from scorching.

YIELD: 1 QUART (1 L)

[LP]

FOR THE ICE CREAM

1 ounce (28 g) almonds, blanched

1 ounce (28 g) walnuts or pecans

1.4 ounces (40 g) raisins

1 cup (250 mL) raw milk
(substitute whole milk; see
notes above)

1 can (14 oz./397 g) sweetened
condensed milk

1 can (14½ oz./411 g) evaporated
milk

PREPARE THE ICE CREAM

Place the nuts in the bowl of a food processor; process until they turn into a smooth paste, 6–8 minutes. Add the raisins and process to incorporate the raisins into the nut paste, 3–4 minutes. Add the raw or whole milk and process to thoroughly combine.

Pour the milk mixture into a large copper saucepan; add the condensed and evaporated milks and stir to combine. Bring the mixture to a boil, then reduce to a simmer; continue cooking at a simmer, stirring frequently, for 1 hour. Strain through a fine-mesh sieve into a heatproof bowl, pressing through as much of the liquid as possible; allow the mixture to cool, cover, and refrigerate for several hours, or preferably overnight.

FREEZE AND FINISH

Process the mixture in an ice cream maker according to the manufacturer's instructions. Place the finished ice cream in a covered container and freeze for 3–4 hours before serving.

[LP]

(left) Santa Clara del Cobre. [LP] *(right)* Copper cauldrons (cazos) just like these—only three times larger—are used by Blanca Vidales Vega to make Carnitas (p. 477), by Nevería La Pacanda to make Nieve de pasta (p. 499), and by Himelda Paredes Sámano to make Conservas de frutas (p. 519). Copper workshops line a couple of streets in the town, and you can frequently hear the tap-tap-tap of coppersmiths giving form to copper in various shapes. The copper museum, Museo Nacional del Cobre, displays masterworks of the art spanning several centuries. [LP]

SANTA CLARA DEL COBRE

JUST 11 MILES (18 KM) from Pátzcuaro, Santa Clara del Cobre is a frequent stop for travelers to the region, tantalized by shops full of glittering copper. Since pre-Columbian times, the P'urhépecha peoples have exploited the rich copper mines found here, and they developed an advanced metallurgy. Bells, axes, masks, jewelry, and other forms of body decoration were crafted, and many exquisite pieces have been found in burial grounds.

Although the indigenous peoples fled the area at the beginning of the conquest, they later returned to continue their traditional work of coppersmithing, now for the benefit of the new ruling class. In exchange for returning, the first bishop of Michoacán, Vasco de Quiroga, gave the P'urhépecha workers the sole right to fabricate *cazos*—large cauldrons used for rendering lard as well as many other purposes. *Cazos* are used throughout Mexico, and they are still fabricated in Santa Clara del Cobre, although copper is no longer mined here; instead, all of the magnificent copper pieces you will see here are now made from recycled items such as electrical cable. Many other culinary tools are also produced, such as sauté pans, saucepans, and comales.

Torta tostada is another offering that contributes to the growing list of unusual sandwich fillings: tamales, chicharrón (p. 397), and in this case, a fried tortilla, or tostada. While the crispy tostada is the raison d'être of the sandwich, it is just one of several other fillings of your choice, including ham, refried beans, head cheese, and/ or Carne apache, with plenty of mayonnaise on the bread. Toppings are shredded cabbage, chopped radishes and onion, and Salsa Valentina, a commercially bottled hot sauce popular throughout the country. The photo is enough of a "recipe" for the sandwich, but following is the recipe for Carne apache. [MC]

CARNE APACHE

STEAK TARTARE "CEVICHE"

I've asked many Mexicans what *carne apache* means to them, and the only consistent answer I receive is that it refers to the Native American people. The Apaches (actually a generic name that the Spanish applied to several groups) were considered fierce and strategic warriors, and indeed they fought Spanish and Mexican troops for centuries starting in the 1600s. Why the name was applied to this raw meat dish shall remain open to interpretation. Although Carne apache may be found in several states of Mexico, Ricardo Muñoz Zurita states that it is principally a food of the eastern zone of Michoacán, particularly Zitácuaro. This recipe for Carne apache—raw steak "cooked" in lime juice—which I found at the *puesto* Tortas y Tostadas "Don Pancho" in Santa Clara del Cobre, appealed to me because it begins with a purée of a ripe, red tomato with the lime juice, lending the finished meat a healthy-looking reddish color rather

FOR THE BEEF

1 medium Roma tomato
(3½ oz./100 g), very ripe red,
quartered

½ cup (125 mL) freshly squeezed
lime juice

1½ pounds (680 g) very lean
sirloin, finely chopped by hand
or pulsed briefly in a processor

FOR FINISHING THE CARNE APACHE

½ medium white onion
(5 oz./137.5 g), finely chopped

2 medium Roma tomatoes
(7 oz./200 g), seeded, cut to
small dice, and placed in a
fine-mesh sieve to drain

1 medium chile perón (substitute
chile manzano or rocoto),
seeded and finely chopped

¼ cup (40 g) pitted green olives,
finely chopped

¼ cup (20 g) cilantro, finely
chopped

2 tablespoons (30 mL) Spanish
olive oil

¼ teaspoon (1.5 g) sea salt

2–3 big grinds fresh black pepper

FOR SERVING

Sandwich ingredients as
suggested above, or tostadas

Shredded cabbage

Radishes, cut into thin julienne
strips

White onion, chopped

Lime wedges

Chile sauce to taste

than the more typical unappetizing gray-brown. Harold McGee explains that the acids in the lime juice help denature the meat's proteins, thereby tenderizing it, and also help prevent the formation of certain harmful bacteria. Avoid ground beef—chop your own—and choose the leanest sirloin you can find. To ensure ultimate freshness, order it from your butcher rather than purchasing the steak in a package.

Prepare-ahead note: Carne apache requires a couple of hours to repose in the lime juice; it should be eaten on the day it is prepared.

YIELD: 6–8 SERVINGS

PREPARE THE BEEF

Place the tomato and lime juice in the jar of a blender and process until thoroughly puréed. Spread the chopped meat over the bottom of a large baking dish; pour the purée over the meat; toss the meat to coat completely with the purée. Leave at room temperature for 2 hours.

FINISH THE CARNE APACHE

Just before serving, transfer the meat to a large mixing bowl and add the remaining ingredients. Toss to combine and serve immediately.

TO SERVE

Use Carne apache as a filling for the *torta tostada*, described above, or simply serve it on a *tostada*. Garnish with some shredded cabbage, chopped onion, and radishes; diners add squeezes of lime juice and chile sauce to taste.

[MC]

Santuario del Carmen. [MC]

TLALPUJAHUA

H ISTORICALLY, TLALPUJAHUA (pronounced "tlal-pooh-HA-wah") was on the border of the competing Aztec and Tarascan Empires, and thus the site of frequent conflicts. After the conquest of the Tarascans in 1522, King Charles V established an *encomienda* that granted mineral rights to Spanish miners; Tlalpujahua continued as a major mining town through the 1930s. Curiously, today the town is known for its production of Christmas tree ornaments and the candied fruits known as *conservas*.

MAZAHUA/HÑATHO

Tlalpujahua is one of the few places in the country with a significant representation of Mazahua peoples. Mazahuas are believed to have descended from Chichimeca groups that settled in the eastern part of present-day Michoacán and the western part of Estado de México. Part of the Mazahua territory extends into the Monarch Butterfly Biosphere Reserve; Mazahuas believe their souls return as monarch butterflies. Today, around 40 percent of the population works in agriculture, growing maize, beans, potatoes, peas, and other vegetables, mostly for auto-consumption. Traditionally, the Mazahuas made clothing from the fibers of maguey leaves, and this is still a practice for bags, belts, and other utilitarian objects. Women's clothing is distinctive and characterized by pleated skirts of satin or lace, richly embroidered blouses and woven sashes. The gastronomy of the Mazahuas is similar to that of the Otomíes: squash and the squash-seed sauce known as *pipián*, wild mushrooms, and a wide variety of *quelites* predominate.

[LP]

MERCADO MUNICIPAL

The 1,200-foot (365 m) climb on the road from Pátzcuaro to Tlalpujahua continued on foot as we scaled flights of stairs from the town's entrance to the market perched on a mountain slope. Some vendors arranged their goods in the two-story covered structure; many more occupied spaces on the ample landings of the Escher-like stairway that zigzags its way up and down and around the market.

The sale of pulque inside the market is prohibited, but the rules are less strict if it is done outside; some vendors do it furtively wherever they may be.

A vendor pours fresh pulque from a jug into a bottle for us. [LP]

ENSALADA DE HABAS

FAVA BEAN AND NOPAL SALAD

TO PREPARE AHEAD

Nopalitos (nopal pad strips)
prepared as described on
page 390

FOR THE SALAD

¼ cup (67.5 mL) freshly squeezed
lime juice

2 tablespoons (30 mL) Spanish
olive oil

1 teaspoon (0.65 g) whole dried
Mexican oregano, lightly toasted

½ teaspoon (3 g) sea salt

3 pounds (1.5 kg) fresh fava beans,
shelled, blanched, peeled, and
steamed until tender

1 cup (108 g) nopalitos

½ medium white onion
(5 oz./137.5 g), finely chopped

2 medium Roma tomatoes
(7 oz./200 g), seeded and cut
into small dice

1 medium chile perón (1.2 oz./33 g;
substitute chile manzano or
rocoto), seeded and finely
chopped

¼ cup (15 g) cilantro, chopped

By all means, try this lovely fresh salad as a filling for tacos or quesadillas as mentioned above, but it also makes a nice side dish or even a main course for a light lunch.

Prepare-ahead note: Ensalada de habas improves with an overnight rest in the refrigerator; it keeps well for 2–3 days.

YIELD: 6 SERVINGS

PREPARE THE SALAD

Place the first four ingredients in the jar of a blender and process until thoroughly incorporated; set aside.

Place the remaining ingredients in a large mixing bowl; pour on the mixture from the blender jar and toss to combine. Refrigerate for a few hours if you wish; bring to room temperature before serving.

On a broad landing at the top of the stairs that led to the market, a long table was spread with a variety of salad and bean dishes that you could order either plated or as fillings for tacos or quesadillas; many people ordered large containers of them to take home. The vendor, Verónica Morales, offered what she called "tacos placeros" (plaza tacos) made from any of the dishes served atop a warm tortilla. Clockwise from top left: Frijoles guisados (p. 509), Ensalada de nopales (p. 390), and Ensalada de habas (recipe above). [LP]

FRIJOLES GUISADOS
JUNE BEANS IN CHILE GUAJILLO MOLE

TO PREPARE AHEAD
Enriched Lard (p. 530)

FOR THE BEANS
1 pound (500 g) frijol de flor de
    junio (substitute pinto beans)
Approximately 16 cups (4 qts./4 L)
    water, divided

FOR THE MOLE
8–10 chiles guajillos (2 oz./60 g
    total)
½ chile chipotle in adobo (5 g),
    drained (optional)
2 medium Roma tomatoes
    (7 oz./200 g), charred
½ medium white onion
    (5 oz./137.5 g), peeled and charred
3 medium cloves garlic
    (¾ oz./18 g), peeled and charred
2 tablespoons (32 g) muscovado
    sugar (substitute dark brown
    sugar)
1 teaspoon (0.65 g) whole dried
    Mexican oregano, lightly toasted
    and crumbled
3 tablespoons (42 g) Enriched Lard
1 cup (250 mL) rich chicken stock,
    or you may use canned broth or
    bouillon
1 tablespoon (15 mL) pineapple or
    apple cider vinegar
⅛ teaspoon (0.25 g) ground cumin
2 teaspoons (12 g) sea salt, or to
    taste

The pale purple bean with cream-colored stripes known as *flor de junio* (June bean) is highly prized by many cooks for certain dishes, like this one. It grows in the Central Highlands and semiarid regions of Mexico—principally in the Bajío—from late June to mid-July. The bean stays firm during cooking, but is meltingly tender on the tongue. It is occasionally available outside of Mexico, or you may substitute pinto beans. The optional *chile chipotle* adds a slightly smoky taste and mild heat. Frijoles guisados will remind you of baked beans, and they may be served similarly as a side dish with a drizzle of *crema* and a dusting of *queso Cotija*; or they may be served in a bowl, topped with chopped onion and cilantro, and eaten like soup or chili.

Prepare-ahead note: Like many bean dishes, Frijoles guisados improves with age; prepare a day or two in advance, refrigerate, and reheat immediately before serving.

PREPARE THE BEANS
Rinse and pick through the beans; place the beans in a large casserole or Dutch oven and cover them with 2 quarts (8 cups/2 L) of the water. Bring to a boil, skimming off any foam; reduce to a simmer and continue cooking until the beans are barely tender, about 1 to 2 hours, depending on your beans, adding more of the water as needed to keep the beans just covered. (Adding boiling water is best so as not to alter cooking time.)

PREPARE THE MOLE
While the beans are cooking, cut the stem off of each chile; slit the chiles open along one side and remove the seeds and veins. Flatten the chiles and lightly toast them on a comal or griddle, or in a heavy skillet, until they are fragrant and slightly darkened, about 1–2 minutes. Place the chiles in a large heatproof bowl and cover them with boiling water. Allow the chiles to soak for 30 minutes.

At the end of soaking time, place the chiles in the jar of a blender, reserving the soaking liquid. Add the next six ingredients, plus 1 cup (250 mL) of the chile soaking liquid. Process until thoroughly liquefied.

Heat the lard in a large heavy skillet until shimmering; add all of the contents from the blender at once: it should splatter and sizzle, so stand back. Cook over medium heat, stirring frequently, for about 20 minutes or until the mixture darkens and thickens considerably (you should be able to see the bottom of the skillet cleanly when you scrape it with a spatula). Add the chicken stock and stir to combine; remove from the heat and set aside.

When the beans are barely tender and in need of more liquid, pour in the chile mixture. Add the vinegar, cumin, and salt, stir to combine, and continue to simmer about another 30 minutes to finish cooking the beans and amalgamate the flavors. Check seasonings and serve.

MALCASADO/BERRO DE AGUA

BOTANICAL: *Berula erecta* (Huds.) Coville/Family Apiaceae
ENGLISH: water parsnip | **P'URHÉPECHA:** *bulhá, chorure*

[LP]

Malcasado acquires its humorous name ("unhappily married") thanks to its distinctive opposite leaf pattern. This *quelite* grows in shallow water at the edges of lakes, marshes, or riparian environments. The plant has a dense root system that helps it remain stable in the water; structural elements remain submerged while the reproductive parts are above the surface of the water. *Malcasado* can grow to heights of 8 to 33 inches (20–85 cm). The edges of the leaves are serrated; the stems are hollow and fragile. From July through September, the plant produces inflorescences composed of many small, white, five-petaled blossoms; fruits are small (0.05–0.07 inch/1.5–2 mm in diameter), round, and flat, each one with a seed. *Malcasado* is native to Eurasia and the Americas. The stems and leaves of the plant are edible, although large quantities may be toxic. In traditional medicine of Michoacán, it is used for treating liver ailments; in Chiapas, it is used to treat dysentery; and in Durango, an infusion is used to purify the blood.

Some of the ingredients of Ensalada de malcasados, clockwise from left: crumbled chicharrón, coarsely chopped malcasados, chopped tomatoes. [LP]

ENSALADA DE MALCASADO

SALAD OF WILD GREENS WITH CHICHARRÓN

TO PREPARE AHEAD

Verduras en escabeche (p. 480)

FOR THE SALAD

6 cups (about 95 g) malcasado, washed, rinsed, and coarsely chopped (substitute mixed greens and herbs as noted below)

2 medium Roma tomatoes (3½ oz./200 g), seeded and cut into medium dice

½ medium white onion (5 oz./137.5 g), chopped

1 cup (150 g) Verduras en escabeche, drained, vinegar reserved

1 medium avocado (9 oz./250 g), seeded, peeled, and cut into medium dice

3½ ounces (100 g) chicharrón, broken into coarse pieces (see photo)

¼ cup (62.5 mL) vinegar from the Verduras en escabeche

1 teaspoon (6 g) sea salt, or to taste

[LP]

Doña Himelda folds some of the salad into a tortilla; a hungry cat waits patiently for an errant bit of chicharrón *to fall to the floor.* [LP]

This quick and easy salad is an occasional offering in the markets; since it was not to be found during our visit, doña Himelda Paredes Sámano, a respected local cook, had her daughter purchase the ingredients from the market around the corner, and in short order we were eating the salad. Since you are not likely to find *malcasado*, use any kind of wild greens—or better yet, a mixture: purslane, dandelion greens, lamb's quarters, wall rocket. Add some more conventional greens, too, if you wish, such as arugula or watercress. To simulate the flavor of *malcasado*, also include equal amounts of parsley and cilantro. The total measure of all the greens combined should be as stated in the instructions; all of the greens should be coarsely chopped. The recipe is easily extended for larger parties. Of course, you may serve this on a plate and eat it with a fork, but the common way in Michoacán—as for so many foods in Mexico—is to eat it like a taco folded into a fresh, warm maize tortilla. The traditional accompaniment for the salad is pulque; if you can't locate it, serve with a sweet, malty beer.

YIELD: 6—8 SERVINGS

PREPARE THE SALAD

Place the first four ingredients in a large salad bowl or platter and toss. To keep the avocado from discoloring and the *chicharrón* from becoming soggy, add them at the very last possible minute before serving. Finish with the vinegar and salt, toss to combine, and serve immediately, either as a plated salad or as tacos as noted above.

Breakfast cooking on the comal at Puesto "Antojito La Hermosa." Clockwise from top center: a sautéed mixture of quelites *(wild greens—*quelites nabo, malcasados, *and* quintoniles); huevos al comal *(a hole is torn from the center of a blue corn tortilla, and an egg is cracked over the opening); charred* chiles perón *and tomatoes for* Salsa de molcajete *(p. 533); and* Sopa aguada *in the large clay pot (recipe follows). The owner's daughter, Luz Neri de Jesús, shared the next three delectable recipes with us.* [LP]

SOPA AGUADA

TOMATO SOUP WITH VERMICELLI

"Watery soup"—the literal translation of the name of this dish—may sound odd until you realize that the name is simply employed to distinguish it from *sopa seca,* "dry soup." To elaborate, both of these are traditional accompaniments to a large Mexican meal with many courses. One of the first courses would be *sopa aguada*—usually some kind of stock or broth that includes a pasta of one kind or another and possibly some vegetables; this soup would immediately be followed by *sopa seca*—a rice pilaf that may contain meats, seafood, or vegetables. The tradition of the serving courses is disappearing, but the individual dishes are not. *Sopa aguada* may be found throughout the republic—even as far away as Chiapas—but it is more common in the central region.

Prepare-ahead note: Sopa aguada keeps well under refrigeration for up to 1 week; reheat before serving.

YIELD: 6–8 SERVINGS

1 pound (500 g) very ripe Roma
tomatoes, charred and quartered

1 medium red onion (10 oz./275 g),
peeled, charred, and quartered

4 medium cloves garlic
(1 oz./24 g), peeled and charred

4 cups (1 L) vegetable or chicken
broth, or bouillon

1 medium chile perón (1.2 oz./
33 g; substitute chile rocoto or
manzano), charred and seeded

2 tablespoons (30 mL)
vegetable oil

½ pound (250 g) vermicelli,
broken into 2-inch (5 cm) pieces

1 tablespoon (15 mL) white
vinegar

1 teaspoon (3 g) sea salt

PREPARE THE SOUP

Working in batches as needed, place the first three ingredients in the jar of a blender with some of the broth; process until thoroughly liquefied; repeat until all of the tomatoes, onion, garlic, and broth have been used. Return some of the mixture to the blender jar, and slowly add pieces of the chile. (*Note*: This soup should leave a pleasant zing at the back of your throat but not be overwhelming. Add quarters of the chile at a time, process, and taste before adding more.) Combine the mixture from the blender jar with the remaining tomato mixture, and taste for heat. To strengthen, add more chile; to weaken, add more tomatoes or broth; set aside.

Heat the vegetable oil in a saucepan or stockpot until shimmering; add the vermicelli and stir frequently, cooking over medium heat, until the vermicelli is pale golden, 3–4 minutes. Pour in the tomato mixture and stir to combine. Continue cooking 6–8 minutes or until the vermicelli is tender and the color of the soup is intensified to a deep red. Add the vinegar and salt and check for seasonings.

[LP]

QUESADILLA DE QUELITES

SAUTÉED WILD GREENS QUESADILLA

[MC]

Create a mix of roughly torn wild herbs and greens as described for Ensalada de mal-casado on page 511. (Spinach, kale, or chard also work well.) Chop some white onion, and sauté the onion and greens in a bit of vegetable oil until the onions are translucent and the greens are tender; sprinkle with salt to taste. Follow the instructions for as-sembling Quesadillas on page 349, using *queso Oaxaca* or Mozzarella. Serve immediately after cooking them; accompany with Salsa de molcajete (p. 533) and wedges of lime.

TACO DE CHILE RELLENO

STUFFED CHILE TACO

The very idea of this taco—not to mention its intoxicating aroma—so tempted me that I took a bite before it could be photographed. It is fascinating to observe how many traditional foods like the chile relleno or even tamales are now being served as tacos or *tortas*; it makes perfect sense for on-the-go foods, since no cutlery is required.

Prepare-ahead note: As they do in the *comedores*, you may prepare the chiles rellenos several hours in advance, and reheat them immediately before serving.

YIELD: 6 SERVINGS

FOR THE STUFFED CHILES

Vegetable oil for frying

6 medium chiles poblanos (about 4¼ oz./120 g each)

5½ ounces (150 g) queso Oaxaca or Mozzarella, coarsely grated

⅓ cup (42 g) *plus* ¾ cup (90 g) all-purpose flour

2 egg whites *plus* 3 large eggs, separated, at room temperature

½ teaspoon (0.325 g) whole dried Mexican oregano, lightly toasted and ground

¼ teaspoon (1.25 g) ground black pepper

1½ teaspoons (9 g) sea salt

PREPARE THE STUFFED CHILES

Pour 2 inches (5 cm) of vegetable oil into a large, deep skillet. Heat the oil to 350°F (176°C). Working two at a time, add the chiles to the hot oil; cook 1–2 minutes per side. Due to the moisture in the chiles, splattering can be rather vigorous, so take care. You are looking for signs that the skin has blistered, which will aid in peeling them. When the skin is well blistered overall, transfer the chiles to paper towels to drain and cool. Turn off the heat, but leave the oil in the skillet: it will soon serve for frying the battered chiles.

When the chiles are cool to the touch, hold them under cold running water and peel them completely: the skin is rather tough, so try to remove as much as possible. Leaving the stem intact, carefully cut a slit along the length of one side of the chile, pry open, and remove the seeds and veins, trying not to tear the chile. Repeat with the remaining chiles. Fill the chiles with approximately 2 heaping tablespoons (25 g) of the shredded cheese and fold and tuck the cut edges tightly closed. Spread ⅓ cup (42 g) of the flour on a large plate; roll each chile in the flour, using the flour as an adhesive to keep the chile tightly closed and to retain its shape; set chiles aside as you finish. (This first coat of flour helps the batter to adhere.)

In a large mixing bowl, beat the 5 egg whites until they form stiff but not dry peaks. Combine the remaining flour, oregano, pepper, and salt in a medium mixing bowl. Beat the egg yolks thoroughly, then beat them into the flour mixture (the mixture will be dry and crumbly). Transfer approximately one-third of the egg whites into the bowl with the egg yolk–flour mixture, and use a handheld mixer to combine, adding a little more of the egg whites if too dry. The resulting mixture will be the consistency of very thick cake batter. Transfer this mixture to the remaining egg whites, and use a rubber spatula to fold gently to incorporate.

Return the oil in the skillet to 350°F (176°C). Roll the filled chiles one at a time in the egg-white mixture, generously coating them, then fry two at a time for 2–3 minutes. Gently lift one chile to check for doneness: it should be golden brown on the bottom; flip to the other side, and cook until golden brown, another 2–3 minutes. Transfer the finished chiles to paper towels to drain.

TO SERVE

Immediately before serving, preheat a comal, griddle, or cast-iron skillet; brush the comal with a bit of vegetable oil or lard. If you prepared the chiles in advance, reheat them for about one minute per side; heat one tortilla on each side for a few seconds until just warmed through. Place the chile atop the tortilla, and serve. Diners add their own salsa and squeezes of lime juice to taste.

[MC]

Directly across the aisle from "Antojito La Hermosa" was a table belonging to the family Ocaña Rodríguez; matriarch Vicky attended us. The lengthy name of their enterprise was tightly squeezed onto the front of their business card: Puesto "Cabeza de Res al Horno en Penca de Maguey" (Beef Head Oven Roasted in Maguey Leaf).

Whole *cabeza de res* (cow's head) is a popular offering in many states; it may be cooked in the style of *barbacoa*, or in Yucatán in the *píib* bathed in fragrant *recado para bistec*, but Vicky told me that her family wraps the head in softened maguey leaves, then roasts it in a baker's wood-burning oven. She easily tempted us with some of the *cachete*—cheek—treasured for its flavorful succulence.

Vicky had just arrived with the head and busied herself with unwrapping it, pulling off some of the meat for customers, then rewrapping it with the leaves to keep it warm. I wasn't sure if she was playing with me, or if this was just some odd part of her work rhythm, but several times she placed, then removed, and replaced the tongue in the hollow where it used to be in the skull. Tongue was our next taco.

LENGUA DE RES

SMOKED AND ROASTED BEEF TONGUE

In talking with Vicky about how her family roasts the cow head, it occurred to me that similar results could be achieved by following the method I offer for Barbacoa de carnero on page 363: lightly smoking the meat first, then roasting it. One tongue is enough to feed a substantial group of people when shredded and served as tacos. Shred only enough for the people you plan to serve; leave the rest whole, refrigerate it, and eat it sliced on sandwiches or as part of a plate of cold cuts.

Prepare-ahead note: For best results, the tongue benefits from a few days' brining, so plan ahead. Cooking takes close to 5 hours. You may prepare the tongue in advance, then coarsely chop or shred while still warm. If desired, reheat the meat in a bit of vegetable oil immediately before serving.

YIELD: 10—12 SERVINGS

FOR THE BRINE

½ cup (145 g) sea salt
½ cup (100 g) sugar
1 gallon (4 L) water
1 medium beef tongue
  (about 3 lbs./1.5 kg)

FOR THE MARINADE AND FINISHING

Ingredients for the marinade for
  Barbacoa de carnero, p. 363

FOR SERVING

Warm maize tortillas
Chopped white onion
Chopped cilantro
Lime wedges
Salsa de chile de árbol (p. 531)

[MC]

BRINE THE TONGUE

Add the salt and sugar to the water; stir well until completely dissolved. Add the tongue and refrigerate for 48 to 72 hours. At the end of the brining time, drain the tongue and rinse; discard the brining solution.

PREPARE THE MARINADE AND FINISH

Follow the instructions for Barbacoa de carnero on page 363 for preparing the marinade. Place the tongue in a large baking dish; pour the chile marinade over the tongue to cover it completely; refrigerate for 2 hours, then proceed with the rest of the recipe, wrapping the tongue in banana leaves, smoking for 30 minutes in a gas or charcoal grill with wood smoking chips or in a stovetop smoker, then finishing the roasting in the oven (place the wrapped tongue in a baking dish and omit the rack instructions). Omit the ingredients and instructions for the *consomé*. At the end of roasting, remove the tongue from the oven and immediately peel it (the tongue must be hot to peel; wear rubber gloves to protect your fingers). With a sharp knife, make an incision at the base and tip of the tongue, and peel the skin as you would remove a glove; discard the skin (it actually is edible, but most people don't care for it, since it is chewy and the taste buds are quite visible). Use a sharp knife to cut away any stubborn pieces.

TO SERVE

While the tongue is still warm, coarsely chop or shred it, and serve atop warm tortillas. Diners add their own garnishes and salsa to taste.

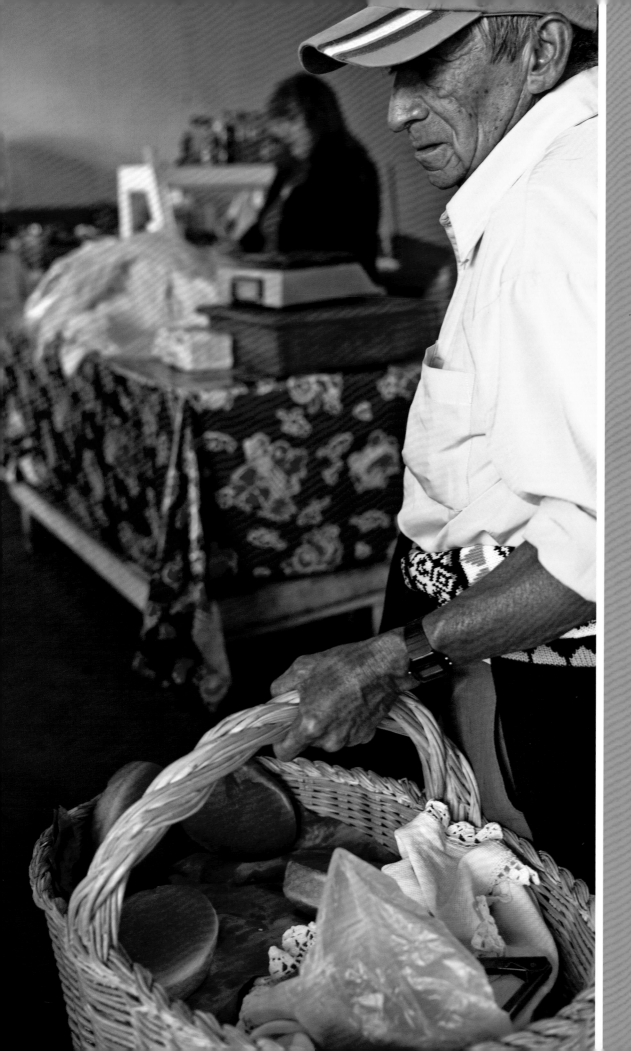

PAN DE CAJA/
PULQUE BREAKFAST BUNS

As we finished our tacos de lengua, a vendor passed through the market selling fresh Pan de caja from a basket. Throughout Mexico, *pan de caja* (box bread) usually refers to bread that is baked in a rectangular tin mold and then sliced for sandwiches, à la Wonder (here, Bimbo). But in Tlalpujahua, we were amused to find that these small ovoid buns had been molded and baked in recycled sardine tins. The vendor—who was also the baker—told me that he uses *asiento de pulque*, the dregs that accumulate at the bottom of the vats in which pulque is fermented. The only difference in taste that I noted between these and Pan de pulque was that these little buns were very buttery and would be wonderful for breakfast, perhaps toasted and served with fruit preserves. Follow the recipe on page 368, but substitute the Enriched Lard for an equal weight of unsalted butter. Butter round, square, or oval molds or cupcake tins (use squat recycled cans, such as those for tuna or sardines, if you have them); fill them halfway with dough, finish the rising time, then bake. [LP]

As in so many of Mexico's tiny pueblos, sacred and profane become unwitting bedmates as they are squeezed together along narrow cobbled streets, blurring spatial and conceptual boundaries between the two. At the topmost landing of the market—right next to an archway that opened to the Santuario del Carmen—was a colorful wagon offering almost twenty types of fruit conserves—*frutas en conserva*.

Conservas are popular in many states of Mexico, but Tlalpujahua is considered to be the capital of the art. Many of the sugary fruits we saw in the Mercado de Dulces in Morelia were prepared here. A couple of steep blocks down from our perch at the market, we visited Himelda Paredes Sámano of the Casa de Conservas, whose family has been in the business since 1933. She and her daughters carry on their grandmother's tradition. She walked us through the steps of preparing one of their most popular *conservas—chilacayote*.

[LP]

(left) Himelda uses a huge curved machete-like knife to whack away the tough rind of the watermelon-sized squash. [LP] *(center) Next, the squash is cut into sections; only tough fibers and sprouted seeds are removed; the rest remains.* [LP] *(right) Himelda stays ever vigilant about skimming any foam that accumulates during cooking.* [LP]

Chilacayote is a large species of the squash family, found from northern Mexico into South America (p. 114). The entire process for making *conserva de chilacayote* takes 48 hours, give or take an hour or two. After a 24-hour soak in a *cal* solution, it is then rinsed and drained and arranged around the walls of a huge copper cauldron. Water and many cones of *piloncillo* are added; it is brought to a boil and monitored vigilantly for another 24 hours until the syrup reaches the thread stage.

CONSERVA DE PERAS

CANDIED PEARS

Doña Himelda preserves many kinds of fruits using her family's method: Old World fruits like figs, apricots, and pears as well as several exotic Mexican fruits such as *tejocote* (*Crataegus mexicana*) and *ciruela* (*Spondias purpurea*). The smaller fruits are preserved whole and displayed in festive pyramid formations atop pedestal plates. The recipes for all are not as labor-intensive as that for *conserva de chilacayote*, but they are time-consuming, since the sugar needs time to absorb into the fruits through and through. However, the recipe for Conserva de peras can be achieved in a mere 16 hours, since the firm consistency of pears means that they do not require a *cal* soak. Start early in the day and finish by early evening. For a different kind of challenge, try the Conserva de melocotón—apricot conserve—which requires soaking in the *cal* solution to maintain the fruit's texture, although it only requires 12 hours of cooking (recipe below). Conserva de peras may be eaten as a dessert or sweet treat any time of day; it is lovely served at the end of a meal with a sliver of aged *queso Cotija*.

[LP]

FOR THE CONSERVA

4 cones piloncillo (about
  2.2 lbs./1 kg; substitute
  2 cups/440 g muscovado sugar)
1 gallon (4 L) water
1 teaspoon (2 g) whole cloves
1 dozen medium Bartlett pears
  (about 6½ lbs./3 kg total. *Note*:
  Choose pears that are just at
  the point of ripening, but still
  quite firm.)

[LP]

Prepare-ahead note: Conserva de peras takes a total preparation time of about 16 hours; active time is only about 1 hour. The finished *conserva* will last indefinitely under refrigeration; bring to room temperature before serving.

PREPARE THE CONSERVE

Place the *piloncillo* in a paper or plastic bag; use a wooden mallet or rolling pin to crush it coarsely. Place the *piloncillo* and water in a large, heavy stockpot, preferably copper. Bring the water to a boil, reduce to a simmer, stirring from time to time, until the sugar dissolves completely. Add the cloves, and continue at a simmer while you peel the pears.

With a paring knife, cut away strips of the peel from the stem to the bottom, leaving spaces between the strips unpeeled (this will help them retain their shape during cooking and also adds a pleasant flavor).

When all the pears have been peeled, carefully lower them into the boiling syrup (Himelda used a long wooden paddle to slide the fruits into the vat.) Return the syrup to a boil, reduce to a simmer, and stir to make sure the pears don't stick to the bottom of the pot. Skim frequently to remove any foam that accumulates on the surface. Maintain the heat at a simmer, stirring from time to time to keep the pears from sticking. After 1 hour, return the syrup to a boil; cook for about 15–20 minutes, then reduce to a simmer, stirring from time to time. Repeat this process, boiling for a few minutes every hour or so, then returning the heat to a simmer. Continue until you have cooked the pears for 15 hours.

At the end of the principal cooking time, raise the heat to boiling, and cook until a candy thermometer reaches the thread stage, 223°F–235°F (106°C–113°C). This should take close to another hour, depending on how much of your original liquid has evaporated.

When the cooking has finished, use a slotted spoon or wok strainer to remove the pears from the syrup. Transfer them to a large platter, and spoon on some of the syrup to cover. Refrigerate until set, and spoon on a bit more of the syrup. Repeat one or two more times, until you can no longer see the flesh of the pears through the syrup. The pears are now ready to eat.

VARIATION

Conserva de melocotón/Apricot Conserve: Choose underripe, firm apricots to the weight specified above. Do not peel the apricots; place them in a large stainless-steel bowl (glass or any other material will be damaged by the *cal* solution). Cover the apricots with water. In a smaller stainless-steel bowl, mix ¼ cup (62.5 mL) of water with 0.2 ounces (6 g) calcium hydroxide. Use a stainless-steel spoon to mix until the powder has dissolved. Pour the mixture into the water containing the apricots, stir briefly to cover the apricots with the solution, and allow the apricots to rest at room temperature for 2 hours. At the end of the soaking time, pour off the calcium hydroxide solution, and rinse the apricots thoroughly until you see no signs of the white-gray powder. Proceed with the recipe above, preparing the syrup first, then cooking the fruits. Cooking time is 12 hours; 1 hour before the finish, stop, and increase the heat as described to reach the thread stage.

ROSCAS DE PUCHA

GLAZED WHOLE WHEAT DIGESTIVES

FOR THE COOKIES

3 large eggs

¾ cup (192 g) muscovado sugar
(substitute dark brown sugar)

2 tablespoons (30 mL) tequila
añejo

1 cup (180 g) almonds, blanched

2 cups (250 g) organic whole
wheat flour

1 teaspoon (4 g) baking soda

1 teaspoon (4 g) tequesquite
(substitute baking powder.
Note: if you do not use the
tequesquite, add a pinch of salt
to the dough.)

FOR THE ICING

1 cup (250 mL) water

4 star anise (approximately 3 g)

1¼ cups (250 g) granulated sugar

1 egg white

Moments before our departure from the market, a woman and her children heaved three hefty baskets brimming with freshly baked sweet breads and cookies and deposited them just to one side of the path we had to cross in order to exit. Even after roundly filling ourselves at stalls inside the market, how could we resist one of these treats as we were leaving? She had several pulque breads, as well as treats made of crispy *bojaldra*. But what interested me most were the little rings known as *puchas*. The early-twentieth-century novelist and journalist Carlos González Peña wrote lovingly of the *puchas digestivas* he saw in the legendary Mexico City bakery Ambriz. Made with whole wheat flour, bicarbonate of soda, and *tequesquite* (p. 405), *puchas* are eaten for their purported health benefits—although I forgot to mention that they also contain tequila and are glazed with a sugary icing. Except for the glaze (which I flavor with a bit of anise), they are pleasantly bland. They are excellent for dunking into tea, coffee, or hot chocolate, in good biscotti fashion—and that is essentially what these are.

Prepare-ahead note: Roscas de pucha need to dry and harden for 24 hours, so plan ahead. The finished cookies last 2–3 weeks in an airtight container.

YIELD: 2 DOZEN

PREPARE THE COOKIES

Preheat the oven to 300°F (149°C); line a baking sheet with baker's parchment.

Break the eggs into the bowl of a stand mixer and add the sugar; beat on medium-high speed until the sugar is dissolved and the mixture is light and creamy; add the tequila and beat for 1 minute; set aside.

Place the almonds in the bowl of a food processor and process until they become a fine powder, about 3–4 minutes. Add the flour, baking soda, and *tequesquite* (or baking powder) and pulse to combine.

Transfer the flour mixture to the bowl containing the eggs and sugar, and beat until thoroughly incorporated, about 1–2 minutes.

Moisten your hands, and form the dough into 24 balls each weighing about 1 ounce (28 g). Use your finger to punch a hole through the center of one of the balls of dough; place it on the baking sheet, and use your fingers to open the hole slightly and form the cookie into a rough doughnut shape. Repeat with the remaining balls of dough.

Bake the cookies for 45 minutes, or until lightly browned and firm. Remove the cookies from the oven and allow them to cool and harden thoroughly at room temperature for 24 hours.

PREPARE THE ICING AND FINISH

Combine the water and the star anise in a small saucepan; bring to a boil, remove from the heat, cover, and allow to steep for 15 minutes; remove and discard the anise. Place a heatproof mixing bowl containing the egg white and a handheld electric beater near the stovetop. Beat the egg white until it forms stiff peaks. Mix the sugar with the water in the saucepan; place over high heat, swirling the pan gently until the sugar dissolves. As soon as the sugar syrup reaches 235°F (115°C) on a candy thermometer, remove the syrup from the heat. Resume beating the egg white; slowly drizzle the syrup in a thin stream into the white as you continue beating. Continue until the mixture begins to thicken and is satiny and shiny, about 1 minute.

Working quickly before the meringue hardens, take one of the cookies with your forefinger in the hole (or you may use the handle of a wooden spoon), and pass the top through the meringue to coat it. Place the cookie on waxed paper and continue with the rest of the cookies. Allow the cookies to dry and harden at room temperature for 24 hours before serving. Store in an airtight container.

[LP]

MARKET

FUNDAMENTALS

ABOUT MAIZE AND MASA

MAÍZ

The corn species broadly grown in Mexico is *maíz dentado* (*Zea mays* L. subs. *Mays indentata*), or "dent corn," named for the small impression marking each kernel. For millennia, the peoples of Mesoamerica have preserved this corn for long-term storage by drying it until it is rock hard. While dehydration is a good preservation strategy, these early peoples also learned that dried corn has at least two distinct disadvantages: it requires concerted effort to grind, and it is difficult to digest.

Nixtamal

To soften the corn, thereby reducing the labor required for grinding and easing its passage through the body, early Mesoamericans developed a method for rehydrating it. By boiling dried corn in water mixed with slaked lime (calcium hydroxide) or wood ashes or sometimes both, the corn softened, and the indigestible pericarp on each kernel dissolved and could be washed away. Unbeknownst to anyone until the advent of modern science, the process also greatly enhances the nutritional value of the corn: calcium content soars a dramatic 750 percent; bound niacin is released; and proteins increase a percentage point or two over raw corn. This rehydrated corn is known as "*nixtamal*," a word from the Nahuatl compound *nextli*, or "ashes," and *tamalli*, "bread of maize dough."

MASA

Masa in Spanish means "dough." There are many kinds of masa, such as those of wheat flour and leavening for making bread, or pastry dough for piecrusts. But the most common use of the word in Mexico refers to dough made of corn. When the rehydrated corn known as *nixtamal* is ground, it becomes a thick, pliable dough: masa. Dough prepared in this way with no other ingredients is the stuff from which tortillas are made. Tamales and other maize breads are also made of this masa, although these will typically include lard, chicken stock, beans, or other enrichments.

Masa Harina

Masa harina—or masa flour—is not cornmeal, nor can the two be used interchangeably. In fact, masa harina is a relative newcomer to Mexican gastronomy. The first successful mass production of masa harina did not occur until one year after the end of World War II, and its sole purpose was for the industrialization of tortilla making in newfangled machines. Masa harina is made in almost the reverse process from which masa is made: masa made of ground rehydrated corn (*nixtamal*) is subsequently dehydrated and finely ground into flour. Cooks then add water or stock to convert it back into dough—masa. In spite of being industrially produced, masa harina does have its uses, and you will find it included in many recipes in this book.

Preparing and Storing Masa

There are two basic methods for preparing corn masa: grinding *nixtamal*-ized corn into a stiff dough, or mixing masa harina with a liquid to create the dough.

Real masa made from *nixtamal* that you purchase at a *tortillería* or elsewhere requires no additional processing other than that described in the recipes found in this book. It should be used as soon as possible after purchase and kept tightly wrapped under refrigeration or frozen until needed.

Masa harina, with brand names like Maseca or Minsa, is widely available in the "ethnic" sections of most supermarkets. It will also say "masa harina" on the label, and it is packaged in small bags much like wheat flour. If you are not combining masa harina with *nixtamal*-ized corn masa (as in the basic recipe for Masa para tamales), you can prepare a basic quantity as follows:

Mix 4 cups (540 g) of masa harina with 2½ cups (625 ml) water and knead briefly to incorporate. Use the masa immediately, or wrap it tightly in plastic wrap and refrigerate or freeze until ready to use. You should have about 2 pounds (1 k) of masa.

PREPARING CORNHUSKS PARA TAMALES

Dried husks are available in most Latin American groceries or online.

Place the husks in a large stockpot, cover with water, and bring to a boil. Keep the husks submerged with a heatproof plate or bowl. Reduce the heat and simmer for 10 minutes. Remove the pot from the heat and allow it to stand for 2 hours. Remove a few husks at a time only when you are ready to use them and pat dry with a towel.

Separate the largest and most pliable husks to use for tamales; cut the smaller ones lengthwise into ¼-inch (6 mm) strips to use as ties.

WORKING WITH BANANA LEAVES

Banana leaves can be found in the freezer section of Asian or Mexican markets.

If you have access to fresh leaves, pass them briefly over an open flame to soften. If using fresh packaged leaves, gently wipe them with a damp towel. Frozen leaves are ready to use after thawing.

While there is no such thing as a standard size in nature, most of the packages of whole fresh leaves I purchase in Yucatán contain leaves that are, on average, 10 inches × 60 inches (25 cm × 150 cm). Frozen leaves are sized similarly. Due to tearing and deformities, you can rarely make use of the entire leaf, but save all but the smallest scraps to use as patches when you are wrapping something and the larger leaf tears.

Cut the sizes you will need all at the same time. Banana leaves are quite fragile, especially after being frozen and thawed, so you must work with them slowly and patiently. If you are not going to use the cut leaves immediately, place them in a resealable plastic bag, folding the largest leaves to fit, and freeze. The ribs also freeze well.

1. Unfold the leaves and place them flat on a work surface.
2. With scissors, cut off the central ribs (the thick "stem" that runs the length of the leaf). Cut or tear the ribs in half lengthwise and set them aside to use as ties.
3. Determine the size leaf you will need based on the kind of food you will be wrapping. Sizes that follow are approximate only, since you will have to conform to the natural contours of your leaves.

COOKING TAMALES

Cooking methods for tamales are as varied as tamales themselves. Most are steamed, but larger tamales are often baked; still others may be cooked over hot coals. In Yucatán, tamales may even be "buried" and cooked in the underground oven known in Mayan as a *píib*. Instructions for specific tamales are included with recipes, but here is a general guide for steaming, the most frequently used method in this book.

STEAMING

It's worth investigating your local Latin American market or online to see if you can find a proper tamale steamer (*vaporera*). These special pots have several advantages:

- They are large. No one in Mexico makes four or five tamales at a time; rather, they are prepared by the dozen or even by the hundreds. *Vaporeras* come in a variety of sizes, accommodating anywhere from thirty to eighty tamales or more. (If you are going to make tamales, remember: go for quantity. They freeze brilliantly and will make you the star of your next impromptu supper party.)
- They have a steam chamber. A convex groove running around the circumference of the interior toward the bottom of the pot provides a resting place for a removable perforated disk. A few inches of space separate the disk from the bottom of the pot; in this space goes the water that produces the steam. Wrapped tamales are stacked on top of the disk.
- They have tight-fitting lids. Actually, the structure of the pot/lid combination is such that the lid almost snaps or locks into place, trapping most of the steam inside. This aids even and thorough cooking.

The virtues of the custom equipment notwithstanding, it is easy enough to retrofit equipment you may already have.

Use a large stockpot fitted with a lid and place a cake rack at the bottom: the rack should be spaced at least 2 inches (5 cm) from the bottom of the pot; if yours isn't that high, you can make simple "booties" of crumpled aluminum foil attached to the rack to create the extra space. Place a weight on the lid during cooking to hold in steam.

BRINING MEATS

The act of soaking meats in salted water to improve flavor and tenderize them can improve their overall flavor and texture, and I recommend it frequently in this book.

Avoid overbrining, since meat proteins that have broken down too much can become mushy. Because brining increases the saltiness of the finished product, all recipes in this book that specify brining have been adjusted for salt content to account for the brining step.

RECOMMENDED BRINING TIMES

Chicken, whole	4–8 hours
Chicken, breast or pieces	2–3 hours
Pork, butt, shoulder, roast	12–48 hours
Pork, loin, chops	4–6 hours
Turkey, whole	12–48 hours
Turkey, breast or pieces	6–8 hours
Venison, roast	12–36 hours
Venison, chops, pieces	6–8 hours

BRINE SOLUTION

1 gallon (4 L) cold water
½ cup (145 g) sea salt
½ cup (100 g) sugar
2 teaspoons (8 g) whole black peppercorns, coarsely crushed
10 whole allspice berries, coarsely crushed

Dissolve the salt and sugar in the water and add the crushed allspice and peppercorns. (I have good luck dissolving the salt and sugar in cold water. It takes a little longer, but I find it is still faster than dissolving it in hot water and then letting the water cool. The water must be cold before adding the meat.) Place the meat in the brine and refrigerate for the specified time. Drain the meat, rinse under cold water, and pat dry with paper towels. Discard the brining solution. (*Note*: For larger cuts, you will double or triple the brine solution recipe, making sure to maintain the exact proportions of water to salt. The solution should completely cover the meat.)

VARIATIONS

For other flavor enhancements, add 2–3 crushed cloves of garlic, a couple of bay leaves, a small stick of *canela* (Mexican cinnamon), and/or 6–8 whole cloves.

SMOKING TECHNIQUES FOR THE HOME COOK

Since so many meats in Mexican markets are cooked over wood fires or coals (or buried among them), smoke is a key flavor in many of the dishes in this book. If you don't have access to a firepit or wood-burning oven, a smoky quality can be imparted to foods by means of the stovetop smoking method, the charcoal grill smoking method, or the gas grill smoking method. Cured meats with a more intense flavor of smoke require slow cooking in a special apparatus.

STOVETOP SMOKING METHOD

You will need the following:

- For large quantities of meat: a large cast-iron Dutch oven or roasting pan with a lid, approximately 9 quarts (9 L). For smaller quantities: a large cast-iron skillet at least 2½ inches (4 cm) deep, fitted with a lid. (*Note*: Because of the intense heat required for this method, enameled iron cookware is not recommended.)
- Heavy-duty aluminum foil
- 10–12-inch (25–30 cm)-diameter cooling rack, or one that fits comfortably in the bottom of your pot or skillet. The cooling rack needs to rest inside the pan or skillet about 1½ inches (4 cm) off the bottom of the pot; if your rack does not have legs, create them with balls of foil.
- 2 tablespoons (⅓ oz./10 g) wood smoking chips, preferably mesquite, dry, not soaked

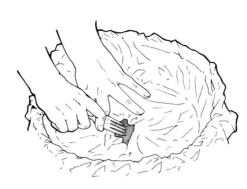

1. *Line the sides and bottom of the interior of a Dutch oven, roasting pan, or skillet with large pieces of foil. Leave at least 6 inches (15.25 cm) of foil extending beyond the edge of the pot on all sides.*

2. *Using a sharp object, cut and tear away a small hole in the foil at the center of the bottom about 3 inches (7.5 cm) in diameter to expose the pot's surface. Wrap the lid with aluminum foil and crimp tightly around the edges.*

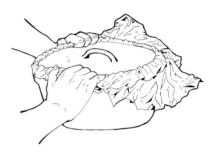

3. *Preheat the uncovered pot without the cake rack over highest heat for 10 minutes. Have food wrapped as per your recipe's instructions at hand. After preheating, place the smoking chips on the exposed surface where you cut away the foil.*

4. *Immediately place the rack at the bottom of the pot. Place the wrapped food on the rack, allowing space around packets so that steam and smoke can circulate. If you have an external-read thermometer, insert it into the meat, avoiding bone.*

5. *Put the lid in place and crimp the edges of the foil tightly all around to seal in the smoke and steam. When the food is done, remove the pot from the heat immediately and uncover to prevent overcooking.*

CHARCOAL GRILL SMOKING METHOD

You will need the following:

- Charcoal
- A shallow metal bowl or disposable aluminum roasting pan full of boiling water (only for meat or poultry)
- ½ cup (1½ oz./40 g) wood smoking chips, preferably mesquite, soaked in hot water for 30 minutes
- A grill or oven thermometer in the grill for an accurate heat reading
- An instant-read thermometer or standard meat thermometer

Preheat the grill, using plenty of charcoal. When the coals are red-hot, spread them to cover the bottom; they should extend from side to side. Place the pan full of water directly on top of the coals; replenish the water during cooking if necessary.

Arrange the prepared food in a grilling basket or tray. Drain the wood chips and spread half of them around the pan (add the remaining chips halfway through cooking time). Place the food on the lowest rack, directly above the pan of water. (*Note:* If you are charring vegetables, place them directly above or even on top of the hot coals, omitting the pan of water.)

Close the lid. For poultry, the internal temperature of the grill should be maintained at 350°F (176°C); you may also use this temperature for faster cooking of pork, beef, or venison. For slower roasting, maintain the grill temperature at 250°F (121°C). Cooking times will naturally vary according to your grill's condition, the cut of meat, and so on; use an instant-read thermometer from time to time to monitor the temperature. (*Note*: Resist the urge to open the lid for at least the first 30 minutes of cooking to avoid losing accumulated steam and smoke.)

GAS GRILL SMOKING METHOD

You will need the following:

- The same tools as for the charcoal grill smoking method, except charcoal
- ½ cup (1½ oz./40 g) wood smoking chips, preferably mesquite, dry, not soaked, loosely wrapped in aluminum foil to form a small pouch

Preheat the grill for 10 minutes. Place a metal pan full of water on the lowest grate, but *not* directly on the burners. Replenish the water during cooking if necessary.

Arrange the prepared food in a grilling basket or tray. Place the wood chip pouch under the grate, on top of a burner shield or as close to the flame as possible. Place the food on a grate directly above the pan of water. (*Note*: If you are charring vegetables, arrange them in a grilling basket and place it on the lowest rack, directly above the flame, omitting the pan of water.)

Refer to the temperatures in the instructions for the charcoal grill smoking method.

CHARRING VEGETABLES

Some cookbooks refer to this process as "toasting," others as "roasting." I call it what it is—charring—since the goal is thoroughly blackened, charred skin over at least 80 percent of the vegetable. The paper of garlic will have mostly burned away; tomatoes will be more black than red; all vegetables will be slightly softened from the cooking process.

Whichever charring technique is used, do not peel away the charred skin of a vegetable unless instructed to do so (as with many chiles) because the charring adds so much flavor. Peel onions before charring, then chop or use them as instructed in a recipe, leaving the charred bits intact. Whole heads of garlic are charred with the paper on; the paper is rubbed off afterward, but the separated cloves retain charring. Individual cloves of garlic are peeled and then charred. Tomatoes are charred whole and never peeled.

On a gas stove: Place onions, tomatoes, and large chiles directly on gas burners and use tongs to turn. Whole heads of garlic, garlic cloves, and smaller chiles can be placed on metal skewers and held directly in the flame. (*Note*: If you prefer to keep the heat-producing capsaicin in chiles from leaching into the food you are preparing, do not place the chiles on a skewer and take care that they do not rupture as you char them.)

On an electric stove: Place a cast-iron skillet or griddle on highest heat for 5 minutes. Arrange the vegetables in one layer on the preheated pan and turn occasionally. (Charring will take a bit longer than directly over a flame.)

On an outdoor grill: Place the vegetables in a perforated grilling basket and locate it either directly on the hot coals of a charcoal fire or close to the flame of a gas grill.

On charring garlic: Depending on the method you use, it can take 10–15 minutes to char a whole head. The ideal method is directly over a flame or on hot coals. The outer paper will catch fire; the garlic should display charring overall, and the paper should be mostly burned away. The head should be cooked and feel slightly soft when you squeeze it. Once the garlic has cooled, rub the black paper off between your palms, separate the head into sections, then into individual whole cloves, which will naturally pull away from any remaining paper. The cloves will have some charring still visible, which is important to the flavor.

ENRICHING LARD

Sadly, the lard (*manteca*) available commercially outside Mexico is highly processed, purified, and sometimes even hydrogenated. Commercial lard is white as snow and about as flavorful. With just a bit of effort, you can render your own; ample instruction for how to do so is available in other volumes or online. A simpler method, however, is to enrich commercial lard to approximate the qualities of lard from *chicharronerías*, which acquires its flavor from frequent boiling and from bits of burned meats that sink to the bottom of the frying vat. To achieve this end, I fry a bit of bacon in the pot as the lard melts and finish by boiling the lard for about 10 minutes more after removing the bacon, which may seem an agonizingly long time as your kitchen fills with smoke! (Be sure your kitchen is well ventilated, or, better yet, prepare it on your outdoor cooker.)

ENRICHED LARD

Prepare-ahead note: Enriched lard will stay fresh for 2–3 weeks under refrigeration. It freezes well and will keep for several months. Make as large a quantity of this recipe as you have storage room for, then divide it into several separate freezer containers.

YIELD: APPROXIMATELY 2 POUNDS (1 KG)

FOR THE LARD
3½ ounces (100 g) smoked slab bacon, cut into 3–4 large
    chunks
2 pounds (1 kg) unhydrogenated lard

PREPARE LARD
Place the bacon and lard in a large, heavy pot, preferably cast iron, over medium heat. As the lard liquefies, continue cooking at a gentle boil until the bacon is thoroughly cooked and browned, about 10 minutes.

    Remove the bacon and discard (or eat!). Raise the heat to high and boil the lard for an additional 8–10 minutes (see note above about smoke). Allow the lard to cool. Strain the cooled lard through a fine sieve into containers and cover. Refrigerate or freeze until ready to use.

MASA PARA TAMALES
MAIZE DOUGH FOR TAMALES

The maize dough for tamales found in Chiapas is particularly rich—a 2:1 ratio of masa:lard. It is so flavorful that I've opted to use this basic recipe for many other maize breads found in this book.

Prepare-ahead note: You may prepare the masa and refrigerate it for one or two days before making the tamales. Bring to room temperature before using.

    TO PREPARE AHEAD
    Enriched Lard (above)

YIELD: 3 POUNDS (1.5 KG)

FOR THE MASA
2 cups (500 g) Enriched Lard, *chilled*
1 tablespoon (12 g) baking powder
2 pounds (1 kg) fresh masa from nixtamal
½ cup (67.5 g) masa harina
½ cup (125 mL) rich chicken stock (substitute 3 Tbsp./36 g
    powdered chicken bouillon, dissolved in ½ cup/125 mL
    hot water)

PREPARE THE MASA
Place the chilled lard and baking powder in the bowl of a stand mixer; beat on high until light and fluffy, about 3 minutes. Add the masa from *nixtamal* a golf-ball-sized chunk at a time. There is no need to go slowly; immediately after adding one ball, add another, until you have added all of the masa. Add the remaining ingredients, and beat on medium for 2–3 minutes to lighten. Cover with a damp towel until ready to form the tamales, or wrap it tightly in plastic wrap to refrigerate or freeze.

FRIJOLES DE LA OLLA
ENRICHED POT BEANS

This is a basic recipe that works for almost any variety of dried bean and can be endlessly adapted.

YIELD: 8–10 SERVINGS

FOR THE BEANS

1 pound (500 g) dried beans

10 cups (2.5 L) water

1 large sprig fresh epazote (substitute 1 Tbsp./4 g dried)

FOR THE ENRICHMENT

½ cup (112 g) Enriched Lard

½ medium white onion (137.5 g), chopped

4 medium cloves garlic (1 oz./24 g), peeled and chopped

1 tablespoon (2 g) dried whole Mexican oregano, lightly
    toasted and ground

½ teaspoon (2.5 g) black pepper, ground

1 teaspoon (6 g) sea salt, or to taste

PARBOIL THE BEANS

Place the beans in a large pot and cover them with the water; add the epazote and bring to a boil. Reduce to a simmer and cook uncovered for about 1½ hours, or until the beans are just tender. Add more water as needed. Remove the epazote and discard.

PREPARE THE ENRICHMENT

Place the lard in a large saucepan and heat over medium-high heat until shimmering. Add the chopped onion and garlic cloves; stir constantly to prevent burning, and cook until the onions are just beginning to caramelize, 6–8 minutes. Add the oregano and pepper and stir to combine.

Transfer the enrichment to the pot with the beans, cook for another 15–30 minutes to integrate the flavors and ensure the beans are very tender. Add salt to taste.

SALSA DE CHILE DE ÁRBOL
FIERY TOMATO AND CHILE TABLE SAUCE

This intensely vinegary and picante salsa accompanies an enormous range of foods.

[MR]

Prepare-ahead note: Due to the high content of vinegar, the salsa keeps well under refrigeration for 2–3 weeks.

YIELD: APPROXIMATELY 2 CUPS (500 ML)

FOR THE SALSA

⅓ ounce (10 g) dried chile de árbol, stems cut off but seeds
    intact

6 medium Roma tomatoes (1⅓ lbs./600 g), quartered

½ medium white onion (5 oz./137.5 g), quartered

1 medium clove garlic (0.2 oz./6 g), peeled

1 cup (250 mL) water

1 tablespoon (15 mL) vegetable oil

¼ cup (62.5 mL) white vinegar

½ teaspoon (3 g) sea salt

PREPARE THE SALSA

Toast the chiles on a comal or in a cast-iron skillet until darkened and fragrant; transfer the chiles to the jar of a blender. Add the next four ingredients to the blender and process until very smooth. Pour the mixture through a fine-mesh sieve placed over a bowl; use a rubber spatula to press as much liquid through as possible; discard any residue. Heat the vegetable oil in a medium saucepan until shimmering; add all of the tomato mixture at once; it should splatter and sizzle, so stand back. Bring the sauce to a boil, reduce the heat to a simmer, and add the vinegar. Continue cooking, stirring frequently, until the sauce thickens slightly and the color intensifies, about 6–8 minutes. Add the salt and check for seasoning.

SALSA VERDE
FRESH SALSA OF TOMATILLOS AND CHILE

Tomatillos (*Physalis philadelphica* Lam.) are especially plentiful in the Central Highlands, and they figured prominently in the economy of the Aztecs. Today, salsa verde is served in markets across the country, though the key ingredient is rarely if ever called "tomatillo" in Mexico; instead, in the Central Highlands and most other regions, you will ask for *tomate*, whereas the red tomato is called *jitomate*; in the Yucatán Peninsula, the red fruit is called *tomate* and the tomatillo is called *tomate verde*. Uncooked, this sauce is eaten with chips as a dip or is spooned onto tacos. When cooked, it can serve as a dressing for foods such as Tlacoyos or Costillitas en salsa verde (p. 112). If the recipe calls for a cooked sauce, simply heat 1 tablespoon (15 mL) vegetable oil in a saucepan; when the oil is shimmering, add the sauce; cook over medium heat, stirring frequently, for another 3–4 minutes or until the sauce reduces and thickens slightly.

Prepare-ahead note: Since so many foods of Mexico call for salsa verde, make extra and freeze; the sauce keeps well frozen for 3–4 months, provided you plan on cooking it (it doesn't survive well for the fresh dip). Just before serving, defrost, stir, and heat as described above.

YIELD: APPROXIMATELY 4 CUPS (1 L)

FOR THE SAUCE
6 large tomatillos (1 lb. 5 oz./600 g), husks removed and discarded, washed
½ medium white onion (5 oz./137.5 g), coarsely chopped
2 medium chiles serranos (¾ oz./20 g), roughly chopped
4 large cloves garlic (1 oz./24 g), peeled and coarsely chopped
¼ cup (15 g) cilantro, coarsely chopped
½ teaspoon (3 g) sea salt

PARBOIL THE TOMATILLOS
Place the tomatillos in a medium saucepan; cover with water, bring to a boil, and cook uncovered 8–10 minutes until barely tender. Remove the tomatillos and reserve the cooking liquid.

PURÉE THE SAUCE AND FINISH
Place ⅓ cup (83 mL) of the reserved cooking liquid in the jar of a blender; discard the remaining liquid. Add the next four ingredients and process until very smooth. Add the tomatillos and purée until smooth. (*Note*: If using the salsa as a dip, process for less time to retain a more rustic texture.) Add the salt and check seasonings. Store in an airtight container and refrigerate; bring to room temperature prior to serving. Because of the mucilaginous properties of the tomatillo, the salsa should be stirred after it rests awhile and just before serving.

SALSA DE JITOMATE
COOKED TOMATO SAUCE

Salsa de jitomate is an indispensable cooked tomato sauce, versions of which appear throughout the republic, and with various uses. Douse tamales with it, bathe tortillas in it for making Entomatadas (p. 206), or use it as the basis for a quick cheese *botana* in Salsa de queso (p. 205). The "heat factor" of this sauce is a matter of taste, and the chiles used vary from region to region such that options are provided below. For a smoky flavor, use a *chile chipotle* in adobo instead. Experiment with your comfort level by adding one, two, or even more pieces of chile at a time until you reach the desired piquancy. The tomato paste is not typical—and therefore listed as an option—but it does help keep the sauce from separating when plated.

TO PREPARE AHEAD
Enriched Lard (p. 530)

YIELD: APPROXIMATELY 4 CUPS (1 L)

FOR THE PURÉE
2 pounds (1 kg) Roma tomatoes, charred and quartered
½ medium red onion (5 oz./137.5 g), peeled and charred

1 cup (250 mL) water

1 tablespoon (15 g) tomato paste (optional)

1 medium blond chile, such as Anaheim, Italian sweet, or banana pepper (1¼ oz./35 g) (substitute serrano or jalapeño chiles), charred, skin intact, and stem removed, or *chile chipotle* in adobo. *Note:* Read notes above about controlling heat.)

FOR FRYING AND FINISHING

½ cup (112 g) Enriched Lard

1 teaspoon (6 g) salt

PURÉE SAUCE

Working in batches as needed, place tomatoes and onion in a blender with the water and optional tomato paste; purée thoroughly. Slowly add slices of the chile through the feed hole until you get the desired heat level.

FRY SAUCE AND FINISH

In a large, heavy stockpot or saucepan with steep sides, heat lard until shimmering. Pour all of the tomato mixture in at once; it should spatter and sizzle, so stand back. Stir to incorporate; continue cooking over moderately high heat, stirring occasionally, about 10 minutes, or until the sauce begins to thicken. Reduce heat to a simmer and continue cooking another 10 minutes, or until sauce has turned a deep red color and reduced by about one-quarter. Add salt and stir to incorporate; check seasonings and serve.

SALSA DE MOLCAJETE
RUSTIC ROASTED TOMATO AND JALAPEÑO SALSA

This sauce is often prepared in and also served from a *molcajete* (a traditional type of stone mortar and pestle). If you have one, it makes a nice presentation. Grinding it in the *molcajete* will give the sauce the requisite rustic texture; otherwise, briefly pulse the ingredients in a food processor, taking care not to overdo it!

Prepare-ahead note: Salsa de molcajete keeps well under refrigeration for about 1 week; bring to room temperature before serving.

YIELD: ABOUT 1½ CUPS (375 ML)

FOR THE SALSA

½ teaspoon (3 g) coarse sea salt

1 large clove garlic (¼ oz./6 g), peeled and charred

2 large chiles jalapeños or 2 chiles manzanos (rocotos; 2½ oz./70 g total), or 4 chiles serranos (1½ oz./40 g total), or 1 medium chile habanero (¼ oz./7 g), charred and peeled, stems removed, seeds intact

6 medium Roma tomatoes (20 oz./600 g), charred and cored, skin intact

1 tablespoon (15 mL) white vinegar

PREPARE THE SALSA

Mash the salt and garlic in a *molcajete* or mortar and pestle until the garlic is completely softened and combined with the salt; add the chiles and mash until they are mostly disintegrated; add the tomatoes and mash until only a few small chunks are left. Add the vinegar, stir, and check the seasonings.

VARIATION

Many states have their own versions of Salsa de molcajete. In Michoacán, it is sometimes composed only of two or three chile varieties, with or without tomato. Experiment!

GLOSSARY

agua fresca. Refreshing drink made of water, puréed fruit, and sugar.

alambre. Literally "metal wire." In Mexico, the term is used to refer to bits of food skewered through a wire or stick for the purposes of grilling or roasting. Kebab, brochette; sometimes also called *brocheta*.

alcaparrado. From *alcaparras* (capers). Generally refers to a mixture of capers, olives, raisins, and sometimes almonds. A Hispano-Arabic introduction found in the cuisines of Cuba, Puerto Rico, and some regions of Mexico, particularly the Yucatán Peninsula.

almuerzo. Mid-morning snack. This is typically consumed between breakfast (*desayuno*) and the large afternoon meal (*comida*), usually around 11:00 a.m. In the United States, the meal might be called "brunch," and in the United Kingdom, "elevenses."

ambulante. Roving vendors not officially affiliated with a market or *tianguis*. Often without even a portable stall, they may be found seated with their wares spread before them on the floor of market interiors around the periphery.

asiento. Tiny meat and fat particles that settle (*asentarse* in Spanish) to the bottom of the pot during the process of rendering slabs of fat into lard.

ate. A kind of fruit paste made of nothing more than puréed fruit and sugar. The mixture is cooked down, much like jam, until it thickens; it is then poured into a mold and left to set. The finished texture is rather like a soft cheese. Several fruits may be used, but the most common are *membrillo* (quince) and *guayaba* (guava).

atole. A thick porridge made by diluting maize masa with water, then cooking it until it lightly thickens. *Atole* has almost limitless expressions, depending on the kind of maize used, the flavorings added, whether it is sweet or savory, and so on.

Aztec/Aztec Empire. The people who settled in the Valley of Mexico and built the great city of Tenochtitlán (now Mexico City) called themselves *Mexica*, origin of the word "Mexico." However, nineteenth-century proto-archaeologists Alexander von Humboldt and William Prescott popularized the name Aztec, referring to Aztlán, the original home (real or mythical) of the Mexica. Even though today it is considered a misnomer, "Aztec" is so commonly used that for the sake of clarity in this book it may be employed more frequently than "Mexica." The term "Aztec Empire" is also misleading and should more appropriately be called the "Mexica Triple Alliance," since this political entity was actually an alliance of three city-states—Mexico-Tenochtitlán, Texcoco, and Tlacopan—that ruled in the Valley of Mexico in the fifteenth and sixteenth centuries.

botana. Appetizer or light snack often served with beer or other alcoholic beverages.

brining. Many vintage Mexican recipes for meat refer to *salmuera*, or brine. However, brining is a strategy not commonly used today. Still, considering the benefits it provides to the flavor and texture of meat, it is recommended as a step in several recipes in this book. For a basic brine solution, use 1 gallon (4 L) water to ½ cup (100 g) salt. Additional flavorings such as crushed garlic, black peppercorns, and allspice may also be included. Brining times under refrigeration vary according to the type and weight of meat; specifications are available in other sources or online. If you do opt for brining, you may wish to adjust the salt quantities specified in the recipe.

café de olla. Coffee sweetened with *panela* or *piloncillo* and flavored with *canela*. It is brewed and kept hot in a large pot (*olla*), traditionally made of clay.

cajeta. A type of caramel sauce typically based on sweetened goat's milk. When mixed with cow's milk or with cow's milk alone, it may be called *dulce de leche* or *leche quemada* in some regions. *Cajeta* may be used as a topping for ice cream, as a filling for crêpes or cookies, or as a spread on bread.

cal. Calcium hydroxide. This white powder or crystal occurs when calcium oxide is mixed with water, a combination known as "slaked lime." *Cal* has many uses in Mexico, including being combined with pigment to form a strongly adherent paint for stucco; mixed with water and a fine aggregate to create cement for building; or to rehydrate dried maize, a process known as *nixtamal*-ization (see below).

caldo. Stock, broth, soup.

campesino. Peasant. Because of the root *campo* (countryside) in the word, it refers simply to someone who lives in the country and does not bear the same pejorative connotation that the word "peasant" does in English.

canela. *Cinnamomum verum*, or "true cinnamon." Also known as Mexican cinnamon or Ceylon cinnamon to distinguish it from its cousin, *Cinnamomum cassia*. True cinnamon is so called because it was the aromatic bark traded on the Asian spice route considered to be of superior quality to cassia and was therefore more expensive; in medieval times and beyond, debates raged as to the distinction between the two, and merchants often tried to pass off the cheaper cassia as Ceylon cinnamon. Botanist Jan Presl (1791–1849) was aware of these debates and assigned binomials to both species to set the issue straight once and for all. Outside of Mexico, *canela* is widely available under the name "Mexican cinnamon." Because it has a lighter, more delicate aroma and flavor, it is recommended for use in the recipes in this book.

carnicería. Butcher shop.

cazo. A large, steep-sided cooking pot often in the form of a truncated cone with a flat bottom and two handles on either side. Usually made of metals such as stainless steel, aluminum, or copper. See photo on page 501.

cazuela. Cooking pot, stew pot, or casserole traditionally made of clay.

central de abasto. Central supply. These are large wholesale warehouses that generally supply many or all of the smaller markets within a region.

charring, charred. Many ingredients used throughout Mexico are charred before being incorporated into a dish. This may be achieved by placing the ingredient directly in a heat source (the flames of a grill or stove) or on a comal or in a cast-iron skillet placed on the highest heat. The finished product should be blackened in patches overall.

chicharrón. Crispy fried pork skin; also known as "cracklings" or "pork rind."

Chichimeca. Historically, a term used by Nahuatl-speaking peoples to refer to several nomadic tribes in northern Mexico. During the colonial period, the Spanish adopted the word to signify "barbarian," particularly since these various tribes occupied mineral-rich lands that the Spanish wanted to conquer; the term therefore served as a rationalization for their conquest. Some of the original tribes, such as Otomí, Tepehuan, Pame, Huichol, and a few others, still occupy parts of modern Mexico, although they each maintain discrete identities. The only ethnolinguistic group still associated directly with the Chichimecas is the Chichimeca-Jonaz, who primarily reside in the modern Mexican states of Guanajuato and San Luis Potosí.

chiffonade. A type of cut used for leafy green vegetables. Stack several leaves of the vegetable, roll tightly, then cut crosswise, perpendicular to the roll, to create narrow "ribbons."

cocina. Related to the French *cuisine*, "cooking," or, alternatively, "kitchen."

cocina económica. Literally "economical cooking." Today, in many regions, the term has come to refer to small family-run restaurants or cafés that operate out of the family home.

colonial. In the case of Mexico, the word refers specifically to the period of the three centuries marked by Spanish rule, from 1521 to 1821.

comal. Round, flat griddle used for cooking tortillas and toasting a wide range of foods. Original comales may have been made of stone; later ones were clay; and, today, they may be of steel or cast iron as well as clay.

comedor. Dining room. In some parts of Mexico, the word refers not only to a particular room in a house but also to eateries located within markets. See also fonda.

crema. Slightly soured and thickened cream, similar to the French crème fraîche. Not to be confused with *media crema*, which has between 15 percent and 18 percent milk fat and is called table cream in some countries.

Creole. As used in this book, a person born in Latin America but of European, usually Spanish, ancestry.

criollo. The Spanish word for "Creole."

dulce. Candy, sweets, or the adjective "sweet."

empanada. Literally "breaded" or "wrapped in bread." Small, filled, wheat-flour or maize-dough pastries typically in a half-moon shape. They may be sweet or savory, baked, fried, or cooked on a comal.

encomienda. During the colonial era, the right granted by the Spanish Crown to exact tribute and forced labor from the native inhabitants of a given area.

Enriched Lard. Most commercial lard you will find beyond Mexico will be insipid. To achieve an excellent flavor, either render your own (ample instruction is offered in other books or online), or else you may "enrich" commercial lard by frying it with some smoked slab bacon. Use approximately 2 pounds (1 kg) of lard to 4 ounces (113 g) bacon. Fry until the bacon is cooked through; remove and put to another use. Continue to boil the lard for 8–10 minutes to darken the color and intensify the flavor. Allow the lard to cool, strain into a container, cover, and refrigerate or freeze until ready to use.

epazote. *Dysphania ambrosioides*, one of Mexico's many wild herbs known as *quelites*. Epazote is broadly consumed throughout the country, often used when cooking beans. It is also a common ingredient in certain quesadillas. Many people beyond Mexico are having luck growing this perennial, and it is increasingly found in farmers' markets in some places. The more widely available dried epazote may be used in cooked foods such as beans, but when the whole leaf will be visible, such as in quesadillas, only fresh should be used.

escabeche. Pickle, from the verb *escabechar*, "to pickle." Any number of foods—vegetables, chiles, even turkey—may be preserved or cooked in acids like vinegar or citrus such as lime or sour orange. *En escabeche* means "pickled."

ethnolinguistic group. Indigenous groups that are linked by language and other cultural characteristics.

fonda. A diner or eatery, often located within the market setting. See also comedor.

guisado/guiso. "Stew" or "casserole"; the term may also be used generally to refer to many types of prepared foods, in-cluding those used as fillings for a variety of maize breads, such as quesadillas or gorditas. May also mean "cooked" or "stewed" as in *hongos guisados* (cooked mushrooms).

hacienda. A plantation or country estate dedicated to the production of any number of agricultural products.

hojaldra. The French *pâte feuilletée*: puffy sheets of paper-thin pastry created by the repetitive folding of alternate layers of flour and butter. Used in the preparation of many baked goods in Mexico, mostly sweet, some savory.

julienne. A culinary term for a knife cut that results in long, thin strips, or "matchsticks."

maguey. Any of a number of species of plant in the genus *Agave*, most particularly *Agave americana*.

maize. The Old English word "corn" derives from the Germanic *Korn*, which means simply "grain." To be accurate, then, wheat, barley, rye, rice, maize, and many other grains are types of "corn." The word as well as the taxonomy *Zea mays* derive from the Antillean Taino word for the grain, *mahís*, which the Spanish transcribed as *maíz*. The word "maize" is used throughout this book interchangeably with "corn" although with greater frequency.

masa. Literally "dough," related to the verb *amasar*, "to knead." In general throughout Mexico, masa most often refers to dough made of ground *nixtamal*, dried field corn that has been rehydrated by cooking it with slaked lime. Maize masa is a major component of the Mexican diet, found in everything from breads like tortillas, tamales, and quesadillas to beverages like *atole* and pozole. It is also used as a thickener. For the recipes in this book, real masa from *nixtamal* is recommended; it may be found in *tortillerías* in Latin neighborhoods or shrink-wrapped in the refrigerated section of Mexican markets. If you cannot locate it, prepare the specified weight of masa using masa harina according to the manufacturer's instructions on the package.

masa harina. A flour made by grinding dehydrated masa made from *nixtamal*. The product was invented in the 1940s as a means of industrializing the production of tortillas. Mixed with water, the resulting masa may be used for tortillas, tamales, and various other maize breads, but the flavor and texture are significantly inferior to real masa from *nixtamal*.

matorral. Scrubland characterized by a Mediterranean climate.

media luna. Literally "half-moon"; a typical way of slicing an onion throughout most of Mexico. Cut the peeled onion in quarters, top to bottom, then thinly slice each quarter top to bottom. Separate the layers of each slice into thin half-moon shapes.

Mesoamerica. "Mesoamerica" is a word you will find in many instances throughout this book. The term was first used in 1943 by the German anthropologist Paul Kirchhoff to describe one of two great civilizations that emerged independently in the Americas: the one he dubbed "Mesoamerica" (Middle America) covered a vast territory ranging roughly from the central Mexican states of Hidalgo and Querétaro, west to Michoacán and east to Veracruz, and south to include the remaining southern Mexican states and parts of Central America; the other great civilization was that of the Incas in Peru. Kirchhoff noted that all of the discrete cultural groups of Mesoamerica were united by several key traits: a sedentary existence based on a sophisticated agricultural system dominated by the production of maize, beans, squash, and chiles; the construction of stepped pyramids; the use of two distinct calendars; an advanced numerical system; pictographic and hieroglyphic writing systems; the so-called Mesoamerican ballgame using a dense rubber ball; a religious complex based on natural deities as well as shamanism and the belief in sacrifice; and several other unifying elements. The expression of the disparate cultural groups that Kirchhoff collected under the umbrella term "Mesoamerican civilization" spanned many centuries, appearing in about 12,000 BCE and ending dramatically in 1521 CE with the conquest of Tenochtitlán by the Spanish.

mestizaje. Miscegenation, interbreeding, commingling—in this book, specifically the mixture of indigenous people with European, particularly Spanish, peoples. The term may also have a culinary application when native and European foods and cooking techniques merge to create something new.

metate. From the Nahuatl *metlatl.* A flat grinding stone used for processing maize, seeds, nuts, chiles, or any of a variety of ingredients.

Mexica. Nahua peoples; speakers of Nahuatl; today erroneously called "Aztecs." A pre-Columbian indigenous group that occupied the great city of Tenochtitlán in the Valley of Mexico and that formed, along with the allied cities of Texcoco and Tlacopan, the powerful Mexica (Aztec) Triple Alliance.

mezcal. A distilled liquor made from the sap or juice of the maguey plant. See page 191.

milanesa. A cut of pork, chicken, or beef that is thinly sliced and/or pounded. The thinness of the cut ensures tenderness and quick cooking.

milpa. The traditional crop field containing domesticated crops such as maize, beans, squash, tomatoes, chiles, and several other species.

mistela. Probably from the Latin *mixtus,* or "mixed." An alcoholic beverage found in several states of Mexico made of aguardiente (literally "burning water") distilled from sweet musts or sugarcane, and flavored with any number of ingredients or fruits such as *canela,* Seville orange peel, anise, *nance* (p. 46), *ciruela,* or mango.

molcajete. From the Nahuatl *mollicaxtli (molli* = "sauce" + *caxtli* = "bowl"). A stone mortar and pestle used for grinding seeds, nuts, spices, and a range of other ingredients.

mole. From the Nahuatl *molli* = "sauce." The generic term for a mixture of ground chiles, nuts, seeds, spices, herbs, and other ingredients used as an accompaniment to or cooking medium for meats or vegetables. Many varieties of mole are found throughout Mexico; the state of Oaxaca claims at least seven. Some feature chocolate; most do not.

muscovado sugar. A dark, unrefined or semirefined sugarcane sugar with high molasses content.

Nahuatl. Language of the Nahua peoples, among whom were the Mexicas, also known as Aztecs. Nahuatl is the indigenous language most extensively spoken in modern Mexico.

nata. Mexican clotted cream. It is the thick cream that congeals and rises to the top of whole milk when it is boiled. *Nata* is used throughout Mexico in many breads and other baked goods.

nixtamal. From the Nahuatl *nextamalli (nextli* = "ashes" + *tamalli* = "maize dough"). Dried field corn that has been rehydrated in a solution of water and slaked lime (calcium hydroxide). The process strips away the indigestible pericarp; unbinds niacin, making it possible for the body to absorb it; and increases the calcium content of the corn by some 750 percent. The resulting corn is also softened and easier to grind than dried maize. The process has been used in Mesoamerica since about 1500 BCE.

nopal; *nopalito.* From the Nahuatl *nopalli (Opuntia* spp., prickly pear cactus; see p. 326). "Nopal" is the generic term for the plant but may also refer to the pads or paddles that are consumed. *Nopalito(s)* generally refers to the prepared pads when they are sliced, cooked, and used in various dishes.

olla. Cooking pot or stockpot made of metal or clay. May also refer to *olla de presión*, or pressure cooker.

Olmec. The first major civilization in Mesoamerica, flourishing roughly from 1500 BCE to 400 BCE. Original development occurred in the Soconusco region of Chiapas (p. 79), but the people later settled in the Gulf Coast lowlands of Tabasco and Veracruz. The Olmecs are believed to have originated many hallmarks of later Mesoamerican culture, including the sacred ballgame, ritual bloodletting, writing, and the Mesoamerican calendar. Artistically, they are known for carving colossal stone heads as well as for fabricating superb jade masks and figures.

orégano. Any one of a number of species of the genus *Lippia*. Native to Mexico and not to be confused with so-called Mediterranean oregano, of the *Origanum* genus. This widely used herb is available beyond Mexico as "Mexican oregano."

panela. Refers to *pan* (bread) because of its loaf shape. In Mexico, *panela* may be a kind of fresh cow's milk cheese, or a molded brick of unrefined sugar high in molasses content (see p. 120).

pasta. Paste. In this book, *pasta* may refer to pastes made of chocolate, puréed beans, or cooked fruit.

penca. The large, fleshy leaf of any of several plant species, particularly *Agave* spp. and *Opuntia* spp.

picadillo. Diminutive of *picado*, "chopped." Typically refers to chopped meats, particularly pork, that are cooked with other ingredients and served over rice, formed into meatballs, or stuffed into sausage casings.

píib. An underground oven used for cooking a wide range of foods, from meats and vegetables to stews and tamales. Foods cooked in a *píib* are smoked and steamed simultaneously.

piloncillo. A cone-shaped block of dark, semirefined or unrefined sugar high in molasses content. In some regions, a block-shaped form of the sugar may be called *panela*. Both sugars are used plentifully throughout the country in the preparation of candies, candied fruits, and other sweets, as well as to sweeten coffee, as in *café de olla* (p. 535).

poblano. The word referring to one who or that which is from the state of Puebla.

Porfiriato. The decades from 1876 until 1911 when Mexico was ruled by the dictatorial president Porfirio Díaz. The era corresponds to the Belle Epoque in Europe and the Gilded Age in the United States. In Mexico, the period saw many sweeping changes, including the widespread development of railroads and a greatly increased focus on public education. Díaz had a passion for all things French, and these years witnessed the introduction into Mexico of many aspects of French culture, including art, architecture, and gastronomy.

portales. Porticos. These are the covered, arched passageways that often trim large public buildings in Mexico. Permanent or provisional markets are often held beneath *portales*.

pueblo. Small town or village. The word may also refer to the people who live in the village.

puesto. For the purposes of this book, a market stall.

P'urhépecha. Sometimes spelled Purépecha. The term is widely used among scholars as the "correct" term for the Tarascans. However, in the sixteenth century, the term was generally translated as the Nahuatl equivalent of *macehualtin*, or "commoner," and thus when P'urhépecha was applied to the language, it meant "language of the commoners." Today, P'urhépecha is the term applied to a language and also to an ethnolinguistic group that resides in Michoacán, with smaller populations in Guerrero and Guanajuato. See page 482.

quelites. From the Nahuatl, *quilitl*. Among the thousands of leafy plant species noted by the indigenous peoples of central Mexico, the ones that they determined to be edible were those they dubbed the generic name *quilitl*. While many Mexican cookbooks describe *quelites* as wild herbs, the description is not wholly accurate: some *quelites* were (and are) used as flavorings much like herbs, yet many others were what we might think of as "leafy green vegetables." It is better to say more broadly that they are a wide variety of edible plants. Those like herbs have small, soft, flexible stems; others are more like bushes; and a few grow to be more like small trees. The common attribute is that the leaves, stalks, flowers, and/or fruits of these plants are consumed. Some investigators estimate that in Mexico there are some five hundred wild species of *quelites*. Most *quelites* grow spontaneously during the rainy season, spreading naturally, and require no tending by humans. A few *quelites*, such as amaranth, were long ago selected for cultivation. Most *quelites* are concentrated in central Mexico and they appear, almost like weeds, in crop fields, in family gardens or orchards, and in woodlands. Some *quelites* that are more or less well known beyond Mexico are Mexican oregano (p. 396), epazote, and *verdolaga* (purslane, p. 400). *Quelites* are employed in a wide variety of ways: as flavorings, or as the equivalent of "green leafy vegetables" in salads, soups, bean dishes, or with cheese in quesadillas. *Quelites* are high in vitamins and minerals; many have antioxidant properties.

rajas. Slices or strips, most typically of chiles such as jalapeños or poblanos.

recado. A spice mixture in powdered or paste form used for seasoning a wide variety of foods. *Recados* are particularly associated with the gastronomy of the Yucatán Peninsula.

salpicón. The word may derive from the French *salmigondis*, or hodgepodge. *Salpicón* refers to any of a range of mixtures of chopped vegetables and sometimes to a chopped vegetable and meat mixture. A *salpicón* of chopped onion and cilantro appears as a common garnish on many foods; often the mixture will also contain chopped chiles. A *salpicón* of shredded cabbage, radish, red onion, cilantro, and *chile habanero* is used frequently in Yucatán in combination with shredded meats such as venison, beef, pork, or chicken to create something rather like a Cobb salad, eaten taco-style atop fresh maize tortillas.

Salsa Valentina. A commercially bottled hot sauce made in Guadalajara, Jalisco, that is popular throughout Mexico and claimed to be the best-selling sauce in the country. It is often doused onto tacos or other foods at the moment of eating, and it is particularly popular sprinkled onto fresh fruits.

sazón. Literally "seasoning." When you say that someone has a good *sazón* in Mexico, it means that they have a knack for cooking.

sofrito. The past participle of the Spanish *sofreír*, "to sauté." Depending on the region, *sofritos* are typically composed of a mixture of onion, garlic, peppers, and tomatoes lightly fried in oil. *Sofritos* serve as the flavoring base for rice, stocks, and a variety of cooked sauces.

stovetop smoking. A method of adding a smoky flavor to foods by placing wood chips with the food in a tightly closed cooking utensil atop the stove. Simple instructions may be found in *Yucatán: Recipes from a Culinary Expedition* as well as in various online sources.

Tarasco, Tarascan. A misnomer applied by the Spanish to the P'urhépecha peoples (see above). The word was a bastardization either of *tarascue*, "in-law," referring to the fact that the Spanish took indigenous women as concubines, or of *tharés*, the native word for "idol." Scholars generally regard it as a completely inappropriate word to describe the culture, and yet its popularity in the common lexicon prohibits avoiding it in this book. The so-called Tarascan Empire occupied much of the modern state of Michoacán and beyond, and the Tarascan people fought fiercely with the Aztecs, whose empire abutted theirs.

terroir. The soil, climate, and other growing conditions that contribute to the unique characteristics of particular foods.

tianguis. From the Nahuatl *tianquiztli*, "marketplace." Today the term may apply to a provisional market with covered stalls arranged in a large, open lot, or it may refer to a regularly occurring outdoor market surrounding a larger market building.

totopos. From the Nahuatl *totopoch*, "well toasted." These are tortillas or fractions of tortillas fried or baked until very crisp. *Totopos*, as pieces, may be used for dips or as garnishes for soups, and when whole (more typically called *tostadas*), as a crispy taco base for a variety of toppings.

vaporera. A large covered pot with a water chamber at the bottom used for steaming tamales. These are commercially available, but you may also use a vegetable steaming basket placed over water in a large stockpot fitted with a lid.

BIBLIOGRAPHY

Adams, Richard E. W., and Murdo J. MacLeod, eds. *The Cambridge History of the Native Peoples of the Americas*. Vol. 2, *Mesoamerica*, Part 2. Cambridge: Cambridge University Press, 2000.

Adams, Ryan. "Offal of the Week: Lungs." *Eat Me Daily* (blog), August 21, 2009. www.eatmedaily.com/?s=offal+of+the+week%3A+lungs.

Alfaro, A. "El chile poblano." *La Prensa*, November 12, 2003. Accessed August 4, 2014. http://impresa.prensa.com/opinion/chile-poblano_0_1058144390.html.

Alonso, R. A., C. Moya, A. Cabrera, Pilar Ponce, R. Quiroga, M. A. Rosales, and J. L. Zuart. "Evaluación *in situ* de la variabilidad genética de los chiles silvestres (*Capsicum spp.*) en la región frailesca del estado de Chiapas, México." *Cultivos Tropicales* 29, no. 2 (2008): 49–55. http://www.redalyc.org/articulo.oa?id=193214882008.

Andrews, Anthony P. "Long-Distance Exchange among the Maya: A Comment on Marcus." *American Antiquity* 49, no. 4 (October 1984): 826–828.

Andrews, Jean. *Peppers: The Domesticated Capsicums*. New ed. Austin: University of Texas Press, 1995.

Arias Toledo, Ariel Alain, María Teresa Valverde Valdes, and Jerónimo Reyes Santiago. "Las plantas de la región de Zapotitlán Salinas, Puebla." Mexico City: Instituto Nacional de Ecología—SEMARNAT, Universidad Nacional Autónoma de México, 2001.

Arreola, Juan José. "Buscan denominación de origen del chile pasilla en Tequisquiapan." *El Universal*, February 19, 2006. http://archivo.eluniversal.com.mx/estados/60247.html.

Attolini, Amalia. "Los mercados más antiguos de México." *Mi México de ayer*, November 13, 2010. http://mimejicodeayer.blogspot.com/2010/11/los-mercados-mas-antiguos-de-mexico.htm.

Baños Ramírez, Othón. "The Decline and Collapse of Yucatan's Henequen Agro-Industry: Neoliberalism Reconsidered." In *Peripheral Visions: Politics, Society, and the Challenges of Modernity in Yucatan*, ed. Edward D. Terry, Ben W. Fallaw, Gilbert M. Joseph, and Edward H. Moseley, 144–169. Tuscaloosa: University of Alabama Press, 2010.

Barros, Cristina, and Marco Buenrostro. "Itacate: Hongos de maíz." *La Jornada*, Sección Cultura, July 12, 2011. http://www.jornada.unam.mx/2011/07/12/opinion/a0601cul.

———. "Itacate: Palmito y coyol." *La Jornada*, Opinión, February 1, 2011. http://www.jornada.unam.mx/2011/02/01/opinion/a0801cul.

Bedoya, Claudia A., and Victor H. Chávez Tovar. "Teocintle: El ancestro del maíz." *Claridades Agropecuarias*, no. 201 (May 2010): 32–42.

"Berro de agua." *Biblioteca Digital de la Medicina Tradicional Mexicana*, UNAM. Accessed November 15, 2014. http://www.medicinatradicionalmexicana.unam.mx/monografia.php?1=3&t=Berro_de_agua&id=7249.

Bishko, Charles Julian. "The Peninsular Background of Latin American Cattle Ranching." *The Hispanic American Historical Review* 32, no. 4 (November 1952): 491–515.

Blanton, Richard E., Gary M. Feinman, Stephen A. Kowalewski, and Linda M. Nicholas. *Ancient Oaxaca*. Cambridge: Cambridge University Press, 1999.

Bonilla-Barbosa, Jaime Raúl, and Betzy Santamaría Araúz. "Plantas acuáticas exóticas y traslocadas invasoras." In *Especies acuáticas invasoras en México*, coord. R. Mendoza and P. Koleff, 223–247. Mexico City: Comisión Nacional para el Conocimiento y Uso de la Biodiversidad, 2013.

Bowen, Sarah, and Ana Valenzuela Zapata. "Geographical Indications, *Terroir*, and Socioeconomic and Ecological Sustainability: The Case of Tequila." *Journal of Rural Studies* 25, no. 1 (January 2009): 108–119. doi:10. 1016/j.jrurstud.2008.07.003.

Bowes, Gemma. "Mexico's Cultural Revolution." *The Guardian*, October 14, 2011.

Bravo Hollis, Helia, and Léia Scheinvar. 1999. *El interesante mundo de las cactáceas*. 2nd. ed. Mexico City: Fondo de Cultura Económica, Colección Sección de Obras de Ciencia y Tecnología, 1999.

Breedlove, Dennis E., and Robert M. Laughlin. *The Flowering of Man: A Tzotzil Botany of Zinacantán*. Vol. 2. Washington, D.C.: Smithsonian Institution Press, 1993.

Bromley, R. J., and Richard Symanski. "Marketplace Trade in Latin

America." *Latin American Research Review* 9, no. 3 (Autumn 1974): 3–38.

Brown, Kendall W. *A History of Mining in Latin America from the Colonial Era to the Present*. Albuquerque: University of New Mexico Press, 2012.

Caballero Nieto, J., A. Martínez, and V. Gama. "El uso y manejo tradicional de la palma de guano en el área maya de Yucatán." *Biodiversitas* (CONABIO) 39 (2001): 1–6. http://www.biodiversidad.gob.mx/Biodiversitas/Articulos/biodiv39art1.pdf.

Carrasco Vargas, Ramón, Verónica A. Vázquez López, and Simon Martin. "Daily Life of the Ancient Maya Recorded on Murals at Calakmul, Mexico." *Proceedings of the National Academy of Sciences of the United States of America* 106, no. 46 (November 2009): 19245–19249.

Cartwright, Mark. "Toltec Civilization." *Ancient History Encyclopedia*. September 9, 2013. http://www.ancient.eu.com/Toltec_Civilization/.

Casas, Alejandro, Alfonso Valiente-Banuet, Juan Luis Viveros, Javier Caballero, Laura Cortés, Patricia Dávila, Rafael Lira, and Isela Rodríguez. "Plant Resources of the Tehuacán-Cuicatlán Valley, Mexico." *Economic Botany* 55, no. 1 (January–March 2001): 129–166.

Castillo Aja, Horacio (coord.). *Recetario indígena de la Sierra Norte de Puebla*. Vol. 6 of Cocina Indígena y Popular. Mexico City: CNCA-DGCPI, Dirección General de Publicaciones, 2003.

Chadwick, Ian. "In Search of the Blue Agave: Tequila and the Heart of Mexico." May 2011. http://www.ianchadwick.com/tequila/pulque.htm.

Cheers, Gordon (publisher). *Botanica: The Illustrated A–Z of Over 10,000 Garden Plants and How to Cultivate Them*. 3rd ed. Cologne, Germany: Könemann, 1999.

Clavigero, Francesco Saverio. *The History of Mexico, Collected from Spanish and Mexican Historians, from Manuscripts and Ancient Paintings of the Indians*. Translated from Italian by Charles Cullen. London: G. G. J. and J. Robinson, 1787.

Clavijero, Francisco Javier. *Historia de la antigua o Baja California*. Mexico City: Secretaría de Educación Pública, 1933.

Cobb, Charles E., Jr. "Mexico's Bajío: The Heartland." *National Geographic* 178, no. 6 (December 1990): 122–144.

Coe, Sophie D. *America's First Cuisines*. Austin: University of Texas Press, 1994.

Comisión Nacional para el Desarrollo de los Pueblos Indígenas. "Mazatecos: Ha Shuta Enima." October 22, 2009. http://www.cdi.gob.mx/index.php?option=com_content&view=article&id=618:mazatecos-ha-shuta-enima-&catid=54:monografias-de-los-pueblos-indigenas&Itemid=62.

CONABIO (Comisión Nacional para el Conocimiento y Uso de la Biodiversidad). "Chipilín (*Crotalaria longirostrata*)." *Naturalista*. http://conabio.inaturalist.org/taxa/161144-Crotalaria-longirostrata.

———. "Guash." http://www.conabio.gob.mx/conocimiento/info_especies/arboles/doctos/44-legum26m.pdf.

———. "Solanaceae: *Capsicum annuum* L.: Chile piquín." http://www.conabio.gob.mx/malezasdemexico/solanaceae/capsicum-annuum/fichas/ficha.htm.

"The Conquest of Tlatelolco." *Historum*, December 13, 2010. www.historum.com/american-history/18557-conquest-tlatelolco.html.

Consejo Nacional para la Cultura y las Artes. *La cocina familiar en el estado de Zacatecas*. Edited by Alfonso de María y Campos. 2nd ed. Mexico City: Océano, 2001.

Cook, Scott, and Martin Diskin, eds. *Markets in Oaxaca*. Austin: University of Texas Press, 1976.

Cortés, Hernán. *The Dispatches of Hernando Cortés, the Conqueror of Mexico, Addressed to the Emperor Charles V, Written during the Conquest, and Containing a Narrative of Its Events*. New York: Wiley and Putnam, 1843.

———. *Letters from Mexico*. Edited and translated by Anthony Pagden. New Haven, CT: Yale University Press, 1986.

Dahlin, Bruce H., Christopher T. Jensen, Richard E. Terry, David R. Wright, and Timothy Beach. "In Search of an Ancient Maya Market." *Latin American Antiquity* 18, no. 4 (December 2007): 363–384.

Davidson, Alan. *The Oxford Companion to Food*. Oxford, UK: Oxford University Press, 1999.

Debouck, D. G. "Beans (*Phaseolus* spp.)." In *Neglected Crops: 1492 from a Different Perspective*, ed. J. E. Hernándo Bermejo and J. León, 47–62. Plant Production and Protection Series No. 26. Rome, Italy: Food and Agriculture Organization of the United Nations (FAO), 1994. http://www.hort.purdue.edu/newcrop/1492/beans.html.

de la Cruz, Juana Inés. *Obras completas de Sor Juana Inés de la Cruz: 1. Lírica personal*. Edited by Antonio Alatorre. Mexico City: Fondo de Cultura Económica, 2009.

———. *Sor Juana Inés de la Cruz Poems: A Bilingual Anthology*. Translated by Margaret Sayers Peden. Tempe, AZ: Bilingual Review Press, 1985.

De la Rosa, M., L. Arce, J. A. Villarreal, L. Ibarra, and J. Lozano. "Germination of Simojovel Pepper Seeds (*Capsicum annuum* L.) Previously Exposed to NaCl and Gibberellic Acid." *Phyton* 81, no. 2 (December 2012): 165–168.

De María y Campos, Alfonso. *La cocina familiar en el estado de Querétaro*. Mexico City: CONACULTA, Editorial Océano de México, 2001.

Díaz del Castillo, Bernal. *The True History of the Conquest of Mexico*. Vol. 1. Translated by Maurice Keatinge. London: Cushing and Appleton, 1803.

Diccionario de la lengua española. 22nd ed. Madrid: Real Academia Española, 2001.

Domínguez Massa, David. "Tiendas de la esquina, vigentes." *Diario de Yucatán*, May 7, 2014.

Drennan, Robert D. "Long-Distance Movement of Goods in the Mesoamerican Formative and Classic." *American Antiquity* 49, no. 1 (January 1984): 27–43.

Dunmire, William W. *Gardens of New Spain: How Mediterranean Plants and Foods Changed America*. Austin: University of Texas Press, 2004.

Durán, Diego. *Book of the Gods and Rites and the Ancient Calendar*. Translated by Fernando Horcasitas and Doris Heyden. Norman: University of Oklahoma Press, 1971.

———. *The History of the Indies of New Spain*. Norman: University of Oklahoma Press, 1994.

Dutton, LaVerne M. "Cochineal: A Bright Red Animal Dye." Master's thesis, Baylor University, Waco, TX, 1992.

Escobar, A. *Recetario del semidesierto de Querétaro*. Vol. 8 of Cocina Indígena y Popular. Mexico City: Consejo Nacional para la Cultura y las Artes, 2003.

Eshbaugh, W. H. 1993. "Peppers: History and Exploitation of a Serendipitous New Crop Discovery." In *New Crops*, ed. J. Janick and J. E. Simon, 132–139. New York: Wiley, 1993.

Ferguson, Bruce G., et al. "Sustainability of Holistic and Conventional Cattle Ranching in the Seasonally Dry Tropics of Chiapas, Mexico." *Agricultural Systems* 120 (September 2013): 38–48. Accessed June 18, 2013. https://doi.org/10.1016/j.agsy.2013.05.005.

Fernández de Oviedo y Valdés, Gonzalo. *La historia general y natural de las Indias*. Madrid: Real Academia de la Historia, 1851–1855.

First Majestic Silver Corp. "Mining History of Mexico." www.firstmajestic.com.

Fitch, Nancy. "The Conquest of Mexico: An Annotated Bibliography." Fullerton: California State University. Accessed June 4, 2013. http://faculty.fullerton.edu/nfitch/nehaha/conquestbib.htm.

Flores y Escalante, Jesús. *Nuestro mero mole: Breve historia de la comida mexicana*. Mexico City: Random House Mondadori, 2013.

Gade, Daniel W. "Hogs." In *Cambridge World History of Food*, ed. Kenneth F. Kiple and Kriemhild Coneè Ornelas, 536–541. New York: Cambridge University Press, 2000. http://www.cambridge.org/us/books/kiple/hogs.htm.

Gálvez, Ramón Jarquín. "Agroecosistemas cafetaleros en Los Altos de Chiapas: Una revisión." *Sociedades Rurales, Producción y Medio Ambiente* 4, no. 7 (December 2003): 83–92.

Gama Maldonado, Roan Raúl. "Tradicional cocina poblana: La oferta gastronómica de la ciudad de Puebla." Tesis de Licenciatura, Escuela de Negocios y Economía, Universidad de las Américas, Puebla, Mexico, 2007.

Gammon, Crystal. "Mexican Monolith Is World's Tallest Freestanding Rock." *Livescience*, May 8, 2013. http://www.livescience.com/29435-mexico-monolith-tallest-rock.html.

García Senosiain, A., P. E. Álvarez Gutiérrez, and B. García Almendarez. "Caracterización genética de cinco poblaciones de timpinchile (*Capsicum annuum*) del estado de Chiapas." Universidad Autónoma de Querétaro, 2008. http://www.uaq.mx/investigacion/difusion/veranos/memorias-2009/11VCRC_46/11_Garcia_Senosiain.pdf.

Gentry, Howard Scott. *Agaves of Continental North America*. Tucson: University of Arizona Press, 1982.

Godoy, Emilio. "Mexico: Agave Sweetens Economic Prospects of Indigenous Women." *Tierramérica* (IPS), February 5, 2011. http://www.ipsnews.net/2011/01/agave-sweetens-economic-prospects-of-indigenous-women/.

González, Arturo H., Carmen Rojas Sandoval, Alejandro Terrazas Mata, Martha Benavente Sanvicente, Wolfgang Stinnesbeck, Jerónimo Aviles O., Magdalena de los Ríos, and Eugenio Acevez. "The Arrival of Humans on the Yucatán Peninsula: Evidence from Submerged Caves in the State of Quintana Roo, Mexico." *Current Research in the Pleistocene* 25 (2008): 1–24. http://www.academia.edu/3610859/The_Arrival_of_Humans_on_the_Yucatan_Peninsula_Evidence_from_Submerged_Caves_in_the_State_of_Quintana_Roo_Mexico.

González Gamio, Angeles. "Puchas digestivas." *La Jornada*, July 14, 2002. http://www.jornada.unam.mx/2002/07/14/036a1cap.php?printver=1.

Gordon, Alice. "Authentic Mexico in the Central Highlands." *Travel + Leisure*, November, 2011. http://www.travelandleisure.com/articles/authentic-mexico-in-the-central-highlands.

Gradie, Charlotte M. "Discovering the Chichimecas." *The Americas* 51, no. 1 (July 1994): 67–88. Berkeley: Academy of American Franciscan History.

Hall, Brian V., Behroz Behnam, and Karen J. Fox. "Royal Mines of Zacualpan, Mexico: 500 Years of Mining History." Impact Silver Corp., July 14, 2011. http://www.impactsilver.com/i/pdf/Royal_Mines_of_Zacualpan_Mexico-500_Years_of%20Mining_History_ESRI_User_Conference_July-14-2011-1.pdf.

Harper, Douglas. *Online Etymology Dictionary*. 2014. www.etymonline.com.

Hassig, Ross. "Periodic Markets in Precolumbian Mexico." *American Antiquity* 47, no. 2 (April 1982): 346–355.

Haviland, John, with Robert M. Laughlin. "Español a raíz tzotzil." University of California/San Diego, Division of Social Sciences, January 2005. http://pages.ucsd.edu/~jhaviland/Laughlin/LaughlinTzotzilEne2005/EspTzoNew.

Henderson, Lucia A. "Blood, Water, Vomit, and Wine: Pulque in Maya and Aztec Belief." *Mesoamerican Voices* 3 (2008): 53–76. http://www.academia.edu/3811531/Blood_Water_Vomit_and_Wine_Pulque_in_Maya_and_Aztec_Belief.

Hernández, Francisco. *Historia de las plantas de Nueva España*. Mexico City: Instituto de Biología, Universidad Nacional Autónoma de México, 1943.

———. *The Mexican Treasury: The Writings of Dr. Francisco Hernández*. Edited by Simon Varey. Stanford, CA: Stanford University Press, 2002.

Hernando Bermejo, J. E., and J. León, eds. *Neglected Crops: 1492 from a Different Perspective*. Plant Production and Protection Series No. 26. Rome, Italy: FAO, 1994.

"Historia de los mercados en México." Sistema de Información Cultural, Consejo Nacional para la Cultura y las Artes. Last updated December 11, 2009. http://sic.cultura.gob.mx/ficha.php?table=gastronomia&table_id=106.

"History and Characteristics of Mexico's Best Wineries." *IN: Riviera Maya and Cancun*, July–August 2013. https://inrivieramaya.com/.

Hutson, Scott R., ed. *Ancient Maya Commerce*. Boulder: University Press of Colorado, 2017.

———. "Carnival and Contestation in the Aztec Marketplace." *Dialectical Anthropology* 25, no. 2 (June 2000): 123–149.

Iber, Jorge. "Vaqueros in the Western Cattle Industry." In *The Cowboy Way: An Exploration of History and Culture*, ed. Paul H. Carlson, 22–24. Lubbock: Texas Tech University Press, 2000.

Instituto Nacional para la Educación de los Adultos. "Geografía del Estado de Querétaro." April 1993. http://bibliotecadigital.conevyt.org.mx/inea%5Cpdf%5C008%5C008004.pdf.

Jenkins, J. A. "The Origin of the Cultivated Tomato." *Economic Botany* 2, no. 4 (October 1948): 379–392.

Karttunen, Frances. *An Analytical Dictionary of Nahuatl*. Norman: University of Oklahoma Press, 1992.

Kaufman, Terrence. 1976. "Archaeological and Linguistic Correlations in Mayaland and Associated Areas of Meso-America." *World Archaeology* 8, no. 1 (1976): 101–118.

Kennedy, Diana. *The Art of Mexican Cooking*. New York: Bantam Books, 1989.

———. *The Essential Cuisines of Mexico*. New York: Clarkson Potter, 2000.

———. *From My Mexican Kitchen*. New York: Clarkson Potter, 2003.

———. *My Mexico: A Culinary Odyssey with Recipes*. Updated ed. Austin: University of Texas Press, 2013.

———. *Oaxaca al Gusto*. Austin: The University of Texas Press, 2010.

Kindscher, Kelly, Quinn Long, Steve Corbett, Kirsten Bosnak, Hillary Loring, Mark Cohen, and Barbara N. Timmermann. "The Ethnobotany and Ethnopharmacology of Wild Tomatillos, *Physalis longifolia* Nutt., and Related *Physalis* Species: A Review." *Economic Botany* 20, no. 10 (2012): 1–13.

Kintzios, Spiridon E., ed. *Oregano: The Genera Origanum and Lippia*. London: Taylor and Francis, 2002.

Kious, W. Jacquelyne, and Robert I. Tilling. *This Dynamic Earth: The Story of Plate Tectonics*. USGS General Interest Publication. Washington, D.C.: U.S. Government Printing Office, 1996. https://pubs.usgs.gov/gip/dynamic/dynamic.html.

Kurlansky, Mark. *Salt: A World History*. New York: Walker Publishing, 2002.

Landa, Diego de. *An Account of the Things of Yucatán: Written by the Bishop of Yucatán, Based on the Oral Traditions of the Ancient Mayas*. Mexico City: Monclem Ediciones, 2000.

———. *Yucatán: Before and After the Conquest*. Translated with notes by William Gates. Toronto: General Publishing Company, 1978.

Las Casas, Bartolomé de. *Historia de las Indias*. Biblioteca de Autores Españoles, Vol. 96. Madrid: Atlas, 1961.

Lascurain Rangel, Maite, Sergio Avendaño Reyes, Citlalli López Binnqüist, Juan Carlos López Acosta, Melissa Covarrubias-Báez, and Rodrigo Duno de Stefano. "Uso y flora leñosa asociada a *Oecopetalum mexicanum* (Icacinaceae): Una especie comestible nativa de la Sierra de Misantla, Veracruz, México." *Botanical Sciences* 91, no. 4 (2012): 477–484.

Laudan, Rachel. *Cuisine and Empire: Cooking in World History*. California Studies in Food and Culture. Berkeley: University of California Press, 2013.

———. "Food and Back Migration: The Cornish Pasty Plot Thickens." Rachel Laudan blog *A Historian's Take on Food and Politics*, March 20, 2015. http://www.rachellaudan.com/2015/03/food-back-migration-cornish-pasty.html.

———. "Where Does Mole Come From? From the Mediterranean or from Mexico?" Rachel Laudan blog *A Historian's Take on Food and Politics*, September 24, 2007. http://www.rachellaudan.com/2007/09/where-does-mole-come-from-from-the-mediterranean-or-from-mexico.html.

Laughlin, Robert M., with John B. Haviland. *The Great Tzotzil Dictionary of Santo Domingo Zinacantán: With Grammatical Analysis and Historical Commentary*. Vol. 2, *English-Tzotzil*. Smithsonian Contributions to Anthropology, No. 31. Washington, D.C.: Smithsonian Institution Press, 1988.

Lesser, Juan M., and A. E. Weidie. "Region 25, Yucatán Peninsula." In *The Geology of North America—An Overview*. Vol. O-2, *Hydrogeology*, ed. William R. Back, Joseph S. Rosenshein, and Paul R. Seaber, 237–241. Boulder, CO: The Geographical Society of America, 1988.

Lira Saade, Rafael, and Salvador Montes Hernández. "Cucurbits (Cucurbita spp.)." In *Neglected Crops: 1492 from a Different Perspective*, ed. J. E. Hernández Bermejo and J. León, 63–77. Rome, Italy: FAO, 1994.

Long-Solís, Janet. *Capsicum y cultura: La historia del chilli*. Mexico City: Fondo de Cultura Económica, 2012.

López Ruiz, Sergio Alejandro. "Historia de Comitán." *Todo Chiapas*, February 14, 2007. http://todochiapas.mx/2007/02/historia-de-comitan/.

Mallén, Patricia Rey. "Mexico's Surprising Wine Industry Is in Trouble." *International Business Times*, November 14, 2013. http://www.ibtimes.com/mexicos-surprising-wine-industry-trouble-1469576.

Markham, Sidney David. *Architecture and Urbanization in Colonial Chiapas, Mexico*. Philadelphia, PA: American Philosophical Society, 1984.

Martínez, Maximino. *Catálogo de nombres vulgares y científicos de plantas mexicanas*. Mexico City: Fondo de Cultura Económica, 1979.

Mayton, Joseph. "Mexico Bans GM Corn in Latest Win against Monsanto and Big AG." *Occupy.com*, October 28, 2013. http://www.occupy.com/article/mexico-bans-gm-corn-latest-win-against-monsanto-and-big-ag.

McGee, Harold. *On Food and Cooking: The Science and Lore of the Kitchen*. New York: Scribner, 1997.

Merino, Isidoro, and Víctor Núñez Jaime. "Próxima parada: América Latina." El Viajero, *El País*, February 15, 2013. https://elviajero.elpais.com/elviajero/2013/02/14/actualidad/1360838917_854438.html.

Mexican Business Web. "SAGARPA Invested $43 Million Pesos in Hydraulic Works in Queretaro." July 17, 2012. https://www.mexicanbusinessweb.mx/eng/?s=SAGARPA+invested+%2443+million+pesos.

Minc, Leah D. "Style and Substance: Evidence for Regionalism within the Aztec Market System." *Latin American Antiquity* 20, no. 2 (June 2009): 343–374.

Minifie, Kemp. "The World of Cilantro." *Gourmet Live*, October 12, 2011. http://www.gourmet.com.s3-website-us-east-1.amazonaws.com/food/gourmetlive/2011/101211/world-of-cilantro.html.

Mizrahi, Yosef, Avinoam Nerd, and Park S. Nobel. "Cacti as Crops." *Horticultural Reviews*. Vol. 18. Hoboken, N.J.: John S. Wiley and Sons, 1997.

Mondragón Pichardo, Juana. "*Portulaca oleraceae* L., Verdolaga." In *Malezas de México*, ed. Heike Vibrans. Mexico City: CONABIO, August 29, 2009. http://www.conabio.gob.mx/malezasdemexico/portulacaceae/portulaca-oleracea/fichas/ficha.htm.

Morton, Julia. "Mexican Husk Tomato." In *Fruits of Warm Climates*, 434–437. Miami, FL: Echo Point Books and Media, 1987.

———. "Passionfruit." In *Fruits of Warm Climates*, 320–328. Miami, FL: Echo Point Books and Media, 1987.

———. "Pito (*Erythrina berteroana*) and Chipilin (*Crotalaria longirostrata*) (Fabaceae), Two Soporific Vegetables of Central America." *Economic Botany* 48, no. 2 (1994): 130–138.

Muehlbauer, F. J., and Abebe Tullu. "*Vicia faba* L." NewCROP

FactSHEET, Purdue University Center for New Crops and Plant Products, 1997. Accessed November 1, 2014. http://www.hort.purdue.edu/newcrop/cropfactsheets/fababean.html.

Muñoz, Ricardo. *Diccionario Enciclopédico de Gastronomía Mexicana*. Mexico City: Editorial Clío, 2000.

Muñoz Saldaña, Rafael. "Frijol, rica fuente de proteínas." *Biodiversitas* (CONABIO) 89 (2010): 7–11. http://www.biodiversidad.gob.mx/Biodiversitas/Articulos/biodiv89art2.pdf.

Mutschlechner, Martin. "The Double-Headed Eagle: The Omnipresent Emblem of the Habsburgs." *The World of the Habsburgs*. 2011. http://www.habsburger.net/en.

Náhuatl Dictionary. Wired Humanities Projects. Accessed November 18, 2014. http://whp.uoregon.edu/dictionaries/nahuatl/.

Neruda, Pablo. *Memoirs/Pablo Neruda*. Translated by Hardie St. Martin. New York: Penguin Books, 1978.

———. "México florido y espinudo." In *Confieso que he vivido*. Barcelona, Spain: Seix Barral, 1974. Translated by Adam Feinstein in *Pablo Neruda: A Passion for Life*. New York: Bloomsbury USA, 2005.

Organización Editorial Mexicana. "Participa el director de 'Avatar' en proyecto para reforestar la Sierra Gorda queretana." *El Sol de México*, June 24, 2010.

Ortiz Guillén, Angel Francisco. *Recetario de Cocina Tradicional Chiapaneca*. Tuxtla Gutiérrez, Mexico: Gas Com, 2011.

Pastrana, Daniela. "Conservation Can Be a Weapon against Poverty." *The Guardian*, July 5, 2010.

Patch, Robert W. *Maya and Spaniard in Yucatán, 1648–1812*. Stanford, CA: Stanford University Press, 1993.

Peel, Derrell S., Rachel J. Johnson, and Kenneth H. Mathews Jr. "Cow-Calf Beef Production in Mexico." Economic Research Service/USDA, November 2010. https://www.ers.usda.gov/publications/pub-details/?pubid=37413.

Pellmyr, Olle. "Yuccas, Yucca moths, and Coevolution: A Review." *Annals of the Missouri Botanical Garden* 90, no. 1 (Winter 2003): 35–55.

Peña, Devon G. "Mayan Farmers Defeat 'Gene Giant' in Latest Court Ruling." *Environmental and Food Justice*, March 15, 2004. https://ejfood.blogspot.com/2014/03/geo-watch-mexican-resistance-to.html t-%E2%80%98gene-giant%E2%80%99-in-latest-court-ruling/.

Pérez Arce, Laura P. "Viva Sierra Gorda." *Earth Island Journal* 21, no. 1 (Spring 2006). http://www.earthisland.org/journal/index.php/eij/article/viva_sierra_gorda1/.

Pérez, Magda Yaneth Culebro, Luvia Adriana Jiménez Rincón, María del Rocío Ortiz Hererra, William Esponda Hernández, and Horacio León Velasco. "El queso crema de Chiapas: Una historia que nos identifica." *Claridades Agropecuarias* 215 (July 2011): 35–42. http://www.infoaserca.gob.mx/claridades/revistas/215/ca215-35.pdf.

Perezgrovas, Raúl. "The Tzotzil Shepherdesses of Chiapas, Mexico, and Their Sacred Wool Sheep." Chiapas, Mexico: Instituto de Estudios Indígenas, 2006.

Perry, Richard D. "Chiapas: Forgotten Missions of the Camino Real." *Exploring Colonial Mexico*. Espadaña Press, 2001. http://www.west.net/~rperry/Chiapas/caminoreal.html.

Peterson, Frederick A. *Ancient Mexico: An Introduction to the Pre-Hispanic Cultures*. New York: Perigee Trade, 1959.

Pilcher, Jeffrey M. *¡Que vivan los tamales! Food and the Making of Mexican Identity*. Albuquerque: University of New Mexico Press, 1998.

Presilla, Maricel E. *Gran Cocina Latina: The Food of Latin America*. New York: W. W. Norton, 2012.

PROFECO. "Chongos zamoranos." Accessed October 21, 2014. http://www.profeco.gob.mx/tecnologias/confite/chongoszam.htm.

Prohens, Jaime, and Fernando Nuez. "The Tamarillo (*Cyphomandra betacea*): A Review of a Promising Small Fruit Crop." *Small Fruits Review* 1, no. 2 (2001): 43–68.

"Proyecto Bicentenario 'Centro Nacional de Recursos Genéticos.'" Gobierno Federal SAGARPA, October 7, 2010. http://www.sagarpa.gob.mx/agricultura/Documents/SistNacRecGen.pdf.

Ramírez Bautista, Jacinta, and Carlos Galindo Leal. *Historias de familias: Quelites*. Mexico City: CONABIO, 2012.

Reilly, F. Kent, III. "Olmec Iconographic Influences on the Symbols of Maya Rulership: An Examination of Possible Sources." In *Sixth Palenque Round Table*, ed. Virginia M. Fields, 151–166. Norman: University of Oklahoma Press, 1991.

Reynolds, Stephen G., and Enrique Arias. *Cactus (Opuntia spp.) as Forage*. FAO Plant Production and Protection Paper 169. Rome, Italy: FAO, 2001.

Roach, John. "Pyramid Tomb Found: Sign of a Civilization's Birth?" *National Geographic News*, May 18, 2010. https://news.nationalgeographic.com/news/2010/05/100518-oldest-pyramid-tomb-zoque-mexico-science/.

Rosas de Oquendo, Mateo. *Sátira hecha por Mateo Rosas de Oquendo a las cosas que pasan en el Pirú, año de 1598*. Edited by Pedro Lasarte. Madison, WI: Hispanic Seminary of Medieval Studies, 1990.

Rzedowski, Graciela C. de, Jerzy Rzedowski, et al. *Flora fanerogámica del Valle de México*. 2nd ed. Pátzcuaro, Michoacán, Mexico: Instituto de Ecología and CONABIO, 2001.

Sabau García, María Luisa. *De México al mundo: Plantas*. Mexico City: Instituto de Ecología, Jardín Botánico del Instituto de Biología del UNAM, and Herbolario de la Asociación Mexicana de Orquideología, 1992.

Sahagún, Bernardino de. *The Florentine Codex: General History of the Things of New Spain*. 12 vols. Translated and with notes by Arthur J. O. Anderson and Charles E. Dibble. Salt Lake City: University of Utah Press, 1982.

———. *Historia general de las cosas de Nueva España*. Colección Sepan Cuántos. Mexico City: Editorial Porrúa, 1999.

Sánchez Cámara, Florencio, ed. "History and Ecology of the Mazahuas as an Example of the Development-Underdevelopment Process in Mexico." In *Concepts for Communication and Development in Bilingual-Bicultural Communities*, 120–122. Berlin: Walter de Gruyter, 1979.

Sánchez Marroquín, Alfredo, and P. H. Hope. "Agave Juice: Fermentation and Chemical Composition Studies of Some Species." *Journal of Agricultural and Food Chemistry* 1, no. 3 (April 1953): 246–249.

Sánchez, Verenise. "Mercados mexicanos, síntesis y germen de cultura." Mexico City: Instituto Nacional de Antropología e Historia, March 22, 2012. http://inah.gob.mx/es/especiales/34-mercados-mexicanos-sintesis-y-germen-de-cultura.

Sangster, D. F. "Geology of Base-Metal Deposits." *Geology* 4 (June 15, 2005): 91–116.

Scheinvar, Léia. *Flora cactológica del Estado de Querétaro: Diversidad y riqueza.* Colección Sección de Obras de Ciencia y Tecnología. Mexico City: Fondo de Cultura Económica, 2004.

Schmal, John P. "The History of Hidalgo." In *History of Mexico.* Houston Institute for Culture, 2004. http://www.houstonculture.org/mexico/hidalgo.html.

———. "The Mixtecs and Zapotecs: Two Enduring Cultures of Oaxaca." In *History of Mexico.* Houston Institute for Culture, 2006. http://www.houstonculture.org/mexico/oaxaca_cultures.html.

Secretaría de Turismo del estado de Chiapas. "Ruta del queso en Ocosingo." N.d. http://llenatedechiapas.com.mx/ruta-del-queso-en-ocosingo/.

SECTUR. "Gastronomic Route, Huastecan Beauties: Hidalgo, Tamaulipas and Veracruz." Rutas gastronómicas, n.d. http://rutasgastronomicas.sectur.gob.mx/en/descargas/rutas/R6/belleza_huastecas.pdf.

Seijas, Susana. "Hidalgo's British Bounty: From Port City to Mountaintop, Cornish Descendants Mine Their Mexican Patrimony." *Inside México,* October 2008. http://insidemex.com/travel/travel/hidalgos-british-bounty.

Shapiro, Leo. "*Vicia faba*: Broad Bean." In *The Encyclopedia of Life.* Accessed November 1, 2014. http://eol.org/pages/703202/hierarchy_entries/50932724/overview.

Sharer, Robert J., with Loa P. Traxler. *The Ancient Maya.* 6th ed. Stanford, CA: Stanford University Press, 2006.

The Silver Institute. "Mine Production." 2017. https://www.silverinstitute.org/mine-production/.

Simons, Gary F., and Charles D. Fennig, eds. *Ethnologue: Languages of the World.* 20th ed. Dallas, TX: SIL International, 2017.

Simpson, Kathleen. *Geography of Mexico.* New Rochelle, NY: Benchmark Education, 2012.

Sistema para el Desarrollo Integral de la Familia del Estado de México. *Los sabores del estado de México.* Biblioteca Mexiquense del Bicentenario. Toluca, Mexico: Sistema para el Desarrollo Integral de la Familia del Estado de México, 2007.

Sluyter, Andrew. "The Hispanic Atlantic's Tasajo Trail." *Latin American Research Review* 45, no. 1 (2010): 98–120.

Smith, Michael E. "The Aztec Marketing System and Settlement Pattern in the Valley of Mexico: A Central Place Analysis." *American Antiquity* 44, no. 1 (January 1979): 110–125.

Snoeks, J., P. Laleye, and T. Contreras-MacBeath. "*Chirostoma attenuatum* (Slender Silverside)." *The IUCN Red List of Threatened Species.* Accessed October 21, 2014. http://www.iucnredlist.org/details/169391/0.

Solís-López, Mariano, Pilar Ponce-Díaz, María de los Ángeles Rosales-Esquinca, Beatriz Xoconostle-Cázares, Delfeena Eapen, and Peggy Elizabeth Alvarez-Gutiérrez. "Análisis de la variabilidad genética de tres poblaciones de timpinchile (*Capsicum annuum* var. *glabriusculum* [Dunal] Heiser & Pickersgill), en la depresión central de Chiapas." Mexico City: V Congreso Internacional de Ingeniería Bioquímica, January 15, 2008. http://www.informatica.sip.ipn.mx/colmex/congresos/chiapas/cdAgropecuaria%5CResumen%5C141219.pdf.

Stone, Cynthia L. *In Place of Gods and Kings: Authorship and Identity in the Relación de Michoacán.* Norman: University of Oklahoma Press, 2004.

Stresser-Péan, G. "Los indios huastecos." In *Huastecos y totonacas,* ed. L. Ochoa. Mexico City: CONACULTA, 1989.

Tainter, Donna R., and Anthony T. Grenis. *Spices and Seasonings: A Food Technology Handbook.* New York: John Wiley and Sons, 2001.

Tamariz, Josefina Martínez. "Papatla (*Heliconia schiedeana*) Leaves Production and Commercialization at San Francisco Town in Huazalingo, Hidalgo." Huejutla de Reyes, Hidalgo, Mexico: Universidad Tecnológica de la Huesteca Hidalguense, August 2011.

Thayer, Warren N. "The Physiography of Mexico." *The Journal of Geology* 24, no. 1 (January–February 1916): 61–94.

Thompson, J. Eric S. *Maya History and Religion.* Norman: University of Oklahoma Press, 1970.

Toovey, Leia Michele. "Silver Mining in Mexico." *Silver Investing News,* October 28, 2010. http://silverinvestingnews.com/4760/silver-mining-in-mexico.html.

Torquemada, Juan de. *Monarquía indiana.* 7 vols. Mexico City: Instituto de Investigaciones Históricas, Universidad Autónoma de México, 1975–1983.

Triberg, Annica. "Smörgåstårta (Sandwich Layer Cake)." *Saveur,* April 1, 2011.

Turner, Jack. *Spice: The History of a Temptation.* New York: Alfred A. Knopf, 2005.

UNESCO World Heritage List. "Prehistoric Caves of Yagul and Mitla in the Central Valley of Oaxaca." 2010. http://whc.unesco.org/en/list/1352.

United States Trade Representative. "Mexico." http://www.ustr.gov/countries-regions/americas/mexico.

Urcid Serrano, Javier. *Zapotec Hieroglyphic Writing.* Washington, D.C.: Dumbarton Oaks Research Library and Collection, 2001.

Valadez-Azúa, R., A. Moreno-Fuentes, and G. Gómez-Álvarez. *Cujtlacochi: El cuitlacoche.* 1st ed. Mexico City: Instituto de Investigaciones Antropológicas, Universidad Nacional Autónoma de México, 2011.

Valadez-Moctezuma, Ernestina, Quetzely Ortiz-Vásquez, and Samir Samah. "Molecular Based Assessment of Genetic Diversity of Xoconostle Accessions (*Opuntia* spp.)." *African Journal of Biotechnology* 13, no. 2 (January 2014): 202–210.

Vázquez Estrada, Alejandro. "Rituales en torno al cerro, el agua y la cruz, entre los chichimeca otomís del semidesierto queretano." *Estudios Sociales, Nueva Época* (Centro INAH, Querétaro) 2 (January 1, 2008): 77–102.

Vela, E. "Los chiles de México: Catálogo visual." *Arqueología Mexicana.* Special Edition, No. 32, 2009.

Vibrans, Heike, ed. "Berula erecta (Huds.) Coville: Palmita de agua." In *Malezas de México.* Last modified July 20, 2009. Accessed November 15, 2014. http://www.conabio.gob.mx/malezasdemexico/apiaceae/berula-erecta/fichas/ficha.htm.

Villanueva Verduzco, Clemente, Efraín Sánchez Ramírez, and Evert Villanueva Sánchez. *El huitlacoche y su cultivo.* Madrid: Mundi-Prensa, 2006.

Villanueva Villanueva, Nancy Beatriz, and Virginia Noemí Prieto. "Rituales de *Hetzmek* en Yucatán." *Estudios de Cultura Maya* (Mérida, Mexico: Universidad Autónoma de Yucatán) 33 (2009): 73–103.

Villegas de Gante, Abraham Z., Arturo Hernández Montes, and Armando Santos Morenos. "El queso crema de Chiapas: Un acercamiento a su caracterización." *Claridades Agropecuarias* 206 (October 2010): 33–38. http://www.infoaserca.gob.mx/claridades/revistas/206/ca206-33.pdf.

Viva Natura. "Mexican Biodiversity." 2017. http://www.vivanatura.org/Biodiversity.html.

Whitaker, Thomas W., and Hugh C. Cutler. "Food Plants in a Mexican Market." *Economic Botany* 20, no. 1 (January–March 1966): 6–16.

Wilford, John Noble. "In an Ancient Mexican Tomb, High Society and Human Sacrifice." *New York Times*, May 17, 2010.

Wine Searcher. "Mexican Tequilas and Wines." Last updated August 13, 2014. https://www.wine-searcher.com/regions-mexico.

Yutzil González, Ixel. "Más de 13.7 millones viven del comercio informal: INEGI." *El Universal*, April 20, 2012. http://www.eluniversal.com.mx/notas/842625.html.

Zadik, Benjamin Joseph. "The Iberian Pig in Spain and the Americas at the Time of Columbus." Master's thesis, University of California, Berkeley, 2005. http://www.bzhumdrum.com/pig/iberianpigintheamericas.pdf.

Zepeda, Sergio. "Cactus, Cactus Everywhere." *AFAR, The Experiential Travel Guide*. https://www.afar.com/places/calle-el-pilancon-cadereyta-de-montes.

INDEX TO RECIPES

BY CATEGORY

GENERAL INDEX

borrego cimarrón (*Ovis canadensis*), 362

botana de viril, 393

botanas (cocktail snacks), 393, *393*, 534

bótil (*Phaseolus coccineus* L.), 86, 88, *88*

brine solution, 527

brining, 534–535

Buenrostro, Marco, 362

Burgoa, Francisco de, 165

Burgos Cetina, Soco, 31, 33, 35, 37, *37*

cacahuates españoles (spicy peanut snack), *393*

cacao: cacao blossoms, *226*; of Chontalpa region, 14, 79, 211, 224, 226; cultivation of, 15; dried cacao beans, *76*; in Gulf Coast region, 210, 211, 214, 224; Maya trade in, 14, 44, 224; in Oaxaca, 155; in Soconusco region, 56, 57, 79. *See also* chocolate

Cacao Route, 213, 224, 226

cactus fruits, of Central Highlands, 3, 290

Cadereyta, Querétaro, 414

café de olla, 80, 535

cajeta, 442, 535

cal. (calcium hydroxide), 535

Calakmul, Campeche, Structure 1, detail of mural, 6, *6*

Calderón, Felipe, 69

caldo, 535

Calvillo, Aguascalientes: guava production in, 291, 293, 300; Mercado "Guel Jiménez," 301, *301*, 302

Camaal Sosa, José, 22

Camino Real de Tierra Adentro (Royal Road of Inner Lands), 293, 294, 421–422

camote (*Ipomoea batatas*), 227, *227*

Campeche, 211

campesino, 535

Cañada, Oaxaca, 148

canela (*Cinnamomum verum*), 80, 535

Cañón del Sumidero, Chiapas, *130*, 132

capers, 15

Carballo Zepeda, Mónica, 81, *81*

Caribbean, 211, 248

Caribbean Sea, 10

carmín, 115, 116, 117, *117*

carnicería, 535

Carnicería La Selecta, *133*

cazos, 501, *501*, 535

cazuelas, 333, *333*, 370, 535

Cecina (salt-cured dried beef), 397, *397*

Celaya, Guanajuato, 310

central de abasto, 535

Central Depression, Chiapas, 130, 133, 136, 138

Central Highlands: characteristics of, 9, 290–291; desert cuisine of, 3, 290; ethnolinguistic groups of, 291; gastronomy of, 290–291; physical environment of, 291; trade of, 224, 226; and Veracruz, 248. *See also* Aguascalientes; Guanajuato (state); Hidalgo; Querétaro; Zacatecas (state)

Central Mexican Plateau, 9, 435

Central Valleys, Oaxaca, 57, 148, 150, 183, 194

chanfaina (organ meat stew), 31

changungas (*Byrsonima crassifolia*), 484

chapulines (*Sphenarium purpurascens*), 156

charales (*Chirostoma attenuatum*), 495, *495*, 496–497

charcuterie, 57, 92

Charles V (king of Spain), 3–4, 248, 504

charrería (horsemanship), 343

charring, charred, 529, 535

chaya (*Cnidoscolus aconitifolius*), 11, 260–261, *260*

chayote (*Sechium edule*), 129, *129*

cheese, 15, 57, 121–122, *122*, 203, 204, *204*, 398, 405–406, *406*, 492

Cheese and Wine Route, 398, 405–406

chepiche (*Porophyllum tagetoides*), 169, *169*

chepil (*Crotalaria* spp.), 169, *169*

Chiapa de Corzo, Chiapas: characteristics of, 130; Church of Santo Domingo, *131*, 132; gastronomy of, 128, 132; Mercado Público Municipal, 132, *132*, *133*, *141*

Chiapas: allspice of, 215; banana production in, 229; beans of, 86–88; cattle of, 133; charcuterie of, 57, 92, *92*; cheeses of, 121–122, *121*; coffee in, 69, 80, *80*, 262; cuisine of, 57, 59; food plants of, 94–98, 114; geological zones of, 57; indigenous rights in, 68–69; language families of, 57, 69; tamales of, 57, 81

chia seeds, 56

chicharrón, 535

chicharrón prensado, 397, *397*

Chichén Itzá, 14, 41

Chichimeca-Jonaz, 291, 535

Chichimecas, 291, 293, 362, 404, 481, 535

chicle, 44

chiffonade, 535

chilacayote (*Cucurbita ficifolia*), 107, 114, *114*, 207, 519, 520

chiles, species of, 3, 15, 149, 150

chiles amashito (*Capsicum annuum* var. *aviculare*), 236, *236*

chiles blanco (*Capsicum annuum*), 136, *136*

chiles blanco en escabeche (pickled blond chiles), 136

chiles chilacates, 442, *442*

chiles chilcostle, 150, *151*

chiles chilhuacles amarillo, *151*

chiles chilhuacles negro, 150, *151*

chiles chilhuacles rojo, *151*

chiles chipotles, 355, *355*

chiles chocolates, 468

chiles de agua (*Capsicum annuum* L.), 150

chiles de árbol de Yahualica, 442, *442*

chiles de chorro (*Capsicum annuum* L.), 330, *330*

chiles de milpa/chiles verdes (*Capsicum annuum*), 20, *20*

chiles de Simojovel (*Capsicum annuum* var. *aviculare*), 91, *91*

chiles en nogada, 290

chiles habaneros (*Capsicum chinense*), 15, 29, *29*

chiles jalapeños (*Capsicum annum*), 272

chiles manzano (*Capsicum pubescens*), 142, *142*

chiles mora (*Capsicum annuum*), 355, *355*

chiles pasillas de Oaxaca, 151

chiles pasillas mixe, 151

chiles piquín (*Capsicum annuum* var. *aviculare*), 91, *91*

chiles poblanos, 330

chiles puyas, 151

chinicuiles (*Hypopta agavis*), 378, *378*

chinín (*Persea schiedeana*), 232, *232*

chipilín (*Crotalaria longirostrata*), 86, 136, *136*, 169

chocolate: and beverages, 45, 77, 79, 98, 192, 215, 275; of Central Highlands, 291; of Chontalpan region, 211, 226; forms of, 79, 155; Museo del Cacao y Chocolatería Cultural, San Cristóbal de las casas, Chiapas, *76*; of Oaxaca, 147, 155, 187; of Villahermosa, 213. *See also* cacao

chocolate de metate (hand-ground chocolate), 155

chocolate mill, 155

Ch'ol, 57, 211

Chong Ovalle, María Leticia "Leti," 72, 117, 140

Chontales of Tabasco, 11, 211, 216, 226

Chontalpa region, Tabasco, cacao production of, 14, 79, 211, 224, 226

chorizo, *92*, *123*

cilantro (*Coriandrum sativum*), 86, 233

cinnamon, 80, 535

Coahuila, 442

Coatepec, Veracruz: characteristics of, 262, *262*; Mercado "Miguel Rebolledo," 263, *263*

PHOTO CREDITS

Most photos not listed here are either tagged with the photographer's intitials (see key to initials on copyright page) or are in the public domain. Every effort was made to determine the correct photographers and sources of photos, but in a few cases the information left behind by the author was incomplete. The publisher welcomes additional information about images.